On th
aroun
New England

860   646   78·2

THOMAS COOK

On 5 July 1841 Thomas Cook, a 33-year-old printer from Market Harborough, in Leicestershire, England, led a party of 570 temperance enthusiasts on a railway outing from Leicester to Loughborough which he had arranged down to the last detail. This proved to be the birth of the modern tourist industry. In the course of expanding his business, Thomas Cook and his son, John, invented many of the features of organised travel which we now take for granted. Over the next 150 years the name Thomas Cook became synonymous with world travel.

Today the Thomas Cook Group employs over 10,000 people worldwide, with more than 1600 locations in over 100 countries. Its activities include travel retailing, tour operating and financial services – Thomas Cook is a world leader in traveller's cheques and foreign money services.

Thomas Cook believed in the value of the printed word as an accompaniment to travel. His publication *The Excursionist* was the equivalent of both a holiday brochure and a travel magazine. Today Thomas Cook Publishing continues to issue one of the world's oldest travel books, the *Thomas Cook European Timetable,* which has been in existence since 1873. Updated every month, it remains the only definitive compendium of European railway schedules.

The *Thomas Cook Touring Handbook* series, to which this volume belongs, is a range of comprehensive guides for travellers touring regions of the world by train, car and ship. Other titles include:

Touring by train
On the Rails around France (Published 1995)
On the Rails around Britain and Ireland (Published 1995)
On the Rails around Europe (Second Edition Published 1995)
On the Rails around the Alps (Publication May 1996)
On the Rails around Eastern Europe (Publication May 1996)
Touring by car
On the Road around California (Published 1994)
On the Road around Florida (Published 1995)
On the Road around Normandy, Brittany and the Loire Valley (Publication March 1996)
Touring by ship
Greek Island Hopping (Published annually in February)
Cruising around Alaska (Published 1995)
Cruising around the Caribbean (Publication September 1996)

For more details of these and other Thomas Cook publications, write to Thomas Cook Publishing, at the address on the back of the title page.

ON THE ROAD AROUND

New England

The definitive
fly-drive guide

Edited by
Stephen H. Morgan

A Thomas Cook Touring Handbook

Published by Thomas Cook Publishing
The Thomas Cook Group Ltd
PO Box 227
Peterborough PE3 8BQ
United Kingdom

Text:
© 1996 The Thomas Cook Group Ltd

Maps and diagrams:
© 1996 The Thomas Cook Group Ltd

ISBN 0 906273 62 5

Managing Editor: Stephen York
House Editor: Kate Hopgood
Map Editor: Bernard Horton
Maps drawn by Amanda Plant

Cover illustration by Michael Bennallack-Hart
Text design by Darwell Holland
Text typeset in Bembo and Gill Sans using
    QuarkXPress
Maps and diagrams created using Aldus
    Freehand and GST Designworks
Printed in Great Britain by Albert Gait Ltd,
    Grimsby

This edition written and researched by
Richard Bourie
Tom Bross
Gunna Bitee Dickson
Patricia Harris and David Lyon
Marjorie Howard
Stephen H. Morgan

Book Editor: **Stephen H. Morgan**
Series Editor: **Melissa Shales**

ABOUT THE AUTHORS

Stephen H. Morgan, Book Editor for this volume, began travel-writing in 1978 for *Yankee Magazine's Guide to New England*. Former Travel Editor of the *Boston Herald*, he has visited six continents and contributed freelance stories to a variety of US newspapers and magazines. He is currently an editor at the *Boston Globe* and a member of the Society of American Travel Writers.

Richard Bourie, whose fondness for New England stems from growing up in Western Massachusetts, wrote the chapters on his home turf as well as on the White Mountains, Nantucket and Martha's Vineyard. He writes a weekly column on adventure travel and outdoor recreation for the *Boston Herald* from his new home near Helena, Montana.

Tom Bross has been a New Englander for 30 years and a freelance travel writer for 25, ever since leaving the 'corporate world' of TV syndicate promotion and public relations. He covers New England, Canada and central and eastern Europe for a number of magazines, guidebooks and US and Canadian newspapers. For this volume he focused on Rhode Island, coastal Connecticut, southern New Hampshire and Vermont.

Gunna Bitee Dickson, who wrote the chapters on New York City and Long Island, is Travel Editor of the New York Daily News.

Patricia Harris and **David Lyon** have collaborated since 1981 on magazine and newspaper articles covering travel, the arts and fine dining. Senior editors of *The Yankee Traveller*, a New England travel newsletter, they covered all of Maine, Cape Cod, the New Hampshire lakes and north woods, as well as Montréal and Québec City for this volume. Raised in Connecticut and Maine respectively, they return from their travels to a home office in Cambridge, Mass.

Marjorie Howard, who focused on Connecticut and Boston's suburbs, has been a reporter at five New England newspapers, writing about its cities, seaside villages, mill towns and suburbs. Her freelance work has appeared in *Boston* magazine, *The New York Times* and *The Boston Globe*.

ACKNOWLEDGEMENTS

The authors and publishers would like to thank the following people and organisations for their assistance during the preparation of this book: Kimberly Adams-Huckman, Addison Associates; Andrews Lodging Bed & Breakfast, Portland, ME; Steve Barba, The Balsams, Dixville Notch, NH; Gilles Bengle, Greater Montréal Convention and Tourism Bureau; Benjamin Prescott Inn, Jaffrey NH; Elizabeth Boardman, Paul Kaza Associates; Breakfast at Tiasquam, Chilmark, MA; Budget Rent-a-Car; Stephen and Karyn Caliri; Roger and Jennifer Cauchi, The Lodge at Moosehead, Greenville, ME; Sonny Cough, Atlantic Eyrie & Atlantic Oakes-By-The-Sea, Bar Harbor, ME; Susan Crowley, Coastal Fairfield County CVB; Alison Cumings, Greater New Haven CVB; Terry Dale, Greater Providence CVB; Caroline Des Rosiers, Hotel La Reine Elizabeth, Montréal; Dexter's Inn & Tennis Club, Sunapee, NH; Jean-Pierre Dion, Québec Hilton, Québec; The Eliot Suite Hotel, Boston; The Forest, Intervale, NH; Richard C. Griffith, Air Canada; Richard F. Hamilton, White Mountains Attractions, N. Conway, NH; The Historic Merrell Inn, South Lee, MA; Kevin Howard, Ocean Edge Resort, Brewster, MA; Inn at Chapel West, New Haven, CT; Inn at Essex, Essex Junction, VT; Inn at Maplewood Farm, Hillsborough, NH; Inn at Montpelier, Montpelier, VT; Dina Jackson, Maine Office of Tourism; Ann Kennard, NH Office of Travel & Tourism Development; Kathleen Kennedy, Mystic, CT, Chamber of Commerce; Jackie LaBella, Connecticut River Valley & Shoreline Visitors Council; Albine Leuthold, Nootka Lodge, Woodsville, NH; Susan Logan, White Mountains Attractions Association, North Woodstock, NH; Sarah Mann and Hope Thurlby, Discover New England; Marilyn Mulholland, Southeastern CT Tourism District; New York City CVB; North Hero House, North Hero, VT; The Old Tavern, Grafton, VT; Ann O'Neill, South County RI Tourism Council; Maplewood Inn, Fair Haven, VT; Sheila Martinez Pina, Bristol County CVB; Rusty McLear, Inn at Bay Point, Meredith, NH; Trevor Pinker and Stephen Mascilo, The Beaconlite Guest House, Provincetown; Marjorie Pritchard; Amy Rafano, Hotel Viking, Newport, RI; Carolyn Rainaud, Diane and Richard Winnick, The Inn on Winter's Hill, Kingfield, ME; Red Brook Inn, Mystic, CT; Charles and Faith Reynolds; Salt Marsh Farm, South Dartmouth, MA; Caroline Sampson, Château Frontenac, Québec; Sheffield House, Block Island; Silvermine Tavern, Norwalk, CT; Suki Scolnick, Chatham Wayside Inn, Chatham, MA; Evan Smith, Newport CVB; Lisa Starr, Block Island Chamber of Commerce; The Tisbury Inn, Vineyard Haven, MA; Pierre A. Tougas, Ministère du Tourisme, Montréal; Candee Treadway, Canadian Consulate General, Boston; Thomas Mott Homestead, Arlburg, VT; The Victorian Inn, Edgartown, MA; The Village Inn, Lenox, MA; The Wauwinet, Nantucket; Westin Hotel, Providence; Barbara Whitten, Portland CVB.

5

CONTENTS

ROUTES AND CITIES

In alphabetical order. Routes are listed in both directions – the reverse route is shown in italics.
See also the Route Map, p. 8, for a diagrammatic presentaion of all the routes in the book.
To look up towns and other places not listed here, see the Index, p. 348.

7

REFERENCE SECTION

8

Key
to route chapters

O   Route start and
    end points

238   Page number of
      route description

Québec, 339

Montréal, 331

CANADA

Maine

Vermont

Fort
Kent

282

Ashland

282

Presque
Isle

Matawamkeag

Bar
Harbor

Acadia
National
Park

282

249

249

Rockland

Moosehead
Lake

269

269

269

269

Augusta

Bethel

259

White
Mountains

Dixville
Notch

204

204

Lincoln

259

North East
Kingdom

238

259

Hanover

216

Montpelier

216

Burlington

216

227

311

Adirondack
Mountains

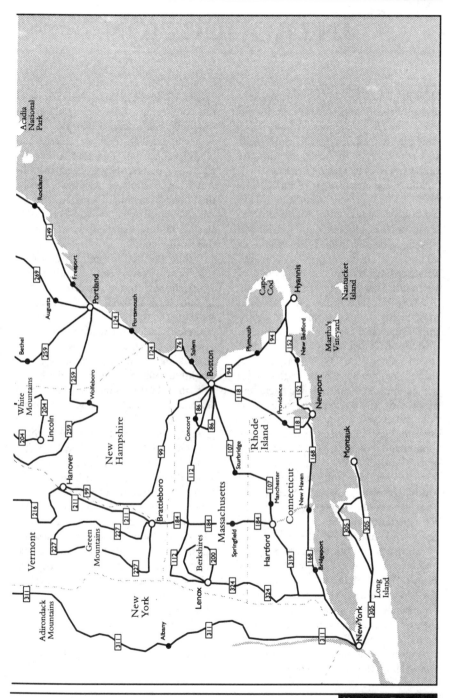

INTRODUCTION

New England is one of the most interesting and beautiful places to visit in the USA. The six-state region is small (by US standards) and compact, with good roads and a temperate, if fickle, climate. Its landscapes vary widely – from the tall buildings and busy streets of its cities to placid village greens; from the rocky, windswept coastline of Maine to the broad beaches of Cape Cod and Rhode Island; from the lush river valleys of Connecticut to the rugged peaks of the White Mountains and deep woods of Vermont. There's even a desert in Maine!

Many travellers prize New England most highly for its fine historical sites – this is after all where America began, in many ways. These states are rich in historical links to the Old World, particularly Britain, whose most restless souls braved the cold North Atlantic beginning in the early 1600s seeking freedom on its wild shores and whose descendants later chose to fight for independence from the motherland. New England's museums and historical sites – including such attractions as Plimoth Plantation, Old Sturbridge Village, Mystic Seaport and Strawbery Banke – give visitors a chance to experience the life of these earlier times and understand the forces and events that led to the Revolution.

And yet there is far more to a New England visit than a lesson in early American history: Fresh-boiled lobster, for example, with steamers and corn on the cob. Whitewater rafting in the north woods of Maine. Band concerts on a village green in the soft light of a summer's eve. Skiing the packed powder of the eastern US's biggest slopes. Bellying up to the counter at a little diner, where the local folks talk in strange accents.

There are high-brow art galleries and low-down jazz joints, elegant dining and hot dogs on the beach. And the all-American pastime of wandering down that narrow ribbon of road just to see what's there. We've tried to give you a taste of all these experiences and more in this small volume.

While the book is primarily written for British travellers – and fellow Anglophones from Australia, Canada, Ireland, New Zealand, South Africa, and so on – it will serve just as well for Americans hitting the road to explore this venerable corner of their own country. Indeed, despite the use of the Queen's English throughout, the viewpoint here is not an Old Englishman's but a New Englander's. That's because this guidebook was researched and written by a group of professional writers from New England and New York, who know the turf well, who live and work here and write about it on a regular basis.

These writers spent six months travelling the highways and byways of their own region, truly 'on the road around New England' (plus a little bit around the edges in New York State and Canada), seeking out the latest details on all the tried-and-trusted attractions of the region and making plenty of new discoveries along the way.

We invite you to do the same.

Stephen H. Morgan
Cambridge, MA

How to Use This Book

ROUTES AND CITIES

On the Road around New England provides you with an expert selection of 24 recommended routes between key cities and attractions of New England (and the alternative gateway city of New York), each in its own chapter. Smaller cities, towns, attractions and points of interest along each route are described in the order in which you will encounter them. Additional chapters are devoted to the major places of interest which begin and end these routes. For large places such as Boston there may be several chapters – e.g. one for the downtown or city centre and one for the greater metropolitan area. These route and city chapters form the core of the book, from page 60 to page 344.

Where applicable, an alternative route which is more direct is also provided at the beginning of each recommended route chapter. This will enable you to drive more quickly between the cities at the beginning and end of the route, if you do not intend to stop at any of the intermediate places. To save space, each route is described in only one direction, but of course you can follow it in the reverse direction, too.

The arrangement of the text consists of a chapter describing a large city or region of interest first, followed by chapters devoted to routes leading from that place to other major destinations; e.g. the first city to be covered is Boston (pp. 60–75), followed by routes from Boston: Boston North Shore (pp. 76–85), West of Boston (pp. 86–93), Boston to Cape Cod (pp. 94–98), Boston to Hanover (pp. 99–106), Boston to Hartford (pp. 107–111), Boston to Lenox (pp. 112–117), Boston to Newport (pp. 118–123) and Boston to Portland (pp. 124–131). Cape Cod is described in chapters following the Boston to Cape Cod route. After the Boston to Newport route comes the chapter on Newport, followed in turn by routes out of Newport to other places, and so on.

The order of chapters thus follows the pattern of your journey, beginning in the south of New England and proceeding generally northwards, ending with routes into Canada. However, you can just as easily work backwards going south. To find the page number of any route or city chapter quickly, use either the alphabetical list on the **Contents** pages, pp. 6–7, or the master **Route Map** on pp. 8–9.

The routes are designed to be used as a kind of menu from which you can plan an itinerary, combining a number of routes which take you to the places you most want to visit.

WITHIN EACH ROUTE

Each route chapter begins with a short introduction to the route, followed by driving directions from the beginning of the route to the end, and a sketch map of the route and all the places along it which are described in the chapter. This map, intended to be used in conjunction with the driving directions, summarises the route and shows the main intermediate distances and road numbers; for a key to the symbols used, see p. 13.

DIRECT ROUTE

This will be the fastest, most direct, and sometimes, predictably, least interesting drive between the beginning and end of the route, usually along major highways.

SCENIC ROUTE

�)◄ This is the itinerary which takes in the most places of interest, usually using ordinary highways and minor roads. Road directions are specific; always be prepared for detours due to road construction, etc.

The driving directions are followed by sub-sections describing the main attractions and places of interest along the way. You can stop at them all or miss out the ones which do not appeal to you. Always ask at the local tourist information centre (usually the Convention & Visitors Bureau or Chamber of Commerce) for more information on sights, lodgings and places to eat at.

⇄ SIDE TRACK

This heading is occasionally used to indicate departures from the main route, or out-of-town trips from a city, which detour to worthwhile sights, described in full or highlighted in a paragraph or two.

CITY DESCRIPTIONS

Whether a place is given a half-page description within a route chapter or merits an entire chapter to itself, we have concentrated on practical details: local sources of tourist information; getting around in city centres (by car, by public transport or on foot as appropriate); accommodation and dining; post and phone communications; entertainment and shopping opportunities; and sightseeing, history and background interest. The largest cities have all this detail; in smaller places some categories of information are less relevant and have been omitted or summarised. Where there is a story to tell which would interrupt the flow of the main description, we have placed **feature boxes** on subjects as diverse as 'The Americas Cup' and 'Covered Bridges'.

Although we mention good independently owned lodgings in many places, we always also list the hotel chains which have a property in the area, by means of code letters to save space. Many travellers prefer to stick to one or two chains with which they are familiar and which give a consistent standard of accommodation. The codes are explained on p. 346, and central booking numbers for the chains are also given there.

MAPS

In addition to the sketch map which accompanies each route, we provide maps of major cities (usually the downtown area, but also the greater metropolitan area in places like Boston), smaller towns, regions, scenic trails, national parks, and so on. At the end of the book is a section of **colour road maps** covering the whole area described in this book, which is detailed enough to be used for trip planning and on the road. The **key to symbols** used on all the types of map in this book is shown on p. 13.

THE REST OF THE BOOK

At the front of the book, **Driving Distances** is a tabulation of distances between main places, to help in trip planning. The use of the **Contents** and **Route Map** pages has already been mentioned above. **Travel Essentials** is an alphabetically arranged chapter of general advice for the tourist new to New England or to the United States, covering a wide range subjects such as accommodation and safety or how much to tip. **Driving in**

New England concentrates on advice for drivers on the law, rules of the road, and so on. **Background New England** gives a concise briefing on the history and geography of this fascinating region. **Touring Itineraries** provides ideas and suggestions for putting together an itinerary of your own using the selection of routes in this book. At the end of the book, the **Conversion Tables** decode US sizes and measures for non-US citizens. Finally the **Index** is the quick way to look up any place or general subject. And please help us by completing and returning the **Reader Survey** at the very end of the text; we are grateful for both your views on the book and new information from your travels in New England.

KEY TO MAP SYMBOLS

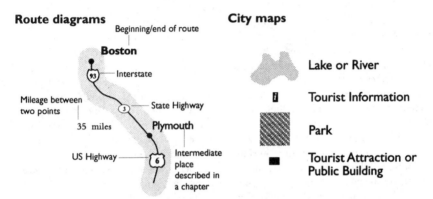

Route diagrams

Beginning/end of route

Boston

(93) — Interstate

Mileage between two points

(3) — State Highway

35 miles **Plymouth**

US Highway — (6)

Intermediate place described in a chapter

City maps

Lake or River

Tourist Information

Park

Tourist Attraction or Public Building

13

KEY TO PRICE DESCRIPTIONS

It is impossible to keep up to date with specific tariffs for lodging and accommodation or restaurants, although we have given some general advice under 'Cost of Living' in the Travel Essentials chapter pp. 14–35). Instead, we have rated establishments in broad price categories throughout the book, as follows:

Accommodation (per room per night)

Budget	Under $35
Moderate	Under $90
Expensive	Under $150
Pricey	$150 and higher

Meal (for one person, excluding drinks, tip or tax)

Cheap	Under $5
Budget	Under $10
Moderate	Under $20
Pricey	Over $20

ABBREVIATIONS USED IN THE BOOK
(For hotel chains, see p. 346)

Bldg	Building (in addresses)	Jan, Feb	January, February, etc.
Blvd	Boulevard	min(s)	minute(s)
Dr.	Drive (in addresses)	Mon, Tues	Monday, Tuesday, etc.
Fwy	Freeway	Rd	Road (in addresses)
hr(s)	hour(s)	Rte	Route, e.g. Rte 450
Hwy	US or State Highway, e.g. Hwy 1	St	Street (in addresses)
I-	Interstate Highway, e.g. I-95	Ste	Suite (in addresses)

TRAVEL ESSENTIALS

The following is an alphabetical listing of helpful tips and advice for those planning a New England holiday.

ACCOMMODATION

New England offers accommodation of every price level imaginable, from five-star hotels and posh resorts to youth hostels and campsites. Local tourist offices can provide accommodation lists and telephone numbers, but generally can't make bookings. Where available, lodging services are noted in the text.

Accommodation can be extremely hard to find in major tourist destinations during high season, which is usually Memorial Day (last weekend in May) to Labor Day (first weekend in Sept), plus weekends and major holidays year-round. Boston, because of its many colleges and universities, is heavily booked also in May for commencement ceremonies and in Sept, when the academic year begins. Maine's high season, in contrast, lasts only from early July through mid to late Aug. In popular skiing areas of New Hampshire, Vermont and Maine, weekend accommodation is heavily booked from early Dec into Mar, and weekday bookings are also heavy during Christmas week and Feb school vacation weeks.

No time is harder to find a room than **foliage season,** mid-Sept–mid-Oct, in Vermont, New Hampshire, Western Massachusetts and some other areas. Many inns and hotels are completely booked *a full year in advance* by regular clients. Travelling spontaneously is always fun, but *call ahead* to reserve a room in foliage season – or risk driving hours out of your way looking for a vacancy.

Thomas Cook or any other good travel agent can handle room bookings when purchasing air tickets and car or other local transportation. All-inclusive fly-drive arrangements and 'do-it-yourself packages' such as Thomas Cook Holidays *America for the Independent Traveller,* can provide hotel coupons, exchangeable at a range of hotel chains, which guarantee a prepaid rate at participating chains, although they do not guarantee rooms – it's up to you to phone ahead as you go or take a chance on availability. It's particularly important to pre-book the first and last nights' stay to avoid problems when connecting with international air flights.

Throughout the book we have indicated prices of accommodation in a comparative way by using terms such as 'moderate' and 'pricey'; see 'How to Use This Book', p. 13, for an explanation of what these descriptions mean in terms of dollars.

Hotels and Motels

US hotel rates are quoted for single or double occupancy; children usually stay cheaply or free with parents.

Most chain hotels and motels have toll-free reservation telephone numbers that can be reached from anywhere in North America. A selection of these, along with the abbreviations used in the text of this book to indicate which chains are present in the town or city being described, can be found on p. 346.

Advance bookings require a voucher or credit card number to be guaranteed. Ask for discounts if you're disabled, a senior citizen, a motoring club member or travelling off season. When checking in, always ask if there's a cheaper room rate than the one you pre-booked. It's often cost-effective to find lodging day by day, especially in off-peak seasons.

Motels are often the best bet. Literally 'motor hotels', motels are one- to three-storey buildings with a modest version of hotel accommodation. Most belong to nationwide chains which enforce service and safety standards. Independent motels may not be quite as fancy but offer even lower prices. Motels fill up fast during high season, but last-minute rooms are usually available in the off-season, especially during the week. The *AAA TourBooks* for *Connecticut, Massachusetts, Rhode Island;* for *Maine, New Hampshire, Vermont* and for *New York* list thousands of motels and hotels; thousands more are just as comfortable and affordable. Check the motels that line major highways entering most cities and towns.

Budget hotels, especially in cities, tend to be dim, dirty and dangerous. Look for a motel or youth hostel instead.

Inns and Bed and Breakfasts
In New England, **bed and breakfasts** can be a more homely alternative to 'cookie-cutter' hotels and motels, but they are seldom the bargain lodgings of their English cousins. In Boston and New York, options range from a room in a private home to an entire luxury apartment (flat) or condominium, with prices on a par with moderate–expensive hotels. In rural or heavy tourism areas such as Cape Cod, where hotels and motels fill up, a bed and breakfast may offer a tidy room with antique furnishings and homespun quilts in a restored 19th-century home, with prices that slightly undercut low-end moderate

motels. Facilities may be private or shared. Some owners offer guests a chance to mingle or watch television in a public parlour. Breakfast is usually the chance to interact with hosts or fellow guests; the meal itself typically includes coffee or tea, orange juice, home-made muffins and cereal.

Country inns are among New England's most enjoyable places to stay. A smaller inn might have the look and feel of a bed and breakfast, but with more rooms and breakfast choices. Bigger inns typically include a full restaurant with hearthside dining, a wide porch with rocking chairs for relaxing, and prices from the expensive range upwards.

Camping
Camping means a tent or a recreational vehicle (RV) in a rural campsite. Those in state parks and forests are often the quietest and most primitive, with firewood available but facilities limited to pit toilets and cold showers. Federal campsites similarly are equipped for those who enjoy the outdoors.

Private campsites vary widely. Some cater to campers but tolerate RVs; others resemble mini-suburbs, with laundry facilities, recreation halls and television antennas on every RV. Standard facilities include a fireplace for barbecues, tent site or electric/sewer hookups, showers and toilets.

Overnight fees range from $8–$30, depending on location and season, at private campsites, $5–$15 at state parks. Many state park campsites can be reserved well in advance by post; indeed, reservations are often required in July and Aug.

Youth Hostels
American Youth Hostels (Hostelling International) was created for tight bud-

15

gets. Most hostels provide a dormitory-style room and shared bath for $10–$15 per night. Some have family rooms, all offer discounts to local attractions. The disadvantage is that there are only a handful of hostels in New England. When two or more people are travelling together, and can share a room, motels may be cheaper.

AIRPORTS

The major airports serving travellers to New England are Boston's Logan International Airport (BOS), New York's John F. Kennedy Airport (JFK) and Newark International Airport (EWR) in New Jersey, just outside New York City. Bangor, Maine, also handles some international arrivals.

Airport information booths cover airport facilities, airport-to-city transport and local accommodation, though no bookings are made (some offer direct phone links to let you make your own bookings).

All major airports have foreign exchange, banking services and car hire facilities. Public transportation to the nearest city is usually available; in Boston, it can be the quickest route into the city centre. Luggage trolleys are free for international arrivals in Boston, but cost $1 at New York's JFK. Specific airport arrival information is given in the chapters dealing with the major airport cities.

BICYCLES

Cycling is popular for countryside touring in New England. Bicycles can be hired by the hour or day in most locations that cater to tourists. Boston is the rare US city that provides a few cycle paths on park land; however, cycle paths along city streets are still a foreign concept, even there. Cycling is easier and less dangerous in slow-paced resort areas and along country roads.

For serious cyclists, tours are available at all levels, with accommodation arranged at campsites or posh inns and a 'sag wagon' carrying heavy gear and worn-out cyclists. Independent bicycle tours are also possible, and distances between towns are not prohibitive. The use of bicycle helmets is always strongly recommended, but usually required only for children.

BORDERS

For travellers from British Commonwealth countries, border inspections are generally routine, as long as you don't fit the 'profile' that Customs and immigration officials are trained to watch out for. Have your passport, visa, proof of support and return ticket in order.

Crossing into Canada can be time-consuming if an official targets you for a car search. If you're not carrying illegal drugs, alcohol, firearms or agricultural products, and if your documents are in order, you should have no difficulty entering the USA or Canada. Carry doctors' prescriptions to prove that any medication is legitimate.

BUSES

Greyhound Bus Lines, *Customer Service, 901 Main St, Dallas, TX 75202; tel: (800) 231-2222,* provides long-distance bus services between major cities nationwide. There are discounts for senior citizens (over 65), disabled travellers and children (under 12) riding with a full-fare adult. The **International Ameripass** offers special discounts for travellers not resident in North America. Greyhound passes are obtainable through Thomas Cook travel shops in the UK.

Thomas Cook publishes bimonthly timetables of US buses in the *Thomas Cook Overseas Timetable,* and a special edition devoted to US (and Canadian) buses and trains, containing much additional travel information, is published annually under the title *Thomas Cook North American Rail and Bus Guide* (full details of these and other publications can be found under 'Useful Reading' on p. 35).

CAMPERS AND RVs

Fly-drive holiday packages usually offer the option of hiring an RV (recreational vehicle), caravan or motorhome. The additional cost can be offset by the economics of assured accommodation for several people, space for meal preparation and eating, and the convenience of comfort items and souvenirs stored nearby.

RVs are cramped, designed to stuff you and your belongings into limited space. The economics work only if advance planning assures that the pricey spur-of-the-moment allure of a hotel shower or unplanned restaurant meal won't overcome RV campers! Account for the cost of petrol – an RV guzzles 3–4 times more than a medium-sized car.

Always get operating manuals for the vehicle and all appliances before leaving the RV hire lot, and ask someone to demonstrate how *everything* works. Systems may be interdependent, or more complex than anticipated.

Be prepared to pre-plan menus and allow additional time each morning and afternoon/evening to level the RV (perfect levelling is essential for correct operation of refrigerators) and to hook up or disconnect electricity, water and sewer hoses, and cable television plugs. As at home, some basic housecleaning must be done; also allow time for laundry at RV parks.

RV travel information: **Recreational Vehicle Industry Association (RVIA)**, *Dept. RK, PO Box 2999, Reston, VA 22090-0999; tel: (703) 620-6003*. To plan RV camping, request *Go Camping America* from **Camping Vacation Planner**, *PO Box 2669, Reston, VA 22090; tel: (800) 477-8669*. Campground directories list private RV park locations, directions, size, number of pitches, hook-ups, laundry, on-premises convenience stores and showers.

CANADA

A valid passport is required for entry into Canada, but no visa is required for citizens of Australia, New Zealand, Republic of Ireland, South Africa or the UK. If returning to the US after a visit to Canada, check with US immigration officials that your visa, if one is required, permits your return.

Canada imposes a 7% **Goods & Services Tax**. In addition, the provinces impose sales taxes of 4%–12% on most goods, meals and lodgings. Visitors may apply for a **rebate** of the GST paid on certain goods they take from Canada and on lodgings of less than 30 days. To qualify for a rebate, your purchases must be for a minimum of $100 ($7 in tax), and you must show your receipts. The rebate application is obtained at Canadian Customs and tourism offices, department stores and hotels. On the same form, visitors can apply for a rebate of Province Quebec's 8% retail sales tax, but not its 4% lodgings tax nor taxes paid to other provinces. Rebates are given at certain duty-free shops or by post: *Revenue Canada, Customs, Excise and Taxation, Visitor Rebate Program, Ottawa, Canada K1A 1J5*.

Canada's national holidays include New Year's Day (1 Jan); Good Friday (Apr); Easter Monday (Apr); Victoria Day (late May); Canada Day (1 July); Labour Day (early Sept); Thanksgiving (mid-Oct); Remembrance Day (11 Nov); Christmas Day (25 Dec) and Boxing Day (26 Dec).

CHILDREN

New England is ideal for travelling with children and its many historical and natural attractions are always welcoming. From museums to transport, check for children's rates, often segmented by age, e.g., under 3 free, 6–12 years $3, 12–18 years $4. A student card must be shown to use student rates.

Any driving destination in New England is equipped for children of all ages, from nappies to video games. Most hotels and motels can arrange for babysitters, though the price may be steep. Many hotel chains allow children under 12, 14, sometimes 18, to stay free in their parents' room. A roll-away child's bed, often called a cot, usually comes at no or minimal cost.

Meals can be difficult, but picnic lunches offer flexibility. It's also a good idea to carry a small cooler filled with ice, cold drinks and snacks, especially in hot weather. Most towns have coffee shops with long hours, childrens' menus and familiar fast-food names. If the children like Mc Donalds at home, they'll like Big Macs in New England.

CLIMATE

New England's weather is known not for its extremes, but for its changeability. Author Mark Twain, who lived many years in Hartford, Conn., joked that he once 'counted 136 different kinds of weather inside of 24 hours'.

In general, expect cold and snow from Dec to Mar, warm days and cool nights from June to Sept. But summer is always cooler and later, winter cooler and earlier, the further north you go. In Hartford, temperatures average 18–35°F in Jan, 38–59°F in Apr, 63–84°F in July, 42–64°F in Oct. Way north in Burlington, Vt., you can take 10 degrees off those winter averages, 5 degrees off the summer figures. Moving to the coast will keep you cooler in summer, warmer in winter – because the ocean moderates the temperature – but a few miles inland you won't feel a difference.

New England is renowned for its harsh winters; indeed, Maine averages 50–70 inches of snow annually along the coast, 90–120 inches in the northern interior. But snowfall is so unpredictable, even in Vermont and New Hampshire, that ski resorts, which depend on the white stuff for their economic survival, must guarantee it with snow-making machines. Still, extreme weather *does* happen, often with

	Boston	Burlington	Bar Harbor	New York City
January				
Highest	36°F/2°C	25°F/-4°C	32°F/0°C	38°F/3°C
Lowest	22°F/-6°C	8°F/-13°C	15°F/-9°C	25°F/-4°C
April				
Highest	56°F/13°C	54°F/12°C	52°F/11°C	58°F/14°C
Lowest	40°F/5°C	34°F/1°C	34°F/1°C	42°F/6°C
July				
Highest	82°F/28°C	81°F/27°C	77°F/25°C	83°F/28°C
Lowest	65°F/18°C	60°F/16°C	56°F/13°C	67°F/19°C
October				
Highest	63°F/17°C	57°F/14°C	58°F/14°C	66°F/19°C
Lowest	47°F/8°C	39°F/4°C	42°F/6°C	48°F/9°C

sudden and devastating consequences. Many summers, a tornado will rip through a small town, smashing houses and tossing cars around. Late summer brings an occasional hurricane from the tropics. Nor'easters lash the coast with wind and rain, sometimes washing away seaside homes or bringing a blizzard.

CLOTHING

Summers are hot and humid, winters cold and damp. In any season, take plenty of layers, from shorts for the beach to jumpers and jackets for the mountains or evenings along the shore. Cotton and wool, worn in layers, are always a safe bet. Adding and removing layers makes it easier to stay comfortable no matter how many times the weather changes a day.

What to pack is a constant question. Except for business, New Englanders dress casually. A wide range of dress is acceptable, even at the ballet or symphony in Boston and New York, and only elegant restaurants require jackets and ties for men. All shops and restaurants, even at the beach, require that shirts and shoes be worn. The bottom line is: when in doubt, leave it at home. New England clothing prices are cheaper than in Britain. But do take good, broken-in walking shoes.

CONSULATES

Australia: *Honorary Consul, 20 Park Plaza, Suite 457, Boston, MA 02116; tel: (617) 542-8655. Consulate General, 630 Fifth Ave, New York, NY 10111; tel: (212) 408-8400.*
Canada: *3 Copley Place, Suite 400, Boston, MA 02116; tel: (617) 262-3760. 1251 Avenue of the Americas, 16th Floor, New York, NY 10020; tel: (212) 596-1600.*
New Zealand: *37 Observatory Circle, NW, Washington, DC 20008; tel: (202) 328-4800.*

Republic of Ireland: *535 Boylston St, Boston, MA 02116; tel: (617) 267-9330. Ireland House, 345 Park Ave, 17th Floor, New York, NY 10154-0037; tel: (212) 319-2555.*
South Africa: *333 E. 38th St, 9th Floor, New York, NY 10016; tel: (212) 213-4880.*
UK: *Federal Reserve Plaza, 25th Floor, 600 Atlantic Ave, Boston, MA 02210; tel: (617) 248-9555. 845 Third Ave, New York, NY 10022; tel: (212) 745-0200.*

COST OF LIVING

While New England and New York have local sales taxes and hotel/lodging taxes, the combined levy is less than the VAT charged in most of Europe. Prices are always marked or quoted without tax, which is added at the time of purchase (see Sales Taxes, p. 29). Petrol prices are a special bargain, about $1.25 per US gallon (4 litres), or about $0.30 per litre. Motel rooms cost $30–$70 per night; hotels from $70 up. Restaurant meals, including soup or salad, main course, dessert, beverage and tax are about $10–$20 per person for lunch, $20–$25 for dinner. Most museums charge $2–$5 per adult, with discounted admission fees for children, senior citizens, college students and others. Some state parks charge a few dollars per car, others are free.

CURRENCY

US dollars are the only currency accepted in New England. Bill denominations are $1, $2 (very rare), $5, $10, $20, $50 and $100. All bills are the same colour, green and white, and the same size. Take great care not to mix them up. The only differences, apart from the denominations marked on them, are the US president pictured on the front and the designs on the back. There are 100 cents to the dol-

19

lar: coins include the copper 1-cent piece (penny), 5-cent nickel, 10-cent dime, 25-cent quarter, 50-cent half-dollar (infrequently used) and the rare Susan B. Anthony dollar.

In Canada, Canadian dollars are the official currency. Coins are similar to US coins but of slightly different sizes and shapes, and include a C$1 and C$2 coin; notes (C$5, C$10, etc.) are all of the same size but different colours.

Outside foreign exchange offices, most New Englanders only have a vague idea that other currencies even exist. Banks are not equipped to exchange foreign currency or travellers' cheques; they will probably refer you to the nearest bank that is, which could be a considerable distance. Better to seek out one of the Thomas Cook locations noted in this book. However, US dollar travellers' cheques, from well-known issuers such as Thomas Cook, are acceptable everywhere and can be used like cash or changed easily. To report Thomas Cook travellers' cheque losses and thefts, call 1-800-223-7373 (toll-free, 24-hour service).

For security reasons, avoid carrying large amounts of cash. The safest forms of money are US dollar travellers' cheques and credit or debit cards. Both can be used almost anywhere. If possible, bring at least one, preferrably two major credit cards such as **Access (MasterCard), American Express** or **Visa.** (Thomas Cook locations will offer replacement and other emergency services if you lose a MasterCard.) Plastic is the only acceptable proof of fiscal responsibility. Car hire companies require a credit card imprint before releasing a vehicle, even if the hire has been fully prepaid. Hotels and motels also require either a credit card imprint or a cash deposit, even if the bill is to be settled in cash.

Some shops, cheaper motels, small local restaurants and low-cost petrol stations require cash. Automated teller machines, or **ATMs,** are a ubiquitous source of cash through withdrawals or cash advances authorised by debit or credit card. **CIRRUS, NYCE** and **Yankee24** are common systems used in New England, but check terms, availability and your PIN (personal identification number) with the card issuer before leaving home.

CUSTOMS ALLOWANCES

Personal duty-free allowances which can be taken into the USA by visitors are 1 US quart (approx. 0.9 litres) of spirits or wine, 300 cigarettes or 50 (non-Cuban) cigars and up to $100 worth of gifts.

On your return home you will be allowed to take the following:

Australia: goods to the value of A$400 (half for those under 18) plus 250 cigarettes or 250 g tobacco and 1 litre alcohol.

Canada: goods to the value of C$300, provided you have been away for over a week and have not already used up part of your allowance that year. You are also allowed 50 cigars plus 200 cigarettes and 1 kg tobacco (if over 16) and 40 oz/1 litre alcohol.

New Zealand: goods to the value of NZ$700. Anyone over 17 may also take 200 cigarettes or 250 g tobacco or 50 cigars or a combination of tobacco products not exceeding 250 g in all plus 4.5 litres of beer or wine and 1.125 litres spirits.

UK: The allowances for goods bought outside the EU and/or in EU duty-free shops are: 200 cigarettes or 50 cigars or 100 cigarillos or 250 g tobacco + 2 litres still table wine + 1 litre spirits or 2 litres sparkling wine + 50 g/50 ml perfume + 0.5 litre/250 ml toilet water.

New England prices for alcohol, tobacco, perfume and other typical duty-

20

free items beat most **duty-free** shops. Follow the locals into chain supermarkets (Star Market, Stop & Shop, A & P, Shaw's and others) and discount stores (K-mart, Lechmere, Caldor, Wal-Mart, Ames, Marshalls, Woolworth and others).

DISABLED TRAVELLERS

Access is the key word. Physically challenged is synonymous with disabled. Physical disabilities should present less of a barrier in the United States than in much of the world. State and federal laws, particularly the Americans with Disabilities Act (ADA), require that all businesses, buildings and services used by the public be accessible by handicapped persons, including those using wheelchairs. Every hotel, restaurant, office, shop, cinema, museum, post office and other public building must have access ramps and toilets designed for wheelchairs. Most cities and towns have ramps built into street crossings and most city buses have some provision for wheelchair passengers. Even many parks have installed paved pathways so disabled visitors can get a sense of the natural world. The bad news is that disabled facilities aren't always what they're meant to be. Museums, public buildings, restaurants and accommodation facilities are usually accessible, but special automobile controls for disabled drivers are seldom an option on hired vehicles.

Some public telephones have special access services for the deaf and disabled. Broadcast television may be closed-captioned for the hearing impaired, indicated by a rectangle around a double cc in a corner of the screen.

US Information: SATH (Society for the Advancement of Travel for the Handicapped), *347 Fifth Ave, Suite 610, New York, NY 10016; tel: (212) 447-7284.*

UK Information: RADAR, *12 City Forum, 250 City Rd, London, EC1V 8AF; tel: (0171) 250 3222,* publish a useful annual guide called *Holidays and Travel Abroad,* which gives details of facilities for the disabled in different countries.

DISCOUNTS

Reductions on entrance fees and public transport for senior citizens, children, students and military personnel are common. Some proof of eligibility is usually required. For age, a passport or driving licence is sufficient. Military personnel should carry an official identification card. Students will have better luck with an *International Student Identity Card (ISIC)* from their local student union than with their own college ID.

The most common discount is for automobile club members. Tour guides from AAA (American Automobile Association) affiliates list hundreds of member discounts for New England and New York State. Always ask about 'Triple A discounts' at attractions, hotels, motels and car hire counters. Most recognise reciprocal membership benefits. Some cities will send high-season discount booklets on request, good for shops, restaurants or lodging.

DRINKING

Hollywood movies to the contrary, you must be 21 years old to purchase or to drink any kind of alcoholic beverage (18 in Connecticut). Licensed establishments are called bars, lounges, saloons, taverns or pubs; state and local laws govern hours, which are generally from morning until 2400, 0100 or 0200.

States regulate sales of beer, wine and liquor; laws vary. In New Hampshire, Maine and Vermont, state-owned stores (and a few independent stores) sell alcohol,

21

but beer and wine are sold at grocery stores. Elsewhere, privately owned liquor (or 'package') stores sell beer, wine and liquor; supermarkets sell beer and wine only, if at all. Connecticut, Massachusetts and Rhode Island prohibit take-away sales on Sun, although bars and restaurants may serve you.

Laws against drinking and driving are very strict and enforced with fines and imprisonment. Every state prohibits carrying any open container of liquor, wine or beer in a vehicle; in some states, such as Maine, any alcohol container must be full, sealed and unopened – or in the boot.

ELECTRICITY

The USA uses 110 volt 60 hertz current. Two- or three-pin electrical plugs are standard. Electrical gadgets from outside North America require plug and power converters. Both are difficult to obtain in the USA because local travellers don't need them. Beware of buying electrical appliances in the US, for the same reason. Few gadgets on the US market can run on 220 v 50 hz power. Exceptions are battery-operated equipment such as radios, cameras and portable computers – or a few dual-voltage models of electric shavers and hair dryers. Tape cassettes, CDs, computer programs and CD-ROMs sold in the USA can be used anywhere in the world.

US video equipment, which uses the NTSC format is *not* compatible with the PAL and SECAM equipment used in most of the rest of the world. *Pre-recorded* video tapes sold in the USA will not work with other equipment unless specifically marked as compatible with PAL or SECAM. *Blank* video tapes purchased in America, however, *can* be used with video recorders elsewhere in the world. Discount store prices on blank video cassettes are very reasonable.

EMERGENCIES

In case of emergency, ring *911* from any telephone; the call is free. Ambulance, paramedics, police, fire brigades or other public safety personnel will be dispatched immediately.

FOOD

American tradition demands huge portions and endless refills of coffee. Copious consumption begins with breakfast. Thinly sliced bacon and eggs cooked to order (fried, scrambled, poached) come with hash browns or home fries (shredded or cubed fried potatoes). Toast, a flat 'English' muffin with butter and jam, or a bagel with cream (farmer's) cheese and lox (smoked salmon slices) may be served alongside. Variations or additions include pancakes, French toast (bread dipped in egg batter and lightly fried) and waffles. Fresh fruit and yogurt, cereal and porridge are other possibilities. A 'continental breakfast' is juice, coffee or tea, and some sort of bread or pastry.

Menus offer similar choices for lunch and dinner, the evening meal. Dinner portions are larger and more costly. Most menus offer appetisers (starters), salads, soups, pastas, entrées (main courses) and desserts.

New England is especially known for its fresh seafood, which is served fried (in batter) or broiled (in butter), sometimes baked, and includes locally caught cod and haddock (often called 'scrod' or 'schrod'), bluefish, tuna, salmon and a variety of more exotic imported fish, such as mahi-mahi. Shellfish appearing on menus include clams (fried whole or as 'strips'), steamers (clams steamed in the shell), quahogs (a round-shell clam), mussels, oysters, scallops and shrimp. New England's unique treat is the lobster, which turns bright red after immersion (live) in boiling water. It is served whole (a challenge to eat without making a mess), in parts (tails and claws) or picked out of the shell for salads or 'lobster roll' sandwiches.

The melting pot of cuisines in major cities includes Brazilian, Cambodian, Caribbean, Chinese, Greek, Indian, Italian, Japanese, Mexican, Middle Eastern, Portuguese, Vietnamese, regional American (such as Dixie-style ribs and barbecue) and many others.

Fast food is quick, economical and impossible to miss. Hamburgers, hot dogs, tacos, fried chicken and barbecue beef are common offerings.

The budget rung of the price ladder includes chain restaurants such as Denny's (common along interstate highways and usually open 24 hours), Friendly's (ice cream, sandwiches and simple meals), Pizzeria Uno and Bertucci's (Italian), Boston Market (roasted chicken), Howard Johnson's (HoJo) and International House of Pancakes (IHoP), which serves all-day breakfast, plus safe, unexciting lunch and dinner choices.

Vegetarians will have little trouble eating well, particularly if they enjoy seafood. In addition, many restaurants offer meatless choices, bountiful salad bars are common and there is a smattering of vegetarian and macrobiotic eateries.

GAMBLING

Gambling is illegal in all New England states. However, all the states have highly advertised lotteries and church halls everywhere run 'casino nights' and 'bingo' or 'beano' games.

New England's only casino is **Foxwoods**, run by the Mashantucket Pequot tribe in Ledyard, Conn. (However, the Wampanoags are negotiating to open a casino in New Bedford, Mass). Betting is legal at thoroughbred horse-racing and Greyhound dog tracks and at jai alai frontons.

HEALTH

Hospital emergency rooms are the place to go in the event of life-threatening medical problems. If a life is truly at risk, treatment will be swift and top notch, with payment problems sorted out later. For mundane problems, 24-hour walk-in health clinics are available in urban areas and some rural communities.

Payment, not care, is the problem. Some form of **health insurance** cover is almost mandatory in order to ensure provision of health services. Coverage provided by non-US national health plans is *not* accepted by New England medical providers. The only way to ensure provision of health services is to carry some proof of valid insurance cover. Most travel agents who deal with international travel will offer travel insurance policies that cover medical costs in New England and the rest of the USA – at least $1 million of cover is essential.

Bring enough prescription medication to last the entire trip, plus a few extra days. It's also a good idea to carry a copy of the prescription in case of emergency. Because trade names of drugs vary from country to country, be sure the prescription shows the generic (chemical) name and formulation of the drug, not just a brand name.

No inoculations are required, and New England is basically a healthy place to visit. Common sense is enough to avoid most health problems. Eat normally (or at least sensibly) and avoid drinking water that didn't come from the tap or a bottle. Assume that most ground water, even in the White Mountains and Maine's north woods, is contaminated with *giardia* and other intestinal parasites. Sunglasses, broadbrimmed sun hats and sunscreen help prevent sunburn, sun stroke and heat prostration. Be sure to drink plenty of non-alcoholic liquids, especially in hot weather.

AIDS (Acquired Immune Deficiency Syndrome) and other sexually transmitted diseases are endemic in New England as they are in the rest of the world. The best way to avoid sexually transmitted diseases (STDs) is to avoid promiscuous sex. In anything other than long-term, strictly monogamous relationships, they key phrase is 'safe sex'. Use condoms in any kind of sexual intercourse. Condoms can be bought in drug stores or pharmacies and from vending machines in some public toilets.

Rabies is another endemic problem in New England. It's most likely to afflict those who are bitten while trying to hand feed the squirrels and chipmunks that haunt many parks. Rabies-infected **raccoons** pass the disease to house pets in suburbs and towns. If bitten by an animal, try to capture it for observation of possible rabies, then go to the nearest emergency medical centre. You must seek *immediate* treatment – if left too late the disease is untreatable and fatal.

All New England states and New York carry a risk of **Lyme disease** from ticks, which can attach themselves to humans who walk through grassy and marshy woodland areas. The disease is passed by brown, pinhead-sized deer ticks. The prevention is to wear light-coloured clothing with long sleeves and a shirt collar, long trousers tucked into socks or boots, a hat and insect repellent containing DEET. Deer ticks are most active from April through October.

Lyme disease is frequently misdiagnosed and usually mistaken for rheumatoid arthritis. Typical symptoms include temporary paralysis, arthritic pains in the hand, arm or leg joints, swollen hands, fever,

fatigue, headaches, swollen glands and heart palpitations. The first symptom is usually a circular red rash around the bite from three to 30 days after contact. Early treatment with tetracycline and other drugs is nearly 100% effective; late treatment often fails. Symptoms may not appear for three months or longer after the first infected tick bite, but the disease can be detected by a simple blood test.

HIKING

Walking is a favourite outdoor activity, especially in park areas. The same cautions that apply anywhere else are good in New England: know the route; carry a map and basic safety gear; carry food and water. Stay on marked trails. Walking off the trail adds to erosion damage, especially in fragile forests, meadows and beaches. It can also get you lost: don't hike off the trail without telling someone, preferably a park ranger.

Hikers should be extremely cautious in areas posted for hunting. Ask locally about hunting seasons for deer and other game before venturing into the woods.

The most common hiking problem is **poison ivy**. The low-growing plant is difficult to identify, although its leaflets, sometimes reddish, always occur in clusters of three. All parts of the plant exude a sticky sap that causes an intense allergic reaction in most people. The most common symptoms are itching, burning and weeping sores. Try to avoid the plant, but if you can't, wash skin or clothing that has come into contact with the plant immediately in hot, soapy water. Drying lotions such as calamine or products containing cortisone provide temporary relief, but time is the only cure.

Wildlife can be a problem. **Mountain lions** (also called bobcats, cougars and pumas) are rumoured to be returning to

New England, but if you can *prove* you saw one, you'll make the nightly news. **Coyotes** and **foxes** are a fact of rural and suburban life, including such unlikely locales as Cape Cod, but are shy of people.

In northern woodlands, especially Maine, **bears** are a more serious threat. They're large, strong, fast-moving, always hungry and smart enough to connect humans with the food they carry. Parks and campsites in bear country have detailed warnings on how to safely store food to avoid attack. When possible, hang anything edible (including toothpaste) in bags well above ground or store in your car. *Never* feed bears; they won't know

---

How To Talk New England

Bubbler Boston-speak for a water fountain.

Buffalo Wings Chicken Wings, usually fried and served with a spicey sauce as an appetiser or bar food.

Chili dog or chili burger Hot dog or hamburger disguised with chili, onions and cheese.

Chips Crisps.

Clam roll Fried clams served usually on a hot-dog roll.

Clam strips Thin pieces of clams without the 'bellies'; a cheaper form of fried clams.

Down East Originally applied to Maine's coastal winds; now it's a place – either Maine or a part of its coast – and an attitude.

Downtown City or town centre.

Frappe Boston-speak for a *milk shake*, i.e., milk blended with ice cream and flavouring.

Fries or french fries Chips.

Holiday A public holiday, such as Labor Day, not a private holiday, which is a *vacation*.

Ivy League A group of eight prestigious universities in the northeastern US, including Harvard, Yale, Dartmouth and Brown in New England, that educate the US 'establishment'.

Micro-brewery or brewpub A tavern that brews its own beer.

Nor'easter A coastal storm or gale blowing from the northeast (i.e., off the ocean), usually bringing heavy rain or snow.

Outlet stores Large stores specialising in factory overruns at reduced prices. Often, they are simply discount stores.

Prep School Preparatory school, a private *High School* for affluent adolescents heading to college.

Preppie A student who attends prep school or who dresses like one who does.

Quahog An edible clam with a hard, round shell (pronounced *kwo-hog* or *ko-hog*, from the Narragansett *poquaûhock*).

Resort A fancy hotel that specialises in leisure activities such as golf, tennis and swimming.

Road kill Literally, animals killed by passing cars, but usually used to describe bad restaurant food.

Soda A soft drink, such as cola, anywhere but Boston.

Tonic A cola or other soft drink, but only around Boston, where it's pronounced *TAW-nick;* anywhere else, it's carbonated water, pronounced normally.

Yankee An old-fashioned New Englander, usually of WASP (White Anglo-Saxon Protestant) heritage, taciturn expression, frugal ways and stern character.

when the meal is over. Unless you come between a mother and her young – or leave food or garbage out – bears generally avoid humans. Making noise usually persuades curious bears to look elsewhere for a meal.

In northern New Hampshire, Vermont and in Maine, watch out for **moose** when driving, especially at night along roads marked for moose crossings. Colliding with a moose is often fatal – for motorists as well as the animal. Be equally careful of motorists stopping suddenly when they spot one. When observing moose, stay in your vehicle; adults are enormous and their movements are unpredictable. Never get between an adult moose (or any other wild animal) and its young.

HITCH-HIKING

In an earlier, more trustful era, hitch-hiking was the preferred mode of transporta-tion for budget travellers. Today, hitch-hiking or picking up hitch-hikers is asking for violent trouble, from theft to physical assault and murder. *Don't do it.*

HUNTING AND FISHING

Licences are required for hunting and freshwater fishing. Check with state tourism offices regarding hunting seasons and where fishing and hunting licences may be purchased. In some places, town halls issue fishing licences.

Massachusetts law prohibits the unli-cenced or unauthorised carrying of firearms; the mandatory penalty is one year in jail. Some states require hunting safety classes before issuing a hunting licence.

INSURANCE

Experienced travellers carry insurance that covers their belongings and holiday invest-ment as well as their bodies. Travel insurance should include provision for cancelled or delayed flights and weather problems, as well as immediate evacuation home in case of medical emergency. Thomas Cook and other travel agencies offer comprehensive policies. Insurance for drivers is covered in more detail in the 'Driving in New England' chapter, p. 42.

LANGUAGE

English is the official language, but recently arrived immigrants speak dozens of languages. Even English can cause non-US visitors a few difficulties, and a selection of commonly encountered terms which may be unfamiliar or have a different meaning in America are set out in the box on p. 25. The next chapter, 'Driving in New England', also provides a glossary of motoring terms for the non-US driver.

LUGGAGE

Less is more where luggage is concerned. Porters don't exist outside the most expensive hotels, and luggage trolleys (baggage carts) are rare. Trolleys are free for international arrivals in Boston, but must be hired for US currency at New York's JFK Airport. Luggage has to be light enough to carry. The normal trans-Atlantic luggage allowance is two pieces, each of 70 lb (32 kg) maximum, per person.

Luggage must also fit in the car or other form of transport around New England. Americans buy the same cars as the rest of the world, not the enormous 'boats' of the 1960s. If it won't fit in the boot at home, don't count on cramming it into a US car.

MAPS

The best all-round maps are produced by the **American Automobile Association,** known simply as AAA ('Triple A'), and distributed through its New England affiliates. State, regional and city maps are available free at all AAA offices, but only to members. Fortunately, most automobile clubs around the world have reciprocal agreements with AAA to provide maps and other member services. Be prepared to show a membership card to obtain service.

Rand McNally road maps and atlases are probably the best known of the ranges available outside the USA, in the travel section of bookshops and more specialist outlets. The most detailed road maps available are produced by **Arrow Map Inc.,** *50 Scotland Blvd, Bridgewater, MA 02324; tel: (508) 279-1177.* Wire-bound and folding Arrow maps are sold at booksellers, news-stands, souvenir shops and airports. Detailed upcountry maps are available from **DeLorme Map Co.,** *Rte 1, Freeport, ME 04032; tel: (207) 865-4171,* and **Jimapco,** *Box 1137, Clifton Park, NY 12065.*

For back-country travel, **US Geological Survey** quadrangle (topographic) maps show terrain reliably; they can be purchased in Boston at the Globe Corner Bookstore (see 'Useful Reading' p. 35). For hiking in the White Mountains or along the Appalachian Trail, maps and guidebooks of **The Appalachian Mountain Club,** *5 Joy St, Boston, MA 02108; tel: (617) 523-0636,* are indispensible.

Before leaving civilisation behind, compare every available map for discrepancies, then check with national forest or park personnel. Most are experienced back-country enthusiasts themselves, and since they're responsible for lost hikers, they have a vested interest in dispensing the best possible information and advice.

OPENING HOURS

Office hours are generally Mon–Fri

0900–1700, although a few tourist offices also keep short Sat hours all year, and weekend hours in summer. Many banks are open from 0900 or 1000 to 1500 or 1600; a few open Mon–Fri 0830–1700, Thur to 1900, Sat 0900–1300. ATMs (cash dispensing machines) are open 24 hours, and are located everywhere.

Small shops keep standard business hours. In major cities, large shops and shopping centres open at 0900 or 1000 Mon–Sat and close at 2000 or 2100, with shorter hours on Sun. Small towns tend to 'roll up the sidewalks' early.

Many museums close on Mon, but most tourist attractions are open seven days a week. Almost everything closes on New Year's Day, Thanksgiving and Christmas Day.

PARKS INFORMATION

For specific national and state parks, monuments and seashores, see the appropriate description among the recommended routes throughout this book. For general information on national parks, monuments and seashores, contact **National Park Service,** *15 State St, Boston, MA 02109; tel: (617) 242-5642.* In New England, these sites include Acadia National Park in Maine, the Cape Cod National Seashore, historical sites in Boston, Lowell and Salem, Mass., and the White Mountain National Forest in New Hampshire. There is a charge for entry to some national and state parks.

PASSPORTS AND VISAS

All non-US citizens must have a valid full passport (not a British Visitor's Passport) and, except for Canadians, a visa, in order to enter the United States. Citizens of most countries must obtain a visa from the US Embassy in their country of residence in advance of arrival.

Citizens of Britain, New Zealand and Ireland may complete a visa waiver form, which they generally receive with their air tickets if the airline is a 'participating carrier'. Provided nothing untoward is declared, such as a previous entry refusal or a criminal conviction, which would make application for a full visa mandatory, the waiver exempts visitors from the need for a visa for stays of up to 90 days. Visitors may make a side-trip overland into Mexico or Canada for up to 30 days and return to the US.

Note: Documentation regulations change frequently and are complex for some nationalities; confirm your requirements with a good travel agent or the nearest US Embassy at least 90 days before your visit.

POLICE

To telephone the police in an emergency, ring *911.* There are many different police jurisdictions within each New England state, each with its own police force. The highways are generally patrolled by the state police. See also under 'Security'.

POSTAL SERVICES

Every town has at least one post office. Hours vary, although all are open Mon–Fri, morning and afternoon. Postal Service branches may be open on Sat or (rarely) on Sun. Some big hotels sell stamps through the concierge. Stamp machines are installed in some stores, but a surcharge may be included in the cost.

For philatelic sales, check major city telephone directories under US Postal Service. Post everything going overseas as Air Mail (surface mail takes weeks or even months). If posting letters near an urban area, they should take about one week. Add a day or two if posting from remote areas.

Poste Restante is available at post offices, without charge. Post should be addressed in block lettering to your name, Poste Restante/General Delivery, city, state, post office's zip (postal) code, United States of America (do not abbreviate). Mail is held for 30 days at the post office branch that handles General Delivery for each town or city, usually the main office.

In Boston, General Delivery mail is handled at *25 Dorchester Ave* (next to South Station), zip code *02205*; in Cambridge, at *Central Sq*, zip code *02139*. Small towns and smaller cities usually have only one post office and one zip code. Identification is required for mail pickup.

PUBLIC HOLIDAYS

America's love affair with the road extends to jumping in the automobile for holiday weekends. Local celebrations, festivals, parades or neighbourhood parties can disrupt some or all activities in town.

The following list of public holidays are celebrated nationally: New Year's Day (1 Jan); Martin Luther King Jr Day (third Mon in Jan); Lincoln's Birthday (12 Feb); Presidents' Day (third Mon in Feb); Memorial Day (last Mon in May); US Independence Day (4 July); Labor Day (first Mon in Sept); Columbus Day (second Mon in Oct); Veterans Day (11 Nov); Thanksgiving Day (fourth Thursday in Nov); and Christmas (25 Dec).

Some others are celebrated statewide or locally: Town Meeting Day (Vermont, first Tues in Mar); Evacuation Day (Boston only, 17 Mar); Patriots Day (Maine and Massachusetts, 19 Apr or third Mon); Rhode Island Independence Day (May 4); Bennington Battle Day (Vermont, 16 Aug).

Post offices and government offices close on public holidays. Some businesses take the day off, though department and discount stores use the opportunity to hold huge sales, well advertised in local newspapers. Petrol stations remain open. Small shops and some grocery stores close or curtail hours.

Call in advance before visiting an attraction on a public holiday as there are frequently special hours.

SALES TAXES

There is no Valued Added Tax or Goods & Services Tax in the USA. Each state imposes its own tax on sales of products and services, itemised separately on every bill. Connecticut: 6% sales tax, 10% admissions tax on most places of amusement. Massachusetts: 5% sales (including meals), 5.7%–9.7% lodgings. New Hampshire: No sales tax, 8% meals and rooms tax, including on beverages. Rhode Island: 7% sales, 5% lodgings. Maine: 6% sales, 7% lodgings. Vermont: 5% sales, 8% lodgings and food, 10% alcohol.

New York State has a 4% sales tax, with additional local sales taxes of up to 4.5%. New York City imposes a rooms tax of 13.25% plus $2, with another tax on rooms over $100. See 'Canada' p. 17 for information on Canada's GST.

Items taxed by states vary. Some exempt clothing, items for babies, takeaway foods. State and federal taxes on petrol, cigarettes and alcoholic beverages are included in the posted price.

SECURITY

Throwing caution to the winds is foolhardy anytime, and even more so on holiday. The US, by history and inclination, permits guns to circulate, both legally and illegally.

However, millions of people travel in perfect safety each year in the USA. So can you if you take the following common sense precautions.

Travelling Safely

Never publicly discuss travel plans or money or valuables you are carrying. Use caution in large cities, towns and rural areas. Drive, park and walk only in well-lit areas. If unsure of roads or weather ahead, stop for the evening and find secure accommodation.

The best way to avoid becoming a victim of theft or bodily injury is to walk with assurance and try to give the impression that you are not worth robbing (e.g. do not wear or carry expensive jewellery or flash rolls of banknotes).

Use a hidden money-belt for your valuables, travel documents and spare cash. Carrying a wallet in a back pocket or leaving a handbag open is an invitation to every pickpocket in the vicinity. In all public places, take precautions with anything that is obviously worth stealing – use a handbag with a crossed shoulder strap and a zip, wind the strap of your camera case around your chair or place your handbag firmly between your feet under the table while you eat.

Never leave luggage unattended. At airports, security officials may confiscate unattended luggage as a possible bomb. In public toilets, handbags and small luggage has been snatched from hooks or from under stalls. Airports and bus and train stations usually have lockers. Most work with keys; take care to guard the key and memorise the locker number. Hotel bell staff may keep luggage for one or more days on request and for a fee – be sure to get receipts for left luggage before handing it in.

Concealing a weapon is against the law. Some defensive products resembling tear gas are legal only for persons certified in their proper use. Mugging, by individuals or gangs, is a social problem in the USA. If you are attacked, it is safer to let go of your bag or hand over the small amount of obvious money – as you are more likely to be attacked physically if the thief meets with resistance. *Never resist.* Report incidents immediately to local police, even if it is only to get a copy of their report for your insurance company.

Driving Safely

Ask someone from the car hire counter to recommend a safe, direct route on a clear map before you leave with the vehicle. Lock all valuables and luggage in the boot or glove box so that nothing is visible to passers-by or other drivers. Don't leave maps, brochures or guidebooks in evidence and don't leave a hotel parking tag in the window – why advertise that you're a stranger in town?

Always keep car doors and windows locked. Do not venture into unlit areas, neighbourhoods that look seedy or off paved roads. *Do not stop* if told by a passing motorist that something is wrong with your car or if someone signals for help with a broken-down car. If you need to stop, do so only in well-lit areas, even if your car is bumped from behind by another vehicle.

If your car breaks down, turn on the hazard lights, and if it is safe to get out, raise the bonnet. Do not split passengers up. Lights on emergency vehicles are red or red and blue, so do not stop for flashing white lights or flashing headlights. Ask directions from police, at a well-lit business area or at a service station.

At night, have keys ready to unlock car doors before entering a car park. Check the surrounding area and inside the vehicle before entering. Never pick up hitchhikers, and never leave the car with the engine running. Take all valuables with you. Fill the petrol tank during daylight hours, and keep it at least half full.

Sleeping Safely

When sleeping rough, in any sort of dormitory, train or open campsite, the safest place for your small valuables is at the bottom of your sleeping-bag. In sleeping cars, padlock your luggage to the seat, and ask the attendant to show you how to lock a compartment door at night. If in doubt, it's best to take luggage with you. In all lodgings, lock doors from the inside. Check that all windows are locked, including sliding glass doors. Ground-floor rooms, while convenient, mean easier access by criminals intent on breaking in. When you leave the room at night keep a light on to deter prowlers.

Use a door viewer to check before admitting anyone to your room. If someone claims to be on the hotel staff or a repair person, do not let the person in before phoning the office or front desk to verify the person's name and job. Money, cheques, credit cards, passports and keys should be with you or secured in your hotel's safe deposit box. When checking in, find the most direct route from your room to fire escapes, elevators, stairwells and the nearest telephone.

Documents

Take a few passport photos with you and photocopy the important pages and any visa stamps in your passport. Store these safely, together with a note of the numbers of your travellers cheques, credit cards and insurance documents (keep them away from the documents themselves). If you are robbed, you will at least have some identification, and replacing the documents will be easier. Apply to your nearest consulate (see 'Consulates').

SHOPPING

Uniquely New England souvenirs include Vermont maple syrup, live Maine lobsters packed for the flight home, 'Boston Harbor tea', Cape Cod saltwater taffy, beach plum jelly, hand-made patchwork quilts, Shaker wooden crafts and the ubiquitous T-shirts. Clothing can be a bargain, particularly at discount or factory outlet stores. Cameras and other photo equipment can be a fraction of UK prices, but do your homework on prices before you go, and shop around. Prices are particularly low in New York City, but some shops sell 'gray market' merchandise; the goods are legitimate, but the warranty may not cover them if you have a problem back at home. When in doubt, don't buy.

Tape cassettes, blank video tapes, CDs, computer programs and CD-ROMs sold in the USA can be used anywhere in the world. For more information on electrical goods, see 'Electricity' in this chapter.

SMOKING

Lighting up is not permitted in public buildings and on public transport. All plane flights in the USA and Canada are non-smoking, and some hire cars are designated as non-smoking. Most hotels/motels set aside non-smoking rooms or floors; bed and breakfasts are almost all non-smoking. Restaurant dining regulations vary by locality; some forbid all smoking, others permit it in the bar or lounge only, some have a percentage of the eatery devoted to smokers. Smoking is prohibited in most stores and shops. Always ask before lighting a cigarette, cigar or pipe. When in doubt, go outside to smoke.

TELEPHONES

The US telephone system is divided into local and long-distance carriers. Depending on the time of day and day of the week, it may be cheaper to call Los Angeles than to call 30 miles away. After

1700 Mon–Fri and all weekend, rates are lower. Useful phone numbers are provided throughout this book.

Public telephones are everywhere, indicated by a sign with a white telephone receiver depicted on a blue field. Enclosed booths are rare; wall-mounted or free-standing machines are more commonly used. If possible, use public phones in well-lit, busy public areas. Cellular telephone use is widespread and rentals are available, but rates are astronomical.

Dialling instructions are in the front of the local white pages telephone directory. For all long-distance calls, precede the area code with a *1*. *Tel: 0* for the operator. For local number information, *tel: 411*. For long-distance phone information, *tel: 1*, then the area code, then *555-1212*. There will be a charge for information calls.

Pay phones take coins, and a local call costs $0.10–$0.25 upwards. An operator or computer voice will come on-line to ask for additional coins when needed. Most hotels and motels add a stiff surcharge to the basic cost of a call, so ask about charges before dialling or find a public telephone in the lobby.

Prepaid phone cards are still a novelty in the USA and availability is only just beginning in Boston and some other areas. Before you travel, ask your local phone company if your phone card will work in America. Most do, and come with a list of contact numbers. However, remember that the USA has the cheapest overseas phone rates in the world, which makes it cheaper to fill pay phones with quarters than to reverse charges. A credit card may be convenient, but is only economical if you pay the bill immediately.

For comparison, local call rates: coin $0.10–$0.25 direct dial, calling card $0.35; operator-assisted, calling card $0.95. Most *800*-numbers are toll-free. Like all long-distance numbers the *800* area code must be preceded by a *1*, e.g. *1-800-123-4567*. Some US telephone numbers are given in letters, i.e. *1-800-23LOGAN*. Telephone keys have both numbers and letters, so find the corresponding letters and depress that key. A few numbers have more than seven letters to finish a business name. Not to worry, US or Canadian phone numbers never require more than seven numerals, plus three for the area code. Numbers in the *900* area code charge the caller a fee for information or other services; rates are often high. Dial an international operator on *00* for enquiries or assistance. For international dialling, *tel: 011-country code-city code* (omitting the first *0* if there is one)-*local number*, e.g., to call Great Britain, Inner London, from the USA, *tel: 011-44-171-local number*. Some country codes:

Australia 61
New Zealand 64
Republic of Ireland 353
South Africa 27
United Kingdom 44

TIME

New England, New York State and the Canadian provinces of Ontario and Quebec share a time zone, GMT minus 5

Time in Boston (EST)	8 a.m.	12 p.m.	5 p.m.	12 a.m.
Time in				
Auckland	1 a.m.	5 a.m.	10 a.m.	5 p.m.
Cape Town	3 p.m.	7 p.m.	12 a.m.	7 a.m.
Dublin	1 p.m.	5 p.m.	10 p.m.	5 a.m.
London	1 p.m.	5 p.m.	10 p.m.	5 a.m.
Perth	9 p.m.	1 a.m.	6 p.m.	1 p.m.
Sydney	11 p.m.	3 a.m.	8 a.m.	3 p.m.
Toronto	8 a.m.	12 p.m.	5 p.m.	12 a.m.

hours, called Eastern Standard Time (EST). From the first Sun in April until the last Sun in October, clocks are pushed forward to Eastern Daylight Time (EDT).

TIPPING

Acknowledgement for good service should not be extorted. That said, tipping is a fact of life, to get, to repeat or to thank someone for service.

Service charges are not customarily added to restaurant bills; the exception, when indicated, is for large groups (such as eight or more people), where experience shows that friends splitting a bill underestimate their share.

Waiters and waitresses expect a tip of at least 15% of the bill before taxes and drinks are added on. If you feel service was extremely good, by all means reward it by increasing the tip to 20%; you can punish truly bad service with a slightly smaller tip, but don't withhold the tip completely unless you speak to the waiter or manager, explaining the service problem and giving them the opportunity to correct it. (Poorly prepared food is the fault of the kitchen, not the waiter, and should be sent back).

In luxury restaurants, also be prepared to tip the maitre d' and sommelier a few dollars, up to 10% of the bill. Bartenders may expect the change from a drink, up to several dollars.

Hotel porters generally receive $1 per bag; a bellperson who shows you the rooms expects several dollars; in luxury properties, tip more. Room service delivery staff should be tipped 10%–15% of the tariff before taxes, unless there's a service charge indicated on the bill. Expect to hand out dollars for most services that involve room delivery.

Tip taxi drivers 10%, unless the service was bad. Tip cloakroom personnel up to $1 per coat unless a service charge is posted.

TOILETS

There is nothing worse than not being able to find one. *Restroom* or *bathroom* are the common terms; *toilet* is acceptable; few people recognise *washroom* or *W.C.* Most are marked with a figure for a male or a female; *Men* and *women* are the most common terms, though ethnic restaurants may use *caballeros* (or *señors*) and *damas, hommes* and *dames* or other variations, and many a waterfront restaurant cannot resist the word play of *buoys* and *gulls*. Occasionally a restroom may be used by both sexes (one person at a time).

Facilities may be clean and well-equipped or filthy. Most businesses, including bars and restaurants, reserve restrooms for clients. Petrol stations provide keys for customers to access restrooms. Public toilets are sporadically placed, but well-marked. Parks and roadside rest stops have toilet facilities. Carry a pack of tissues in case paper is lacking.

TOURIST INFORMATION

In the USA, each state is responsible for its own tourism promotion. Address requests for information well in advance. **Connecticut Department of Economic Development, Tourism Division,** *865 Brook St, Rocky Hill, CT 06067-3405; tel: (800) CT-BOUND.* **Maine Publicity Bureau,** *P.O. Box 2300, Hallowell, ME 04347-2300; tel: (207) 623-0363.* **Massachusetts Office of Travel and Tourism,** *100 Cambridge St, 13th Floor, Boston, MA 02202; tel: (800) 447-MASS, ext 300.* **New Hampshire Office of Vacation Travel,** *PO Box 586, Concord, NH 03301; tel: (603) 271-2666.* **Rhode Island Tourism Division,** *7 Jackson Walkway, Providence, RI 02903; tel: (800)*

33

556-2484 or (401) 277-2601. **Vermont Department of Travel and Tourism,** *134 State St, Montpelier, VT 05602; tel: (802) 828-3236.*

Although it is *not* a New England state, New York is frequently on the itinerary of New England visitors: **New York State Department of Economic Development,** *One Commerce Plaza, Albany, NY 12245; tel: (518) 474-6950.*

The six New England states have combined their resources to establish an overseas marketing organisation, which provides information and brochures, maps and itinerary planning: **Discover New England,** handled in Britain by *Boston Fox Tigue, Trac House, 34 Francis Grove, Wimbledon, London SW19 4DT; tel: (01732) 742777.* In the USA, the address is *Heritage Place C-3A, Worcester Court, Falmouth, MA 02540; tel: (508) 540-8169.* This book also gives contact details of tourism offices in regions, cities and towns along specific routes.

For Canadian tourism information, contact the province or territory you plan to visit. Parts of two Canadian provinces are covered in this book. **Ontario Travel,** *Queen's Park, Toronto, Ont. M7A 2R9 Canada; tel: (416) 314-0944, fax: (416) 314-7372.* **Tourisme Quebec,** *P.O. Box 20 000, Quebec, PQ G1K 7X2 Canada; tel: (514) 873-2015.*

TRAINS

Amtrak is the official passenger train transportation company in the US; *tel: (800) 872-7245.* The main New England route runs from Boston to New York City, with stops at Providence and points along the Connecticut shoreline. The ride takes up to five hours, with long delays at New Haven, Conn., to switch from diesel to electric engines; prices vary according to time and day of travel.

From New Haven, another route serves Hartford, Conn., and Springfield, Mass. A special train, the **'Montrealer'**, follows this route, stopping at points in Vermont, then switches to buses to cross the border into Canada and continue on to Montreal. The **'Cape Codder'** runs between New York City and Hyannis on Cape Cod. Boston–Chicago service is available, though infrequent.

New England offers several scenic railroads of tourist, rather than transportation, interest; these are detailed under sightseeing throughout the text.

TRAVEL ARRANGEMENTS

Given the fact that many of the world's international airlines fly into Boston – and *all* of them fly into New York City – and the ease of hiring cars at airports, New England is an ideal destination for independently minded travellers. However, the many types of air ticket and the range of temporary deals available on the busy routes make it advisable to talk to your travel agent before booking, to get the best bargain.

In fact, taking a fly-drive package such as one of Thomas Cook's own, or one of the many others offered by airlines and tour operators, is usually more economical than making all your own arrangements. All include the air ticket and car hire elements; some also follow set itineraries which enables them to offer guaranteed and pre-paid en route accommodation at selected hotels.

Programmes such as Thomas Cook Holidays' *America for the Independent Traveller* allow the flexibility of booking the airline ticket at an advantageous rate and then choosing from a 'menu' of other items, often at a discounted price, such as car hire, hotel coupons (which pre-pay accommodation but do not guarantee

34

availability of rooms) and other extras such as excursions.

USEFUL READING

Most British and international colour-illustrated guidebook series feature a volume on New England. If you are arranging your own accommodation as you travel, a comprehensive guide such as the *AAA Tourbooks* for *Connecticut, Massachusetts and Rhode Island,* for *Maine, New Hampshire and Vermont* and for *New York* or the *Mobil Travel Guide: Northeast,* which covers New England, New York State and all of Eastern Canada, can often be obtained through specialist travel bookshops outside the USA.

Thomas Cook Travellers: Boston and New England and *New York* (both £7.99) are available from bookshops in the UK and in Ireland, Canada, Australia, New Zealand and South Africa.

Books you can buy in New England include:

In and Out of Boston with (or without) Children, by Bernice Chessler, 1992, Globe Pequot Books, Old Saybrook, CT.

Car-Free in Boston: The guide to public transit in Greater Boston and New England, 1995, Association for Public Transport, Boston.

AMC White Mountain Guide, 25th Ed. 1992, Appalachian Mountain Club, Boston. Also AMC's *Maine Mountain Guide,* 1993, and river and canoe guides.

The Berlitz Traveller's Guide to New England, 1993, Berlitz Publishing Co., New York.

Michelin Green Guide to New England, 6th Ed., Michelin Travel Publications, Greenville, SC.

Comprehensive general guides to areas covered in this book as well as maps and more specialised books on New England history, culture and lore may be purchased at **The Globe Corner Bookstore,** *1 School St, Boston, MA 02108; tel: (617) 523-6658 or (800) 358-6013,* or its two branch shops: *500 Boylston St, Boston,* and *28 Church St, Cambridge.*

WEIGHTS AND MEASURES

Officially, the USA is converting to the metric system, in truth little has changed. Some road signs show miles and kilometres. The non-metric US measures are the same as Imperial measures except for fluids, where US gallons and quarts are five-sixths of their Imperial equivalents. Conversions of weights, measurements and temperatures are given on p. 347.

WHAT TO TAKE

Absolutely everything you could ever need is available, so don't worry if you've left anything behind. In fact most US prices will seem low: competition and oversupply keeps them that way. Pharmacies (chemists), also called drug stores, carry a range of products, from medicine to cosmetics to beach balls. Prepare a small first aid kit before you leave home with tried and tested insect repellent, sun-screen cream, and soothing, moisturising lotion. Carry all medicines, glasses, and contraceptives with you, and keep duplicate prescriptions or a letter from your doctor to verify your need for a particular medicine.

Other useful items to bring or buy immediately upon arrival are a water-bottle, sunglasses, a hat or visor with a rim, a Swiss Army pocket knife, a torch (flashlight), a padlock for anchoring luggage, a money belt, a travel adaptor, string for a washing line, an alarm clock and a camera. Those planning to rough it should take a sleeping bag, a sheet liner, and an inflatable travel pillow. Allow a little extra space in your luggage for souvenirs.

35

DRIVING IN NEW ENGLAND

This chapter provides hints and practical advice for those taking to the states' roads, whether in a hire car or RV, or in their own vehicle.

ACCIDENTS AND BREAKDOWNS

Holidays should be trouble-free, yet should a **breakdown** occur, pull off to the side of the road where visibility is good and you are out of the way of traffic. Turn on hazard lights or indicators and, if it is safe, get out and raise the bonnet. Change a tyre only if you're out of the traffic flow.

Dial 911 on any telephone to reach state or local police, fire or medical services. Emergency phone boxes are placed at frequent intervals on some interstate highways. Report your phone number, location, problem and need for first aid. Do not abandon your car and attempt walking for help on the interstates; wait for police patrols to stop.

If involved in a **collision**, stop. Call the state police (if the accident occurs on a state or interstate highway) or local police if there are injuries or physical damage to either vehicle. Show the police and involved driver(s) your driver's licence, car registration, car insurance coverage, address and contact information. Other drivers should provide you with the same information.

Collisions have to be reported to your car hire company. Injuries or death must be reported to the police at the time of the accident. Collisions with injuries, death or accidents resulting in property damage of more than $500 or $1000 (the amount varies between states), must also be reported in writing to the state Depart-

ment of Motor Vehicles (except in Connecticut); reports must be filed within 48 hours in Maine, 72 hours in Vermont, five days in Massachusetts, 10 days in Rhode Island and New York, 15 days in New Hampshire.

Fly-drive travellers should bear in mind the effects of **jet-lag** on driver safety. This can be a very real problem. The best way to minimise it is to spend the first night after arrival in a hotel at the airport or in the city and pick up your hire vehicle the next day, rather than take the car on the road within hours of getting off the plane.

CANADA

Motorists travelling between the USA and Canada must pass through customs at the border, which often involves a vehicle inspection for illegal firearms, drugs or agricultural materials. You will need a copy of your car hire contract showing that use of the vehicle in Canada is authorised by the hire agency.

Visitors are advised to obtain a Non-Resident Inter-Provincial Motor Vehicle Liability Insurance Card before entering Canada. The minimum liability insurance limit is $200,000, except in Québec, where it is $50,000.

Seat belt use is mandatory for drivers and passengers. Possession of radar detection devices is illegal in most Canadian provinces, including Québec. Petrol and motor oil are sold by the litre; petrol grades are the same as those in the USA, but prices are significantly higher, sometimes double the US price. Speed limits and distances are given in kilometres; signs are in English and French.

CAR HIRE

Hiring a car or RV (camper) gives you the freedom of the road with a vehicle you can leave behind after a few weeks. Whether booking a fly-drive package with an agency or making independent arrangements, plan well in advance to ensure you get the type and size of vehicle you require. Free, unlimited mileage is common with cars, less so with RVs.

Sheer volume in airport rental car turnover means that in the USA it's usually cheaper to pick up the vehicle from an airport than from a downtown site and to return it to the airport. A surcharge (called a drop fee) may be levied if you drop the car off in a different location from the place of hire. When considering an RV, ask about one-way and off-season rates.

You will need a valid credit card as security for the vehicle's value. Before you leave the hire agency, ensure that you have all documentation for the hire, that the car registration is in the glove compartment and that you understand how to operate the vehicle. For RVs, also get instruction books and a complete demonstration of all systems and appliances and how they interconnect. Avoid hiring a car that exhibits a hire company name on a window decal, on the fender (bumper) or on licence plate frames. It's advertising for criminal attention.

Car size terminology varies, but general categories range from small and basic to all-frills posh: sub-compact, compact, economy, mid-size or intermediate, full-size or standard, and luxury. Sub-compacts are rarely available. Expect to choose between two- or four-door models. The larger the car, the faster it accelerates and consumes petrol. Some vehicles are equipped with four-wheel drive (4WD), unnecessary except for off-road driving (not covered in this book).

Standard features on US hire cars usually include automatic transmission, air conditioning (especially useful for July and Aug driving) and cruise control, which sets speeds for long-distance highway driving, allowing the driver to take the foot off the accelerator.

DIFFICULT DRIVING

Winter

In winter visibility can be nil due to high winds and blowing snow. Because of slower speed limits and slippery roads, plan on more time to get to and through areas with snow-covered streets. Local radio stations broadcast weather information.

Interstates and other major highways are plowed promptly and kept clear with sand and salt. In areas of Vermont, New Hampshire and Maine where skiing is a major recreational industry, secondary roads are generally cleared quickly to allow skiers to get to the slopes.

If you get stuck while driving in snow, don't spin the wheels; rock the car gently back and forward. Gently pump the brakes when slowing or stopping; if the car skids on slippery roads, turn the steering wheel in the direction of the skid. Snow chains can be useful in mountainous or remote areas, but snow tyres or regular all-season tyres are usually adequate for most winter driving conditions in southern New England.

Useful items are an ice scraper, a small shovel for digging out, warm sleeping bags, blankets and extra clothing in case of long delays. Keep the petrol tank at least half-filled if possible, in case you're stuck for a while.

If you get stuck in a snowstorm: *Stay in the vehicle* until help arrives, put a red flag on the radio antenna or door handle and keep warm with blankets; run the engine and heater only until the car is warm, then turn it off. Open windows a little to give ventilation and prevent carbon monoxide poisoning. *Do not go to sleep.*

Fog and Rain

Fog can occasionally be heavy in low-lying areas and is treacherous to drive in. Turn on the headlights, but use only the low beams to prevent blinding oncoming drivers as well as yourself with reflective glare. Lower your speed; look for reflective road markings to guide you.

Heavy downpours can begin suddenly, making driving dangerous. When travelling on the interstate, it may be advisable to pull over into a rest stop until bad weather passes. The risk of 'hydroplaning' increases on rain-slicked roads and bridges between 35–55 mph; lower your speed when roads are wet, and pump your brakes gradually when slowing or stopping.

DISTANCES

Unlike much of the USA, point-to-point driving distances in New England are not great, except in far-northern Maine. One of the most-travelled routes, from Boston to New York City along the interstate highways, is a 230-mile drive, which takes four to five hours, depending on traffic. Plan on 50 miles per hour *direct* driving time, without stops, longer in cities and in the mountains. Use the sample driving distances and times on p. 345 as guidelines but allow for delays and stops.

DOCUMENTATION

In New England and New York State, your home country's driver's licence is valid. The minimum driving age is 16. Car hire companies may have higher age requirements, typically 21 or over (with additional charges for under-25 drivers).

INFORMATION

Automobile club membership in your home country can be invaluable. AAA clubs provide members of corresponding foreign clubs traveling to North America the reciprocal services that AAA members are eligible to receive abroad. Auto club services include emergency road service and towing; maps, tour guide books and specialist publications; touring services; road and camping information; discounts to attractions and hotels. The rule of thumb is, if it's free at home, it should be free in the USA, too. The AAA may charge for some services, like maps and tour books.

The emergency breakdown road service may not be available to some non-North American club members. For information on reciprocal clubs and services, contact your own club or request *Offices to Serve You Abroad, American Automobile Association, 1000 AAA Drive, Heathrow, FL 32746-5063; tel: (407) 444-7700.* Carry your own club membership card with you at all times.

MOTORCYCLES

If *Easy Rider* is still your idea of America, so be it. Motorcycles provide great mobility and a sense of freedom. Luggage will be limited, however; vast distances can make for days in the saddle; and remember that potholes, gravel, poor roads, dust, smog and sun are a motorcyclist's touring companions. You can hire motorcycles locally by finding a telephone directory listing. Helmets are required by law for both driver and passenger in most states; foreign visitors must have a valid licence to operate a motorcycle in their home country. By custom (and in some states by law), most motorcyclists turn on the headlight even in the daytime to increase their visibility. Cars can share lanes with motorcycles, though this is unsafe and is not to be recommended.

PARKING

Public car parks are indicated by a blue sign showing P with a directional arrow. Prices are sign-posted at the entrance. Some city centre garages charge high rates, but give discounted evening parking for shoppers and theatre-goers who get their sales receipts or tickets validated.

In civic centres, shopping and downtown areas and financial districts, coin-operated parking meters govern kerbside parking. Charges and time limits vary with the locality. Compare garage and meter charges for the most economic choice. Kerbs may be colour-coded: *yellow* is a loading zone, generally for lorry deliveries; *red* is no stopping or parking. No parking is allowed within 10–15 ft (varying between states) of a fire hydrant, near a disabled person pavement ramp, a bus stop area, intersection or crosswalk (pedestrian crossing), on a sidewalk, in front of a driveway or on a state or interstate highway except in emergencies. Precise parking prohibitions vary between states, so you need to be alert to the signs posted.

If you park in violation of times and areas marked on signs nearby, or let the parking meter expire, expect to be issued with a citation – a ticket that states the violation, amount of fine and how to pay it. If you do not pay it, the car hire company may charge the ticket amount (and any penalties) against your credit card. Fines range from a few to several hundred dollars, depending on the violation and the area. Valet parking at garages, hotels, restaurants and events may be pricey, and the parking attendant will expect an additional tip of $1 or $2 when returning the car. The valet attendant will return the car keys with the car.

PETROL

Petrol (gas) is sold in US gallons (roughly four litres per gallon). Prices including tax are shown in cents, for instance, 121.9 (=$1 and 21.9 cents) per gallon. Prices can vary from 100 to 165 cents per gallon, depending on location and on fluctuations in the petroleum market. In areas with many stations there can be strong price competition. Near urban areas, prices tend to be lower. In mountain or remote rural areas, prices can be much higher. Some stations offer full service – filling the petrol tank, washing the windscreen and checking motor oil, usually for about $0.20 more per gallon. Most motorists use the more economical self-service.

Most US cars require unleaded petrol, and due to environmental controls, leaded is not available in most areas. The three fuel grades are regular, super and premium: Use regular petrol unless the car hire company indicates otherwise. A few vehicles use diesel fuel, which is not available at all filling stations.

When petrol stations are more than a few miles apart on interstate highways or other major routes, normally a road sign will state the distance to the next services. Open petrol stations are well lit at night; many chains stay open 24 hours. Most stations accept cash, credit cards and US dollar travellers' cheques. Self-service stations in urban areas usually require advance payment before filling the tank; many have petrol pumps with automated credit-card readers.

POLICE

Police cars signal drivers with flashing blue or red-and-blue lights and sometimes a siren. Respond quickly, but safely, by moving to the side of the road. Roll the driver's side window down but stay in the vehicle unless asked to get out.

39

You have the right to ask an officer – politely – for identification, though it should be shown immediately anyway. Make sure your driver's licence and car registration papers are ready for inspection when requested. Officers normally check computer records for vehicle registration irregularities and the driver for theft, criminal record or other driving violations. If cited, do not argue with the officer, as a bad situation can only get worse.

If a police officer suspects that you are intoxicated, you may be asked to take a 'breathaliser' test to measure your alcohol level from a breathing sample. Some experts claim the tests are inaccurate and can result in a false conviction for drunken driving. Nevertheless, although you have the right to refuse to take the test, refusal will usually result in arrest and the confiscation of your driver's licence. You are legally drunk if your blood alcohol content is 0.08% or higher (0.10% in some states).

The fine for littering the highway is $1000 in some states.

ROAD SIGNS

International symbols are used for directional and warning signs, but many are different from European versions; all language signs are in English, some are bilingual near the border of Canada's French-speaking Québec province. Signs may be white, yellow, green, brown or blue. (A selection of signs is included in the Planning Maps colour section at the back of this book.)

Stop, Yield, Do Not Enter and Wrong Way signs are *red and white*. *Yellow* is for warning or direction indicators. *Orange* is for roadworks or temporary diversions. *Green* indictes highway directions. *Brown* is an alert for parks, campsites, hiking, etc. *Blue* gives non-driving information, such as radio station frequency for traffic or park

information or services in a nearby town. Speed limits and distances are primarily shown in miles, not kilometres. Dual-system signage is occasionally posted in National Parks and near the Canadian border. Speed limit signs are *white* with black letters.

Traffic lights are red, yellow and green. Yellow indicates that the light will turn red; stop, if it is safe to do so, before entering the intersection.

A favourite (and highly illegal) New England trick is to jump the red light; that is, enter the intersection when the signal is yellow and about to turn red. Police can cite you if you enter an intersection and you will not be clear of the intersection before the light turns red.

It is permitted to turn right at a red traffic light – after coming to a full stop – if there is no traffic coming from the left, i.e. as if it were a 'give way' sign, unless there is a sign specifically forbidding it (No Turn on Red), which is common in urban areas. (Note: In New York City, turning on red is *not allowed* unless a sign permits it). A flashing yellow light, or hazard warning, requires drivers to slow down; flashing red means stop, then proceed when safe. A green arrow showing with a red light indicates you may turn in the direction indicated.

Massachusetts has two unusual uses of traffic lights: A flashing green light indicates a pedestrian crossing in use; proceed with caution, prepared for the light to change. Solid red and yellow lights showing together require cars to stop; pedestrians may cross the street.

ROAD SYSTEM

The US Interstate Highway System was built in the 1950s to streamline cargo transportation across the country. Federal funds maintain the interstates, which have limited access and are usually the smoothest roads available. The interstate highways, designated I-(number) in the text, are the straightest and usually the least scenic (and least commercialised) route from point to point. East-west interstate route numbers end in 0, e.g., I-90, I-80; north-south routes numbers end in 5 or occasionally other odd numbers, e.g., I-95, I-91; some three-digit route numbers, e.g., I-295, I-495, circumnavigate large cities; others, e.g., I-195, I-395, connect routes.

In the northeastern USA, some interstate highways are toll roads, including the Massachusetts Turnpike (I-90), the New York State Thruway (I-87 and I-90) and the Maine Turnpike (I-95). Roads called *expressway, highway, turnpike* or *parkway* are usually dual-carriageways with limited access.

Rest areas, common along highways, usually have restrooms with toilets and public telephones and are often landscaped. Picnic tables are provided in scenic areas, and rest stops of historic or geographic interest give explanatory signs and maps.

US, state, county and local routes can range from satin-smooth to pitted, depending on local spending; some are heavily commercialised, others very scenic. Dirt roads indicated on maps or described in this text may be treacherous. Ask locally about road conditions before venturing on. Car hire companies may prohibit driving on unpaved roads.

RULES OF THE ROAD

Lanes and Overtaking

Drive on the right. Vehicles are left-hand drive. The lane on the left is fast; the right is the slowest, and cars enter or leave traffic from the right (unless otherwise shown by signs). Overtake other vehicles on the left side. *Cars may and will pass you on both sides in a multi-lane road.* For many drivers from the UK, this is the most unexpected and confusing feature of US roads. Use your indicators, but don't be surprised if other drivers don't.

Make right turns from the right-hand lane after stopping at stop signs or traffic lights. Turn left from the most left-hand of lanes going in your direction, unless the turn is prohibited by a no-turn sign. Enter bike lanes (where they exist) only if making a right turn.

Overtaking on a two-way road is permitted if the yellow or white line down the centre is broken. Overtake on the left. Highways, especially in mountainous areas or long, narrow stretches of road, have occasional overtaking areas. Overtake only when oncoming traffic is completely visible, and avoid overtaking in fog or rain. Two solid yellow or white lines means no overtaking and no turning unless into a private driveway or for a legal U-turn. On three-lane roads, overtaking is permitted in the middle lane; signs and/or broken lines indicate in which travel direction overtaking is allowed. Driving or parking on pavements is illegal.

Right of way

Main road drivers have the right of way over cars on lesser roads. At the junction of two minor roads, the car to the right has the right of way when two cars arrive at the same time. At a four-way stop, the car arriving first may go first. School buses are usually large and yellow, but occasionally smaller vehicles display a 'School Bus' sign. All vehicles in both directions must stop for school buses displaying flashing red lights. Allow emergency vehicles with sirens to get through traffic by pulling over to the right and stopping.

41

Drivers entering a roundabout (rotary or traffic circle) must give way to cars already in the circle.

Highway Driving

An 'exit' or 'off ramp' is the ramp (slip road) leading off the highway; an 'entrance' or 'on ramp' leads into the highway.

When highway traffic does flow, it flows smoothly and quickly. The speed limit of 55 mph is widely ignored; 70–75 mph is common in the fast (left) lane. The safest speed is to match the general traffic flow in your lane, no matter how fast or slow.

The far-left lane is for the fastest-moving traffic; stay to the right unless overtaking. Signal a lane change and move left, if it is safe to do so, to allow cars entering the highway from the 'on ramp' to merge into traffic. However, don't be surprised if other drivers don't grant the same courtesy. When entering a highway, use your signal and accelerate as you merge into the traffic flow.

Some expressways have carpool lanes for vehicles carrying several passengers; signs will specify the number of passengers required to access those speedier lanes and the effective hours. **Carpool** lanes, also known as diamond lanes or HOV (high occupancy vehicle) lanes, are marked on the roadbed with a white diamond symbol. Special bus lanes will be marked.

Pedestrians

Pedestrians generally have the right-of-way over vehicles – but they may risk their lives asserting that right, especially in Boston. Pedestrians must cross at intersections and crosswalks (pedestrian crossings) and must wait for the 'Walk' at crossings governed by lights; they always have the right of way at these crossings. Some cities and towns may cite pedestrians for jaywalking.

Speed Limits

The standard speed limit on highways is 55 mph but 65 mph or faster is allowed on rural stretches of the interstates. Traffic may flow faster or slower than those limits, but state and local police can ticket anyone going faster than the limit. You may not see the patrols, as radar guns are used from a distance to track speeds and some state police use unmarked vehicles.

Regardless of speed limits, the *Basic Speed Law* allows police to cite motorists for driving faster than is safe. The speed limit is generally 20 mph around schools, 30 mph in residential districts. To go much faster than the speed limits for mountain driving and when taking bends is to court disaster.

Seat Belts

All states *recommend* using seat belts. They are *required* for use by the driver and front-seat passengers in Connecticut, New York, Rhode Island and Massachusetts, by all passengers in Vermont. Children under 4 years old (5 years in Vermont) must ride in an approved child safety seat; older children generally must wear seat belts even where it is not required for adults.

Vehicle Insurance

Requirements for minimum third-party liability insurance coverage vary between states; to ensure you have enough insurance anywhere in New England, obtain coverage of $20,000 for death or injury to any person, $40,000 for death or injury to more than one person and $10,000 for property damage. In New York, minimums are $50,000/$100,000/$5000. (New Hampshire does not require insurance, making it even more necessary for visitors, who risk collision with uninsured drivers.) In practice, considerably more coverage is desirable, and overseas visitors hiring a car are strongly recommended to take out top-up liability cover, such as the Topguard Insurance sold by Thomas Cook in the UK, which covers liability up to $1 million. (This is not to be confused with travel insurance, which provides cover for your own medical expenses – see Travel Essentials p. 23 and p. 26.).

Car hire agencies will also ask the driver to take out collision damage waiver, or CDW (sometimes called loss damage waiver, LDW). Refusing CDW makes the renter personally liable for damage to the vehicle. CDW is strongly recommended for drivers from outside the USA and is often insisted upon as part of a fly-drive package. Sometimes it is paid for when booking the car hire abroad, sometimes it is payable locally on picking up the car. Occasionally special car hire rates will include CDW.

US and Canadian drivers using their own cars should ask their insurance company or auto club if their coverage extends to New England, New York State and Canada and meets their minimum coverage requirements. If not, arrange for insurance before signing the car hire contract.

Vehicle Security

Lock it when you leave, lock it when you're inside, and don't forget the windows. Never leave keys, documents, maps, guidebooks and other tourist paraphernalia in sight. Be mindful of anyone lurking in the back seat or house part of the RV, especially at night. Watch other drivers for strange behaviour, especially if you're persistently followed. Never leave an engine running when you're not in the vehicle. Keep car keys with you at all times. And always park in well-lit areas.

Some New England Driving Terms

Big rig or 18-wheeler A large lorry, usually a tractor pulling one or more trailers.

Boston stop: Slowing at a stop sign, but not stopping.

Bumper-to-bumper: Slow-moving, heavy traffic with little space between cars.

Connector: A minor road connecting two highways.

Divided highway: Dual carriageway

DUI or DWI: Driving Under the Influence of alcohol or drugs, or Driving While Intoxicated, aka Drunken Driving. The blood alcohol limit in New England states varies from 0.08% to 0.10% and is very strictly enforced.

Fender: Bumper

Garage or parking garage: Car park

Gas(oline): Petrol

Grade: Gradient, hill

Highway: Parkway, motorway

Hit-and-run: Illegally leaving the scene after being involved in a collision.

Hood: Bonnet

Motor home: Motor caravan

Ramp: Slip road

Rent: Hire

Rubberneck(er): Slowing down to peer while driving past the scene of an accident.

RV: Motor caravan

Shoulder: Verge

Sidewalk: A UK 'pavement'

Speed bump: A road hump intended to make motorists slow down.

(Stick)shift: Gear lever

Tailgating: Driving too closely to vehicle immediately in front.

Tow truck: Breakdown lorry

Traffic cop: Traffic warden

Truck: Lorry

Trunk: Boot

Windshield: Windscreen

Yield: Give way

43

BACKGROUND
NEW ENGLAND

GEOGRAPHY

New England is the USA's only distinct region, comprising the six northeastern states of Connecticut, Massachusetts, Vermont, Rhode Island, Maine and New Hampshire. It is bordered on the north by Canada, the west by New York, the south by Long Island Sound and the east by the Atlantic Ocean, enclosing a total land area of 66,608 square miles – about 40 per cent the size of California, or two-thirds the United Kingdom.

Geologically, the landscape is old. Its mountains – only a few up north really deserve the name – were long ago worn down in the age of glaciers, which as they receded left some notable coastal islands (including Nantucket and Martha's Vineyard), a multitude of inland lakes, vast deposits of sand and gravel, and a poor, rocky soil. The latter defeated many New England settlers, who gave up and headed west – seeking land, yes; but land with topsoil!

Those too tough – or proud – to leave forged their struggle with the geography into the prototypical Yankee character: hardy, flinty, taciturn, independent and upright.

New England's only great river, the slow, meandering Connecticut, bisects the region from north to south. Its upper reaches form the only natural border between states (Vermont-New Hampshire). Its lower half floods each spring, creating the region's richest farmland, which is still, though to a diminishing

extent, devoted to growing the expensive and delicate tobacco leaves which wrap cigars. The region's highest point is Mt Washington in New Hampshire – at 6288 ft also the tallest peak in the northeastern US; for quite a way inland from the coastline, the land rises no more than a few hundred feet above sea level.

Settlers in the 1600s confronted a vast wilderness, a land of plenty; today virtually all the virgin forest they found has been cleared. Yet, the region is more heavily forested now than then. Travelling northward, the land becomes less populated and more mountainous, with spruce-fir forests predominating. Only in far-northern Maine does the land give way to barren Canadian landscape resembling tundra.

New England is surprisingly far south – Boston lies near the same latitude as Rome. But the weather is generally cool and humid – and very changeable. In northern Maine, the winters are long and cold, with deep snow, the summers short and cool; northern temperatures in July average only in the 70s Fahrenheit, while winter can bring 40–60 days below zero inland, 10–20 days on the coast. Southern New England is more temperate, with summer temperatures generally in the 70s and 80s°F., winter from the 20s–40s°F.

However, short spells of extreme weather are possible: The 'Arctic Express' roaring in from Canada can brings a week or more of near-zero temperatures anywhere in the region. Along the coast, a 'Nor'easter' means blizzard conditions in winter and wind-lashed rain in the warmer seasons. Late summer sends hurricanes up the Eastern Seaboard from the Caribbean, often as far as New England. July and Aug usher in 'dog days' with sweltering humidity and mercury in the high 90s°F.

HISTORY

The earliest known residents of the region, going back at least 3500 years, were Indians of the Algonquian language group, who became known to Europeans by a variety of tribal names: Passamaquoddy, Penobscot and Abenaki in Maine; Pennacook in New Hampshire; Mahican, Pocomtuc and Nipmuc in north-central areas; Massachuset, Wampanoag and Nauset along the south-eastern coast; Narrangansett and Niantic in Rhode Island; Pequot and Mohegan in Connecticut.

These early settlers hunted and gathered food in the forests, cultivated crops in the open areas and fished along the coast. They lived in bands – several of which would make up a tribe, and governed themselves by consensus. Indians of this area generally lived in wigwams, a framework of poles covered with bark, reeds or woven mats, and they dressed in skins and furs, sometimes embroidered with shells and tubular shell beads, called wampum.

The first Europeans to arrive were probably the Norsemen, exploring the coast around 1000 AD from their bases in Greenland. Others fished the waters off New England in the 1500s.

French explorer Samuel de Champlain mapped the coastline in 1605, and Capt John Smith of the Virginia colony explored from Maine to Cape Cod in 1614; it was his journal that named the area New England. Europeans brought the Indians manufactured goods for trade, but also diseases for which they had no resis-

tance; one early epidemic spread through New England killing many Indians in 1616–17, not long before the Pilgrims arrived.

COLONIAL PERIOD

The first permanent English settlement of North America was at Virginia in 1607. Indeed, it was to that warmer climate that the Pilgrims were heading when they left England seeking religious freedom in 1620. The Pilgrims were a group of separatists from the Church of England who practiced congregational self-government. Many escaped persecution to Holland, where they planned the voyage to the New World. On receiving royal permission to start a colony, they set sail for Virginia in Sept 1620 aboard the *Mayflower*. They were blown off course by storms and landed instead on 21 Nov at the tip of Cape Cod, anchoring in Provincetown's sheltering harbour. Here, lacking a charter to settle in New England, they drew up the Mayflower Compact, an agreement on governing their group (and restricting those who disagreed).

A month later, the 102 settlers moved across the bay to more hospitable lands at Plymouth, yet the first winter was so harsh that half the settlers died. In the spring, with help from the Wampanoag Indians and under the leadership of Gov. William Bradford and Capt Myles Standish, they began to thrive. Following the first harvest in 1621, colonists and Indians held a three-day feast to celebrate their bounty; Americans mark this event each year as Thanksgiving, on the fourth Thursday in Nov.

Other groups of English settlers arrived to the north, mainly in Salem. These were not separatists, but Puritans, who wanted to reform the church from within. In 1629, granted a charter by Charles I to

45

trade and colonise between the Charles and Merrimack rivers, they founded the Massachusetts Bay Company with John Winthrop as governor. In 1630, they acquired a small peninsula of land at the mouth of the Charles River, known by the Indians as Shawmut and occupied by a lone white man, the Rev. William Blackstone; this became Boston.

The Puritans came to the New World to practise religious freedom – but not to grant it to others. It wasn't long before groups, tired of their strict theocracy, broke away. In the 1630s, expelled from Salem, Roger Williams took his followers to Rhode Island, and Thomas Hooker left Cambridge for Hartford and founded Connecticut. In 1692, the religious fervor of Salem was so intense that charges of witchcraft levelled at several young women led to the imprisonment of 150 people and the hanging of 19.

The Puritans' excesses led the crown to revoke their charter. Following the Glorious Revolution in England, William and Mary granted a new charter in 1691 to the Province of Massachusetts Bay, which included the 'Old Colony' of Plymouth and the territory of Maine. Theocracy was ended, and the power of taxation was given to the provincial legislature.

During the 1600s, there was increasing friction between Indians and waves of English immigrants, who delved deeper into the wilderness to settle, resulting in the devastating King Philip's War of 1675–76. Massasoit, the grand sachem, or inter-tribal chief, of the Wampanoags, had maintained peace and trade with the early settlers. He visited the Pilgrims at Plymouth in 1621 and shared Indian ways of planting and fishing. The peace was first broken with the Pequot War of 1637, in which the Puritans and rival bands decimated that tribe.

After Massasoit died in 1661, his son Metacom (known as King Philip) brought most of the New England tribes together into an alliance. The execution of three Wampanoags sparked bloodshed, which led to Indian raids on frontier settlements in Massachusetts, Connecticut and Rhode Island, followed by retaliation on Indian villages by the colonial militia.

The Indians were winning until their crops were destroyed in spring 1676; Philip died that Aug. The war left 600 settlers and 3000 Indians dead. Fifty towns were raided, a dozen destroyed, but the Indians got the worst of it: Whole villages were killed, tribes wiped out and survivors driven off their land, leaving southern New England to the Europeans.

REVOLUTION

The late 1700s was a time of increasing conflict between the crown and its subjects – many by now American born – in Massachusetts and the other colonies. Underlying that conflict was the 1689–1765 struggle for empire between Britain and France; the American phase included the French and Indian War (1754–63), which resulted in Britain's annexation of Canada.

Following its costly victory over France, Britain stepped up enforcement of trade regulations and sought to raise new revenues, with first the 1764 Sugar Act, then the unpopular 1765 Stamp Act, which levied a tax on newspapers, pamphlets and commercial and legal documents.

In Boston, Samuel Adams, John Hancock and James Otis formed committees of correspondence to encourage protest; boycotts in Philadelphia and New York led to repeal of the acts.

However, in 1767 the Townshend Acts imposed a new set of levies on imports, which sparked further protests and anti-British sentiment, culminating on 5 Mar 1770 in the so-called Boston Massacre, in which five colonists were shot dead by soldiers facing a taunting mob. A period of calm followed until 1773, when the Tea Act and its related tax sparked the famous Boston Tea Party. King George III responded by closing Boston's port and instituting other controls, including altering the 1691 provincial charter to replace the elected governing council with an appointed one. The Massachusetts legislature countered by remaking itself into an independent 'provincial congress', and the several colonies together formed a Continental Congress at Philadelphia in 1774, whose original aim was to pressure Britain to redress the grievances and restore colonial autonomy.

However, events at Lexington and Concord led the colonies to war against Mother England and eventually independence (see feature box pp. 50–51).

THE STATES

CONNECTICUT

Only 90 miles long by 55 miles wide – Connecticut is the third smallest state in the Union, with an area of only 4872 square miles. Yet it's one of the most densely populated states, with 3.2 million people, and has one of the highest incomes per capita.

Dinosaurs walked the muddy plains during the Jurassic period, 185 million years ago, leaving their fossilised footprints (now a tourist attraction) in Rocky Hill.

By the time Europeans arrived, Indians were well settled, comprising about 16 separate tribes with 5000–7000 members. History records that relations were good between Indians and the early English set-

tlers. Of course, by then Massachusetts Puritans aided by rival Indians had already wiped out 'the most warlike' tribe in the Pequot War of 1637, America's first massacre of native peoples. Today, Indian place names are ubiquitous; 'Connecticut' itself means 'land beside the long tidal river'.

Puritans who found Boston 'too liberal' came to the Connecticut River's valley in 1633, founding Windsor, Wethersfield and Hartford, and colonised the coast by 1638. The Fundamental Orders of 1639, which organised Connecticut Colony, is considered the world's first written constitution, thus giving the state its nickname, Constitution State.

Later, its 1662 royal charter was the subject of intrigue, when the governor tried to seize it; the document was hidden in an oak tree, memorialised now as the Charter Oak. Connecticut was one of the 13 original states.

Today, the state has an ethnically diverse population, and great extremes of rich and poor. The big cities of Bridgeport (pop. 141,000), New Haven (home of Yale University) and even Hartford, the capital, have some depressing, rundown neighbourhoods best avoided by outsiders. In contrast are comfortable Fairfield County's white-collar dormitory towns for New York City and the affluent suburban belt ringing Hartford. The state's easternmost third, mostly rural, has some of New England's prettiest countryside.

Manufacturing has been the key to the state's wealth for two centuries. In New Haven in 1794, Yale-educated Eli Whitney invented the cotton gin, which revolutionised textile mills. He later developed the concept of mass production in his Hamden musket factory. The principle of interchangeable parts was also used in clockmaking, another Connecticut prod-

47

uct. At places likeWaterbury, brassware, hats and fine silver built the state's economy. Today. its mainstays are defence menufacuring (aircraft engines, helicopters, submarines and firearms) and insurance.

In the 1970s, the few remaining Mashantucket Pequots sparked the tribe back to life. They won recognition from the US government (thus gaining sovereignty) in 1983 and founded Foxwoods casino, which has become a 1990s economic powerhouse in southeastern Connecticut.

MAINE

Jutting out into the North Atlantic in the northeastern corner of the US, Mainers are the first Americans to see the sunrise each day. Their state is New England's largest, measuring 330 miles by 210 miles at the longest and widest points – indeed, its 33,265 square miles roughly equal the other five states combined. Yet Maine is comparatively small, ranking 39th among the 50 states. With only 1.2 million people, it's the most sparsely populated state east of the Mississippi River – and among the poorest and least developed.

Archaeologists have found remnants showing that Stone Age people lived in Maine. Later, along with neighbouring Vermont, New Hampshire and eastern Canada, Maine became home to as many as 20 tribes of a branch of the Algonquian nation, known as the Abenaki ('living at the sunrise'). When Giovanni da Verrazzano made the first recorded exploration along Maine's rocky 3,500-mile coast in 1524, the Abenakis he encountered had already seen Europeans. By 1630, there were permanent English settlers on Monhegan Island, the Isles of Shoals and other coastal sites; in 1635, the territory was granted to Sir Ferdinando

Gorges, 'Lord of New England'. In the mid-1600s, it came under the charter of Massachusetts Bay.

The first naval encounter of the American Revolution occurred 12 June 1775 in Machias, when townspeople captured the armed British schooner *Margaretta.* That same year, the British burned Falmouth (now Portland), and Col Benedict Arnold led an expedition up the Kennebec River and through the northern woods in an unsuccessful attempt to capture Québec and bring the French and Indians into the Revolution. Maine separated from Massachusetts and was admitted to the Union as the 23rd state in 1820.

Today, nearly 90 percent of Maine's land is forested, much of it with evergreens, lending the nickname Pine Tree State. The vast north woods, largely controlled by lumber companies, offers little access, save on narrow logging roads, and few people. Hardy visitors can, however, hunt and fish, observe moose and other wildlife, and shoot the rapids in the Allagash wilderness. Timber for paper and paper products remains the largest industry, with trade, tourism and service industries out pacing such historical mainstays as fishing, shipbuilding, mining and agriculture.

The state capital is upstate at tiny Augusta, pop. 21,000, but half the population lives in the four counties of the southwestern tip, from Portland, pop. 64,000, down to the New Hampshire border. Most tourists hug the coastline, exploring the little villages 'down east', camping amid pine forests and boating offshore.

MASSACHUSETTS

New England's most populous state, with 6 million of the region's 13 million people, is quite small in area. At 8284 square miles, it is only the fourth largest state in New

48

England and 45th among the 50 states, while ranking 11th in the US in terms of population.

What it lacks in size, however, Massachusetts makes up for in power and impact. America's 'Cradle of Liberty' is also the birthplace of America's Industrial Revolution and home of its first schools, Boston Latin School (1635) and Harvard College (1636).

Capt John Smith in 1614 named the area for the Massachuset tribe (wiped out by smallpox in 1633), who lived 'near the great hill' – believed to be Blue Hill, south of Boston. Following the Revolution (see feature box), Massachusetts was a centre of fishing and trade, with ships out of Boston and Salem opening trade routes to China. When whale oil and baleen were paramount, Nantucket and later New Bedford, after 1840, were the world's whaling centres.

Francis Cabot Lowell opened the first US textile mill in 1814 in Waltham, then applied English mill techniques to the new mill city at Lowell; with mills at Lawrence, Chicopee, Fall River and New Bedford, Massachusetts was a leader in the textiles market, which dominated the economy until its collapse in the 1920s. Later, the boot and shoe industry rose to prominence, then machinery and tools. Since World War II, electronics and science-oriented industries (especially biotech in the 1990s) have led the economy.

The Bay State also has a rich literary tradition, beginning with the poetry of Anne Bradstreet and Jonathan Edwards in colonial times. In Concord from 1830–1855 lived a community of writers identified by their belief in an idealistic system of thought called Transcendentalism. Among their circle were Ralph Waldo Emerson, Henry David Thoreau, Margaret Fuller and Bronson Alcott.

Other literary giants have included Herman Melville, Henry Wadsworth Longfellow, Emily Dickinson, Horatio Alger, poet Robert Lowell and many more, up to novelist John Updike today.

New England's only really big city is the Massachusetts capital, Boston, with a modest population of 574,000, although the metropolitan area has a hefty 3 million.

While the state is very built up, a 30-minute drive from Boston Common will nevertheless yield a quiet walk in the woods or a day at the beach. A three-hour drive brings you to the Berkshires, where nature and culture pleasantly coexist.

NEW HAMPSHIRE

Slightly smaller than Vermont at 9297 square miles, but with twice the population (1.1 million), New Hampshire has a bit of a split personality. Despite its agricultural, rural image, it is among the most industrialised states in the US. Although ugly commercialism mars many roadside landscapes, the Granite State's small towns are rich in charm and its natural areas offer much untarnished beauty.

New Hampshire was originally the home of two distinct tribal groups, both of the Algonquian nation. Along the coast were the Nashaway, Piscataqua, Squamscot and others (whose Anglicised place names exist today). To the north were Western Abenaki, among them the Amoskeag, Pennacook, Winnepesaukee, the Pequacket and Sokoki. By 1725, depleted by war and disease, the survivors had withdrawn north into Canada. Now New Hampshire is a bastion of White Anglo-Saxon Protestants (WASPs), with French Canadians the second largest ethnic group; African-Americans account for less than one percent, Asians even fewer.

English settlement began in 1623 at Portsmouth and Dover under the author-

49

New England's role in the American Revolution

5 March 1770: Boston, Mass. – Angry over the presence of British troops in the city, a mob converged on the **Customs House** and became violent. Soldiers opened fire killing five people. Known as the **Boston Massacre**, the incident is marked by a circle of cobblestones in front of what is now the **Old State House**. The five casualties lie buried in Boston's **Old Granary Burying Ground**.

16 Dec 1773: Boston – Under cover of night, townsmen dressed as Indians rowed out to three ships in Boston Harbor and dumped their cargo of tea overboard. This **Boston Tea Party** prevented the East India Company from selling the tea at a price that undercut American importers, and thus aided the longstanding protest against a tax on tea.

18 Apr 1775: Boston to Concord, Mass. – With signal lanterns hung in Boston's **Old North Church**, two late-night riders set out to warn Patriot leaders of British troop movements. Paul Revere, a silversmith who had been one of the anonymous 'Indians' of the BostonTea Party, rowed across the river to Charlestown, then went on horseback through Medford to Lexington. His compatriot William Dawes rode off the then tiny peninsula of Boston via Boston Neck (now *Washington St*) and through Cambridge.

Both messengers were captured by the British, but not before heading off the arrest of rebel leaders John Hancock and Samuel Adams, alerting 'every Middlesex village and farm' to the British advance and recruiting Dr Samuel Prescott to ride onward to Concord, where the militia kept its military stores.

Revere, a longtime activist in the resistance to British rule, won his place in history when Henry Wadsworth Longfellow penned the 1861 poem which begins, 'Listen, my children and you shall hear/ Of the midnight ride of Paul Revere...'

19 Apr 1775: Lexington, Mass. – Maj Gen Thomas Gage, ordered to act vigorously against the rebels, sent Lt Col Francis Smith with 700 British regulars to destroy military supplies at **Concord** and arrest the Patriot leaders.

An advance guard led by Maj John Pitcarn ran across 77 colonial Minutemen, led by Capt Jonas Parker, who had been warned by Revere and Dawes the previous night. The resulting skirmish on **Lexington Green** left eight Americans dead, ten wounded. One redcoat was wounded.

19 Apr 1775: Concord, Mass. – Later the same day, Lt Col Smith carried out his mission to destroy the supplies at Concord. But a covering party was confronted by 350 Minutemen at the **North Bridge**, where three regulars were killed and eight wounded. Ralph Waldo Emerson in 1837 immortalised that confrontation as 'the shot heard around the world'.

The battles – actually brief skirmishes – at Lexington and Concord aroused thousands of Massachusetts 'Patriots', who pursued and harassed the British troops all the way back to Boston. The day is marked with an official holiday, **Patriots Day**, in Massachusetts and Maine.

10 May 1775: Ticonderoga, N.Y. – Ethan Allen and his 83 Green Mountain Boys captured the British garrison at Fort Ticonderoga, without firing a shot. The next day Crown

Point, N.Y., was captured, giving the Americans control of **Lake Champlain** and an entry point to Canada. Leading the rebels with Allen was Benedict Arnold, who later betrayed the Patriot's cause, becoming a traitor in US history, a hero to Britain.

25 May 1775: Boston – Gen Gage received reinforcements from England as Maj Gens William Howe, John Burgoyne and Henry Clinton arrived aboard the frigate Cerberus. However, Gage's forces still numbered only 6000, while 7500 Americans had enlisted against them.

17 June 1775: Charlestown, Mass. – The misnamed **Battle of Bunker Hill**, which actually took place on nearby Breed's Hill, was a victory for the British, though a Pyrrhic one. Gen William Howe, attempting to break the seige of Boston, where his troops had been surrounded since the rout on 19 April, led about 2200 regulars against a force of as many as 4000 Americans, commanded by Col. William Prescott, who ordered his men, who were short of ammunition 'Don't fire until you see the whites of their eyes'. Howe suffered 100 casualties to the Americans' 400 while gaining an outpost of little value.

3 July 1775: Cambridge, Mass. – Gen George Washington and other officers, appointed earlier by the Continental Congress, took command of the new Continental Army in a ceremony on **Cambridge Common**.

30 Dec 1775: Québec City, Canada – About 1000 Americans attempting to invade Canada were defeated by 1200 British troops led by Guy Carleton. More than half the Americans were killed, wounded or captured and the American leader, Brig Gen Richard Montgomery, later died of his wounds. The British regained control of an invasion route into New York, and the colonials abandoned their ambitions to conquer the north.

4 March 1776: Dorchester, Mass. – Captured cannons and supplies were hauled from Fort Ticonderoga, N.Y., by Col Henry Knox's men and placed on Dorchester Heights, where they threatened British troop ships in Boston Harbor.

17 March 1776: Boston – Gen William Howe evacuated British troops from Boston and relocated them to Halifax, Nova Scotia. The day is still marked as **Evacuation Day** and is an official holiday in Suffolk County.

The permanent British abandonment of Boston concluded the early stage of the American Revolution. The colonists' resolve to separate from England became official with the **Declaration of Independence** in Philadelphia on 4 July 1776.

After that date, the hard fighting of the revolution began. New England military units played a major role in the struggle (and British troops remained in Newport R.I.), though no major battles took place on New England soil.

The closest were the **Battle of Bennington**, fought in New York 4 miles northwest of Bennington, Vt., on 16 Dec 1777, and the **Battle of Freeman's Farm** at Saragota, N.Y., on 7 Oct 1777.

Major battles were fought in New Jersey, Pennsylvania, New York, North and South Carolina, in the 'West' (present-day Illinois and Indiana) and at sea. The Revolution ended when Lord Cornwallis surrendered to George Washington after the Battle of Yorktown in Virginia on 19 Oct 1781.

The British crown accepted **American Independence** in a peace treaty signed in Paris in 1783.

ity of the Council for New England in London; their purpose was to fish and trade for furs with the Indians. Exeter and Hampton were settled in 1638–39 by ministers from Massachusetts, and the name New Hampshire was in use for the area between the Piscataqua and Merrimack rivers by 1629.

In the Revolutionary period, unrest boiled over 14 Dec 1774, when an armed mob of 400 stormed Fort William and Mary in Portsmouth harbour and carried away first the gunpowder, then on the next night the fort's 16 cannons, 60 muskets and other stores. The following summer, New Hampshire's Minutemen joined the Battle of Bunker Hill after hearing of the skirmishes at Lexington and Concord. New Hampshire's provincial congress voted unanimously for independence 19 days before the Declaration of Independence on 4 July 1776.

New Hampshire is known for its staunch conservatism and Yankee temperament, expressed in the state motto, 'Live Free or Die', which is emblazoned on auto licence plates.

Frugality in government is matched with a resistance to broad-based income and sales taxes and costly government services. Instead, revenues are raised with a lottery, state liquor sales, a hefty business profits tax, licence fees and – as visitors learn – taxes on meals, lodgings and petrol.

One of the smallest US states in both size (44th) and population (42nd), New Hampshire has only moderate suburban sprawl, mostly along the Massachusetts border. The state capital, Concord, has only 36,000 people; the biggest city, Manchester, only 100,000. The state relies heavily on its manufacturing, with the paper industry in the north country a strong second, plus granite quarries, dairy farms and business services. The moun-

tains, forests and 1,300 lakes, much more than the 18-mile coastline, are a lucrative tourist draw, summer and winter.

RHODE ISLAND

'Little Rhody', the smallest state in the Union, is only 48 miles long by 37 miles wide. With one million people on 1212 square miles – two-thirds of which are farm, forest or undeveloped land – Rhode Island is the second most densely populated US state. Yet, even its biggest city, Providence, a cultural centre as well as state capital, is faulted more for its sleepiness than its bustle. Low-lying (the highest point is only 812 ft above sea level) and heavily suburbanised, Rhode Island takes a seaward aspect, calling itself Ocean State for its pricey water frontage and miles of nice beaches.

The west side of Narragansett Bay and its islands were originally inhabited by Indians of the same name (also given to the state's best surfing beach and a brand of beer), while the eastern shore was home to the Wampanoags, with Niantics along the southern coast and Nipmucs to the northwest. In 1524, it was visited by Giovanni da Verrazzano, who compared present-day Block Island to Rhodes, inadvertently giving a name to the area and the state, which comprises many islands, but is not itself an island.

European settlement started in 1636 with English clergyman Roger Williams, who was kicked out of Massachusetts Bay Colony by the Puritans for his 'dangerous' religious views. Leading his flock southward, Williams bought a sizable piece of land from the Indians and founded Providence Plantation, later obtaining a royal charter for the colony, which became a haven of religious freedom for Anabaptists, Quakers and others. Today, the state is still officially called The State of

Rhode Island and Providence Plantations. In the Revolution, Rhode Island was the first colony to renounce its allegiance to King George III, on 4 May 1776. British troops occupied Newport later that year and remained until 1779, despite a combined French-American effort to oust them. Rhode Island was one of the 13 original states.

Rhode Island's economy was built on agriculture, but also on its maritime trade, which for a time involved the colony in the infamous 'triangular trade' of importing molasses from the Caribbean, distilling it into rum and bartering the rum for slaves from Africa. Some slaves even laboured on the plantations of southern Rhode Island. After the Revolution, Pawtucket Falls supplied power for mills in the textile industry, which fed into the China trade. Cotton kept Rhode Island prosperous into the 1920s, then US Navy bases into the 1970s. Today, important art and culinary schools and ivy-league Brown University help give Providence a vibrant atmosphere.

A wide-ranging ethnic mix, from Italian, Jewish, Portuguese to Eastern Europeans, Hispano-Americans and Southeast Asians, make the state a cultural melting pot.

VERMONT

New England's only landlocked state takes its name from the French words, *vert mont*, for the Green Mountains that form its spine. With only 9614 square miles of land and 560,000 people (fewer than the city of Boston), Vermont is among the smallest US states in both area (43rd) and population (48th).

Vermonters joke that they have 'more cows than people'. Yet, the state's bucolic charm, untrampled natural beauty and well-developed recreational attractions (including some of the best skiing in the eastern US) draw many tourists.

The Abenaki Indians, Vermont's first inhabitants, were driven out in the 16th century by the Iroquois, who used the area as a hunting ground. In 1609, French explorer Samuel de Champlain sailed into the huge lake (now the border with New York State) and gave it his name, but it wasn't until 1666 that the French established Fort Ste Anne on Lake Champlain's Isle de la Motte. Not until 1724 did English settlers arrive, setting up Fort Dummer in the Connecticut River Valley near Brattleboro. British success in the French and Indian War of 1754–63 brought even more settlers.

News in 1775 of Lexington and Concord unified hostile factions in New York and Vermont against the Crown, and the outlaw group of Ethan Allen and the Green Mountain Boys took Fort Ticondera from the British (see feature box).

Briefly an independent republic after the Revolution, Vermont joined the Union in 1791 as the 14th state.

The Green Mountain State today is about 60 percent forested and mostly rural. It's also quite mountainous – except along the Connecticut River Valley to the east and Lake Champlain to the west, where the elevation dips to only 95 ft – however, the highest peak, Mt. Mansfield, which contains a ski resort, is a mere 4393 ft.

The state's biggest city Burlington, numbers only 39,000 (131,000 in the metrpolitan area), and the capital, Montpelier, only 8200. Vermont hides its manufacturing (machines, tools, electrical and computer equipment) and its mining (marble) well. To all eyes, its a land of dairy farms, Christmas trees and maple sugaring, with a hefty component of outdoor tourism.

53

TOURING ITINERARIES

Much of the pleasure of a driving holiday lies in tailoring your itinerary to match your tastes and interests. By dividing New England into recommended routes, this book is intended to make it easy and pleasurable to plan your ideal tour. By linking several of our routes you can create a trip that will suit your tastes, and you can be confident of following a tried and tested path that introduces you to the best that the route has to offer.

This chapter begins with some practical advice on tour planning, followed by two ready-made itineraries designed to show you as much as possible of New England's variety in a two- or three-week trip. Feel free to vary our suggestions, using the full range of information contained in the route descriptions. The remaining pages list features of New England that you can use to create a self-planned 'themed' tour using the routes noted.

PRACTICAL HINTS

Here are a few tips to make practicable routes easier to plan and more fun to follow:

1. Use the most detailed maps available. The colour map section at the end of this book is useful for planning itineraries and will enable you to follow the routes while driving, but a more detailed road map will be invaluable, especially if you intend to vary the routes we have recommended. If you

haven't already acquired a good road map or atlas, stop at the nearest AAA office as soon as possible after arriving in New England and pick up maps for the areas you will be touring. For even more detail, buy the bound or folding maps published by Arrow or DeLorme and sold at major booksellers.

2. Don't schedule too much driving each day. Allow a conservative 50 miles (80 km) per hour of highway driving, 40 miles (64 km) each hour on secondary roads to allow for stretch breaks and the inevitable unplanned stops. It's better to have more time to explore along the way than be pressed to arrive by mealtime each evening. Each route description in this book gives information not only about mileage but also likely driving times.

3. Check weather and road reports. Most paved roads are open all year, but a few secondary roads through mountain passes, such as Rte 108 through Smugglers Notch, Vt., close in winter. Unusually heavy snow or seasonal flooding can occasionally close roads. Road construction and heavy traffic around large cities are the most common obstacles.

4. Unless accommodation is pre-booked, plan to arrive each night with enough time to find a place to sleep. In some areas, particularly Boston, New York City, Acadia National Park and small towns with few motels, advance bookings are essential.

5. Build in time at the end of the trip to get back to the departure city (usually Boston or New York) the day before a scheduled flight home. Airlines don't hold entire planes for one car-load of late arrivals, and passengers travelling on cheap fares who miss a flight may be faced with buying a new ticket home – at full price.

6. Give serendipity a chance by not planning in too much detail. Allow time to spend an extra few hours – or an extra day – in some unexpected gem of a town or to turn down an interesting side road. Anyone who wants their days preplanned in 15-minute increments will be happier on a fully escorted package coach tour than a self-drive holiday.

THE BEST OF NEW ENGLAND

The following tours start and end in Boston, but since they're circular, can be picked up in New York City, which is the region's largest international port of entry, or any other convenient spot.

The tours combine many recommended routes, with a few digressions and short-cuts added. Suggested overnight stops are in **bold type.** Adapt the tours freely or use the same cut-and-paste idea to combine several routes for a more personal itinerary.

14 DAYS

For those who want (or need) to 'do' New England in one whirlwind bout of driving. It *can* be done, but allow a few days at home to recover before returning to work.

Day 1: **Boston** (p. 60).

Day 2: Boston to Lexington and Concord and back to **Boston** (West of Boston, p. 86).

Day 3: Boston to Plymouth to Sandwich to the Cape Cod National Seashore at **Orleans** (Boston–Cape Cod, p. 94; Cape Cod, p. 132).

Day 4: Cape Cod to New Bedford to **Newport** (Cape Cod, p. 132; Cape Cod–Newport, p. 152; Newport, p. 158).

Day 5: Newport to Mystic to **New York City** (Newport–New York, p. 168).

Day 6: **New York City** (pp. 286).

Day 7: New York to Litchfield to Stockbridge and **Lenox** (New York City–Lenox, p. 324; Lenox and the Berkshires, p. 192; Berkshires Loop, p. 200).

Day 8: Lenox to Williamstown to Bennington, then meandering in a northerly loop through the Green Mountains or directly east to **Brattleboro** (Lenox and the Berkshires, p. 192; Boston–Lenox, p. 112; Green Mountains Loop, p. 204).

Day 9: Brattleboro to Hanover to **North Woodstock-Lincoln** in the White Mountains (Brattleboro–Hanover, p. 211; Portland to New Hampshire Loop, p. 259; White Mountains, p. 222).

Day 10: **White Mountains** and White Mountains Circuit, pp. 222–231.

Day 11: Lincoln to Lake Winnepesaukee to Sebago Lakes to **Portland** (Portland–New Hampshire Loop, p. 268).

Day 12: Portland northward to Freeport to Camden/Rockport and back to **Portland** (Portland, p. 243; Portland– Bar Harbor, p. 249).

Day 13: Portland southward to Kennebunkport and Ogunquit to Kittery and **Portsmouth** (Boston–Portland, p. 124).

Day 14: Portsmouth to Newburyport to Gloucester to **Boston** (Boston's North Shore, p. 76).

21 DAYS

Three weeks is a more realistic time frame

55

to see most of New England. If possible, add another week to see the more remote and less travelled northern reaches of Vermont and Maine, to wander farther afield in New York State (including Niagara Falls or Long Island) or to visit Québec and Montréal.

Day 1: **Boston** (p. 60).

Day 2: **Boston.**

Day 3: Boston to Lexington and Concord and back to **Boston** (West of Boston, p. 86).

Day 4: Boston to Plymouth to Sandwich to **Harwich** or **Orleans** on Cape Cod (Boston–Cape Cod, p. 94; Cape Cod, p. 132).

Day 5: Cape Cod circuit north to Cape Cod National Seashore and Province-town, south to Chatham, west to **Hyannis** or **Falmouth** (Cape Cod, p. 132).

Day 6: Ferry from Hyannis to **Nantucket** or Falmouth to **Martha's Vineyard** (Nantucket, p. 148; Martha's Vineyard, p. 144).

Day 7: Ferry back to Cape Cod, drive to New Bedford and **Newport** (Cape Cod–Newport, p. 152; Newport, p. 158).

Day 8: From Newport along shores of Narragansett Bay – north to Bristol and Providence, then south to Warwick and Narragansett – and on to **Mystic** (Newport, p. 158; Boston–Newport, p. 118; Newport–New York, p. 168).

Day 9: Mystic to Old Saybrook and Essex, then to New Haven and **New York City** (Newport–New York; side-track to Essex in Hartford chapter, p. 178).

Day 10: **New York City** (p. 286).

Day 11: New York to Hartford, then via Rte 44 and Rte 202 to Litchfield, then to **Lenox** (New York–Hartford, p. 319; New York–Lenox, p. 324; Lenox and the Berkshires, p. 192; Berkshires Loop, p. 200).

Day 12: Lenox to Williamstown to Bennington, meandering through the **Green Mountains** in southern Vermont (Boston–Lenox, p. 112; Green Mountains Loop, p. 204).

Day 13: From Middlebury in the Green Mountains via Rte 7 to Burlington and **Lake Champlain** (p. 232).

Day 14: Burlington to Montpelier to St. Johnsbury to Littleton, then via I-93 to **North Woodstock-Lincoln** in the White Mountains (Hanover–Burlington, p. 216; North-east Kingdom Loop, p. 238).

Day 15: **White Mountains** and White Mountains Circuit (p. 222–p. 231).

Day 16: White Mountains via I-93 to Littleton, then north and west into Maine to **Rangeley** (Portland–New Hampshire Loop, p. 259).

Day 17: Rangeley via Rte 4 to Farmington, then Rte 2 to Bangor and on to Bar Harbor and **Acadia** (p. 274).

Day 18: **Acadia.**

Day 19: From Acadia south along to the coast to **Portland** (Portland–Bar Harbor, p. 249).

Day 20: Portland to Kennebunkport to Ogunquit to Kittery to **Portsmouth** (Boston–Portland, p. 124).

Day 21: Boston's North Shore (p. 76) to **Boston.**

THE MAJOR CITIES

Small towns and countryside define the New England experience far more than do big cities. Indeed, only Boston (ranked 20th) is among the 100 largest US cities, although top-ranked New York City lies conveniently nearby. New England's major cities are of the medium-to-small variety, and they vary widely in character and appeal.

The cities are listed in alphabetical order, identifying the recommended routes from this book that lead to and from them. By studying the chapters that describe the cities in full (also cross-referenced below) and the other recommended routes you can omit those places that don't interest you and mix in some non-city routes for a taste of forest, mountain or coastal scenery.

BOSTON

History and culture are the main attraction in New England's only big city (pop. 574,000). Many visitors also proclaim it the most European of US cities. That's partly because of its older, red-brick architecture, its narrow streets and lovely parks and green spaces, but also because it is so compact and 'walkable' – unlike the rest of automobile-dominated America.

The Freedom Trail as well as other historical sites and museums in Boston and neighbouring Cambridge provide touchstones for the beginnings of the American Revolution and many other important points in the nation's political, literary, scientific and intellectual development (Boston, p. 60; West of Boston, p. 86).

BURLINGTON

Only by Vermont standards could the nation's 761st-largest city, Burlington (pop. 39,000), be called 'major'. This pleasant, thriving small city on the shores of Lake Champlain offers a fine hub for exploring the region's prodigious natural charms (Burlington and Lake Champlain, p. 232; New York City–Burlington, p. 311; Hanover–Burlington, p. 216).

HARTFORD

Capital of Connecticut as well as of the US insurance industry, Hartford is a somewhat neglected urban island in a sea of suburbs. A top-notch art museum, the Wadsworth Atheneum, and the homes of authors Mark Twain and Harriet Beecher Stowe

are the main attractions in this medium-sized (pop. 140,000) city, which gives access to some lovely and far more interesting areas in the hinterlands (Hartford, p. 178; Boston–Hartford, p. 107; New York–Hartford, p. 319).

NEW YORK CITY

Leaving quiet New England to visit the largest US city (pop. 7.3 million), you can get a jolt of big-city adrenalin, 24 hours a day.

Though US television beams a California-based view of America abroad, the Big Apple is still the US business and cultural capital. You name it – theatre, art, museums, restaurants, shopping, traffic, even crime – New York is where it's at: bigger, better, classier, costlier than anywhere else (Newport–New York, p. 168; New York City, p. 286).

PORTLAND

Maine's only sizeable city (pop. 64,000) puts on no big-city airs – and that's its charm. This old sea dog – Portland was a major Victorian shipping and shipbuilding centre – bristles with refurbished shops, taverns and restaurants in the Old Port area.

Nightlife is low-key and folksy. Meanwhile, the islands of Casco Bay and the forests are only minutes away (Portland, p. 243; Boston–Portland, p. 124; Portland–Bar Harbor, p. 249).

PROVIDENCE

A college town and business centre as well as capital of the state of Rhode Island, this medium-sized city (pop. 160,000) has a vibrant art, theatre and cultural scene. It's conveniently close to historic mill towns, factory outlet shopping and beachside attractions along Narragansett Bay (Boston–Newport, p. 118).

TOP HISTORIC SIGHTS

Boston National Historical Park and the **Freedom Trail**, *Boston; tel: (617) 242-5642.* A 3-mile walking tour through Boston's centre gives visitors a glimpse of 350 years of history. The federal government administers seven of the Freedom Trail's sites plus the monument at Dorchester Heights, where cannons from Fort Ticonderoga convinced British troops to leave Boston in 1776 (Boston, p. 60).

Historic Deerfield, *Deerfield, Mass.; tel: (413) 774-5581.* A dozen historic homes built in the 1700s and 1800s, shown on guided tours, give a taste of early American life. The town was an English outpost in the 1660s (Hartford–Brattleboro, p. 184).

Lowell National Historical Park, *Lowell, Mass.; tel: (508) 970-5000.* Preserved 1820s textile mills, workers' homes and a canal system tell the story of the Industrial Revolution in the first US company town (Boston–Hanover, p. 99).

Minute Man National Historical Park, *Concord, Lincoln* and *Lexington, Mass; tel: (617) 862-7753.* Scene of the first battles of the American Revolution on 19 April 1775. Battle Road was where Minute Men harassed and fired upon Gen Gage's retreating Redcoats for 20 miles from Concord to Boston. North Bridge was the site of a skirmish known as 'the shot heard 'round the world' (West of Boston, p. 86).

Mystic Seaport, *Mystic, Conn.; tel: (860) 572-0711.* Historic homes, shops and commercial buildings show the life of the seaport in the mid-19th century. The *Charles W. Morgan* is the last of the wooden whaling ships (Newport–New York, p. 168).

Old Sturbridge Village, *Sturbridge, Mass.; tel: (508) 347-3362.* A 200-acre living-history museum that recreates New England village life in the 1830s (Boston–Hartford, p. 107).

Plimoth Plantation, *Plymouth, Mass.; tel: (508) 746-1622.* The Pilgrims' village life of 1622 is recreated by costumed interpreters who portray its residents and interact with visitors. Even the farm animals are bred to resemble those of the period (Boston–Cape Cod, p. 94).

Salem Maritime National Historic Site, *Salem, Mass.; tel: (508) 745-1470.* Wharves and buildings of the 17th-, 18th- and 19th-century seaport are preserved. Also of interest: The House of Seven Gables, which inspired the novel by Nathaniel Hawthorne, the Peabody & Essex Museum (see Top Museums) and exhibits on the 1692 Salem Witch Trials (Boston's North Shore, p. 76).

Strawbery Banke, *Portsmouth, N.H.; tel: (603) 433-1100.* On the site of the original waterfront settlement, 40 historic buildings are preserved to show lifestyles and architecture over a 350-year span (Boston–Portland, p. 124).

TOP MUSEUMS

Currier Gallery of Art, *Manchester, N.H.; tel: (603) 669-6144.* European painting and sculpture from the 13th to 20th centuries, American painting and furnishings (Boston–Hanover, p. 99).

John F. Kennedy Library and Museum, *Boston; tel: (617) 929-4523.* A memorial to JFK's life and short presidency, displayed in rooms resembling the White House; the museum's dramatic setting provides a sweeping panorama of the city and harbour (Boston, p. 60).

Metropolitan Museum of Art, *New York City; tel: (212) 535-7710.* One of the world's great art museums, with collections from ancient Egypt to the 20th century (New York City, p. 286).

Museum of Fine Arts, *Boston; tel: (617) 267-9300.* American, European, Asiatic, Egyptian and Classical collections displayed in 200 galleries (Boston, p. 60).

Norman Rockwell Museum, *Stockbridge, Mass.; tel: (413) 298-4100.* Studio, costumes and props used by the most famous illustrator of small-town American life, plus 504 of his original paintings and drawings (Lenox and the Berkshires, p. 192).

Peabody & Essex Museum, *Salem, Mass.; tel: (508) 745-9500.* More than 350,000 artifacts and works of art illustrating the Colonial, Federal and Victorian periods, maritime history and the China trade (North Shore, p. 76).

Shelburne Museum, *Shelburne, Vt.; tel: (802) 985-3346.* A collection of 37 restored historic buildings, such as 18th- and 19th-century homes, lighthouses, barns, schoolhouses, which were moved from all over New England. Inside are collections of Americana; European and American art (Burlington and Lake Champlain, p. 232).

Sterling and Francine Clark Art Institute, *Williamstown, Mass.; tel: (413) 458-9545.* Eclectic collection of 15th- to 20th-century paintings, sculpture, drawings, prints by well-known European and US artists (Boston–Lenox, p. 112).

Wadsworth Atheneum, *Hartford, Conn.; tel: (860) 247-9111.* The nation's oldest public art museum, with 40,000 works including Hudson River landscapes, two period rooms, Colonial furniture, 16th- and 17th-century European painting (Hartford, p. 178).

Whaling Museum, *New Bedford, Mass.; tel: (508) 997-0046.* One of the world's largest museums on whaling in the age of sailing ships, located in a small city that was once the world's whaling capital (Cape Cod–Newport, p. 152).

TOP PARKS

Acadia National Park, approx. 45 miles south-east of Bangor via Rte 1A, then Rte 3; *tel: (207) 288-3338.* This 41,000-acre nature preserve within 108-sq-miles of Mount Desert Island on Maine's rocky coast includes 120 miles of walking trails and a 27-mile scenic driving loop (Bar Harbor and Acadia, p. 274).

Baxter State Park, approx. 45 miles via back roads north-east from Greenville; approx. 80 miles north of Bangor via I-95, then back roads; *tel: (207) 723-5140.* A 200,000-acre wilderness tract in Maine's north woods; location of 5267-ft Mt Katahdin, terminus of the Appalachian Trail (Portland–Moosehead, p. 269; Bar Harbor–Fort Kent, p. 282).).

Cape Cod National Seashore, 90–120 miles south-east from Boston via Rte 3, then Rte 6; *tel: (508) 349-3785.* A 40-mile stretch of Atlantic Ocean beaches, fragile dunes, marshes, cranberry bogs and cedar forest covering 27,000 acres between Chatham and Provincetown (Cape Cod, p. 132).

Green Mountain National Forest, Rte 7 and scenic Rte 100 parallel the mountain range north-south; Rte 9 crosses the lower region from Brattleboro to Bennington; *tel: (802) 773-0300.* The US Forest Service maintains 340,000 acres of woodland covering this range of moderate-sized peaks, which extend 100 miles from the Massachusetts border through central Vermont (Green Mountains Loop, p. 204; Hanover to Burlington, p. 216).

White Mountain National Forest, 143 miles from Boston via I-93; approx. 65 miles from Portland via Rte 302; *tel: (603) 528-8721.* Well-maintained hiking trails give access to the dense forest and rugged peaks of this 725,000-acre preserve in northern New Hampshire (White Mountains, p. 222 and p. 227).

59

BOSTON AND CAMBRIDGE

Boston is 'The Hub' – a name bestowed in 1858 by Oliver Wendell Holmes, who wrote that Bostonians considered their city 'the Hub of the Universe'. Learning and culture rank high in this Athens of America, where the first school was built in 1636 and 25-odd colleges and universities thrive today. The oldest US city, founded 1630, Boston was once a Brahmin town (Boston's social elite) – 'the home of the bean and the cod, where the Lowells speak only to Cabots, and the Cabots speak only to God'. There's still a Yankee establishment, but it's matched by an Irish one, and ethnic diversity is on the rise.

You can do the Freedom Trail in a matter of hours, but allow a week to see all the sights in and out of town. The compact size of Boston's centre surprises visitors, who find they can get nearly everywhere on foot.

TOURIST INFORMATION

The Greater Boston Convention and Visitors Bureau, *PO Box 490, Prudential Tower, Suite 400, Boston, MA 02199; tel: (617) 536-4100 or (800) 888-5515*, operates the Boston Common Visitor Information Center, *146 Tremont St on Boston Common* (T: *Park St*), and the Prudential Center Visitor Information Center, *Center Court, Prudential Center*, both are open Mon–Fri 0900–1700, Sat–Sun 1100–1800. GBCVB does not book rooms. National Park Service Visitor Center, *15 State St, Boston, MA 02109* (T: *State St*); *tel: (617) 242-5642*, open daily 0900–1700, has tours, brochures, helpful rangers and public toilets; also a good bookshop on local history.

WEATHER

Boston has a generally cool, wet climate. July is the warmest month, averaging 65–82°F with occasional hotter, 'muggy' spells. Mid-Dec to mid-Mar is cold (averaging 23–36°F in Jan) with moderate snowfall. Spring is slow to warm up; trees don't 'leaf out' until mid–late May. Bostonians love fall's crisp, cool temperatures (47–63°F in Oct) and its warm, 'Indian summer'.

ARRIVING AND DEPARTING

Airport
Logan International Airport is in East Boston, directly across the harbour from downtown, 20–30 mins from the city centre by public transport ($0.85). Free shuttle to Airport subway station on the T's Blue Line.

By car (tunnel toll $2), the 3-mile trip can take 15 mins to 2 hours depending on traffic, time of day and weather. Taxi to downtown hotels $8–$12, shuttle bus $7.50.

The **Airport Water Shuttle** makes a seven-minute trip to **Rowes Wharf** downtown; *tel: (617) 330-8680 or (800) 235-6426*, Mon–Fri 0600–2000, Sun, holidays 1200–2000, $8. Free shuttle to rental car location and airport hotels. Suburban express buses; *tel: (617) 23-LOGAN*. Terminal E handles all international arrivals and most departures. Free Massport shuttle to Terminals A–D for domestic connections. Airport shops sell live lobsters packaged to fit under an airline seat ($12 per pound).

By train
Amtrak; *tel: (617) 482-3660 or (800) 872-7245,* has services to Providence, New York City and nationwide from **South Station,** *Summer St at Atlantic Ave,* via **Back Bay Station.**

By bus
All bus lines operate from a new terminal adjacent to South Station. **Greyhound**; *tel: (617) 526-1808 or (800) 231-2222,* serves major cities in New England and nationwide. **Peter Pan Trailways**; *tel: (800) 343-9999,* serves Western Massachusetts, Hartford and New York. **Plymouth & Brockton Street Railway Co.**; *tel: (617) 773-9401,* goes to Cape Cod. **Bonanza Bus Lines**; *tel: (617) 720-4110,* goes to Cape Cod and Providence.

By boat
Bay State Cruise Co., *67 Long Wharf; tel: (617) 723-7800,* operates one daily round-trip passenger ferry to Provincetown mid-June–early Sept; Sat, Sun only (early June and Sept–Oct). Ocean-going cruise liners dock at the **Black Falcon Cruise Terminal** in South Boston; *tel: (617) 330-1500.* MBTA passenger ferries operate between *Long Wharf* and **Charlestown Navy Yard,** Mon–Fri 0630–2000, $1, and between *Rowes Wharf* and **Hingham** on the South Shore, Mon–Fri 0600–1930, $4.

By car
Reconstruction of the **Central Artery** (John F. Fitzgerald Expressway) will disrupt traffic patterns in downtown Boston until the year 2004. The Artery, an elevated motorway that shunts north-south traffic through the city centre and serves Logan Airport via the outbound **Callahan** and inbound **Sumner tunnel** is being relocated below ground. Consequently, precise driving directions are subject to change; avoid the Artery if possible, especially during morning and evening rush hours.

From the west: The **Massachusetts Turnpike (I-90)** is the most direct route in or out of Boston. Use Exits 18–20 (Cambridge/Allston) for Charles River locations, Exit 22 (Prudential Center/Copley Sq.) for Back Bay, Theatre District and Boston Common, Exit 24 for downtown or the Expressway north and south.

From the south: All routes funnel into **I-93** to enter Boston. Use the *Kneeland St*/Chinatown exit for Back Bay, Theatre District, Boston Common and downtown; use Callahan Tunnel exit for Logan Airport. From the north: **I-95** connects with **Rte 1,** which enters and leaves Boston via the **Tobin Bridge.** I-93 south feeds into the Central Artery for downtown or *Storrow Dr* for Back Bay, Beacon Hill, Boston Common.

GETTING AROUND
Boston's narrow, winding and one-way downtown streets are said to follow colonial cowpaths of the 1600s, and its drivers are known for rudeness and for their sudden, dangerous and illegal traffic manoeuvres. Take advantage of the city's reputation as America's most walkable city and see as much as you can on foot or via public transport.

Most areas frequented by tourists present few problems in street safety. After dark, be cautious walking in the Chinatown/Theatre District area, the South End and *Central Sq.,* Cambridge,

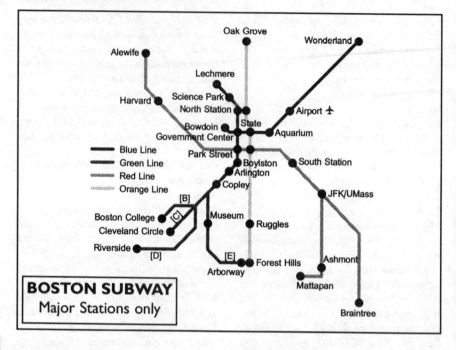

BOSTON SUBWAY
Major Stations only

62

and avoid any areas that are rundown, dimly lit or solitary, including Boston Common and other large public parks.

Taxi stands are located at the airport, South and North Stations, hotels and major squares and intersections. Passing cabs will stop when hailed. Fares are metered; tolls, baggage handling and a $1 fee from the airport are extra. An alarming number of Boston cabbies require directions in order to find your destination.

Neighbourhoods

'Downtown' means the Financial District and adjacent shopping areas, while 'the neighbourhoods' are the large residential tracts away from the downtown where most Bostonians live and few tourists visit. These include streets of one- or two-family homes, 'three-deckers' and tenements, usually of plain wood construction, in such places as Allston-Brighton, Dorchester, Jamaica Plain, Roslindale, Roxbury, South Boston and West Roxbury. A few neighbourhoods closer to downtown offer interesting sightseeing. **Beacon Hill,** one of the oldest parts of the city, is the small rise above Boston Common where a signal beacon once stood; it's a European-looking warren of narrow streets and brick townhouses, which includes **Louisburg Sq.,** Boston's poshest address.

Boston originally was a tiny peninsula (called **Shawmut** by the Indians) with three small hills (hence, the name of *Tremont St*). Two were cut down and used for landfill. One of the filled areas, the **Back Bay,** was a foul-smelling mudflat until the 1800s. Now its alphabetically named streets are lined with classy townhouses, many occupied by schools, consulates and condominiums. The city's prettiest promenade is here: tree-lined

Commonwealth Ave shows its finest colours in May with cherry, apple and magnolia blossoms.

At the tip of Boston proper is the **North End,** an Italian enclave with trattorias and *cannoli* shops. Southeast of the Common is tiny **Chinatown,** with Asian shops and restaurants and a large dragon gate, squeezed in between the **Theatre District** and the *Mass. Pike.* Beyond the Pike is the **South End,** a multicultural melting pot with restored townhouses on one street, urban blight on the next.

Public Transport

All major attractions are accessible by the **Massachusetts Bay Transportation Authority (MBTA);** *tel: (617) 222-3200 or (800) 392-6100.* Always called the **'T,'** it operates bus, streetcar and subway lines in Boston and nearby suburbs, plus commuter rail lines to towns as distant as 60 miles. Service daily 0500–0100, every 3–15 mins; Sun and holidays 0540–0100 with less frequency. Subway tokens cost $0.85 ($0.40 children 5–11, $0.20 seniors) and permit one continuous ride; some lines charge extra fares to and from distant points. Four colour-coded lines serve the downtown and outlying neighbourhoods. The direction **Inbound** always means toward the centre (**Park St** or **Downtown Crossing**); **Outbound** always means away from the centre. (If you ride the Red Line through *Park St,* you transfer from an Inbound to an Outbound train without leaving your seat.)

Unlike the three rapid-transit lines (**Red, Blue** and **Orange Lines**), the **Green Line** operates **streetcars** (below ground in the city centre). It is not one, but four ploddingly slow streetcar lines. You can ride any Green Line train in and around Boston's centre, but when heading outbound in a southerly direction, take

notice of which line goes to your destination. The **Arborway ('E')** line splits off after **Copley Sq.** down *Huntington Ave* (Symphony Hall and the Museum of Fine Arts are here) to Jamaica Plain. Three more lines split beyond **Kenmore Sq.**: The **'B'** line along *Commonwealth Ave* through Boston University is, oddly enough, named after **Boston College,** its terminus. The **'C'** line follows **Beacon St** to **Cleveland Circle.** The **'D'** line runs through Brookline en route to **Riverside** in suburban Newton. T buses cost $0.60 (exact change or subway token only) and operate along numbered routes on surface streets. The T's **Boston Passport,** valid on all trains, streetcars and buses ($5 one day, $9 three days, $18 seven days), is sold at Downtown Crossing station and Bostix booths, or call the T for information. Transport maps are posted in stations.

MBTA **Commuter Rail** (Purple Line) trains run from **North Station** (connecting to Green Line) to Fitchburg, Lowell, Haverhill, Rockport and Ipswich; from South Station (Red Line) and **Back Bay Station** (Orange Line) the trains go to Framingham, Worcester and Providence.

Driving

If driving is unavoidable, stay alert to unpredictable moves by other drivers. At traffic light changes, often one, two or three drivers will attempt to 'beat' the red light, endangering motorists on the cross-street who have the green. 'Rotaries' (roundabouts) are especially tricky: Cars entering must yield to those already in the circle, but few local drivers know, or heed, the rule.

A Massachusetts oddity: names of cross streets are usually well marked, but main thoroughfares rarely are, thus making it difficult to know what street you are travelling along. Boston's poor directional signs are famous for confusing visitors.

Metered parking spaces, generally $0.25 per 15 min, are limited downtown; resident-only permit parking is in effect in many neighbourhoods. Garages and car parks (look for blue 'P') offer the easiest, most secure parking.

STAYING IN BOSTON

Accommodation

All major chains are represented, either in Boston or suburban locations within a 30–40 min drive from downtown.

Most hotels in the Back Bay or downtown are pricey. These include Boston's venerable **Ritz-Carlton,** *15 Arlington St, Boston, MA 02117; tel: (617) 536-5700 or (800) 241-3333,* and its modern competitor, likewise facing the Public Garden, the **Four Seasons Hotel,** *200 Boylston St, Boston, MA 02116; tel: (617) 338-4400 or (800) 332-3442.* Boston tradition is upheld at the pricey **Omni Parker House,** *60 School St, Boston, MA 02108; tel: (617) 227-8600 or (800) 843-6664,* which gave its name to a favourite American dinner roll and has long served as a political meeting place.

Back Bay hotels include Boston's *grande dame,* **The Copley Plaza,** *138 St. James Ave, Boston, MA 02116; tel: (617) 267-5300,* in *Copley Sq.,* pricey, and the **Lenox Hotel,** *710 Boylston St, Boston, MA 02116; tel: (617) 536-5300 or (800) 225-7676,* expensive.

A more intimate choice is 96-room **The Eliot Suite Hotel,** *370 Commonwealth Ave, Boston, MA 02215; tel: (617) 267-1607 or (800) 44-ELIOT,* at the far end of Back Bay but near *Newbury St* shopping. Pricey.

Also well located are the 143-room **Copley Square Hotel,** *47 Huntington Ave, Boston, MA 02116; tel: (617) 536-9000,* expensive, and the moderate–expensive low-rise **MidTown Hotel,** *220 Huntington Ave, Boston, MA 02115; tel: (617) 262-1000 or (800) 343-1177.* The moderate **Tremont House (QI),** *275 Tremont St, Boston, MA 02116; tel: (617) 426-1400 or (800) 331-9998,* in the Theatre District, is good value.

If price matters more than location or parking, try the newly opened **Shawmut Inn,** *280 Friend St, Boston, MA 02114; tel: 720-5544,* at North Station, whose 66 moderate–expensive rooms have kitchenettes.

Most hotels offer lower-cost packages, especially out of the summer-fall peak season. Also, try *Hd, HJ* or *BW,* with several locations, moderate–expensive.

Several small guesthouses offer moderate rooms in Brookline along the *Beacon St* Green Line. The nicest is the 11-room Victorian-style **Beacon Inn,** *1087 Beacon St, Brookline, MA 02146; (617) 566-0088;* which has a second, less ornate 14-room house at *1750 Beacon St.*

Budget choices include **Boston International AYH,** *12 Hemenway St, Boston, MA 02115; tel: (617) 536-9455,* in the Fenway neighbourhood.

For women only, there's the **Berkeley Residence/Boston YWCA,** *40 Berkeley St, Boston, MA 02116; tel: (617) 482-8850,* in the South End near Back Bay Station.

A Bed & Breakfast Agency, *47 Commercial Wharf, Boston, MA 02110; tel: (617) 720-3540 or (800) 248-9262,* reserves moderate–expensive rooms in local homes, including waterfront lofts. **Citywide Reservation Service,** *25 Huntington Ave, Boston, MA 02116; tel: (617) 267-7424 or (800) 468-3593,* books rooms in hotels, inns, guesthouses and bed and breakfasts.

64

Eating and Drinking

In the old days, Boston seafood restaurants invented the word 'scrod' (or 'schrod') for the freshest catch (cod or haddock) rather than change their menus every day. Today, scrod, bluefish, lobster and clams are the staples of waterfront eateries. Try **Durgin-Park,** *5 Faneuil Hall Marketplace; tel: (617) 227-2038,* for hearty New England fare, including seafood, prime rib of beef and Indian pudding. Moderate.

All around it in **Faneuil Hall Marketplace** are other restaurants and food stalls offering everything from pizza and hot dogs to Greek and Chinese cuisine to seafood. Cheap–pricey.

For fresh-from-the-boat seafood in no-nonsense atmosphere there's **No Name Restaurant,** *15½ Fish Pier off Northern Ave, S. Boston; tel: (617) 338-7539,* budget–moderate. Expect to wait for a table at popular **Legal Sea Foods,** locations at *35 Columbus Ave; tel: (617) 426-4444,* also at *Copley Place, Kendall Sq. in Cambridge, Chestnut Hill* and *Logan Airport.* Moderate–pricey.

For good, basic Italian fare in the North End at a budget–moderate price, there's the bustling **European,** *218 Hanover St; tel: (617) 523-5694,* on the Freedom Trail. For quieter dining, explore the small moderate–pricey trattorias along *Hanover, Salem* or *North Sts.* Then linger for *cappuccino* and *dolce* at **Mike's Pastry Shop,** *300 Hanover St; tel: (617) 742-3050,* cheap. Boston's best Italian pizza is at **Regina Pizzaria,** *11½ Thatcher St; tel: (617) 227-0765.* Cheap–budget.

In the South End, gourmet Italian **Appetito,** *1 Appleton St; tel: (617) 338-6777,* is worth its pricey menu, and there are a variety of moderate–pricey eateries along *Tremont St* and *Columbus Ave.* Near North Station is a cavernous brewpub,

The **Commonwealth Brewing Co.**, *138 Portland St; tel: (617) 523-8383,* offering salads, steaks and sandwiches, budget–moderate. On the waterfront, summer al fresco dining is the only way to see the water, but **The Chart House,** *60 Long Wharf; tel: (617) 227-1576,* pricey, has a cosy atmosphere indoors.

In Chinatown, try **Peking Cuisine,** *10 Tyler St; tel: (617) 542-5857,* plus a variety of storefront Chinese and Vietnamese eateries along *Harrison Ave, Tyler* and *Beach Sts.* Cheap–budget. Fans of the TV programme *Cheers* are drawn to its touristy real-life model, the **Bull & Finch Pub,** *84 Beacon St; tel: (617) 227-9605,* for sandwiches and burgers. Budget–moderate.

In the Theatre District, dark wood-panelled **Jacob Wirth,** *33–37 Stuart St; tel: (617) 338-8586,* is dyed-in-the-wool Bostonian, with a budget German menu and Boston-brewed Samuel Adams and Harpoon beers. If you visit Arnold Arboretum, stop at **Doyle's,** *3484 Washington St, Jamaica Plain; tel: (617) 542-2345,* whose noisy pub atmosphere is pure Boston. Budget–moderate.

Communications

The US Postal Service operates more than 50 branches in the Boston area; main office is the **J.W. McCormack Station,** *Post Office Sq., downtown Boston.* There's a 24-hour service available at the **General Mail Facility,** *25 Dorchester Ave* (T: *South Station); tel: (617) 451-9922.*

Money

Thomas Cook Foreign Exchange, *160 Franklin St, Boston, MA 02110; tel: (617) 695-0269,* open Mon–Fri 0900–1700, Carrying travellers cheques in US dollars is advisable, as exchange offices are rare.

65

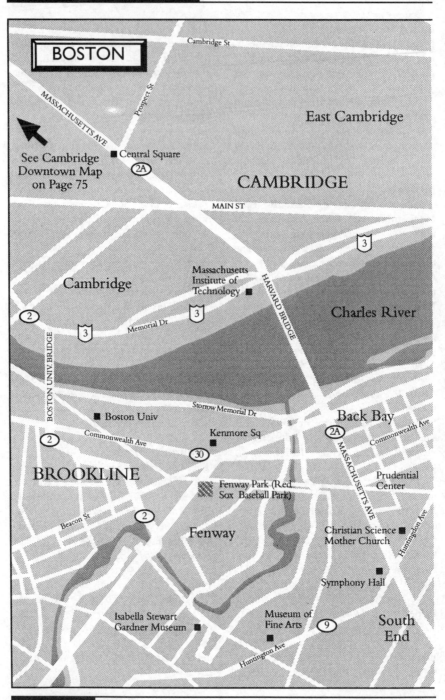

BOSTON

Cambridge St

MASSACHUSETTS AVE

Prospect St

See Cambridge
Downtown Map
on Page 75

East Cambridge

Central Square

(2A)

CAMBRIDGE

MAIN ST

3

Massachusetts
Institute of
Technology

HARVARD BRIDGE

Charles River

Cambridge

(2)

3

Memorial Dr

3

BOSTON UNIV. BRIDGE

Storrow Memorial Dr

Boston Univ

Back Bay

(2A)

Commonwealth Ave

(2)

Commonwealth Ave

Kenmore Sq

(30)

MASSACHUSETTS AVE

Prudential
Center

BROOKLINE

Fenway Park (Red
Sox Baseball Park)

Beacon St

(2)

Fenway

Christian Science
Mother Church

Huntington Ave

Symphony Hall

Isabella Stewart
Gardner Museum

Museum of
Fine Arts

(9)

South
End

Huntington Ave

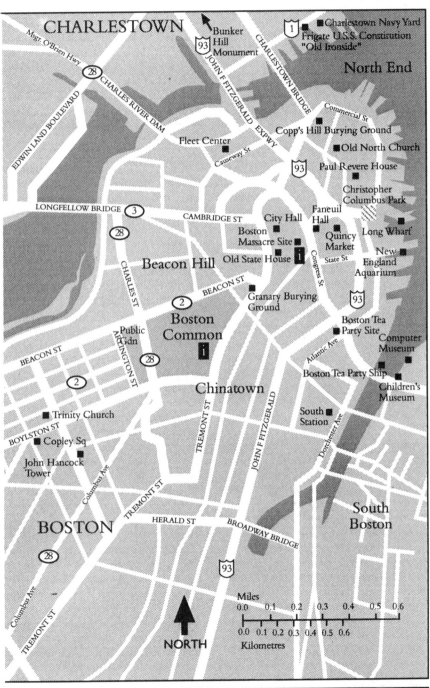

CHARLESTOWN

Msgr. O'Brien Hwy

Bunker Hill Monument

CHARLESTOWN BRIDGE

JOHN F FITZGERALD EXPWY

Charlestown Navy Yard
Frigate U.S.S. Constitution "Old Ironside"

North End

CHARLES RIVER DAM

EDWIN LAND BOULEVARD

Commercial St

Copp's Hill Burying Ground

Fleet Center

Causeway St

Old North Church

Paul Revere House

Christopher Columbus Park

LONGFELLOW BRIDGE

CAMBRIDGE ST

City Hall

Faneuil Hall

Boston Massacre Site

Quincy Market

Long Wharf

CHARLES ST

Beacon Hill

Old State House

State St

Congress St

New England Aquarium

BEACON ST

Granary Burying Ground

Public Gdn

ARLINGTON ST

Boston Common

Boston Tea Party Site

Computer Museum

BEACON ST

Atlantic Ave

Chinatown

Boston Tea Party Ship

Children's Museum

Trinity Church

BOYLSTON ST

Copley Sq

TREMONT ST

JOHN F FITZGERALD

South Station

Dorchester Ave

John Hancock Tower

Columbus Ave

TREMONT ST

BOSTON

HERALD ST

BROADWAY BRIDGE

South Boston

Columbus Ave

TREMONT ST

NORTH

Miles
0.0   0.1   0.2   0.3   0.4   0.5   0.6

0.0 0.1 0.2 0.3 0.4 0.5 0.6
Kilometres

67

ENTERTAINMENT

Boston is the big time, such as it is, for arts and theatre in New England. See the 'Calendar' section in Thursday's *Boston Globe*, 'Scene' in Friday's *Boston Herald* or the weekly *Boston Phoenix* for listings of what's happening. Bi–weekly *Panorama* is available free in hotels.

Theatre

Once a top theatre try-out town, Boston now gets mostly tried-and-true block-busters in the Theatre District, *Tremont* and *Boylston Sts*, but it has a thriving small-theatre scene. Downtown houses are the **Wang Center for the Performing Arts**, the **Colonial, Wilbur** and **Emerson Majestic** theatres and **The Charles Playhouse**. Performing classic and contemporary drama are the **Lyric Stage**, *140 Clarendon St; tel: (617) 437-7172*, and **Huntington Theatre Company**, *264 Huntington Ave; tel: (617) 266-0800*, open Sept–June. Half-price same-day tickets are sold, cash only, at **Bostix;** *Faneuil Hall* and *Copley Sq.; no phone*, open Mon–Sat 1000–1800, Sun 1100–1600 (Faneuil Hall booth closed Mon).

Music

Boston Symphony Orchestra plays at 2600-seat **Symphony Hall,** *301 Massachusetts Ave, Boston, MA 02115; tel: (617) 266-1492* (information) or *266-1200* (tickets), early Oct–mid-Apr; at Tanglewood in Lenox (see Berkshires) in summer. **The Boston Pops** plays at Symphony Hall mid-May–early July and gives free concerts at the **Hatch Shell** on the Esplanade in early July.

Boston Ballet; *tel: (617) 695-6955 (tickets)*, performs at the Wang Center mid-Oct–end May. **Boston Lyric Opera,** *114 State St, Boston, MA 02109; tel: (617) 248-8660*, performs at Emerson

Majestic Theatre mid-Oct–end Mar. The **Handel & Haydn Society**; *tel: (617) 266-3605*, is the oldest continuing US arts organization; varied locations. **Harborlights,** *Fan Pier, Northern Ave, S. Boston; tel: (617) 931-2000 or 737-6100*, is a June–Aug waterfront concert series. **Great Woods** is a summer concert stage in Mansfield (see p. 119).

Clubs

Near the Theatre District are several comedy clubs, plus dancing at the Roxy and Zanzibar. In **Kenmore Sq.**, **The Rat** and other clubs draw a raucous young crowd. Nearby, clubs on **Lansdowne St**, behind Fenway Park, vary their clientele with theme nights (gay, Asian, international). **Harvard St** in **Allston** has a variety of youth-oriented clubs, among which **Harpers Ferry**, *158 Brighton Ave*, is a blues standout. The **piano bar** crowd can head to big hotels or **Lily's** at Faneuil Hall Marketplace.

Ideas

Befitting the Athens of America, Boston and Cambridge excel in the quality and variety of their public lectures. The renowned **Ford Hall Forum**; *tel: (617) 373-5800* (end Sept–mid-Nov and mid-Mar–mid-May); plus poetry and prose readings, art gallery exhibits and children's events. See local media for listings.

Events

On **17 Mar,** Boston city offices and schools close for **Evacuation Day,** marking the 1776 departure of British troops from Boston; it's also **St. Patrick's Day,** an occasion for parades and mass consumption of beer in heavily Irish-American South Boston. Thousands of runners and their fans fill the streets (and hotels) for the **Boston Marathon,** held on **Patriots Day** (**19 Apr** or the nearest Mon), a celebration of the Revolutionary War battles of Lexington and Concord. **Boston Harborfest** celebrates Independence in early July, with Old Ironsides' annual Turnaround Cruise, a **Chowderfest** contest on City Hall Plaza and a **Fourth of July Concert** (attendance: 500,000 or more) by the Boston Pops orchestra at the Hatch Shell on the Charles River Esplanade, accompanied by New England's biggest fireworks display. College rowing teams fill the river in late Oct for the **Head of the Charles Regatta.** On New Year's Eve, **First Night** opens Boston's downtown streets to alcohol-free revelry, with musical, theatre and children's performances.

Sports

Boston has teams in four professional sports. The **Boston Red Sox** play baseball Apr–early Oct, with home games at **Fenway Park,** *4 Yawkey Way, Boston, MA 02215* (T: *Kenmore*); *tel: (617) 267-1700.* Tickets, $8–$20, are often easy to obtain on game day. Tickets are more expensive and harder to get for the **Boston Celtics** basketball team (Nov–late Apr); *tel: (617) 523-3030,* and the **Boston Bruins** hockey team (Oct–end Apr); *tel: (617) 227-3200,* both of which play home games at the **FleetCenter** (T: *North Station*) a brand-new facility which opened for the 1995–96 season, replacing **Boston Garden.** The **New England Patriots** play football home games Aug–early Jan at **Foxboro Stadium,** *Rte 1, Foxborough, MA 02035; tel: (800) 543-1776* for tickets.

Thoroughbred horse-racing, with pari-mutuel betting, is held at **Suffolk Downs,** *111 Waldemar Ave (off Rte 1A), East Boston, MA 02128; tel: (617) 567-3900,* Oct–June (TV 'simulcasting' from other tracks year round). Greyhound dog-racing is held at **Wonderland Greyhound Park,** *Rte 1A, Revere, MA 02151; tel: (617) 284-1300,* year round.

SHOPPING

The pedestrian mall at Downtown Crossing, corner *Washington* and *Winter Sts* (T: *Downtown Crossing*), is the main shopping area, with **Filene's, Macy's** and a variety of smaller shops. **Filene's Basement,** which pioneered 'automatic markdowns', is a bargain shopper's mecca.

Shops along the Back Bay's **Newbury St** range from posh Burberry, Cartier and Brooks Brothers near *Arlington St* and the Ritz-Carlton Hotel to the funkier Patagonia, Urban Outfitters and Tower Records near *Mass. Ave.* In between is a people-watcher's paradise amid boutiques, galleries and cafés. **Waterstone's Booksellers,** corner *Newbury* and *Exeter Sts,* has a multi-storey shop at the centre.

Paralleling *Newbury St* is a mile-long indoor concourse with moderate–pricey shops and varied restaurants: The 70-shop **Prudential Center** mall is connected by a walkway to 100-shop **Copley Place,** letting you walk, shop and eat indoors all the way from the Sheraton Boston Hotel to *Copley Sq.* Boston's biggest redevelopment success is **Faneuil Hall Marketplace,** which is crowded with tourists and local people day and night (T: *Haymarket*). Three renovated 1825 market buildings, supplemented by newer structures house 125 shops, restaurants, food stalls and pubs. Some of the best shopping is from local artisans' pushcarts.

SIGHTSEEING

Walking tours

Four self-guided walking trails show different aspects of Boston history. Best-

69

known is the 2.5-mile **Freedom Trail,** marked with a red-brick line along the sidewalk. The 14 sites, comprising 350 years of history, are separately owned and some charge admission fees. Pick up a free map at the Boston Common Visitors Information Center (T: *Park St*) where the trail begins; the National Park Service Visitors Center, halfway along the trail, has a better one.

First stop is 50-acre **Boston Common,** bounded by *Park, Tremont, Boylston, Charles* and *Beacon Sts,* America's oldest park, which was laid out in 1634 as common pasture land. The trail leads through the Common to the 1797 **State House,** *Beacon St; tel: (617) 727-3676,* tours weekdays 1000–1600, designed by Charles Bulfinch, with its landmark 23-carat gilded dome. This is where the General Court (state legislature) of the Commonwealth of Massachusetts meets and the Governor's office is located.

Park St Church, *1 Park St, corner Tremont St; tel: (617) 523-3383,* is where abolitionist William Lloyd Garrison first spoke out against slavery (1829) and the hymn *America* was first sung (1831). Open Tues–Sat 0830–1600 (July–Aug), by appointment Sept–June; Sun services all year. A few steps away, the small 17th-century **Old Granary Burying Ground,** *Tremont St,* open 0800–1600, holds the graves of revolutionary leaders John Hancock and Samuel Adams, Patriot Paul Revere, the five casualties of the 1770 Boston Massacre and nursery rhymester 'Mother Goose'. The large Franklin monument is for Benjamin Franklin's parents; their famous Boston born son rests in Philadelphia.

The 1754 **King's Chapel,** *58 Tremont St; tel: (617) 227-2155,* open Mon–Sat 0930–1600, Sun 1300–1500, free, was Boston's first Anglican church (in 1785 it

became Unitarian), and it has the oldest US pulpit in continuous use. Beside it is Boston's oldest **Burial Ground,** where Puritan Gov. John Winthrop and Mary Chilton, the first woman Pilgrim to land at Plymouth, are buried.

Around the corner on *School St* is the site of Boston's **First Public School** (Boston Latin, built 1635), where Benjamin Franklin, Samuel Adams and Cotton Mather learned their lessons. On the site today is the 1862 **Old City Hall,** where Boston mayors, including the legendary James Michael Curley, held sway from 1865 to 1969; refurbished, it now houses offices and a pricey French restaurant, **Maison Robert.**

The Old Corner Bookstore, *School and Washington Sts,* was a gathering place for early 1800s writers such as Ralph Waldo Emerson, Nathaniel Hawthorne and Harriet Beecher Stowe, whose presence gave Boston fame as 'the Athens of America'. Earlier on this site was the home of **Anne Hutchinson,** a Puritan fighter for women's rights; the small brick building now houses the **Globe Corner Store,** specialising in New England and travel books.

Diagonally opposite the bookshop is the 1729 Georgian-style **Old South Meeting House,** *Washington and Milk Sts; tel: (617) 482-6439,* open daily 0930–1700 (Apr–Oct), and Mon–Fri 1000–1600, Sat–Sun 1000–1700 (Nov–Mar), $2, a colonial church where the Boston Tea Party was launched. Across *Milk St,* look for the building with a bust of Benjamin Franklin, marking it as the statesman-scientist's 1706 birthplace.

The 1713 **Old State House,** *206 Washington St* (T: *State St*)*; tel: (617) 720-3290,* open daily 0930–1700, $3, was the seat of British government from 1713–76; the eastern end still bears the royal lion and

Boston Tea Party

In the 1760s, having defeated France in the Seven Years' War, Britain sought to defray the war's costs through taxes on British colonists in North America. The 1765 Stamp Act and 1767 Townshend Act provoked boycotts and were repealed, but an import duty on tea stood. Colonists protested against it, instead buying cheaper tea smuggled from Holland.

Then in May 1773 Parliament agreed to let the faltering East India Company dispose of its tea surplus in North America. Parliament would refund the shilling-per-pound duty, thus helping the company to undercut smugglers.

The *Dartmouth* arrived in Boston Harbor with the first shipment in Nov 1773, followed by the *Eleanor* and *Beaver*. Patriot leaders John and Samuel Adams, John Hancock and Josiah Quincy were determined to stop the tea from landing, knowing that its low price would lure colonists into breaking the boycott. Gov Thomas Hutchinson insisted the cargo be unloaded.

After a rally at Old South Meeting House, 50 to 100 men dressed up as Mohawk Indians on 16 Dec 1773 and boarded the three ships at Griffin's Wharf. They tore open the 342 chests of tea, valued at £18,000 and dumped them into the harbour. Similar acts of rebellion followed in New York and other ports. Parliament punished the colonies with harsh measures that only served to unite the colonists and set the stage for revolution.

Boston's waterfront was gradually filled in, leaving the site of Griffin's Wharf near South Station on dry land. The replica ship *Beaver II* and a small museum at Congress St Bridge recount the history for visitors.

unicorn. Inside is a collection of colonial and maritime memorabilia. Outside is a circle of cobblestones marking the site of the 1770 **Boston Massacre,** in which British sentries fired on a mob protesting taxes and killed five.

There's a statue of Patriot leader Samuel Adams outside **Faneuil Hall,** *Merchants Row* (T: *Government Center, State St, Haymarket); tel: (617) 242-5642,* a 1742 colonial meeting house and market known as the 'Cradle of Liberty' for its role in the planning of the Revolution; open daily 0900–1700, free historical talks every half-hour. The hall (it's pronounced *FAN-yew-ul)* once stood on the waterfront, which is now half a mile away. Facing it is Faneuil Hall Marketplace. The Freedom Trail leads next through the **Blackstone Block,** the only part of Boston that approximates the look of the 1700s.

Further on, amid the North End's narrow streets, stands the circa-1680 **Paul Revere House,** *19 North Sq.; tel: (617) 523-2338,* open daily 0930–1715 (mid-Apr–end Oct), 0930–1615 (Nov–mid-Apr); closed Mon (Jan–Mar), $2.50. In the 1770s it was home to silversmith Paul Revere, famed for the midnight ride of 18 Apr 1775 to warn Patriot leaders at Lexington and Concord of British troop movements.

On nearby *Hanover St* is a landmark statue of Revere on horseback, and the small park leads to 1723 **'Old North Church'** (*Christ Church*), *193 Salem St; (617) 523-6676,* open daily 0900–1700, from whose steeple two lanterns were hung as a signal ('one if by land, two if by sea') on the night of Revere's ride.

Uphill from the church, is **Copp's Hill Burial Ground,** where Cotton Mather and other Puritans were laid to rest. **Bunker Hill Monument,** *Monument Sq., Charlestown* (T: *Community College*); *tel: (617) 242-5641,* open daily 0900–1630, is a 221-ft obelisk marking the site of the 17 June 1775 battle (actually on Breed's Hill), in which British troops attempted to end the rebel siege of Boston.

At Charlestown Navy Yard **Bunker Hill Pavilion,** *55 Constitution Rd, Charlestown; tel: (617) 241-7575,* open daily 0930–1600 (Apr, May, Sept–Nov), 0930–1700 (June–Aug), $1.50–$3, has a multi-media show about the battle, in which the American commander told his Minutemen, 'Don't fire until you see the whites of their eyes!'

The Freedom Trail concludes at Pier 1 with **'Old Ironsides' (USS Constitution);** *tel: (617) 426-1812,* open daily 0930–sunset (guided tours available until 1545) a 52-gun frigate and the world's oldest commissioned warship, whose solid oak hull repelled cannonballs during the War of 1812. The ship's history is told in the **USS Constitution Museum,** *Building 22, Charlestown Navy Yard, Charlestown, MA 02129; tel: (617) 426-1812,* open daily 0900–1800 (June–early Sept), 1000–1700 (early Sept–end Nov and Mar–end May), 1000–1500 (Dec–Feb), $4.

Boston's other walks feature different sites. The **Black Heritage Trail** is a 1.6-mile self-guided walking tour around Beacon Hill, highlighting the history of Boston's 19th-century African-American community, including stops on the Underground Railroad, which shepherded runaway slaves from the South to Canada. Most of these sites are closed to the public.

Pick up a map at the Boston Common Visitor Center or the **Museum of Afro-American History,** *46 Joy St, Boston,* *MA 02110* (T: *Park St*); *tel: (617) 742-1854,* open Mon–Fri 1000–1600, Sat–Sun by appointment, free. The trail starts at **The Robert Gould Shaw and 54th Regiment Memorial,** corner *Beacon* and *Park St* on Boston Common, a sculpture by Augustus Saint-Gaudens depicting the first black regiment of the US Civil War and its white commander.

The **Women's History Trail** leads through Chinatown, Beacon Hill, Downtown and the North End, revealing the history of some of Boston's prominent women, including author Louisa May Alcott, Quaker Mary Dyer, who was banished and hanged for her beliefs, and political matriarch Rose Fitzgerald Kennedy. The fourth trail, **Harborwalk,** begins at the Old State House and guides you to a history of the waterfront, ending at the Boston Tea Party Ship.

Guided Tours

Three companies offer narrated trolley tours of Downtown, Back Bay and Charlestown tourist areas, with stops at major attractions and free re-boarding. Routes and prices ($16) are similar for **Beantown Trolley,** *tel: (617) 236-2148;* **Blue Trolley,** *tel: (617) TROLLEY (876-5539),* and **Old Town Trolleys,** *tel: (617) 269-7010.* All sell tickets near the New England Aquarium and on Boston Common. **Dicover Boston,** *73 Tremont St, Boston, MA 02108; tel: (617) 742-1440,* runs multi-lingual trolley tours.

The most unusual trips are those of **Boston Duck Tours,** *tel: (617) 723-DUCK (723-3825),* $18, which takes passengers aboard renovated World War II amphibious landing vehicles ('ducks') through city streets followed by a short ride on the Charles River. Apr–Nov; tours begin at the Aquarium.

You can take in the whole town at

once from observatories atop the **John Hancock Tower,** *Copley Sq.; tel: (617) 572-6429,* open Mon–Sat 0900–2300, Sun 1000–2300 (May–Oct) 1200–2300 (Nov–Apr), $3.75, or the **Prudential Center;** *tel: (617) 236-3318,* open Mon–Sat 1000–2200, Sun 1200–2200, $2. **Harbour cruises** operate from waterfront points, particularly Long Wharf and *Rowes Wharf.*

Museums

The **Boston Tea Party Ship and Museum,** *Congress St Bridge, Boston, MA 02210* (T: *South Station*); *tel: (617) 338-1773,* takes you aboard the *Beaver II,* a replica of one of the ships from which colonists tossed tea into the harbour in 1773. Open daily 0900–1700 (Mar–May and Sept–Dec), 0900–1800 (end May–early Sept), closed Dec–end Feb, $3.25–$6.50.

Across a small plaza, the world's only **Computer Museum,** *300 Congress St, Museum Wharf, Boston, MA 02210; tel: (617) 426-2800,* open Tue–Sun 1000–1700 (Sept–May), daily 1000–1800 (July, Aug), $5–$7, has vintage computers and hands-on exhibits, but its centrepiece is a giant walk-through computer that explains how all the parts function. Next door is the the **Children's Museum,** *300 Congress St, Boston, MA 02210; tel: (617) 426-8855,* completely designed to entertain and educate kids. Open Tues–Sun 1000–1700, Fri 1000–2100 (Sept–June); open Mon in summer and school vacation weeks, $6–$7; Fri 1700–2100, $1.

Also on the waterfront is **New England Aquarium,** *Central Wharf, Boston, MA 02110* (T: *Aquarium*); *tel: (617) 973-5200,* where you follow a winding walkway around a four-storey glass ocean tank, watching fish, sea turtles and sharks swim in and out of a coral reef.

Open Mon, Tue, Fri 0900–1800, Wed, Thur 0900–2000, Sat, Sun, holidays 0900–1900 (July–early Sept); slightly earlier closings rest of year, $4.50–$8.50. The Aquarium has whale-watch cruises Apr–Oct, $24.

Yet another site with kids in mind is the **Museum of Science,** *1 Science Park, Boston, MA 02114* (T: *Science Park*); *tel: (617) 723-2500,* which reveals the secrets of everything from anthropology to space exploration, with an excellent **Charles Hayden Planetarium** show and giant-screen 70mm films shown in the **Mugar Omni Theater.** Open daily 0900–1700, Fri 0900–2100 (Sept–July), Sat–Thur 0900–1900, Fri 0900–2100 (July–Sept), $6–$8, planetarium and theatre extra.

Nearby in CambridgeSide Galleria mall is the **Sports Museum of New England,** *100 CambridgeSide Pl, Cambridge, MA 02141; tel: (617) 621-0520,* which details the city's infatuation with sports. Open Mon–Sat 1000–2130, Sun 1100–1800, $4.50–$6.

Boston has a trio of top-notch art museums. For an all-encompassing look at paintings, prints, sculpture and other artworks from a wide range of periods, there's the **Museum of Fine Arts,** *465 Huntington Ave, Boston, MA 02115* (T: *Museum*); *tel: (617) 267-9300.* Of special note is its Asiatic art. Open Tue–Sun 1000–1645, Wed 1000–2145, West Wing only Tue, Thur 1700–2145, $3.50–$8; Wed 1600–2145 free. A short walk from the MFA is Boston's jewel, the **Isabella Stewart Gardner Museum,** *280 The Fenway* (mailing address: *2 Palace Rd*), *Boston, MA 02115; tel: (617) 566-1401,* open Tue–Sun 1100–1700, $3–$7. The eclectic collection of a 19th-century socialite includes works by Rembrandt, Botticelli and Titian, along with tapestries and Graeco-Roman statuary. The rooms

73

overlook an ornate courtyard of trees, flowering plants and artworks at the centre of a re-created 15th-century Venetian palazzo.

In the Back Bay is the smaller **Institute of Contemporary Art**, *955 Boylston St, Boston, MA 02115* (T: *Hynes/ICA*); *tel: (617) 266-5152*, with changing exhibits of photography, painting, sculpture and performance art in a former police station. Open Wed–Sun 1200–1700, $2.25–$5.25; Thur 1700–2100 free.

South of the city centre in Dorchester, with a sweeping view of Boston Harbor and Dorchester Bay, is the **John F. Kennedy Library and Museum**, *Columbia Point, Boston, MA 02125* (T: *JFK/UMass*, then free shuttle every 20 mins); *tel: (617) 929-4523*, which celebrates and explains the life and career of Boston's most recent US president. Open daily 0900–1700, $2–$6.

Further away, but also worth a visit, is the **John F. Kennedy Birthplace National Historic Site**, *83 Beals St, Brookline, MA 02146; tel: (617) 566-7937*, tours Wed–Sun 1000–1630 (May–Oct), $2, the 35th president's modest boyhood home (T: *Coolidge Corner* on the *Beacon St* ('C') streetcar).

Architecture

In *Copley Sq.*, the 1877 brownstone **Trinity Church**, the Romanesque Revival masterpiece of architect Henry Hobson Richardson, is well worth a look. So is the 1895 **Boston Public Library**, directly across the square, which – aside from the literary treasures within – has a superb marble main staircase and a lovely central courtyard.

Parks

From 1884–96, Frederick Law Olmsted designed a system of nine parks, which

were to be like an **'Emerald Necklace'** around the city; they still form a greenbelt for walking or bicycling through Boston. The system begins with Boston Common, the first US park (1834), and the adjacent **Public Garden**, the first US botanical garden (1837), where swan boat rides have soothed summer afternoons since 1877. It continues down **Commonwealth Ave Mall Park** to the **Back Bay Fens**, then along the Muddy River and the Riverway. Next are **Leverett Pond, Olmsted Park** and **Jamaica Pond** along *The Jamaicaway* in Jamaica Plain. Next is **Arnold Arboretum**, main entrance *125 Arborway, Jamaica Plain* (T: *Forest Hills*); *tel: (617) 524-1718*, whose 265 acres include gardens with 7,000 varieties of trees, shrubs and flowers, all labelled, plus lots of open space for quiet relaxation.

Olmsted said the 'Crown Jewel in the Emerald Necklace' was 527-acre **Franklin Park**, *Circuit Dr.* off *Blue Hill Ave* or *Morton St; tel: (617) 635-7383*, about 20 min from downtown by car. Within it is 72-acre **Franklin Park Zoo**; *tel: (617) 442-4896*, open Mon–Fri 0900–1700, Sat, Sun, Mon holidays 0930–1730, $3–$5.50. The parks are open sunrise to sunset, free; they are unsafe after dark.

CAMBRIDGE

Tourist Information: The Cambridge Office for Tourism, *18 Brattle St, Room 352, Cambridge, MA 02138; tel: (617) 441-2884*, operates a **Visitors Information Booth,** *Harvard Sq.* (T: *Harvard Sq.*), open daily 0900–1700.

STAYING IN CAMBRIDGE

Accommodation

Cambridge has *BW, HJ, Hy, Ma, Sh* and *Su*. **The Charles Hotel,** *1 Bennett St, Harvard Sq., Cambridge, MA 02138; tel:*

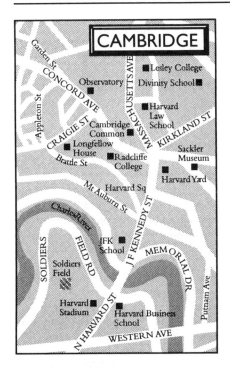

Bombay Club, *57 John F. Kennedy St* (in the Galeria mall); *tel: (617) 661-8100,* has some of the best Indian food around, moderate. Cheap and budget eateries abound in this student haven, where convenience outweighs quality. **John Harvard's Brew House,** *33 Dunster St; tel: (617) 868-3585,* is a studenty brewpub.

Central Sq. is very well known for its budget–moderate ethnic restaurants (Chinese, Thai, Indian, African, Middle Eastern) and a rougher edge to the street life. **Green Street Grill,** *280 Green St; tel: (617) 876-1655,* has an eclectic menu in a funky atmosphere, moderate. **Carberry's Bakery and Coffee House,** *74–76 Prospect St; tel: (617) 576-3777,* sells the hearty fresh-baked bread that most of America lacks.

Kendall Sq. has a **Legal Sea Foods,** *5 Cambridge Center; tel: (617) 864-3400.* At *Inman Sq.,* is **S&S Deli,** *1334 Cambridge St; tel: (617) 354-0620,* budget, with burgers and basic American fare. Storefront restaurants ranging from barbecue to Chinese, Indian, Portuguese and Brazilian can also be found.

(617) 864-1200 or *(800) 882-1818,* pricey, with 296 rooms, is right next to *Harvard Sq.* and the river. Even closer to Harvard Yard is 113-room **The Inn at Harvard,** *1201 Massachusetts Ave, Cambridge, MA 02138; (617) 491-2222,* expensive. The expensive 400-room **Royal Sonesta Hotel,** *5 Cambridge Pkwy, Cambridge, MA 02142; tel: (617) 491-3600,* stands on the riverbank near the Museum of Science. A more intimate choice is the 17-room **A Cambridge House Bed & Breakfast Inn,** *2218 Massachusetts Ave, Cambridge, MA 02140; tel: (617) 491-6107* or *(800) 232-9989,* moderate–expensive.

Eating and Drinking

In *Harvard Sq.,* the **Harvest,** *44 Brattle St* (in courtyard); *tel: (617) 492-1115,* is a Cambridge literary hangout, moderate.

ENTERTAINMENT

Nationally known **American Repertory Theatre,** *Loeb Drama Center, 64 Brattle St, Cambridge, MA 02138; tel: (617) 547-8300,* adds lustre and a contemporary twist to Boston's theatre offerings. **Hasty Pudding Theatre,** *12 Holyoke St, Cambridge, MA 02138; tel: (617) 495-5205,* stages student productions and professional musical comedies.

In *Harvard Sq.,* **Regattabar** in the Charles Hotel is a top venue for jazz performances, while **House of Blues,** *96 Winthrop St,* shares the glitz of the *Blues Brothers* film starring John Belushi and part-owner Dan Aykroyd. **Club Passim,**

47 *Palmer St; tel: (617) 492-7679,* has led the folk music scene since Bob Dylan and Joan Baez. There are dance and music-only clubs in *Central Sq., Inman Sq.* offers jazz and Irish joints. Among the hottest clubs is **Johnny D's,** *17 Holland St, Somerville* (T: *Davis Sq.*); *tel: (617) 776-9667.* There are several first-run movie theatres, but the **Brattle Theatre,** *40 Brattle St; tel: (617) 876-6837,* is unique, with a rear-projection screen and a roster of art and classic films. The **Harvard Film Archive,** *Carpenter Center for the Visual Arts, 24 Quincy St; tel: (617) 495 4700,* shows art-house and foreign films.

SIGHTSEEING

Derided as 'The People's Republic of Cambridge' for its politics, this small city across the Charles River functions as Boston's 'Left Bank', with bookshops, cafés, arty denizens and an intellectual air that is driven by its two big universities. **Harvard Sq.,** once funky and counter-cultural, now has the well-kept look of a shopping mall; however, it's still the main place for people-watching and hanging out, and it has the greatest concentration of bookshops in the USA.

The Square is also has some sites of historic interest. **Harvard University,** which now sprawls well beyond ivied Harvard Yard, was America's first US college (1636), and its presence dominates the city. **Cambridge Common** is where Gen George Washington took command of the First Continental Army on 3 July 1775, an event duly noted with a plaque. Cambridge's oldest church, **Christ Church,** *Zero Garden St,* a 1761 Tory house of worship used as a Revolutionary War barracks, and 1833 Unitarian **First Church,** *11 Garden St,* embrace the **Old Burying Ground,** where early residents lie. Amidst the man-

sions along **Brattle St** (formerly Tory Row) is the **Henry Wadsworth Longfellow House,** *105 Brattle St, Cambridge, MA 02138; tel: (617) 876-4491,* open for tours Wed–Sun 1000–1630 (May–Oct), $2. This was Gen Washington's headquarters in 1775–76 and poet Longfellow's home 1837–1882. Nearby **Brattle House** stands on the former site of a village blacksmith's shop 'under the spreading chestnut tree' celebrated by Longfellow.

Along the verges of Harvard Yard are the university's three interconnected art museums. The **Fogg Art Museum,** *32 Quincy St, Cambridge, MA 02138; tel: (617) 495-9400,* features European and American masterpieces. The **Busch-Reisinger Museum,** same entrance, is known for its 20th-century German collection. And the **Sackler Museum,** *Quincy St and Broadway; tel: (617) 495-9400,* houses Asian and Islamic collections. All are open daily 0900–1700, $5 for all. A short walk away, at the **Harvard University Museums of Natural and Cultural History,** entrances at *24 Oxford St* and *11 Divinity Ave; tel: (617) 495-3045,* are another four collections within one building: a botanical museum, with a unique 'glass flowers' exhibit, a comparative zoology museum with dinosaur skeletons and stuffed animals, an archaeology museum with Mayan and Southwest Indian artifacts and a topnotch mineral and geology collection. Open Mon–Sat 0900–1630, Sun 0100–1630, $4.

The **Massachusetts Institute of Technology** occupies the portion of Cambridge closest to Boston, and the riverside promenade here commands the finest **view of the Boston skyline** anywhere, with sailboats in the foreground and tall buildings dwarfing the State House's golden dome beyond.

BOSTON NORTH SHORE

Boston's North Shore encompasses some of the finest scenery and most spellbinding history in New England. Among its treasures are a rocky coast line, grand mansions and charming seaside towns. Salem was once the centre of luxury trade with the Far East while the gritty seaport of Gloucester echoes with the sound of seagulls following ships in from a long day out at sea. Perhaps the most enduring legacy is the Salem witch trials of 1692, which struck terror into the hearts of its residents. The trials still resound in American history and are often cited as an example of how mass hysteria can result in great injustice.

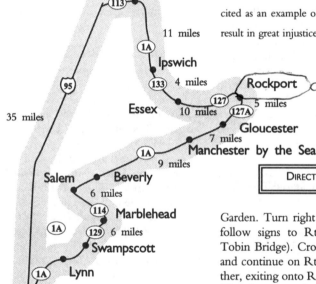

DIRECT ROUTE: 35 MILES

Garden. Turn right onto *Storrow Dr.* and follow signs to Rte 1 north (Exit 27, Tobin Bridge). Cross the **Tobin Bridge** and continue on Rte 1 about 3 miles farther, exiting onto Rte 16 **(Revere Beach Pkwy)** eastbound. After 1.5 miles on Rte 16, take Rte 1A north through a primarily unattractive landscape, following signs toward Lynn. After 4.3 miles, bypass the fork bearing left for Downtown Lynn, continuing instead 0.5 miles on the Carroll Pkwy to a rotary where you'll see a sign for Marblehead and **Swampscott.** From the rotary take the scenic ocean view drive along *Lynn Shore Dr.*

Drive 0.9 miles through Swampscott, then another 0.7 miles to a fork and a traffic light. Bear left onto Rte 129 (*Atlantic*

ROUTE

Reconstruction of the **Central Artery (I-93)** through downtown Boston will make the most direct route out of town (via I-93 to the Callahan Tunnel) troublesome well into the next century.

A simple alternative, from **Boston Common,** is to take *Beacon St* west to *Embankment Rd* at the corner of the Public

77

Ave) and drive another 1.5 miles into **Marblehead**. After 1.4 miles, you can turn off for a scenic four-mile loop around **Marblehead Neck** by making a right onto *Ocean Ave*. It's 1.5 miles from this point to Castle Rock and another 0.5 miles to Chandler Hovey Park and Marblehead Light. Return via *Harbor Ave* to *Ocean Ave* and turn right back onto *Atlantic Ave*; continue 1.5 miles into Marblehead centre and turn right onto *Washington St*, where you'll see a sign for *Front St* and the harbour to visit Marblehead's **Old Town**. Leaving Marblehead, follow *Washington St*, which becomes *Pleasant St* (Rte 114). Take this route west into **Salem**, where it joins Rte 1A. Continue to *Derby St*, where you'll see signs for the Salem Visitor Center and parking. Follow signs to the garage; the Visitor Center is across the street. From Salem take Rte 1A (*Bridge St*) north into Beverly and then Rte 127 north. Follow this leisurely, scenic drive through Beverly, Manchester-by-the-Sea, the Magnolia section of Gloucester and into **Gloucester**.

Make a five-mile loop through East Gloucester, bringing you to Rocky Neck and scenic Bass Rocks, then follow Rte 127A north five miles to **Rockport**. Drive 2.5 miles from *Main St* to *Beach St* to *Granite St* and follow Rte 127 to *Gott Ave* and **Halibut Point**. Make a right from *Gott Ave*, go 8.7 miles and turn onto Rte 128 south. At Exit 14 (about 2 miles), take Rte 133 west four miles to **Essex** and another five miles toward **Ipswich**. At *Northgate Rd* turn right, then right again onto *Argilla Rd* and follow it to **Crane Beach**; or you can stay on Rte 133 to Rte 1A and continue into Ipswich. If you visit Crane Beach, return via *Argilla Rd* all the way to Rte 1A, turn right (north) and go 0.5 mile into the centre of Ipswich.

Follow 1A north through the towns of Rowley, Newbury and into **Newburyport**, a total of 12 miles. Returning to Boston, leave Newburyport on **Rte 113** (*High St*) west to **I-95** south; at Exit 46 take Rte 1 into Boston (via the Tobin Bridge), a total of 35 miles.

MARBLEHEAD

Tourist Information: Marblehead Chamber of Commerce, *62 Pleasant St, Marblehead, MA 01945; tel: (617) 631-2868*, does not book rooms. An information booth is open end May– mid-Oct, intersection of *Pleasant* and *Spring Sts*.

ACCOMMODATION AND FOOD

Marblehead has numerous bed and breakfasts, ranging from one room to 12. Some offer ocean views and many are furnished with antiques. Try the moderate three-room **Stillpoint B&B**, *27 Gregory St, tel: (617) 631-1667*, which serves breakfast on a deck overlooking the harbour. The three-room **Harborside House**, *23 Gregory St, tel: (617) 631-1032*, is conveniently located in the historic district, moderate. **The Seagull Inn**, *106 Harbor Ave, tel: (617) 631-1893*, is half a block to the ocean and harbour; moderate to pricey. The 20-room **Harbor Light Inn**, *58 Washington St, tel: (617) 631-2186*, has a pool.

For a great sitdown Italian meal there's **Rosalie's Restaurant**, *20 Sewall St; tel: (617) 631-5353*, located in a 100-year-old brick factory. Reservations are recommended. Pricey. For seafood try the moderate to pricey **The Landing**, *81 Front St; tel: (617) 631-1878*, located on Marblehead Harbor, or the funkier **Barnacle**, *141 Front St; tel: (617) 631-4236*, owned by a lobsterman. **The King's Rook**, *12 State St; tel: (617) 631-9838*, is excellent for a sandwich or salad lunch and an elegant dessert or iced drink. Budget. **The Driftwood**, *63 Front St; tel: (617) 631-1145*, is a local favourite, specialising in huge all-day breakfast, fish and chowder. Budget.

SIGHTSEEING

Settled by fishermen from Cornwall and the Channel Islands in 1629, Marblehead is known for its lovely harbour, narrow streets and as a sailing community. Most people mean **Old Town** when they refer to Marblehead, and the best way to see this pleasantly congested area is to park the car on the outskirts and walk along *Hooper* and *Washington Sts* and along the waterfront on *Front St*. Along these streets are an assortment of interesting antique stores including **Old Town Antique Corp**, *108 Washington St; tel: (617) 631-9728*.

Abbot Hall, *Washington St; tel: (617) 631-0528*, open Mon, Thurs and Fri 0800– 1700, Tues and Wed 0800–2100, Sun 1100-1800, free, is the 1876 Victorian town hall towering above Marblehead and home of the famous painting, 'Spirit of '76', in which two drummers and a fife player march with the American flag after a battle with the British. The **Jeremiah Lee Mansion**, *161 Washington St; tel: (617) 631-1069*, open Mon–Sat 1000–1600, Sun 1300–1600 (mid-May– mid Oct), $4, is a Georgian mansion built in 1768 by a wealthy merchant whose fleet traded with the West Indies and Europe.

For outdoor activity drive a loop on Marblehead Neck and clamber on the rocks at **Castle Rock** or take a walk at **Chandler-Hovey Park**. Each offers fine vistas and benches from which to see them. In Old Town **Crocker Park** at the south end of *Front St* and **Fort Sewall** at the north will give you views, sea air and benches for a picnic.

SALEM

Tourist Information: Salem Chamber of Commerce, *32 Derby Sq., Old Town Hall, Salem, MA 01970, tel: (508) 744-0004*, open Mon–Fri 0900–1700, does not book rooms but will provide referrals. The **National Park Service Visitor Center**, *2 Liberty St, Salem, MA 01970; tel: (508) 741-3648*, open daily 1000– 1700 (winter), 0900–1800 (summer). **North of Boston Convention and Visitors Bureau**, *P.O. Box 642, Beverly, MA 01915; tel: (800) 742-5306*.

ACCOMMODATION

Salem offers a choice of elegantly restored inns and bed and breakfasts, most within walking distance of downtown sights. The 1845 Greek Revival **Amelia Payson Guest House**, *16 Winter St; tel: (508) 744-8304*, is convenient and non-smoking; moderate. The moderate 11-room **Coach House Inn**, *284 Lafayette St; tel: (508) 744-4092* or *(800) 688-8689*, is a Victorian Mansion built by a sea captain and is a ten-min walk to downtown. The expensive **Hawthorne Hotel**, *18 Washington Sq. West; tel: (508) 744-4080, (800) 729-7829* is on Salem Common. The 22-room **Salem Inn**, *7 Summer St; tel: (508) 741-0680*, is an 1834 Federal-style sea captain's home just off Salem Common. Expensive to pricey.

The expensive **Inn at Seven Winter Street**, *7 Winter St; tel: (508) 745-9520*, is an 1870 French Victorian building with antiques and canopy beds and within walking distance of downtown. Adjacent to the Witch Musem is the eight-room **Stepping Stone Inn**, *19 Washington Sq. North; tel: (800) 338-3022*, built in 1846; moderate to expensive. The four-room 1808 **Suzanna Flint House**, *98 Essex St; tel: (508) 744-5281 or (800) 752-5281*, has a garden sitting area; moderate.

79

For a more mundane but modern experience, there's the comfortable 125-room *QI*, moderate to expensive. In the same category is the 367-room **Tara Ferncroft Conference Resort,** *50 Ferncroft Rd, Danvers; tel: (508) 777-2500 or (800) 544-2242;* expensive. Both are a short drive from Salem.

Winter Island Maritime Park, *50 Winter Island Rd; tel: (508) 745-9430,* with 41 RV sites and tent pitches, is open May–end Oct and offers a beach, boat launch and pier.

EATING AND DRINKING

Salem has good seafood restaurants but for a quick snack try **Pickering Wharf,** *Derby St; tel: (508) 745-9540,* which has a dozen sandwich, pizza, snack shops and restaurants. Salem's best known restaurant is the **Lyceum,** *43 Church St; tel: (508) 745-7665,* the building from which Alexander Graham Bell called Boston, making the first long–distance phone call. Now it's a beautifully decorated restaurant specialising in grilled seafood. For a beer and a burger or Mexican food there's **In a Pig's Eye Restaurant,** *148 Derby St; tel: (508) 741-4436;* budget.

SHOPPING

Souvenirs, food and gifts are easy to find at **Pickering Wharf,** *Derby St; tel: (508) 745-9540,* a renovated area on the waterfront with 35 shops and restaurants.

Ye Olde Pepper Companie, *122 Derby St; tel: (508) 745-2744,* open daily 1000-1700, is America's oldest candy company, established in 1806. For unusually delicious chocolates there's **Harbour Sweets,** *85 Leavitt St; (508) 745-7648,* open Mon–Fri 0830–1630, Sat 0900–1500. **Crow Haven Corner,** *125 Essex St; tel: (508) 745-8763,* open daily 1030–1900, is owned by Laurie Cabot,

Salem's official witch, and features herbs, crystals and other paraphernalia necessary to practice witchcraft.

SIGHTSEEING

Salem calls itself 'Witch City' and enjoys playing up its role in the 1692 witch trials even though the accusations actually began in Danvers, then called Salem Village. A more enlightened segment of its history is its sea trade with the Far East which brought exotic goods and made Salem the richest American city per capita in 1790. Many of the museums, homes and exhibits celebrating Salem's history are located near the splendid Salem Common surrounded by beautiful Federal homes, making this an excellent place for a walking tour.

The **National Park Service Visitor Center,** provides free maps of the 1.7 mile Heritage Trail which takes you to major sites along a clearly marked, red path on the sidewalk. The center also has a 30-min film on the history of Essex County which includes an explanation of why so many place names come from England.

If you'd rather not walk, ride the **Salem Trolley,** *9 Pickering Way; tel: (508) 744-5469,* with one-hour narrated tours, stopping at most major sites on the trail; $8 adults, $20 family of four or more. There are numerous trail stops to choose from. The 1642 **Witch House,** *310½ Essex St, Salem, MA 01970; tel: (508) 744-0180,* open daily 1000–1630 (mid-March–end June), 1000–1800 (July–early Sept), 1000–1630 (early Sept–1 Dec), $5, is the restored home of Jonathan Corwin, one of the judges of the Salem witch trials and the site of preliminary examinations of the accused. The **Witch Dungeon Museum,** *16 Lynde St, Salem, MA 01970; tel: (508) 741-3570,* open daily 1000–1700 (Apr–end Nov); $4, employs professional actors to re-enact a witch trial.

Peabody Essex Museum, *East India Sq.; tel: (508) 745-9500,* open Tues–Sat 1000–1700, Sun 1200–1700 (end May–end Oct); $7, or $18 for family of four or more, was founded in 1799 and is the oldest continuously operating museum in America. On display are many of the luxury items brought back by Salem seafarers as well as exhibits on whaling and fishing. **The Salem Witch Museum,** *Washington Sq.; tel: (508) 744-1692,* open daily 1000–1700 (Sept–June); 1000–1900 (July and Aug); $4, is a bit corny but offers a dramatic explanation of the trials through dioramas, narration and displays.

The **Salem Maritime Historic Site,** *174 Derby St; tel: (508) 740-1660,* open daily 0900–1700, free, has a slide show and tours including a stop at the Custom House. Or you can wander on your own, amid the restored wharves, once bustling with activity, and warehouses and the nearby **West India Goods Store,** brimming over with sugar, molasses and tropical fruits from the Caribbean. **The House of the Seven Gables,** *54 Turner St, Salem, MA 01970; tel: (508) 744-0991,* open daily 0900–1800 (early July–end Oct), 1000–1630 (Nov–end June), closed Jan, $7, is the 17th-century mansion made famous by Nathaniel Hawthorne's story of the same name. The house where he was born in Salem was moved to this site.

Just south of the city on Rte 1A is **Pioneer Village,** *Forest River Park; tel: (508) 744-0991,* open Mon–Sat 1000–1700, Sun 1200–1700 (end May–end Oct); $4.50 per adult, $12 for family of four or more, where authentically costumed actors recreate 17th-century Salem and explain Puritan village life. The **East India Cruise Company,** *Pickering Wharf; tel: (508) 741-0434,* has daily 90-min narrated cruises of the North Shore coastline departing daily 1300, 1500, 1800 (end May–early Sept); Sat and Sun 1300 and 1500 (early Sept–mid-Oct), $7.

History Alive!, *Old Town Hall, Derby Sq.; tel: (508) 741-8689,* open daily, 1130, 1330 and 1500 (mid-June–end Oct), $5, presents 'Cry Innocent: The People vs Bridget Bishop', a re-enactment of a witch trial. **Dracula's Castle,** *New Derby St; tel: (508) 741-0280,* open daily 1200–1700 (5 July–1 Sept and in Oct), $5, is a family oriented haunted house with a trail of eerie chambers leading to Dracula's haunted crypt.

MANCHESTER-BY-THE-SEA

Manchester is a lovely seaside town worth stopping in primarily if you are interested in spending a few hours at scenic **Singing Beach** at the end of *Beach St,* where the sand supposedly makes a musical noise underneath one's footsteps. Arrive early to find a parking space and be prepared to walk. The small car park at the beach is $15 a day or try Masconomo Park off *Beach St,* with free, unlimited parking and a 0.5 mile walk or behind Town Hall, which has two-hour, free parking and a 1.1 mile walk.

GLOUCESTER

Tourist Information: Cape Ann Chamber of Commerce, *33 Commercial St, Gloucester, MA 01930; tel: (508) 283-1601,* does not book rooms but provides referrals.

ACCOMMODATION

Gloucester offers plenty of choices, including a mix of older homes and more modern lodgings with ocean views. The 48-room *BW* **Bass Rocks Ocean Inn,** *107 Atlantic Rd; tel: (508) 283-7600,* was originally an 1899 summer mansion for a wealthy family. In the 1960s a motel was added. All rooms have ocean views;

81

expensive. **Cape Ann Campsite,** *80 Atlantic St; tel: (508) 283-8683,* has 300 shaded tent pitches and trailer sites overlooking a river and is a mile from Wingaersheek Beach. The 29-room **Cape Ann Motor Inn,** *33 Rockport Rd; tel: (508) 281-2900 or (800) 464-VIEW,* is on Long Beach and all rooms have an ocean view; moderate to expensive. **Cape Ann's Marina Resort,** *75 Essex Ave; tel: (508) 283-2116,* has 52 rooms with views of the water; moderate to expensive. **Spruce Manor,** *14 Essex Ave; tel: (508) 283-0614,* is a 20-room Victorian home with 11 other motel units, located on the way to Ipswich. Moderate to expensive.

EATING AND DRINKING

Gloucester's restaurants specialise in seafood platters and chowder. Try **The Gull,** *75 Essex St; tel: (508) 281-6060,* moderate. For a fancier meal try the moderate to pricey **White Rainbow,** *65 Main St; tel: (508) 281-0017,* offering such fare as a lobster burrito and scallops in Japanese barbecue sauce. For a wacky experience there's the moderate **Evie's Rudder,** *73 Rocky Neck Ave; tel: (508) 283-7967,* which has great food, a kooky atmosphere and spontaneous entertainment including an invisible flaming baton twirling act.

SIGHTSEEING

This working class city has been an important fishing centre since the 1620s but was also a turn-of-the-century playground for rich people from Boston who built massive seaside 'cottages' on the water. It's easy to while away time watching the fishing boats or enjoying a nearby beach. For the latter, try **Good Harbor Beach** near Rockport or **Wingaersheek Beach** on Ipswich Bay.

The Magnolia section of the city is home of the **Hammond Castle Museum,** *80 Hesperus Ave; tel: (508) 283-2080,* open Wed–Sun and Mon holidays 1000–1700, $5.50. Eccentric inventor John Hays Hammond built this re-created medieval castle in 1926. It's known for its 8600-pipe organ in the Great Hall. The Chamber of Commerce has a guide to the **Gloucester Maritime Trail** offering four scenic and historic walking trails. The 1.1 mile Downtown Loop includes a US Coast Guard Station, historic homes and the 70-year-old *The Gloucester Adventure, tel: (508) 281-9079* a two-masted, 121-foot fishing schooner, open Thurs–Sun 1000–1600 (end May– end Sept) or by appointment; $3. Have breakfast on board Sun 0900–1200 all year round, $5. The historic loop focuses on **Stage Fort Park** on Rte 127 including a beach and a rocky ocean ledge. Note the statue on *Stacey Blvd* called **The Gloucester Fisherman,** known locally as **The Man at the Wheel,** commissioned in 1923 to mark the city's 300th anniversary.

The two-mile Vessels View walk takes you to a fish pier and the 1.1 mile Painters Path goes to **East Gloucester** and **Rocky Neck.** The art colony along *Rocky Neck Ave* is a colourful hotchpotch of galleries, studios and restaurants.

The **Beauport Sleeper-McCann House,** *75 Eastern Point Blvd; tel: (508) 283-0800,* open Mon–Fri 1000–1600 (mid-May–mid-Oct); Mon–Fri 1000–1600, Sat and Sun 1300–1600 (mid-Sept–mid Oct); $5, was built in the 1920s as a 'summer cottage' and is now an antique filled museum.

Gloucester offers plenty of chances to head out to sea. Try **Yankee Whale Watch,** *75 Essex St; tel: (800) 942-5464 or (508) 283-0313,* which also offers full- and half-day fishing trips; **Cape Ann Whale Watch,** *415 Main St; tel: (800) 877-5110 or (508) 283-5110,* **Capt. Bill's**

Whale Watch and Deep Sea Fishing, *9 Traverse St; tel: (800) 33-WHALE,* or **Seven Seas Whale Watch,** *Seven Seas Wharf, 63 Rogers St; tel: 800-238-1776 or (508) 283-1776.* Most trips are about four hours and cost $21. Reservations are recommended.

ROCKPORT

Tourist Information: Rockport Chamber of Commerce, *3 Main St, Rockport, MA 01966; tel: (508) 546-6575.* It does not book rooms but will provide referrals and operates an information booth on *Upper Main St* (Rte 127) Mon–Sat 1100–1700; Sun 1300–1700 (mid-May–Oct).

ACCOMMODATION

Rockport has everything from the standard dull-but-comfortable motels to arty and antique–filled inns and bed and breakfasts. The moderate **Bearskin Neck Motor Lodge,** *74 South Rd; tel: (508) 546-6677,* has eight motel units and is perched on a narrow spit of land jutting into the water. The eight-room, expensive **Seacrest Manor,** *131 Marmion Way; tel: (508) 546-2211,* has spacious grounds and gardens. Smoking is not allowed and owners discourage bringing children. **The Yankee Clipper Inn,** *96 Granite St; tel: (800) 545-3699 or (508) 546-3407,* has 26 rooms, some in the 1840 Greek Revival building and others in the modern Quarterdeck. There is a marvellous ocean view and a heated salt water pool; expensive to pricey. For convenience there is expensive **Captain's Bounty Motor Inn,** *1 Beach St; tel: (508) 546-9557,* with 24 rooms on the beach near the center of town. The **Addison Choate Inn,** *49 Broadway; tel: (800) 245-7543, (508) 546-7543,* is a 19th-century house with beautifully decorated rooms; expensive.

EATING AND DRINKING

Rockport has fine restaurants but this is also a good place to walk and snack, mostly along **Bearskin Neck,** which has ice-cream, fried dough, chowder and other goodies. Note that Rockport is a dry town, meaning there are no liquor stores and alcohol is not served in restaurants. You can bring your own bottle, however, and restaurants will gladly provide glasses. For a lobster dinner there's the moderate **Lobster in the Ruff,** *Bearskin Neck; tel: (508) 546-RUFF.* **The Seaside Restaurant,** *21 Dock Sq.; tel: (508) 546-3905,* features ocean views and a children's menu; budget to moderate. **The Peg Leg Restaurant and Inn,** *18 Beach St; tel: (508) 546-3038,* has seafood and traditional American fare; moderate. **Ellen's Harborside,** *T-Wharf; tel: (508) 546-2512,* has seafood platters; budget.

SHOPPING

Bearskin Neck juts out into the harbour and is jammed with gift, craft and souvenir shops as well as places to snack. It's also often jammed with people. For quieter shopping, stroll in the centre of town and you'll find art galleries and stores including shops at **Dock Square.** A traditional treat is **Tuck's Candies,** *7 Dock Sq.; tel: (508) 546-2840.* **Sun Basket,** *8½ Bearskin Neck, tel: (508) 546-7546,* has North American Indian crafts.

SIGHTSEEING

Rockport has something for everyone: a boat–filled harbour, ocean vistas, art galleries and plenty of shopping. Park in the town car park at the information booth on Rte 127, a mile before town. It costs $6 but there are shuttle buses to town on weekends, saving you lots of aggravation.

Soak up the atmosphere of art and ocean by merely strolling around town and dropping into a few galleries. Mixed in with the shops are rough hewn lobster shacks and fishermen's homes. Make sure you notice **Motif Number 1,** a red lobster shack at the harbour covered with colourful buoys. It got its name because it's considered the favourite subject of American painters and photographers.

The Rockport Chamber of Commerce has information on three scenic walking tours that take you to wharves, historic sites and old burial grounds.

The **Paper House,** *Pigeon Hill St; tel: (508) 546-2629,* open by appointment only, $1, is a home with furniture made of 100,000 copies of Boston newspapers. It took 20 years to construct.

Halibut Point State Park, *Gott Ave; tel: (508) 546-2997,* is on the outskirts of town and well worth the drive to take a walk along a sloping granite coast with splashing waves. Walk amidst its 54 acres on your own or take a guided tour along the park's water-filled granite quarry, Sat 0930 (mid-May–late Oct).

ROCKPORT TO NEWBURYPORT

This pleasant drive takes you along the Essex River, and past green farmland and well maintained colonial homes. **Essex** is known for antiques shops and its regionally famous restaurant **Woodman's,** *Route 133; tel: (508) 768-6451,* which serves plump fried clams and huge onion rings. It's big, noisy and fun; budget.

Ipswich has **Chipper's River Café,** *Caldwell's Block; tel: (508) 356-7956,* a local hangout with great food, known especially for huge breakfasts and muffins; budget. It also boasts one of the most beautiful beaches in Massachusetts. The four-mile **Crane Beach** has sand dunes and also, unfortunately, greenheads, a bug that stings, usually in late July and early

Aug. Officials post signs if they're bothersome. Parking is $8. Overlooking the beach is **Castle Hill,** *290 Argilla Rd; tel: (508) 356-4351,* open 1300–1600, days vary so call ahead, $5, a 59-room mansion built in the early 1900s by Richard Crane, a plumbing fixture magnate. Note the sterling silver bathroom fixtures. Scenes from *The Witches of Eastwick, Flowers in the Attic* and *The Next Karate Kid* were filmed here. The grounds are open in spring and summer for various concerts.

For kids there's **New England Alive,** *163 High St; tel: (508) 356-7013,* open Mon–Fri 1000-1700, Sat–Sun 0930-1800 (May–Nov), $5, a petting farm and nature study centre with wild and domestic animals. The **Ipswich River** offers excellent canoeing, especially for families. You can rent a canoe from **Foote Brothers,** *230 Topsfield Rd; tel: (508) 356-9771,* open daily 0800–1800 (early Apr–end Oct), $25 for a four-hour gentle ride. Stop in **Rowley** to browse for antiques in the shops around Rte 1A.

NEWBURYPORT

Tourist Information: Greater Newburyport Chamber of Commerce & Industry, *29 State St, Newburyport, MA 01950; (508) 462-6680;* does not book rooms but provides information.

ACCOMMODATION

There are bed and breakfasts in town and a variety of motels and hotels in the vicinity. **The Garrison Inn,** *Brown Sq.; tel: (508) 465-0910,* built in 1809 has 24 rooms including six two-level suites; moderate to expensive. The six-room **Windsor House,** *38 Federal St; tel: (508) 462-3778,* is an 18th-century federal mansion conveniently located and owned by Britons who serve a Cornish breakfast and afternoon tea; moderate to expensive.

ENTERTAINMENT

The **Firehouse Center for the Visual and Performing Arts,** *Market Sq.; tel: (508) 462-7336,* has an art gallery as well as theatre and music.

EATING AND DRINKING

Seafood restaurants and sandwich and ice cream shops abound. **David's Restaurant at the Garrison Inn,** *11 Brown Sq.; tel: (508) 462-8077,* has childcare for $5 a child (including a meal) while you dine on the light menu of pasta and fish downstairs or the fancier dishes upstairs; budget to moderate. **Scandia,** *25 State St; tel: (508) 462-6271,* is known for veal and lobster; moderate. **The Grog,** *13 Middle St; tel: (508) 465-8008,* is a long-time local hangout; budget. The moderate **Michael's Harborside,** *Tournament Wharf; tel: (508) 462-7785,* offers seafood and a view of the harbour.

Jonah's In The Whale, *26 Market St; tel: (508) 463-8668,* has chowder, burgers, onion rings and three kinds of fries; budget. **Fowles Luncheonette,** *17 State St; tel: (508) 463-8675,* looks the same as it did in 1944, with a vintage soda fountain; cheap. **Ciro's,** *The Firehouse Center, Market Sq.; tel: (508) 463-3335,* has gourmet pizzas and Italian specialties, moderate.

SHOPPING

Once down-at-heel, Newburyport was beautifully restored in the 1970s and now has bricklined paths, a pleasant outdoor seating area and plenty of giftshops. On weekends the town is bustling with tourists. **Santa Fe Expressions,** *2 Market Sq.; tel: (508) 463-2003,* has items from the Southwest. **Newburyport Printmaker,** *12–16 Inn St; (508) 462-6021,* features pictures of New England and the sea. Visitors homesick for England often wander into **Best of British,** *22 State St;*

tel: (508) 465-6976 which carries imported foods and goods. For kids there's **The Ink Pad Plus,** *2 Threadneedle Alley, (508) 462-8040* which carries a vast array of ink pads and stickers.

SIGHTSEEING

The Chamber of Commerce has information on a walking tour that includes the **Old Jail,** built in 1823, the **Garrison Inn,** named for abolitionist William Lloyd Garrison who was born here, and the 1835 **Custom House,** designed by Robert Mills, who also designed the Washington Monument in Washington, D.C.

Newburyport is known for the early-1800 mansions lining **High St,** many with 'widow's walks' – small porches on the roof that allowed the stay-at-home-wife to scan the horizon for her husband's ship which she hoped was returning from a long sea voyage.

85

⤴ SIDE TRACK FROM NEWBURYPORT

Follow *Water St* to Plum Island Turnpike and the **Parker River National Wildlife Refuge,** *Northern Blvd, Plum Island, Newburyport, MA 01950; tel: (508) 465-5753,* open daily sunrise–sunset, beach sometimes closed seasonally to protect endangered birds (April–end June) $5 per car.

Considered one of the best bird-watching sanctuaries in the US, this 6.5 mile beach is the southern two-thirds of Plum Island, a barrier island and salt marsh. Come early in the day to find parking at this popular spot for swimming, walking, picnicking and observing nature. Even if the beach is closed the refuge is open. There's also access to the public beach from Plum Island's tiny centre; beach is free, private car parks charge about $5. ⬛

WEST OF BOSTON

On 19 Apr 1775, British forces marched from Boston toward Concord for what they thought would be an easy task: to confiscate caches of arms owned by the increasingly restless colonists. Instead they met with the first armed resistance from local militia. The ensuing battles were the start of the American Revolution. A trip along Battle Rd, with stops in Lexington and Concord, provides a vivid lesson in US and British history. In addition, Concord also reveals important literary history – in the mid-19th century, it was home to a flourishing community of writers and philosophers. The route finishes with a country ramble through some of Greater Boston's prettiest towns. Because of the rich political and literary history in this area, this is a popular route for tourists and may carry heavy traffic. Allow a full day or even two in order to stop at the many attractions.

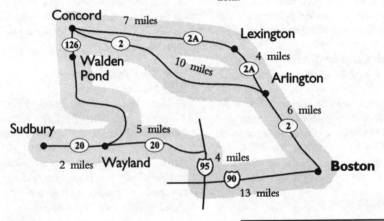

DIRECT ROUTE: 51 MILES

ROUTE

From Boston Common, follow *Beacon St* west 1 mile to *Massachusetts Ave*. Make a right and cross the Charles River to **Cambridge** and the **Massachusetts Institute of Technology**. From MIT follow '*Mass. Ave*' (Rte 2A) 5 miles through interesting but congested Cambridge to **Arlington Center**.

As a slightly longer but quicker alternative, take *Beacon St* from Boston Common and turn right onto *Berkeley St*, then left onto *Storrow Dr.*, which follows the river and becomes *Soldiers Field Rd*. Look for signs to Arlington and Rte 2 bearing right. Follow Rte 2 through part of Cambridge and into Arlington; take Exit 59 and turn right onto Rte 60 (*Pleasant St*), which takes you to Arlington Center, where a left turn rejoins the slower route at *Mass. Ave*. From Arlington Center follow *Mass. Ave* (leaving Rte 2A) 5 miles to the **Battle Green** in **Lexington**. From there bear left, continuing on *Mass. Ave* 1.8 miles to the start of *Battle Rd* (locally called *Great Rd*, again designated Rte 2A), which goes 4.6 miles into **Concord Center**.

After seeing the many sights here, depart via *Main St* and turn left onto *Walden St* (Rte 126) to visit **Walden Pond**. From here you can backtrack 0.2 miles to Rte 2 East for the return trip to Boston.

Or, to see some countryside instead, continue 0.8 miles south and make a left onto *Baker Bridge Rd* and go another half-mile to the Bauhaus-style **Gropius House**. Continue on *Baker Bridge Rd* to the end 0.6 miles, turn right onto *Sandy Pond Rd* and you'll see an entrance 0.2 miles on the left for the **DeCordova Museum**.

Another half-mile beyond, turn right onto *Lincoln Rd* and go 1.6 miles, then right onto *Codman Rd* and go 0.3 miles to the **Codman House**.

From here, make a right turn and return to Rte 126, following it through Wayland to Rte 20. Turn right and follow Rte 20 through **Sudbury** until you see the signs for the Wayside Inn on the right. This route returns to Boston by taking Rte 20 to Rte 128/I-95 South. Take the *Massachusetts Turnpike* (I-90) to downtown Boston (Exit 22) for Copley Place/ Prudential Center.

ARLINGTON

Tourist Information: Arlington Chamber of Commerce, *1 Whittemore Park, Arlington, MA 02174; tel: (617) 643-4600*. The chamber does not book rooms.

Despite the fact that the bloodiest battle of the first day of the American Revolution took place here, Arlington has not capitalized on tourism like its better-known neighbours, Lexington and Concord. Still, it's worth a stop for history buffs. At the corner of *Mystic St* and *Mass. Ave* in Arlington Center is a monument to **Uncle Sam**, the rugged symbol of the United States best known from a World War I recruiting poster. A man named Sam Wilson was born in Arlington in 1766 and eventually moved to Troy, N.Y., where he became a meatpacker. His casks of beef and pork, sent to American troops during the War of 1812, were stamped with the federal monogram, 'U.S.' A legend grew that the letters were for Uncle Sam Wilson, and he became famous as the symbol of America.

At the same corner is the entrance to the **Minuteman Bikeway**, a pleasant, flat 11-mile trail through Arlington, Lexington and Bedford. Only 0.3 miles further west on *Mass. Ave* is the **Jason Russell House**, *7 Jason St, Arlington, MA 02174; tel: (617) 648-4300*, open Mon–Sat 1300–1700 or by appointment; $2 adults, $0.50 children. Of the 49 Minutemen killed on 19 Apr 1775, nearly half died here, and bullet holes are still visible.

LEXINGTON

Tourist Information: Lexington Visitor Center, *1875 Massachusetts Ave, Lexington, MA 02173; tel: (617) 862-1450*, open daily 0900–1700. **Battle Road Visitor Center**, *Rte 2A, Lexington, MA 02173; tel: (617) 862-7753*, open daily 0830–1730 (mid-Apr–end Oct).

ACCOMMODATION

While this route is easily done as a day trip from Boston, there are plenty of choices should you want to make an overnight

87

stay. Be advised to book early, as this is a popular tourist area, especially in the autumn. The 96-room **Battle Green Motor Inn**, *1720 Massachusetts Ave, Lexington, MA 02173; tel: (617) 862-6100*, in the centre of town is dowdy but convenient for shopping, dining and touring Lexington Green; moderate. There's a *Sh*, with 119 rooms, adjacent to *Battle Rd*, and *TL*, with 171 rooms; both moderate. The three-room **Mary Van and Jim's 'This Old House' Bed and Breakfast**, *12 Plainfield St, Lexington, MA 02173; tel: (617) 861-7057*, was the subject of a makeover for a public television programme and provides a charming atmosphere and a substantial breakfast. Moderate.

EATING AND DRINKING

Lexington offers a variety of good restaurants, all within walking distance of the town centre. **Bel Canto**, *1709 Massachusetts Ave; tel: (617) 861-6556*, is not your standard, greasy American pizza parlour, offering outstanding calzones and pizzas as well as Italian specialties; budget. **Lemon Grass**, *1710 Massachusetts Ave; tel: (617) 862-3530*, serves Thai food ranging from the mild to the extra hot; moderate. **Mario's Italian Restaurant**, *1733 Massachusetts Ave; tel: (617) 862-3006*, provides hearty food in a casual atmosphere, budget. **One Meriam**, *1 Meriam St; tel: (617) 862-3006*, dishes up standard American breakfast and lunch; cheap. **Goodies to Go**, *1734*

Massachusetts Ave; tel: (617) 863 1704, is a good spot for take-away lunches and snacks; cheap. Lines often form at **Steve's Ice Cream**, *1749 Massachusetts Ave; tel: (617) 863-1484*, where you can custom design your ice cream cone with candy, nuts and other munchies; cheap.

EVENTS

Patriot's Day, a Massachusetts holiday, is celebrated the third Mon in Apr. The day begins at 0600 with the re-enactment of the historic battle on Lexington Green, followed by a sunrise parade down *Mass. Ave* and a ceremony on the green. At 1300, as the bell in the **Old Belfrey** is rung, a horseman dressed as Paul Revere rides down *Mass. Ave*, shouting, 'The British are coming! The British are coming!' before yet another parade at 1400.

SHOPPING

Lexington Center along *Mass. Ave* and its side streets have souvenir and gift shops and art galleries. **The Crafty Yankee**, *1838 Massachusetts Ave; tel: (617) 863-1219*, features handcrafted items.

SIGHTSEEING

Lexington and the road to Concord are rich in historic sites. Allow plenty of time to leave the car in order to visit buildings and to meander through the attractive town centres, both of which offer good shopping and dining.

The first lesson in American Revolutionary history is at the **Museum of Our National Heritage**, *33 Marrett Rd; Lexington, MA 02173; tel: (617) 861-6559*; bear left off *Mass. Ave* at the sign about 3.5 miles from Arlington Center. A useful ongoing exhibit called 'Let it Begin Here' explains the origins of the American Revolution. Open Mon–Sat 1000–1700, Sun 1200–1700, free.

Another half mile on the left along *Mass. Ave* stands **Munroe Tavern**, *1332 Massachusetts Ave, Lexington, MA 02173; tel: (617) 862-1703*, which was used by the exhausted British as a field hospital during their retreat on 19 Apr 1775. The Tavern houses the office of the **Lexington Historical Society**, *tel: (617) 862-1703*. Buy a combination ticket here for tours of the Munroe and two historic sites in Lexington Center, **Buckman Tavern** and the **Hancock-Clarke House**. All three are open Mon–Sat 1000–1700, Sun 1300–1700 (mid-Apr–Oct). Tickets cost $3 per house, $7 combination; children $1–$2. Prices include a guided tour; first tour 1000, last 1630. In Lexington Center, leave the car alongside **Battle Green** or in the car park behind the shops on the north side of *Mass. Ave*. Everything is within walking distance. Start at the Visitor Center, just east of Battle Green where a diorama explains the events.

Battle Green, also referred to as **Lexington Green**, is considered the site of the first conflict of the American Revolution. Here 77 'Minutemen' – they could be 'ready at a minute's warning' – lined up planning to make merely a symbolic stand. When the 700 British soldiers advanced, a shot was fired – no one knows from which side. British soldiers began firing on the Minutemen and when they finished, eight Americans were dead. The British troops continued on toward Concord. On the green stands the heroic **Minuteman statue**. Opposite the green is **Buckman Tavern**, *1 Bedford St, Lexington, MA 02173; tel: (617) 862-5598*, where the Colonial militia gathered just before dawn to await the British. Alerted by the beating of a drum and the ringing of an alarm bell, the men left the tavern for the green. A short walk from

the tavern is the **Hancock-Clarke House**, *36 Hancock St, Lexington, MA 02173; tel: (617) 861-0928*, a parsonage where Revolutionary leaders John Hancock and Samuel Adams were guests on the night of 18 Apr 1775. Fearing they would be captured by the British, supporters sent William Dawes and Paul Revere to stop at the house on their way from Boston that night to warn citizens of Lexington and Concord of the impending British march.

Across from the green on *Clark St*, just off *Mass. Ave*, is **Belfrey Hill** and the Old Belfrey. Here the bell was rung to warn the Minutemen of the approach of the British.

From Battle Green, continue on past some of Lexington's fine, old Victorian homes on the way to **Battle Road**, located in the 750-acre **Minute Man National Historical Park**, which has a Visitor Center just off Rte 2A. Further along the way toward Concord, you'll come to the **Capture Site** where Paul Revere was arrested by the British, the **William Smith House**, a restored 18th-century house typical of the period and home to the captain of the Lincoln Minutemen, and 1754 **Hartwell Tavern**, a popular local gathering place, on the way past farm stands, fields and private homes to **Meriam's Corner**. Here the Meriam House and barn gave cover to the militia, allowing them to get close enough to the British to fire on them. From here British troops – having already been outgunned at North Bridge in Concord (see below) – began an arduous retreat back to Boston, coming under attack along the way.

CONCORD

Tourist Information: Concord Chamber of Commerce, *2 Lexington Rd, Concord, MA 01742; tel: (508) 369-*

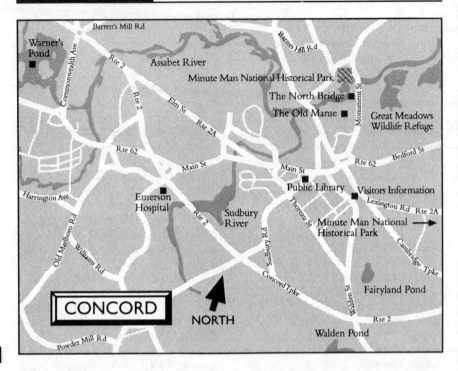

3120. The chamber does not book rooms. **North Bridge Visitor Center,** *174 Liberty St, Concord, MA 01742; tel: (508) 369-6993,* is open daily 0900–1600. The **Visitor Information Booth,** *Lexington Rd* and *Heywood St (no telephone),* is open Mon–Fri 1000–1500, Sat–Sun and holidays 0930–1630 (Apr); daily 0930–1630 (May–end Oct).

ACCOMMODATION

Autumn is the busiest time of year, so make sure you phone in advance. There are several historic homes and inns in the area. The **Anderson Wheeler Homestead,** *154 Fitchburg Turnpike; Concord, MA 01742; tel: (508) 369 3756,* offers bed and breakfast and Victorian lawn games; moderate. **The Colonel Roger Brown House,** *1694 Main St, Concord, MA 01742; tel: (508) 369-9119* or toll-free

(800) 292-1369, also moderate, was built in 1775 and is on the National Historic Register. The expensive 60-room **Colonial Inn,** *48 Monument Sq., Concord, MA 01742; tel: (508) 369 9200,* was built in 1716 and is in the centre of Concord. Its central portion was used as a storehouse during the Revolution. The seven-room **Hawthorne Inn,** *462 Lexington Rd, Concord, MA 01742; tel: (508) 369-5610,* is a cheerful bed and breakfast built in 1870. expensive–pricey. *HJ* is not near town but is convenient to Rte 2, moderate. **North Bridge Inn,** *21 Monument St, Concord, MA 01742; tel: (508) 371-0014,* has newly renovated rooms. Moderate.

EATING AND DRINKING

Concord has a variety of restaurants offering foreign food as well as traditional American fare. **Aigo Bistro,** *84 Thoreau*

St (in the Concord Depot); *tel: (508) 371-1333*, moderate, is Provence style and known for its garlic soup. the **Colonial Inn Dining Room**, *48 Monument Sq.; tel: (508) 369-9200*, offers full American style meals, afternoon tea, brunch on Sunday; pricey.

The **Sally Ann Food Shop**, *73 Main St; tel: (508) 369-4558*, is open daily at 0730 and offers muffins, scones and budget take-away lunches. West Concord, a short distance west of Concord Center via Rte 62, is known for a shop called **Concord Teakcakes**, *59 Commonwealth Ave; tel: (508) 369 7644*, a bakery specialising in scones, muffins and the 'Black' cake made and written about by poet Emily Dickinson; budget.

SHOPPING

There are three separate shopping areas featuring souvenirs, books and gifts. Concord Center, adjacent to *Monument Sq.* and near historic sites, has some interesting bookshops with rare, out-of-print and New England books, plus handicrafts and gift shops.

The Depot is an area around an old train station; notable is the **Stationers**, *85 Main St; tel: (508) 369-1692*, for Massachusetts-made Crane's paper. In West Concord, **Bear-in-Mind**, *53 Bradford St; tel: (508) 369-1167*, is the world's oldest and largest catalogue company devoted to the Teddy Bear; you can visit their warehouse outlet.

EVENTS

While the rest of the state celebrates **Patriots Day** on the closest Mon, Concord always sets aside the actual day, 19 Apr, for a Dawn Salute at 0600 at the **North Bridge**, followed by a remembrance ceremony and the arrival of the Sudbury militia. On the state holiday, there's a parade from **Concord Armory**, *Stowe* and *Everett Sts*, to North Bridge.

Colonial Weekend at Minuteman National Park in early Oct features an 18th-century military encampment, folksinging and hayrides.

SIGHTSEEING

Allow a lot of time for Concord, which offers history and nature in a charming setting. It's a bustling place in summer, popular with tourists and with bicyclists who often take a break at *Monument Sq.*

On the way in from Lexington are three sites that come up in quick succession. **Grapevine Cottage**, *491 Lexington Rd*, now a private home that cannot be visited, was once the home of Ephraim Bull, who developed the Concord grape made famous by a jam and jelly company called Welch's. **The Wayside**, *455 Lexington Rd, Concord, MA 01742; tel: (508) 369-6975* (hours subject to change, so call ahead), was the home of author Nathaniel Hawthorne, best known for *The Scarlet Letter*, written in 1852.

Nearby is **Orchard House**, *399 Lexington Rd, Concord, MA 01742; tel: (508) 369-4118*, open Mon–Sat 1000–1630, Sun 1300–1630 (Apr–end Oct); Mon–Fri 1100–1500, Sat 1000–1630, Sun 1300–1630 (Nov–end Mar); closed 1–15 Jan. This was Louisa May Alcott's family home from 1858–77 and the setting for her most popular book, *Little Women* (1868). Her father, Bronson Alcott, was a philosopher, educator and writer, whose Transcendalist ideas were considered ahead of his time. Along with philosophers and writers Ralph Waldo Emerson, Henry David Thoreau and Nathaniel Hawthorne, Alcott was part of an important literary circle in Concord.

Less than half a mile further on the left is the **Concord Museum**, *200 Lexington*

91

Rd, Concord, MA 01742; tel: (508) 369-9609, open Mon–Sat 1000–1700, Sun 1300–1700; $3–$6, whose exhibits include the lantern hung in the steeple of the Old North Church in Boston on the night of Paul Revere's famous ride. Across the street is **Emerson House**, 28 Cambridge Turnpike, Concord, MA 01742; tel: (508) 269-2236, open Thurs–Sat 1000–1630 (mid-Apr–end Oct), $3, where the author lived from 1835 until his death in 1882.

In **Concord Center**, park along the square or in the parking area on Keyes Rd; both are within walking distance of several points of interest. **The Old Hill Burying Ground** on Lexington Rd was the burial site of the first settlers and of several Revolutionary families. Across the street is **Wright Tavern**, 2 Lexington Rd; tel: (508) 369-3120, the headquarters of the Minutemen before dawn on 19 Apr 1775. Later that day it became the headquarters of the British. Now it's the Chamber of Commerce office. Next door, the **Meetinghouse of the First Parish in Concord** was the site of the First and Second Provincial Congress of 1774.

Down Main St at the corner of Keyes Rd is the **Main St Burying Ground**, burial site of earliest Concord families and Revolutionary soldiers. Across the street is the **Concord Free Public Library**, which has collections dealing with early Concord history and its authors. **Sleepy Hollow Cemetery**, to the northwest of Monument Sq. along Rte 62 (Bedford St), includes an area called **Author's Ridge**, containing the graves of the town's famous literary figures. It's also the site of the **Melvin Memorial**, a monument to three Concord brothers who died in the Civil War, done by American sculptor Daniel Chester French.

A short car ride out of Concord Center north on Monument St is the town's most significant historical place, a replica of **The North Bridge**, which is considered the site of the first battle of the American Revolution. When the British arrived in Concord on 19 Apr 1775 they began searching house to house for arms. Seven companies were sent across a bridge over the narrow Concord River to seize supplies hidden on a farm. Here, by 'the rude bridge that arched the flood' – as Ralph Waldo Emerson later put it in his 1837 Concord Hymn – the American militia engaged the British and for the first time fired a volley – 'the shot heard round the world' – into the ranks of British soldiers. Outnumbered, the British retreated into Concord Center, then all the way to Boston; an inscription here honours two unknown British soldiers who died 'to keep the Past upon its throne'.

There's a small car park on Monument St opposite the path to the bridge. Half a mile beyond, turn left onto Liberty St for the North Bridge Visitors Center, which houses exhibits and activities on the start of the war and a bookshop.

Heading back toward Concord Center, on the right you'll see **The Old Manse**, Monument St, Concord, MA 01742; tel: (508) 369-3909, open Mon, Wed, Thurs, Fri 1000–1700, Sun and holidays 1300–1700 (mid-Apr–end Oct). This was home to Concord's early ministers and later to authors Hawthorne and Emerson.

Walden Pond, Rte 126, 0.2 miles off Rte 2 (open daylight hrs, parking $2), is where philosopher and naturalist Henry David Thoreau wrote Walden, based on his observations while living alone in a small cabin in the woods here from 1845–47. Today the beach is mobbed during the summer, but you can quickly escape the crowds by taking a leisurely walk around the pond, stopping at the site of the cabin.

There's a replica of the cabin at the **Thoreau Lyceum**, *156 Belknap St, Concord, MA 01742; tel: (508) 369-5912,* open Mon–Sat 1000–1700, Sun 1400–1700 (closed Jan, open weekends in Feb), the headquarters of the Thoreau Society, located off *Main St* near Concord Depot.

RECREATION

The **Concord** and **Sudbury Rivers** offer easy canoeing and scenic views of the North Bridge and other sites. Canoes can be hired at **South Bridge Boat House**, *496 Main St, Concord, MA 01742; tel: (508) 369-9438.* Guided tours are available by appointment.

Great Meadows National Wildlife Refuge, *Monsen Rd; tel: (508) 443-4661,* is a 250-acre portion of a 3000-acre refuge featuring a variety of wading birds. Get a panoramic view from the tower near the entrance, then take the short walking loop. Look carefully and you may see turtles, frogs, snakes and muskrat.

LINCOLN

Lincoln is a quiet New England town that prides itself on preserving its rural character and is sometimes considered a bit snooty by outsiders. Nevertheless, this affluent community with its fields, stone walls and large homes is popular for Sunday drives from Boston and Cambridge not only for its beauty but for its rich cultural offerings.

Gropius House, *68 Baker Bridge Rd, Lincoln, MA 01773; tel: (617) 259-8843,* was the family home of and the first US building by Bauhaus architect Walter Gropius when he arrived in 1937. Open Fri–Sun 1200–1700 (June–mid-Oct); Sat and Sun 1200–1700 on the first full weekend of each month (Nov–end May); $5.

DeCordova Museum and Sculpture Park, *51 Sandy Pond Rd, Lincoln,* *MA 01773; tel: (617) 259-8355,* a museum of 20th-century art in a turreted brick building, also features a 35-acre sculpture park with 40 large-scale contemporary sculptures overlooking **Flint's Pond**. Open Tues–Fri 1000–1700, Sat–Sun 1200–1700; $4.

The 1740 **Codman House**, *Codman Rd, Lincoln, MA 01773; tel: (617) 259-8843,* originally a Georgian mansion, was more than doubled in size in 1797 by merchant John Codman to imitate an English country residence. Open Wed–Sun, tours hourly 1200–1600 (June–mid-Oct); $4.

SUDBURY

Not the place to plan to sightsee or shop, Sudbury does boast a historic inn and a small town centre. With sparkling white churches and a town hall, Sudbury looks like the essence of New England.

The Wayside Inn, *Wayside Inn Rd, Sudbury, MA 01776; tel: (508) 443-1776,* has ten guest rooms that fill up early, so call well in advance; expensive. Most people come here for a meal: traditional Yankee fare such as Nantucket Bay scallops, pot roast and Indian pudding. Lunch served Mon–Sat 1130–1500, dinner 1700–2100, Sun 1200–2000; reservations advised.

Sometimes called Longfellow's Wayside Inn – poet Henry Wadsworth Longfellow made the inn famous with his 1863 book, *Tales of a Wayside Inn* – the structure was built in 1716 as a tavern on the *Boston Post Rd*, the main thoroughfare to New York. Indians lived on this spot as much as 3000 years ago.

Nearby is the **Carriage House Inn**, *738 Boston Post Rd, Sudbury, MA 01776; tel: (508) 443-2223,* a 37-room modern building; expensive. A breakfast buffet is included and non-smoking rooms are available.

BOSTON–CAPE COD

Meandering along the scenic South Shore will take you past enchanting harbours, cranberry bogs and beautifully kept homes. Many residents trade the commute into Boston for the seaside and charm. Aside from the loveliness of the area, it's an important part of American history. This is where the Pilgrims settled in 1620 after an arduous ocean voyage from England; here is where they spent their first difficult winter and where survivors settled.

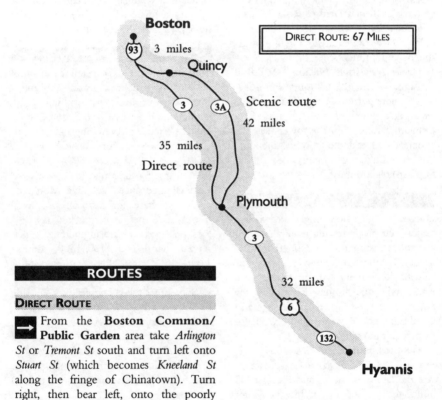

Boston

93   3 miles

Quincy

3   3A

Scenic route
42 miles

35 miles
Direct route

Plymouth

3

32 miles

6

132

Hyannis

DIRECT ROUTE: 67 MILES

94

ROUTES

DIRECT ROUTE

➡ From the **Boston Common/ Public Garden** area take *Arlington St* or *Tremont St* south and turn left onto *Stuart St* (which becomes *Kneeland St* along the fringe of Chinatown). Turn right, then bear left, onto the poorly signed Fitzgerald Expressway (I-93) south. In Quincy, about 1 mile south of the exit for Furnace Brook Parkway (Exit 8), the road splits. Bear left, following signs for Rte 3 South. Follow Rte 3 to Plymouth, a total of 35 miles from Boston, and remain on Rte 3 to the **Sagamore Bridge**, another 15 miles. Rte 3 ends here but connects with Rte 6. Follow Rte 6 over the bridge for 17 miles, then Rte 132 into **Hyannis**, a total of 67 miles from Boston.

SCENIC ROUTE

Follow the direct route onto I-93 south and go 8 miles, exiting at Furnace Brook Parkway (Exit 8). Go 1.5 miles and turn right onto *Adams St,* passing the Adams mansion at 1.5 miles. Follow *Adams St* to the end and turn left onto *Hancock St.* Go two blocks to the **National Park Service Visitor Center** and sites in **Quincy.** Follow Furnace Brook Parkway northeast less than one mile and turn right on to Rte 3A (Southern Artery) where you'll see signs to Cape Cod.

Follow Rte 3A seven miles through Weymouth and **Hingham** to the rotary at *Summer St* and bear left for **Nantasket Beach.** Turn left onto *George Washington Blvd* and follow it three miles to the beach and into **Hull.**

From Hull take Rte 228 south and turn left on to *Atlantic Ave,* about a half mile from the beach. Go one mile across a peninsula with the ocean on the left and Straits Pond on the right.

At the end of the road bear left on to *Jerusalem Rd* in **Cohasset,** past ocean vistas and lavish homes. Bear left onto *Atlantic Ave* and follow it for about three miles along the coastline to Cohasset harbour, onto *Elm St* and into the centre of town.

Return to Rte 3A via *Sohier St* from the centre and take a leisurely drive south to **Plymouth.** At **Scituate,** enter the waterfront area via *First Parish Rd.* Return to 3A and take it through the towns of **Marshfield, Duxbury** and **Kingston.** Look for *Samoset Rd* (Rte 44) and a sign saying Downtown Harbor District and make a left into the centre of Plymouth.

After leaving Plymouth turn left on *Sandwich St* (Rte 3A), and go 2.2 miles to **Plymouth Beach** and **Plimoth Plantation.** From the plantation, take Plimoth Plantation Highway to Exit 4 on

Rte 3 and go south to the Sagamore Bridge. Cross the bridge and follow Rte 6, then Rte 132 to **Hyannis.**

BOSTON TO PLYMOUTH

Starting in Quincy you'll still be in a congested, urban setting. Quincy is the birthplace of two early presidents, John Adams and and his son, John Quincy Adams. **The Quincy Presidential Trail,** a 10.5-mile journey to sites associated with the lives of the Adams family is noted with signs on *Hancock St,* as is a shorter walking tour. The Adams family made major intellectual and political contributions to the US, with diplomats, writers and historians as well as presidents among its members.

Adams National Historic Site, includes a mansion, library, flower garden, greenhouse and pond. Tours leave from the **National Park Service Visitor Center,** *1250 Hancock St, Quincy, MA 02169; tel: (617) 770-1175,* $2 for the mansion and nearby Adams birthplaces, open daily 0900–1700 (mid-Apr–mid Nov).

Hingham boasts a beautiful, tree-lined **Main St,** site of the historic **Old Ship Church,** *99 Main St; tel: (617) 749-1679,* phone for opening hours, free. It was built in 1681, making it the oldest wooden church in continuous use in the US. .

The Old Ordinary, *Lincoln St; tel: (617) 749-0013,* open Tues–Sat 1330–1700 (mid-June–early Sept), $5, built in 1680, was a tavern on the highway from Plymouth to Boston. The town of **Nantasket** has a gorgeous beach set against the backdrop of a shabby but pleasant arcade with games, ice cream, pizza and french fries.

Take a ride on a restored 1928 carousel with a Wurlitzer organ spinning out tunes. Follow *Nantasket Ave* to the end for a visit to **Fort Revere Park,** an area used for

95

defence since the 1600s. The fort is covered with grafitti but the park has a view of the Boston skyline, **Boston Harbor Islands** and the **Boston Lighthouse**.

Cohasset likes to boast that it has one of the most beautiful town commons in America; Hollywood took note by using it as the setting for scenes from *The Witches of Eastwick*, based on the book by New England author John Updike.

Scituate is a lovely seaside town with restaurants and several bed and breakfasts. In **Duxbury** the **King Caesar House**, *120 King Caesar Rd, Duxbury, MA 02332; tel: (617) 934-6106*, open Wed–Sun 1300–1600 (mid-June–early Sept), Fri and Sat 1300–1600 (Sept), $3, was the home of a 19th–century shipping magnate.

The **John Alden House**, *105 Alden St, Duxbury, MA 02332; tel: (617) 934-9092*, open weekends 1000–1700 (mid-May–end June and early Sept–mid-Oct), Tues–Sun 1000–1700 (end June–early Sept), $2.50, built in 1653, was home to the early colonist known in the poem, 'The Courtship of Myles Standish', by Henry Wadsworth Longfellow.

Duxbury has the five mile **Duxbury Beach**, open daily 0800–2000; from Rte 3A take Rte 139 north and turn right at *Canal St* and follow signs.

As you drive through **Kingston** and **Marshfield** and enter **Plymouth**, keep an eye out for cranberry bogs, which have been cultivated here since the 1600s, and are a deep red in the fall at harvest time.

PLYMOUTH

Tourist Information: Plymouth Visitor Information, *130 Water St, Plymouth, MA 02360; tel: (800) 872-1620* or *(508) 747-7525*, will book rooms and tours. They offer several packages which include admission to various sites and gift shop discounts.

ACCOMMODATION

Plymouth has motels, campgrounds and bed and breakfasts. All bed and breakfasts are in the moderate range. Two convenient ones are **In-Town Bed and Breakfast**, *23 Pleasant St, Plymouth, MA 02360; tel: (508) 746-7412*, which includes a walking tour of the area and **Hall's Bed & Breakfast**, *3 Sagamore St, Plymouth, MA 02360 (508) 746-2835*, an 1872 Victorian home. **Myles Standish State Forest**, *P.O. Box 66, S. Carver, MA 02366; tel: (508) 866-2526*, is a 14,000-acre preserve with 475 tent pitches, plus ponds, bathhouses, beaches and bridle and bike paths.

The most convenient motels are the 94-room **Governor Bradford Motor Inn**, *98 Water St, Plymouth, MA 02360; tel: (800) 332-1620* or *(508) 746-6200*, where some rooms have ocean views. Expensive. There's a *Sh* on *Water St* with 175 rooms, expensive. The 79-room **John Carver Inn**, *25 Summer St, Plymouth, MA 02360; tel: (800) 274-1620* or *(508) 746-7100*, has a restaurant and outdoor pool. Moderate. Just south of the centre is **Pilgrim Sands Motel**, *150 Warren Ave, Plymouth, MA (02360); tel: (800) 729-SANDS* or *(508) 747-0900*, with two pools, a private beach and located across from Plimoth Plantation. Expensive.

EATING AND DRINKING

There are plenty of places to get a quick snack or eat a seafood meal. **The Lobster Hut**, *Town Pier; tel: (508) 746 2270*, is casual. Dine on lobster, chowder or fish and chips indoors or on picnic tables overlooking the harbour. Budget to moderate. **Wood's Seafood Market & Restaurant**, *Town Pier; tel: (508) 746-0261* or *(800) 626-1011*, is informal and offers broiled and fried seafood plates as well as sandwiches; cheap to budget. For a fancier meal there's **The Inn for All Seasons,** *97 Warren Ave; tel: (508) 746-8823,* south of Plymouth centre and located in the former summer residence of a wealthy coal magnate; moderate.

EVENTS

Each Friday in Aug at 1800 you can watch **Pilgrim's Progress,** in which marchers representing Mayflower Pilgrims who survived the first winter gather at Plymouth Rock and march to **Burial Hill.** Public **Thanksgiving Day** festivities are held the fourth Thursday in Nov, including a processional from Plymouth Rock, a service at First Parish Church and a feast with turkey all the traditional trimmings.

SHOPPING

Cordage Park, *Court St, Rte 3A, Plymouth, MA 02360; tel: (508) 746-7707,* open daily 1000–1900, Sun 1200–1800; is a restored 19th-century rope mill with 50 stores including 25 factory outlets.

SIGHTSEEING

Plymouth likes to call itself 'America's Hometown' because this is where the Pilgrims first settled in the New World after their voyage from England in 1620. The sites to mark this event are all located within walking distance in the busy centre of town and along the harbour. The **Plymouth Rock Trolley Co.**, *22 Main St, Plymouth, MA 02360; tel: (508) 747-3419,* provides a narrated tour as well as the opportunity for unlimited boarding privileges for a day from any of the sites including Plimoth Plantation, $6.

The best known monument is **Plymouth Rock,** near the state pier on *Water St,* believed to be the place where the first Pilgrims set foot ashore. The rock may be a letdown since it's merely a big stone surrounded by a monument on the

waterfront. But its symbolic value as the origin of a settlement where people came to find freedom is great.

Nearby the **Mayflower II,** *State Pier; tel: (508) 746-1622,* open Mon–Sun 0900–1700 (Apr–end Nov), $5.50, is a replica of the 1620 **Mayflower** that brought the Pilgrims here. The rooms and deck are small, and it's hard to believe 102 passengers spent two cramped months aboard. Buy a combination ticket to also see **Plimoth Plantation** for $18.50. Note the statue of **Massasoit** across the street from Plymouth Rock and walk up Cole's Hill for a view of Plymouth Harbor and to see where the colonists buried those who died during the difficult first winter.

For the real flavour of Pilgrim life **Plimoth Plantation** is a must *P.O. Box 1620, Rte 3A, Plymouth, MA 02362; tel: (508) 746-1622,* open daily 0900–1700 (Apr–end Nov); adults $15, children $9. Children will enjoy this re-created 1627 Pilgrim village where actors dressed as Pilgrims cook, harvest, tend farm animals, make crafts, play games and speak to you about their lives in authentic dialect. Everything you'll see and hear has been authenticated. Part of the fun is that actors stay in character, so if you mention that your plane landed at Logan Airport, they'll profess to have no idea what you're talking about.

Next to the village is a Wampanoag home site where you'll learn about cooking, dugout canoes and crafts and the guidance the Indians gave the Pilgrims. Allow several hours to visit.

The **Plymouth National Wax Museum,** *16 Carver St, Plymouth, MA 02360; tel: (508) 746-6468,* open daily 0900–1700 (March–end Nov), 0900–2100 (July and Aug), 0900–1900 (June, Sept and Oct); $5.50, depicts the Pilgrims' story of persecution in England,

97

the trip across the ocean and the settlement in New England in 26 scenes with life-size figures using light and sound. **Pilgrim Hall Museum**, *75 Court St, Plymouth, MA 02360; tel: (508) 746-1620*, open daily 0930–1630, $5, has a collection of artifacts, furniture and maps used by the pilgrims.

The **Richard Sparrow House**, *42 Summer St, Plymouth, MA 02360; tel: (508) 747-1240*, open daily except Wed 1000–1700, (end May–25 Dec), $2, built in 1640, is the oldest house in Plymouth.

The area is famous for growing cranberries. **Cranberry World**, *225 Water St, Plymouth, MA 02360; tel: (508) 747-2350*, open daily 0930–1700 (May–end Nov), free, has a demonstration bog, a display of antique and contemporary harvesting tools, cooking demonstrations and free cranberry refreshments. The **Plymouth**

Bay Winery, *170 Water St, Plymouth, MA 02360; tel: (508) 746-2100*, open Mon–Sat 1000–1800, Sun 1200–1700 (early Sept–end May), Mon–Sat 1000–2100, Sun 1200–1700 (June–early Sept), free, has tours and tastings, emphasising wine made from cranberries and other local fruit.

The **Children's Museum of Plymouth**, *46–48 Main St; (508) 747-1234*, open Fri and Sat 1000–1800, Sun 1200–1800, (spring, fall and winter), Mon–Sat 1000–1800, Sun 1200–1800 (mid Apr–early Sept), $3.50, has a variety of activities for kids to experience including learning about a lighthouse, a whale watch, a bank, sports and radio. **Plymouth Beach** is on a 3.5-mile jut of land and has lifeguards, a bathhouse and a concession stand along with parking for 200 cars.

98

Pilgrims

In the early 1600s a group of religious dissenters – many from the northern English village of Scrooby – rebelled under the numerous rules and rituals set forth by the Church of England. Led by William Brewster and William Bradford, these Separatists were hunted and arrested for their beliefs. Some left England for Holland but became worried they were losing their English way of life. A group decided to go to America where they believed they could have religious freedom while remaining English.

On 16 Sept 1620, 102 passengers and a crew of 26 began the long and difficult journey across the cold Atlantic. The ship was only 100 feet long and 25 feet wide and, because of the late start, encountered seasonal bad weather. The passengers spent much of their time below deck in cramped quarters, weathering wind and storms. The 3000-mile voyage took 67 days.

The Pilgrims had planned to sail for Virginia but a storm blew them north where they stepped ashore, first at Provincetown on Cape Cod on 21 Nov, then at Plymouth on 16 Dec. Scurvy and extremely harsh weather claimed the lives of about half the Pilgrims during the first grueling winter.

With the help of Native Americans, especially Massasoit, grand sachem of the Wampanoags, and a man called Squanto, the Pilgrims learned how to grow vegetables, fish and hunt. The Pilgrims and Native Americans joined together for a Harvest Feast in 1621, which today Americans celebration as Thanksgiving Day on the fourth Thurs in Nov.

BOSTON–HANOVER

Lowell, Mass., and Manchester, N.H., display the textile mills that put those Merrimack Valley cities in the forefront of the US Industrial Revolution. New Hampshire's south-western corner offers church-steeple communities and abundant outdoor recreation. Hanover, home of Dartmouth College, is New England's northernmost bastion of Ivy League intellectualism. Those are the disparate elements of direct and scenic drives, beginning in Massachusetts and ending at the crossroads of New Hampshire and Vermont in the Upper Valley of the Connecticut River.

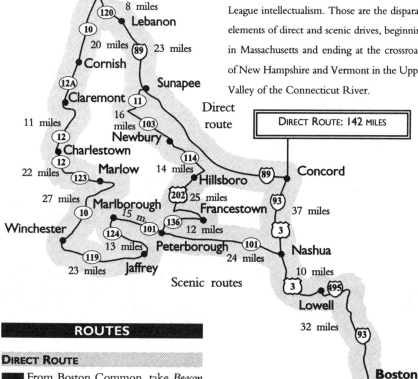

DIRECT ROUTE: 142 MILES

99

ROUTES

DIRECT ROUTE

From Boston Common, take *Beacon St* west to *Embankment Rd* at the corner of the Public Garden. Turn right onto *Storrow Dr* and follow signs to Expressway North (I-93).

Drive 22 miles on I-93 to Exit 44B, then take I-495 south to Exit 36 and get on the **Lowell Connector,** a spur of Rte 3; from there follow the **National** Historical Park signs to **Lowell** centre. Leaving Lowell via the Lowell Connector, take Rte 3 north into New Hampshire; bypass Nashua to reach **Manchester.** Rte 3 between Nashua and Concord becomes the **Everett Turnpike,** where motorists encounter two toll plazas ($0.75 each).

Just beyond Manchester, the Everett Turnpike joins I-93 north, and you'll have a chance to stop at a **Tourist Information Center,** open 24 hrs daily. After 17 miles from Manchester, on the outskirts of Concord, I-89 splits from I-93 (which continues north to the White Mountains; see pp. 222); take I-89 northbound, following signs to the Dartmouth/ Lake Sunapee Region.

Visit **Concord** either by taking I-93 north to Exit 14 or by taking I-89 Exit 2 onto *Clinton St* for 2.5 miles towards *Main St* in the city centre; return to I-89 by reverse direction. For **Lake Sunapee** use Exits 11, 12 or 12A, or continue the 52-mile drive from Concord to **Lebanon.** From Exit 18, go 5 miles via Rte 120 into **Hanover.**

The distance from Boston to Hanover totals 142 miles, which can be covered non-stop in 3 hours or so. Chain hotels are located along I-495 in Massachusetts and between Nashua and Concord in New Hampshire. Along I-89 the only petrol directly on the highway is at Exit 10 near Lebanon.

SCENIC ROUTE

▅▅▶ Make that plural, for you can decide between a good-sized meander through south-western New Hampshire into the Lake Sunapee region or a longer, looping drive westward through the Monadnock region then north along the Connecticut River. Both are great in foliage season.

The former begins at Exit 7 off Rte 3 in **Nashua** for a 24-mile drive on Rtes 101A/101 to **Peterborough.** (If you wish, side-track 2 miles on Rte 45 to **Temple,** a picturesque hill village.) Upon reaching Peterborough, head north on Rte 123, then north-east on Rte 136 via

Greenfield to **Francestown,** a total of 12 miles. Drive 7 miles from Francestown west to Bennington, followed by a northbound journey of 18.5 miles on Rtes 202 and 9 to **Hillsborough,** then on to **Henniker.**

From Henniker take Rte 114 to **Bradford** and **Newbury,** where Rte 103B brings you to the west side of **Lake Sunapee** for quick access to Sunapee Harbor. Go 4 miles via Rte 11 to I-89 to rejoin the direct route to Hanover. This scenic route amounts to 86.5 miles if you include the short side trip to and from Temple.

For an even longer (124-mile) scenic route extension: At Peterborough, instead of turning north, stay on Rte 101 west another 15 miles through **Dublin** to **Marlborough.** Turn left onto Rte 124 in order to backtrack eastward, thus reaching the entrance to **Monadnock State Park,** followed by **Jaffrey Center** and **Jaffrey.** A 7-mile drive south from that town via Rte 202 reaches Rte 119 for a westward drive through **Fitzwilliam** to **Winchester,** where the northbound leg of your journey begins.

Take Rte 10 from Winchester to **Keene** (11 miles), then to **Marlow** (16 miles). From that tiny place, head 14 miles west on rural Rte 123 through **Alsted** to reach the Connecticut River at Rte 12. Drive 8 miles north to **Charles-town** and on into **Claremont,** where Rtes 12 and 103 intersect by twists and turns.

From downtown Claremont, follow Rte 103 west towards riverside Rte 12A for a 5-mile northbound drive to **Cornish,** where the prime off-highway attraction is the **Saint-Gaudens National Historic Site.** Return to Rte 12A. After 10 miles by way of **Plainfield,** you'll reach I-89, but head north on Rte 10 to arrive in **Hanover.**

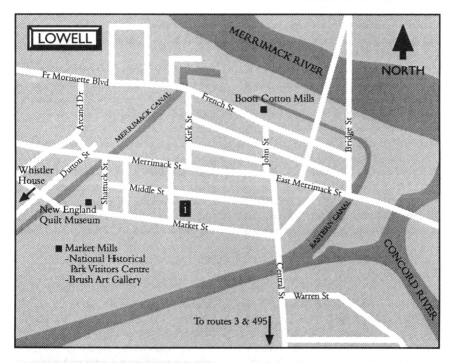

LOWELL

Tourist Information: Greater Merrimack Valley Convention & Visitors Bureau, *18 Palmer St, Lowell, MA 01852; tel: (508) 459-6150,* open Mon–Fri 0830–1700. **Lowell National Historical Park,** *246 Market St, Lowell, MA 01852; tel: (508) 970-5000,* operates the **Market Mills Visitors Center,** open daily 0900–1700, and provides general as well as national park information; free parking.

ACCOMMODATION AND FOOD

Sh is conveniently central. **Commonwealth House,** *87 Nesmith St; tel: (508) 452-9071,* is a moderate Victorian bed and breakfast. **Cobblestone's,** *91 Dutton St; tel: (508) 970-2282,* features innovative US cuisine, moderate. Try Thai, Laotian, Cambodian and Vietnamese specialties at

moderate **Southeast Asian Restaurant,** *343 Market St; tel: (508) 452-3182.* Seafood and steaks are moderate–pricey at the **Press Club,** *31 Central St; tel: (508) 453-8564,* with a sports bar serving Lowell's micro-brewed Mill City beer.

SIGHTSEEING

Mindful of the pioneering millworks in Rhode Island, Boston entrepreneurs looked to the cascading confluence of the Merrimack and Concord rivers. Francis Cabot Lowell copied England's Manchester power looms, which led to the mighty 1820s mills of the first US company town in the Industrial Revolution. Decades after regional textile manufacturing's drastic decline, two mills have been restored as focal points of the **Lowell National Historical Park.** Get oriented in the **Market Mills Visitor**

Center, with exhibits and free parking. The building also contains a budget café and Brush Hill Art Gallery & Studios, open Mon–Sat 1100–1700, Sun 1200–1600. Across downtown in the Boott Cotton Mills Museum, 88 looms and shuttles raise a clattering racket for some sense of bygone working conditions (there were 4000 here in the Weave Room a century ago); open daily 0900–1700, $3 ($10 combination admittance also includes a canal-boat ride and mill-to-mill transit aboard an 1887 trolley). The Patrick J. Mogan Cultural Center was an 1835 company boarding house where the legendary 'mill girls' lived. Period rooms and displays recall the details of their hardworking existence.

Moviedom's Bette Davis and 'Beat Generation' writer Jack Kerouac (On the Road) both came from Lowell. Eight granite pillars in Eastern Canal Park are inscribed with excerpts from Kerouac's auto-biographical musings, and his grave in Edson Cemetery, off Gorham St, is a magnet for fans. The birthplace of local painter James McNeill Whistler is now the Whistler Museum of Art, 243 Worthen St, Lowell, MA 01852; tel: (508) 452-7641, open Tues–Sat 1100–1600 and Sun 1300–1600 (June–Aug); Wed–Sat 1100–1400 and Sun 1300–1600 (Mar–May and Sept–Dec), $2.

The bank where millhands deposited their savings has been recycled into the New England Quilt Museum, 18 Shattuck St, Lowell, MA 01852; tel: (508) 452-4207, open Mon–Sat 1000–1700, Sun 1200–1700, $3. This gritty, multi-ethnic city whoops it up annually in late July during the Lowell Folk Festival.

MANCHESTER

Tourist Information: Greater Manchester Chamber of Commerce, 889

Elm St, Manchester, NH 03101; tel: (603) 666-6600, open Mon–Fri 0800–1700.

ACCOMMODATION AND FOOD

Hd is right downtown; DI is across the river. Down in the stone depths of a former mill, moderate Café Pavone, 75 Arms Park Dr; tel: (603) 622-5488, is an Italian eatery with an umbrella-shaded patio. In an adjacent mill building, Stark Mill Brewery, 500 Commercial St; tel: (603) 623-3260, is a budget eatery and brewpub serving Amoskeag Golden Ale and Sheila's Red Tail Ale. Budget Sunburst Café, 1117 Elm St; tel: (603) 627-6420, is a bright spot on Manchester's rather humdrum main thoroughfare.

SIGHTSEEING

Emulating down-river Lowell, drowsy Derryfield was reborn as the Manchester of America with prolific output from the world's largest-ever cotton-mill complex, covering more than a mile of Merrimack riverfront. At its peak in the 1920s, the Amoskeag Manufacturing Company's 17,000 millhands were turning out 4 million yards of cloth weekly. Enquire about guided mill tours at the Manchester Historical Association, 129 Amherst St; tel: (603) 622-7531, open Tues–Fri 0900–1600, Sat 1000–1600.

Manchester's cultural gem is the Currier Gallery of Art, 192 Orange St, Manchester, NH 03101; tel: (603) 669-6144, with a stellar collection including early US silver, pewter, textiles and furnishings, open Tues–Sat 1000–1600, also Thurs 1000–2100 and Sun 1300–1700, $4.

Architect Frank Lloyd Wright designed the Zimmerman House in his 'Usonian' style, including the furniture. Tours Thur–Fri 1400, Sat 1315 and 1430, Sun 1330 and 1500. Reached by van from the art gallery, $6 for combined Currier/Zimmerman admittance.

CONCORD

Tourist Information: Concord Area Chamber of Commerce, *244 N. Main St, Concord, NH 03301; tel: (603) 224-2508,* Mon–Fri 0800–1700.

ACCOMMODATION AND FOOD

HI is in-town. **Phil A. Buster's,** *1 Eagle Sq; tel: (603) 228-1982,* is an amiable restaurant and tavern. There's a comparably relaxed ambience at **Thursday's,** *6–8 Pleasant St; tel: (603) 224-2626.* Both moderate.

SIGHTSEEING

Self-guided tours of the **State House,** New Hampshire's capitol, are free, Mon–Fri 0800–1630; *tel: (603) 271-2154.* Concord stagecoaches played a key role in 'winning the West'. One of these flawlessly crafted conveyances is in the **Museum of New Hampshire History,** *Eagle Sq, Concord, NH 03301; tel: (603) 225-3381,* Tues–Sat 0930–1700, also Thurs 1700–2300 and Sun 1200–1700, $3.50.

NASHUA TO PETERBOROUGH

The westward drive from Nashua takes you primarily past suburbs and shopping malls, but the hilltop village of **Temple,** 2 miles south of Rte 101 along Rte 45, is worth a side trip. Close to **Temple Mountain's** modest ski slopes and cross-country trails, it features an idyllic green surrounded by a church, meeting house, general store and old burying ground. Also overlooking the green is the comfortable **Birchwood Inn,** *Temple, NH 03084; tel: (603) 878-3285,* originally a stagecoach stop, moderate.

In **Peterborough,** sharing space with the town cinema is the region's trendiest restaurant, pricey **Latacarta,** *6 School St; tel; (603) 924-6878.* The enchanting **New England Marionette Opera,** *Main St, Peterborough, NH 03458; tel: (603) 924-4333,* gets rave reviews for its performances of bravura puppetry. Worth noting, but not open to visitors, is the **MacDowell Colony,** an artists' retreat where Leonard Bernstein wrote his *Mass* and many literary works have been been crafted in splendid solitude.

PETERBOROUGH TO HILLSBOROUGH

Greenfield State Park offers nature trails, Otter Lake swimming and boat rentals; *tel: (603) 547-3497.* Scenic Greenfield centre's **Carbee's Corner** houses a craft gallery, candy store and coffee shop; *tel: (603) 547-3322.* Reached by a winding drive through forested terrain, **Francestown** and **Bennington** are photogenic too.

HILLSBOROUGH AND HENNIKER

Henniker's moderate **Daniel's** overlooks the Contoocook River, *Main St; tel: (603) 428-7621.* Tops regionally for moderate–expensive lodging and/or dinner is **Colby Hill Inn,** off *Western Ave, Henniker, NH 03242; tel: (603) 428-3281.* Vintage radios are amongst the antiques in the moderate **Inn at Maplewood Farm,** *447 Center Rd, Hillsborough, NH 03244; tel: (603) 464-4242,* a bed and breakfast downhill from exceptionally beautiful **Hillsborough Center.**

Local niceties include a covered bridge and 1889 apothecary. The 14th US president grew up in the **Franklin Pierce Homestead,** *Rte 31, Hillsborough, NH 03244; tel: (603) 478-3165,* open

Mon–Sat 1000–1600, Sun 1300–1600 (July–mid-Oct), $2.

SUNAPEE REGION

Tourist Information: Contact the **Lake Sunapee Business Association**, *tel: (800) 258-3530*, for advance enquiries. **New London Area Chamber of Commerce**, *Main St, New London, NH 03257; tel: (603) 526-6575*, open Mon–Fri 1000–1630. An **information booth** on Rte 11 in **Lower Sunapee Village** opens late June–early Sept; *tel: (603) 763-2201*.

ACCOMMODATION AND FOOD

Tennis courts and a swimming pool are perks at expensive–pricey **Dexter's Inn & Tennis Club**, *Stagecoach Rd, Sunapee, NH 03872; tel: (603) 763-5571 or (800) 232-5571*. BW is close to the lake and state park. The laid-back, moderate **Anchorage** has a lakeside deck in Sunapee Harbor; *tel: (603) 763-3334*.

With an ideal location facing a remarkably spacious green, the moderate **New London Inn** is a circa-1792 landmark, *8 Main St, New London, NH 03257; tel: (603) 526-2791*. New London's **Gourmet Garden**; *tel: (603) 526-6656*, is a budget deli café. Also budget are the breakfasts and lunches at lace-curtained **Foot Hills Restaurant**, *Main St, Warner; tel: (603) 456-2140*.

SIGHTSEEING AND RECREATION

The *Sunapee II* departs Sunapee Harbor on narrated lake excurions, daily at 1000 and 1430 (mid-May–Nov); *tel: (603) 763-4030*. Buffet dinner is served aboard the *Kearsarge* during summertime lake cruises; *tel: (603) 763-5477*. A winter skiing destination, **Mt Sunapee State Park** draws hikers, campers and picnickers in other seasons. Chairlift ascent to the mountain's

2743-ft summit opens onto New Hampshire and Vermont highland vistas.

Native American artifacts fill the **Mt Kearsarge Indian Museum**, *Kearsarge Mountain Rd, Warner, NH 03278; tel: (603) 456-600*, open Mon–Sat 1000–1700, Sun 1300–1700 (May–Oct), $5. The region's most 'photogenic' villages are **Bradford**, neighbouring **Bradford Center** and **New London**, affluent home of Colby-Sawyer College, plus the summer-stock **Barn Play-house**, *209 Main St; tel: (603) 526-4631*.

PETERBOROUGH TO JAFFREY

Heading deeper into the Monadnock region, there's a quicker way from Peterborough to Jaffrey along Rte 202 south, but Rte 101 takes you through tiny **Dublin**, the home of *Yankee Magazine* and the *Old Farmer's Almanac*, which keep New England traditions alive for millions of readers worldwide. Forty miles of easy-to-challenging trails make 3165-ft **Mt Monadnock** a hikers' heaven; *tel: (603) 532-8862*.

Little **Jaffrey Center** is a classic with its white spired 1775 meeting house and cemetery, burial place of author Willa Cather (*My Antonia, Death Comes to the Archbishop*). The moderate **Benjamin Prescott Inn**, *Rte 124 East, Jaffrey, NH 03452; tel: (603) 532-6657*, is a farmhouse bed and breakfast. Also moderate, **Michael's Jaffrey Manor**, *E. Main St; tel: (603) 532-8555*, is recommended for New England-style meals.

JAFFREY TO WINCHESTER

Fitzwilliam surrounds a triangular green, locale of the moderate, vintage **Fitzwilliam Inn**, *Fitzwilliam, NH 03447; tel: (603) 585-9000*. Three miles farther west, bushes amidst pine groves and wildflower trails reach full bloom towards mid-July in **Rhododendron State Park**; *tel: (603) 532-8862*. Stop at the **Swanzey Historical Museum & Information Center**, *Rte 10, West Swanzey, NH 03469; tel: (603) 352-4579*, open Mon–Fri 1300–1700, Sat–Sun 1000–1700, for directions to five covered bridges nearby.

KEENE

Tourist Information: Monadnock Travel Council, *8 Central Sq, Keene, NH 03431; tel: (603) 352-1308*, open Mon–Fri 0800–1700, has details on all the small towns in the region.

ACCOMMODATION AND FOOD

Near Keene State University, the moderate **Carriage Barn Guest House**, *358 Main St, Keene, NH 03431; tel: (603) 357-3812*, is an in-town alternative to outlying BW, DI and S8. You'll find eateries around downtown's common and along one of New England's widest main thoroughfares. Amongst several moderate choices is the **Stage Restaurant & Café**, *30 Central Sq; tel: (603) 357-8389*, adorned with theatrical memorabilia.

ENTERTAINMENT AND SHOPPING

Keene's **Colonial Theater**, *95 Main St; tel: (603) 352-2033*, is a movie and live-entertainment showplace. What was originally an 1838 woollen mill has been transformed into the **Colony Mill Marketplace**, with shops, crafts gallery, antiques centre and a food court.

KEENE TO CLAREMONT

Tourist Information: Greater Claremont Chamber of Commerce, *Tremont Sq, Claremont, NH 03743; tel: (603) 543-1296*, open Mon–Fri 0830–1730.

ACCOMMODATION AND FOOD

Two moderate bed and breakfasts are bargains with their elegance and sumptuous breakfasts. **Maple Hedge** features Edwardian decor, *Rte 12, Charlestown, NH 03603; tel: (603) 826-5237*. **Goddard Mansion** was a tycoon's summer estate, *25 Hillstead Rd, Claremont, NH 03743; tel: (603) 543-0603*.

All light-meal choices are tempting at Claremont's genuinely old-time Italian **George Boccia**, *66 Tremont Sq; tel: (603) 542-9816*. **Jean Marie's Candy Works** replicates a 1950s soda fountain and ice-cream parlour, *26 Tremont Sq; tel: (603) 542-3338*. North Charlestown's moderate–pricey **Indian Shutters**; *tel: (603) 826-4366*, is an historic restaurant and tavern with splendid valley and mountain views.

SIGHTSEEING

Farm stands, wetlands, maple-syrup 'sugar houses' and, across a lily pond, **Marlow's** church and meeting house are seen along Rte 10 beyond Keene. Then Rte 123 passing Lake Warren and through **Alsted** covers rural, up-and-down topography. Cornfields are prevalent during the Rte 12 drive up the fertile Connecticut River Valley, with Mt Ascutney looming on the Vermont side.

Fifty-three of 64 commercial, religious and domestic buildings along **Charlestown's** mile-long *Main St* are on the state's historic register. The plunging Sugar River waterfalls virtually pre-ordained Claremont's 19th-century milltown prosperity. Ask at the chamber of commerce for a descriptive walking-tour map of the **Claremont Village Industrial District**.

CORNISH AND PLAINFIELD

Doubtlessly photographed a zillion times, the 460-ft **Cornish-Windsor covered**

105

bridge is the longest US wooden bridge and the world's longest two-lane span, connecting New Hampshire with Windsor, Vt. (see p. 213).

The Cornish area's **Saint-Gaudens National Historic Site** is 1.5 miles uphill from Rte 12A; tel: (603) 675-2175; open daily 0830–1630 (late May–Nov), $2. This was sculptor Augustus Saint-Gaudens' villa and studio during the town's 20th-century 'Cornish Colony' period, when creative luminaries including US novelist Winston Churchill worked here. Full-scale models of Saint-Gaudens' major public works are displayed in garden pavilions amidst white birches and Lombardy poplars. Among these is a replica of the monumental Robert Gould Shaw Memorial on Boston Common.

Magazine illustrator Maxfield Parrish, another 'Cornish Colony' crony, lived in nearby **Plainfield,** a valley hamlet on whimsically named Blow-me-down Brook. Employing his inimitable deep-blue tones, he painted the Town Hall's stage set – an ethereal rendition of north-country forests, Mt Ascutney and the shimmering Connecticut River.

HANOVER

Tourist Information: Hanover Area Chamber of Commerce, 37 S. Main St, Hanover, NH 03755; tel: (603) 643-3115, open Mon–Fri 0900–1600.

ACCOMMODATION

As historic, prestigious and pricey as the college that owns it, the **Hanover Inn,** On the Green, Hanover, NH 03755; tel: (800) 443-7024, is unsurpassed for service and cuisine.

Rooms in the moderate **Chieftain Motor Inn,** 84 Lyme Rd, Hanover, NH 03755; tel: (603) 643-2550, overlook the Connecticut River. Or cross the river to

the moderate **Norwich Inn,** 225 Main St, Norwich, VT 05055; tel: (802) 649-1143.

FOOD AND DRINK

Café Buon Gustaio is a zesty, moderate Italian trattoria; 72 S. Main St; (603) 643-5711. Students and families like moderate, non-smoking **Molly's Balloon,** 43 S. Main St; tel: (603) 643-2570. Neighbouring Norwich's pricey **La Poule à Dents,** Main St; tel: (802) 649-2922, is haute French.

SIGHTSEEING AND ENTERTAINMENT

Hanover owes its zip and verve to Dartmouth College, whose immense campus quadrangle doubles as the town common.

The white 18th-century buildings along 'Dartmouth Row' are quintessentially Greek Revival. See José Clemente Orozco's Epic of American Civilization murals inside **Baker Memorial Library,** painted when he was Dartmouth's artist in residence during the early 1930s. This steepled brick building contains priceless Shakespeare folios and fine examples of early US portraiture, open Mon–Fri 0800–2400, Sat–Sun 0900–2400; tel: (603) 646-2560.

Collections in Dartmouth's boldly modernistic **Hood Museum of Art,** Hanover, NH 03755; tel: (603) 646-2006, open Tues–Sat 1000–1700, Sun 1200–1700, free, which is also facing the quadrangle, cover a broad spectrum of international painting and sculpture.

The adjoining **Hood Center;** tel: (603) 646-2422, architectural forerunner of New York City's Metropolitan Opera House, is a superlative performing-arts centre, scheduling drama, dance, avant-garde films and Dartmouth Symphony Orchestra concerts, also containing a budget cafeteria.

BOSTON-HARTFORD

A dull, two-hour (110-mile) drive from one state capital to another can be livened up with stops at Old Sturbridge Village, a re-created New England town of the 1830s, or in Worcester, which boasts a fine art museum. If you're not in a hurry, take a brief detour through northeastern Connecticut's lovely countryside.

> DIRECT ROUTE: 110 MILES

107

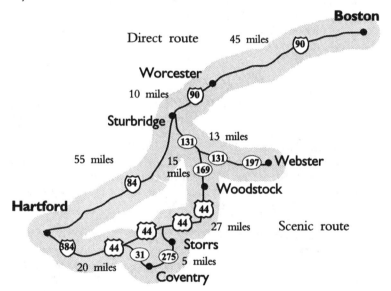

Direct route · 45 miles · Boston · 90 · Worcester · 10 miles · 90 · Sturbridge · 13 miles · 131 · 55 miles · 15 miles · 131 · 169 · 197 · Webster · 84 · Woodstock · Hartford · 44 · 44 · 44 · 27 miles · Scenic route · 384 · 44 · 44 · 31 · 275 · Storrs · 5 miles · 20 miles · Coventry

ROUTES

DIRECT ROUTE

From the area of the **Boston Common and Public Garden,** follow *Arlington St* five blocks south to signs for an entrance to the **Massachusetts Turnpike.** Turn right and follow the Mass. Pike (I-90) west

about 55 miles to Exit 9 (Sturbridge). After the toll, follow I-84 another 55 miles to Hartford. Use Exit 49 for Civic Center, Exit 47 for Mark Twain House.

For stopovers along the way, follow the Mass. Pike 45 miles to Exit 10 (Auburn and Worcester), then I-290 east into **Worcester** and get off at Exit 16 for downtown. To **Sturbridge,** take the Mass. Pike to Exit 9 (I-84) toward

Hartford and New York. After the toll booth take the first exit (3B), which takes you to Rte 20 west. After 1.5 miles, **Old Sturbridge Village** is on the left.

SCENIC ROUTE

▶ Leaving Old Sturbridge Village, go east on Rte 20 to the junction with Rte 131 and bear right. Follow Rte 131 through an uninteresting residential and commercial landscape and through the mill town of **Southbridge**.

After 4.6 miles from Old Sturbridge Village, bear right on Rte 169 south. This is a beautiful country route past farms, New England stone walls and rolling hillsides. Follow it 3.9 miles into **Woodstock** and another 6.1 miles to **Roseland Cottage** in the centre of town.

Rte 169 joins with Rte 44 for about five miles. Stay on Rte 44 where it turns west and go 3.7 miles to **Mashamoquet Brook State Park**.

Continue on Rte 44 which becomes less rural and less charming and go about 17 miles to Storrs and the **University of Connecticut**. Return to Rte 44 and go 7.4 miles, watching carefully for a sign on the right marked **Nathan Hale Homestead**.

Turn left at the sign (*Silver St*) and go less than a mile to **Caprilands**. From here, go to the end of *Silver St* and make a left on to *South St* to the Hale Homestead in Coventry, a total of 3.5 miles.

Return to Rte 44 and follow it to Bolton Notch to I-384 which turns into I-84. Follow this into Hartford.

WORCESTER

Tourist Information: Worcester County Convention and Visitors Bureau, *33 Waldo St, Worcester, MA 01608; tel: (508) 753-2920*, does not book rooms. Worcester is the state's second largest city and has many claims to fame: the country's first park was created here as was the first wire-making company and the first carpet loom. The city is also known for its political background having played a role in the female suffrage movement and seen the growth of the Free Soil Party, now better known as the Republican Party.

ACCOMMODATION AND FOOD

Worcester has *Hd, Ma, RI* and *TL*.

In 1906 the Worcester Lunch Car company began manufacturing railroad car restaurants, the prototype for the diners which used to dot the US landscape in large numbers.

Worcester still boasts some ten diners where the food may not be pretty but it is hearty and plentiful. Try the **Boulevard Diner**, *155 Shrewsbury St; tel: (508) 791-4535*; budget. For an elegant meal there's **Beechwood Restaurant**, *363 Plantation St; tel: (508) 754-5789*, featuring dining on the terrace; pricey.

In between is the moderate **Maxwell Silverman's Toolhouse**, *25 Union St; tel: (508) 755-1200*, in a restored factory building.

SHOPPING

The city is proud of its newly opened **Worcester Common Fashion Outlets**, *100 Front St; tel: (508) 798-2581*, with more than 100 bargain shops including designer outlets and a large food court.

SIGHTSEEING

Although Worcester isn't considered a major tourist stop, it does have several excellent museums.

The best is the **Worcester Art Museum**, *55 Salisbury St, Worcester, MA 01609; tel: (508) 799-4406*, open Tues–Fri 1100–1600, Sat 1000–1700, Sun

1300–1700, $5. It's the second largest in New England and one of the more exciting with everything from Egyptian antiquities to Pop Art. Of particular interest is the large collection of 17th-, 18th- and 19th-century American art, including works by John Singleton Copley, Winslow Homer and John Singer Sargent. The **Higgins Armory Museum**, *100 Barber Ave, Worcester, MA 01606, tel: (508) 853-6015*, open Tues–Sat 1000–1600, Sun 1200–1600, $4.75, displays weapons and armour from ancient Greece and Rome, medieval Europe and feudal Japan, in a Gothic setting.

The **Goddard Exhibition** in Clark University's Goddard Library, *950 Main St, Worcester, MA 01610; tel: (508) 793-7572*, open Mon–Fri 1000–1600, free, houses memorabilia of Robert Goddard, the father of US rocketry, who was born in Worcester.

Salisbury Mansion, *40 Highland St, Worcester, MA 01609; tel: (508) 753-8278*, open Thurs–Sun 1300–1600, $2,2, was built in 1722 and beautifully restored in 1830. The **New England Science Center**, *222 Harrington Way, Worcester, MA 01604; tel: (508) 791-9211*, open Mon–Sat, 1000–1700, Sun 1200–1700, $6, is a 60-acre science park excellent for youngsters, with a planetarium, observatory and wildlife centre. A small tourist train circles the grounds.

STURBRIDGE

Tourist Information: Sturbridge Information Center, *380 Main St, Sturbridge, MA 01566; tel: (800) 628-9379* or *(508) 347-7594*, will not make reservations but will provide information and let you make free phone calls to find a room.

ACCOMMODATION

Because so many families spend a full day

or two at the village, there is plenty of accommodation and restaurants in the area. Oct is the busiest month and reservations are recommended.

Sturbridge Village has its own lodgings known as **The Old Sturbridge Village Lodges and Oliver Wight House**, *Route 20 west, Sturbridge, MA 01566; tel: (508) 347-3327*. This 59-room complex consists of a 200-year-old house with ten rooms and smaller buildings, all made to resemble a small New England village. Prices are moderate–expensive during the week and slightly higher at weekends.

The nine-room **Sturbridge Country Inn**, *530 Main St, Sturbridge, MA 01566; tel: (508) 347-5503*, has a fireplace and whirlpool tub in each room and some rooms have four-poster beds; Expensive; higher rates in Oct.

The **Publick House Historic Inn**, On the Common, *P.O. Box 187 (Rte 131), Sturbridge, MA 01566; tel: (800) PUBLICK or (508) 347-3313*, has 17 rooms decorated in Colonial style; expensive.

There's *BW* and *QI* in Sturbridge and *Rm* in **Auburn**, about 20 miles away. The tourist information lists 20 bed and breakfasts in the area.

The closest campground to the village is **Yogi Bear's Sturbridge Jellystone Park**, *Box 600, Sturbridge, MA 01566; tel: (508) 347-9570*, (Exit 2 off I-84, then follow signs) which is geared for kids, with a pool, waterslide, lake, nightly entertainment, petting zoo and more. There are 399 sites; slightly more costly than most sites, though still budget.

EATING AND DRINKING

For a quick bite there's chain fast-food on Rte 20 right outside the village, including Massachusetts-based **Friendly's**.

Try **Rom's Restaurant**, *Rte 131-*

Sturbridge Rd, Sturbridge, MA 01566; tel: (508) 347-3349, which serves big Italian meals; budget to moderate. **Publick House**, On the Common, Rte 131, Sturbridge, MA 01566; tel: (800) PUB-LICK or (508) 347-3313, serves standard American fare such as chicken and fish in a New England inn setting; moderate.

SIGHTSEEING

Old Sturbridge Village, 1 Old Sturbridge Village Rd, Sturbridge, MA 01566; tel: (508) 347-3362, open daily 0900–1700 (Apr–end Oct), Tues–Sun 1000–1600 (Nov–Dec and Feb–Mar), weekends only in Jan; adults $15, children $7.50; tickets valid for two days.

Families, school children and history buffs have long enjoyed this re-created village showing what daily life was like in New England in 1830. Spread out over 200 acres, the village comprises some 40 structures making up a small town including a blacksmith shop, carding mill (where wool is prepared for spinning), school and meeting house.

Costumed actors demonstrate the life and work of the village and join in with community celebrations. The village changes with the seasons: planting crops in spring, harvesting in fall, indoor activities in winter to prepare for spring. It is particularly realistic during the winter months, when there are fewer tourists. Numerous seasonal events take place; call for information.

Although there are modern amenities (restaurant, restrooms, areas for changing babies), the village does an excellent job of bringing the past to life. You might hear a choir practising at the meetinghouse or watch shoppers make their purchases at Mr. Knight's store or see an oxcart move slowly over a roadway.

Special demonstrations include weav-

ing, basket-making, broom making and using herbs. Youngsters especially enjoy the working farm and the one-room schoolhouse.

Brimfield, 8 miles west, has heavily attended antiques flea markets on Rte 20 during weekends in May, July and Sept and the area becomes extremely busy. For information on antiques shows tel: (413) 283-6149.

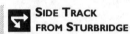

SIDE TRACK FROM STURBRIDGE

WEBSTER

Take Rte 131 heading south-east from Sturbridge and join Rte 197 leading into Webster. Here you'll find a small industrial town bordering the largest natural body of water in Massachusetts. The lake's official name is Lake Chargoggagoggmanchauggagoggchaubnunagungamaug meaning, in the Nipmuc dialect, 'you fish on your side, I fish on my side, no one fishes in the middle'. However, it's usually known as Lake Webster.

As well as having the longest and most complicated name in US geography, the lake, with its trout, perch and pike, is also a paradise for those keen on fishing. A side trip is certainly recommended. 🔺

STURBRIDGE TO HARTFORD

The inauspicious start from Sturbridge becomes a tranquil country ride past rolling farmland and through small, rural towns. Promoted as Connecticut's 'Quiet Corner', this is an area where it's best to slow down and enjoy small pleasures. For help in booking accommodation, tel: (800) CT-BOUND, open round the clock.

In Woodstock, stop in the centre of

town across from the well-tended green to tour **Roseland Cottage**, *556 Rte 169; tel: (860) 928-4074,* open Wed–Sun 1200–1700 (mid-May–mid-Sept) and Fri–Sun 1200–1700 (mid-Sept–mid-Oct), $4, make reservations for tea (June–Sept). This pink, Gothic revival home, built in 1846, has lovely grounds and rather unusual interiors.

The 22-room **Inn at Woodstock Hill**, *94 Plaine Hill Rd, Woodstock, CT 06267; tel: (860) 928-0528,* is on 14 acres and has spacious rooms, many with fireplaces; moderate–expensive. It's also known for its pricey restaurant. **Fox Hunt Farms Gourmet Shop**, *290 Rte 169, Woodstock, CT 06267; tel: (860) 928-0714,* has a café and wonderful desserts; budget.

In S. Woodstock stop at **Tea Room at the Livery**, *Junctions of Rtes 169 and 171; tel: (860) 963-0161,* which serves lunch as well as tea and pastry; budget.

In Pomfret, home of the posh **Pomfret** School, **The Vanilla Bean Café**, *450 Deerfield Rd; tel: (860) 928-1562,* serves homemade soups and hearty sandwiches.

Three convenient bed and breakfasts, all moderate and all located on Rte 169, are the **Cobbscroft**, *349 Pomfret St, Pomfret, CT 06258; tel: (860) 928-5560,* with four rooms filled with antiques; **Karinn**, *330 Pomfret Rd, Pomfret, CT 06259,* with five rooms, fireplaces and gardens; and **Clarke Cottage**, *354 Pomfret St, Pomfret, CT 06258; tel: (860) 928-5741,* with four rooms, located on a former estate.

If you're interested in antiques, drive three miles east on Rte 44 from Pomfret to **Putnam**, which calls itself the 'antiques district'. Many of the shops are within walking distance of each other along Main or *Front Sts.*

Mashamoquet Brook State Park,

on *Rte 44, Pomfret, CT 06259; tel: (860) 928-6121,* is a good place to swim and have a picnic. On the grounds are the **Brayton Grist Mill** and **Marcy Blacksmith Museum**, open weekends 1400–1700 (end May–Sept), free.

The **University of Connecticut** is a sprawling campus. Stop at the information booth for a visitor permit. Two places of note are the **William Benton Museum of Art**, *245 Glennbrook Rd, Storrs, CT 06269; tel: (860) 486-4520;* open Tues–Fri 1000–1630, Sat and Sun 1300–1630 (closed between exhibitions so call ahead), free, and the **Connecticut State Museum of Natural History**, *University of Connecticut, Wilbur Cross Building, Rte 195, Storrs, CT 06269; tel: (860) 486-4460,* open Mon and Thur–Sat 1200–1600, Sun 1300–1600, free, has exhibits of fossils and Indian artifacts.

For a treat, go to the campus **Dairy Bar**, open Mon–Fri 1000–1700, Sat and Sun 1200–1700, which serves delicious ice cream made by students at the agricultural school.

Coventry is known for the **Nathan Hale Homestead**, *2299 South St, Coventry, CT 06238; tel: (860) 742-6917;* open daily 1300–1700 (mid-May–mid-Oct), $4, the home of a young American who spied on the British during the Revolution and was hanged.

Nearby is **Caprilands**, *534 Silver St, Coventry, CT 06238; (860) 742-7244,* a herb farm with an 18th-century farm house, book shop and information center, gallery and 31 gardens with 300 varieties of herbs. The shop is open daily 0900–1700 except for major holidays.

Special Joys Doll & Toy Museum, *41 N. River Rd, Coventry, CT 06238: (860) 742-6359,* open Wed–Sun 1100–1700, free, has antique dolls and unusual toy furniture.

BOSTON–LENOX

This journey begins in the region's largest city and ends in a classic New England village in the state's highest hills. The history of the Shakers comes alive at several locations; the route passes through mill towns that played a part in the industrialisation of the USA and winds along the Mohawk Trail, a 63-mile touring road from Orange to Williamstown that follows a legendary Indian footpath.

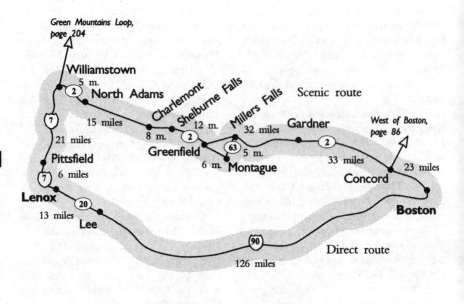

DIRECT ROUTE: 138 MILES

112

Green Mountains Loop, page 204

West of Boston, page 86

ROUTES

DIRECT ROUTE

➡ From the Boston Common/Public Garden area, follow *Arlington St* five blocks south to signs for an entrance to the Massachusetts Turnpike. Turn right and follow the 'Mass. Pike' (I-90) west 126 miles to Exit 2 at Lee. The toll for autos is $5.20. Take Rte 20 west 3.8 miles, through downtown Lee, 9 miles to *Walker St* (Rte 183 south) in Lenox. Turn left and drive one mile into the village.

➤ From Boston Common, follow *Beacon St* west to *Berkeley St*, turn right, then left onto *Storrow Dr.*, which hugs the Charles River and becomes *Soldiers Field Rd*. Bear right and cross the river via the Eliot Bridge, then bear left to join Rte 2 west, which passes through parts of Cambridge, then Arlington, Lincoln and Concord (for details on these towns see West of Boston, p. 86).

West of Concord, take Rte 111 west at Exit 43. The exit is beyond a traffic light. Do not bear left until you have passed through the light and reached the exit sign. Follow Rte 111 eight miles to the Harvard Common, then take Rte 110 west (left) 0.9 mile to *Madigan Lane*, turning right. At the end, turn right onto *Prospect Hill Rd*, which provides a view of the Nashoba Valley and Wachusett Mountain to the west. Further up the hill on the left is the entrance to the Fruitlands Museums. After the museum, continue on *Prospect Hill Rd*, which turns to *Shirley Rd* 1 mile from the museum, to the end of the road. Turn left, cross above Rte 2 and return to the highway headed to Gardner, 23 miles west.

Continue on Rte 2 into the valley of the **Millers River**. A rest area 28 miles west of Gardner on the south side of Rte 2 gives access to the river. Use caution in bearing left 1.2 miles west of the rest area at a sign pointing 'to Rte 63 south.' Follow Rte 63 through Millers Falls and 4.3 miles south to a green sign to Montague Center at *Central St*. Take *Central St* into **Montague**, continuing past the church and town hall, turning right where *Central* meets *School St*. Cross the river and turn left onto *Greenfield Rd*.

Follow *Greenfield Rd* 4.2 miles, turn left and cross the Connecticut River. Turn left and head into **Greenfield**, merging onto

Rtes 5 and 10 north. After 1.1 miles, turn right under the train trestle and into the center of Greenfield. At the top of the hill, turn left (west) onto Rte 2A (*Main St*). Rte 2A crosses under I-91 at a roundabout and rejoins Rte 2.

Follow Rte 2 eight miles and turn left onto Rte 2A to **Shelburne Falls**. After crossing the **Deerfield River**, with the **Bridge of Flowers** just upstream, follow Rte 2A back to Rte 2. Continue west on Rte 2 through **Charlemont**. Further west, the road crosses the Deerfield River and passes a statue of a Mohawk Indian, which has become the symbol of the **Mohawk Trail**.

The trail climbs along the **Cold River** to the town of **Florida** and crosses three summits, two occupied by souvenir shops, one by an inn and restaurant. Nonetheless, the views are panoramic and worth a stop or three. The middle summit, Whitcomb, is the highest – 2173 feet. The western-most summit offers a view of the **Greylock Range**, New York's **Taconic Range**, Vermont's **Green Mountains** and the mill cities of **North Adams** and **Adams**. This view reminds at least one British expatriate of the landscape of the Yorkshire Dales. Here begins a precipitous descent through a hairpin turn and into **North Adams**. Continue on Rte 2 to **Williamstown**, where it joins Rte 7 and turns south, just past **Williams College** and the town green. Rte 7 north leads to **Bennington, Vt**, and into the Green Mountains (See Green Mountains Loop, p. 204). Stay on Rte 7 south after Rte 2 turns off to the west. **Mount Greylock State Reservation** is best reached by turning left at a reservation sign 13.6 miles south of Williamstown. Rte 7 continues south to **Pittsfield**, where it circles halfway around the green and continues toward **Lenox**. Bear right onto Rte 7A

113

5.5 miles from the Pittsfield green and drive one mile into the village.

BOSTON TO GARDNER

On Rte 111, 0.2 mile from Rte 2, turn left on Rte 27 and drive 1 mile south to reach the **Discovery Museums**, *177 Main St, Acton, MA 01720 tel: (508) 264-4200.* One is for children 6 and under; the other lets older children explore science. Call for opening times, both are closed Mon; $5 per museum, $8 for both. Budget accommodation is available nearby at the **Friendly Crossways Hostel**, *Whitcomb Ave, P.O. Box 2266, Littleton, MA 01460; tel: (508) 456-3649.*

HI members can get free passes for admission to the **Fruitlands Museums,** *Prospect Hill, Harvard, MA 01451 tel: (508) 456-3924.* Open Tues –Sun and Mon holidays 1000 –1700 (mid-May –mid-Oct), except tea room and museum store, which remain open until just before Christmas; $6. The museums are named for the farm where Transcendentalist Bronson Alcott and others conducted a brief 1843 experiment in utopian living.

GARDNER

Tourist information: Worcester County Convention & Visitors Bureau, *33 Waldo St, Worcester, MA 01608; tel: (508) 754-8560.* **Greater Gardner Chamber of Commerce**, *55 Lake St, Gardner, MA 01440; tel: (508) 632-1780,* publishes a map and guide to the downtown and to local furniture factory outlets.

ACCOMMODATION AND FOOD

There's an **S8** at *22 Pearson Blvd, tel: (508) 630-2888.* **Skip's Blue Moon Diner,** *102 Main St; tel: (508) 632-4333,* has a marble lunch counter and many original fixtures. Cheap to budget. **The Garden**

Café & Deli is at the back of **Happy Trails Natural Food Store**, *24 Main St; tel: (508) 632-4076,* and serves vegetarian sandwiches and soups, cheap, Tues–Fri 1000–1500 and live music Sat until late night. Closed Mon. No music during the summer. No alcohol served, but you can bring your own beer or wine. **Sully's**, *74–76 Parker St; tel: (508) 632-7457,* is a good family restaurant, with music on Fri and Sat nights, comedy on Sat. Moderate.

SIGHTSEEING

Beginning in 1805 with one chairmaker and continuing to this day, the furniture industry has formed the economic base of this working–class town, nicknamed 'The Chair City'. The industry's heyday was in the 1920s, but furniture stores are still numerous. Silversmithing has played a lesser but noted role.

Gardner Heritage State Park Visitors Center, *26 Lake St, Gardner, MA 01440; tel: (508) 630-1497,* has exhibits on the furniture industry as well as the immigrants who contributed to it. Call for hours and programs. **Chair City Steam Bath**, *286 West St, Gardner, MA 01440; tel: (508) 632-1630,* has offered moist solace to the weary or stressed for more than 70 years, originally popular among the Finnish immigrants. Despite its age, it's in good shape. Private rooms. $6 for 45 mins. Drive 1 mile north of downtown on Rte 68.

GARDNER TO SHELBURNE FALLS

There's good swimming, a campsite and mountain laurel at **Laurel Lake** in **Erving State Forest**, up *Church St* from Rte 2; *tel: (508) 544-3939.* Budget. **Outdoor Centre of New England**, *10 Pleasant St, Millers Falls, MA 01349; tel: (413) 659-3926,* offers private or group instruction in white water canoeing and kayaking. **The Book Mill**, *440 Greenfield Rd at Depot Rd, Montague, MA 01351; tel: (413) 367-9206*, has an impressive choice of used books, perched above the **Sawmill River**. See Hartford to Brattleboro route (p. 184) for the town of **Greenfield**. Gould's Sugar House, *Rte 2, Shelburne, MA 01370; (413) 625-6170*, produces maple syrup in Mar and Apr and sells it from then until Oct, except May, which is planting season. Breakfast and lunch served. Cheap.

SHELBURNE FALLS TO CHARLEMONT

Tourist Information: Village Information Center, *75 Bridge St, Box 42-B, Shelburne Falls, MA 01370*; tel: (413) 625-2544. **Mohawk Trail Association**, *P.O. Box 722, Charlemont, MA 01339; tel: (413) 664-6256.*

ACCOMMODATION

A lodging brochure of area bed and breakfasts is available from the **Bed and Breakfast Association**, *P.O. Box 5, Buckland, MA 01338*. **The Charlemont Inn**, *Rte 2, Charlemont, MA 01339; tel: (413) 339-5796* is more than 200 years old. Nothing fancy. Budget to moderate. **Springbrook Family Camp Area**, *RFD 1, 32 Tower Rd, Shelburne, MA 01370; tel: (413) 625-6618*. Open May–mid-Oct. Budget.

EATING AND DRINKING

Copper Angel Café, *2 State St, Shelburne Falls, MA 01370; tel: (413) 625-2727.* Budget. **McCusker's Market and Deli**, *3 State St, Shelburne Falls, MA 01370; tel: (413) 625-9411*, bakes heavenly breads and sells organic produce. Cheap. Charlemont Inn serves tavern and Mexican cuisine. Moderate.

SIGHTSEEING AND SHOPPING

The pride of Shelburne Falls is a wonderful mix of engineering and botany: the **Bridge of Flowers**, a graceful concrete span. It's best enjoyed in spring or summer. Once it carried trolleys across the **Deerfield River**; now it's essentially a huge planter. Vehicles use the span just downstream. Below the dam are the **Glacial Potholes**, carved out of granite by stones spinning in whirlpools. To the chagrin of the town fathers, swimmers, sunbathers and the curious are drawn to the rock riverbed like magnets, but they visit at their own risk. A horn sounds to warn them before the flood gates are opened.

Charlemont is up the river. A covered bridge, built in 1951, spans **Mill Brook**, just 0.3 mile up Rte 8A from Rte 2.

The proprietors of **Wandering Moon**, *59 Bridge St, Shelburne Falls, MA 01370; tel: (413) 625-9667*, are anachronists, medievalists motivated by the art and history of the pre-industrial ages. They sell swords, chain mail, Celtic jewellery, music, books and other unusual wares. At **Bald Mountain Pottery**, *28 State St, Shelburne Falls, MA 01370; tel: (413) 625-8110*, you can watch the potters at their wheel, with a good view of the river. You can also see glassware being blown at **North River Glass**, *Deerfield Ave, Shelburne Falls, MA 01370; tel: (413) 625-6422*. Watch all you want; just don't talk to the glass blowers.

CHARLEMONT TO WILLIAMSTOWN

Two miles west of Charlemont centre is a rest area in the true sense of the word. Look for the 18th- and 19th-century gravestones, some fallen. **Zoar Outdoors**, *Mohawk Trail, Charlemont, MA 01339; tel: (800) 532-7483*, offers

115

kayaking, canoeing and rafting on the Deerfield, one of the state's prime whitewater rivers. **Mohawk Trail State Forest**, *Rte 2, Charlemont, MA 01339; tel: (413) 339-5504*, and **Savoy Mountain State Forest**, *Rte 2, Florida, MA 01247; tel: (413) 663-8469*, have picnicking, swimming, hiking and tent pitches for $6 a night, cabins for $8.

If all goes well, the **Massachusetts Museum of Contemporary Art** will open its doors in 1997 in an old mill building on *Marshall St* in North Adams. Hd is visible from Rte 2 in downtown.

The best cure for hunger along this stretch is a five-mile detour south on Rte 8 to **Miss Adams Diner**, *53 Park St, Adams, MA 01220; tel: (413) 743-5300*. Typical diner fare shares the stage with vegetarian dishes, including 'Fake BLT' made with tempeh, a fermented soybean cake, instead of bacon. The crowd is a nice mix. In Nov and Dec, persimmon pudding is a special offering. Closed Mon. Cheap. Call ahead to see if dinner is served.

Look for wooden, brick, stone and Tudor cottages in the arts and crafts style passing from North Adams to Williamstown. The private mobile home park on the north side of Rte 2 is probably the only one in the world with huge twin concrete lions guarding the entrance.

WILLIAMSTOWN

Tourist Information: Williamstown Board of Trade, *P.O. Box 357, Williamstown, MA 01267; tel: (413) 458-9077*. Information booth at the town green, Rtes 2 and 7.

ACCOMMODATION

The Orchards, *222 Adams Rd, Williamstown, MA 01267; tel: (413) 458-9611* or *(800) 225-1517*, is a luxurious inn, pricey in summer and fall, expensive the rest of the year. Meals are moderately priced.

River Bend Farm Bed and Breakfast, *643 Simonds Rd, Williamstown, MA 01267; tel: (413) 458-3121*, is a 1770 Georgian colonial home on the Hoosic River, one mile north of Williams College on Rte 7. Expensive.

You can find moderately priced motels east of the centre of town on Rte 2. At the **1896 Motels**, *Rte 7, Williamstown, MA 01267; tel: (413) 458-8125*, one may choose a brookside bed and breakfast or a pondside room. Moderate. An apartment for six rents for $125 a night.

Bascom Lodge, *P.O. Box 1800, Lanesboro, MA 01237; tel: (413) 743-1591*, a rustic stone building on top of Mount Greylock, is managed by the Appalachian Mountain Club. Hike in or drive. Budget bunkrooms. Private rooms priced moderate. Family-style dinners, budget. The lodge also serves breakfasts and packs trail lunches for $4.50. Open mid-May–late Oct.

EATING, DRINKING AND SHOPPING

Explore *Spring* and *Water Sts*, across Rte 2 from the college, for a variety of shops and restaurants.

Robin's Restaurant is at the end of *Spring St; tel: (413) 458-4489*. Moderate. **Hot Tomatoes**, *100 Water St; tel: (413) 458-2722*, serves take-out specialty pizzas. Take them out to the picnic tables by the river in back. Moderate.

Next door is **Green River Books**, *96 Water St; tel: (413) 458-0058*, another heavenly reading room on a stream, with general and scholarly titles.

The Store at Five Corners, *Rtes 7 and 43; tel: (413) 458-3176*, serves gourmet foods and lunches that can be enjoyed beside the Green River.

The home of **Williams College**, this village is tucked into a corner of the state and was first settled in the 1750s by soldiers from the Northwest Outpost of the Massachusetts Bay Colony. The college's **Chapin Library**, in *Main St's* **Stetson Hall**, has one of four extant contemporary copies of the Declaration of Independence. **Williamstown Theatre Festival**, *P.O. Box 517, Williamstown, MA 01267; tel: (413) 597-3377* or *597-3400*, stages excellent plays on the Williams campus with well known actors from late June–Aug. **The Clark Art Institute**, *225 South St, P.O. Box 8, Williamstown, MA 01267; tel: (413) 458-9545*, shows the works of Renoir, the Old Masters, Degas, Toulouse-Lautrec, Winslow Homer and others in a museum small enough to enjoy in a single visit. The collection also includes 16th- to 19th-century silver from England, the US and the Continent. Open Tues–Sun 1000–1700, free.

Williams College Museum of Art, *Main St* between *Spring* and *Water Sts; tel: (413) 597-2429*, has American, contemporary and non-Western art. Open Tues –Sat 1000–1700, Sun 1300–1700, free.

WILLIAMSTOWN TO LENOX

Mount Greylock State Reservation, *Rockwell Rd, Lanesboro, MA 01237; tel: (413) 499-4262*, contains the state's highest peak, at 3491 feet. **Overlook Trail** is a good family hike. Walking from **Jones Nose** to the **Appalachian Trail** is moderately difficult. **Roaring Brook Trail** ascends or descends 1,200 ft in two miles, depending on where you start. Take *North Main St* and *Rockwell Rd* two miles to the **Visitor's Center**; *tel: (413) 443-0011*, eight more to the top of the mountain and the **War Memorial Tower**. The campsite is near the top. Budget. **Whippletree**

Bed and Breakfast, *Rte 7, Lanesboro, MA 01237; tel: (413) 442-7468*, is in the shadow of Mount Greylock and gets motorists, some hikers and bicyclists.

Shakers

Because they danced fitfully, shook, trembled, jerked, whirled and sometimes screeched during the course of their worship of the Lord, they were called Shakers.

The Shakers were a society of devout Christians, 5,000 to 6,000 members strong in the mid-19th century when the sect was at its zenith. After coming from Manchester, England, in the 1770s, a small group recruited converts and established settlements at scattered sites in New England, New York and other states, where they practiced communal living and a simple, agrarian way of life. The Shakers are remembered at several of these sites – Pittsfield and Harvard, Mass.; Sabbathday Lake, Maine, and Canterbury and Enfield, N.H. – where remnants of their architecture, agriculture and handicraft have been preserved or restored.

The members believed they should live separately from non-Shakers and share their goods and possessions. They also believed in equality of the sexes, the sanctity of work and the second coming of Christ. Relations of any kind between the sexes, even conversation, was strictly forbidden. This celibacy, combined with the industrialisation and urbanisation of America, eventually spelled the doom of the Shakers. We are left with their works – meeting halls with separate entries for men and women; oval boxes, chairs and cabinets, unembellished yet elegant, and simple labour-saving machines.

117

BOSTON–NEWPORT

A combination of highways connecting Boston with Providence, then a scenic drive in south-central Rhode Island, amounts to a 75-mile direct route from Boston to Newport. Side-trip meandering would add 10–15 miles to your journey. The trip combines a short inland portion of Massachusetts, the urban attractions of Rhode Island's capital city for a recommended stop-over and finally the western shoreline region alongside Narragansett Bay.

Boston

93

48 miles

95

Pawtucket

3 miles

Providence

95

14 miles

1

E Greenwich

1

8 miles

1A **Wickford**

14 miles

1A **Newport**

138

118

DIRECT ROUTE: 75 MILES

ROUTE

From Boston Common take *Tremont St* south and turn left onto *Stuart St* (which becomes *Kneeland St*). After five blocks along the fringe of Chinatown, turn right, then bear left onto the poorly signed Fitzgerald Expressway (I-93) southbound. After 10 miles, follow signs onto Rte 128 north, then take Exit 1 onto I-95 south toward Pawtucket (Exit 29) and **Providence** (Exit 22).

After Providence, drive south on I-95 to Exit 17, where *Elmwood Ave* becomes Rte 1. Fourteen miles beyond Providence, you'll arrive in **East Greenwich**. From there, stay on Rte 1 for 5.5 miles to a fork in the road where Rte 1 meets Rte 1A. A left turn onto 1A brings you to the centre of **Wickford**.

Continue on 1A for a 4-mile drive to Rte 138; turn right for a short detour to visit the **Gilbert Stuart Birthplace** in

Saunderstown. After returning to Rte 138, an eastward crossing of the **Jamestown Bridge** (free) and a 1-mile cross-island drive direct to the **Newport Bridge** ($2 toll) brings you into Newport.

BOSTON TO PROVIDENCE

Fourteen miles from the I-93/I-95 interchange in Massachusetts, accommodation on Rte 140 South (Exit 7A) on the **Mansfield** outskirts includes *CM, DI, Hd, M6* and *QI*. Mansfield's economic lifesaver is **Great Woods**, a covered open-air amphitheatre with a mid-June–Sept concert schedule ranging from classical to jazz to rock; *tel: (508) 339-2333*.

Twenty-six miles from I-93/I-95, Exit 29 in Rhode Island leads to downtown **Pawtucket** and the locale of America's first commercially workable cotton textile factory (1793), now the **Slater Mill Historic Site**, *Roosevelt Ave, Pawtucket, RI 02862; tel: (401) 725-8638*, open Tues–Sat 1000–1700, Sun 1300–1700 (June–early Sept), $5. With the Blackstone River falls generating water power, Samuel Slater duplicated British methods of converting raw cotton to thread to finished cloth, as demonstrated in the yellow clapboard mill building. There's a pleasant riverside park here, and CI accommodation is a few blocks away. Continue south from Pawtucket for 4.5 miles; take Exit 22 to reach downtown Providence.

PROVIDENCE

Tourist Information: Greater Providence Convention & Visitors Bureau (GPCVB) *30 Exchange Terrace, Providence, RI 02903; tel: (401) 274-1636 or toll-free (800) 233-1636*, open Mon–Fri 0830–1700, has information, maps, brochures and accommodation listings. **Rhode Island Tourist Promotion**

Division, *7 Jackson Walkway, Providence, RI 02903; tel: (401) 277-2601 or (800) 566-2484*, is a useful source of state-wide information.

ARRIVING AND DEPARTING

From Providence Station, *100 Gaspee St; tel: (800) 872-7245*, **Amtrak** connects the city with Boston's South Station, also New York. **Bonanza Bus,** *1 Bonanza Way (Exit 25 off I-95); tel: (401) 751-8800*, serves downtown Boston, Logan International Airport, New York and a number of smaller cities throughout southern New England.

GETTING AROUND

I-95's splitting of Providence into East Side/West Side results in easy orientation. You'll undoubtedly spend most of your time on the East Side, which includes a compact downtown district, the Rhode Island state capitol building and College Hill.

Public Transport

Kennedy Plaza is where **Rhode Island Public Transit Authority (RIPTA)** buses fan out for extensive metropolitan service. Basic fare is $0.85, each transfer en route $0.15; *tel: (401) 781-9400* for day and evening schedules.

By Car

After exiting off I-95, avoid immediate misery by steering clear of inner downtown's cluster of narrow, one-way streets and construction detours. Reaching the heights of **College Hill** becomes a choice between walking up steep streets or climbing them by car; the latter option can result in searching for a rare parking space or at best a 30-minute meter. Choose instead after exiting I-95 to turn right and enter the Convention Center garage,

119

where the long-stay rate is $8.50 per day.

ACCOMMODATION

Providence has no lack of centrally located hotels. Newest and best, expensive–pricey, is the 25-storey **Westin**, *1 West Exchange St, Providence, RI 02903; tel: (800) 228-3000*. The **Omni Biltmore**, *Kennedy Plaza, Providence, RI 02903; tel: (800) 843-6664*, is moderate–expensive. Also in-town: *DI, Hd* and *Ma*. **State House Inn**, *43 Jewett St, Providence, RI 02908; tel: (401) 785-1235*, is a moderate bed and breakfast in a West Side neighbourhood. Its East Side counterpart is a 10-room Italianate beauty, **Old Colony Bed & Breakfast**, *144 Benefit St, Providence, RI 02903; tel: (401) 751-2002*. Moderate–expensive.

EATING AND DRINKING

Downtown's *haute cuisine* and therefore pricey French restaurant, is **Pot au Feu**, *44 Custom House St; tel: (401) 273-8953*. American food with a creative flair is featured at moderate–pricey **Angels**, *125 N. Main St; tel: (401) 273-0310*. Finicky food critics praise **New Rivers**, *7 Steeple St; tel: (401) 751-0350*, moderate. Nearby and also small and moderate, is **Bluepoint Oyster Bar & Restaurant**, *99 N. Main St; tel: (401) 272-6145*, where seafood is the speciality. Basic, budget–moderate Italian trattorias line *Atwells Ave* in the West Side's Federal Hill district (Exit 21 off I-95). Two brewpubs serve good budget–moderate meals accompanied by their eclectic house brands of beer and ale: **Trinity Brewhouse**, *186 Fountain St; tel: (401) 453-2337*, and **Union Station Brewery**, *Capital Center (at Kennedy Plaza); tel: (401) 274-2739*.

ENTERTAINMENT

Providence possibly features a thicker con-

centration of serious art and culture than any other US city. For decision-making, consult the daily 'What's Happening' section of the *Providence Journal* and more comprehensive listings in two free, hip alternative tabloids: the *Phoenix* and the *Nice Paper*.

A nationally renowned award winner, the **Trinity Repertory Company**, *201 Washington St; tel: (401) 351-4242*, produces classic and contemporary works. The extra-large stage at the **Providence Performing Arts Center**, *220 Weybosset St; tel: (401) 421-2787*, accommodates touring versions of the blockbuster Broadway musicals.

'Home hall' of the **Rhode Island Philharmonic** is Veterans Memorial Auditorium, *Brownell St; tel: (401) 831-3123*.

Providence has much to offer in the farther-out realm of jazz, folk, blues, country and rock. Various combos play in the **Pork Chop Lounge** at **AS220**, *115 Empire St; tel: (401) 831-9327*. Another multi-musical venue is **CAV**, *14 Imperial Pl; tel: (401) 751-9164*, while rock concerts and dance parties pack 'em in at **Lupo's Heartbreak Hotel**, *239 Westminster St; tel: (401) 272-5876*.

The **Festival Ballet**, *5 Hennessey Ave, N. Providence; tel: (401) 353-1129*, offers classical, jazz and modern dance, programmed mainly in downtown's Performing Arts Center. **Brown University Dance Extension**, on campus in the *Ashamu Studio; tel: (401) 863-3285*, is a touring company with autumn and spring concerts. **Groundwerx Dance Theater**, *95 Empire St; tel: (401) 454-4564*, concentrates on offbeat, cutting-edge choreography. During the second weekend of June, a **Festival of Historic Houses** home and garden tour is sponsored by the **Providence**

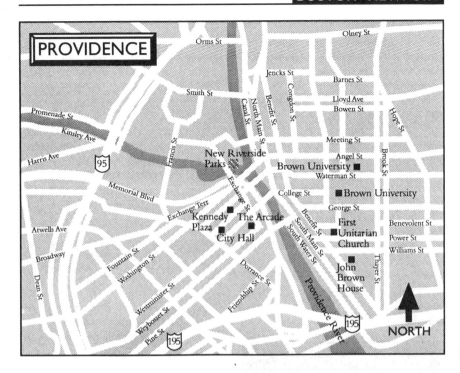

Preservation Society, *21 Meeting St, Providence, RI 02903; tel: (401) 831-7440.*

The GPCVB publishes a free *Stroll Through Providence* walking-tour map with capsule descriptions of primary attractions.

Rhode Island's colossal **State Capitol,** front entrance at *82 Smith St,* is topped by the world's second-largest marble dome after St. Peter's Basilica. Free tours Mon–Fri 0830–1630; *tel: (401) 277-2357.*

Rows of colonial, Federal and Victorian houses distinguish the brick-paved **Benefit St** 'Mile of History', which includes Providence's Greek Doric-style, 1838 **Athenaeum** library. *Benefit St* meets **Wickenden St,** so pop-arty that wacky sculptures hang on the telephone poles. The steeple of the **First Baptist Meeting House** on *N. Main St* was designed by a student of Sir Christopher Wren, with the interior illuminated by a 1792 Waterford crystal chandelier. A statue of founding father **Roger Williams** overlooks Providence from high up on *Congdon St's* **Prospect Terrace**. Williams was kicked out of Massachusetts Bay Colony by the Puritans for his 'new and dangerous opinions'. In 1636 he moved south and founded a plantation settlement dedicated to religious freedom. The smallest US state is still officially named the State of Rhode Island and Providence Plantations.

Downtown's skylit, 1828 **Arcade,** between *Weybosset* and *Westminster Sts,* ranks as America's first indoor market-place. Interconnected **Waterplace Park** and **Providence River Park** enhance the city centre with footbridges, walk-ways, ornamental lamps and pleasure-boat moorings.

Museums

The elite **Rhode Island School of Design** (called Rizz-dee in student jargon), founded 1877, injects a lively buzz of intellectual activity to the city. Its **Museum of Art**, *224 Benefit St; tel: (401) 454-6500*, open Tues, Wed, Fri, Sat 1030–1700, Thur 1200–2000, Sun 1400–1700, $2, is among the best in New England. The *Pendleton House* wing showcases an outstanding assemblage of Early American furniture and decorative arts. A rich merchant's Georgian mansion built in 1786, the **John Brown House**, *52 Power St; tel: (401) 331-8575*, $2.50, open Tues–Sat 1100–1600, Sun 1300–1600 (Mar–Dec), Sat 1100–1600, Sun 1300–1600 (Jan–Feb), displays porcelain, glassware, paintings and furnishings amassed during the China Trade's maritime heyday.

PROVIDENCE TO EAST GREENWICH

Point-to-point distances are short in Rhode Island, merely twice the size of Greater London, so minimal time is lost by favouring a scenic Rte 1/1A route soon after leaving Providence. Petrol, food and strip-mall shopping opportunities are plentiful once you've reached Rte 1. You'll see *CI*, *Rd* and *Sh* accommodation, and the western shore of Narragansett Bay is always nearby.

EAST GREENWICH

Tourist Information: East Greenwich Chamber of Commerce, *5853 Post Rd, East Greenwich, RI 02818; tel: (401) 885-0020*. Near the **Kent County Courthouse** (1750) dominating *Main St*, the **General Varnum House**, *57 Peirce St; tel: (401) 884-4110*, open Thur–Sat 1300–1600 (mid-June–Aug), Sat 1300–1600 (Sept), $2, is an 18th-century mansion built by a Revolutionary War commander. Towards the south end of town, go left on *Forge Rd* to reach the opposite side of the cove and **Goddard State Park** with its 8 miles of walking/biking trails.

Turn downhill where *Main* meets *King St* to reach *Water St* for views of Greenwich Cove. Three moderately priced seafood restaurants with outdoor decks are situated here: **Blue Parrott Café**; *tel: (401) 884-2002*, **Twenty Water Street**, *tel: (401) 885-3703* and **Harbourside Lobstermania**; *tel: (401) 884-6363*.

EAST GREENWICH TO WICKFORD

BW and random budget accommodations are en route as you proceed south on Rte 1 past the **Quonset Point Naval Air Station,** where quonset huts originated. These metal prefab structures were ubiquitous during World War II – but few people know the name was taken from a dwelling used by Indians in Rhode Island. Then, less than a mile down Rte 1A, comes one of Rhode Island's prettiest villages, unsullied by mass tourism.

WICKFORD

Tourist Information: South County Tourism Council, *4808 Tower Hill Rd, Wakefield, RI 02879; tel: (401) 789-4422* or *(800) 548-4662*. Elm-shaded *Main St* leading to the fishing-boat dock epitomizes colonial USA with its parallel rows of clapboard dwellings and two churches. Several antiques and handicraft shops are located towards the village centre's *Main St/Brown St* crossroad. The **Wickford Art Festival** is a major outdoor event, with the works of some 275 artists displayed along village streets during the second weekend of July, 1000–dusk. The village's utterly New Englandy, moderate category bed and breakfast is **Narragansett House,** *71 Main St, Wickford, RI 02852; tel: (401) 294-3593.* You'll find three small, cheap–budget restaurants, the nicest of which is **Peaches' Tea Room,** *16 West Main St, Wickford, RI 02852; tel: (401) 294-5771.*

WICKFORD TO JAMESTOWN

Depart Wickford by staying on Rte 1A. Upon reaching Rte 138, look for the sign leading to the **Gilbert Stuart Birthplace,** 2 miles away on a hilly side road lined with two-century-old stone fences. The artist-to-be was raised here in his father's gambrel-roofed snuff mill prior to London tutelage by Benjamin West and ensuing fame as painter of the George Washington portrait reproduced on the US $1 bill. The site at *Gilbert Stuart Rd, Saunderstown, RI 02874; tel: (401) 294-3001,* $3, is open Thur–Mon 1100–1630 (Apr–mid-Nov).

After returning to Rte 138, you're less than a mile from the 1.5-mile toll-free bridge that brings you onto Conanicut, a pastoral island, measuring merely 9 miles long and 1 mile wide.

JAMESTOWN (CONANICUT ISLAND)

Tourist Information: Newport County Convention & Visitors Bureau, *23 America's Cup Ave, Newport, RI 02840; tel: (800) 326-6030.*

ACCOMMODATION AND FOOD

There are three moderate bed & breakfasts in Jamestown, the island's only village. Best of the trio, with private baths, is the **Lionel Champlin House,** *20 Lincoln St, Jamestown, RI 02835; tel: (401) 423-2782.* A huge, shingle-sided and pricey resort hotel, the **Bay Voyage,** *150 Conanicus Ave, Jamestown, RI 02835; tel: (401) 423-2100,* has a superb dining room.

Regional Italian cuisine has drawn attention to pricey **Trattoria Simpatico,** *13 Narragansett Ave; tel: (401) 423-3731.* Moderate **Oyster Bar & Grill,** *22 Narragansett Ave; tel: (401) 423-3380,* specialises in fresh seafood. Also moderate, **Schoolhouse Café,** *14 Narragansett Ave; tel: (401) 423-1490,* serves creative American meals. Or shop for picnic supplies at cheap-budget **Ferry Market & Deli,** *47 Conanicus Ave; tel: (401) 423-1592.*

SIGHTSEEING

Like Wickford, Jamestown is an unspoiled seaside community (population 5,000). Stop at the Town Hall on Narragansett Ave for a copy of the Village Association's *Discover Jamestown* folder, with its street map, list of miscellaneous establishments and descriptions of island attractions. The avenue ends at waterfront *Conanicus Ave,* where Newport can be seen across Narragansett Bay. For some sidetrack driving beyond the village, head for Conanicut Island's southernmost tip by crossing the Mackerel Cove causeway to reach **Beavertail State Park** and its 1856 lighthouse, with a **Lighthouse Museum;** *tel: (401) 423-1771,* free, open Wed–Sun 0900–1700 (summer only).

On the eastern waterfront via *Shore Rd,* a 1-mile trail winds through the **Conanicut Sanctuary** wildlife habitat. On pastureland in the island's midsection, you'll see the 1787 **Jamestown Windmill,** *North Rd; tel: (401) 423-1798,* free, open mid-June–Sept. Getting back on Rte 138 is a necessity, for it continues east over the 2-mile toll bridge connecting Conanicut Island with urban Newport.

123

BOSTON–PORTLAND

These routes offer the extremes of driving in New England – a fast and rather dull express route on the interstate highways or a meandering drive through the seaside villages and towns of the New Hampshire and Maine coasts. The scenic route captures much of what people seek on the New England coast: historic towns, picturesque fishing villages, the best swimming in northern New England and the last two great honky-tonk beach towns in the region. Unfortunately, this concentration of quintessential New England attractions elicits a parallel concentration of travellers on the coastal roads. Traffic becomes slow and heavy during the summer and the scenic parts are occasionally interrupted by stretches of ugly strip development, a characteristically American architecture that reaches its nadir between interstate and ocean.

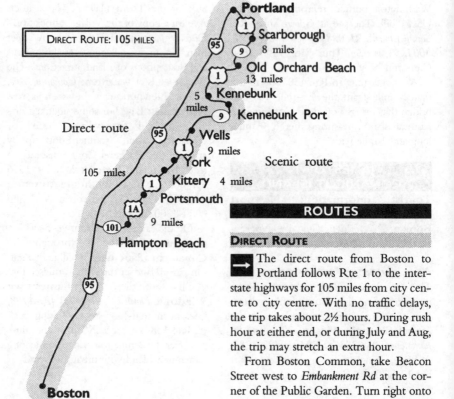

DIRECT ROUTE: 105 MILES

Portland

Scarborough
8 miles

Old Orchard Beach
13 miles

Kennebunk
5 miles

Kennebunk Port

Direct route

Wells
9 miles

York

Scenic route

105 miles

Kittery 4 miles

Portsmouth

9 miles

Hampton Beach

Boston

ROUTES

DIRECT ROUTE

→ The direct route from Boston to Portland follows Rte 1 to the interstate highways for 105 miles from city centre to city centre. With no traffic delays, the trip takes about 2½ hours. During rush hour at either end, or during July and Aug, the trip may stretch an extra hour.

From Boston Common, take Beacon Street west to *Embankment Rd* at the corner of the Public Garden. Turn right onto

Storrow Dr. and follow signs to Rte 1 north (Exit 27, Tobin Bridge). Continue 13 miles north on Rte 1 to I-95 North exit, marked 'New Hampshire-Maine' (the second I-95 exit, not the first). Continue on I-95 North to New Hampshire Turnpike to Maine Turnpike to Exit 6A on Maine Turnpike (I-295, Downtown Connector). Take Exit 4 or 7 for Portland waterfront, 5 or 6 for downtown.

SCENIC ROUTE

The scenic route follows the direct route to the New Hampshire Turnpike, departing at Exit 2, Rte 101 (formerly 51) to **Hampton Beach**. (For a more scenic drive through Massachusetts, see North Shore chapter, p. 77) At the tollbooth, bear left on Rte 101 East to Hampton Beach.

Leaving Hampton Beach, follow Rte 1A north, keeping the ocean in sight along the New Hampshire coast to **Portsmouth**. At Portsmouth, follow signs to Strawbery Banke or Downtown. Leaving Portsmouth, cross the Memorial Bridge (Rte 1 north) to **Kittery**; in less than one mile, turn right onto Rte 103. Follow Rte 103 to Rte 1A to wander through the coastal villages of **the Yorks**. Rte 1A rejoins Rte 1 shortly before **Ogunquit**, which is followed on Rte 1 by **Wells Beach** and **Wells**.

Turn right on Rte 9 to **Kennebunk Beach, Kennebunkport and Cape Porpoise**. At Cape Porpoise, retrace your route to Kennebunk Lower Village, turn right onto Rte 9A for 5 miles to **Kennebunk** and turn right onto Rte 1. Continue north on Rte 1 for 13 miles to Rte 5 in **Saco**; turn right toward **Old Orchard Beach**. From Old Orchard Beach, follow Rte 9 east through Pine Point in **Scarborough** to Rte 1. Continue on Rte 1 to **Portland**, veering right onto Rte 1A, which leads directly to the waterfront and Old Port district.

HAMPTON BEACH

The beach portion of New Hampshire's Town of Hampton, known as Hampton Beach, sports unusually extensive swimming beaches for New England and has evolved as a populist summer destination for inland New Englanders and many Canadians, especially from Québec.

Tourist Information: Hampton Beach Area Chamber of Commerce, *836 Lafayette Rd, Hampton, NH 03842; tel: (603) 926-8717 or (800) GET-A-TAN,* open Mon–Sat 0900–1700. **Tourist Information Center,** *180 Ocean Blvd,* open daily 0900–2130 (mid-June–early Sept), Sat–Sun (Apr–mid-June and early Sept–end Oct).

ACCOMMODATION

Many motels in various price ranges line *Ocean Blvd, Ashworth Ave* and adjacent streets. In general, this is one of the lower-priced areas along the New England coast. **Hampton Beach State RV Park,** *Ocean Blvd; tel: (603) 926-8990,* along the tidal Hampton River, is part of Hampton Beach State Park and is the only RV park directly on the New Hampshire coast: 20 first-come, first-served sites in a prime spot south of the main part of the beach on Rte 1A with miles of sandy beaches, a park store and saltwater fishing. Budget.

ENTERTAINMENT

The town sponsors almost nightly concerts and Wed and holiday evening fireworks in July and Aug at the Sea Shell Bandstand at **Hampton State Beach**. The **Hampton Beach Casino Ballroom**, *Ocean Blvd; tel: (603) 929-4100,* is an 1800-seat cabaret summer concert hall 'where the beach meets the stars'. **Hampton Playhouse,**

357 Winnacunnet Rd; tel: (603) 926-3073, produces summer theatre.

SIGHTSEEING

Deep-sea fishing, whale-watching expeditions and sightseeing cruises are available from **Hampton State Pier at the State Marina,** *Rte 1A*, south of the main beach area at the Hampton-Seabrook bridge.

RYE BEACH

Rye Beach has both rocky overlooks and sandy beaches, officially open sunrise to sunset. Best of the rocky areas is **Ragged Point Picnic Area,** *Rte 1A*. **Wallis Sands State Park,** *Rte 1A*, has the smoothest sand bottom for swimming of the New Hampshire beaches and fewer sunbathers per square foot. **Odiorne Point State Park,** *Rte 1A*, open daily (early May–late Oct), is the largest undeveloped stretch of shore on New Hampshire's 18-mile coast. It has picnic areas and extensive walking/cycling trails through an array of habitats. The **Seacoast Science Center,** *Odiorne Point State Park; tel: (603) 436-8043*, open daily 1100–1700, 1000–1800 (summer), is a perfect introduction to coastal and marine environments in this area of New England; free.

PORTSMOUTH

Originally settled in 1623 as Strawbery Banke, Portsmouth became a town in 1631. It has been a major shipbuilding centre since the 17th century, but the industry is recently moribund. Great care has been taken to preserve the historic flavor of the community as it has grown into the region's largest city.

Tourist Information: Greater Portsmouth Chamber of Commerce, *500 Market St, Portsmouth, NH 03802-0239; tel: (603) 436-1118; Exit 7 from NH*

Turnpike, open Mon–Fri 0830–1700, Sat–Sun 1100–1600 (end May–mid-Oct), has publications featuring the entire New Hampshire seacoast. At the **Information Kiosk,** *Market Sq.*, open end May–mid-Oct, staff answer questions and provide directions. Does not help with lodging. Round-the-clock information available by tuning car radio to 98.9 FM in front of the Chamber building for brief message about Seacoast area accommodations, restaurants and events.

ACCOMMODATION

Several chain hotels are represented: *DI, Hn, HJ, Sh, Su*. There are three good bets for bed and breakfast, all moderate to expensive: the Victorian **Sise Inn,** *40 Court St, Portsmouth, NH 03801; tel: (603) 433-1200;* the elegant and romantic **Governor's House,** *32 Miller Ave, Portsmouth, NH 03801; tel: (603) 431-6546;* and lodgings in a former brewery, **Bow Street Inn,** *121 Bow St, Portsmouth, NH 03801; tel: (603) 431-7760.*

EATING AND DRINKING

Best eating and drinking is in the old port area (*Market, Bow, Ceres* and *Congress Sts*). **The Blue Strawbery,** *29 Ceres St; tel: (603) 431-6420*, pioneered gourmet prix fixe meals in the area; Pricey. Other eateries fall into the moderate range. **Portsmouth Gas Light Company,** *64 Market St; tel: (603) 430-9122*, has casual American food upstairs and great pizzas from wood-fired brick ovens downstairs. **Portsmouth Brewery,** *56 Market St; tel: (603) 431-1115*, is a credible brewpub.

The Dolphin Striker, *15 Bow St; tel: (603) 431-5222*, features continental preparations and fine local fish right across from the tugboat dock.

Oar House, *55 Ceres St; (603) 436-*

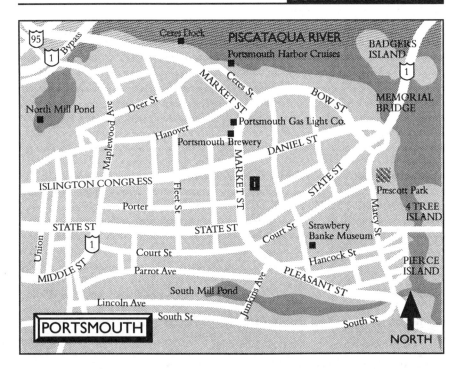

4025, has a good fish-oriented menu and its seasonal waterfront dock tables are great for a drink or light meal.

ENTERTAINMENT

Seacoast Repertory Theatre, *125 Bow St; tel: (800) 639-7650, (603) 433-4472,* is a professional regional theatre with main stage Sept–June, summer series July–Aug.

SHOPPING

The old port area is also a good strolling district of small boutiques. **N.W. Barrett Gallery,** *53 Market St; tel: (603) 431-4262,* displays very high quality fine crafts.

SIGHTSEEING

The Information Kiosk provides a map for an ambitious walking tour of six properties notable for history and architectural detail. Hours vary but houses are generally open from mid-June–mid-Oct, each charging a separate admission of $4.

Of special interest are the **Governor John Langdon House,** *143 Pleasant St; tel: (603) 436-3205,* one of the finest 18th-century homes in New England; **The John Paul Jones House,** corner *Middle* and *State Sts; tel: (603) 436-8420,* especially rich in nautical history; and the **Wentworth-Gardner House,** *Market St; tel: (603) 436-4406,* perhaps America's best example of Georgian architecture. **Strawbery Banke Museum,** Visitors' Center on *Marcy St; tel: (603) 433-1100,* open daily 1000–1700 (May–Oct, Thanksgiving weekend and first two weekends of Dec), illustrates 350 years of architectural and social change through furnished houses, exhibitions, period gardens, traditional crafts and special programs; $10.

Nine furnished houses and six exhibit houses built 1695–1943 reflect a wide range of architecture and life-styles. **Prescott Park;** *tel: (603) 431-8748,* along the *Marcy St* waterfront contains a large formal garden with fountains – a mecca for flower lovers. Its spectacular All-American Trial Garden boasts a living catalogue of more than 500 varieties of annuals.

At the **Port of Portsmouth Maritime Museum – Albacore Park,** *Market St Extension; tel: (603) 436-3680,* open daily 0930–1600, you can walk through the experimental submarine, *U.S.S. Albacore,* built at the Portsmouth Naval Shipyard in 1953; $4.

EVENTS

Prescott Park Arts Festival features live theatre and concerts almost daily in July and Aug.

SIDE TRACK FROM PORTSMOUTH

The Isles of Shoals comprise nine small islands with a total land area of 200 acres. Four of the islands – Lunging, Seavey, Star and White – are part of New Hampshire. Appledore, Cedar, Duck, Malaga and Smuttynose belong to Maine.

Star Island, owned by the Unitarian Church, is the only island in the group open daily to the public. Daytrips to visit the islands are available daily mid-June–early–Sept from **Star Island Stopover Cruises,** *Barker Wharf, 315 Market St; tel: (800) 894-5509* or *(603) 431-5500* ($16.50), and mid-June–Oct from **Portsmouth Harbor Cruises,** *Ceres St Dock; tel: (800) 776-0915* or *(603) 436-8084;* $7–$12. Regular ferry service to Star ($16.50) is available on weekends beginning in Apr and daily mid-June–early Sept on **Isles of Shoals Steamship Company,** *Barker Wharf, 315 Market St; tel: (800) 441-4620* or *(603) 431-5500.* Sailings are on the *MV Thomas Laighton,* a 90-foot replica of a turn-of-the-century steamship. The narrated cruise to the island includes a three-hour stopover on Star.

An hour-long historical walking tour of Star departs at 1300 from the **Oceanic House,** an old-fashioned white-clapboard resort hotel. You can also wander along island paths unescorted, but watch your step, as brush along the paths often shelters gull chicks or eggs. Only guests may order meals at the hotel, but the snack bar is open for everyone. Stayovers are possible only if you're registered with one of the conferences at the hotel centre; **The Star Island Corporation,** *110 Arlington St, Boston MA 02116-5320.*

Appledore Island, the largest of the nine islands, is accessible on request from the **Shoals Marine Laboratory,** *Cornell University, Ithaca NY 14853; tel: (607) 255-3717.* During the late 19th century, Appledore's resort hotel attracted noteworthies in the arts. The garden of the hotel's hostess, Celia Thaxter, has been restored to its 1893 glory. Tours of Ms Thaxter's garden are offered Wed mid-June–early Sept. ⬛

KITTERY

The scenic route bypasses the **factory outlets** along Rte 1. You may not want to; there are more than 150 brand-name outlet stores with savings of 20–70 percent. Otherwise, if you stick to the scenic route, **Fort McClary State Memorial Park,** *Rte 103; tel: (207) 439-2845,* which dates from 1715, is a grand rocky overlook with stone beaches and waterside walking trails.

THE YORKS

Tourist Information: Chamber of Commerce, *Rte 1 and I-95 connector, York, ME 03909; tel: (207) 363-7104,* is open daily 0900–1700 (extended summer hours). Four distinct villages of the Town of York lie north from Kittery along Rte 1A: **York Beach, Cape Neddick, York Harbor** and **York Village.**

The Yorks are more a summer community than a tourist destination, so best lodging bets are for campers. **Libby's Oceanside Camp,** *Rte 1A, York Harbor, ME 03911; tel: (207) 363-4171,* and **Camp Eaton,** *Rte 1A, York Harbor ME 03911; tel: (207) 363-3424,* both lie directly on **Long Sands Beach.** Libby's has RV hookups only; Camp Eaton also has tent pitches and housekeeping cabins. All along the Maine coast, every community with fishermen tends to have clam bakes and lobster pounds and the Yorks are no exception. Most famous locally is **Foster's Lobster & Clambake,** *Rte 1A, York Harbor; tel: (207) 363-3255.*

York Village has a beautiful green with historic homes, a monument to the Civil War dead with a statue of a soldier dressed in a Confederate uniform (the corresponding Union statue is somewhere in South Carolina, and neither town wanted to pay the freight to exchange them).

Old York Historical Society, *York St and Lindsay Rd (140 Lindsay Rd); tel: (207) 363-4974,* open Tues–Sat 1000–1700, Sun 1300–1700 (mid-June–Sept), has seven historical buildings (admission $2 per building) dating from the mid-18th century: **Jefferds Tavern,** built in 1759, with house 'rules' admonishing guests to 'abhor all oaths, cursing and blasphemy'; the **Old School House** with hard wooden benches, tiny windows and a prison-like ambiance; the **Emerson Wilcox House;** the **Old Gaol** with wooden stocks on the hill out front; the **John Hancock Warehouse and Wharf;** the **George Marshall Store;** and the **Elizabeth Perkins House.**

York Harbor is the area's fishing centre with historic inns, antiques shops and art galleries. **Town Dock no. 2** is home to several boating and fishing excursions; one of the more peculiar is **Lobstering Trips;** *tel: (207) 363-3234,* in which you putter out on a 22-foot skiff to watch a few traps being hauled; call between 1700 and 1800; $6.50. The road continues to the aptly named **Long Sands Beach** and the village of **Cape Neddick,** which has fine old homes and picturesque views of the ocean.

From the north end of the beach a local road leads east to the tip of Cape Neddick and **Nubble Point Light,** one of the most photographed lighthouses in New England. Backtracking to Rte 1A leads through **York Beach,** a lively spot with beachside amusements and taffymaking (the making of a type of sweet sold along the New England seashore).

OGUNQUIT

Tourist Information: Chamber of Commerce, *Rte 1S at Obed's Lane, Box 2289, Ogunquit, ME 03907; tel: (207) 646-2939;* also, summers *tel: (207) 646-5533,* open daily (July–Aug), limited hours (Sept–June). Ogunquit is impossible for drivers in the summer. Park your auto in a designated long-stay lot and use one of the old-fashioned trolleys that run every few minutes from mid-May–mid-Oct (Columbus Day weekend).

Ogunquit is known as an artists' colony and a particularly hospitable area for same-gender couples. The Indian name means 'Beautiful Place By the Sea'. It's true – the beach runs for about three miles and has three entrances. The Main Beach at *Beach*

129

St has a boardwalk, shops and restaurants. Other entrances are north of town at the Footbridge and Moody Beach. Each has its own car park. **Marginal Way** – a scenic, rose-lined footpath on a bluff – connects the village along the shoreline to **Perkins Cove,** a manmade inlet made famous by artists who come here during the summer. The cove features small shops, galleries, restaurants and variety of scenic cruises on small boats from Barnacle Billy's Dock.

Seacoast Tours, *Perkins Cove; tel: (207) 646-6326,* offers an amusing 2½-hour minibus tour narrated by 'an eighth generation Mainer'; $12.50. The **Ogunquit Playhouse,** *Rte 1; tel: (207) 646-2402 or (207) 646-5511,* is a famed venue of professional summer theatre, offering three musicals and two plays each ten-week season from end June–early Sept.

WELLS/WELLS BEACH

Tourist Information: Wells Information Center, *Rte 1, Moody/Wells, ME 04090; tel: (207) 646-2451,* is open Tues–Sat 1000–1600, Sat–Thur 0900–1700 and Fri 0900–2000 (summer).

Turn off Rte 1 down *Mile Rd* for **Wells Beach,** a seven-mile stretch of wide, flat sandy beaches with outlet stores, speciality shops and boutiques, rare book stores, antique shops and flea markets. **Wells Auto Museum,** *Rte 1; tel: (207) 646-9064,* open daily (mid-June–Sept), displays more than 130 antique automobiles, plus an outstanding collection of nickelodeons, vintage arcade games, license plates and toys; $3.50.

Rachel Carson Wildlife Refuge, *Rte 9 East; tel: (207) 646-9226,* open daily sunrise-sunset, consists of 1600 acres of wetlands. Secluded walking paths wind through the refuge and several species of bird live on the safe sanctuary grounds.

The one-mile Rachel Carson Trail offers vistas and closeup views of the salt marsh.

KENNEBUNK
KENNEBUNKPORT
KENNEBUNK BEACH

Tourist Information: The Kennebunk-Kennebunkport Chamber of Commerce, *P.O. Box 740, Kennebunk, ME 04043; tel: (207) 967-0857,* operates the **Tourist Information Center** in Kennebunk Lower Village, open Mon–Fri 0900–1700 and additional weekend hours (end May–mid-Oct).

This isn't a place you'd normally stop, especially on a budget, but it boasts one of the finest inns and dining rooms in Maine: **The White Barn Inn,** *Beach St, Kennebunkport; tel: (207) 967-2321.* The 24 guest rooms include suites with fireplaces and whirlpool baths and the restaurant is hailed for its New England regional haute cuisine. Pricey, but this Relais & Chateaux property is the only AAA 5-Diamond dining north of Boston. The villages of Kennebunk, Kennebunk Beach and Kennebunkport comprise an area which caters to many 'summer folk' – artists, writers and former President George Bush, who may sometimes be spotted at the wheel of his racing boat off Walker's Point. **Lower Kennebunk Village** is a crossroads for getting to the other villages, but has its own charms, including summer brewery tours at **Kennebunkport Brewery at Shipyard Shops,** *8 Western Ave (Rte 9); tel: (207) 967-4311.*

Kennebunkport was once an important shipbuilding centre and **Dock Square** is the active business and shopping area of the 'Port'. Along the quiet residential streets and avenues of town, lovely 18th- and 19th-century homes peep out from under shady trees. Deep-sea fishing trips and whale-watching cruises leave daily from the Dock Square wharf. Across the river, the silver strip of sand signifying Kennebunk Beach is visible. **Seashore Trolley Museum,** *Log Cabin Rd, off Rte 9; tel: (207) 967-2800,* daily May–late Oct, has the world's largest collection (225) of trolleys and offers rides on antique electric trolleys; $6.

The inland town of Kennebunk exemplifies early American tradition, with its stately business district and well-kept residential areas. **Brick Store Museum,** *117 Main St; tel: (207) 985-4802,* open Tues–Sat 1000–1630, has historical and fine and decorative arts exhibitions in restored 19th-century buildings as well as a museum shop; $3, $4 with adjacent **Taylor-Barry House,** open Tues–Fri 1300–1600 (June–Sept), an 1803 sea captain's home with four period-furnished rooms and a 20th-century artist's studio.

Just north of Kennebunkport the quaint fishing village of **Cape Porpoise** has both the popular resort colony of Goose Rocks Beach and miles of uncrowded beaches within a 15-minute drive of downtown.

OLD ORCHARD BEACH

Tourist Information: Chamber of Commerce Information Center, *P.O. Box 600, First St, Old Orchard Beach, ME 04064; tel: (800) 365-9386, (207) 934-2500,* open Mon–Fri 0900–1700, daily 0900–1700 (July–Aug). This festive summer resort town is a must for families travelling with children. The seven-mile stretch of sandy beaches at Old Orchard Beach have made the town a summer destination since the mid-19th century, when the Grand Trunk Railroad brought vacationers from Canada. It remains one of the last beach towns with both great swimming beaches and innumerable honkytonk amusements. **Old Orchard Ocean**

Pier has been going strong since 1898 with its arcades, shops and boutiques adjacent to **Funtown U.S.A.**, a traditional amusement park with flashy rides. **Wonderland Arcade** claims to be the first amusement arcade in New England. The downtown has been recently renovated with wide brick sidewalks, park benches, foliage plantings and a new bathhouse – all designed to add an air of neo-Victorian decorum to the carnival atmosphere.

Speaking French can be an advantage in some establishments, as Old Orchard Beach is the top New England destination for Québec tourists. Shuttle transportation runs every half hour July–Aug. Along Rte 9 south of Old Orchard is the calmer 100-acre **Ferry Beach State Park.** Old Orchard Beach has **fireworks** displays every Thur at 2130, July–Aug, at the Palace Playground and during the Canada/USA Festival, 30 June–4 July. The festival celebrates the independence days of Canada and the USA and effectively launches the high season for the resort town.

SCARBOROUGH

Shortly before and after the turn of the century, American artist Winslow Homer lived here on **Prout's Neck,** painting some of his best seascapes and watercolours. Largely absorbed by Greater Portland in recent years, Scarborough retains a few grand wild spots.

The **Scarborough Marsh Nature Center,** *Pine Point Rd, Scarborough, ME 04074; tel: (207) 883-5100,* a 3,000-acre wildlife refuge and wetlands study area superb for birdwatching, offers regular tours and canoe trips June–early Sept. **Scarborough Downs Race Track,** *Rte 1; tel: (207) 883-4331,* offers day and evening harness racing during summer.

131

CAPE COD

Cape Cod is one of the first areas settled by Europeans, yet remains in many parts rural or even wild. This arm-shaped land jutting into the North Atlantic is defined less by its soil than by the waters around it. Fishing and shellfishing remain major economic pursuits, topped only by tourism to the vast sandy beaches and pine-glade interior. The light that suffuses the landscape has long drawn artists as well. Millions of visitors flock to Cape Cod from July–Oct, but spring is slow and many places stay closed until late May. Fall can be busy into Nov. Reservations are advised in every season.

TOURIST INFORMATION

Cape Cod Chamber of Commerce, *junction Rtes 6 and 132, Hyannis, MA 02601; tel: (508) 362-3225.* Open Mon–Fri 0830–1700 (year-round), also Sat–Sun (mid-May–mid-Oct). Seasonal **information booths,** open daily 0900–1700 (late-May–mid Oct), stand on the Cape side of Sagamore Bridge, at the Sagamore roundabout, and in Bourne on the Cape side of the Bourne Bridge on Rte 28 South (toward Falmouth). Local information centres supplement the Cape-wide centre. While most answer telephone messages and mail throughout the year, they welcome visitors daily July–Aug, weekdays late May–June and Sept–mid-Oct.

WEATHER

Cape Cod enjoys a cool and extended spring, a temperate summer and golden, lingering autumns. Daytime summer highs range 60–80°F., and winter highs 25–45°F.

ARRIVING AND DEPARTING

Airports
Commercial air service is available in Hyannis at **Barnstable County Municipal Airport** and in Provincetown at **Provincetown Municipal Airport.** Daily Provincetown–Boston service is via **Cape Air;** *tel: (800) 352-0714 or (508) 771-6944.* Hyannis is served from Boston, Nantucket and Martha's Vineyard on **Cape Air** and from New York-LaGuardia daily and Newark daily in the summer on **Colgan Air;** *tel: (800) 272-5488 or (703) 368-8880.* Taxi from either airport to village centre is approximately $5 per person.

By ferry
Martha's Vineyard & Nantucket Steamship Authority, *Reservation Bureau, 509 Falmouth Rd, Suite 1C, Mashpee, MA 02649; tel: (508) 477-8600,* is the sole all-year ferry and sole vehicle ferry between Woods Hole and Martha's Vineyard, Hyannis and Nantucket and between the islands. Vehicle reservations essential.

Hy-Line Cruises, *Ocean St Dock, Hyannis, MA 02601; tel: (508) 778-2600,* operates daily summer passenger service from Hyannis to both Nantucket and Martha's Vineyard. **Bay State Cruise Co.,** *67 Long Wharf, Boston, MA 02110; tel: (617) 723-7800,* operates one daily round-trip passenger ferry between Boston and Provincetown mid-June–early Sept, weekend trips in early June and Sept–Oct.

By Bus

Bonanza Bus Lines; *tel: (800) 556-3815 or (401) 331-7500,* provides service between Boston or Providence and Bourne, Falmouth, Woods Hole and Hyannis. **Plymouth & Brockton Street Railway Co.**; *tel: (508) 746-0378,* provides service between Boston and Sagamore, Barnstable, Yarmouth, Dennis, Brewster, Orleans, Wellfleet, Truro and Provincetown.

GETTING AROUND

Natives divide Cape Cod into the **Upper Cape** (shoulder), the **Mid Cape** (upper arm) and the **Outer Cape** (the forearm and fist). Each is treated with separate listings for lodging, dining and attractions.

Village nomenclature can be confusing, in that many of the 15 towns have several villages treated locally as discreet entities (see map).

Three major highways run through Cape Cod to its 'elbow'. **Rte 28**, nicknamed the 'Freeway to Fun', is mostly stop-and-go with many traffic lights but also most of the main commercial activity. It skirts the west end and the south coast. **Rte 6A**, the Old Kings Highway, rated as one of the ten 'most scenic byways' in the US, traverses the north coast. **Rte 6** is bland highway until it joins 6A and 28 in Orleans, continuing as the narrow and difficult Rte 6 to the tip of Provincetown.

These limited roads make driving a test of patience. Summer travel a few miles from one town to the next can take an hour. Village parking is slim; beach parking usually requires a permit purchased at Town Hall.

STAYING ON CAPE COD

Accommodation

Cape Cod lodgings tend toward independent motels, pre-World War II vacation cabins, small bed and breakfasts and renovated inns from stagecoach days. **Bed & Breakfast Cape Cod**, *P.O. Box 341, W. Hyannisport, MA 02672; tel: (508) 775-2772,* represents more than 90 properties at all price ranges. **House Guests Cape Cod**, *Box 1881, Orleans, MA 02653; tel: (800) 666-HOST,* represents 100 locations on Cape Cod and nearby islands. It offers a free 50-page lodging directory.

ENTERTAINMENT

The Friday *Cape Cod Times* carries extensive activity listings in *Cape Week.*

Sports

The venerable **Cape Cod Baseball League** launches many collegiate players on professional careers. Falmouth, Bourne, Cotuit, Hyannis, Brewster, Dennis-Yarmouth, Orleans, Chatham and Wareham have teams. The *Cape Cod Times* sports section lists dates and times.

There are 25 **public golf courses** on Cape Cod; pick up 'Golfers' Map to Cape Cod' at information booths; *tel: (800) TEE-BALL.* **Fishing** is a major avocation as well as vocation. Non-resident licences are available from city and town clerks and some sporting goods stores. No licence is required for angling in salt water, but local permits are required for shellfishing. The Chamber provides a *Fresh and Saltwater Fishing Guide.*

Events

Annual Cape Cod Canal Striped Bass Fishing Tournament in late May offers prizes up to $1000. Registration required.

Contact **Cape Cod Canal Chamber of Commerce;** *tel: (508) 759-6000,* for details. The **Barnstable County Fair**, *Barnstable County Fairgrounds, Rte 151, E. Falmouth, MA 02536; tel: (508) 563-3200,* in late July is a celebration of the Cape's agriculture.

SHOPPING

Cape Cod's **largest flea market** sets up on weekends and Mon holidays mid-(Apr–Sept), also Wed–Thur (July–Aug), at **Wellfleet Drive-In Theatre**, *Rte 6A* at the Wellfleet-Truro town line; *tel: (800) 696-FLEA or (508) 349-2520.* The Cape is known for fine glass, pottery and art. Three major glass makers are **Cape Cod Glass Works,** *845 Sandwich Rd (Rte 6A), Sagamore; tel: (508) 888-9262,* maker of paperweights, perfume bottles and glass rods of entwined colours known as ribbon canes; **Pairpoint Crystal Co.,** *851 Sandwich Rd, Sagamore; tel: (508) 888-2344,* maker of hand-blown crystal; and **Chatham Glass Co.,** *17 Balfour Lane* off Rte 28 (*W. Main St*); *tel: (508) 945-5547,* maker of art glass. Both potters and antiques shops flourish on the north shore of the Mid Cape along Rte 6A and the Outer Cape along Rte 6. The brochure, *Cape Cod Potters,* is available at information centres. Wellfleet and Provincetown, long summer havens for the New York art crowd, have world-class galleries.

CAPE-WIDE SIGHTSEEING

Cape Cod Scenic Railroad, *252 Main St, Hyannis, MA 02601; tel: (800) 872-4508 or (508) 771-3788,* offers scenic tours between Hyannis and Sagamore Bridge all year and dinner train rides spring–fall. **Cape Cod Rail Trail** follows an abandoned railroad right-of-way for about 25 miles through Dennis, Harwich, Brewster, Orleans and Eastham, where it connects with the bicycle trails of the **Cape Cod National Seashore.** The trail crosses highways at several points and passes through a variety of ecosystems. A trail map is available at information booths.

UPPER CAPE

Close to the canal is the quieter, more traditional part of the Cape – far from the honky-tonk of Hyannis or the dramatic sweep of the Cape Cod National Seashore. Its historic villages have low-key beaches, tidy harbours and a wealth of ponds and streams.

STAYING ON UPPER CAPE COD

Accommodation
Hotel chains include *BW, HJ, Rm, QI;* bed and breakfasts dominate. **Cape Cod Canalside Bed and Breakfast,** *7 Coastal Way, Bourne Village, MA 02532; tel: (508) 759-6564,* has a great canal view and loans bicycles; moderate. **Wood Duck Inn,** *1050 County Rd, Cataumet, MA 02534; tel: (508) 564-6404,* has sweeping views of a working cranberry bog (Oct harvest), moderate.

Several moderate–expensive bed and breakfasts occupy historic houses in Sandwich Village, including **The 1829 Captain Ezra Nye House** *152 Main St, Sandwich, MA 02563; tel: (508) 888-6142,* the **Isaiah Jones Homestead,** *165 Main St, Sandwich, MA 02563; tel: (508) 888-9115* and **The Village Inn at Sandwich,** *4 Jarves St, Sandwich MA 02563; tel: (508) 833-0363.*

The classic Falmouth town green is surrounded by several moderate–expensive bed and breakfasts: **The Palmer House Inn,** *81 Palmer Rd, Falmouth, MA 02540; tel: (800) 472-2632 or (508) 548-1230,* **Village Green Inn,** *40 Main St, Falmouth, MA 02540; tel: (508) 548-5621,*

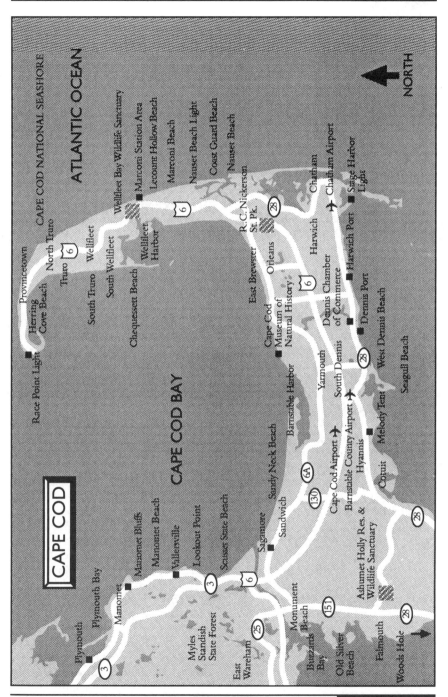

and **Inn at One Main**, *One Main St, Falmouth, MA 02540; tel: (508) 540-7469*. Motels are comparably priced. The plain and clean **Sandy Neck Motel**, *669 Rte 6A, East Sandwich, MA 02537; tel: (508) 362-3992*, is neatly situated at the entrance to Sandy Neck Beach. Falmouth has a motel 'strip' along the town beach area in Falmouth Village. **Sands of Time and Harbor House**, *Woods Hole Rd, Woods Hole, MA 02543; tel: (800) 841-0114 or (508) 548-6300*, overlooks the inner harbour.

State-run **Scusset Beach Reservation**, *PO Box 1292, Buzzards Bay, MA 02532; tel: (508) 888-0859*, has camping close to Scusset Beach, the Cape Cod Canal and a fishing pier. **Peter's Pond Park**, *Cotuit Rd, Box 999, Sandwich, MA 02563; tel: (508) 477-1775*, sits on a large spring-fed pond. **Sippewissett Campground and Cabins**, *836 Palmer Ave, Falmouth, MA 02540; tel: (508) 548-2542*, is a family-oriented camping and cottage colony.

Eating and Drinking

Imaginative cuisine is found at moderate–pricey **Coonamessett Inn**, *Jones Rd and Gifford St, Falmouth; tel: (508) 548-2300*; and **Regatta of Falmouth-By-The-Sea**, *Scranton Ave, Falmouth harbour; tel: (508) 548-5400*. A more casual (budget–moderate) restaurant, run by a Wampanoag chief, features outstanding Native American seafood: **The Flume**, *Lake Ave, Mashpee; tel: (508) 477-1456*, open Apr–Nov. **Landfall Restaurant**, *Luscombe Ave, Woods Hole; tel: (508) 548-1758*, adjacent to the Martha's Vineyard Steamship Authority; open April–Nov; budget– moderate.

Shuckers, *91 Water St, Woods Hole; tel: (508) 540-3850*, is a dockside bar-restaurant known for its raw shellfish. It also serves sandwiches, steamed seafood, grilled chicken, fish and beef; budget–moderate.

SIGHTSEEING

Excursion

OceanQuest, *Water St, Woods Hole, MA 02543; tel: (800) 37-OCEAN or (508) 547-0508*, variable summer schedule, adults $14, offers a fascinating hands-on introduction to marine science.

Beaches and Natural Areas

Bourne's best facility is the state-run **Scusset Beach** on Cape Cod Bay near the Sagamore Bridge. On Buzzards Bay, the well-sheltered **Monument Beach** adjoins the Bourne Marina; the entrance via *Emmons Rd* has no sign. Diving, sport fishing, sightseeing and overnight charters are available at the **Bourne Marina**, *tel: (508) 759-2512*. Eight miles of paved roads along the Cape Cod Canal offer the state's longest uninterrupted bicycle trail and a chance to view cruise ships, tankers, sailboats and tugs passing through the Canal.

Sandwich's **Town Neck Beach** is reached by the **Sandwich Boardwalk** over Mill Creek. Blue herons feeding in the shallows are often spotted from the walkway. Sandwich's best beach for surf casting is at *East End Beach Rd* on **Scorton Creek**. Sandwich provides the access road for **Sandy Neck**; *tel: (508) 362-8300*, a magnificent barrier beach with lofty dunes. Sandy Neck, which actually lies in Barnstable, is a conservation area with hiking and birdwatching.

Wakeby Lake, the largest freshwater pond on the Cape, straddles Sandwich and Mashpee. Sandwich maintains a sandy beach at the **Ryder Conservation Land** off *Cotuit Rd*. The 700-acre lake is bisected by a peninsula containing the

Lowell Holly Reservation, *tel: (617) 821-2977,* open daily 0900–1700 (late-May–mid-Oct). Take Rte 130 exit off Rte 6 to *South Sandwich Rd.* Falmouth has six public beaches. Best for swimming is **Surf Drive**; best for sunsets is **Old Silver.** Each year, about 125 species of birds visit **Ashumet Holly & Wildlife Sanctuary,** *286 Ashumet Rd, East Falmouth; tel: (508) 563-6390,* open daily sunrise–sunset, adults $3. High count on a single day is 75 species.

The **Shining Sea Bikeway** connects Falmouth village and Woods Hole on a 3.5-mile auto-free path along beaches, marshes and woodlands; it connects to another 24 miles of marked bicycle routes.

Museums and Historic Attractions

Aptucxet Trading Post Museum, *24 Aptucxet Rd, Bourne Village, MA 02532; tel: (508) 759-9487,* open Mon–Sat 1000–1700, Sun 1400-1700 (May–mid-Oct), adults $2, off *Shore Rd* in Bourne, is a replica 1627 wooden trading post where Pilgrims traded with the Dutch and Native Americans.

In Sandwich, pick up a *Walking Guide of Historic Sandwich Village* at the **Town Hall,** junction *Rtes 6A* and *130.* **Sandwich Glass Museum,** *129 Main St, Sandwich, MA 02563; tel: (508) 888-0251,* open daily 0930–1630 (Apr–Oct), Wed–Sun 0930-1600 (Nov–Dec and Feb–Mar), adults $3.50, displays highly collectible Sandwich glass, an industry launched in 1825. **Dexter's Grist Mill** beside Town Hall is a working restoration of the town's 17th-century grist mill. Bring empty bottles to fill with drinking water from the adjacent spring. The 76-acre grounds of **Heritage Plantation of Sandwich,** *Grove and Pine Sts, Sandwich, MA 02563; tel: (508) 888-3300,* open daily 1000-1700 (mid-May–late Oct),

adults $7, sport more than 1000 varieties of trees, shrubs and flowers. Most notable are the rhododendrons, which bloom mid-May–mid-June. Separate structures house military and art museums. Best known is the reproduction Shaker round barn with vintage automobiles. **Thornton Burgess Museum,** *Rte 130 on Shawme Pond, Sandwich, MA 02563; tel: (508) 888-4668,* open Mon-Sat 1000-1600, Sun 1300-1600 (call for winter hours), $1, has books, original artwork and memorabilia pertaining to the children's book author and conservationist.

Much of Mashpee belongs to the Wampanoag tribe. The **Wampanoag Indian Museum,** *Rte 130, Mashpee, MA 02649;* call Tribal Council for information, *tel: (508) 477-1536,* displays artifacts, clothing, tools and furniture. **Indian Meeting House and Burial Ground** on Rte 28 are remnants of Native culture.

Falmouth Historical Society, *55–65 Palmer Ave, Falmouth, MA 02540; tel: (508) 548-4857,* Mon–Fri 1400–1700 (mid-June–mid-Sept), adults $2, operates a house museum built in 1790 by a doctor who was a medical corpsman during the American Revolution. The Society also produces a self-guided walking tour of the town's historic sites.**Woods Hole Oceanographic Institute Exhibit Center,** *15 Market St, Woods Hole, MA 02543; tel: (508) 457-2000, ext. 2252,* open Tues–Sat 1000–1630, Sun 1200–1630, adults $1, has historical exhibits on marine research and films of, among other subjects, the wreck of the *Titanic.* **National Marine Fisheries Service Aquarium,** *Albatross and Water Sts, Woods Hole, MA 02563; tel: (508) 548-5123,* open daily 1000–1600 (mid-June–early Sept), Mon–Fri 1000–1600 (early-Sept–mid-June), free, has seals and tanks of locally important fish.

137

MID CAPE

The Mid Cape is the most densely populated portion of Cape Cod, with the village of Hyannis (part of Barnstable) the densest of all. It's peaceful along Rte 6A on the north shore, bustling along Rte 28 to the south.

STAYING ON MID CAPE COD

Accommodation

Hotel chains include *BW, DI, EL, Hd, HJ, Rm*. Rte 28 in Yarmouth and Dennis has the broadest variety of lodging. Independent motels are most affordable, but some beachfront accommodations on *South Shore Dr* in South Yarmouth are moderate. Unadvertised beach motels can be found on small fingers of land off *Lower County Rd* in Dennis, which parallels Rte 28 along the ocean.

Rte 6A is rich in bed and breakfast lodgings (moderate–expensive). Three Yarmouth Port properties on the National Register of Historic Places are **Wedgwood Inn**, *83 Main St, Yarmouth Port, MA 02675; tel: (508) 362-5157,* **Liberty Hill Inn**, *77 Main St, Yarmouth Port, MA 02675; tel: (800) 821-3977 or (508) 362-3976.* and **One Centre Street Inn**, *1 Centre St, Yarmouth Port 02675; tel: (508) 362-8910.*

Camper's Haven, *Old Wharf Rd, Dennisport, MA 02639; tel: (508) 398-2811,* and **Grindell's Oceanview Park,** *Old Wharf Rd, Dennisport, MA 02639; tel: (508) 398-2671,* accommodate RVs.

Eating and Drinking

For the best pricey dining on the Mid Cape try the **Regatta of Cotuit,** *Rte 28, Cotuit; tel: (508) 428-5715,* in an elegant Federal mansion. **Mill Way Fish & Lobster,** *276 Mill Way (off Rte 6A), Barnstable; tel: (508) 362-2760,* is a fresh fish market and casual take-away where one of the owners trained at the top US culinary arts school. For contemporary Italian using local seafood, try **abbicci,** *43 Main St, Yarmouth Port; tel (508) 362-3501.* Great, inexpensive fried seafood has been served since 1933 at **Kream 'N' Kone,** *Rte 28* and *Sea St, Dennisport.*

ENTERTAINMENT

Cape Cod Melody Tent, *West Main St at West End Rotary, Hyannis; tel: (508) 775-0899,* open July–Aug, is the top tourist attraction on Cape Cod – Las Vegas acts have to go somewhere in the summer. **Cape Cod Performing Arts Association;** *tel: (508) 362-3364,* brings chamber music ensembles to Yarmouth for summer concerts at Thirwood Place on *North Main St* in South Yarmouth and the First Congregational Church in Yarmouth Port. **Cape Cod Symphony Orchestra;** *tel: (508) 428-3577,* performs throughout the year at Mattacheese School in West Yarmouth. Summer pops (popular orchestral music) concerts draw 8000 to 10,000 people.

Cape Playhouse, *Main St (Rte 6A), Dennis; tel: (508) 385-3838, (508) 385-3911* for box office, is the oldest summer theatre in the country (since 1927) and runs a ten-week season from end June–early Sept. Bette Davis was an usher the first season, an actress the second. **Cape Cinema;** *tel: (508) 385-2503,* on the same property, shows art and repertory films. Off-season films move into **Cape Museum of Fine Arts;** *tel: (508) 385-4477,* on same grounds.

SIGHTSEEING

Excursions

Whale watches sail only from Barnstable and Provincetown. **Whale Watcher**

Cruises, *Barnstable Harbor; tel: (508) 775-1622 or (800) 287-0374,* adults $15–$22, has daily cruises. **Hy-Line Hyannisport Harbor Cruises;** *tel: 508 778-2600,* offers trips around the Kennedy compound (adults $8), among other cruises. Canoeing and kayaking are excellent on the Bass River. **Cape Cod Boats,** *Bass River Bridge, West Dennis; tel: (508) 394-9268),* rents the necessary gear. For aerial sightseeing: **Hyannis Air Service,** *Barnstable Municipal Airport,* East Ramp, off Rte 28 on *Mary Dunn Rd; tel: (508) 775-8171.*

Beaches and Natural Areas

Nantucket and Vineyard Sounds feature the warmest waters and gentlest currents. Beaches along the north shore of the Mid Cape tend to be smaller (with the exception of Sandy Neck) with colder water. Many 'beaches' are small sandy patches next to extensive marshlands.

Sandy Neck Beach (see Upper Cape) in West Barnstable extends across Barnstable harbour from the west. This eight-mile barrier beach is part of a 100-acre habitat for many wildlife species. The **1776 South Conservation Area,** off Rte 149 north of *Church St, Barnstable; tel: (508) 790-6245,* is the most diverse conservation land in the town: 226 acres of freshwater and saltwater marshes, fields and uplands.

Gray's Beach (and Bass Hole Beach), end of *Centre St* off Rte 6A, Yarmouth, has a boardwalk over salt marshes. The sunset view is stunning. The 2.4-mile **Callery-Darling Trail,** north of Rte 6A in Yarmouth Port, stretches from *Homers Dock Rd* to the salt marshes west of *Centre St,* ending at the Gray's Beach boardwalk (access for the disabled). Great blue herons, marsh hawks, quail, pheasants, foxes, rabbits and deer can be seen.

Of Yarmouth's 14 public beaches, the most popular is **Seagull Beach** in Bass River (between South and West Yarmouth). Along *South Shore Dr* are **Bass River Beach** in South Yarmouth, adjacent **Thatcher Town Beach** and **Parkers River Beach.**

Museums and Historic Attractions

Every town has historic villages worth visiting for ambiance. South Yarmouth (and Bass River, a sub-village) along *Old Main St* and Yarmouth Port along Rte 6A are listed in the National Register of Historic Districts, as is South Dennis.

The photo and audio exhibits at **The John F. Kennedy Museum,** *397 Main St, Hyannis, MA 02601, no phone,* open Mon-Sat 1000-1600 and Sun 1300-1600 (summer), Sat 1000-1600 (winter), adults $1, open a window on JFK's days on Cape Cod. Said Kennedy, 'I always come back to the Cape and walk on the beach when I have a tough decision to make. The Cape is one place I can think and be alone'.

Cahoon Museum of American Art, *Rtes 28 and 130, Cotuit, MA 02635; tel: (508) 428-7581,* open Tues-Sat 1000-1600 (Apr-Dec), free, highlights 'naive' Cape Cod painters, especially Ralph Cahoon, who died in 1982. His paintings of mermaids in old Cape Cod settings sold for a few hundred dollars at his death but now fetch tens of thousands.

Captain Bangs Hallett House, *2 Strawberry Lane, Yarmouth Port, MA 02675; tel: (508) 362-3021,* open Sun 1300–1600 (June–Sept), Thur-Fri 1300–1600 (July–Aug), adults $3, was the home of a prosperous China Trade sea captain. A 1.25-mile nature trail (donation $1) leads across the property.

ZooQuarium, *674 Rte 28, West Yarmouth, MA 02673; tel: (508) 775-8883,*

139

open daily 0930-1700 (mid-Feb–late Nov), 0930–1830 (late-June–early Sept), adults $7.50, children $4.50, has dolphins, sharks and sea lions as well as llamas, lions and New England wildlife.

Scargo Hill Observatory, *Scargo Hill Rd off Rte 6A, Dennis,* built in 1902, is a rude stone tower providing spectacular views of Cape Cod Bay.

Cape Museum of Fine Arts, *Rte 6A, Dennis, MA 02638,* on grounds of Cape Playhouse; *tel: (508) 385-4477,* open Tues–Sat 1000–1700, Sun 1300–1700, adults $2, shows the work of Cape artists.

OUTER CAPE

The Outer Cape is a country unto itself, as much water as land. Once densely forested, its shores became engulfed in sand once settlers felled the trees. In both landscape and sociology, the Outer Cape represents Cape Cod's most extreme expression.

STAYING ON OUTER CAPE COD

Accommodation

Hotel chains include *BW, Hd, Sh.* Reservations systems include **Harwich Accommodations Association,** *P.O. Box 655H, Harwichport, MA 02646; tel: (508) 432-7166,* and **Orleans Bed & Breakfast Associates,** *Box 1312C, Orleans, MA 02653; tel: (800) 541-6226 or (508) 255-3824,* which represents properties near the National Seashore. **In Town Reservations (Provincetown);** *tel: (800) 67-PTOWN,* brokers rooms, while **Provincetown Reservation System;** *tel: (800) 648-0364,* handles rooms, tickets and restaurant seats. The latter is sponsored by the Provincetown Business Guild, which promotes gay tourism. Provincetown is one of the chief gay tourism destinations in the US.

Ocean Edge Resort and Conference Center, *2907 Main St, Brewster, MA 02631; tel: (508) 896-9000,* a seaside golf resort, rents pricey but commodious one- and two-bedroom units by the night.

Quiet Harwichport has superb lodgings, mostly moderate in spring and fall, expensive July–Aug. **Beach House Inn,** *4 Braddock Lane, Harwichport, MA 02646; tel: (800) 870-4405 or (508) 432-4444,* has its own private beach. **Sandpiper Beach Inn,** *16 Bank St, Harwichport, MA 02646; tel: (800) 433-2234 or (508) 432-0485,* has a stunning beach view.

Chatham is an expensive but beguiling town at the elbow of Cape Cod. With summer traffic, it's essential to bunk near the historic district or the beach. Best in-town bets are newly renovated **Chatham Wayside Inn,** *512 Main St, Chatham, MA 02633; tel: (800) 391-5734 or (508) 945-5550,* next to a town park and bandstand, and **The Cranberry Inn,** *359 Main St, Chatham, MA 02633; tel: (508) 945-9232,* next to nature trails through a cranberry bog. Both are moderate–expensive. Beachside lodging runs to extremes. The **Chatham Bars Inn,** *Shore Rd, Chatham, MA 02633; tel: (800) 527-4884 or (508) 945-0096,* is a very pricey landmark resort. **Inn Among Friends,** *207 Main St, Chatham, MA 02633; tel: (508) 945-0792,* offers moderate–expensive lodging near the Chatham Lighthouse.

Moderate–expensive choices at Nauset Beach include **Nauset Beachside Motel and Cottages,** *Nauset Beach, P.O. Box 121, East Orleans, MA 02643; tel: (508) 255-3348,* and the less expensive **Ship's Knees Inn,** *186 Beach Rd, P.O. Box 756, East Orleans, MA 02643; tel: (508) 255-1312.* Motels and housekeeping units line Rte 6 from Eastham to Truro. Rte 6A (Beach Point) in North Truro has a few motels on Cape Cod Bay.

Wellfleet has quieter, moderately priced bed and breakfasts: **Brehmer Graphics Art Gallery Bed and Breakfast,** *Commercial St, Wellfleet, MA 02667; tel: (508) 349-9565,* and **B&B In the Dunes,** *7 Cliff Rd, Wellfleet, MA 02667; tel: (508) 349-1236,* on a popular surfing beach.

Bed and breakfasts abound near Provincetown's *Commercial St.* A best buy (moderate–expensive) is **The Beaconlite,** *12 Winthrop St, Provincetown, MA 02657; tel: (800) 696-9603 or (508) 487-9603,* an English-style country house with common rooms.

It's impossible to beat the location of **Dyer's Beach House,** *173 Commercial St, Provincetown, MA 02657; tel: (508) 487-2061,* five motel rooms on piles on the harbour; moderate Sept–May, expensive June–Aug. Cheapest lodging (moderate) is **The Outermost Hostel,** *28–30A Winslow St, Provincetown, MA 02657; tel: (508) 487-4378,* open mid-May–mid-Oct with 30 beds in five dormitory cabins.

Nickerson State Park, *3488 Main St, Brewster, MA 02631; tel: (508) 896-3491,* has 420-plus pitches on 2000 acres. Reservations accepted late-May–mid-Sept, six months–14 days before arrival; *tel: (508) 896-4615, reservations only.* **North Truro Camping Area,** *Highland Rd, North Truro, MA 02652; tel: (508) 487-1847,* has 350 pitches near National Seashore's Highland Beach; reservations by mail only.

Eating and Drinking

Best buys are casual dining on great fish. **Thompson's Clam Bar,** *Wychmere Harbor, Harwichport; tel: (508) 432-3595,* is a dockside institution. **Sea in the Rough,** *Rte 28, Chatham; tel: (508) 945-1700,* is a budget–moderate spot to sample Chatham's shellfish, perhaps the best in

New England. **Hatch's Fish Market,** *Main St* behind Town Hall, Wellfleet; *tel: (508) 349-2810,* steams lobster and smokes its own fish and mussels. For lobster in the rough, visit **Bayside Lobster Hut,** *91 Commercial St, Wellfleet; tel: (508) 349-6333.* At the **Dancing Lobster,** *Fisherman's Wharf, Provincetown; tel: (508) 487-0900,* a local restaurant family scion went renegade to serve budget price gourmet seafood.

Provincetown has the lion's share of bistros and fine restaurants. Foodies favour **Front Street,** *230 Commercial St; tel: (508) 487-9715,* and **Martin House,** *157 Commercial St; tel: (508) 487-1327.* Less precious but superb bistro food is found at **Gallerani's Cafe,** *133 Commercial St; tel: (508) 487-4433.* **The Moors,** *Bradford St Extension, Commercial St; tel: (508) 487-0840,* serves Portuguese style seafood amongst authentic shipwreck and whaling decor.

ENTERTAINMENT

Town band concerts occur every Friday late June–early Sept at the Kate Gould Park bandstand in Chatham. **Wellfleet Drive-In Theatre,** *Rte 6 at Eastham-Wellfleet line; tel: (508) 349-7176,* late May–early Sept, is the last operating drive-in theatre in Massachusetts. **Wellfleet Harbor Actors Theater,** *Kendrick Ave, Wellfleet harbour; tel: (508) 349-6835,* presents six avant garde plays spring–early winter.

SIGHTSEEING

Excursions

Among boat tours from Saquatucket Harbor, **Freedom Cruise Line,** *Rte 28, Sasquatucket Harbor, Harwichport; tel: (508) 432-8999,* takes day cruises to and from Nantucket; adults $27 round-trip, bicycle

$9.50. Mainland parking is free for first day, $8 per day afterwards. **Cape Cod Divers,** *815 Main St, Harwichport; (508) 432-9035,* operates a dive boat in Nantucket Sound for experienced scuba divers; $50 for two dives or $90 package with gear rental; daily mid-May–Oct.

Chatham's shifting patterns of sand and water are best viewed from the air. **Cape Cod Flying Circus,** *Chatham Airport, George Ryder Rd, Chatham; tel: (508) 945-2363,* offers three-passenger scenic flights starting at $30.

Art's Dune Tours, *Provincetown; tel: (508) 487-1950; reservations required, prices vary,* provides beach buggy tours through dunes of the National Seashore Park. Several companies operate whale-watching cruises from Provincetown June–Oct, all in the same price ranges and boat classes. The three boats of **Dolphin Fleet of Provincetown;** *tel: (508) 349-1900 or (800) 826-9300 for reservations (advised),* adults $16.50–$17.50, are guided by naturalists from the **Center for Coastal Studies**.

Beaches and Natural Areas

Brewster has several warm-water beaches off Rte 6A on Cape Cod Bay; one of the best is **Linnell Landing Beach** (with access for disabled people). **Brewster Flats** is an excellent clamming area, with flats exposed almost a mile at low tide.

Cape Cod Museum of Natural History, *Rte 6A, Brewster, MA 02631; tel: (508) 896-3867,* has three nature trails through wetlands, beech forest and salt marsh. The **Herring Run,** *Satucket Rd,* is a wonderful place to see the spring migration of herring, which spawn at inland ponds, late Apr–mid-May. The 2000-acre **Nickerson State Park,** *3488 Main St, Brewster; tel: (508) 896-3491,* has motorboating, picnicking, birdwatching and

trails for cycling, hiking and horseback riding. Chatham is a webbed network of constantly shifting sand and sea. Best swimming is at **South Beach,** created a few years ago when a hurricane severed a barrier island. **Oyster Pond Beach** is popular for protected swimming. **Monomoy Island,** a 2710-acre national wilderness area spanning two barrier beach islands offshore from Chatham, lies on a classic bird migration route.

South Monomoy is accessible through tours run by the **Cape Cod Museum of Natural History** and the **Wellfleet Bay Wildlife Sanctuary.** Water taxis (about $20) run from **Stage Harbor Marina** to North Monomoy; *tel: (508) 945-1860.* During the fall migration, as many as 20 species of birds have been spotted simultaneously on North Monomoy's single tree.

Two Orleans beaches represent the best of the Cape: **Skaket Beach** off Rte 6A is a warm-water beach on Cape Cod Bay, with a nine-foot tidal change. At the end of *Nauset Rd* off Rte 6 in East Orleans is the huge expanse of dunes called **Nauset Beach.** The 1,000-car lot fills by 0900 June–Aug. **Nauset Marsh** is ideal for canoeing and kayaking. Rentals from **Goose Hummock Shop,** *Rte 6A, Orleans; tel: (508) 255-0455,* begin at $20 per half day.

Wellfleet Bay Wildlife Sanctuary, *291 State Highway Rte 6, South Wellfleet, MA 02663; tel: (508) 349-2615,* trails open daily 0800–dusk ($3), **visitors centre** open Tues–Sun 0830–1700, covers 1,000 acres with six trails featuring almost every Cape Cod habitat from deciduous forest to tidal flats. This critical spot on the North American flyway is regional headquarters of the Massachusetts Audubon Society. More than 260 bird species have been recorded at the sanctuary and more than 60 species nest here.

The Cape Cod National Seashore

Established in 1961 along a 40-mile stretch between Chatham and Provincetown, the National Seashore protects the fragile environments of the forearm and fist of the Cape. Within its boundaries are 27,000 acres of fragile dunes, rolling beaches, fertile marshes, cranberry bogs and cedar forest. It is administered by the **National Park Service,** South Wellfleet, MA 02663; tel: (508) 349-3785.

Salt Pond Visitor Center, Rte 6, Eastham; tel: (508) 255-3421, open daily mid-March–Dec, and **Provincelands Visitor Center,** Rte 6, Provincetown, MA 02657; tel: (508) 487-1256, open daily late-May–early Sept, have exhibits, audiovisual programs, publications, and information services. From late-June–early Sept, lifeguards patrol the National Seashore's six beaches: **Coast Guard Beach** (good surfing), **Nauset Light Beach** (good surfing and surf casting), **Marconi Beach, Head of the Meadow Beach, Race Point Beach** (most spectacular dunes and lifesaving centre) and **Herring Cove Beach** (sheltered swimming beach that faces into the sunset). Seashore parking is $5 per day, $15 for a summer pass for all beaches; car parks, however, fill early in the morning. Several other beaches under town control lie within the park boundaries but are subject to town regulations.

The Seashore has many self-guided nature trails, with brochures on each available at the visitors centres. Rangers offer daily interpretive trail walks. Three bicycle trails ranging 1.6–7.3 miles provide challenging terrain.

At **Old Harbor Lifesaving Museum** at Race Point, rangers demonstrate surf boat rescues Thur afternoons July–Aug. Many ships foundered off the Cape, and there were once 13 Lifesaving Service stations. The museum is the last one standing. The **Marconi Station Site** marks the spot where Gugleimo Marconi made the first trans-Atlantic radio signal from the US in 1901. Five lighthouses still stand in the National Seashore; the **Three Sisters,** Cable Rd, North Eastham, are open for tours July–Aug.

143

Museums and Historic Attractions

The **Cape Cod Museum of Natural History**, Rte 6A, Brewster, MA 02631; tel: (508) 896-3867, open Mon–Sat 0930–1630, Sun 1230-1630, adults $4, has displays as well as the self-guided walks.

The Old Atwood House Museums, 347 Stage Harbor Rd, Chatham MA 02633; tel: (508) 945-2493, open Tues–Fri 1300–1600 (mid-June–Sept), adults $3, are a jumble of local history in the main buildings. The separate Stallknecht Murals, painted 1931–43, depict Christ in modern garb interacting with Chatham townspeople. **The Pilgrim Monument and Museum,** Bradford St, Provincetown, MA 02657; tel: (508) 487-1310, open daily 0900–1700 (mid-March–Nov), adults $5, commemorates the first landing of Pilgrims in 1620. Its 255-ft tower provides a panoramic view. Among the museum exhibits are the treasures of the only pirate ship ever excavated, the Whydah, which sank off Wellfleet in 1717.

Provincetown has long attracted artists in the summer and the **Provincetown Art Association and Museum,** 460 Commercial St, Provincetown, MA 02657; tel: (508) 487-1750, open Sat-Sun 1200-1600 (all year), daily 1200-1700 and 1900-2100 (July–Aug), adults $3, celebrates their work.

MARTHA'S VINEYARD

On this island, a community of sailors, fishermen, farmers, artists and a few literary lions brace themselves every spring for a deluge of visitors who stay through mid-autumn. The six towns are as diverse as the population. Compare the somewhat honky-tonk Oak Bluffs with the old architecture and affluence of Edgartown. Vineyard Haven strikes a happy medium between those two. West Tisbury, Chilmark and Gay Head are rural and lovely.

TOURIST INFORMATION

Martha's Vineyard Chamber of Commerce, *P.O. Box 1698, Beach Rd* (between *Main* and *Water Sts*), *Vineyard Haven, MA 02568; tel: (508) 693-0085,* publishes comprehensive guides. **Dest-Innations,** *P.O. Box 1173, Osterville, MA 02655; tel: (508) 428-5600,* books reservations on the island and other parts of New England. Free fax service from United Kingdom for itineraries or information; *tel: 0800-89-8627.*

ARRIVING AND DEPARTING

By ferry
Martha's Vineyard & Nantucket Steamship Authority, *P.O. Box 284, Woods Hole, MA 02543; tel: (508) 477-8600; TDD 540-1394,* makes a 45-min crossing from **Woods Hole** on Cape Cod to **Vineyard Haven** (all year) and to **Oak Bluffs** (end May–Nov). Make reservations by early spring if you plan to take your car across during the summer. Without a reservation, you and your car

will wait in a standby line. Autos $38, adults $4.75, children 5–12 $2.40, bicycles $3. The Steamship Authority car park in Woods Hole costs $7.50 per day; free shuttle bus to the dock. Passenger-only ferries operate between Oak Bluffs and **Falmouth,** *tel: (508) 548-4800* (end May–mid-Oct), adult $10 RT; **Hyannis,** *tel: (508) 778-2600* (May–end Oct), adult $11 one-way; and **Nantucket,** *tel: (508) 693-0112* (June–mid-Sept), adults $11 one-way. Also between Vineyard Haven and **New Bedford,** *tel: (508) 997-1688* (end May–early Oct), adults $9 one-way.

By air
Martha's Vineyard Airport, *Airport Rd,* has service from Boston, Hyannis, New Bedford and Nantucket via **Cape Air and Nantucket Airlines;** *tel: (800) 352-0714.*

GETTING AROUND

Taxis are available at ferry docks and the airport and can take you anywhere on the island. From spring to fall, tour buses also meet the ferries from mid-morning to mid-afternoon, giving tours that last approximately 2.5 hours, visiting all six towns and stopping at the Gay Head cliffs. Adults $11.50, children $3; *tel: (508) 627-TOUR.*

Shuttle buses are the cheapest form of transport on the island in summer. A down-island bus connects Vineyard Haven, Oak Bluffs and Edgartown. The three towns are best explored on foot. An up-island shuttle runs from the three towns to **Gay Head;** *tel: (508) 693-1589.*

Vineyard Classic Cars, across from

144

the carousel in Oak Bluffs; *tel: (508) 693-5551*, hires convertibles, mint old cars and Harley Davidson motorcycles for those who like to ride in style. Find other cars for hire at the airport or near ferry docks in Vineyard Haven and Oak Bluffs.

Mopeds are for hire but are frowned upon by many island residents. You'll be somewhat safer and much more welcomed if you rent a bicycle. **Vineyard Bike & Moped**, across from the carousel in Oak Bluffs; *tel: (508) 693-7886*.

Up-island route

This route begins and ends at the Steamship Authority dock in Vineyard Haven, and takes the motorist or well-conditioned bicyclist up-island. From the dock, take a left onto *Water St* and drive to a stop sign at **Five Corners**. Turn right, then bear left up the hill onto *State Rd*. Bear right after 3 miles, continue 2.6 miles to a traffic island and bear left onto *South Rd*, which leads to the centre of **West Tisbury**. In the town centre, turn right onto *Music St* or continue straight on *South Rd*, which offers some distant ocean views. If you choose Music, turn left after 0.6 mile onto *Middle Rd*, an inland pastoral route which meets *South Rd* at **Beetlebung Corner**.

From *Middle Rd*, continue straight at the stop sign, thus rejoining *South Rd*, which turns left at Beetlebung Corner and leads 6 miles to the **Gay Head Lighthouse** and cliffs. Return to Beetlebung Corner and turn left onto *Menemsha Cross Rd*. Bear left at a traffic island after 0.9 mile and drive 0.5 mile down the hill to **Menemsha**, a small fishing village. Turn right at a gift shop onto *Basin Rd*, which ends at **Menemsha Beach**. Return to the traffic island and drive straight onto *North Rd*. Follow it 5.6 miles then bear left, retracing the 5.5 miles

back into Vineyard Haven. Turn left at Five Corners to the ferry dock.

VINEYARD HAVEN

Choose from inns and bed and breakfasts along *Main St* or further removed from the village (all addresses *Vineyard Haven, MA 02568*). **Crocker House Inn**, *4 Crocker Ave, P.O. Box 1658; tel: (508) 693-1151 or (800) 772-0206*, is within walking distance from the ferry and a beach but quiet. Moderate–expensive. **Martha's Vineyard Family Campground**, *265 Edgartown Rd, Box 1557; tel: (508) 693-3772*, accepts caravans. Budget. Open mid-May–mid-Oct.

The wait is typically long for an over-rated, overpriced dinner at **The Black Dog Tavern**, *Beach St Extension; tel: (508) 693-9223*, but it's the hands-down best-in-town for breakfast. Budget. **The Scottish Bake House**, *State Rd (on the way to W. Tisbury); tel: (508) 693-1873*, sells blueberry scones, Cornish pasties, clotted cream and more.

Gosnold's Cruises, *33 Beach Rd; tel: (508) 693-8900*, offers cruises focusing on lighthouses and lunch, lobsters, wildlife, maritime history, sunset or Sunday brunch, $10–$40. Public restrooms are located on *Cromwell Lane*, above the A&P supermarket car park and at the ferry dock.

OAK BLUFFS

Tourist Information: Oak Bluffs Association, *P.O. Box 1521, Oak Bluffs, MA 02557*. Just west of the busy shops of *Circuit Ave* and south of *Lake Ave*, the **Martha's Vineyard Methodist Campground Association** was the site of summer religious camp meetings and revivals in the mid-1800s. At first, members stayed in tents but those gave way to the colourful Victorian cottages, adorned

145

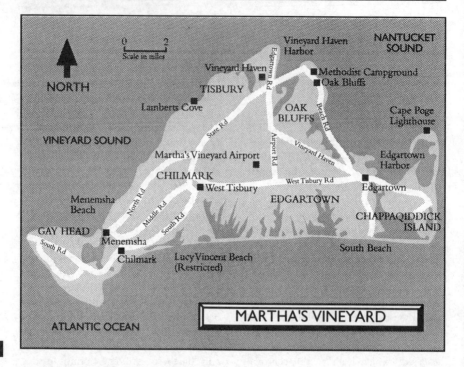

with 'gingerbread' trim, now standing. At the centre of the neighbourhood is the **Tabernacle**, built in 1879 to replace a large tent where meetings took place. Oak Bluffs has a strong, affluent African-American community.

The Flying Horses Carousel, *Lake* and *Circuit Aves*, is said to be the oldest working carousel in the USA. **Oak Bluffs Inn**, *Circuit* and *Pequot Aves*, *P.O. Box 2477, Oak Bluffs, MA 02557; tel: (508) 693-7171 or (800) 955-6235*, has a cupola and off-season package deals. Expensive. **Attleboro House**, *11 Lake Ave, Box 1564; tel: (508) 693-4346*, has rooms with a view of the harbour. Moderate. Of the island's two campsites, **Webb's Camping Area**, *Barnes Rd, Oak Bluffs; tel: (508) 693-0233* (postal address: *RD 3, Box 100, Vineyard Haven, MA 02568)*, is best suited for campers and

popular among bicyclists. Open mid-May–mid-Sept. Reservations strongly suggested. Budget. **Two Fabulus Guys, One Swell Buritow**, *164 Circuit Ave; tel: (508) 646-6494*, serves delicious Mexican food, including vegetarian 'buritows'. Eat al fresco. Moderate. **Jimmy Seas Pasta Restaurant**, *332 Kennebec Ave; tel: (508) 696-8550*, makes its red sauce by simmering lobster bodies all day in tomatoes, herbs and spices. Dinners – seafood, chicken, pasta – are served fresh in the pan. Several bars, some with live music and dancing are dotted along *Circuit Ave*. Public restrooms are on *Kennebec Ave*, north of *Park St*.

EDGARTOWN

This historic town has the island's oldest houses, most shops and highest prices (all addresses *Edgartown, MA 02539)*.

The **Old Whaling Church**, *89 Main St; tel: (508) 627-4442*, has a Greek Revival exterior and an antique interior. **The Dr. Daniel Fisher House**, *99 Main St; tel: (508) 627-8017*, is in the Federal style. Tours of both buildings are given at 1100, 1200, 1300 and 1400, beginning from **The Vincent House Museum**, the island's oldest residence, which is behind the church; *tel: (508) 627-8017*. **Holly's Tours**, *(508) 627-9201 or (508) 693-9321*, does a ghost tour.

Some say room 12 at **The Victorian Inn**, *S. Water St; tel: (508) 627-4784*, is haunted, but it has what the enthusiastic innkeeper calls 'a Mary Poppins view' of Edgartown rooftops. The inn is highly recommended. A four-course breakfast is served on the patio. Expensive. **Meeting House Inn**, *40 Meeting House Way, P.O. Box 2420; tel: (508) 627-6220 or (800) 627-2858*, is a pastoral bed and breakfast two miles out of town.

If you've had too much sun, **The Newes from America**, *23 Kelly St; tel: (508) 627-7900*, is good – a colonial pub with food and microbrewed beers, ales. Open 365 days a year. Budget. Hear jazz after 2200 in the basement pub at **Andrea's**, *137 Upper Main St; tel: (508) 627-5850*. Open Apr–Oct and Christmas.

A trolley (actually an open air shuttle-bus) leaves *Main* and *Church Sts* every 15 min for **South Beach**, 0900–1730, hourly in bad weather, $1.50 one way. Mid-June–mid-Sept.

To escape the madding crowds, ride the **'On Time'** ferry ($1–$4.50) to **Chappaquiddick Island**. Explore the barrier beach, sand dunes and salt marsh of **Cape Poge Wildlife Refuge**, the rolling heath of **Wasque Reservation** and **Mytoi**, a preserve of hiking trails, a pond and Japanese gardens, 0.3 mile down unpaved *Dyke Rd*.

WEST TISBURY

Music St got its name after a whaling captain brought home a piano, neighbours followed his example and the road filled with the sounds of children practising on the keyboards. **Hosteling International–Martha's Vineyard**, *Box 158*, is 1 mile west of town on *Edgartown Rd, W. Tisbury, MA 02575; tel: (508) 693-2665*. Budget.

CHILMARK

Breakfast at Tiasquam, off *Middle Rd, Chilmark, MA 02535; tel: (508) 645-3685*, is a bed and breakfast which offers seclusion, thrown clay sinks, skylights, lobster bakes and a jocular host who can cook with the best. Expensive–pricey. **The Yard**, *Middle Rd* at Beetlebung Corner, *P.O. Box 405, Chilmark, MA 02535; tel: (508) 645-9662* holds workshops and dance and theatre performances late May–Aug.

GAY HEAD-MENEMSHA

The town of **Gay Head** is the home and tribal land of the **Wampanoag Indians** but is also home to white landowners. Waves crash into the clay cliffs below the **Gay Head Lighthouse** and the water turns red. Nude bathing is permitted near the cliffs. Don't climb on the delicate cliffs, and refrain from the popular habit of removing clay and painting your skin – it abets the erosion of the cliffs. In **Menemsha**, get a boiled lobster 'to go' from the fish markets at **Dutcher Dock** or from the back door of **Home Port**, *Basin Rd; tel: (508) 645-2679*, and eat it on the beach at sunset. **Menemsha Inn**, *Box 38, North Rd, Menemsha, MA 02552; tel: (508) 645-2521*, has nice rooms, suites and cottages and provides a pass to **Lucy Vincent Beach**, a sublime stretch of shoreline, but only open to Chilmark residents.

147

NANTUCKET

This island has cobblestones in its harbour village and heaths and cranberry bogs inland. Thousands of daffodils bloom in the spring, planted in the 1970s and 1980s by the garden club. Nantucket is the manicured, genteel cousin to the free-spirited Martha's Vineyard. Its early fortunes were made in whaling, and many of the buildings that resulted from that money are still standing, most notably in the village.

TOURIST INFORMATION

Nantucket Island Chamber of Commerce, *48 Main St, Nantucket, MA 02554; tel: (508) 228-1700 or 228-3643*, open Mon–Fri 0900–1700, has brochures on lodging, restaurants and recreation. **Nantucket Information Bureau**, *25 Federal St; tel: (508) 228-0925*, keeps tabs on lodging vacancies. Call at least a week before your arrival. It also operates **information kiosks** at docking areas and the airport.

ARRIVING AND DEPARTING

By ferry
Martha's Vineyard & Nantucket Steamship Authority, *P.O. Box 284, Woods Hole, MA 02543; tel: (508) 477-8600; TDD 540-1394*. The crossing from South St Dock in **Hyannis** to Nantucket village takes 2 hrs, 15 min. Adults one-way $10, children $5, bicycles $5; autos by reservation only $105 RT (mid-May–mid-Oct), $66.50 (mid-Oct–mid-May). Leave your car in the

Steamship Authority car park in Hyannis, $7.50 per day; Nantucket village is best enjoyed on foot and good bike trails can take you to outlying areas and beaches. If you must take a car, make ferry reservations by early spring.

Passenger-only ferries (bicycles permitted) operate from **Hyannis**; *tel: (508) 778-2600*, and **Harwichport**; *tel: (508) 432-8999* (each 1 hr, 45 mins). Also from **Martha's Vineyard** June–mid-Sept (2 hrs, 15 mins); *tel: (508) 693-0112 or 778-2600*.

By air
Nantucket Memorial Airport has flights from Boston, Hyannis, New Bedford and Martha's Vineyard via **Cape Air and Nantucket Airlines**; *tel: (800) 352-0714*.

GETTING AROUND

Taxi stands can be found at the docks, airport and at the **Pacific Club Building** at the foot of *Main St*. Besides renting bicycles, motor scooters, cars and Jeeps, **Young's Bicycle Shop**, *6 Broad St; tel: (508) 228-1151*, offers a free map of streets and cycle paths, the only map you'll need here. Young's Jeeps come with permits and instructions for 'four-wheeling' on designated beaches.

Watch for colour-coded route signs that point the way to bike paths and beaches, or consult Young's map. The cobblestones are best avoided by road bikes but can be negotiated on mountain bikes. Police will cite you for biking or skating the wrong way on one-way streets. If you're on foot, bicycle or

148

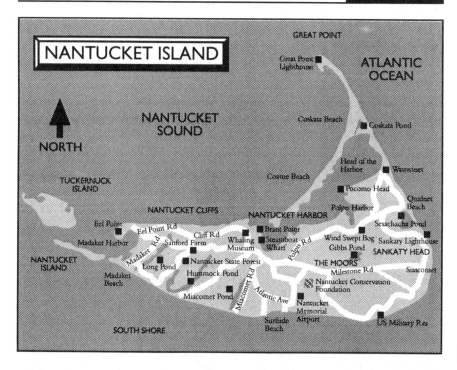

NANTUCKET ISLAND

GREAT POINT

Great Point Lighthouse

ATLANTIC OCEAN

NORTH

NANTUCKET SOUND

Coskata Beach — Coskata Pond

TUCKERNUCK ISLAND

Head of the Harbor — Wauwinet

Coatue Beach

Pocomo Head

Quidnet Beach

NANTUCKET CLIFFS

Polpis Harbor

Sesachacha Pond

NANTUCKET HARBOR

Eel Point — Eel Point Rd

Brant Point

Madaket Harbor — Cliff Rd — Sanford Farm

Whaling Museum — Steamboat Wharf — Wind Swept Bog — Gibbs Pond — Sankaty Lighthouse

SANKATY HEAD

NANTUCKET ISLAND

Long Pond — Nantucket State Forest

THE MOORS

Milestone Rd — Siasconset

Madaket Beach — Hummock Pond

Nantucket Conservation Foundation

Miacomet Pond

Surfside Beach — Nantucket Memorial Airport

US Military Res.

SOUTH SHORE

skates, leave curving, congested *Washington St* to the autos.

ROUTE

After landing at Steamboat Wharf, drive straight onto *Broad St* and take the third left, just past the **Whaling Museum**, a red brick building on the right. (Feel free to curse the island's street signs, most of which can only be read from one side.) After the road becomes cobblestone, turn right onto *Main St.* Head up the hill, turn left onto *Orange St*, continuing one mile to a rotary (roundabout).

Circle two-thirds of the roundabout, following the sign to **'Sconset** and **Polpis** onto *Milestone Rd*, paralleled by a cycle path. Continue for 6.5 miles. *Milestone Rd* becomes *Main St* in **Siasconset** (called 'Sconset in local slang). Traffic flows around a ship's mast

in the centre of the village, a good place to park and stroll some of the side streets. Ask directions for a walk to *Evelyn St*, which runs between small cottages whose roofs are covered with trellis work and, in the warm months, a blanket of roses. You can also walk along the water on *Ocean Ave* and **'Sconset Beach**. From the ship's mast, drive between the tennis courts and post office and continue to the end, turning left onto *Broadway*, so named because several New York theatre actors stayed along this lane.

Broadway joins *Sankaty Ave.* Follow the signs to **Quidnet, Wauwinet** and **Polpis** and a sign to **Nantucket Center**. A digression after 0.2 mile onto *Butterfly Lane* and *Baxter Rd* leads 1.2 miles to **Sankaty Light**, a Coast Guard lighthouse. Watch for a hedge shaped to resemble a spouting whale beside a house on the right. On the way back from the light, turn right onto *Bayberry Lane* and right onto *Sankaty Ave*, which becomes *Polpis Rd* and continues past **Sesachacha Pond**. The road curves to the west (left). Look to the left for **Windswept Bog**, where walking trails lead into the moors.

Polpis merges with *Milestone Rd*. Bear right, returning to the roundabout, circle two-thirds of it and follow the sign to **Madaket** and **Surfside** onto *Sparks Ave*, which curves to the right. Keep to the right, merging onto *Pleasant St*, which continues past a triangle. Do not follow *Williams St*.

Pleasant St ends at the cobbles of *Main St*. Turn right and go downhill, turning left in front of the **Pacific National Bank**, a brick building, onto *Centre St*. Follow it to the front door of the **Jared Coffin House**, the former home of a wealthy ship owner, now an inn. Turn right onto *Broad St* and proceed down the hill to Steamboat Wharf. The route is just under 20 miles long.

STAYING IN NANTUCKET

Accommodation
Inns abound in and outside the village. Rates may begin in the moderate range but expensive and pricey accommodation are the rule. Request the lodging guide published by the Chamber of Commerce and Visitor Services and Information Bureau.

In the village: **House of Orange**, *25 Orange St; tel: (508) 228-9287*, welcomes gay guests but not exclusively. Expensive. **The Nesbitt Inn**, *21 Broad St; tel: (508) 228-0156*. Moderate. **Stumble Inne**, *109 Orange St; tel: (508) 228-4482*. Moderate–expensive.

Out of the village: **The Wauwinet Inn**, *P.O. Box 2580, Wauwinet Rd,* *Nantucket, MA 02584; tel: (508) 228-0145 or (800) 426-8718*, is the last bit of civilisation before you reach the least inhabited part of the island, Great Point, and how civilised! The host leads excellent natural history tours. Pricey. **Hostelling International** runs a hostel in an old life-saving station with a lively Victorian exterior and a typical hostel interior, just west of Surfside Beach at *31 Western Ave; tel: (508) 228-0433*, three miles from town. Open late-Apr–mid-Oct. Reservations essential in July, Aug and on all weekends. Budget. There are no campsites on the island.

Eating and Drinking
The Chanticleer, *9 New St, Siasconset; tel: (508) 257-6231*, is a showcase, noted for its French dishes. Pricey. **The SeaGrille**, *45 Sparks Ave; tel: (508) 325-5700*, serves excellent salads, seafood, a vegetarian platter, Nantucket bouillabaisse and more. Moderate. **The Boarding House**, *12 Federal St; tel: (508) 228-9622*, is a restaurant and bar popular among many types, including gays. Moderate–pricey. The sandwiches at **Something Natural**, *50 Cliff Rd; tel: (508) 228-0504*, come on slabs, not slices, of homemade breads, all delicious, especially the herbed. Cheap.

Communications
The main post office is at *5 Federal St; tel: (508) 228-1067*. All addresses are *Nantucket, MA 02554* unless noted otherwise.

ENTERTAINMENT

The **Community Band** plays concerts early each Sun evening in the summer at Children's Beach. Contemporary bands play and patrons drink, dance and eat pizza, burgers and sandwiches at **The**

Muse, *40 Surfside Rd; tel: (508) 228-6873.* Cover charge most nights.

Events

The **Daffodil Festival** in late Apr includes a parade of antique cars festooned with the flowers and the Garden Club's Daffodil Show. The Christmas season, known here as **Nantucket Noel**, begins the day after Thanksgiving. Make reservations early.

SHOPPING

The core of the village is filled with shops, most of which sell gifts or clothes. Explore **Old South Wharf**, a row of restored sea shanties that house artist studios and galleries. Dogs sniff their way to **Cold Noses**, *Straight Wharf; tel: (508) 228-KISS*, a shop catering to their needs, where they can follow painted paw marks along the floor to the counter and get a free dog biscuit.

SIGHTSEEING

Great Point Natural History Tours, postal address: *RFD 319X, Wakeman Center, Vineyard Haven, MA 02568; tel: (508) 228-6799*, offers three hours of natural history on a ride along the barrier beach of **Coskata-Coatue Wildlife Refuge** to what seems like the end of the world but is the northernmost tip of the island. See plovers, terns, oyster catchers, sea ducks and possibly a whale or seal along the way. **Gail's Tours**, *P.O. Box 3270, Nantucket, MA 02584; tel: (508) 257-6557*, are run by a bubbly, sixth-generation islander who knows the prettiest spots and the homes of the rich and famous. At 1000, 1300 and 1500 daily.

The **Whaling Museum**, *Broad and South Beach St; tel (508) 228-1736*, is home to a 43-foot whale skeleton and collections of whaling implements and

scrimshaw. Open weekends beginning in late Apr; seven days from late May. Adults $5, children $3. Climb the tower of **The First Congregational Church & Old North Vestry**, *62 Centre St*, for good views of the village and island.

Public beaches

North shore, Nantucket Sound: **Jetties Beach** is a favourite family beach, with swimming lessons for children 6 and older from 4 July–early Sept. A shuttle bus connects it to town. **Children's Beach** is on the harbour, just north of the Steamboat Wharf. Good for small children. **Dionis Beach** is also good for families, but not as crowded as those closer to the village. Follow *Eel Point Rd* and look for a white rock, parking lot and portable toilets to the right. **Brant Point** is better for channel watching than swimming. No lifeguard and strong currents.

South shore, open Atlantic: **Surfside** offers great waves, swimming and surf casting, at the end of *Surfside Rd*. At the western tip of the island, six miles from town, **Madaket Beach** is the place to be at sunset.

The surf also gets heavy at **Siasconset Beach**, on the southeastern shore.

Recreation

Wind surfing is best at **Pocomo Head**, toward the head of Nantucket Harbor. **Sanford Farm**, *Madaket Rd east of Cliff Rd*, is preserved by the **Nantucket Conservation Foundation**, *118 Cliff Rd; tel: (508) 228-2884*. Hike along a self-guided trail, observe bird life or take a long walk to the sea. Mountain biking is discouraged there, but encouraged on the sandy roads that criss-cross the moors off *Polpis Rd*. Vegetation is fragile. Stay on the roads. Contact the Foundation for information on other preserves.

151

CAPE COD-NEWPORT

After leaving Cape Cod, the direct route to Newport comprises a 41-mile drive via the completely featureless I-195 motorway to Fall River, Mass., then an additional 18 mile drive on the southbound highway with more enjoyable Rhode Island countryside panoramas. Travelling nonstop gets you from the bridge to Newport in 2–2½ hours. The scenic route is considerably more meandering, due to ragged coastal geography in this part of Massachusetts and much of Rhode Island. It combines busy, commercialised Rte 6 with looping, twisting country roads, some of which ultimately lead to ocean shores. Depending upon how many loops and twists you choose to follow, you'll cover anywhere between 60 and 80 miles, amounting to a full-day or easygoing two-day journey.

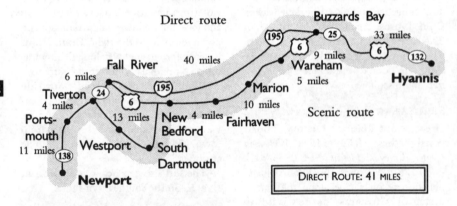

152

DIRECT ROUTE: 41 MILES

ROUTES

DIRECT ROUTE

➡ From Hyannis, take Rte 132 to Rte 6, then drive 12 miles westbound, leaving the Cape via the Sagamore Bridge. Continue westbound on Rte 6 another 4 miles alongside the Cape Cod Canal to the Bourne Bridge traffic circle, then an additional 17 miles via Rte 25 to reach I-195. A dozen I-195 exits en route to **Fall River** provide access to petrol and food, both especially prevalent in the **New** **Bedford, North Dartmouth** and **Fall River** vicinities.

Upon reaching Fall River, take Exit 8B onto Rte 24 South for a 6-mile journey crossing the Massachusetts-Rhode Island state line. You'll reach the toll-free bridge at **Tiverton** for a cross-over onto **Aquidneck Island**. Continue south for 12 miles on Rte 138 past **Portsmouth** and **Middletown** for arrival in **Newport**.

SCENIC ROUTE

At the Bourne Bridge, you must negotiate a formidable roundabout for access to the portion of Rte 6 on the outskirts of **Buzzards Bay** village. Weekend traffic on Rte 6, the spine of this slower route, is invariably 'wicked heavy' in regional terminology. So, if possible, avoid travelling mid-afternoon Fri to late-evening Sun. On the other hand, most of our suggested off-highway roadways are relatively uncrowded at all times.

From Buzzards Bay village, take Rte 6 for 10 miles to **Wareham,** where it becomes *Main St,* then follow the **Onset** sign for 2 miles of side-road driving past cranberry bogs and salt marshes to reach this village overlooking **Onset Bay.** Back on Rte 6, travel 5 miles to **Marion;** turn left onto *Main St* for a village visit. Then, back on Rte 6 (now concurrently *Fairhaven Rd*), proceed westward for another 5 miles to **Mattapoisett,** another charming bayview community.

The distance from Mattapoisett to **Fairhaven** is 5 miles, with Rte 6 locally co-named *Huttleston St.* Fairhaven and **New Bedford** are connected by two successive Rte 6 bridges crossing the Acushnet River for a distance of 3 miles between the two city centres.

New Bedford to Fall River is a 12-mile trip on Rte 6. But a haphazard street plan makes Fall River 'driver-unfriendly' for newcomers.

At the southern outskirts, take Exit 8B (the Rte 24 interchange) for cloverleaf access onto I-195, then traverse the city's full east-to-west width for unflustered arrival at well-marked **Heritage State Park.**

After seeing the sights, get back on the direct-route course by taking Exit 8A on Fall River's southern outskirts for travelling down Aquidneck Island to Newport.

VERY SCENIC ROUTE

If time permits, your alternative to touring cities is a southerly country road ramble through pasturelands and along miles of old stone fences, reaching estuaries and the ocean, augmented by 'side-door' access to easternmost Rhode Island. Use the **Dartmouth** sign on Rte 6 as an indicator for this optional drive. Tiny Massachusetts communities to seek out within the **South Dartmouth** and **Westport** townships are **Pandanaram Village, Russell Mills Village, Central Village** and **Westport Point,** all dating from US colonial times.

Cornell Rd north of Westport Point curves west to the invisible Massachusetts -Rhode Island state line. The three most photogenic villages in this littlest sliver of little Rhode Island are **Adamsville, Little Compton Commons** and **Tiverton Four Corners** as you drive south and then swing north towards the bridge between **Tiverton** and Aquidneck Island on your way to Newport.

TOURIST INFORMATION

Bristol County Convention & Visitors Bureau (BCCVB), *PO Box 976, New Bedford, MA 02741; tel: (508) 997-1250 or (800) 288-6263,* is an all-encompassing facility for the entire Bourne-to-Newport coastal region. **Canal Region Chamber of Commerce,** *70 Main St, Buzzards Bay, MA 02532; tel: (508) 759-6000,* located in a former rail station, provides information for Bourne, Buzzards Bay, Wareham, Onset and Marion.

CAPE COD TO FAIRHAVEN

South-coastal Massachusetts beyond the bridge is often referred to as Off Cape, an apt term because of Cape Cod atmospherics that spread over to this western portion

153

of the Buzzards Bay shoreline, with ocean waters warmed by the same branch of the Gulf Stream. You'll see hundreds of the typical wood-frame houses with their cedar shingles weathered from original brown to silvery gray. Cape Cod similarities extend to cranberry bogs, juniper bushes, scrub pine, wildflowers and splendid beaches. Food and petrol would be primary reasons for a stop-over prior to Rte 6. If early breakfast is a necessity , the low-cost crack of dawn portion of a seafood reastaurant on the roundabout opens at 0500: **Quinlal's**; *tel: (508) 759-7222.* Buzzard Bay village's most prominent landmark is the steel girder, trans-canal **Railroad Bridge**, erected in 1935. After passing through **Wareham** (birthplace of film star Geena Davis), take a short country detour towards **Onset,** a placid Victorian village overlooking **Onset Bay**.

The public beach at **Fort Independance** is appealing, with stands selling saltwater taffy, hamburgers and hot dogs during the summer. Full meals are served in the bayview **Holland Inn Restaurant**, *8 S. Water St; tel: (508) 295-8442,* moderate–pricey. Close by, an 1890s mansion has been transformed into the **Onset Pointe Inn**, *9 Eagle Way; tel: (508) 295-8442,* moderate–expensive.

From early spring to mid-Oct, 2- and 3-hr **Cape Cod Canal Cruises** depart from Onset's town pier; *tel: (508) 295-3883* for schedules and fares.

Returning from Onset to Rte 6 via East Wareham, you'll be driving a short distance before coming to **Marion,** the most affluent community on the west shore of Buzzards Bay, with a sizable millionaire population and, on *Front St*, the 1872 **Beverly Yacht Club,** second oldest in the US after its counterpart in New York City.

Sailboats fill Sippican Harbor; across the inlet, East Marion's sprawling estates occupy prime bay frontage on Allen's Point. Around the turn of the century, Marion became a summer haven for writers, artists and show-business personalities - among them Henry James, Augustus Saint Gaudens and Ethel and Lionel Barrymore. Marion's only bona-fide restaurant is on the moderate–pricey side: **Harriet's,** *7 Cottage St; tel: (508) 748-2053.*

Roaming Marion's narrow streets puts you in close touch with impeccably maintained white clapboard houses. On *Main St*, the 1841 **First Congregational Church** has a steeple clock with gilded hands. The town hall on *Spring St* features elaborate Italianate Victorian architecture; next door, the **Elizabeth Taber Library** is a Greek Revival classic, with a small **Natural History Museum** upstairs. Marion's Art Centre, encompassing a gallery and community theatre on *Pleasant St*, was originally a circa-1830 Universalist church. From Marion, continue via Rte 6 towards the next noteworthy town, **Mattapoisett** Aside from petrol stations, budget motels and fast-food franchises, an advantage of returning to the highway comes in the unchanged 1940's look of the **Mattapoisett Diner**, *81 Fairhaven Rd; tel: (508) 758-9555*, cheap–budget.

Most of New Bedford's whaling vessels were built here between 1752 and 1878 – 350 barks, brigs, sloops and schooners, launched at six shipyards. On one of them, the *Acushnet*, Herman Melville's sea duty in 1841 inspired his novel *Moby Dick*. Early 19th-century shingle-sided houses line *Water St*. Accommodation, food and drink all are attractively provided in the oldest US seaside resort, dating from 1799: the **Mattapoisett Inn**, *13 Water St; tel: (508) 758-4922*, moderate–expensive.

154

FAIRHAVEN

Tourist Information: Fairhaven Chamber of Commerce, *40 Center St, Fairhaven, MA 02179; tel: (508) 979-4023.*

The only in-town lodging is the hospitable, moderate **Edgewater Bed & Breakfast,** *2 Oxford St; tel: (508) 997-5512.* Rte 6 traversing Fairhaven is locally named *Huttleston St* after Standard Oil tycoon Henry Huttleston Rogers, a native son who became a civic benefactor. Look for the **Fairhaven Center** sign, your cue for a left-hand turn onto *Main St* and from there to *Center St.* Here's where Henry's generosity becomes evident in the enormous 1892 **Town Hall,** resembling a red-brick Flemish castle and – directly across the street – the equally flamboyant 1893 **Millicent Public Library,** an Italian Renaissance showpiece inside and out.

Continue west on *Center St* to *Old Fort Rd,* where you'll reach a waterfront park and the local beach – flanked by the site of **Fort Phoenix,** bristling with six Revolutionary War cannons; here US militiamen repulsed British invaders on 7 Sept 1778. High ground affords panoramic views of Buzzards Bay and, across the Acushnet River, New Bedford's harbourfront.

NEW BEDFORD

Tourist Information: The BCCVB runs a **Visitor Center** at *47 N. Second St, New Bedford, MA 02740; tel: (508) 991-6200,* open Mon–Sat 0900–1600, Sun 0930–1600. Same hours for a smaller **Waterfront Visitor Center** on Fishermen's Wharf.

GETTING AROUND

Most points of tourism interest lie within a compact, walkable area. You'll want a comfortable pair of shoes to navigate the cobblestone streets in the Waterfront Historic District. The wisest tactic is to park your car in the centrally located garage on *Elm St,* where the hourly rate is $0.30 and the full-day rate is $2.50.

Southern Regional Transit Authority (SRTA) buses run regularly, not only throughout New Bedford, but connecting to Fairhaven and Fall River. For timetables and fares, enquire at the Visitor Center or contact the transit office, *tel: (508) 999-5211.*

ACCOMMODATION AND FOOD

Despite its seafaring and touristic prominence, New Bedford has no recommendable in-town hotels or inns. Rely instead upon *DI* on Hathaway Road, closer to I-195 than downtown, and *CI* (Exit 12, I-195) in S Dartmouth, both moderate.

The Historic District's stand-out restaurant, in a rock-solid recycled bank building, is **Freestone's,** *41 William St; tel: (508) 993-7477.* Tops for budget–moderate seafood, sandwiches, salads and fish and clam chowder, plus its pub bar. For breakfast and light lunch, consider **Spearfield's,** *1 Johnny Cake Hill; tel: (508) 994-4848,* budget.

SIGHTSEEING

By 1830, New Bedford had surpassed Nantucket as the world's leading whaling centre, home port to 329 whaling ships at the height of activity in 1857. Herman Melville's allegorical masterpiece, *Moby Dick,* immortalised the city and the era. Today, though economically depressed New Bedford still has one of the largest commercial fishing fleets in the eastern US. The Visitor Center sponsors free one-hour summertime **walking tours** of the Waterfront Historic District, 1000–1500 daily. Included are the oldest **US Custom House** in continuous use (1836) and the

155

Seamen's Bethel (1832) a chapel with a pulpit shaped like a bowsprit, described by Melville in *Moby Dick*. At Fishermen's Wharf, the 1894 wooden schooner Ernestina can be boarded from May–end Oct. The Visitor Center has detailed brochures for three **self-guided walking tours** of the *County St* area, an in-depth way to learn about 19th-century residences spanning a wild array of architectural styles.

The **New Bedford Whaling Museum**, *18 Johnny Cake Hill; tel: (508) 997-0046*, open Mon–Sat 0900–1700, Sun 1300–1700 (1100–1700 July–Aug), $4.50, should be your main destination while in the city. Devoted to local maritime history, its centrepiece is a walk-on half-scale model of the fully rigged whaling bark *Lagoda*. **Rotch-Jones-Duff House & Garden Museum**, *396 County St; tel: (508) 997-1401*, $3, open Tues–Sat 1000–1600, Sun 1300–1600, is a 22-room Greek Revival mansion built by a Quaker merchant in 1834, reflecting the life and times of three outrageously rich families.

FALL RIVER

Tourist Information: BCCVB **Visitors' Center**, *Heritage State Park, 200 Davol St West, Fall River, MA 02720; tel: (508) 675-5759*, open daily, 1000–1600.

ACCOMMODATION AND FOOD

DI (Exit 5, I-195) is the only in-town lodging, located on the west side of Mt. Hope Bay; out of town there's Fall River-Westport **Hampton Inn** (Exit 10), *tel: (800) 426-7866*, moderate. Fall River, like New Bedford, has a large ethnic Portuguese population, with two pertinent restaurants worthy of recommendation: **Sagres**, *181 Columbia St; tel: (508) 675-7018*, and **Estoril**, *1577 Pleasant St; tel: (508) 677-1200*. Both moderate.

Informal **Waterstreet Café**, *36 Water St; tel: (508) 672-8748*, is situated amidst the city's major visitor attractions in the Heritage State Park vicinity, budget. Also convenient because it's right in the park, **Heritage Outlook Bistro** is a cheap–budget eatery.

ENTERTAINMENT

Summer productions of the **Little Theater of Fall River** are on stage at *340 Prospect St*, with fall and winter performances in the **Arts Center**, *Bristol Community College, Elsbree St*.

SHOPPING

New England's largest **factory-outlet complex** consists primarily of three converted mills totalling 70 discount bazaars. The boggling slew of cut-rate merchandise includes clothing, shoes, cookware, jewellery, sunglasses, books, luggage, even chocolates. Each building also has a cheap-price café. The trio of outlets, on the *Quarry St-Quequechan St* side of town, is not easily reachable by foot from Heritage State Park. Drive instead, taking Exit 8A off I-195.

SIGHTSEEING

Fall River attained prominence as America's busiest centre of cotton textile manufacturing from 1811 until the Great Depression. Now some of the massively long mills have been made into factory-outlet shopping warehouses. The city remains best known for an unsolved 1892 axe murder allegedly perpetrated by Fall Riverian Lizzie Borden on her father and stepmother. She was tried and acquitted.

Heritage State Park, with its waterside esplanade, is a four-part attraction. The structure housing Visitors' Center facilities also contains textile-mill historical exhibits. A nearby building features an antique, hand-painted **Carousel**, and the park is 'home port' of the full-scale *HMS Bounty* replica, constructed for the 1962 Marlon Brando movie.

Dwarfing all else is **Battleship Cove;** *tel: (508) 678-1100*, open 0900–sunset, $8.50, where the World War II battleship *USS Massachusetts*, the destroyer *USS Joseph P. Kennedy Jr.* and the *USS Lionfish* submarine can be boarded. The Visitors' Center has maps for self-guided **walking tours** of Fall River's **Maritime Heritage Trail**, extending uphill from the park to the business district and factory-outlet warehouse area. Two museums are located a block from Battleship Cove. The **Marine Museum**, *70 Water St; tel: (508) 674-3533*, $3, open Mon–Fri 0900–1700, Sun 1200–1600 (May–Oct), contains the world's largest assemblage of *RMS Titanic* artifacts and memorabilia, plus the 28-foot scale model made for the 1953 film. The **Old Colony & Fall River Railroad Museum**, outdoors at *Central at Water Sts; tel: (508) 674-9340*, $1.50, open 1000–1700 (closed Jan–Mar), features vintage locomotives and carriages.

The **Fall River Historical Society**, *451 Rock St; tel: (508) 679-1071*, $3, open Tues–Fri 0900–1630, Sat–Sun 1300–1700 (closed Jan–Mar) concentrates on decorative arts, accessories and furnishings in an 1854 Greek Revival mansion. Its best-known exhibit is devoted, inevitably, to details of the infamous Lizzie Borden case.

NEW BEDFORD TO NEWPORT

If you follow the Very Scenic Route, the beach at Massachusetts' **Demarest Lloyd State Park** and a shoreline **Audubon Bird Sanctuary** are south of Russells Mills Village via two-lane rural roads. In the village itself, look for the showroom and workshop of **Salt Marsh Pottery**, *1166 Russells Mills Rd; tel: (508) 636-4813*, and the 1793 **Davoll's General Store**, *1288 Russells Mills Rd; tel: (508) 636-4530*. Two dozen shingle-sided 1770s houses line Westport Point's *Main Rd*, leading to a lobster-boat dock and the high sand dunes of 2-mile-long **Horseneck Beach State Reservation.**

This pastoral area's best bed & breakfast, 6 miles south of Rte 6, is **Salt Marsh Farm**, *322 Smith Neck Rd, S Dartmouth, MA 02748; tel: (508) 992-0980*, a colonial dwelling with two rooms on homestead fields cultivated since 1727, moderate. **Westport Camping Grounds** are at *346 Old County Rd; Westport, MA 02790; tel: (508) 636-2555*. Fresh-caught seafood and a perch on a wharf are double attributes of Westport Point's **Moby Dick**, *1 Bridge St; tel: (508) 636-6500*, moderate–pricey.

On the Rhode Island segment of this southerly terrain, wine tasting is offered daily at **Sakonnet Vineyards**, off Rte 77 at *162 W. Main Rd, Little Compton RI; tel: (401) 635-8486*. Vintages have such jaunty names as Eye of the Storm, Rhode Island Red and Spinnaker White. Folksy and inexpensive, the **Commons Restaurant** overlooks the village green in Little Compton Commons, RI; *tel: (401) 635-4388*. On Rte 77, Little Compton's **Country Harvest** is a moderate–pricey restaurant with commanding across-the-water views of Aquidneck Island; *tel: (401) 635-4579*. From Tiverton Four Corners, drive 7 miles north on Rte 77 to **Tiverton**. At the end of *Lawton Rd*, **Fort Barton** was a Revolutionary War redoubt, now a park with spectacular panoramics of the Sakonnet River and Aquidneck Island. Crossing the bridge at Tiverton, you return to the direct route to Newport which becomes *East Main Rd* in Portsmouth. Moderate-priced lodgings include *Rm* and *HJ*.

157

NEWPORT

This city's eminence as an oceanfront resort dates back to the early 18th century, when plantation owners from the Carolinas and West Indies travelled north to escape humidity and malaria. By the 1850s, New Yorkers able to pay the fare could reach Newport via overnight passage on the Fall River Steamship Line. And so began a seasonal influx of millionaire families personifying the Gilded Age and commissioning celebrity architects to design their palatial 'summer cottages' along and near Bellevue Ave. Rhode Island's most southerly town of appreciable size became high society's 'in' place to spend it and certainly show it off.

TOURIST INFORMATION

Newport County Convention & Visitors Bureau, *23 America's Cup Ave, Newport, RI 02840; tel: (401) 849-8048 or (800) 326-6030.* Facilities at the bureau's **Gateway Visitors Center** (same address and phone numbers), open Mon–Thur 0900–1700, Fri–Sat 0900–1900, include an enquiry counter, literature racks and a photo-mural exhibit with number-coded descriptions of city landmarks. Tickets for tours, attractions and special events can be purchased here. **Cellet Travel Services Ltd** is Newport County's information bureau in the UK, at *George House, 121 High St, Henley-in-Arden, Solihull, West Midlands B95 5AU; tel: 056-479-4999.*

ARRIVING AND DEPARTING

For motorcoach travel, **Bonanza Bus,** *Gateway Center, 23 America's Cup Ave, Newport, RI 02840; tel: (401) 846-1820,* has morning and afternoon connections between Boston and Newport, $12 one-way for a 90-min trip with stops in Portsmouth and Middletown, R.I., and Fall River, Mass. **Rhode Island Public Transportation Authority (RIPTA)** public-transit buses make frequent daily 1-hour runs between Providence and Newport for $2.50 one-way fare; *tel: (401) 781-9400* for specifics.

GETTING AROUND

Newport's tiny downtown centre is squeezed between *Washington Sq.* on the north and *Memorial Blvd* on the south. The longest and swankiest portion of *Bellevue Ave* runs due south from there. *Bellevue Ave*, in turn, leads to an **Ocean Drive** loop around the southernmost tip of Aquidneck Island (see Sightseeing).

Public Transport
RIPTA provides wide-spread, efficient in-town service for basic fare of $0.85.

Driving
Access to Newport depends upon the direction you've taken to get there. The speediest way from Cape Cod entails exiting I-195 at Fall River, Mass., followed by a drive south through Portsmouth and Middletown, RI. Taking the 75-mile direct route from Boston means you'll drive on I-95 through metro Providence, then on Rtes 1/1A to Rte 138 which crosses the toll-free Jamestown-Verrazzano Bridge and then the Newport Bridge ($2 toll). This, too, is the double-

bridge approach if you are coming from New York and Connecticut.

Immediately upon exiting the 2-mile Newport Bridge (New England's longest suspension span), turn right onto Rte 238, (Farewell St) bear right onto *America's Cup Ave*. Then you'll see the modernistic Visitors Center. Due to scant space, short-term meters and resident-only permits, overnight on-street parking is a virtual impossibility, especially in summer. Rely instead upon the sizeable long-stay facility alongside the Visitors Center, where the 24-hour rate is $10.

Bicycling

While the combined *Bellevue Ave/Ocean Ave* distance of nine to ten miles ordinarily necessitates driving (see Sightseeing), an alternative is bicycle rental from a downtown source: **Ten Speed Spokes**, *18 Elm St; tel: (401) 847-5609*. Rates are $5 hourly, $25 daily.

STAYING IN NEWPORT

Accommodation

In-town lodging runs the gamut from slick hotels (including a pricey harbourfront *Ma*) to cute New Englandy inns tucked away on tree-shaded side streets. Costs vary widely from off-season to the peak May–Oct period, with 'bargain time' covering Nov–Mar. Be advised that peak-period weekend bookings should be made four or five months in advance. Brochures and room-rate listings are plentiful at the Visitor Center, where you can also dial direct (no charge) to any of 200-plus establishments. Three chain motor hotels are on Newport's northern fringe: *BW*, *CM* and *HJ*.

Alongside mainland yacht moorings, **Newport Harbor Hotel & Marina**, *49 America's Cup Ave, Newport, RI 02840; tel:*

(800) 955-2558, is expensive–pricey. Similar cost range and nautical locale pertains to **Harbourside Inn**, *Christie's Landing, Newport, RI 02840; tel: (401) 846-6600*. In a quiet residential location three blocks up from downtown, the vintage (1926) **Hotel Viking**, *1 Bellevue Ave, Newport, RI 02840; tel: (800) 556-7126*, moderate–expensive, features the genteel **Vanderbilt Restaurant** and views from a rooftop patio bar at Newport's highest point, plus the huge advantage of complimentary guest parking.

There's no charge for bookings arranged by **Taylor-Made Reservations**, *16 Mary St, Newport, RI 02840; tel: (401) 848-0300 or (800) 848-8848* – a useful service when trying to decide amongst all the possibilities. Newport's recommendable bed and breakfasts with private bath are moderate–expensive. Of these, consider **La Forge Cottage**, *96 Pelham St, Newport, RI 02840; tel: (401) 847-4400*, close to downtown in what's locally known as the Historic Hill District. In the north waterfront Point neighbourhood, what had been a summer mansion, then a convent is now the **Stella Maris Inn**, *91 Washington St, Newport, RI 02840; tel: (401) 849-2862*.

Shared-bath lodgings are in the moderate category – among them the **Marshall Slocum Guest House**, *29 Kay St, Newport, RI 02840; tel: (401) 841-5120*, **Melville House**, *39 Clarke St, Newport, RI 02840; (401) 847-0640*, and **Hydrangea Inn**, *16 Bellevue Ave, Newport, RI 02840; tel: (401) 846-4435*, all in Historic Hill.

Eating and Drinking

Dinners are invariably pricey but well worth it for cuisine and ambiance in two widely known restaurants. **White Horse Tavern**, on the corner of *Marlborough St*

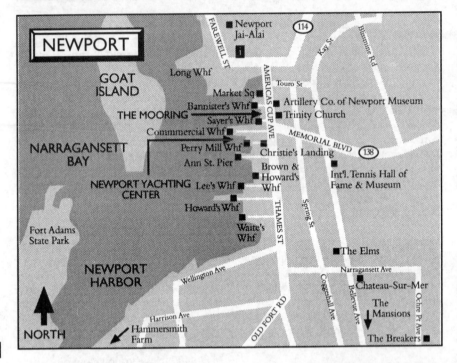

and *Farewell St; tel: (401) 849-3600*, ranks as the nation's oldest in continuous operation. Venerable, too, **The Black Pearl**, *Bannister's Wharf; tel: (401) 846-5264*, is a dockside eatery, more expensive in the Commodore Room than the black-painted tavern, where lunchtime meals are budget–moderate.

Fillet of sole with crabmeat and scallops is a house speciality at the **Brick Alley Pub & Restaurant**, *140 Thames St; tel: (401) 849-6334*, moderate, with a copious soup and salad buffet amidst a colourful mix of antiques. (Newporters rhyme their downtown main street, Thames, with James).

Nearby and also moderate, the **Music Hall Café**, *250 Thames St; tel: (401) 848-2330*, specialises in south-western Tex-Mex food and drink. Pricey and Victorian by contrast, with Châteaubriand carved tableside, **La Forge Casino Restaurant**, *186 Bellevue Ave; tel: (401) 847-0418*, features an outdoor porch overlooking the former casino's tennis courts, also a warm-weather sidewalk café.

Desirable waterfront settings, saloon-size bars and budget–moderate price ranges are good reasons to order lunch at **Christie's**, *Christie's Landing, off lower Thames St; tel: (401) 847-5400*, and **The Mooring**, *Sayer's Wharf; tel: (401) 846-2260*. Petite **Muriel's**, *58 Spring St; tel: (401) 849-7780*, budget–moderate, has Belgian waffles on its breakfast menu and cooks up what many regard as Newport's best seafood chowder.

The Place, *28 Washington Sq.; tel: (401) 847-0125*, a wine bar with vegetarian specials, is the chic, pricey portion of **Yesterday's** pub with its 26 brands of micro-brewed beer.

In the *Lower Thames St* waterfront area, Welsh heirlooms and a brick patio add to the charm of **Elizabeth's**, *Brown & Howard Wharf; tel: (401) 846-6862*, tops in town for its prodigious bouillabaise feast. Moderate.

Communications

The main post office is at *320 Thames St* – in this city where the first US postal office opened in 1829.

ENTERTAINMENT

Refer to updated listings in the *Newport Daily News* and a free tabloid, *Newport This Week*. In addition, there's a 24-hour *Newport Activity Line; tel: (401) 848-2000 in Rhode Island, (800) 263-4636* from anywhere beyond.

Music

Along with 'mansion row', Newport's claim to international fame is mid-Aug's **JVC Jazz Festival**, a mega-event at **Fort Adams State Park**; *tel: (401) 847-3700*. Same location, phone number for the early-Aug **Newport Folk Festival**.

Weekend jazz gigs are a big summertime draw at **The Red Parrott**, *348 Thames St; (401) 847-3140*, while **Christie's** jumps to the nightly beat of various bands, and karaoke sing-alongs are popular at **Cobblestones**, *206 Thames St; tel: (401) 846-4285*. **Callahan's Café Zelda**, *528 Thames St; tel: (401) 849-4002* resounds with rhythm and blues Wed evenings, rock music on Thurs.

In a milder vein, each July's **Newport Music Festival** features classical chamber-ensemble and choral concerts in the fabled **Bellevue Ave Mansions**; *tel: (401) 846-1133*. The Lounge at **La Forge Casino Restaurant**, *186 Bellevue Ave; tel: (401) 847-0418*, becomes an easy-listening piano bar on weekend evenings.

On Stage

Theatre department students at **Salve Regina University**, *100 Ochre Point Ave, Newport, RI 02840; tel: (401) 847-6550*, perform in dramas and musical comedies each spring and fall. The **Newport Playhouse & Cabaret**, *102 Connell Hwy, Newport, RI 02840; tel: (401) 848-7529*, is a dinner theatre presenting adaptations of Broadway musicals; Thursdays are murder-mystery nights, open to all, although it's best to call in advance. Studios of **The Island Moving Company**, an avant-garde ballet troupe, are at *3 Charles St, Newport, RI 02840; tel: (401) 847-4470*.

Cinema

Two theatres showing first-run films are virtually side-by-side: **Jayne Pickens Theatre**, *48 Touro St; tel: (401) 846-5252*; **Opera House Cinema**, *19 Touro St; tel: (401) 847-3456*.

Sports

Wagering on fast-paced Spanish Basque pelota action gets hot and heavy at outlying **Newport Jai Alai**, *150 Admiral Kalbfus Rd, Newport, RI 02840; tel: (401) 849-5000*, where simulcast horse-racing and video slot machines and card games are additional ways to efficiently lighten your wallet.

During the second week of July, top-seeded pros direct from Wimbledon compete in the mens' **Miller Lite Hall of Fame Tennis Championships** on the grass courts at the International Tennis Hall of Fame. It's immediately followed by the womens' **Virginia Slims Hall of Fame Invitational**.

Among numerous sailing regattas, sloops competing each Aug in the Plymouth-to-Newport transatlantic race arrive in the harbour. This is also the season for New England regional croquet

161

championships at the International Tennis Hall of Fame, plus all-American baseball games at cozy little Cardine's Field on *America's Cup Ave.*

Events

Two food fests take place at the Newport Yachting Center, *America's Cup Ave.* First the **Great Chowder Cook-off** in mid-June, $8, then **Taste of Rhode Island** over the last weekend of Sept, $2.50. In early Aug, an **Arts & Crafts Festival** draws onlookers to Touro Park.

America's Cup

By history and tradition, Newport remains virtually synonymous with the America's Cup – referring of course to the world's most prestigious yacht-racing trophy.

Although the first race in 1851 was held around the Isle of Wight, the New York Yacht Club put together a remarkably long string of consecutive US victories, beating every America's Cup challenger between 1870 and 1980. Newport hosted the races from 1930 to 1983.

The winning streak was snapped that year when the Australians captured the cup. Then in 1987, Californian Dennis Conner beat the Aussies, brought the trophy back to the US, and wounded proud old Newport by moving subsequent races to his home town San Diego Yacht Club.

New Zealand's team trounced Conner's in 1995, resulting in a return contest 'Down Under'. Newporters will be paying close attention. A US victory could bring the America's Cup championship race back to where they're convinced it belongs – in 2003.

SHOPPING

Two of Newport's salty old boat piers have become something-for-everyone retail bazaars: **Bannister's Wharf** and **Bowen's Wharf**. The nearby **Brick Market Place** encompasses 30 stores, galleries and clothing boutiques. You'll find cubbyhole establishments along *Thames St*, whilst two flashy *Bellevue Ave* shopping malls, located where 'mansion row' begins, prove that the patrician Gilded Age has indeed vanished. Historic Hill's **Spring St** exudes small-scale mercantile charm with shops devoted to such miscellanea as antiques, pottery, quilts and ship models. **The Coop,** *99 Spring St; tel: (401) 848-2442,* is a crafts cooperative representing local artisans.

SIGHTSEEING

The **Newport Historical Society** (see Museums) sponsors $5 walking tours of the city centre Fri and Sat mornings, mid-June–Sept. Narrated bus excursions and harbour cruises can be booked at **Viking Tours** in the Visitors Center, *tel: (401) 847-6921.* For two-hour harbour and bay sailing cruises aboard a 70-ft schooner, call on **Yankee Boat Peddlers,** *Christie's Landing; tel: (401) 849-3033.*

Notably photogenic streets in the very walkable **Historic Hill** enclave include Pelham, Division, Hill, Mill, Corne, Spring, Clarke, Cross, Duke and Charles. Among US 'firsts and oldests' are **Touro Synagogue** and the **Seventh Day Baptist Meeting House** (both on *Touro St*), the Quakers' **Friends Meeting House** (corner of *Farewell/Marlborough Sts*), and **Redwood Library** (*Bellevue Ave*). In the **Old Colony House** facing *Washington Sq.,* George Washington and Count Rochambeau planned the war-winning Battle of Yorktown, and rebellious Rhode Island's legislature foreswore allegiance to George III on 4 May 1776. Services celebrating the 250th anniversary of white-steepled **Trinity Episcopal Church** at *Queen Anne Sq.* were attended by Elizabeth II and the Archbishop of Canterbury in 1976. Art Nouveau windows in two *Pelham St* churches – **Channing Memorial** and **Newport Congregational** – are by US stained-glass maestro John La Farge. Flimsy legend has it that Touro Park's **Old Stone Mill** was erected by Norse Vikings long before Christopher Columbus crossed the Atlantic; less carried-away theorists place what might have been a grain silo closer to 1644.

Unless you've overdosed on Historic Hill's extensive and remarkably intact colonial architecture and gardens, the equally old district of **the Point** merits a walk-around. It begins at *Marsh St*, a brief stroll north of the Visitors Center, and ends 10 blocks away at *Van Zandt Ave*, close to the Newport Bridge's exit ramp. *Washington St*, the Point's main north-south thoroughfare, runs north-south alongside Narragansett Bay. The neighbourhood's Battery Park has a fine western exposure over the bay.

Cliff Walk, a 3.5-mile pathway, combines high, craggy promontories and sweeping ocean panoramas with close-up views of mansion terraces and manicured lawns. Wild roses burst into full bloom through June–July. The curving walk extends from *Memorial Blvd* to the southerly end of *Bellevue Ave.*

The looping seven-mile route around a windswept peninsula along *Ocean Ave*, *Ridge Rd* and *Harrison Ave* passes some of North America's costliest real estate, with private domains overlooking granite promontories and the crashing surf. **Brenton Point State Park** is a pleasant midway stop-over for picnicking; views of

the town and harbour are dramatic from **Fort Adams State Park**. But the foremost landmark is the 50-acre **Hammersmith Farm**, *Ocean Ave, Newport, RI 02840; tel: (401) 846-0420*, bayfront estate of the Auchincloss family, which included Jacqueline Bouvier. This is where she and John F. Kennedy had their wedding reception. Open daily 1000–1900 (Apr–mid-Nov); $7.

The Mansions

Collectively, Newport's paramount tourism attraction consists of eight open-to-the-public 'summer cottages'. Six – The Breakers, Chateau-sur-Mer, the Elms, Kingscote, Marble House and Rosecliff – are maintained by the **Preservation Society of Newport County,** *424 Bellevue Ave, Newport, RI 02840; tel: (401) 847-1000*. This is a direct source for admittance tickets, but they're also available at the Visitor Center. Prices for combination tickets range from $12.50 (any two mansions) to $28 (all six). The six mansions are open daily 1000–1700 (May–Sept), plus Sat 1000–1800 at the Breakers. The Breakers, Chateau-sur-Mer and the Elms, decked out in Christmas decor, open 1000–1600 in Dec (closed 24–25 Dec). Check ahead for different time periods during other months of the year.

The Breakers, *Ochre Point Ave*, $10, emulating a 16th-century Italian palazzo, totalling 72 rooms and overlooking the ocean, was built for railroad tycoon Cornelius Vanderbilt in 1895.

Chateau-sur-Mer, *Bellevue Ave*, $6.50, dating from 1852, is one of the outstanding examples of over-the-top Victorian architecture and design in the US.

The Elms, *Bellevue Ave*, $7.50, a Pennyslvania coal-mining magnate's summer residence, resembles a French chateau

163

complete with a Carrara marble grand staircase and formal sunken gardens.

Kingscote, *Bellevue Ave at Bowery St*, $6.50, completed in 1839 and thus the street's first summer mansion, is a Gothic Revival showpiece with early Rhode Island furnishings and Chinese art.

Marble House, *Bellevue Ave*, $6.50, in neoclassical style inspired by the Petit Trianon at Versailles, features a Chinese tea house and past owner William K. Vanderbilt's yachting memorabilia.

Rosecliff, *Bellevue Ave*, $6.50, with the largest ballroom of all the 'cottages', 22 bedrooms and a heart-shaped limestone staircase, was where Mia Farrow and Robert Redford romanced in the cinema version of *The Great Gatsby*.

Apart from the Preservation Society's realm, two additional mansions can be visited: **Belcourt Castle**, *657 Bellevue Ave; tel: (401) 846-0669*, $6.50, another of the Vanderbilt clan's turn-of-the-century digs, contains such perks as a gilded coronation coach, an imperial Russian hand-cut crystal chandelier, 2,000 pieces of fine art and features the world's first-ever indirect lighting, installed by Thomas Edison in 1894. Opens daily 1000–1600 (Feb–Apr) and 0900–1700 (Sept–mid-Oct); Mon–Sat 1000–1500 (Dec–early Jan).

Beechwood, *580 Bellevue Ave; tel: (401) 846-3772*, $8, puts a different twist on mansion tours with costumed guides and performers enacting the free-spending era of Caroline Astor, 'grand dame' of Newport society. Open Fri–Sun 1000–1600 (Feb–mid-May), daily 1000–1700 (mid-May–Nov), 1000–1600 (Nov–mid-Dec).

Museums

The **International Tennis Hall of Fame**, *194 Bellevue Ave, Newport, RI 02840; tel: (401) 849-3990*, in what was originally Newport's shingle-style casino, became in 1881 the first tournament home of what is now the US Open. The museum is the world's largest of its kind, and its 13 courts are the country's only competition grass courts available for public play. Open daily 1000–1700; $6.

The **Museum of Newport History** in the Brick Market at *120 Thames St, Newport, RI 02840; tel: (401) 846-0813*, $5, Mon and Wed–Sat 1000–1700, Sun 1300–1700. It provides overviews of local history and accomplishments through artifacts, displays and illustrations, plus high-tech interactive computers and videos.

The America's Cup Gallery is the star attraction at the **Museum of Yachting**, *Fort Adams State Park, Newport, RI 02840; tel: (401) 847-1018*, $3, open daily 1000–1700 (mid-May–Oct).

Newport's **Naval College War Museum,** *Coasters Harbor Island, Newport, RI 02840; tel: (401) 841-4052*, open 1000–1600 year-around and Sat–Sun 1200–1600 (summer), free, covers the global history of war at sea, with emphasis on US Navy exploits in Narragansett Bay. The first US torpedo, Newport-made in 1869, is on view.

New England paintings and sculptures are highlighted in two landmark buildings occupied by the **Newport Art Museum,** *76 Bellevue Ave, Newport, RI 02840; tel: (401) 848-8200*, open Tues–Sun 1000–1700 (June–Sept), 1000–1600 (Oct–May), $5. Early US portraiture, glassware, furniture and locally crafted silver and pewter are exhibited at the **Newport Historical Society,** *82 Touro St, Newport, RI 02840; tel: (401) 846-0813*, open Tues–Fri 0930–1630, Sat 0930–1200 (also Sat 0930–1630 in summer). Free. This organisation sponsors $5 walking tours of Newport's 'ye olde' centre, Fri–Sat mornings, mid-June–Sept.

Children enjoy the **Rhode Island Fishermen & Whale Museum,** *18 Market Sq, Newport, RI 02840; tel: (401) 849-1340,* open daily 1000–1700 except Wed (summer), and except Tues–Wed during the rest of the year. $2.50. Sharks and other marine creatures swim in the museum's new aquarium at Easton's Beach; $3.50.

Newport's oldest surviving dwelling, from 1675, is the **Wanton-Lyman-Hazard House,** *17 Broadway, Newport, RI 02840; tel: (401) 846-0813,* open Thur–Sat 1000–1600, also Sun 1300–1600 (mid-June–Aug); $4. The house is an outstanding US example of Jacobean architecture and includes an 18th-century rose garden.

OUT OF TOWN

Tourist Information: Bristol County Chamber of Commerce, *654 Metacom Ave, Warren, RI 02885; tel: (401) 245-0750.*

For a short-distance East Bay diversion, depart Newport by driving 1.5 miles north on Rte 138 to reach Rte 114. Head north, first by commercialised dual carriageway but soon through villages and pastureland to reach the Mt. Hope Bridge ($0.30 toll), thereby leaving Aquidneck Island for arrival in **Bristol**, 10.5 miles from Newport. Rte 114 concurrently becomes *Hope St* in Bristol. Continuing four miles on Rte 114 brings you to the centre of **Warren**. The latter town is merely 3.5 miles from the I-195 motorway, should you decide upon speedy travelling east towards Cape Cod or west to Providence.

In addition to petrol and food along Rte 114, tent spaces ($13) and full RV hookups ($22) are available at **Melville RV Campground,** *181 Bradford Ave, Portsmouth, RI 02871; tel: (401) 849-8212.*

Eight miles from Newport and three miles prior to reaching the bridge leading into Bristol County, a left turn onto Cory's Lane in Portsmouth leads to **Green Animals Topiary Gardens,** *Corey's Lane, Portsmouth, RI 02871; tel: (401) 683-1267,* a great-for-kids layout with sculpted animals and birds, plus geometric forms made from English boxwood and a next-door Victorian toy museum. Open daily 1000–1700 (May–Nov); $6.50.

Bristol, one of Rhode Island's prettiest towns, is at the southern terminus of the 14.5-mile **East Bay Pike Path** to East Providence, with $12 per-day rentals available at **Bay Path Cycles,** *13 State St; tel: (401) 254-1277.*

Once a Pennsylvania millionaire's summer estate, 33-acre **Blithewold Mansion & Gardens,** *101 Ferry Rd, Bristol, RI 02809; tel; (401) 253-2707,* sprawls alongside Narragansett Bay. Mansion open daily 1000–1600 (Apr–Oct), grounds and arboretum daily 1000–1700 (year-round), $7.50 to tour the 45-room mansion and grounds; $4 grounds only. **Linden Place,** *500 Hope St, Bristol, RI 02809; tel: (401) 253-0390,* oozes Federal-style opulence on an in-town site that also features a carriage barn, circa-1750 summer cottage and rose arbours. Open Thur–Sat 1000–1600, Sun 1200–1600 (late May–mid-Oct); $4.

On Bristol's northern outskirts, look for statues of two charging bulls at the main auto entrance into **Colt State Park,** *Rte 114, Bristol, RI 02809; (no telephone),* open daily all year. In addition to spacious picnic grounds, there's a three-mile biking-hiking trail. Park acreage includes the **Coggeshall Farm Museum,** off *Poppasquash Rd, Bristol, RI 02809; tel: (401) 253-9062,* a working farmstead relying solely upon 18th-century agricultural methods, including seasonal sheep-shearing and maple sugaring. Open 1000–1800 (summer), 1000–1600 (winter, closed Jan).

165

Herreshoff Marine Museum, 7 *Burnside St, Bristol, RI 02809; tel: (401) 253-5000*, focuses on the boat works where eight winning America's Cup defenders were built between 1893-1934. Among 35 vessels on display is the oldest US yacht, launched here in 1859. Opens Mon–Fri 1300–1600, Sat–Sun 1100–1600 (May–Oct); $3.

A white Greek Revival 'wedding cake' built in 1809, **Rockwell House Inn**, *610 Hope St, Bristol, RI 02809; tel: (401) 253-0040*, is a moderate-range bed and breakfast right in Bristol centre.

Cruise *Hope St* to find a convenient grocery store, bagel shop, the **Café la France** coffee-pastry hangout and a cheap-eats luncheonette. All this plus Danish-German **Redlefsen's Rotisserie & Grill**, *425 Hope St; tel: (401) 254-1188*, for moderate–pricey meals. A somewhat pricier seafood restaurant, the **Lobster Pot**, *119-21 Hope St; tel: (401) 253-9100*, overlooks Bristol's yacht harbour.

The short drive from Bristol to Warren is mainly worthwhile for those interested in antiques and collectible Americana. Pertinent shops line *Water St*. For one-stop browsing, dozens of dealers show their wares in the former Lyric Theatre, now the **Warren Antique Center**, corner *Main* and *Miller Sts; tel: (401) 245-5461*, open Mon–Sat 1000–1700, Sun 1200–1700. Moderate-priced country cuisine is served in the 1795 **Nathaniel Porter Inn**, *125 Water St; tel: (401) 245-6622*. Warren is on the bike path.

 SIDETRACK FROM NEWPORT

BLOCK ISLAND

Though much less publicised than Nantucket and Martha's Vineyard, this offshore haven, seven miles long and three miles wide, is beguiling to urban-ites seeking refuge from their frazzled lifestyles. The year-round population is 850 or so; stoplights, parking meters and house numbers don't exist and 25 percent of the island is environmentally protected by the US Nature Conservancy.

Tourist Information: Block Island Chamber of Commerce, *Water St, Block Island, RI 02807; tel: (401) 466-5200 or (800) 383-2474*. Ask for the all-purpose *Block Island Travel Planner*.

ARRIVING AND DEPARTING

Interstate Navigation Co., *P.O. Box 482, New London, CT 06320; tel: (203) 442-7891 (in Connecticut) or (401) 783-4613 (recorded information)*, operates once-daily service for the 20-mile crossing from Newport's Fort Adams to Old Harbor on Block Island at 1030, return 1545 (late June–early Sept); adults $6.45 one-way, $9.25 same-day return (passengers only, no cars).

Year-round service, with frequent daily summer sailings, runs between the island and the State Pier in *Galilee, RI*, 12 miles from Newport via the Newport and Jamestown bridges, then a southbound drive on Rtes 1 and 108. One-way fare for the 12-mile, 70-minute crossing from Galilee is $20.25 per auto, $6.60 per adult with or without a car. (Service also available from New London, Conn.). Should you wish to bring your car on board, advance reservation is absolutely essential – and, in fact, should be made at least a month ahead during summer peak season.

Daily, year-round flights from Westerly, RI, to Block Island take 12 mins aboard **New England Airlines**; *tel: (401) 596-2460*.

Both are plentiful except in winter, when residents have the place mostly to themselves. For visitors' needs in the immediate Old Harbor vicinity, they maintain 40-plus bed and breakfast inns and guest houses along with several dowager Victorian resort hotels. Three of the latter, moderate–expensive in summer, are on *Water St* facing the ferry-boat landing: **Harborside Inn**; *tel: (401) 466-5504 or (800) 892-2022*, the **National Hotel**; *tel: (401) 466-2901 or (800) 225-2449*, and **Inn at Old Harbour**; *tel: (401) 466-2212*. *Spring St* leads uphill to the pricey **Hotel Manisses**; *tel: (401) 466-2421 or (800) 626-4773*, and the **Spring House Hotel**; *tel: (401) 466-5844 or (800) 234-9263*.

Bed and breakfast stays are generally moderate in summer. Its central location on a quiet village side street makes this one especially recommendable: **Sheffield House**, *High St; tel: (401) 466-2494*. For closer access to Block Island's terrific east-shore beaches, consider **The Sullivan House**, *Com Neck Rd; tel: (401) 466-5020*. When mid-year holiday makers disembark, the Old Harbor area is abuzz with ice-cream parlours, take-out sandwich joints, snack bars and upscale eateries.

Baked goods and country produce are sold Sat 1000–1200 at a **Farmer's Market**, *Negus Park on Ocean Ave*. Menu choices in an English Tudor setting are on the pricey side at **Winfield's**, *Com Neck Rd; tel: (401) 466-5856*, same for dining rooms in the vintage hotels. Best on *Water St* for budget–moderate seafood meals are **Finn's**, *tel: (401) 466-2473*, and the **Mohegan Café**, *tel: (401) 466-5911*. **The Beachhead**, *Com Neck Rd; tel:* *(401) 466-2249*, is a budget burgers-and-beer gathering place.

Full-day bicycle rentals cost $8–$12; $50–$60 for mopeds (which the locals love to hate). Chatty taxicab drivers offer roundabout island tours; usually $25 total for up to five passengers. Horseback trail rides start at **Rustic Rides Farm**, *West Side Rd; tel: (401) 466-5060*. From late June–mid-Sept, the Nature Conservancy sponsors free 1–1½-hour **nature walks**; *tel: (401) 466-2129*. To prep for self-guided hiking, ask for the Conservancy's $1.50 trail map at the Chamber of Commerce. It details five scenic and pristine walking trails, exceeding 20 miles overall.

Touring beyond Old Harbor by whatever means opens onto grassy moors, bayberry shrubs and blackberry patches, hedge roses, salt marshes, fresh-water ponds and ocean vistas, with 400 miles of three-century-old stone fences crisscrossing the terrain. The south-coastal **Mohegan Bluffs** – resembling West Ireland's Cliffs of Moher – tower above rocky coves. From the overlook, a 151-step wooden stairway clambers down to a pocket beach. Atop this headland: Block Island's brick 'Cottage Gothic' **Southeast Lighthouse** was recently moved 275 feet inland from the eroding cliff.

Birdwatchers prefer an autumn visit, when several hundred thousand migratory birds travelling the 'Atlantic Flyway' make a stop-over en route to South America. Springtime brings countless yellow daffodils into full bloom, and white billows of shadblow blossoms cover the island.

NEWPORT–NEW YORK CITY

The 160-mile direct journey through Rhode Island and Connecticut to the New York state line can be covered non-stop in three hours or so. Much of the slightly longer scenic alternative follows the original course of the Boston Post Road, mile-posted in 1672 for mail delivery between Boston and New York City. Present-day contrasts are striking – a mixed bag of seascapes, beaches and marinas, marshlands and nature sanctuaries, lighthouses, village greens, dowager-Victorian resorts, Ivy League academia, backyard-barbecue suburbia, nasty patches of urban blight, the per-capita richest US county (Fairfield in Connecticut) and something-for-everyone tourist attractions.

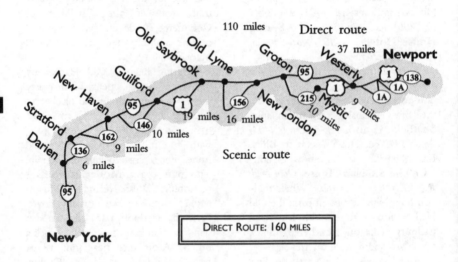

168

DIRECT ROUTE: 160 MILES

ROUTES

DIRECT ROUTE

➡ Cross the **Newport Bridge** ($2 toll), then the **Jamestown-Verrazano Bridge**. Continue west on Rte 138 for 2.5 miles to Rte 1; head 37.5 miles south-southwest to **Westerly** and

the **Pawcatuck River bridge** at the Rhode Island/Connecticut state line. In Connecticut, drive 2.5 miles north on Rte 2 towards the I-95 motorway for your westward journey to the New York state line, a distance of 110 miles.

In New York State, continue on I-95 (the New England Thruway) to Exit 6 for southbound access onto Rte 278 (the Bruckner Expressway). Cross the **Triboro Bridge** ($3 toll); exit upon seeing the **Manhattan/FDR Drive** sign. Proceed south on *Franklin D. Roosevelt Dr (East River Dr)* to *42nd St*; exit onto that crosstown thoroughfare. Stay on *42nd St* past *Park* and *5th Aves* for arrival at **Times Square**.

I-95 rush-hour traffic becomes intense in the metro areas, especially along the Bridgeport-Stamford 'commuter corridor'. At the first Connecticut exit upon leaving Rhode Island (Exit 92), a motorists' **Welcome Center** is open daily 0900–1700. I-95 is designated north-south rather than geographically sensible east-west on its Connecticut portion. It helps to remember that I-95 extends from far-northern Maine to far-southern Florida.

SCENIC ROUTE

▶ In Rhode Island

Depart Newport by crossing the two bridges; drive 8 miles south on Rte 1A to **Narragansett Pier,** then 2 miles west towards **Wakefield** for southbound access onto Rte 1, rejoining the direct route. Turn left upon reaching another segment of Rte 1A (*Shore Rd*), running 13 miles to **Watch Hill**. Backtrack 6 miles north on 1A to **Westerly**. South off Rtes 1 and 1A between Newport and Westerly, some of New England's best beaches fringe **Block Island Sound**. Especially: **East Matunuck State Beach** (west of biblically named **Jerusalem** and **Galilee**) and **Misquamicut State Beach** near Watch Hill.

In Connecticut

From Westerly/Pawcatuck, drive 4 miles on Rte 1 to **Stonington Borough** and a further 5 miles to the seaport city of **Mystic**. From here a **side track** is possible to Foxwoods Casino, or continue 3 miles south on Rte 215 to **Noank**. From that idyllic hamlet, take Rte 215 north for 7 miles to reach I-95 at **Groton**; cross the **Thames River Bridge** to **New London**. Head south from there for a 16-mile Rte 156 shore drive through **Niantic** past **Rocky Neck State Park** towards **Old Lyme**.

Return to I-95 near Old Lyme and cross the **Connecticut River** to reach **Old Saybrook**. Then proceed onto Rte 1 for touring through **Westbrook, Clinton, Madison** and **Guilford**. Old Saybrook-Guilford distance is 19 miles. Petrol stations, motels and budget eateries are plentiful.

From Guilford, choose Rte 146 for a super-scenic 10.5-mile jaunt with coves and salt marshes in view – passing through **Leetes Island** and **Stony Creek** en route to **Branford,** then resume travelling on I-95 to **New Haven**. Then take Exit 42 onto Rte 162 for 9 miles, 're-connecting' with I-95 at the **Housatonic River bridge** near **Stratford**.

Stay on the motorway for 15.5 miles to Exit 17 for a 6-mile Rte 136 drive to the boat-harbour village of **Rowayton**, on the Fivemile River prior to rejoining I-95 at **Darien**. After **Stamford**, cross the Connecticut/New York State line and follow the Direct Route into Manhattan.

NARRAGANSETT PIER AND WAKEFIELD

Tourist Information: South County Tourism Council (SCTC), *4808 Tower Hill Rd, Wakefield, RI 02879; tel: (401) 789-4422 or (800) 548-4662,* has information by mail on most of southern Rhode Island. **Wakefield Chamber of**

169

Commerce, *368 Main St, Wakefield, RI 02880; tel: (401) 783-3878,* is open to walk-in visitors Mon–Fri 0900–1700.

ACCOMMODATION AND FOOD

The expensive **Village Inn,** *1 Beach St, Narragansett Pier, RI 02882; tel: (800) 843-7437,* is biggest and best locally. Enquire about numerous bed and breakfasts at the information facility. Neighbouring Wakefield's hospitable, moderate–expensive **Larchwood Inn** serves New Englandy meals, *521 Main St, Wakefield, RI 02879; tel: (401) 783-5454.*

Considering the ocean views and its setting in what had been an 1888 life-saving station, moderate-priced lunches, dinners and copious Sunday buffets are bargains at the **Coast Guard House,** *40 Ocean Rd; tel: (401) 789-0700.* For budget fare, seek out the **Whale Rock Deli,** *9 Pier Marketplace; tel: (401) 783-6640.*

SIGHTSEEING

While New York's upper crust favoured Newport in summer, Philadelphians 'discovered' Narragansett Pier. Hence the elegant summer homes along *Ocean Rd.* Another 'Gilded Age' left-over is **The Towers,** sole remains of a casino that was high society's watering hole before a 1900 fire destroyed it. Today the mile-long beach predominates, and surfers 'hang ten' on the Eastern Seaboard's wickedest waves.

MID-COAST SOUTH COUNTY

Tourist Information: Charlestown Chamber of Commerce, *Old Post Rd, Charlestown, RI 02813; tel: (401) 364-3878,* is open daily 0900–1800 (summer only); or write to SCTC.

This general area encompasses state and township beaches, salt-water ponds and random tacky villages.

ACCOMMODATION AND FOOD

The General Stanton Inn, *Rte 1A, Charlestown, RI 02813; tel: (800) 397-0100,* expensive, is a rambling old-timer. Proximity to East Matunuck State Beach is a perk at the expensive **Admiral Dewey Inn,** *668 Matunuck Beach Rd, South Kingstown, RI 02879; tel: (401) 783-2090.* Pricier: **Shelter Harbor Inn,** *10 Wagner Rd, Westerly, RI 02891; tel: (800) 468-8883.* Tent pitches are available mid-April–Oct on Watchaug Pond's shore in **Burlingame State Park,** *Park Rd; tel: (401) 322-7994.*

Locale and food are unbeatable at the **South Shore Grille,** *210 Salt Pond Rd; tel: (401) 782-4780,* moderate, overlooking a cove and yacht marina. In East Matunuck, **Cap'n Jack's,** *584 Succotash Rd; tel: (401) 789-4556,* packs 'em in for seafood feasting.

ENTERTAINMENT

Near the state beach, **Theatre-By-The-Sea,** *364 Card's Pond Rd, Matunuck, RI 02879; tel: (401) 782-8587,* features summer-stock productions.

WESTERLY/WATCH HILL

Tourist Information: Greater Westerly-Pawcatuck Area Chamber of Commerce, *74 Post Rd, Westerly, RI 02891; tel: (401) 596-7761,* open Mon–Fri 0900–1700; or SCTC above.

ACCOMMODATION AND FOOD

In Watch Hill (Westerly's 'rich aunt'), pride of place belongs to the **Watch Hill Inn,** *38 Bay St, Watch Hill, RI 02891; tel: (800) 356-9314,* moderate–pricey in summer. Close to Misquamicut State Beach, a moderate–expensive choice is the **Breezeway Motel,** *70 Wimpanaug Rd, Misquamicut, RI 02891; tel: (800) 462-8872.* Westerly's cheap–budget 'in' place is

Woody's Café, *43 Broad St; tel: (401) 596-1991.* Best downtown for fish and steaks is **Dylans,** *2 Canal St; tel: (401) 596-4075,* moderate. Also moderate, the **Olympia Tea Room,** *74 Bay St; tel: (401) 348-8211,* has existed near the peninsular tip of Watch Hill since 1916.

Along with another of Rhode Island's terrific beaches, Watch Hill has the circa-1867 **Flying Horse Carousel,** with each steed sculpted out of a single piece of wood.

MYSTIC AND STONINGTON

Tourist Information: Southeastern Connecticut Tourism District, *P.O. Box 89, 27 Masonic St, New London, CT 06320; tel: (860) 444-2206 or (800) 863-6569,* has details on coastal attractions from the Rhode Island border to Old Lyme and well inland. **Mystic Chamber of Commerce,** *16 Cottrell St, Mystic, CT 06355; tel: (860) 572-9578,* is open Mon–Fri 0900–1700.

Book early, since Mystic Seaport is Connecticut's most-visited tourist attraction; the Chamber of Commerce is a useful referral source. *HJ, Hn, BW, DI, CI* and *RI* are near I-95 access. For bed and breakfast comfort in a colonial dwelling, opt for the **Red Brook Inn,** *2750 Gold Star Hwy, Mystic, CT 06372; tel: (860) 572-0349.* Lauren Bacall and Humphrey Bogart honeymooned in the expensive–pricey **Inn at Mystic,** *Rtes 1 and 27, Mystic, CT 06355; tel: (860) 237-2415.* Similar rates at the **Whaler's Inn,** *20 E. Main St, Mystic, CT 06355; tel: (800) 243-2588.* **Seaport Campgrounds,** *Campground Rd, Mystic, CT 06372; tel: (860) 536-4044,* opens mid-Apr–late Oct.

Downtown has much budget–moderate variety for meals and pub socialising. **S&P Oyster Co,** *1 Holmes St; tel: (860) 536-2674,* overlooks Mystic's 1922 bascule drawbridge. Same inspiration for **Drawbridge Inn,** *34 W. Main St; tel: (860) 536-9653.* **Seamen's Inne,** *105 Greenmanville Ave; tel: (860) 536-9649,* is closest to Mystic Seaport for meals and pubs.

Blessedly un-Disneyfied **Mystic Seaport,** *75 Greenmanville Ave, Mystic, CT 06355; tel: (860) 572-5315,* is the preeminent US maritime museum with its re-created 19th-century aura. This includes a whaling ship, square-rigger and fishing schooner, shipyard goings-on, working craftspeople, Mystic River steamboat cruises, the largest-anywhere nautical bookstore and galleries of ship models, figureheads and seafaring paintings. Open daily 0900–1700 (Apr–June and Sept–Oct), 0900–1800 (late June–early Sept), 0900–1600 (Nov–Dec), 1000–1600 (Jan–Mar), $15.

Seals, penguins and leaping dolphins and whales cavort at **Mystic Marinelife Aquarium,** *55 Coogan Blvd, Mystic, CT 06355; tel: (860) 536-3323,* daily 0900–1730 (July–Aug), 0900–1630 (Sept–June), $9.50.

Ask at the Chamber of Commerce about **windjammer cruises** – day trips and longer sailings.

Connecticut's only commercial fishing-fleet port is at **Stonington Borough,** an almost unbelievably pretty village where *Water St* leads to a beach and a granite lighthouse. Amongst several moderate restaurants are **Noah's,** *113 Water St; tel: (860) 535-3925,* and **Skipper's Dock,** *66 Water St; tel: (860) 535-2000,* which jumps each Sun to Dixieland jazz.

171

NOANK

In the opposite direction from Mystic via Rte 215, this is another picturesque charmer, perched on a rocky land's end. **Abbott's**, *117 Pearl St; tel: (860) 536-7719*, boils full-fledged New England shore dinners (clam chowder, steamers, corn on the cob, lobster) May–Oct. The moderate–pricey Victorian **Palmer Inn**, *25 Church St, Noank, CT 06340; tel: (860) 572-9000*, has been meticulously restored.

⇄ SIDE TRACK FROM MYSTIC

FOXWOODS RESORT CASINO

Away from the coast, southern Connecticut is hilly and forested, with drowsy villages here-and-there. So nothing prepares first-timers for the sudden appearance of **Foxwoods Casino** after a very scenic 11.5-mile drive from Mystic via Rte 27 to 201 and then Rte 2 for arrival at the **Mashantucket Pequot Reservation**. Here the Native American citizenry owns the world's biggest go-for-broke gambling colossus.

The spread also includes restaurants, big-name entertainment, shops galore, video arcades and cinemas. Plus the glitzy, expensive–pricey **Foxwoods Resorts Hotel** and more subdued **Two Trees Inn. Foxwoods**, *Rte 2 West, P.O. Box 410, Ledyard, CT 06339; tel: (800) 752-9244*; if you want to reserve a room *tel: (800) 369-9663*. ⬛

GROTON AND NEW LONDON

Tourist Information: **Southeastern Connecticut Tourism District (SCTC)**, *27 Masonic St, New London, CT 06320; tel: (860) 444-2206 or (800) 863-6569*; open Mon–Fri 0830–1630, has information on the entire region.

ACCOMMODATION AND FOOD

There's a downtown *Rd* and outlying *Hd* in New London; Groton has *BW, QI* and *S8*. Overlooking Long Island Sound, the expensive–pricey **Lighthouse Inn**, *6 Guthrie Pl, New London, CT 06320; tel: (860) 443-8411*, was a steel tycoon's summer estate. New London's **Thames Landing Oyster House**, *2 Captain's Walk; tel: (860) 442-3158*, is choicest for seafood, while **O'Brien's on Bank**, *52–54 Bank St; tel: (860) 442-3420*, offers enjoyable outdoor dining. Both moderate.

SIGHTSEEING

The mouth of the Thames River (pronounced *Thaymz*, not *Temz)* divides these two seaport cities. Visitors are welcome at the **US Coast Guard Academy**, *Mohegan Ave, New London, CT 06320; tel: (860) 444-8327*, daily 0900–1700 (May–Oct); Sat–Sun 1000–1700 (Apr), free. Playwright Eugene O'Neill (*Long Day's Journey Into Night* and *The Iceman Cometh)* grew up in **Monte Cristo Cottage**, *325 Pequot Ave, New London, CT 06320; tel: (860) 443-0051*, open Mon–Fri 1300–1600 (Apr–Dec), $3. Fine art along with dolls, dollhouses and antique toys are in the **Lyman Allyn Art Museum**, *625 Williams St, New London, CT 06230, tel: (860) 443-2545*, open Tues–Sat 1000–1700, Wed 1000-2100, Sun 1300–1700, $3.

USS Nautilus, the world's first nuclear-powered sub, can be boarded at the **US Naval Submarine Base**, *Groton, CT 06349; tel: (800) 343-0079*, open Wed–Mon 0900–1700, Tues 1300–1700 (mid-Apr–mid-Oct); Wed–Mon 0900–1600 (mid-Oct–mid-Apr), free.

Rocky Neck State Park, *Rte 156, Niantic, CT 06357; tel: (860) 739-5471,* has a mile-long, crescent-shaped beach, one of the best around, plus camping.

OLD LYME AND OLD SAYBROOK

Tourist Information: Old Saybrook Chamber of Commerce, *146 Main St, Old Saybrook, CT 06475; tel: (860) 388-3266,* open Mon–Fri 1000–1500. SCTC (above) has Old Lyme information; for Old Saybrook, write **Connecticut River Valley & Shoreline Visitors Council (CRV&SVC),** *393 Main St, Middletown, CT 06457; tel: (860) 347-0028 or (800) 486-3346.*

ACCOMMODATION AND FOOD

The moderate–pricey **Old Lyme Inn,** *85 Lyme St, Old Lyme, CT 06371; tel: (860) 434-2600,* exudes vintage charm and has an award-winning grill room. Gourmet cuisine, too, at the pricier **Saybrook Point Inn,** *2 Bridge St, Old Saybrook, CT 06475; tel: (800) 243-0212.* West of Old Saybrook on Rte 1, lower-cost lodgings include *CI* and *DI*.

Old Saybrook's cheeriest restaurant is **Wine and Roses,** *150 Main St; tel: (860) 388-9646.* Moderate, as is **Dock & Dine,** *Saybrook Point; tel: (860) 388-4665,* for seafood and Connecticut River delta panoramics.

SIGHTSEEING

The two towns, dating from early 17th-century English settlement, are on opposite banks at the mouth of the Connecticut River. Ask at the Chamber of Commerce for an Old Saybrook walking-tour brochure that includes a crash course in early-US domestic architecture.

Old Lyme's standout attraction in the past was a vastly influential turn-of-the-century Impressionists' art colony, representative paintings are in the **Florence Griswold Museum,** *96 Lyme St, Old Lyme, CT 06371; tel: (860) 434-5542,* Tues–Sat 1000–1700, Sun 1300–1700 (June–Oct), Wed–Sun 1300–1700 (Nov–May), $4.

WESTBROOK AND CLINTON

Tourist Information: Clinton Chamber of Commerce, *1630 House, Rte 1, Clinton, CT 06413; tel: (860) 669-8500,* is open Mon–Fri 0900–1300. Or write to CRV&SVC above.

ACCOMMODATION AND FOOD

Two 'ye-olde' moderate-niche bed and breakfasts are recommendable. **Captain Dibbell House,** *21 Commerce St, Clinton, CT 06413; tel: (860) 669-1646,* and **Captain Stannard House,** *138 S. Main St, Westbrook, CT 06498; tel: (860) 399-4634.*

Watch for a cluster of budget–moderate clam-shack joints in Westbrook's harbour vicinity. The most acclaimed is **Lenny & Joe's Fish Tale,** *86 Boston Post Rd; tel: (860) 669-0767.*

MADISON

Tourist Information: Madison Chamber of Commerce, *22 Scotland Rd, Madison, CT 06443; tel: (203) 245-7394,* Mon–Fri 0900–1500, or write to CRV&SVC.

ACCOMMODATION AND FOOD

Affluent Madison's priciest lodging is the **Tidewater Inn,** *949 Boston Post Rd, Madison, CT 06443; tel: (203) 245-8457.* The **Madison Beach Hotel,** *94 W. Wharf Rd, Madison, CT 06443; tel: (203) 245-1404,* moderate–expensive, stands right on the waterfront.

Moderate–pricey **Café Lafayette,** *725*

173

Boston Post Rd; tel: (203) 245-7773, features *nouvelle* cooking and Madison's most convivial bar.

RECREATION
Connecticut's longest public beach (2 miles) is in **Hammonasset Beach State Park**, also featuring nature trails and campsites, off Rte 1; *tel: (203) 245-2785*.

GUILFORD AND BRANFORD
Tourist Information: CRV&SVC covers these two towns in addition to **Guilford Visitors Bureau**, *32 Church St, Guilford, CT 06437; tel: (203) 458-0408*, open Sat 1000–1600, Sun 1200–1600 (Apr–Dec), and **Branford Chamber of Commerce**, *152 Montowese St, Branford, CT 06405; tel: (203) 488-5500*, open Mon–Fri 0900–1630.

Guilford was settled in 1639 by Puritans from Ockley near London. Its 14-acre village green is straight out of a lithograph by Currier and Ives, a famed team of 19th-century printmakers. Standing tall on Branford's green, **Trinity Episcopal Church** has dazzling Tiffany stained-glass windows.

ACCOMMODATION AND FOOD
Inexpensive *DI* and *M6* are near Branford centre. Dine amidst walls hung with modern art in Guilford's moderate **Bistro on the Green**, *25 Whitfield St; tel: (203) 458-9059*. Branford's literally little **Le Petit Café**, *225 Montowese St; tel: (203) 483-9791*, is the very essence of a French bistro, serving $18.50 *prix-fixe* dinners.

NEW HAVEN
Tourist Information: Greater New Haven Convention & Visitors Bureau, *1 Long Wharf Dr, New Haven, CT 06511; tel: (203) 777-8550 or (800) 322-7829*, open Mon–Fri 0830–1700.

ACCOMMODATION
The Inn at Chapel West, *1201 Chapel St, New Haven, CT 06511; tel: (203) 777-1201*, is pricey and luxurious. Less costly but equally central: **Colony Inn**, *1157 Chapel St, New Haven, CT 06511; tel: (800) 458-8810*. *Hd* is near the university, *HJ* near the waterfront.

EATING AND DRINKING
A hip, eclectic restaurant scene is inevitable in this collegiate city. 'Yalies' mingle at non-smoking, vegetarian **Claire's Corner Copia**, *1000 Chapel St; tel: (203) 562-3888*. For another dose of academia, have breakfast at the **Atticus Bookstore Café**, *1082 Chapel St; tel: (203) 776-4040*. Epicureans frequent **Consiglio's**, *165 Wooster St; tel: (203) 865-4489*. **Scoozi**, *1104 Chapel St; tel: (203) 776-8268*, and the **Union League Café**, *1032 Chapel St; tel: (203) 562-4299*.

Two budget landmarks are famously historic. **Louis' Lunch**, *261 Crown St; tel: (203) 562-5507*, is the legendary birthplace of the all-American hamburger. And in New Haven's Italian neighbourhood, **Frank Pepe Pizzeria Napoletana**, *157 Wooster St; tel: (203) 865-5762*, takes credit for concocting the first-ever US pizzas, in 1925.

SIGHTSEEING
Elite **Yale University** makes New Haven tick. Free tours begin daily at **Yale Visitor Information Center**, *149 Elm St; tel: (203) 432-2300*.

Yale University Art Gallery is North America's oldest university art museum, *1111 Chapel St, New Haven, CT 06520; tel: (203) 432-0600*, open Tues–Sat 1000–1700, Sun 1400–1700, free. The largest collection of British art outside the UK is in the **Yale Center for British**

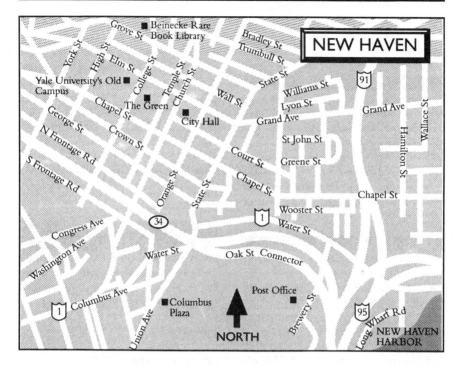

NEW HAVEN

Art, *1080 Chapel St, New Haven, CT 06520; tel: (203) 432-2800,* open Tues–Sat 1000–1700, Sun 1200–1700, free. Yale's **Peabody Museum of Natural History** *170 Whitney Ave, New Haven, CT 06520; tel: (203) 452-5050,* ranks among the world's best, with dinosaur bones and Connecticut Indian exhibits. Open Tues–Sat 1000–1700, Sun 1200–1700, $4; free Tues–Sat 1500–1700.

A sunken sculpture garden graces the university's **Beinecke Rare Book & Manuscript Library,** *121 Wall St, New Haven, CT 06520; tel: (203) 432-2977,* with its Gutenberg Bibles, Charles Dickens manuscripts and rare Audubon bird prints. Open Mon–Fri 0830–1700, Sat 1000–1700, free.

ENTERTAINMENT

A show-biz town, New Haven is home of the **Yale Repertory Theatre,** *222 York St; tel: (203) 432-1234.* The **Shubert Performing Arts Center,** *247 College St; tel: (203) 562-5666,* is best-known for en-route-to-Broadway shows. Major dramas have premiered at **Long Wharf Theatre,** *222 Sargent Dr; tel: (203) 787-4282.*

NEW HAVEN TO BRIDGEPORT

What looks like a concrete air-raid bunker is actually a pari-mutuel gambling emporium, the **Milford Jai-alai** fronton, reached via Exit 40 off I-95; *tel: (203) 877-4242,* open Apr–Jan. Milford produces two well-known consumer products: Bic pens and Schick shavers.

A replica of London's Globe Theatre in Stratford has, alas, fallen into disrepair. But its locale, the **American Shakespeare**

175

Theatre State Park, remains a well-kept recreational space on the Housatonic riverfront.

BRIDGEPORT

The prime reason for a Bridgeport stop-over is the bizarre, neo-Byzantine-Romanesque **Barnum Museum**, *820 Main St, Bridgeport, CT 06604; tel: (203) 331-9881*, recalling the past-century career of 'Three-Ring Circus' impresario P.T. Barnum. Open Tues–Sat 1000–1630, Mon 1000–1630 (July–Aug), Sun 1200–1630, $5.

FAIRFIELD AND WESTPORT

Tourist Information: Coastal Fairfield County District, *297 West Ave, Gate Lodge-Mathews Park, Norwalk, CT 06850; tel: (203) 854-7825 or (800) 866-7925*, handles the region from Bridgeport to Greenwich. **Westport Chamber of Commerce**, *180 Post Road East, Westport, CT 06881; tel: (203) 227-9234*, open Mon–Fri 0900–1700.

Now, rather suddenly, comes the Fairfield County 'Gold Coast' of top-dol-lar homes, up-market boutiques, preppy private schools and a typically Yankee kind of discreet classiness. Joanne Woodward and Paul Newman live in Westport. Sightsee by roaming residential side streets and gentrified country lanes in Westport and neighbouring, waterfront **Southport**. Wealth begets culture, so enquire about concerts, art exhibits and theatrical performances.

ACCOMMODATION

Downtown's pricey **Inn at National Hall**, *2 Post Rd West, Westport, CT 06880; tel: (203) 221-1351*, is ultra-luxe. The more countrified **Inn at Longshore**, *260 Compo Rd South, Westport, CT 06880; tel: (203) 226-3316*, is a notch cheaper.

EATING AND DRINKING

Westport's bounty makes the mind bog-gle, eased by getting to know the town centre. Swanky options include **Restaurant Zanghi**, *2 Post Rd West; tel: (203) 221-7572*, and **Les Bistro des Amis**, *7 Sconset Sq.; tel: (203) 226-2647*. The hoi-polloi find **Glynn's Café**, *199 Post Rd; tel: (203) 226-3008*, and **Onion Alley**, *41 Main St; tel: (203) 226-0794*, much less uppity. **Gregory's**, *1599 Post Rd; tel: (203) 259-7417*, moderate, is a chic Euro-US bistro in Fairfield.

NORWALK/SOUTH NORWALK

Tourist Information: Coastal Fairfield County Information Center, *297 West Ave, Norwalk, CT 06850; tel: (203) 854-7825 or (800) 866-7925*, open Mon–Fri 1000–1700; also Sat–Sun 1100–1600 (July–Oct).

ACCOMMODATION AND FOOD

The Norwalk Inn, *99 East Ave, Norwalk, CT 06851; tel: (800) 873-2392*, moderate, is centrally located. Tucked away in north-suburban Silvermine, his-toric **Silvermine Tavern**, *194 Perry Ave, Norwalk, CT 06850; tel: (203) 847-4558*, moderate–expensive, soothes with canopy beds and creaky floorboards.

Though still rough around the edges, revitalised South Norwalk (a.k.a. SoNo) has become 'restaurant row', with new-comers popping up. For example, **Savoy Supper Club**, *15 N. Main St; tel: (203) 831-0900*, and **Amberjacks**, *99 Washington St; tel: (203) 853-4332*. Both moderate.

New England Brewing Co., *13 Marshall St; tel: (203) 866-1339*, is this area's brewpub – a century younger than the saloon oldie **Jeremiah O'Donovan's**, *138 Washington St; tel: (203) 838-3430*.

SIGHTSEEING

Oceanic miscellanea fills SoNo's **Maritime Center,** *10 N. Water St, Norwalk, CT 06854; tel: (203) 852-0700,* open daily 1000–1700; to 1800 in summer, $7.50. Uptown in Norwalk, 33 **WPA murals** funded by the federal Works Progress Administration during the Great Depression are in **City Hall,** *125 East Ave, Norwalk, CT 06851; tel: (203) 866-0202,* open Mon–Fri 0900–1700, free.

OUT OF TOWN

NEW CANAAN

Tourist Information: New Canaan Chamber of Commerce, *111 Elm St, New Canaan, CT 06840; tel: (203) 966-2004,* open Mon–Fri 0900–1200.

The 'Gold Coast' extends inland, as becomes evident by a 5-mile diversion north on Rte 123 to this well-heeled community. Two pricey retreats are side-by-side: **Roger Sherman Inn,** *195 Oenoke Ridge, New Canaan, CT 06840; tel: (203) 966-4541,* and **Maples Inn,** *179 Oenoke Ridge, New Canaan, CT 06840; tel: (800) 959-6477.* Lunch downtown won't bankrupt you at **Hay Day Express,** *97 Main St; tel: (203) 972-8200,* nor at **Gates,** *10 Forest St; tel: (203) 966-8666.* Fish-and-pasta selections are moderate at the **Blue Water Café,** *15 Elm St; tel: (203) 972-1799.*

STAMFORD AND GREENWICH

Tourist Information: Coastal Fairfield County Information Center, *297 West Ave, Norwalk, CT 06850; tel: (203) 854-7825 or (800) 866-7925,* open Mon–Fri 1000–1700; also Sat–Sun 1100–1500 (July–Oct). **Thomas Cook** has a **Foreign Exchange** office at *107 Broad St, Stamford, CT 06901, tel: (203) 348-7725.*

ACCOMMODATION

Quite a number of firms have moved their corporate headquarters from New York to Stamford, thus creating a mini-Manhattan loaded with hotels, including *Rd, Rm, Ma, Sh* and *S8.* More genteel Greenwich offers expensive–pricey alternatives, among them **Greenwich Harbor Inn,** *500 Steamboat Rd, Greenwich, CT 06830; tel: (203) 661-06830,* and **Stanton House Inn,** *76 Maple Ave, Greenwich, CT 06830; tel: (203) 869-2110.*

Posh, sylvan Old Greenwich has a knockout-spectacular *HY,* built where Condé Nast used to publish its glossy magazines.

EATING AND DRINKING

Restaurants are virtually wall-to-wall in Greenwich centre, so decide according to preference and budget. *Haute* French is prevalent, led by **Bertrand,** *253 Greenwich Ave; tel: (203) 661-4459,* and **Le Figaro Bistro de Paris,** *372 Greenwich Ave; tel: (203) 622-0018.* **Terra,** *156 Greenwich Ave; tel: (203) 629-5222,* is tops for Italian meals.

The less rarerefied category includes **Thataway Café,** *499 Greenwich Ave; tel: (203) 622-0799,* also Old Greenwich's **Boxing Cat Grill,** *1392 E. Putnam Ave; tel: (203) 698-1995.*

SIGHTSEEING

Stamford's cultural showpiece is its branch of New York's **Whitney Museum of American Art,** *1 Champion Plaza, Stamford, CT 06921; tel: (203) 358-7630,* open Tues–Sat 1100–1700, free.

One of coastal Connecticut's largest nature sanctuaries, covering 485 acres crisscrossed by 15 miles of trails, is the **Audubon Center of Greenwich,** *613 Riversville Rd; tel: (203) 869-5272,* open Tues–Sun 0900–1700 all year, $3.

177

HARTFORD

The one-time home of writers Mark Twain and Harriet Beecher Stowe, Hartford has a proud past. Today, although it has fine museums and historic sites, it is considered somewhat stuffy because it is dominated by insurance companies. Yet Hartford has its surprises: excellent restaurants, unusual architecture and good shopping.

TOURIST INFORMATION

Greater Hartford Tourism District, *One Civic Center Plaza, Hartford, CT 06103; tel: (860) 520-4480 or toll-free (800) 793-4480.* **Greater Hartford Convention & Visitors Bureau, Inc.** *One Civic Center Plaza, Hartford, CT 06103; or (860) 728-6789 or toll-free (800) 446-7811.*

Hartford is eager to help tourists, so take advantage of the city's assistance. There are **welcome centres** at the **Old State House,** *800 Main St; tel: (860) 522-6766,* open Mon–Fri 1000–1800, Sat 1000–1700, the **Hartford Civic Center Mall,** *1 Civic Center Plaza; tel: (860) 275-6456,* open Mon–Fri 1000–1930, Sat 1000–1800, Sun 1200–1700, and the **Connecticut State Capitol,** *Capitol Ave; tel: (860) 240-0222,* Mon–Fri 0900–1500.

The **Hartford Guides,** dressed in khaki, red and white uniforms and red golf caps, are stationed around the city. They can give you directions and provide information on events, attractions, shopping and restaurants, and they will escort you to your bus, car or any other downtown destination. If it's raining, they'll be wearing bright red windbreakers and will escort you with an umbrella. If you need a guide and don't see one, *tel: (860) 293-8105.*

For toll-free hotel and motel reservations anywhere in Connecticut, *tel: (800) CT-BOUND,* daily, around the clock.

ARRIVING AND DEPARTING

By air
Bradley International Airport is located in Windsor Locks, 12 miles north of Hartford. Despite the name, it has no customs services, so all international travellers arrive via connecting flights after clearing customs at a US port of entry.

Allow 20–30 mins for the drive to the city centre; take Rte 20 east, then I-91 south to exits for downtown Hartford. Car hires are available through courtesy phones located at the baggage claim area. Taxi $21. The **Airport Connection;** *tel: (860) 627-3000,* $9, is a van service to Hartford hotels and Union Station.

By bus and train
Union Station, operated by the **Greater Hartford Transit District;** *tel: (860) 247-5329,* is within walking distance of downtown and is open 24 hrs. Bus service to Boston, Rhode Island and New York is provided by **Peter Pan Trailway;** *tel: (800) 343-9999,* **Greyhound;** *tel: (860) 522-9267,* and **Bonanza Bus Lines;** *tel: (800) 556-3815.*

Amtrak; *tel: (800) USA-RAIL (872-7245),* operates trains north to Springfield, Mass., and Vermont, south to New Haven, where travellers connect for Boston and New York's Penn. Station.

GETTING AROUND

Hartford's city bus service is **Connecticut Transit;** *tel: (860) 525-9181.* Fares $0.95–$1.45.

STAYING IN HARTFORD

Accommodation

Hartford has *Hd, Rm, Sh, S8, Su,* with *CI, HJ, M6, QI* in towns nearby. The 124–room **Goodwin Hotel,** *Goodwin Square, One Hayes St, Hartford, CT 06103, tel: (860) 246-7500 or (800) 922-5006,* is conveniently located across from the Civic Center. The former mansion of industrialist J.P. Morgan, it has turn of the century charm; expensive– pricey.

Eating and Drinking

Hartford has great Italian restaurants located in the city's South End. One of the best known is **Carbone's,** *588 Franklin Ave, tel: (860) 296-9646;* moderate. For fun there's **Brown, Thomson & Co.,** *942 Main St; tel: (860) 525-1600,* located in a former 1877 department store designed by New England architect Henry Hobson Richardson. The menu is vast and the setting spectacular. Budget–moderate. **Truc Orient Express,** *735 Wethersfield Ave; tel: (860) 296-2818,* has excellent Vietnamese food; moderate. The indoor **Hartford Civic Center Mall,** *1 Civic Center; tel: (860) 727-8010,* has about a dozen restaurants as well as places for ice-cream and snacks. With about 50 shops, the mall is also a major focus for shoppers.

Events

A Taste of Hartford, the largest food festival in New England, is held in early June at **Constitution Plaza.** Some 60 restaurants participate, and there's live music and a party-like atmosphere.

ENTERTAINMENT

Local hockey fans are crazy about their **Hartford Whalers,** who play at the Civic Center from Oct–May; *tel: (860) 728-3366* or toll-free *(800) WHALERS.* The **Hartford Stage Company,** *50 Church St; tel: (860) 527-5151,* is highly regarded venue for drama and often is reviewed by out-of-town critics. Performances Oct–June. **Bushnell Memorial Hall,** *166 Capitol Ave; tel: (860) 246-6807,* is a performing arts centre with more than 300 events each year from Sept–June.

SIGHTSEEING

Hartford's slightly dull reputation comes from serving as the home of major insurance companies, founded here in the early 19th century to protect the shipping industry in the Connecticut River Valley. The office buildings are mixed in with state government buildings since Hartford is also the state capital. The city is known for shutting down at night because most insurance and government workers live in the suburbs, leaving behind a mostly poor, minority population of 140,000. Nevertheless there are some outstanding historic and cultural offerings, many of which can be seen downtown by foot.

The **Wadsworth Atheneum,** *600 Main St, Hartford, CT 06103; tel: (860) 247-9111,* open Tues–Sun 1100–1700, $5, has more than 45,000 works and features 19th-century impressionists and an excellent contemporary art collection.

A few miles west from downtown is where two important American writers made their homes. The **Mark Twain House,** *351 Farmington Ave, Hartford, CT 06105, tel: (860) 493-6411,* open Mon–Sat 0930–1700, Sun 1200–1700 (end May–mid-Oct and Dec); Mon and Wed–Sat 0930–1700 (rest of year), $6.50, is a 19-room Victorian Gothic home built

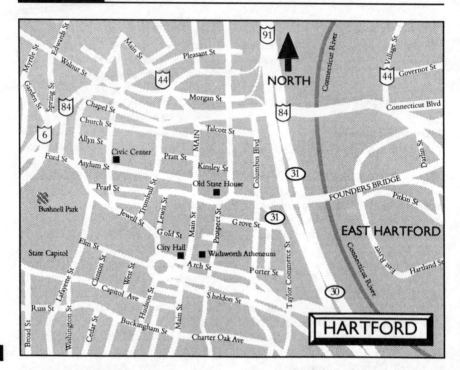

in 1873 with elaborate woodwork and stencils. Twain lived here for 17 years and published *Tom Sawyer* and *Huckleberry Finn* during this time. Next door is the **Harriet Beecher Stowe House,** *73 Forest St, Hartford, CT 06105; tel: (860) 525-9317,* open Mon–Sat 0930–1600, Sun 1200–1600 (end May–mid Oct and Dec), Tues–Sat 0930–1600 (rest of year), $6.50, where the author of *Uncle Tom's Cabin* lived from 1873–96.

The **Old State House,** *800 Main St, Hartford, CT 06103; tel: (860) 522-6766,* open Mon–Sat 1000–1700, Sun 1200–1700, free, was designed by Charles Bulfinch, the architect of Boston's State House. Built in 1796, it is the oldest state capitol building in the nation and is now an elegant private museum with a gift shop. The state legislature no longer meets there but instead bangs the gavel at the

Connecticut State Capitol, *210 Capitol Ave, Hartford, CT 06106; tel: (860) 240-0222,* open Mon–Fri 0700–1700; free hourly tours Mon–Fri 0915–1315 (all year), also on Sat 1015–1415 (Apr–Oct). This is a gaudy, 1879 wedding cake building made of Connecticut marble with a gold leaf dome. Adjoining the capitol grounds is **Bushnell Park,** designed by Frederick Law Olmsted, who designed New York City's Central Park and Boston's Emerald Necklace parks. In the park is the **Bushnell Park Carousel** *on Jewell St; tel: (860) 246-7739,* open Tues–Sun 1100–1700 (May–Aug), Sat and Sun 1100–1700 (Sept), $0.50, which has a 1914 hand-carved carousel with 48 horses and a 1925 Wurlitzer organ.

Elizabeth Park Rose Gardens, *915 Prospect Ave, Hartford, CT 06105;* open daily dawn–dusk, free, has 15,000 plants.

Peak blooming season is late June–early July. Greenhouses are open Mon–Fri 0800–1500, Sat–Sun 1000–1400, free. **Travelers Tower,** *700 Main St, Hartford, CT 06103; tel: (860) 277-2431,* open Mon–Fri (early May–end Oct), is 527-ft high and offers a view of the city. Be prepared to climb 72 steps at the top. Free.

Center Church, *675 Main St, Hartford, CT 06103; tel: (860) 249-5631,* open by appointment, was built in 1807 and modelled after St Martin-in-the-Field in London. The church traces its history to a meetinghouse established in 1636. Inside are six windows depicting religious events which were designed by Louis Comfort Tiffany, a founder of the Art Nouveau movement and known for stained glass windows and lamps in the late 19th and early 20th centuries. Adjacent to the church is the **Ancient Burying Ground,** *60 Gold St,* dating back to 1663, where the city's early founders are buried.

 SIDETRACK FROM HARTFORD

CONNECTICUT RIVER VALLEY

Tourist Information: Connecticut River Valley & Shoreline Visitors Council, *393 Main St, Middletown, CT 06457; tel: (860) 347-0028 or (800) 486-3346.*

A short drive south of Hartford along the Connecticut River Valley will take you to some of the state's prettiest towns and most interesting attractions, making for an enjoyable day trip that concludes at the Connecticut shore. The Connecticut River runs 410 miles through four states from its source near the border of Canada and New Hampshire. Native Americans of the

Algonquian nation named the river *Quinnetukut,* meaning 'land beside the long tidal river.' From the 18th century on, river landings became ports for schooners and West Indies traders and ship building was an important industry, especially in the town of Essex.

In front of the state capitol building on *Capitol Ave,* make a left in front of Bushnell Auditorium and follow signs to I-91, keeping right to go south. Take Exit 26 to **Old Wethersfield.** Make a right at the bottom of the exit and follow signs to the **Webb-Deane-Stevens Museum,** *211 Main St, Wethersfield, CT 06109, tel: (860) 529-0612,* open Wed–Mon 1000–1600 (May–Oct), Sat and Sun 1000–1600 (Nov–Apr), $6. Tours leave every hour; last tour at 1500. This is the site of three 18th-century houses furnished to provide a glimpse of that period in America. Here Gen George Washington planned the battle that led to the American victory at Yorktown in 1783.

Return to I-91 south and take Exit 23 to Rocky Hill. Turn from the exit and go less than one mile to **Dinosaur State Park,** *400 West St, Rocky Hill, CT 06067; tel: (860) 529-8423,* park open daily 0900–1630, free; casting area open daily 0900–1530 (May–Oct); exhibit centre open Tues–Sun 0900–1630. Giant prehistoric reptiles once roamed the Rocky Hill region, and their footprints and fossils can still be found. Visitors can make casts from actual dinosaur tracks by bringing their own materials.

Return to I-91 south and go about a mile to Rte 9 and follow it 18.5 miles for a pleasant, leafy drive to Exit 7 (Rte 82). Follow Rte 82 east to the Connecticut River. You may have a

181

wait for the drawbridge which often backs up traffic. To the right, before the bridge, is **Camelot Cruises**, *1 Marine Park, Haddam, CT 06438; tel: (860) 345-8591*, offering a variety of river trips, ranging from two hours ($12.85) to day-long trips downriver and across Long Island Sound to New York State ($24.75).

On the other side of the bridge is the 1876 Victorian **Goodspeed Opera House**, *Rte 82, East Haddam, CT 06423; tel: (860) 873-8668;* tours are offered Mon 1300–1500, Sat 1100–1330 (early June–mid-Oct), $2, with performances Apr–Dec. The opera house was restored in 1963 and has since staged vintage and original musicals, some of which go on to Broadway.

The white, ornate opera house is in a charming riverside town. Take a stroll around the shops and restaurants across the street. Get a take-away sandwich and excellent coffee at **Café Pronto**, *2 Norwich Rd; tel: (860) 873-8100*, eat at the park next to the opera house and watch the sailboats go by. Dine or stay at six-room **Gelston House**, *8 Main St, East Haddam, CT 06423; tel: (860) 873-1411*, built in 1853, is expensive–pricey, while the restaurant serves elegant meals; moderate–pricey. Reservations recommended. If you have opera house tickets, the restaurant will make sure you are served in time for the performance.

Continue on Rte 82, following signs for **Gillette Castle State Park** noting the ornate gingerbread houses in East Haddam. The castle is 2.7 miles from the opera house; keep an eye out for the sign where you make a right and drive 1.5 miles to the entrance. The wooded park is open 0800–1900, free,

and is filled with trails and picnic areas, but the big attraction is **Gillette Castle**, *67 River Rd, East Haddam, CT 06423; tel: (860) 526-2336*, open daily 1000–1700 (end May–mid-Oct), Sat–Sun 1000–1600 (mid-Oct–Christmas), $4. Built in 1919, this was the home of actor William Gillette, famous for his portrayal of Sherlock Holmes. The outside is a craggy stone building and inside are hand-carved fixtures created by Gillette. It's worth a visit if only to see the exterior with its sweeping view of the Connecticut River.

Return to Rte 82 and follow it east on a lovely drive past antiques shops, older homes and tall trees, and turn right onto Rte 148. Go 2.7 miles to the **Chester-Hadlyme Ferry**, *Rte 148; tel: (860) 566-7635*, open daily 0700–1845 (Apr–mid-Dec), $2.25 one way for car and driver plus $0.75 per passenger, carries only nine cars. The pleasant trip across the river is only about four minutes. Look back at the shoreline from the boat and you'll see the castle hovering above.

On the other side of the river, take Rte 148 one mile to **Chester**, one of the prettiest towns in Connecticut, where the best thing to do is simply walk around the small town centre. Drive to the end of *Main St*, turn right and you're on Rte 154. Follow it about two miles and turn left on *Main St* into **Ivoryton**, which boasts the 13-room **Copper Beech Inn**, *46 Main St, Ivoryton, CT 06442; tel: (860) 767-0330*, a lovely country inn with an excellent restaurant.

Originally the home of an ivory merchant (the town used to produce ivory keys for pianos) the inn boasts a stunning copper beech tree on the front lawn. Accommodation and meals are pricey but the decor and food are outstanding.

Follow *Main St* out of Ivoryton about a mile east to the **Essex Steam Train & Riverboat Ride,** *The Valley Railroad Co., Railroad Ave, P.O. Box 452, Essex, CT 06426; tel: (860) 767-0103.* Travel 19th-century steam trains on trips through the Connecticut River Valley, ranging from one hour, $8, to a 2½-hour ride connecting with a riverboat, $14. Departures daily 1000–1615, Sat 1000–1730 (early June–early Sept); boat-train departures Wed–Sun 1000–1445 (early Sept–end Oct), Wed, Sat, Sun (early May–early June).

Continue another mile east to **Essex,** a pleasant, busy riverside town which at one time had eight shipbuilding yards and for many years served as a steamboat stop from New York to Hartford. Each year in mid-May, the town has a Burning of the Ships Parade at noon to mark the burning of the Essex fleet by British mariners during the War of 1812. Nearly everything is clustered along *Main St.* Head toward the river. Along the way, you'll find plenty of shops, restaurants and places to eat. The **Clipper Ship Bookshop,** *12 North Main St; tel: (860) 767-1666* or *(800) 822-6650,* housed in an 1820 shop, is happily crammed with 15,000 books. Try a sandwich and dessert from **Ken's Coffeehouse,** *51 Main St; tel: (860) 767-8454.* Rest on a bench outside the shop at **Griswold Square,** a small garden on *Main St,* or sit by the river and watch the variety of boats, people and birds on the water.

At the foot of *Main St* is the **Connecticut River Museum,** *67 Main St, Essex, CT 06426; tel: (860) 767-8269,* open Tues–Sun 1000–1700, $4, which has exhibits of ship models and tools used in navigation and shipbuilding. In the boathouse is a reproduction of the first submarine and small craft used in fishing and yachting.

The best known restaurant and accommodation is at the **Griswold Inn,** *36 Main St, Essex, CT 06426; tel: (860) 767-1776,* built in 1733. Known as 'The Gris', the inn has 26 rooms and features an art collection of steamboat prints and memorabilia, a library of firearms and marine paintings. Rooms are expensive–pricey and meals moderate–pricey. The inn features a a 'hunt breakfast' buffet Sun for $12.95. Reservations are advised.

From Essex, follow Rte 9 south to **Old Saybrook,** where you connect with the Newport to New York City Route (See p. 168). ▲

HARTFORD-BRATTLEBORO

The Connecticut River plays faithful accompanist to this route and so does an intermittently conspicuous ridge of basalt which resisted the erosional forces of the river as it cut a course through the region's sedimentary rock. Like the blade of a giant hockey stick, the ridge curves east at the Massachusetts mill city of Holyoke, forming the Mt. Holyoke Range on the east side of the river, extending out toward the Pelham hills. The route takes the same eastward digression before returning to the river and following it to Brattleboro. Along this route, which touches three states, lie the birthplace of basketball, diverse college towns, farms and a preserved colonial village.

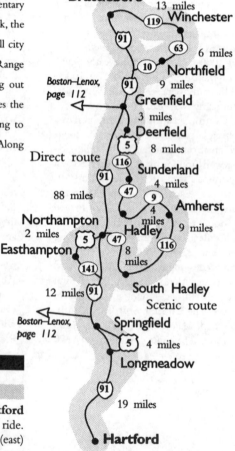

184

DIRECT ROUTE: 88 MILES

Boston–Lenox, page 112

ROUTES

DIRECT ROUTE

I-91 runs due north from **Hartford** to **Brattleboro**, an 88-mile ride. Take Exit 2 in Vermont and turn left (east) into Brattleboro.

Also note: I-91 intersects the Boston to Lenox route (see pp. 112–117) at two points. At W. Springfield, exit onto I-90 (Massachusetts Turnpike) for a direct drive east to Boston or west to Lenox and the Berkshires. At Greenfield, take the slower, more scenic Rte 2 to the same destinations.

SCENIC ROUTE

To begin this route, just under 120 miles long, follow I-91 from Hartford 19 miles to Exit 49 at **Longmeadow**, the first town in Massachusetts. From the exit turn right onto Rte 5, which passes several historic colonial homes on the town green. After 3.8 miles, the road descends toward the Connecticut River and the city of Springfield, passing Forest Park.

Rte 5 returns to I-91. Follow I-91 to Exit 17B, then take Rte 141 west toward **Easthampton**. This climbs up and over a shoulder of **Mt. Tom**, offering a view of Easthampton and **Southampton** to the north and west. After descending, take the first right onto *East St* and follow it to Rte 5 at the Connecticut River. Turn north (left) and follow Rte 5 2.5 miles into **Northampton**.

At the city's main intersection, turn right onto Rte 9 east and drive two miles, crossing the river to the junction of Rte 47. Turn right and follow Rte 47 to South Hadley, 8.3 miles, skirting the **Holyoke Range**. Look out for a signpost on the left documenting the crest of floods.

In the centre of South Hadley, turn left onto Rte 116 north. Keep left at a triangular island near the **Mount Holyoke College** campus. Rte 116 then curves to the right and left on its way up to **the Notch**. Rte 116 is quite steep and curving as it drops into Amherst. Use care and a low gear, if needed. After passing **Hampshire College** on the left and **Amherst College** on the right, Rte 116 reaches the Amherst town common. Turn left onto joined Rtes 9 and 116. Stay on Rte 9 for 4 miles to the centre of **Hadley** and turn right (north) onto Rte 47, which runs along tobacco, onion, potato and strawberry fields and the Connecticut River on its way to **Sunderland**.

In the centre of Sunderland, turn left onto Rte 116 and cross the river, with **Mt. Sugarloaf** looming above. Follow Rte 116 to the intersection of Rtes 5 and 10. Turn right (north), continuing on Rtes 5 and 10 for 5 miles to a sign for **Historic Deerfield**. Turn left, then bear right after 0.1 mile for a visit to 'The Street'. This goes a mile through the village before it turns right, back to the highway. Turn left onto Rtes 5 and 10 and continue to **Greenfield**, 2.5 miles.

After passing a raised railway bed atop a block wall, turn right and drive under the railroad overpass and uphill. Turn left at the intersection and follow Rte 2A west, bearing left after downtown, still on 2A, to a roundabout (rotary) at I-91. Take the first ramp to your right onto I-91 north. After 7.5 miles, take Exit 28A and turn right, following Rte 10 to **Northfield**. Where Rte 10 joins Rte 63, turn left and head into the town centre. Remain on Rte 63 after it bears left and passes through **Winchester, N.H.**, on the way to **Hinsdale, N.H.**, where it meets Rte 119. Turn left (west) and follow 119 until it crosses the Connecticut River into **Brattleboro**.

HARTFORD TO SPRINGFIELD

Tourist Information: Connecticut's North Central Tourism Bureau, *111 Hazard Ave, Enfield, CT 06082; tel: (860) 763-2578 or toll-free (800) 248-8283.*

Chain hotels and motor inns can be found at most interchanges along I-91 between Hartford and Springfield.

Two attractions are reached from I-91 Exit 40. The **New England Air Museum**, *Rte 75, Windsor Locks, CT 06096; tel: (860) 623-3305*, at Bradley International Airport, contains two hangars full of historic aircraft. Open daily 1000–1700, $6.50. **Old New-gate**

185

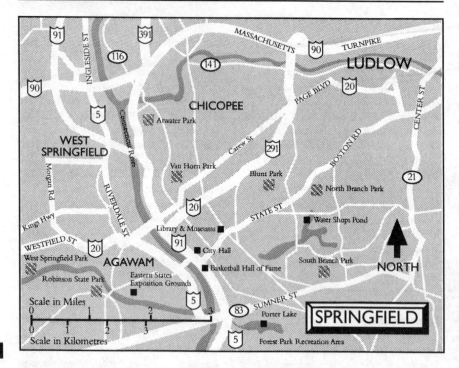

186

Prison, *Newgate Rd, E. Granby, CT 06026; tel: (860) 653-3563 or 566-3005*, began as a copper mine in 1707 but later became a prison for Tories and convicts in 1773. Though they probably didn't see it, the view of a valley outside the prison is pleasing. Open Wed–Sun 1000–1630 (mid-May–Oct), $3.

Riverside Park, *1623 Main St, Agawam, MA 01001; tel: (413) 786-9300*, is the largest amusement park in New England, featuring rides, stock car races and rock concerts. Open daily, hours vary (early Apr–late Oct), $12–$22. From I-91, take Exit 47W in Connecticut or Exit 3 in Massachusetts.

SPRINGFIELD

Tourist Information: Greater Springfield Convention & Visitors Bureau, *34 Boland Way, Springfield, MA*

01103; tel: (413) 787-1548 or toll-free (800) 723-1548.

ACCOMMODATION

Sh, Ma and more affordable *Hd* are in Springfield; other chain hotels are on Rte 5 (*Riverdale St*) in W. Springfield, across the river.

EATING AND DRINKING

The Student Prince and Fort, *8 Fort St; tel: (413) 734-7475*, offers German and American fare and has a large collection of steins (earthenware beer mugs) and glassware. Moderate. **Sitar**, *1688 Main St; tel: (413) 732-8011*, serves Indian and Pakistani dishes, including vegetarian. Delicious breads. Dinner is budget–moderate, weekday lunch specials, cheap.

The Tavern, *53 W. Gardner St at W. Columbus Ave; tel: (413) 736-0456*, next to the highway, is casual and convenient. Budget– moderate.

ENTERTAINMENT

The Springfield Symphony performs at **Symphony Hall**, *Court St; tel: (413) 787-6600*, beside the 300-foot **Campanile** tower, both facing **Court Square**, off I-91 Exit 6. **Stage West**, *1 Columbus Center; tel: (413) 781-2340*, is the home of a theatre company presenting US and English drama, comedies and musicals, two blocks north.

EVENTS

The Eastern States Exposition, 'the Big E,' New England's largest state fair, a collaborative effort between the states, is held mid-Sept in W. Springfield.

SIGHTSEEING

Two art museums, a science and a history museum ring a quiet quadrangle behind the city library at *State* and *Chestnut Sts* and constitute **The Springfield Museums**, *220 State St, Springfield, MA 01103; tel: (413) 739-3871*, open Thur–Sun 1200–1600; Wed–Sun (June–Aug), $4 admission to all four. **The Basketball Hall of Fame**, *1150 W. Columbus Ave, Springfield, MA 01101; tel: (413) 781-6500*, open daily 0900–1700 (Sept–June); 0900–1800 (July–early Sept), $7, is a shrine to the sport invented in this city in 1891. A college athletics professor, James Naismith, was given two weeks to devise a game that would bring into line a group of rugby and football players studying to become executive secretaries. He hung a peach basket in the gym and told them to throw a ball into it.

The small **Indian Motocycle Museum**, *33 Hendee St, Springfield, MA 01139; tel: (413) 737-2624*, open daily 1000–1700, $3, is best enjoyed by motor-cycle enthusiasts. 'Indians' were manufactured here beginning in 1901. Indian owners and fans from all over the US gather each July for a rally. There's a small-arms collection on display at the **Springfield Armory**, *1 Armory Sq; tel: (413) 734-8551*, open daily 1000–1700, free. Gen. George Washington chose this site for the first US arsenal in 1777. It later became an armoury and the manufacturing site of the famed Springfield rifle.

SPRINGFIELD TO NORTHAMPTON

The shops along *Riverdale St* (Rte 5) in W. Springfield can meet your needs for travel supplies. From I-91 Exit 13B, take Rte 5 south. There's a *HI* in Holyoke at I-91 Exit 15.

Nick's Nest, *1597 Northampton St, Holyoke; tel: (413) 532-5229*, is a tiny hot dog shop worth visiting, if only to see how the employees manage to open the door for you without leaving their post behind the counter. No electronics involved. Cheap. Take I-91 Exit 17A to Rte 5 and go right at the traffic light. **The Log Cabin**, *500 Easthampton Rd, Rte 141, Holyoke; tel: (413) 536-7700*, moderate–pricey, and **Harvest Valley Restaurant**, next door; *tel: (413) 532-1664*, moderate, offer dining with a valley view.

Mt. Tom State Reservation, *Rte 141, Holyoke; tel: (413) 527-4805*, has 30 miles of hiking trails, good views. **Mt. Tom Ski Area**, *Rte 5, Holyoke, MA 01040; tel: (413) 536-0416*, offers modest ski slopes in winter, a water slide and wave pool in summer.

NORTHAMPTON

Tourist information: Northampton Chamber of Commerce, *62 State St, Northampton, MA 01060; tel: (413) 584-1900*, runs a booth on *King St* across from

187

the Hotel Northampton, open Tues–Sun 0900–1700 (late May–mid-Oct). **Berkshire Bed & Breakfast Homes**, P.O. Box 211, Williamsburg, MA 01096; tel: (413) 268-7244, fax: (413) 268-7243, can make reservations for home stays or bed and breakfasts in the valley.

ACCOMMODATION

The **Hotel Northampton**, 36 King St; tel: (413) 584-3100, is the best location for those who want to stay in the heart of this small city. Expensive. For a quieter location, try **The Autumn Inn**, 259 Elm St; tel: (413) 584-7660, which has a secluded pool, but also a two-night minimum Apr–Oct. Moderate to expensive. There's also a DI.

EATING AND DRINKING

East of Rte 5, Main St has become 'Restaurant Row'. Choose from Greek, Japanese and sushi, regional Italian, Thai, pizza slices, Indian and authentic Mexican food or the French country deli. **Northampton Brewery**, 11 Brewster Ct; tel: (413) 584-9903, serves sandwiches and pub fare along with ales, lagers, stout, Bock and bitter.

Paul and Elizabeth's, Thorne's Market, 150 Main St; tel: (413) 584-4832, offers natural foods, vegetarian lunches and dinners, fish. Budget–moderate. West of Look Park on Rte 9 is the **Look Restaurant**, 410 N. Main St, Leeds; tel: (413) 584-9850, which serves good breakfast with homemade bread. Cheap.

Continue further west to try **Squires Smoke and Game Club**, 132 Main St, Haydenville; tel: (413) 268-7222, which smokes or grills beef, rabbit, squab, duck, even vegetarian dishes. Heed the writing on the wall: 'When a man or woman meets their maker, they will have to account for those pleasures of life they have failed to experience.' The restaurant is located by a waterfall behind the Brassworks building, six miles west of downtown Northampton on Rte 9. Moderate.

The city's finest restaurant is **Green Street Café**, 64 Green St; tel: (413) 586-5650, a relaxed bistro where food is taken seriously and the decor is a mix of sophistication and whimsy. Note the Nixon table, whose surface is laminated with Watergate-era news clippings. Moderate.

ENTERTAINMENT

Pleasant Street Theatre, 27 Pleasant St; tel: (413) 586-0935, and **The Academy of Music**, 274 Main St; tel: (413) 584-8435, keep the city abreast of recent cinema. The Academy is a grand, old opera house where the Swedish soprano Jenny Lind performed in 1851 and called the city the 'Paradise of America'.

Pearl Street, 10 Pearl St; tel: (413) 584-7771, offers live, boisterous music some nights, disco dancing on others, retro nights and gay nights. **Fire and Water**, 5 Old South St; tel: (413) 586-8336, presents performance art and music, poetry readings; serves salads, vegetarian sandwiches and soups. Cheap.

SIGHTSEEING AND SHOPPING

Northampton is the home of **Smith College**, one of the foremost US women's colleges. The community derives its personality equally from students, young professionals, hippies nearing retirement, a proud lesbian, gay and bisexual population, and plain old folks. Writers, artists, a few transvestites and street musicians add to the mix. Tolerance runs high.

Many former patients from a state hospital for the mentally ill, now closed, have come to depend on the social services and support found here and have made it their home. They roam the streets, some homeless, most harmless. Expect requests for philanthropy.

Words and Images Museum, *140 Main St; tel: (413) 586-8545,* pays tribute to comic book art, which made the founder, one of two artists who created the Teenage Mutant Ninja Turtles, a millionaire. The art pleases both children and adults. Open Tues–Sun 1200–1700, Thur to 2100, Sat to 1800, $3.

Smith College Museum of Art, *Tryon Hall, Elm St at Bedford Terrace; tel: (413) 585-2760,* includes works by Matisse, Picasso, Seurat, Gauguin, Monet and more. Open Tues–Sun 1200–1600 (July–Aug); earlier openings rest of year, free.

The botanical gardens around **Lyman Plant House,** on the Smith College campus, *tel: (413) 585-2748,* were designed by Frederick Law Olmsted (1822-1903), the landscape architect who designed Boston's parks and New York's Central Park.

Sample the city's art and craft galleries along *Main St,* which feature many local artists who have won wider acclaim in the art world. Antiques enthusiasts can find several dealers operating from **The Antiques Center,** *9½ Market St,* and elsewhere along *Market St,* but don't miss the boats, canoes and offbeat finds at the **Ross Brothers,** *28 N. Maple St.* It's worth a trip to Florence, a section of Northampton, 2.5 miles west of downtown on Rte 9.

Northampton Film Festival presents independent film-makers and their works in late Oct or early Nov, after the leaves have fallen. For information, contact **Northampton Film Associates;** *tel: (413) 586-3471.*

Norwottuck Rail Trail is a paved bicycle path, starting above the western bank of the Connecticut River at **Elwell State Park,** just north of I-91 Exit 19, and running east through Hadley, ending a few miles beyond the campus of Amherst College. **Look Memorial Park,** *N. Main St, Florence; tel: (413) 584-5457,* has tennis courts, picnic areas, a playground, pedal boats, a children's train and family concerts during the summer; $2 per car.

Soak your muscles and bones at **East Heaven Hot Tubs,** *33 West St; tel: (413) 586-6843,* which has a soothing, Japanese atmosphere, lots of teak and indoor and outdoor tubs; $11–$12.50 per person for 30 mins.

NORTHAMPTON TO AMHERST

A former hotel on **Mt. Holyoke** affords stunning views, especially in the autumn, when trees are ablaze with colour. The white structure seen in the north is the Peace Pagoda, a shrine built by a local Buddhist community. The old hotel is now a visitor centre at **Skinner State Park,** *Rte 47, P.O. Box 91, Hadley, MA 01035; tel: (413) 586-0350.* Park open Mon–Fri 0800–sunset, Sat–Sun 1000–sunset; auto road open Apr–Nov, $2 per auto Sat, Sun 1000–1930. The **Metacomet-Monadnock Trail** follows the ridge west to the river and east to **The Notch Visitor Center** in **Holyoke Range State Park,** *Rte 116, South Hadley; tel: (413) 253-2883,* open daily 0800–1630; closed Tues–Wed (Nov–Apr), free.

Shops and eateries can be found at **The Village Commons,** at the junction of Rtes 47 and 116 in South Hadley, which is the home of **Mount Holyoke,** another exclusive women's college. **Musicorda**

Festival, *P.O. Box 557, S. Hadley, MA 01075; tel: (413) 538-2590* stages classical music concerts on Fri and Sun eves, late June–early Aug, on the Mount Holyoke College campus, Rtes 47 and 116. **Summer Theater at Mount Holyoke College**, *S. Hadley 01075; tel: (413) 538-2632*, stages plays for children in an outdoor amphitheatre, $4, and for adults in a tent, $16–$18.

AMHERST

Tourist Information: Amherst Chamber of Commerce, *11 Spring St, Amherst, MA 01002; tel: (413) 253-0700*, prints a brochure of inns and bed and breakfasts in Hampshire County and runs an information booth on the town common, open daily 1100–1600 (May–Oct).

ACCOMMODATION AND FOOD

The **Lord Jeffery Inn**, *30 Boltwood Ave, Amherst, MA 01002; tel: (413) 253-2576*, a country inn on the common, is named for Baron Jeffery Amherst, a British army officer (1717-97). Moderate–expensive. In the next town, **The Tin Roof**, *P.O. Box 296, Hadley, MA 01035; tel: (413) 586-8665*, is a budget bed and breakfast with shared bathrooms, lovely gardens and an exercise room. The clientele are all women, predominantly lesbian. Reservations required. Head out of town for great barbecued food. From Rte 9, take Rte 116 north to Sunderland and **Bub's Bar-B-Q**, *Amherst Rd; tel: (413) 548-9630*. Budget–moderate.

SIGHTSEEING AND RECREATION

Amherst is a college town, location of the main campus of the huge, state-owned **University of Massachusetts** and **Amherst College**, a small, prestigious liberal arts college. The town centre has an array of shops, cafés, bookstores and

restaurants, stretching 0.4 mile north of the common on or near *Pleasant St.*

Park at the town common and walk 0.2 mile east to the **Emily Dickinson Homestead**, *260 Main St, Amherst; tel: (413) 542-8161*. This house once constituted the world of one of America's greatest poets and recluses, known as 'the Belle of Amherst'; now it's a residence for Amherst faculty. Grounds open daily 1000–1700; selected rooms are open for tours, by appointment only, Wed–Sat 1330–1600 (May–Oct); Wed and Sat only (Oct–mid-Dec and Mar–May), $3.

The **Hitchcock Center**, *525 S. Pleasant St, Rte 116; tel: (413) 256-6006*, is a nature and environmental education centre, with short hiking trails. Amherst has established an extensive system of conservation land. Contact the conservation office in town hall for a map and information; *tel: (413) 256-4045*.

ENTERTAINMENT

The main campus of The University of Massachusetts is northwest of the town centre. Its **Fine Arts Center**; *tel: (413) 545-2511 or (800) 999-8627*, presents theatre, dance, orchestral, jazz and rock concerts and other cultural attractions.

Katina's, *Russell St, Rte 9, Hadley; tel: (413) 586-4463*, is a nightclub for those who like their rock hard. Parking is on the other side of Rte 9, which presents the challenge of crossing in the dark without getting killed. Several have failed. Use extreme caution.

AMHERST TO GREENFIELD

Tourist Information: In Springfield; also: **Massachusetts Department of Food and Agriculture**, *100 Cambridge St, Boston, MA 02202; tel: (617) 727-3018*, ext. 171, distributes an agricultural tourism directory of 150 sites, some of which welcome visitors for farm stays. **The Deerfield Inn**, *The Street, Deerfield, MA 01342; tel: (413) 774-5587*, places you at the centre of a preserved museum town. Expensive–pricey. Buy candles or learn the art of the chandler in a free tour at **Yankee Candle Company**, *Rte 5, S. Deerfield; tel: (413) 665-2929*. Santa Claus is here, too, in a Bavarian Christmas Village. **Mt. Sugarloaf**, *off Rte 116, S. Deerfield; tel: (413) 665-5587*, offers a panoramic view of the valley. A road goes to the summit. Open daily 0800–sunset (May to Oct).

Walk through **Historic Deerfield**, *Box 321, Deerfield, MA 01342; tel: (413) 774-5581*, and take guided tours of 14 museum houses. This preserved community opens its doors so people can get a look at life on the frontier of New England in the 17th and 18th centuries. Most of the remaining homes, though, date from the 18th and 19th centuries. The homes are filled with antiques and works of decorative arts.

Museum houses and the information centre, across from the Deerfield Inn, are open daily 0930–1630, $5 per house. **Memorial Hall Museum**, *Memorial St, Deerfield, MA 01342; tel: (413) 774-7476*, tells the town's story, including an attack and kidnapping by French and Indian forces in 1704.

GREENFIELD

Tourist Information: Franklin County Chamber of Commerce, *395 Main St, P.O. Box 790-W, Greenfield, MA 01301; tel: (413) 773-5463*, publishes an accommodation list and runs an information booth at the Howard Johnson motor lodge, just south of I-91 on Rte 2. Open daily 1000–1700 (mid-June–mid-Oct); Sat–Sun (late-May–mid-June). Find motels on Rte 2 just north of I-91. Restaurants

and coffee shops dot Greenfield's *Main St* and extend north on Rte 2A. **Green Field's Market**, *144 Main St; tel: (413) 773-9567*, is a natural foods co-op with excellent baked goods and deli menu.

GREENFIELD TO BRATTLEBORO

Penfrydd Farm, *RR1, Box 100A, Colrain, MA 01340; tel: (413) 624-5516*, a bed and breakfast in a 19th-century house, is west of Greenfield, off the route, but well worth the trip for a farm-stay; moderate.

Monroe and Isabel Smith AYH-Hostel, *51 Highland Ave, Box 2602, Northfield, MA 01360; tel: (413) 498-3505* mid-June–Sept, *498-5983* rest of year. Reservations essential on weekends. Budget.

Northfield Mountain Recreation and Environmental Center, *99 Millers Falls Rd, Northfield, MA 01360; tel: (413) 659-3714*, offers tours to **Powerhouse Cavern**, where a hydroelectric plant generates power from water falling from a reservoir on top of the mountain, plus exhibits, 25 miles of trails and a cross-country ski centre. It's located 5.3 miles south of the junction of Rtes 10 and 63. Open Wed–Sun 0900–1700 (May–mid-Oct), free.

The riverboat at **Quinnetukut II** cruises 12 miles of the Connecticut, leaving from **Riverview Picnic Area**, *across Rte 63 from the centre; tel: (413) 659-3714*. The 90-min tours are hosted by a naturalist; departures Wed–Sun 1100, 1315, 1500.

Watch live greyhound racing and simulcasts of dog, thoroughbred and harness racing at **Hinsdale Greyhound Park**, *Rte 119, Hinsdale, NH 03451; tel: (800) 648-7225*. Open all year. Two restaurants.

191

LENOX AND THE BERKSHIRES

Fortunately for all the travellers who are drawn every summer to the Berkshires, these hills also exert a strong pull on artists, dancers, writers and actors. The cultural calendar on any summer night offers a wealth of possibilities and is likely to frustrate only those who want to see it all. The area lately has also become a mecca for the New Age movement. You can spend a day at a yoga centre, find sustenance in a natural foods store, or indulge yourself with a therapeutic massage or aromatherapy.

Lenox is the well preserved New England village at the heart of the Berkshires and its culture. Stockbridge has been home to several artists, from the illustrator Norman Rockwell, who captured optimistic scenes of Americana (using locals as models) to Daniel Chester French, the sculptor whose seated Abraham Lincoln is one of Washington, D.C.'s most popular monuments.

West Stockbridge is far less manicured but just as occupied with art as Stockbridge, while Pittsfield, with a population close to 50,000, is the Berkshires' only city with downtown stores, hotels and a minor-league baseball team.

TOURIST INFORMATION

Berkshire Visitors Bureau, *Berkshire Common, Pittsfield, MA 01201; tel: (800) 237-5747,* publishes several guides including one for disabled travellers. **Pittsfield Information Booth** is downtown on *Bank Row,* open Mon–Thu 0900–1700, Fri–Sat 0900–2000, Sun 1000–1400. **Lenox Chamber of Commerce,** *75 Main St, P.O. Box 646, Lenox, MA 01240; tel: (413) 637-3646 or (800) 25-LENOX,* offers a lodging referral service.

The **West Stockbridge Tourist Information** kiosk is in the car park next to the Shaker Mill Tavern, across the bridge from the junction of Rtes 102 and 41. Open late May–12 Oct. **Stockbridge Chamber of Commerce,** *P.O. Box 224, Stockbridge, MA 01262; tel: (413) 298-5200.*

Help yourself to information at the booth on *Main St* in the centre of the village. **Stockbridge Lodging Association,** *Box 224, Stockbridge, MA 01262; tel: (413) 298-5327,* publishes a brochure of member inns. Lee also has a booth at the bottom of *Main St.* **Lee Chamber of Commerce,** *Railroad St, P.O. Box 345, Lee, MA 01238; tel: (413) 243-0852.* **Great Barrington-Southern Berkshire Chamber of Commerce,** *362 Main St, Great Barrington, MA 01230; tel: (413) 528-1510.*

GETTING AROUND

Berkshire Regional Transit Association, *67 Downing Pkwy, Pittsfield, MA 01202; tel: (800) 292-2782,* connects Pittsfield, Lenox, Stockbridge and Great Barrington. Write or call for timetables.

Aarow Taxi, *tel: (413) 499-8604,* serves Pittsfield and Lenox. **Rainbow**

Taxi, tel: (413) 499-4300, Pittsfield. Lenox. **Park Taxi**, tel: (413) 243-0020 and **Abbott's Limousine & Livery**, tel: (413) 243-1645, serve Lee. **Stockbridge Livery**, tel: (413) 298-4848, Stockbridge. **Taxico**, tel: (413) 528-0911, Great Barrington.

If you're driving, invest $3.25 in a **Jimapco Road Map** of Berkshire County, which includes 14 detailed maps of communities with virtually every road labelled. They're available in convenience stores and bookstores, or contact **Jimapco**, Box 1137, Clifton Park, NY 12065; tel: (518) 899-5091.

STAYING IN LENOX AND THE BERKSHIRES

Accommodation

Inns abound in Lenox, Stockbridge and surrounding towns. Most fall in the expensive to pricey range. More economical motels, including QI, S8, Su and TL, can be found on and near Rtes 20 and 7. You'll find Hn in Pittsfield, expensive. If you plan on a summer or fall visit, make reservations during the previous winter or early spring.

The Red Lion Inn, Main St, Stockbridge, MA 01262; tel: (413) 298-5545 is a geographical and historical benchmark where Rte 7 leaves Rte 102 and heads south to Great Barrington. The inn has hosted guests since 1773. It's popular and crowded during the summer and fall. The best seats in the house are the rockers on the porch. Expensive.

The Historic Merrell Inn, 1565 Pleasant St, Rte 102, South Lee, MA 01260; tel: (413) 243-1794, is an old stagecoach inn where the milk is still delivered to the front porch in bottles Tues and Fri mornings. Though the quality remains high, the innkeepers have reduced their prices. Always enquire about special rates. Moderate to expensive.

Sunset Farm Bed and Breakfast Inn, 74 Main Rd, Tyringham, offers lodging in an old farmhouse far from the crowds, with shared bath and a restaurant open Fri and Sat for lunch and dinner. Mailing address is 74 Tyringham Rd, Lee, MA 01238; tel: (413) 243-3229. Moderate.

Olde White Horse Inn, 378 South St, Pittsfield, MA 01201; tel: (413) 442-2512, is a bed and breakfast on a main thoroughfare but set back, built in 1907. Moderate to expensive. **The Williamsville Inn**, Rte 41, W. Stockbridge, MA 01266; tel: (413) 274-6118. keeps a sculpture garden from June–Oct. Storytellers and poets entertain at Sunday dinner from Nov–Apr. Expensive.

The Old Inn on the Green & Gedney Farm, Rte 57, Star Rte 70, New Marlborough, MA 01230; tel: (413) 229-3131, is a restored 18th-century inn and a barn with two-storey suites. Moderate to pricey. **The Village Inn**, 16 Church St, Lenox, MA 01240; tel: (800) 253-0917 or (413) 637-0020, serves an afternoon tea with scones and clotted cream. During the winter, the inn, which went into business in 1815, holds several authentic English high teas with chamber music. The tavern downstairs, formerly a stables, features poetry readings and music. Expensive. **Amadeus House**, 15 Cliffwood St, Lenox, MA 01240; tel: (413) 637-4770. Moderate to pricey.

The Egremont Inn, Old Sheffield Rd, S Egremont, MA 01258; tel: (413) 528-2111, dates to 1780 but has pool and tennis courts. Moderate to expensive.

Blantyre, 16 Blantyre Rd, Lenox; tel: (413) 637-3556 (summer), (413) 298-3806 (winter), is a baronial Tudor mansion built in 1902 and restored in the 1980s to an inn

193

with gourmet restaurant, swimming pool, tennis courts and croquet lawn. It was modelled after a home in Blantyre, a village east of Glasgow, Scotland. Pricey for both lodging and meals. Closed Nov–mid-May.

The best camping is at state forest campsites. However, be warned that because of state budget cutbacks, phone calls often get no reply, especially off-season. **October Mountain State Forest**, *Woodland Rd, Lee, MA 01238; tel: (413) 243-1778*, has 50 tent pitches and RV sites, dump stations for trailers and RVs. **Pittsfield State Forest**, *Cascade Rd, Pittsfield, MA 01201; tel: (413) 442-8992*, and **Beartown State Forest**, *Blue Hill Rd, Monterey, MA 01245; tel: (413) 528-0904*, are better for car and tent camping. For those who want to leave the car behind, **Mt Washington State Forest**, *East St, Mt Washington, MA 01258; tel: (413) 528-0330*, has 15 wilderness pitches.

Eating and Drinking

Several establishments in Lenox and Stockbridge serve picnic lunches or dinners that can be enjoyed before an arts performance, beside a lake or along a hiking trail. **Loeb Foodtown**, *42 Main St, Lenox, MA 01240; tel: (413) 637-0270*, sells budget picnics with sandwiches or barbecued chicken and salads as well as beer, wine and produce. **Crosby's Catering**, *56 Church St, Lenox 01240; tel: (413) 637-3396*, packs upscale picnic boxes. Moderate.

Naji's, *40 Main St, Stockbridge, MA 01262; tel: (413) 298-5465*, is a tiny café down an alley off *Main St* where you can order Middle Eastern food, sandwiches or pizza, cheap to moderate, or choose from a variety of picnic baskets: taboulli, baba ganouj and grape leaves to filet mignon and marinated artichoke salad. Moderate.

Call ahead to give them appropriate time to prepare your choice.

In Lenox, **Suchèle Bakers**, *31 Housatonic St; tel: (413) 637-0939*, makes tea loaves, tarts, tortes and, in summer, fresh fruit pies. Coffee lovers converge on **The Berkshire Coffee Roasting Company**, *52 Main St; tel: (413) 637-1606*.

The Church Street Cafe, *65 Church St; tel: (413) 637-2745* is a bistro with good canned music and excellent food. Moderate to pricey. Just down the street is **Café Lucia**, *90 Church St; tel: (413) 637-2640*, an intimate Italian restaurant. Moderate. **Candlelight Inn**, *53 Walker St; tel: (413) 637-1555*, has a backyard garden where you can have lunch or dinner. Moderate to expensive. Also open for drinks and dessert after evening concerts.

Dakota, *Rte 7* on the Lenox-Pittsfield town line; *tel: (413) 499-7900*, is a rustic family restaurant with an extensive salad bar, with decor from the American West. Moderate.

Lee has two good ethnic restaurants. **Cactus Café**, *54 Main St, Lee, MA 01238; tel: (413) 243-4300*, serves authentic Mexican food, especially pleasing to those who like it hot. Moderate. **Paradise of India**, *5 Railroad St; tel: (413) 243-0500*. Budget to moderate.

Besides making varied flavours of homemade ice-cream, the dairy farmer who owns **The Berkshire Ice Cream Co.**, *4 Albany Rd, Rte 2, W. Stockbridge, MA 01266; tel:(413) 232-4111*, sells stock in his cows. Word has it that his livestock pay handsome dividends. Open all year. Pizza, muffins and other foods are also available at the shop, on the mill pond. Cheap. Also in W. Stockbridge, **Truc Orient Express**, *Harris St; tel: (413) 232-4204*, serves gracious Vietnamese lunches and dinners, offering respite from the New

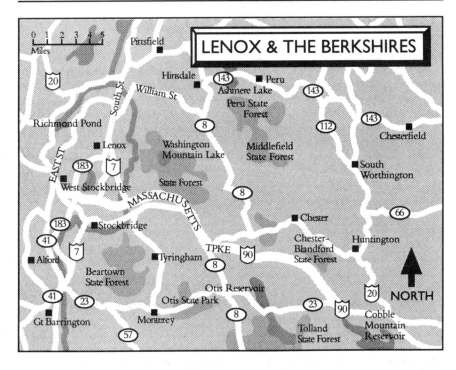

England Americana that characterizes most of this village, with al fresco dining. Budget–moderate. **La Bruschetta Ristorante**, *1 Harris St; tel: (413) 232-7141*, serves continental and Italian dinners, open Fri–Sun in winter, closed Wed in spring, summer and fall. Moderate.

A meal at **Jack's Grill & Restaurant**, *Main St, Housatonic, MA 01236; tel: (413) 274-1000*, must be accompanied by a scenic ride on Rte 183 along the Housatonic River. Budget to moderate.

ENTERTAINMENT

The Boston Symphony Orchestra played its first concert on the grounds of a Lenox mansion called Erskine Park in Lenox in 1936. Now, the orchestra's summer home is **Tanglewood,** a 500-acre estate on *West St* where visitors can bring a picnic and sprawl on a blanket beneath the stars

to hear the music. During concert season, July–Aug; *tel: (413) 637-5165*. From Sept–June, write or call *Symphony Hall, 301 Massachusetts Ave, Boston, MA 02115; tel: (617) 266-1492*.

The Finnish architect Eliel Saarinen was commissioned in 1937 to design a permanent structure for the concerts on the Tanglewood estate. His design was more expensive than fund-raisers could afford, though. The committee wanted something simpler. Saarinen is said to have retorted 'If you build it that way, you'll end up with nothing but a shed!' The BSO did just that. Stockbridge engineer Joseph Franz simplified the design and the structure has ever since been lovingly referred to as 'the Shed'. If you want to see the musicians, get a seat in the Shed. It's more expensive, but not as fun.

A new music hall opened on the

grounds in 1994, supplementing the Shed. The grounds are open for a stroll except during concerts and an hour beforehand. A weekend of jazz concerts typically closes the season in early Sept. **South Mountain Concerts**, *Rtes 7 and 20, P.O. Box 23, Pittsfield, MA 01202; tel: (413) 442-2106*, presents chamber music on the top of a mountain.

The National Music Center, *40 Kemble St, Lenox, MA 01240; tel: (413) 637-4718*, is the home of the non-profit National Music Foundation. The centre holds educational workshops and lectures and serves as a retirement home for professional musicians.

Author Edith Wharton set her novel *Ethan Frome* in Starkfield, a fictional town closely resembling Lenox Village. The sledging incident in the story is based on a similar event that took place around the turn of the century on the hill that begins at the monument in the centre and runs down *Stockbridge Rd*. Wharton's home, **The Mount**, south of the junction of Rtes 7 and 7A; *tel: (413) 637-1899*, a mansion built in 1902, is under restoration and open for tours; $4.50–$6.

On summer afternoons and evenings, Shakespearean and contemporary plays are performed on the grounds and indoors by an acclaimed troupe, **Shakespeare & Co.**, *tel: (413) 637-1199* or summer box office *(413) 637-3353*. Adaptations of Wharton's shorter works are performed in the mansion's drawing room.

The Berkshire Theater Festival, *E. Main St, Box 797, Stockbridge, MA 01262; tel: (413) 298-5536* or summer box office *(413) 298-5576*, is one of the oldest summer theatre companies in the US. Katharine Hepburn, James Cagney and Dustin Hoffman are only a few of the players who have trodden its boards since 1928. Major works have been performed,

by playwrights such as Tennessee Williams, Lillian Hellman and Eugene O'Neill.

The Berkshire Museum's Little Cinema, *39 South St, Pittsfield; tel: (413) 443-7171*, shows foreign and US films, steering blissfully clear of mainstream Hollywood fare.

Some of the world's best dance companies make summer stops at **Jacob's Pillow Dance Festival**, *George Carter Rd, off Rte 20, Becket, P.O. Box 287, Lee, MA 01238; tel:* (seasonal box office) *(413) 243-0745*. Besides featured performances in an intimate auditorium, free performances take place on an outdoor stage and visitors can watch choreography taking shape in rehearsal studios.

Eat al fresco at the **Pillow Café** or bring your own refreshments to the picnic area.

When you're sated with all this highbrow culture, take yourself out to the ball game. You won't, however, manage to escape the Berkshires' scenic splendour. **Wahconah Park**, home of the **Pittsfield Mets**, *105 Wahconah St, P.O. Box 328, Pittsfield, MA 01202; tel: (413) 499-6387*, a minor league team affiliated to the New York Mets, is a rare find – a ball park with a view of the mountains, and one of few parks where the game is regularly delayed when the setting sun shines into the eyes of the batter, catcher and umpire. A family of four can see a game for less than $25. The season runs from mid-June–Aug and includes a fireworks display on or near the Fourth of July.

There are corners of the Berkshires where music other than classical flourishes. Several of these corners are in southern Berkshire County. **Bucksteep Manor**, *Washington Mountain Rd, Becket, MA 01223; tel: (800) 645-2825*, tends toward country bands and eclectic music. **The**

Lion's Den, is a downstairs pub at the Red Lion Inn in Stockbridge that has a regular schedule of blues, folk, jazz and country. *Tel: (413) 298-5545.* **Jay's**, *1220 North St, Pittsfield, MA 01201; tel: (413) 442-0767*, offers various rock bands and comedians.

Events

The Lenox Tub Parade looks back to a turn-of-the-century tradition, a procession of flower-bedecked, pony-drawn carts through the village. The tradition has lately been revived each autumn. The Chamber of Commerce can provide the precise date; *tel: (800) 255-3669.*

A **Harvest Festival**, at the **Berkshire Botanical Garden**, *Rtes 102 and 183, Stockbridge, MA 01262; tel: (413) 298-3926*, in early Oct is the time to buy plants, seeds, pumpkins, apple cider, doughnuts and local crafts. Fifteen acres of herb, perennial and vegetable gardens. The centre is open daily May–Oct; $5.

SHOPPING

The Lenox House Country Shops, *55 Pittsfield-Lenox Rd*, are upmarket, in a faux-New England village setting off busy Rtes 7 and 20. **1884 House**, *Main St, Stockbridge, MA 01262; tel: (413) 298-5159*, a small brick building which was the original town hall, offers a touch of home. The shop sells Scottish cashmere, Donegal and Harris tweeds, wellies and regimental ties. **Mad Dogs & Englishmen**, *24 Walker St, Lenox, MA 02140; tel: (413) 637-0667*, is a gift shop and a tad offbeat. **Anneegoodchild**, next door at *22 Walker St; tel: (413) 637-0700*, is downright off-the-wall, with nice American primitive art and objects.

Across the street in the Curtis Shops is **The Hand of Man**, *tel: (413) 637-0632*, a craft gallery with products ranging from jewellery and birdhouses to children's toys such as jack-in-the-boxes.

Expect the unexpected at the **Ute Stebich Gallery**, *104 Main St, Lenox, MA 02140; tel: (413) 637-3566*, a wonderfully offbeat series of small rooms where one finds folk art from the US, Europe, the Caribbean and other corners of the world. Open daily 1100–1700 (late June–mid-Sept), Thurs–Sat 1100–1700 (rest of the year), or by appointment.

SIGHTSEEING

Berkshire Hiking Holidays, *P.O. Box 2231, Lenox, MA 01240; tel: (413) 637-4442*, offers inn-based walking vacations that combine outdoor adventure with arts outings at Tanglewood, the Mount, Jacob's Pillow and more.

Besides its American pieces, **The Berkshire Museum**, *39 South St, Pittsfield, MA 01201; tel: (413) 443-7171*, has European works from the 15th to 19th centuries, a regional history collection and a natural science collection. Open Mon 1000–1700 (July and Aug), Tues–Sat 1000–1700, Sun 1300–1700; $3. **Arrowhead**, *780 Holmes Rd, Pittsfield, MA 01201; tel: (413) 442-1793*, besides being the home of Herman Melville, where he wrote *Moby Dick*, is the headquarters of the Berkshire County Historical Society. Open daily 1000–1700 from late May–early Sept, open Fri–Mon in Sept and Oct, by appointment in winter; $3–$4.50.

Hancock Shaker Village, *junction of Rtes 20 and 41, P.O. Box 898, Pittsfield, MA 01202; tel: (413) 443-0188*, is a testament to the life and beliefs of a self-sufficient religious community (See feature box, p. 117). These people were artisans of the highest calibre in a simpler time. Twenty-one buildings have been restored, including a round stone barn. Open

197

Apr–Nov. Ninety-minute tours begin on the hour from 1000–1500. Special events, including antiques sales and craft shows, take place throughout the season. The museum opens occasionally for winter programs; $5–$10, $25 for families. **The Norman Rockwell Museum**, *Rte 183, P.O. Box 308, Stockbridge, MA 01262; tel: (413) 298-4100*, holds the world's largest collection of this popular illustrator's works. Open weekdays 1100–1600, weekends 1000–1700 (Nov–Apr), daily 1000–1700 (May–Oct). Visit the artist's studio on the grounds of the museum; $2–$8.

Chesterwood, *4 Williamsville Rd, Stockbridge, MA 01262; tel: (413) 298-3579*, is the estate of Daniel Chester French, a famous American sculptor, where visitors can take a guided tour of his Colonial Revival house, studio and gardens. An antique auto show is held in May, a flower show in July and an outdoor sculpture exhibit runs July–Oct. The estate is open daily May–Oct, 1000–1700; $6.50. **Naumkeag**, *Prospect Hill Rd, Box 792, Stockbridge, MA 01262; tel: (413) 298-3239*. The summer mansion of a lawyer and diplomat, designed by noted American architect Stanford White, completed in 1886. The gardens are well worth a summer visit but Christmas decorations make Naumkeag a popular stop in Dec; $4–$6.

The Berkshire Scenic Railway Museum, *Housatonic St and Willow Creek Rd, Lenox, MA 01240; tel: (413) 637-2210*, is housed in a restored depot along the Housatonic River. Several train cars, also restored, are on display. Open weekends and holidays, June–Oct. Free admission.

Avid readers should not miss the public libraries in Lenox and Stockbridge. At the **Lenox Library**, *18 Main St, Lenox, MA 01240; tel: (413) 637-0197*, rest your feet in the reading room, which has a stunning array of periodicals, or close your eyes and listen to a recording in the music room. The book collection numbers 75,000 volumes. Novelist Edith Wharton was once a docent here. Open Mon–Sat 1000–1700 (rest of the year). The **Stockbridge Library**, *Main St, Stockbridge, MA 01262; tel: (413) 298-5501*, boasts a salon-style reading room and a historical collection that includes memorabilia of Indians and residents who came along later. Open Tues–Fri 0900–1700, Sat 0900–1600.

Recreation

Stockbridge might be a quiet New England town if it weren't overrun by tourists in the summer and fall. The best way to see its sights and perhaps avoid some of the hordes is to hike or bike along six trails described in a free *Hike and Bike Guide* published by the Laurel Hill Association. Pick up a copy at the *Town Hall, W. Main St, Stockbridge, MA 01262; tel: (413) 298-4714*.

Among the notable destinations are **Bowker's Woods**, on a bend in the Housatonic River; **Ice Glen**, a narrow gorge where you can walk among huge boulders and hemlocks; **Laura's Tower**, which offers magnificent views from on high; and **Butler Bridge**, a footbridge over the Housatonic.

Main Street Sports & Leisure, *48 Main St, Lenox, MA 01240; tel: (413) 637-4407*, rents road and mountain bikes, canoes, in-line skates, tennis racquets and cross-country skis. Ski trails begin just two blocks north and up *Aspinwall Rd* in **John Drummond Kennedy Park**. There is no trail fee.

The same trails wind behind **The Arcadian Shop**, at *Lenox House Country Shops, 55 Pittsfield-Lenox Rd, Lenox, MA*

01240; tel: (413) 637-3010, another good recreational sports shop that rents skis. **Pleasant Valley Wildlife Sanctuary,** on *West Mountain Rd* in Lenox, and **Canoe Meadows Wildlife Sanctuary,** on *Holmes Rd* in Pittsfield, are owned and managed by the Massachusetts Audubon Society. For information on both, contact the society at *472 W Mountain Rd, Lenox, MA 01240; tel: (413) 637-0320.* They are open year round, except Mon and major holidays. Both have cross-country ski trails.

Canoe Meadows is 260 acres of woods, fields, marshes and ponds, only a mile and a half from downtown Pittsfield. Pleasant Valley lies in the shadow of Lenox Mountain. Observe beavers at work in Pike's Pond.

Downhill skiers have several slopes to choose from, mid-Dec–end Mar. **Bousquet,** *Dan Fox Dr, Pittsfield, MA 01201; tel: (413) 442-8316,* is close to downtown Pittsfield, with 21 trails, five lifts and a half-pipe for snowboarders. Open daily 1000–2200, except Sun when it closes at 1600. **Catamount,** *Rte 23, S Egremont, MA 01258; tel: (413) 528-1262,* has 24 trails, six lifts. Open 0830–1600 weekends and holidays; 0900–1600 weekdays. Night skiing, Wed–Sat 1700–2200. **Jiminy Peak,** *Corey Rd, Hancock, MA 01237; tel: (413) 738-5500.* 28 trails, eight lifts. Open weekdays 0900–2230, weekends 0830–2230. **Butternut,** *Rte 23, Great Barrington, MA 01230; tel: (413) 528-2000.* 22 trails, eight lifts.

When enough snow falls, the cross-country skiing is good at **Bucksteep Manor,** *Washington Mountain Rd, Becket, MA 01223; tel: (413) 623-5535,* with 25 km of trails, and at **Beartown** and **Mt Washington** state forests. (See addresses under Accommodation p. 193).

Hike to the top of **Monument Mountain** in Great Barrington and you'll be following in the footsteps of authors Herman Melville and Nathaniel Hawthorne, who met for the first time on a hike in 1850 shortly after Hawthorne finished *The Scarlet Letter.* They are said to have drunk several bottles of champagne on the way to the summit. We suggest just water.

Trail maps available from **The Trustees of Reservations,** *The Mission House, Main St, Stockbridge, MA 01262; tel: (413) 298-3239.* The trustees also manage **Bartholomew's Cobble,** *Weatogue Rd, Ashley Falls,* where more than 700 species of plants grow among the marble and quarzite hills or cobbles on the Housatonic River, and **Tyringham Cobble,** *Jerusalem Rd, Tyringham,* a hillside and rock outcroppings above a picturesque hamlet. For more information on the cobbles, contact the Trustees at the Mission House.

Bash Bish Falls State Park, in Mt Washington State Forest, is difficult to reach in the southeast corner of the state but well worth the trip. Stop and get a map at the state forest headquarters on East St. Signs will also help. The two cascades here cut a gorge 275 ft deep and flow into New York. Legends hold that Bash Bish was an Indian princess who was driven insane by demons and either leapt to her death from the top of the falls and was followed by her lover or was tied to a canoe and pushed off by her father, who disapproved of the lover.

The Kripalu Yoga and Health Center, *Rte 183, Stockbridge, MA 01262; tel: (413) 448-3400,* stands on a 300-acre site above Stockbridge Bowl, a lake, and is blessed with one of the most breathtaking views in the Berkshires. Fittingly, people come here to find spiritual and physical rejuvenation in residential or day programs, which can be had for as little as $25.

BERKSHIRES LOOP

This 120-mile route heads well off the beaten paths of the Berkshires, down country roads and through 'the hill towns' on the border of Berkshire and Hampshire counties. In the stretches between listed attractions lie some of the finest back roads from which to view fall foliage in Massachusetts. Petrol stations and restaurants are rare along parts of this route. Fill up with food and fuel in Great Barrington before starting the loop.

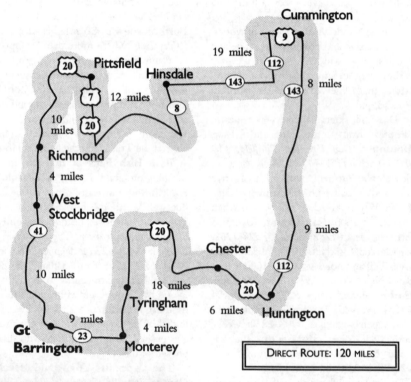

Cummington

19 miles

8 miles

Pittsfield

Hinsdale

12 miles

10 miles

Richmond

4 miles

West Stockbridge

9 miles

10 miles

Chester

18 miles

Tyringham

9 miles

4 miles

6 miles

Huntington

Gt Barrington

Monterey

DIRECT ROUTE: 120 MILES

ROUTE

The loop begins in **Great Barrington** at the **Southern Berkshire Information Center**. Follow *Main St* north through the centre of town, turn right and take Rte 23 east to the centre of **Monterey**, about 9 miles. Turn north (left) and follow *Tyringham Rd* 3.8 miles, turn left onto *Main Rd*, which takes you into **Tyringham**. A Shaker settlement thrived from 1792–1875 in this picturesque valley, drained by **Hop Brook**. On a hill across the valley from the present village, Shaker houses still stand. Continue through the village 4.2 miles to Rte 102. If you're thirsty, draw cold water from a spring pipe at 3.5 miles. Donations accepted in a metal box with a coin slot. Turn right at Rte 102 and bear right onto Rte 20 east. Bear left where Rte 8 north joins Rte 20 east and continue on Rte 20 as it drops and winds into **Chester,** along the West Branch of the Westfield River. In **Huntington,** turn left onto Rte 112, heading up to where the river's Middle Branch and East Branch meet, about a mile north.

Follow Rte 112 to *Ireland St* in **South Worthington.** Turn right and take *Ireland St* three miles to a triangle. Along the way are views of the Berkshire foothills to the west. Bear right and continue on the road. It descends to *River Rd* on the right, which offers access to **Chesterfield Gorge,** carved from granite by glacial ice and the East Branch of the Westfield. Admission: $1.50. No swimming. A mile north of the gorge, cross Rte 143 onto *Cummington Rd* and follow it to *Fairgrounds Rd*. Turn right and continue to Rte 9. Cross onto **Cummington's** *Main St*, which rejoins Rte 9 after 0.7 mile. Turn right and go 0.4 mile to Rte 112 south.

Rte 112 turns, curves and runs a gauntlet of huge sugar maples. After 2.3 miles, leave Rte 112 and take *Cummington Rd* to Rte 143. Turn north and stay on 143, which offers a view to the southwest after about two miles, then splits **Ashmere Lake** on the way to **Peru** and **Hinsdale.** At Hinsdale's traffic light, turn south onto Rte 8. Turn right after 3.3 miles onto *Pittsfield Rd,* which becomes *Kirchner Rd.* At **Burgner's Farm Products,** turn left onto *Williams St.* After 2.1 miles, turn south (left) onto *Holmes Rd.* Follow it past **Arrowhead.** At joined Rtes 7 and 20, turn north (right) and run a gauntlet of a different kind – motels, restaurants, petrol

stations and discount factory outlets. After 0.7 mile of this, turn left on *Dan Fox Dr,* which jogs left and right around **Pittsfield Airport.** Turn left onto *Barker Rd.* Entering **Richmond,** Barker becomes *Swamp Rd.* Follow it 0.2 miles and turn left on *East Rd,* unpaved but easily passable and offering sweeping views of New York State's **Taconic Range.** At the end, turn right onto *Lenox Rd,* then left onto *Swamp Rd,* which continues 3 miles to **West Stockbridge.** Turn left onto the *Main St* of the village and follow Rte 41 for 3.5 miles. Turn right onto *Cobb Rd,* which curves left and becomes *East Alford Rd.* Continue south, bearing left after the village centre onto *Alford Rd,* which becomes *Taconic Ave.* Drive under the railroad trestle and you have returned to the start of the loop.

GREAT BARRINGTON

Tourist Information: Great Barrington Southern Berkshire Chamber of Commerce, *362 Main St, Great Barrington, MA 01230; tel: (413) 528-1510,* makes lodging referrals.

ACCOMMODATION

You'll find it less expensive to stay here than in **Lenox, Stockbridge** and among the pricey inns in the area, but many places have a two- or occasionally a three-night minimum on weekends. Choices, all moderate, include **Mountain View Motel,** *304 State Rd (Rte 23), Great Barrington, MA 01230; tel: (413) 528-0250.* **Littlejohn Manor,** *1 Newsboy Monument Lane (Rte 23), Great Barrington, MA 01230; tel: (413) 528-2882,* serves a full English breakfast and afternoon tea with homemade scones and Scottish shortbread. **Barrington Court Motel,** *400 Stockbridge Rd (Rte 7), Great Barrington, MA 01230; tel: (413) 528-2340,* drops its rate to $50–$60 in the fall. A five-minute drive off the route is **Hidden Acres**, *35 Tremont Dr, Alford, MA 01230; tel: (413) 528-1028*, a bed and breakfast in a pastoral setting, 6 miles from Great Barrington.

EATING AND DRINKING

20 Railroad St, *same address; tel: (413) 528-9345*, seems known as much for its convivial mix of patrons as for its 28-foot-long mahogany bar. Budget to moderate. **Kintaro**, *286 Main St; tel: (413) 528-6007*, Japanese meals. Moderate. The fare at **Hickory Bill's Bar-B-Que**, *405 Stockbridge Rd; tel: (413) 528-1444*, tastes spicy and smoky but you can eat it at a table beside the river. Budget to moderate.

ENTERTAINMENT

The Aston Magna Festival, *323 Main St, P.O. Box 1035, Great Barrington, MA 01230; tel: (413) 528-3595*, presents baroque, classical and early Romantic chamber music during July and Aug at **St. James Church**, across *Main St* from the information booth.

Bogie's, *935 S. Main St: tel: (413) 528-5959*, is a restaurant that also offers a driving range for golfers, a swimming pool and live music on the weekends, a good place for the youthful. **The Mahaiwe Theater**, *14 Castle St; tel: (413) 528-0100*, has been hailed as the Cinema Paradiso of these parts. It's an old movie house that shows first runs, old clips and kids' matinees and hosts film festivals.

SIGHTSEEING AND SHOPPING

This was the first town in the USA to get electric streetlights and the last town in the USA where a British court was convened. A plaque on *Church St* marks where civil rights pioneer **W.E.B. DuBois** was born in 1868. Up in the second-floor corridor of **Town Hall**, *334 Main St*, is a treasure

– a gallery of 17 photographs, all by the French photographer **Lucien Aigner**, now in his 90s and transplanted here since 1955. His subjects include **Albert Einstein, Winston Churchill, Marlene Dietrich** and **Louis Armstrong**. Closed at weekends. **Crystal Essence**, *39 Railroad St, Great Barrington, MA 01230; tel: (413) 528-2595*, has everything you need for passage into the New Age – gemstones, meditation tapes, books, jewellery.

GREAT BARRINGTON TO WORTHINGTON

Tyringham Art Gallery, *75 Tyringham Rd, Tyringham, MA 01264; tel: (413) 243-0654*, is a building of stone and wood that Hansel and Gretel might have stumbled across. Trails lead through sculpture gardens. Open daily 1000–1700 (late May–early Oct), $1.

From the centre of town, take *Jerusalem Rd* 0.3 mile south to entrance of **Tyringham Cobble**. A two-mile loop trail leads to **Cobble Hill**, about 400 feet above town. Rte 20, after crossing under the Massachusetts Turnpike twice, begins an uphill climb known as **Jacob's Ladder**, with **Jacob's Pillow**, a summer showcase for dance (See p. 196), occupying the upper rung. They pack them in at **Walker Island Campground**, *27 Rte 20, Chester, MA 01011; tel: (413) 354-2295*, but the location is nice. Budget.

The Miniature Theatre of Chester, *Box 487, Huntington, MA 01050; tel: (413) 354-7770*, performs in the auditorium of the Chester Town Hall, where Vincent Dowling, former director of Dublin's Abbey Theatre, has brought world-class theatre to Chester. Performances Thurs–Sat 2000, Wed, Sun matinees 1400 (mid-July–early Sept), $12. **The Old Kelso Homestead**, *Bromley Rd, Chester, MA 01011; tel: (413) 667-3251*, is an uncommonly beautiful farm where you can pick your own blueberries.

WORTHINGTON TO CUMMINGTON

Tourist Information: Besides providing lodging referrals **Hampshire Hills Bed & Breakfast Association**, *P.O. Box 553, Worthington, MA 01098*; lists local attractions in its brochure.

ACCOMMODATION

Lodging in the hill town bed and breakfasts is also less expensive than in Lenox, Stockbridge and other Berkshire towns. **Swift River Inn**, *151 South St, Cummington, MA 01026; tel: (800) 532-8022*, was a gentleman's dairy farm at the turn of the century. Mountain biking and rock climbing during the summer, cross-country skiing in the winter. No smoking.

EATING AND DRINKING

Little River Café, at the corner of *Rte 112 and Ireland St; tel: (413) 238-5837*. Open Wed–Sun 1700–2130, cocktails from 1600. Budget to moderate. Choose from restaurant, tavern or skiers' cafeteria at Swift River Inn (address above). Budget to moderate. Sunday brunch.

ENTERTAINMENT AND SIGHTSEEING

Worthington has forests, fields of potatoes, apple orchards, sugar houses and a musical family that stages intimate summer concerts in a wooden hall beside a brook. **The Sevenars Concerts**, *1190 Huntington Rd, Worthington, MA 01098; tel: (413) 238-5854*, are staged by the Schrades, a New York family of mostly concert pianists who spend summers here. Three generations play in a family concert the second Sun in July. A donation of $10 is requested but no admission is charged. Visiting musicians and choral groups perform in

the small hall across *Ireland St* from the Little River Café, an idyllic setting, on Fri evenings and Sun afternoons. Homemade refreshments served. **Stone Pool Pottery** fires works in a wood-fired kiln and sells them in a gallery on a historic homestead at the end of *Conwell Rd; tel: 238-5362*. Irregular hours, so call ahead.

Cummington is favoured by poets, artists, cows and sheep. **William Cullen Bryant Homestead**, *Bryant Rd, Cummington, MA 01026; tel: (413) 634-2244*, was the summer home of a vigorous poet (1794–1878) who also translated Homer, practiced law and edited the *New York Post*. Antiques here include Staffordshire and Wedgwood plates. Open Fri–Sun 1300–1700 (late June–early Sept), Sat, Sun only from early Sept–mid-Oct. Craft fair held third weekend of July. Open for a weekend at every other Christmas. Phone for admission fee. **The Old Creamery Grocery**, *445 Berkshire Trail, Cummington, MA 01026; tel: (413) 634-5560*, has a wood stove and a great deli; it sells *Bart's Ice Cream* and *My Dad's Cereal*, both locally made. Try them.

CUMMINGTON TO GREAT BARRINGTON

This section is mostly landscape. The resident artist sets his works on the lawn at **John Stritch Gallery**, *Rte 143, Hinsdale, MA 01235; tel: (413) 655-8804*. **Burgner's Farm Products**, *Dalton-Division Rd, Pittsfield, MA 01201; tel: (413) 445-4704)*, and **Bartlett's Orchard**, *575 Swamp Rd, P.O. Box 43 Richmond, MA 01254; tel: (413) 698-2559*, are good stops for apples, cider, baked goods. Bartlett's season is from late Aug to late May. See pp. 192–199 for information on **Arrowhead** and **West Stockbridge**. **Alford** has a town hall and church at its centre.

GREEN MOUNTAINS LOOP

New England's most rural and only landlocked state is dominated by various ranges of the Green Mountains. Make seasonal considerations a part of your vacation planning. Vermont's summertime appeal actually plays second fiddle to autumn foliage, normally reaching peak colour late Sept to mid-Oct – resulting in peak traffic, peak room rates and an absolute need to plan a 'leaf-peeping' visit well in advance.

DIRECT ROUTE: 265 MILES

204

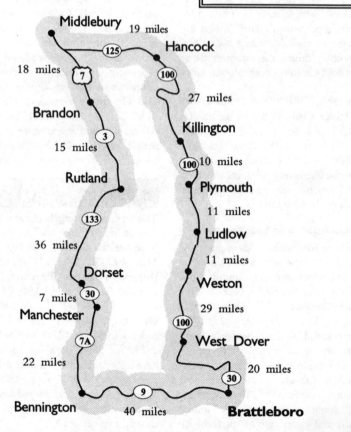

Middlebury — 19 miles — Hancock

125

18 miles — 7

100

27 miles

Brandon

3

Killington

15 miles

100 — 10 miles

Rutland

Plymouth

133

11 miles

36 miles

Ludlow

Dorset

11 miles

7 miles — 30

Weston

Manchester

29 miles

7A

100

22 miles

West Dover

30

20 miles

Bennington — 40 miles — **Brattleboro**

9

ROUTE

Depart **Brattleboro** by heading west on Rte 9 for a 40-mile drive, traversing the southern portion of the **Green Mountain National Forest** via **Wilmington** to **Bennington**. Choose the more scenic northbound Rte 7A rather than Rte 7 for a 14-mile journey onward to **Arlington** and a further 8 miles to **Manchester Village**. From **Manchester Center**, drive 7 miles north on Rte 30 to **Dorset**, then 9 miles through the pastoral **Mettawee River Valley** to **Pawlet**. The Rte 133 journey between that hamlet and big (for Vermont) **Rutland** totals 27 miles. Next comes a 4-mile jaunt via Rte 3 to **Proctor**. Rtes 3 and 7 connect at Pittsford; follow the latter road 11 miles north to **Brandon**, then 17.5 miles to **Middlebury**. Rte 125 from the town centre and **East Middlebury** becomes the high-altitude, 15.5-mile **Robert Frost Memorial Drive**, curving through the national forest's northern segment. You will arrive in **Hancock** for a southbound turn onto Rte 100 and a 27-mile journey alongside forested foothills via Rochester and Pittsfield to the Killington area – best known for winter skiing, but also popular for year-round recreation. Continue 9.5 miles on Rte 100 to **Plymouth Union** and an additional 11 miles to **Ludlow**, another skiers' mecca because of its proximity to Okemo Mountain.

The 11-mile drive from Ludlow south to **Weston** gets you to the eastern flank of the forest's lower segment. Stay on Rte 100 to **Londonderry, Jamaica, Wardsboro** and **West Dover** – altogether 29 miles. Leave Rte 100 upon seeing the **East Dover** sign, your cue for a 13-mile trip on a country road (no route number) through **South Newfane** to **West Dummerston**. You'll reach Rte 30; turn south towards Brattleboro, 7 miles away, for the completion of our recommended 265-mile loop.

TOURIST INFORMATION

Vermont Department of Travel & Tourism, *134 State St, Montpelier, VT 05602; tel: (802) 828-3236*, open Mon–Fri 0800–1630, is a pre-trip resource. Chambers of commerce in numerous towns augment their services with centrally located information booths, usually open late May–Nov, including weekends. Though they supply accommodation listings, making reservations is a do-it-yourself affair. Some of Vermont's typical village and country inns require a minimum two-night stay on booked-solid weekends and holidays during summer and autumn. And many offer extended-stay packages.

BRATTLEBORO

Tourist Information: Brattleboro Area Chamber of Commerce, *180 Main St, Brattleboro, VT 05301; tel: (802) 254-4565*, open Mon–Fri 0830–1700.

ACCOMMODATION AND FOOD

The **Latchis Hotel**, *50 Main St, Brattleboro, VT 05301; tel: (802) 254-6300*, moderate, is the Art Deco mainstay of a mini-complex including a restored movie palace and moderate-priced restaurant combined with the Windham brewpub. *DI, M6* and *S8* are on Brattleboro's northern outskirts. Downtown's nicest budget–moderate restaurant is **Walker's**, *132 Main St; tel: (802) 254-6046*.

SIGHTSEEING

Superannuated hippies from the tie-dyed Age of Aquarius have made Brattleboro an arty, jazzy place. A 1916 rail station houses the **Brattleboro Museum & Art Center**, *Canal and Bridge Sts, Brattleboro,*

205

VT 05301; tel: (802) 257-1024, open Tues–Sun 1200–1800 (mid-May–Nov), $2. Displays include photos of British author Rudyard Kipling's hillside manse in nearby West Dummerston, where he and his US-born wife lived for four years in the late 1900s; here Kipling wrote the two *Jungle Books* and *Captains Courageous*.

BRATTLEBORO TO BENNINGTON

Amongst this westward drive's attractions are **Marlboro**, whose college since 1951 has been the locale of **Marlboro Music**, a world-class July–Aug chamber-music festival, and **Wilmington**, a riverside village packed with shops and eateries.

BENNINGTON

Tourist Information: Bennington Area Chamber of Commerce, *Veterans Memorial Dr., Bennington, VT 05201; tel: (802) 447-3311*, open daily 0900–1700.

ACCOMMODATION

You'll find *BW* and *Rm*, plus moderate-range motels. Best of the bunch for downtown proximity is the **Paradise Motor Inn**, *141 W. Main St, Bennington, VT 05201; tel: (802) 442-8351*. **Woodford State Park**, *Bennington, VT 05201; tel: (802) 447-7169*, has a campsite and hiking trails overlooking the national forest's Adams Reservoir.

EATING AND DRINKING

In a refurbished 1897 rail station, steak and seafood dinners are moderate at **Bennington Station**, *Depot St; tel: (802) 447-1080*. Green Mountain Coffee complements fresh scones at the **South Street Café**, *105 South St; tel: (802) 447-2433*.

SIGHTSEEING

Two Chamber of Commerce walking-

tour maps enable you to 'do' the town and its college. The 306-ft **Bennington Battle Monument**, Vermont's tallest structure, commemorates the 16 Dec 1777 victory over Gen Burgoyne's Redcoats.

The Bennington Museum, *W. Main St, Bennington, VT 05201; tel: (802) 447-1571*, open daily 0900–1700, $5, contains historic local pottery and regional Americana, also paintings by Grandma Moses, the patron saint of US country-primitive art. Bennington is just 13 miles up Rte 7 from Williamstown (see p. 218), so Vermont touring can be combined with the Berkshire Hills of western Massachusetts.

ARLINGTON AND MANCHESTER

Tourist Information: In Bennington, but also: **Manchester and the Mountains Chamber of Commerce,** *2 Main St, Manchester, VT 05255; tel: (802) 362-2100*, Mon–Fri 0900–1700, Sat 0900–1600, Sun 1000–1400.

ACCOMMODATION

Top for comfort and Greek Revival stateliness is the expensive–pricey **Arlington Inn**, *Rte 7A, Arlington, VT 05250; tel: (802) 375-6532 or (800) 443-9422*. Or head 6 miles on Rte 313 and cross an 1852 covered bridge approaching the expensive **Inn on Covered Bridge Green**, *River Rd, W. Arlington, VT 05250; tel: (802) 375-9489 or (800) 726-9480*, once a home of Norman Rockwell.

Manchester Village's upper-crust resort (including two 18-hole golf courses) is **The Equinox**, *Rte 7A, Manchester, VT 05254; tel: toll-free (800) 362-4747*. Four expensive–pricey inns are close by. **The Seth Warner Inn**, *Rte 7A, Manchester Center, VT 05255; tel: (802) 362-3830*, is a budget–moderate bed and breakfast.

EATING AND DRINKING

For variety, Manchester outshines Arlington. **The Quality Restaurant**, *735 Main St; tel: (802) 362-9839*, is a budget oldie. Beef lovers home in on the **Sirloin Saloon**, *Rtes 11/30; tel: (802) 362-2600*, moderate. Fancier and pricier: the **Black Swan**, *Rte 7A; tel: (802) 362-3807*.

SIGHTSEEING AND SHOPPING

Arlington's tourism overload stems from the fact that a long-time resident was Norman Rockwell, the Rembrandt of idealised *Saturday Evening Post* magazine-cover illustrations. See what the fuss is all about by browsing the **Norman Rockwell Exhibition and Gift Shop**, *Rte 7A, Arlington, VT 05250; tel: (802) 375-6423*, daily 0900–1700 (May–Oct), 1000–1600 (Nov–Apr), $1.

Contrast that with 24-room **Hildene**, *Rte 7A, Manchester Village, VT 05255; tel: (802) 362-1788*, the sumptuous summer estate of President Abraham Lincoln's son, Robert Todd Lincoln; open for tours daily 1000–1600 (mid-May–end Oct), $6. You can view the fishing tackle of such personages as Dwight Eisenhower, Ernest Hemingway and Bing Crosby at the **American Museum of Fly Fishing**, *Rte 7A, Manchester Center, VT 05254; tel: (802) 362-3300*, open daily 1000–1600 (May–Oct), Mon–Fri (Nov–Apr), $2.

For smashing panoramics, drive 5-plus miles to the 3825-ft summit of **Mount Equinox** via $6 toll road. Watch for the sign on Rte 7A midway between Arlington and Manchester. Daily 0800–2200 (May–Nov); *tel: (802) 362-1114*.

DORSET AND PAWLET

With its impeccable green and white clapboard houses, marble church and antiques shops, **Dorset** is right up there amidst Vermont's 'picture-prettiest' villages. All this plus summer's **Dorset Theatre Festival**, *P.O. Box 519, Dorset, VT 05251; tel: (802) 867-5777*. Tinier, humbler **Pawlet** features two pottery studios, an ex-hotel that's now Machs' General Store and, for low-budget breakfast or lunch, the **Station Restaurant & Ice Cream Parlor**, *School St; tel: (802) 325-3041*. With dairy farms and hay fields bordered by wooded slopes, the **Mettawee River Valley** between Dorset and Pawlet amounts to a pleasantly scenic drive. Then, switching north-eastward via Rte 133, you'll swoop over rolling terrain.

RUTLAND AND PROCTOR

Tourist Information: Rutland Region Chamber of Commerce, *256 N. Main St, Rutland, VT 05701; tel: (802) 773-2747*, open Mon–Fri 0800–1700.

ACCOMMODATION AND FOOD

Fairly sizable Rutland (pop. 18,000), a useful stop-over for petrol and other essentials, has *BW, CI, DI, Hd* and *HJ*.

A worthwhile, moderate downtown choice with a gigantic something-for-everyone menu is **Pappy's Restaurant & Ordinary**, *128 Merchant's Row; tel: (802) 775-7489*.

RECREATION AND SIGHTSEEING

Information about trekking and camping in the wondrously vast **Green Mountain National Forest** is plentiful and mostly free at the Forest Supervisor's Office, *231 N. Main St, Rutland, VT 05701; tel: (802) 747-6700*, open Mon–Fri 0800–1630.

Washington, D.C.'s Lincoln Memorial and US Supreme Court owe their classical whiteness to Vermont-quarried marble. See it being sculpted at the **Vermont Marble Exhibit**, *Main St, Proctor, VT*

05765; tel: (802) 459-3311, open daily 0900–1730 (mid-May–mid-Oct), Mon–Sat 0900–1600 (mid-Oct–mid-May), $3.50.

BRANDON

Virtually all of this Neshobe River town is listed in the National Register of Historic Places; explore side streets (especially Park and Franklin) for a passing parade of Federal, Greek Revival and Italianate residential architecture. A descriptive booklet is available at an information kiosk on *Central Sq*, staffed daily 0900–1700 June–Oct.

ACCOMMODATION AND FOOD

The moderate–expensive **Moffett House**, *69 Park St, Brandon, VT 05733; tel: (800) 752-5794*, is a Victorian bed and breakfast. The town centre's rambling, moderate **Brandon Inn**, *20 Park St, Brandon, VT 05733; tel: (802) 247-5766 or (800) 639-8685*, is run by a hospitable lady from Hertfordshire and her Austrian-chef husband, responsible for dining-room cuisine. **Patricia's Restaurant**, *18–20 Center St; tel: (802) 247-3233*, is a lunch and dinner eatery for budget-conscious patrons. Listen to the locals gossiping over breakfast at **The Cook Stove**, *25 Center St; tel: (802) 247-3929*.

MIDDLEBURY

Tourist Information: Addison County Chamber of Commerce, *2 Court St, Middlebury, VT 05753; tel: (802) 388-7951*, open daily 0900–1700 (July–Oct), Mon–Fri 0900–1700 (Nov–June).

ACCOMMODATION

When parents come to check up on their kids attending exclusive **Middlebury College**, they're apt to stay at the dowa-ger **Middlebury Inn**, *14 Courthouse Sq., Middlebury, VT 05753; tel: (802) 388-4961 or (800) 842-4666*, moderate–expensive. Moderate **Brookside Meadows**, *RD 3, Box 2460, Middlebury, VT 05753; tel: (802) 388-6429 or (800) 442-9887*, is a mountain-view bed and breakfast located 3 miles from town.

Vermont innkeepers are part of US folklore – so much so that eccentricities in the 'Stratford Inn' became a TV sitcom starring Bob Newhart. It's really the **Waybury Inn**, *Rte 125, East Middlebury, VT 05740; tel: (802) 388-4015 or (800) 348-1810*, moderate.

EATING AND DRINKING

Students keep Middlebury buzzing, with jaunty restaurants and locally brewed Otter Creek ale, suited to their tastes. Regarding Otter Creek, a deck hanging over it distinguishes **Woody's**, *5 Bakery Lane; tel: (802) 388-4182*, specialising in seafood, moderate. Comparable cost category fits steak or chicken dinners at **Fire & Ice**, *26 Seymour St; tel: (802) 388-7166*.

SIGHTSEEING AND SHOPPING

Morgan horses, the first US light thoroughbreds, go through their paces at the University of Vermont's **UVM Morgan Horse Farm**, *R.D. 1, Middlebury, VT 05753; tel: (802) 388-2011*, daily 0900–1600 (May–Nov), $3.50.

Craftspeople show their wares down by Otter Creek Falls, once the power source of Middlebury's stone mill buildings. Focal point of this bustling activity is the **Vermont State Craft Center at Frog Hollow**. A footbridge spanning the waterway gets you to shops in the recycled **Marble Works**. Picnic tables overlook the falls; likewise for the laid-back **Storm Café**, *Frog Hollow Mill; tel: (802) 388-1063*.

ROBERT FROST MEMORIAL DRIVE

This Rte 125 highland traversal through the national forest crosses Vermont's north-south hiking heaven, the **Long Trail**, and plunges through the **Middlebury Gap**. Weather permitting, you'll see the Adirondack Mountains. The scenic road's name honors the revered naturalist poet, who from 1940-63 summered in a farm cabin close to the route's minuscule village of **Ripton**. The **Robert Frost Wayside Trail** combines picnic areas and an interpretive pathway sign-marked with Frost poems.

THE WHITE RIVER VALLEY

Here's another hill-and-dale topographical treat, for Rte 100 skirts the very edge of the national forest as you drive south alongside verdant meadowlands. Choicest of wide-apart communities is **Rochester**, with Wed bake sales, summer bandstand concerts and a Sept harvest fair on the green. For moderate lodging and dining in a country setting, pick the **Huntington House**, *On the Green, Rochester, VT 05767; tel: (802) 767-4868.*

KILLINGTON

Tourist Information: Killington & Pico Areas Association, *P.O. Box 114, Killington, VT 05751; tel: (802) 773-4181,* open Mon–Fri 0830–1630. Befitting its eminence as the eastern US's largest winter-sports destination, the six-mountain Killington region's amenities include dozens of lodgings covering a broad cost spectrum, dozens more eating places, plus nightspots for après-ski carousing. *The Mountain Times* includes a Dining Guide listing. For full coverage regarding accommodation, food, recreation and special events, ask for the *Killington-Pico-Rutland Visitor's Guide.*

The flurry of happenings extends beyond snow season. For instance, this is a superb area for hiking and mountain biking, golf and tennis. An aerial gondola ride to the 4241-ft summit of **Killington Peak** opens onto sensational views, while the **Pico Peak Alpine Slide** offers the opposite-direction screamer of a 3410-ft summit-to-base sled descent. Killington hosts a July–Aug chamber-music festival and Green Mountain Guild theatricals.

PLYMOUTH UNION PLYMOUTH NOTCH

In a fateful triple-header, Calvin Coolidge was born, sworn in as 30th US president and buried in Plymouth Notch, a hilltop speck located 1 mile from Plymouth Union's Rtes 100/100A junction. That makes the **Plymouth Notch Historic District** historically significant; *tel: (802) 672-3773,* open daily 0900–1730 (late May–mid-Oct), $4.

The layout includes Coolidge's 1872 birthplace, the Plymouth Cheese Factory established by his father in 1890 (and still operating) and a creaky-floor general store. Once a tavern, the Wilder House now functions as a budget lunchroom. Built in 1830 as a stagecoach stop, moderate **Salt Ash Inn,** *Plymouth, VT 05056; tel: (802) 672-3748,* oozes rustic charm.

LUDLOW AND WESTON

Tourist Information: Ludlow Area Chamber of Commerce, *Okemo Marketplace, Ludlow, VT 05419; tel: (802) 228-5830,* daily 0730–1900.

ACCOMMODATION AND FOOD

Ski-town Ludlow has *BW*, motels and lodges, also bed and breakfasts. North of town, moderate **Echo Lake Inn,** *P.O. Box 154, Ludlow, VT 05149; tel: (800) 356-6844,* dating from 1840, features ten-

209

nis, swimming and New England-style dining. In quietly charming Weston, gracious inns are the norm, typified by the moderate **1830 Inn on the Green**, *P.O. Box 104, Weston, VT 05161; tel: (802) 824-6789*. Ludlow's breakfast-lunch cheapie is **The Hatchery**, *164 Main St; tel: (802) 228-2311*. Weston's **Country Picnic Deli**, *Main St at the Millyard; tel: (802) 824-6909*, turns out budget soups, salads and sandwiches.

SHOPPING AND ENTERTAINMENT

It's fun to poke around in Weston's **Vermont Country Store** on the triangular common. Across the maple-shaded lawn, the colonnaded **Weston Playhouse**, *tel: (802) 824-8167*, is a summerstock theatre and Oct locale of Vermont's oldest antiques show.

WESTON TO WEST DOVER

Now Rte 100 twists and squiggles close to three ski mountains – **Bromley, Stratton** and **Mt. Snow** in north-to-south sequence – as you pass through **Londonderry** and then plain and simple **Rawsonville, Jamaica** and **Wardsboro**.

At Londonderry's Rte 100/11 crossroads, **The Garden Market**, **tel: (802) 824-6021**, is strategically situated for deli take-aways, and there's a down-home general store in Jamaica. Windhall Brook tent pitches are in **Jamaica State Park**, *Jamaica, VT 05343; tel: (802) 874-4600*, mid-May–Oct.

WEST DOVER TO BRATTLEBORO

The trip's last leg begins in **West Dover**. At that village, equidistant between Mt. Snow and Haystack Mountain, leave Rte 100 for a purely rural drive through **East Dover, South Newfane** and **Williamsville** (three blinks and they're gone).

Maple Syrup

When crochety Vermonters mention 'mud season', they're grumbling about the consequence of snowmelt that brings gloominess and goo when daytime temperatures begin to rise, usually towards late February or early March. But night-time chill counteracts the thaw, causing sap in the state's gazillion sugar maples to rise.

So mud season is tapping time – meaning extraction of the sap, hauled to sugar houses (or newfangled evaporator plants) for boiling, which concentrates the sugar to turn it into syrup. Vermont's production, largest in the US and second only to Québec's, exceeds 500,000 gallons yearly. But it doesn't come easily, considering the tree-to-tree slogging and the fact that each gallon of syrup requires 40–50 gallons of sap.

The 'maple-sugaring' still goes full steam throughout springtime, in case you're making a PM (post-mud) visit. It's impossible to come in any season and not find maple syrup – in A-B-C grades, priced accordingly – for sale at shops and farm stands.

Learn about the process at the **New England Maple Museum** in Pittsford, north of Rutland but with a Rutland address/phone: *Rte 7, Rutland, VT 05701; tel: (802) 483-9414*, daily 0830–1730 (late May–Nov), 1000–1600 (Nov–late Dec and late Mar–late May); closed Jan–Feb, $1.75.

Arrival at **West Dummerston** brings you to Rte 30 in traffic-jammed, shopping-malled suburban Brattleboro for a short drive to the downtown centre (or access onto I-91), thereby closing the Green Mountains Loop.

BRATTLEBORO–HANOVER

Go-it-alone Vermonters are happy to be separated from New Hampshire by the wide Connecticut River. Moreover, the efficient interstate highway (I-91) is on their side of the stream. Choose it if you want to zip quickly northward towards a cross-over into New Hampshire's Ivy League college town. Or take extra time to meander through the Green Mountain State's southeastern countyside.

Hanover

12 miles

89

4

Woodstock

91

13 miles

106

Scenic route

131

Proctorsville

Direct route

8 miles

103

Chester

35

68 miles

7 miles

Grafton

16 miles

35

Townshend

30 91

17 miles

Brattleboro

DIRECT ROUTE: 68 MILES

211

ROUTES

DIRECT ROUTE

➡ The 68-mile distance means you can drive non-stop from Brattleboro to **Hanover** in little more than an hour. I-91 stays close to the river, occasionally visible depending upon gaps in Vermont's omnipresent woodland. Fuel up in advance; petrol stations are non-existent on this uncommercialised route. True to statewide fervour for unspoiled natural beauty, advertising billboards are banned on I-91 and, in fact, on every other Vermont road.

Take I-91 as far as **Norwich** and cross the Ledyard Bridge to Hanover. If interstate travel doesn't thrill you, the slower Rte 5 parallels I-91, with direct-access to petrol, shops and eating places. Some riverside communities might be worth a stop-over, depending upon your curiosity level and available time. We've detailed several that could be interesting.

SCENIC ROUTE

▪▪▪▶ From Brattleboro (or I-91 Exit 2), drive 12 miles north on Rte 30 past West Dummerston to picture-postcard **Newfane**, then another 5 miles to **Townshend**.

After reaching the village, turn onto Rte 35 for a 16-mile journey – through a river valley with flocks of sheep and even a llama ranch – to **Grafton**. Continue north for 7 hilly miles to another little charmer, **Chester**, which brings you to Rte 103. Head 8 miles north to **Proctorsville**, where Rte 103 meets Rte 131. Eastward bound, go through **Cavendish** for 7 miles to the Rtes 131/106 crossroads.

Now comes a beautiful 12.5-mile drive via Rte 106, passing dairy farms and horse ranches as you proceed north through quaint-but-affluent **South Woodstock** and into cosmopolitan **Woodstock**. Then 7.5 miles east on Rte 4 to the bridge spanning the **Quechee Gorge**.

Four miles further east, you'll come to I-89 – disconcerting after all those lazy two-lane down-state roads. Drive 3.5 miles south on I-89 towards **White River Junction** for another encounter: the I-89/I-91 interchange snarl, meaning arrival at the direct route, with different ways to reach Hanover from this point. Take I-91 to Norwich and the bridge. Or cross the river into New Hampshire and go 4 miles north via Rte 10 to Hanover.

The scenic route covers 90–100 miles, best enjoyed with overnight stays along the way.

Some but definitely not all villages have information booths, open summer and autumn only. The chambers of commerce in Brattleboro, Bellows Falls, Windsor and White River Junction provide year-round regional tourism services.

Amtrak's New York-Montréal **Vermonter** train stops at Brattleboro, Bellows Falls White River Junction and St. Albans (where passengers transfer to coaches); *tel: (800) 872-7245.*

BELLOWS FALLS

Tourist Information: Great Falls Regional Chamber of Commerce, *55 Village Sq, Bellows Falls, VT 05101; tel: (802) 463-4280*, open Mon–Fri 1000–1600 (Sept–June); daily (late June–early Sept). Get the lowdown on Bellows Falls' turn-of-the-century hellcat, Hetty Green, the filthy-rich 'Witch of Wall Street'.

ACCOMMODATION AND FOOD

A bed and breakfast north of town, **Horsefeathers**, *16 Webb Terrace, Bellows Falls, VT 05101; tel: (802) 463-9776*, overlooks the river; moderate. **Terra Verde**, *14 On the Square; tel: (802) 463-3006*, is a vegetarian/natural foods deli.

SIGHTSEEING

The Green Mountain Flyer, a vintage old-time steam train, chugs a 26-mile excursion route between here and **Chester Depot** mid-June–mid-Oct. *Bellows Falls, VT 05101; tel: (802) 463-3069*, $10 round-trip.

At New England Power's waterfall station alongside the first navigable US canal (1802), spawning Atlantic salmon can be seen swimming past underwater windows, free, at the **Fish Ladder and Visitors**

Center, *Bridge St; tel: (802) 463-3226,* open Thur–Mon 0900–1700 (late May–mid-Oct).

Classic English motorcars can be seen 3 miles south of Bellows Falls in the **MG Car Museum**, *Rte 5, Westminster, VT 05158; tel: (802) 722-3708,* open Tues–Sun 1000–1700 (Jun–mid-Oct), $3.50.

WHITE RIVER JUNCTION AND WINDSOR

Tourist Information: White River Chamber of Commerce, *15 Main St, White River Junction, VT 05001; tel: (802) 295-6200,* Mon–Fri 0900–1700, Sat–Sun 1300–1700 (July–Aug). **Windsor Area Chamber of Commerce**, *Main St, Windsor, VT 05089; tel: (802) 674-5910,* Mon–Fri 0900–1700.

ACCOMMODATION AND FOOD

Along with *CI, Hd, HJ, S8* and *Su,* White River Junction has the restored railroad-era **Hotel Coolidge**, *White River Junction, VT 05001; tel: (800) 622-1124,* moderate. The hilltop **Juniper Hill Inn**, *R.R. 1, Windsor, VT 05808; tel: (802) 674-5936 or (800) 359-2541,* is a moderate–expensive ex-mansion. Both serve lunches and dinners. All-organic ingredients draw nutrition-minded clientele to White River Junction's **Itas'ca**, *2 N. Main St; tel: (802) 295-0125.* **Windsor Station**, *Depot Ave; tel: (802) 674-2052,* harking back to Windsor's heyday on the Connecticut River Valley's rail line, offers copious menu choices. Moderate.

SIGHTSEEING AND ENTERTAINMENT

Tours and beer tastings are free at the **Catamount Brewing Company**, *58 Main St, White River Junction, VT 05001; tel: (802) 296-2248,* open Mon–Sat 1900–1700, Sun 1300–1700.

Starting in the mid-19th century, a Windsor armoury fabricated machine tools and perfected the 'American system' of interchangeable parts with mass production of famous Enfield rifles. This Yankee-ingenuity workplace has become the **American Precision Museum**, *196 Main St, Windsor, VT 05808; tel: (802) 677-5781,* open Mon–Fri 0900–1700, Sat–Sun 1000–1400 (mid-May–Nov), $3.

Feisty Vermont was an honest-to-goodness independent republic for 14 years beginning in 1777. The declaration was made (over drinks, we suspect) in a tavern, now the **Old Constitution House** historical museum, *16 N. Main St, Windsor, VT 05808; tel: (802) 672-3773,* free.

The **Vermont State Craft Center** occupies two floors of Windsor House, the state's largest Greek Revival building, *54 Main St, Windsor, VT 05089; tel: (802) 674-6729.*

The **Windsor-Cornish covered bridge** over the Connecticut River is longer than dozens of others throughout Vermont and New Hampshire.

For Jun–Aug show biz, there's the **White River Theatre Festival**, *Briggs Opera House, White River Junction, VT 05001; tel: (802) 296-2505.*

NEWFANE

Tourist Information: Pick up a Newfane orientation folder at the **Windham County Historical Society**, across from the common, open Wed–Sun 1200–1700 (late May–late Oct).

ACCOMMODATION AND FOOD

Ambience and meals are terrific in two close-together, moderate–expensive establishments on the town common, **Old Newfane Inn**; *tel: (802) 365-4427,* and **Four Columns Inn**; *tel: (802) 365-7713.*

213

Both Newfane, VT 05345. Pop into the **Newfane Store**; *tel: (802) 365-7775*, for luncheon take-aways.

SIGHTSEEING AND SHOPPING

If ever a Vermont village seemed to be posing for a picture it's here. Surrounding a perfect green with its Victorian fountain and Civil War monument, the white ensemble includes the two inns, two country Gothic churches, Newfane's 1832 Union Hall and Windham County's colonnaded courthouse.

Antiques shops and a country store crammed with goods ranging from cheese and chocolates to toys and exquisitely hand-made quilts can be found nearby.

Two miles north on Rte 30, a block-buster al fresco flea market draws crowds every Sat–Sun, dawn to dusk (May–late Oct).

TOWNSHEND

This is another stopped-in-time village, with a bandstand on the two-acre common. Townshend's 1790 Congregational church towers over it and, on the opposite side, are an apothecary and corner grocery store.

Head beyond the village to the **Windham Hill Inn**, *R.R. 1, West Townshend, VT 05359; tel: (802) 874-4080*, pricey. Centrally located **Boardman House**, *Townshend, VT 05353; tel: (802) 365-4086*, budget– moderate, is a five-room Bed and Breakfast. You can rough it in **Townshend State Park**, *Townshend, VT 05353; tel: (802) 365-7500*, with tent pitches, a cold-water dam for swimming and Bald Mountain hiking trails.

Although it's closed to auto traffic, West Townshend's covered bridge is worth a 'photo stop' during your Rte 30 drive. Built in 1870, the lattice-frame

structure extends 166 ft over the West River, this is Vermont's longest single-span covered bridge.

GRAFTON

Author Rudyard Kipling, naturalist-philosopher Henry David Thoreau and US President Woodrow Wilson have all stayed at **The Old Tavern**, *Grafton, VT 05146; tel: (802) 843-2231 or (800) 843-1801*; it's expensive–pricey, but moderate with special offers in May–Sept. The excellent dining room is the only place in the village serving meals.

Soapstone from local quarries was the stuff of indestructible stoves in the 19th century. Long after that boom went bust, the Windham Foundation (a New Jersey banker's legacy) funded painstaking renewal alongside the Saxtons River, hence today's pristine look. Windham maintains the hostelry, hiking trails, a general store, art gallery and a cheese company producing award-winning Covered Bridge cheddar.

CHESTER

Amongst the eye-catching 'gingerbread' style buildings along the linear town green is moderate **Inn Victoria**, *Chester, Vt 05143; tel: (802) 875-2208*. Same category and address, the circa-1780 **Chester House**, *P.O. Box 708, Main St, Chester, VT 05143; tel: (802) 875-2205*, is a relaxing bed and breakfast.

Have lunch or tea out on the porch at **Raspberries and Tyme** *on the green; tel: (802) 875-4486.*

The tiny rail station in **Chester Depot** is the western terminus of the **Green Mountain Flyer** (see Bellows Falls). Vermont food specialities and scads of 'a little bit of this and that' stuff an 1871 country store on the green, **Carpenter's Emporium**; *tel: (802) 875-3267.* Stone

Village on *North St* is a double row of 30 pre-Civil War dwellings constructed of rough-hewn stone, used as 'station stops' by runaway slaves on their south-to-north Underground Railway route.

CHESTER TO WOODSTOCK

This 27.5-mile drive covers Rtes 103, 131 and 106. If you're in a city mood, go 7.5 miles from Chester to **Springfield** and its red-brick downtown district at Black River Falls. From Springfield, you can curve north and then west to Rte 103.

Cavendish, on Rte 131, is inauspicious but noteworthy. After his 1974 exile, Russian author/emigré Alexander Solzhenitsyn lived here for nearly two decades. Moneyed **South Woodstock**, on the other hand, *is* auspicious. The expensive–pricey **Kedron Valley Inn**, *Rte 106, South Woodstock, VT 05071; tel: (802) 457-1473*, has its own equestrian centre.

WOODSTOCK

Tourist Information: Woodstock Area Chamber of Commerce, *4 Central St, Woodstock, VT 05091; tel: (802) 457-3555*, open Mon–Fri 1000–1600 (June–Nov), Tues–Thur 1000–1600 (Nov–May). Its *Window on Woodstock* booklet is comprehensive. The chamber conducts walking tours Mon–Wed, Fri and Sat at 1030 (late May–mid-Oct), $2.50.

ACCOMMODATION

The huge **Woodstock Inn and Resort**, *14 The Green, Woodstock, VT 05091; tel: (802) 457-1100 or (800) 448-7900*, is pricey and replete with ritzy amenities. Below that stratosphere, moderate lodgings include the **1830 Shire Town Inn**, *31 South St, Woodstock, VT 05091; tel: (802) 457-1830*, and **The Woodstocker**

61 River St; tel: (802) 457-3896 or (800) 457-3896.

EATING AND DRINKING

Eateries in all price ranges are abundant. For saloon atmosphere, burgers and moderate dinners, try **Bentley's**, *3 Elm St; tel: (802) 457-3232*. The moderate–pricey **Prince and the Pauper**, *24 Elm St; tel: (457-1818)* is candlelit and romantic. In addition to serving sandwiches and pastries, **Mountain Creamery**, *33 Central St; tel: (802) 457-1715*, scoops out irresistible home-made ice-cream.

SIGHTSEEING

Revitalised by millions from the Laurence Rockefellers, who own the Woodstock Inn and have other ties to the area, Woodstock's 'Vermontish' ingredients include its village green, church bells cast by Paul Revere, in-town covered bridges, fresh-painted clapboard at every turn, arts and crafts shops and nearby ski slopes. But chic boutiques and a rather slick aura dilute the charm to some extent.

Delve into Vermont's rural essence at the **Billings Farm and Museum**, *Rte 12 and River Rd, Woodstock, VT 05091; tel: (802) 457-2355*, daily May–Nov, $6, with Jersey cows, sheep-shearing and cheese-making among the agrarian attractions.

QUECHEE GORGE

Glacial action carved this 165-ft chasm on the Ottauquechee River, making the overhead Rte 4 bridge an immensely popular viewing site. Along with picnic facilities, **Quechee Gorge State Park**; *tel: (802) 295-2990*, has exhilarating hiking trails leading past sugar maples, hemlocks, spruce, birch and pine trees right into the depths of the gorge. Quechee's mid-June hot-air balloon festival is a colourful annual attraction.

215

HANOVER–BURLINGTON

Vermont's vertical shape results in a rather short east-to-west interstate highway trip across the state – the Connecticut River and Lake Champlain aren't really very far apart. Short traversal time, however, should be gauged against some of the most beautiful terrain and irresistible villages in New England. These can only be appreciated close-up, by means of leisurely country-road meandering – even impulsive detours when you spot a white church spire poking through the trees or crowning a hill. Hence the following travel alternatives: quick and direct or slow and scenic.

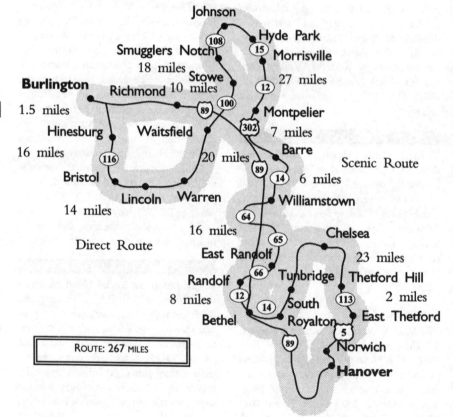

Johnson
Smugglers Notch
(108)
Hyde Park
(15) Morrisville
18 miles Stowe
27 miles
(12)
Burlington
Richmond 10 miles
(89) (100)
1.5 miles
Montpelier
Hinesburg Waitsfield
(302) 7 miles
16 miles
(116)
20 miles Barre
(89)
Scenic Route
Bristol
(14) 6 miles
Lincoln Warren
Williamstown
14 miles
(64)
Direct Route
16 miles
(65)
Chelsea
East Randolf
23 miles
Randolf
(66) Tunbridge Thetford Hill
8 miles
(12)
(113) 2 miles
(14) South
Bethel
Royalton East Thetford
(5)
(89) Norwich

Hanover

ROUTE: 267 MILES

216

ROUTES

DIRECT ROUTE

➡ From Hanover centre, follow the Norwich sign by driving west on *Wheelock St* across the Connecticut River bridge into Vermont. Go south on I-91 to Exit 12 for access onto I-89 North. Cross Vermont via I-89 to Exit 1, then go north on Rte 7 to reach downtown Burlington. Total I-89 distance across Vermont is 91 miles, so you can reach Burlington from Hanover in less than two hours. There are no petrol stations directly on I-91 or I-89, so prepare accordingly prior to leaving Hanover.

SCENIC ROUTE

➡ Drive 1.5 miles from Hanover to Norwich, then 10 miles north on Rte 5 to East Thetford and 2 miles west via Rte 113 to Thetford Hill and another 23 miles to reach Chelsea. From that town, head south on Rte 110 past Tunbridge to South Royalton, then take Rtes 14 and 107 westward for 7 miles (crossing I-89) to Bethel, thus reaching Rte 12 for an 8-mile drive north to Randolph, followed by a short drive on Rte 66 (again crossing I-89) to Randolph Center and East Randolph.

Next go 9 miles north on Rte 14 to East Brookfield and 2 miles west to Brookfield; crossing that village's floating bridge brings you onto Rte 65 for a north-bound drive to Northfield Center. Head 7 miles east via Rte 64 to Williamstown, then 6 miles via Rte 14 to Barre and 7 miles on Rte 302 to Montpelier, the state capital.

Take Rte 12 north from Montpelier to Morrisville (27 miles), then Rte 15 to Hyde Park, Johnson and Jeffersonville to reach Rte 108 for an 18-mile drive south through Smugglers Notch (closed in winter) to Stowe and 10 miles south via Rte 100 from there to Waterbury. Staying on Rte 100 for 20 miles (crossing I-89) brings you to Waitsfield and then Warren. Drive west through the Lincoln Gap to Bristol (14 miles). (Bristol connects via Rte 17 west to the New York City to Burlington route at Chimney Point, see p. 311, and via Rte 116 south to the Green Mountains Loop at East Middlebury, see p. 204). From Bristol go 16 miles north via Rte 116 through Starksboro and Hinesburg, followed by an 8.5-mile drive over an unnumbered rural road through Mechanicsville and Rhode Island Corners to Richmond. Turn left onto Rte 2; after 1.5 miles, you'll reach the interstate. Take I-89 north to downtown Burlington.

The total distance of this looping, to-and-fro route is 267 miles. Since it crosses I-89 at several points, you can easily parcel the journey into shorter segments, according to time and inclination.

Vermont Department of Travel & Tourism, *134 State St, Montpelier, VT 05602; tel: (802) 828-3236,* open Mon–Fri 0800–1630, is a state-wide information resource for advance planning. Information booths, open summer and autumn, are found in the centres of only a few villages and towns.

NORWICH TO CHELSEA

Norwich's village green, fronting the inevitable white-steepled church, is the first of many you'll see during this off-the-interstate drive. Norwich and East Thetford are linked by a road flanking the Connecticut River's west bank, followed by a climb to Thetford Hill, whose 1787 Congregational church is Vermont's oldest meeting house in continuous use.

Then comes the saw-mill village of Post Mills, followed by West Fairlee

217

and **Vershire** prior to reaching **Chelsea**, a crossroads town in the midst of dairy-farm country.

A farmers' market occupies Chelsea's North Common lawn each Wed 1500–1800 from mid-May to mid-Oct. Thetford Hill's Grange Hall is home of the long-standing **Parish Players** community-theatre company; *tel: (802) 785-4344.*

Guests can borrow bicycles at the 1832 red-brick **Shire Inn,** *Main St, Chelsea, VT 05038; tel: (802) 685-3031,* moderate–expensive. **Rest 'n Nest Campground** welcomes RV travellers, *Latham Rd, Thetford Center, VT 05075; tel: (802) 785-2997,* open Apr–Nov.

The choicest place for a budget meal along this section of the scenic route is unpretentious **Dixie's II,** *Main St, Chelsea; tel: (802) 685-3000.*

CHELSEA TO RANDOLPH

Tourist Information: Randolph Chamber of Commerce, *66 Central St, Randolph, VT 05060; tel: (802) 728-9027,* open Mon–Fri 0900–1600.

Of five covered bridges spanning the White River in the **Tunbridge** vicinity, the flower-festooned 1879 Howe Bridge is especially close to Rte 110. **South Royalton** features one of central Vermont's largest village greens, complete with a bandstand; south of town in Sharon, off Rte 114, is a monument marking the birthplace of Joseph Smith, who founded the Mormon church. Browse through **Bethel's** circa-1890 Brick Store with its antique soda fountain.

Vermont Law School students order such un-Yankee budget–moderate fare as Cuban chicken with rice and Spanish gazpacho soup at **Hanna's Café,** *On the Green, South Royalton; tel: (802) 763-2626.* **Three Stallion Inn** nestles on 1300 pas-

toral acres adjacent to the Montague Golf Club, *Stock Farm Rd, Randolph, VT 05060; tel: (802) 728-5575,* moderate. Dinners are mostly moderate at **August Lion Restaurant,** *36 Main St, Randolph; tel: (802) 728-5043.* The **Porter Music Box Museum & Gift Shop,** *Sunset Hill, Randolph, VT 05060; tel: (802) 728-9694,* opens Mon–Sat 0930–1700, $2.50.

An early Aug Opera Festival and late Aug Chamber Music Festival take place in elegant **Chandler Music Hall,** *71–73 Main St, Randolph, VT 05060; tel: (802) 728-9878.*

RANDOLPH TO WILLIAMSTOWN

Brookfield's **floating bridge**, the only one like it east of the Mississippi River, bobs and soaks as motorists splash across Sunset Lake en route to a back-road hilltop drive alongside Sunny Brook.

Two 19th-century hillside dwellings overlooking the bridge comprise the moderate–expensive **Green Trails Inn,** *Brookfield, VT 05036; tel: (802) 276-3412.* The **Autumn Crest Inn,** *Rte 64, Williamstown, VT 05679; tel: (802) 433-6627,* gets high marks for both lodging and cuisine.

BARRE AND MONTPELIER

Tourist Information: Central Vermont Chamber of Commerce, *Stewart Rd, Barre, VT 05641; tel: (802) 229-5711,* open Mon–Fri 0900–1700.

ACCOMMODATION

Among plentiful budget–moderate motels, Barre has *DI* and *HJ,* with *CI* in Montpelier. The patrician **Inn at Montpelier,** *147 Main St, Montpelier, VT 05602; tel: (802) 223-2727,* is moderate–expensive and centrally located. Also downtown: moderate **Capitol Plaza**

218

Hotel, *100 State St, Montpelier, VT 05602; tel: (802) 223-5252 or (800) 223-5252.*

EATING AND DRINKING

With local headquarters, New England Culinary Institute runs Montpelier's excellent moderate–pricey **Main Street Grill & Bar**, *118 Main St; tel: (802) 223-3188.* Moderate **Chadwick's**, *52 State St; tel: (802) 223-2384*, has a saloon atmosphere. Budget **Horn of the Moon Café**, *8 Langdon St; tel: (802) 223-2895*, is a natural-foods eatery with hippie overtones. Best of Barre's slim pickings is the **Green Mountain Diner**, *240 N. Main St; tel: (802) 476-6292*, budget–moderate.

SIGHTSEEING AND ENTERTAINMENT

Barre (pronounced 'Barry') claims to be the world's granite capital and proves it with the **Rock of Ages Quarry**, 475 ft deep and 50 acres big.

The **Visitors Center**, *Graniteville, Rte 14; tel: (802) 476-3119*, opens Mon–Sat 0830–1700, Sun 1200–1700 (May–Oct); Sun 0830–1700 (mid-Sept–mid-Oct), free. Narrated tours Mon–Fri 0930–1500, $3.50. Montpelier (population 9000) is the smallest US state capital.

Its Greek Revival **Vermont State House**, *State St; tel: (802) 828-2228*, has free half-hour guided tours Mon–Fri 1000–1530, Sat 1100–1430 (July–mid-Oct).

Vermont Historical Society exhibits are next door in the 'Steamboat Gothic' **Pavilion Building**, *109 State St, Montpelier, VT 05602; tel: (802) 828-2291.* Open Tues–Fri 0900–1630, Sat 0900–1600, Sun 1200–1600, $3.

For eye-catching examples of granite stonecutters' gravesite artistry, explore Barre's **Hope Cemetery**, *Merchant St (Rte 14).* The **Barre Opera House**,

upstairs at City Hall, *Prospect St, Barre, VT 05641; tel: (802) 476-8188*, is an acoustically fine-tuned performing-arts centre.

MONTPELIER TO JEFFERSONVILLE

Tourist Information: **Lamoille Valley Chamber of Commerce**, *Sunset St, Morrisville, VT 05661; tel: (802) 888-7607*, open Mon–Fri 0830–1600.

ACCOMMODATION AND FOOD

The four-room, moderate **Windridge Inn**, *Main St, Jeffersonville, VT 05464; tel: (802) 644-5556*, a bed and breakfast, is right in the centre of a charming village. Walk downstairs to its pricey, epicurean French restaurant, **Le Cheval d'Or**.

Students attending the local state college, one of four in Vermont, enliven Johnson, a woollen-mill town in a verdant river valley. Their favoured budget–moderate eating/socialising havens are **Plum & Main**, *Main St; tel: (802) 635-7596* (originally Johnson's post office), and the **French Press Café**, *Main St; tel: (802) 635-2638*. **Dinner's Dunn** is a combined bakery and moderate lunch and dinner restaurant in Jeffersonville, *Main St; tel: (802) 644-8219.*

RECREATION AND ENTERTAINMENT

Rte 12 north beyond Montpelier follows the curve of a lofty ridge, with forested mountains to the left and eastward pastures grazed by Holstein cows; you'll see a farm with a round barn. **Elmore State Park**; *tel: (802) 888-2982*, with its lakeside beach, picnic benches and Mt Elmore hiking trails, opens mid-May–mid-Oct.

Hyde Park exemplifies small-town Vermont's cultural vitality with its white 1911–12 Opera House, where the **Lamoille County Players**, *Main St, Hyde Park, VT 05655; tel: (802) 888-*

219

4507, stage musicals and dramas May–Nov.

SMUGGLERS NOTCH

Rte 108 becomes a thriller of a drive beginning 12 miles south of Jeffersonville when it narrows into corkscrew turns squeezed between rocky escarpments. So, understandably, this roadway through the notch (Vermontese for a glacier-carved mountain gap) closes to auto traffic during snow season, usually late Nov–late May.

Vermont hiking country's 265-mile north-south **Long Trail**, which follows the ridge line of the Green Mountains from Massachusetts to the Canadian border, slithers into and around Smugglers Notch, attracting outdoor enthusiasts of all endurance levels.

The **Green Mountain Club**, *RR 1, Box 650, Rte 100, Waterbury Center, VT 05677; tel: (802) 244-7037*, open Mon–Fri 0900–1630, publishes the *Guide Book of the Long Trail ($9.95)*, plus maps and other hiking guides. **Smugglers' Notch** ski area; *tel: (802) 644-8851* or *(800) 451-8752*, offers 56 trails and six lifts on three inter-connected mountains, open end Nov–mid-Apr.

STOWE

Tourist Information: Stowe Area Association, *Main St, Stowe, VT 05672; tel: (802) 253-7321* or *toll-free (800) 247-8693*, open Mon–Fri 0900–1700 (0900–2000 in winter), also Sat–Sun 1000–1700 year-round, functions as a central reservations service.

ACCOMMODATION AND FOOD

Stowe, rivalling Killington (see Green Mountain Loop) as Vermont's premiere all-seasons mountain resort, fills visitors' needs with over 60 lodgings of all types and prices. For in-town convenience and past-century charm, consider the expensive–pricey **Green Mountains Inn**, *Main St, Stowe, VT 05672; tel: (802) 253-7301* or *(800) 445-6629*.

Among outlying choices closer to highland recreation, the most famous is the **Trapp Family Lodge** (founded by the real-life *Sound of Music* clan), moderate-expensive depending upon Main or Lower Lodge and time of year; *42 Trapp Hill Rd, Stowe, VT 05672; tel: (802) 253-8511 or (800) 826-7000*.

Eating places are in bountiful supply, too. Three 'recommendables', all on *Mountain Rd*, are the **Cactus Café** for Tex-Mex fare; *tel: (802) 253-7770*, **Mr. Pickwick's Pub & Restaurant**; *tel: (802) 253-7558*, and the **Partridge Inn**, specialising in seafood and steaks; *tel: (802) 253-8000*. **Mother's** is a deli-bakery with a sidewalk terrace in the village centre, *Main St; tel: (802) 253-9044*.

RECREATION AND ENTERTAINMENT

Proximity to Mt Mansfield – at 4393 ft, Vermont's loftiest peak – and vast Mt Mansfield State Forest explains Stowe's popularity.

A 5.5-mile pathway leads from the village church over the Little River and up to mountain foothills. Downhill and cross-country skis, bicycles, also canoes for paddling on the Waterbury Reservoir can be rented at **Action Outfitters**, *Mountain Rd; tel: (802) 253-7975*.

Equestrian trail rides are available through **Topnotch Stables**, *Mountain Rd; tel: (802) 253-8585*. You'll find public tennis courts on *School St*, and the **Stowe Theatre Guild**, *Main St; tel: (802) 253-3961*, schedules summertime productions.

Stowe Mountain Resort; *tel: (802) 253-7311 or (800) 247-8693*, has 45 trails on 487 acres, with 11 lifts, plus cross-country skiing and varied other activities, both winter and summer.

STOWE TO WARREN

Tourist Information: Sugarbush Chamber of Commerce, *Village Sq, Waitsfield, VT 05673; tel: (802) 496-3409,* Mon–Fri 0900–1700, with a lodging reservation facility.

ACCOMMODATION

Originally a lumber baron's Victorian homestead, **Thatcher Brook Inn,** *Rte 100, Waterbury, VT 05676; tel: (802) 244-5911,* is moderate–expensive. The **Old Stagecoach Inn,** *18 N. Main St, Waterbury, VT 05676; tel: (802) 244-5065,* is an old-fashioned bed and breakfast, moderate. Gorgeous landscaping and a round barn distinguish the expensive–pricey **Inn at Round Barn Farm,** *E. Warren Rd, Waitsfield, VT 05673; tel: (802) 496-2276.*

EATING AND DRINKING

Waitsfield's **RSVP** stands for Richard's Special Vermont Pizza and also has a sandwich menu and salad bar, *Bridge St; tel: (802) 496-7787.* Nearby **Bridge Bakery,** *Bridge St; tel: (802) 496-0077,* overlooking Vermont's oldest continuously used covered bridge (1833), is enjoyable for sandwiches, soup and beverages. Both budget.

SIGHTSEEING AND RECREATION

Two of Vermont's top visitor attractions are on Rte 100 south of Stowe. At **Ben & Jerry's** ice-cream kingdom, *Waterbury, Vt 05676; tel: (802) 244-5641,* $1, you can watch the rich stuff being whipped up during a 30-min plant tour, Mon–Sat 0900–1400.

In addition to its made-on-the-spot apple cider, **Cold Hollow Cider Mill,** *Waterbury Center, Vt 05677; tel: (802) 244-*

8711, stocks every conceivable Vermont food product, merchandise item, book and souvenir, open daily 0800–1800.

In addition to epitomising rural Vermont, the very scenic **Mad River Valley** is quite comparable to Stowe for all manner of year-round outdoor activities, focused on the ski areas – **Sugarbush;** *tel: (802) 583-2381,* and **Mad River Glen;** *(802) 496-3551* in terrain nearly as high as Mt Mansfield.

WARREN TO RICHMOND

Westward departure via Warren's covered bridge leads directly to a steep ascent through the **Lincoln Gap** (closed in winter) towards its 2424-ft crest inside the northern edge of the Green Mountain National Forest. Then a downward plunge to tiny **Lincoln,** where there's a pottery studio and maple-sugar house.

The drive continues through the **New Haven River Gorge** approaching **Bristol,** with a spacious green, and budget **Main Street Diner,** *24 Main St; tel: (802) 453-2430.* North of town, **Mary's at Baldwin Creek,** *Rte 116; tel: (802) 453-2432,* is a gourmet-calibre, moderate–expensive restaurant.

Once past Hinesburg, an unnumbered farmland road by way of Mechanicsville and Rhode Island Corners reaches a junction; turn right and downhill into **Richmond,** almost within view of I-89 east of metro Burlington. You'll come upon this pretty village's unique 1813 **Old Round Church,** actually a 16-sided polygon topped with a belfry. It's open Mon–Fri 1000–1600 (early July–early Sept and late-Sept–early Oct); *tel: (802) 434-2556,* free.

Budget food including fresh-baked maple bread is tempting at the **Bridge Street Café & Eatery,** *Bridge St; tel: (802) 434-2233.*

221

WHITE MOUNTAIN NATIONAL FOREST

New Hampshire's White Mountains, formed 300–350 million years ago, are the highest in New England and by far the most rugged. In the White Mountain National Forest, 725,000 acres of peaks and woodlands are protected by federal law. The forest's trails can lead a few metres off the highway to a lovely waterfall or for miles deep into a remote wilderness. Moose sightings are likely; bear sightings are possible. British visitors have compared the White Mountains to the Inverness region of Scotland.

222

TOURIST INFORMATION

New Hampshire Office of Travel and Tourism, *172 Pembroke Rd, Box 1856, Concord, NH 03302-1856; tel: (603) 271-2343*, is a resource for pre-trip planning. **White Mountains Attractions**, *Box 10, Rte 112, N. Woodstock, NH 03262; tel: (603) 745-8720 or (800) 346-3687*, provides information about tourist attractions and places to stay at its **White Mountains Visitor Center**, *Rte 112 at I-93 Exit 32, Lincoln, tel: (603) 745-8720 or (800) 346-3687*, open daily 0830–1700 (mid-Oct–late May), 0830–1730 (rest of year). **New Hampshire Bed & Breakfast Reservation Service**; *tel: (800) 582-0853*.

Country Inns in the White Mountains, *P.O. Box 2025, N. Conway, NH 03860; tel: (603) 356-9460 or (800) 562-1300*. **Ski 93**, *P.O. Box 517, Lincoln, NH 03251; tel: (603) 745-8101 or (800)*

937-5493, provides information to skiers and can make lodging reservations.

The **Appalachian Mountain Club (AMC)**, *5 Joy St, Boston, MA 02108; tel: (617) 523-0636*, is a non-profit group, 60,000 strong, dedicated to conservation, recreation and environmental education. Membership costs $40 per person, $65 per family. The serious hiker or backpacker may wish to head directly to the **AMC Visitor Center and Lodge**, ten miles north of Jackson on Rte 16 at **Pinkham Notch** (mailing address: *P.O. Box 298, Gorham, NH 03581*); *tel: (603) 466-2727*, to purchase guide books, maps, brochures. *The AMC White Mountain Guide* ($16.95) is an indispensable tool for exploring this area, nearly 500 pages worth but small enough to fit in a pocket. Mail orders, *tel: (800) 262-4455*; also sold at AMC in Boston and in bookstores.

AMC also runs the **Crawford Notch Station Information Center**; *tel: (603) 466-7774*, at a former rail stop on Rte 302. Open daily 0900–1600 (late May–early Sept). **US Forest Service**, *Box 638, 719 N. Main St, Laconia, NH 03247; tel: (603) 528-8721*, also offers excellent information at its visitors centres and at **Saco Ranger Station**, *Rte 112* near the junction of joined Rtes 16 and 113, *Conway; tel: (603) 447-5448*. Open daily 0800–1700.

DeLorme Publishing Co., *Rte 1, Freeport, ME 04032; tel: (207) 865-4171*, makes the best general map of the region, *Trail Map & Guide to the White Mountain National Forest*.

WEATHER

Winter in these mountains is often severe. Average Jan temperatures range from 6–26°F; expect extreme variations in temperatures and wind speeds, heavy snows and freezing rains. Average winter snowfall is 100 inches. Motorists should consider waiting out icy conditions.

In summer, the weather changes just as quickly. Average July high is 78°F, the low 36°F. Snow and ice are not uncommon above tree line. In any season, these mountains demand that visitors, especially hikers, be well prepared for a wide range of weather conditions.

ARRIVING AND DEPARTING

By Bus

Concord Trailways, *tel: (800) 639-3317*, serves Lincoln, North Conway, Jackson, Glen, Franconia and Pinkham Notch from Boston and Logan International Airport. The Boston to Conway trip costs $47.50 return.

By Car

I-93 connects Boston to Lincoln, approximately 120 miles. From Portland, Maine, take Rte 302 approximately 70 miles to North Conway.

GETTING AROUND

The AMC operates a hiker shuttle bus between Pinkham Notch and Franconia Notch, stopping at trail heads and visitor centres, June–early Oct, $6–$8. Reservations recommended; *tel: (603) 466-2727*.

STAYING IN THE NATIONAL FOREST

Accommodation

AMC huts are part of a system of back country lodgings along the Appalachian Trail, in the European hut tradition, and accessible only by foot. Lodging fees are moderate at the eight huts in the White Mountains. All eight are open for full service (staff on hand, two cooked meals a day) early June to early Sept, but some remain open longer into the autumn, and two, **Zealand Falls** and **Carter Notch**, operate during the winter on a self-service basis. Winter visitors must bring their own food and a warm sleeping bag.

Lakes of the Clouds Hut, the highest, largest and most popular, is 4.5 miles up the **Tuckerman Ravine Trail** from Pinkham Notch, but can also be reached from the west on the Ammonoosuc Ravine Trail. **Carter Notch Hut**, reached via the Wildcat Ridge Trail or the Nineteen-Mile Brook Trail, is about 1000 ft below the 4422-ft Wildcat Mountain. The **A to Z Trail**, reached via the Avalon Trail, which starts behind the Crawford Notch station, leads to the **Zealand Falls Hut**. The most remote of the huts is **Galehead** at 3800 ft.

Caretakers also charge $5 a night at eight of 13 **AMC shelters**. The rest are free. The shelters are small, three-sided buildings, occupied on a first-come, first-served basis. Bring along a small tent or tarpaulin in case there's no room. To the backpacker or mountaineer, the **AMC Visitor Center and Lodge** (address p. 222) is a mecca, marketplace, *pension* and point of departure. Break bread in the cafeteria; budget. Meals served family style, except for the Fri dinner buffet. Sleep in shared bunkrooms in **Joe Dodge Lodge**; budget. Essential information – guide books, maps and sage advice – is available here. So are showers, on the lower level. Store open daily 0630–2200 all year round. **Crawford Notch Hostel**, *Rte 302, Crawford Notch; tel: (603) 864-7773 or 466-2727*, is an AMC facility,

223

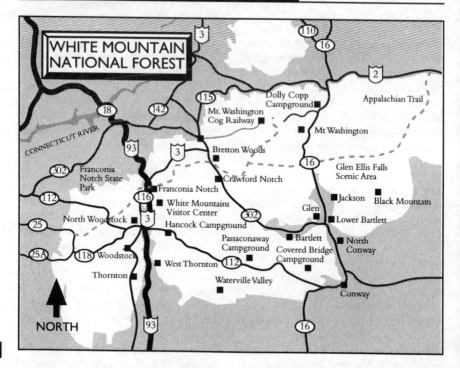

providing budget accommodation and a self-service kitchen. Most campsites operated by the US Forest Service do not have a phone or mailing address. All offer budget accommodation. For information on these sites, write to **Forest Supervisor**, *Box 638, Laconia, NH 03247; tel: (603) 528-8721,* or visit the Saco Ranger Station. **Hancock Campground** is along the Kancamagus Highway on the East Branch of the Pemigewasset River, accommodating tents and RVs. Also along the Kancamagus (and the Swift River), **Passaconaway Campground** is relatively primitive; **Jigger Johnson Campground** offers more services. Disabled travellers can fish at **Covered Bridge Campground**, on *Dugway Rd*, over the bridge from the Kancamagus (Rte 112). Brook trout can be found in **Russell Pond** and cooked at the campsite

there on *Tripoli Rd, Campton* (take I-93 Exit 31 or Rte 175), to the south. **Dolly Copp**, north of Pinkham Notch on Rte 16, is one of the largest campsites in the National Forest Service system, able to accommodate more than 1000 campers. **Zealand Recreation Area**, east of Twin Mountain on Rte 302 includes three campsites and picnicking. The road south leads to the **Zealand, Hale Brook** and **Lend-A-Hand** trails.

In **Franconia Notch State Park**, *Rte 3, Franconia, NH 03580; tel: (603) 271-3254,* **Lafayette Place** is a budget campsite, with coin-operated showers and a small store in the lodge. The trail to **Lonesome Lake**, a glacial tarn with an AMC hut on the shore, begins in the campsite. The hut is popular among hiking families because it's only 1.5 miles from the trail head.

EATING AND DRINKING

Hikers and campers should stock up on groceries at stores along Rte 112 in Lincoln or along joined Rtes 302 and 16 in North Conway (on the strip south of the village). There is one small grocery market in Franconia. Campers at Pinkham Notch can resupply in the town of Gorham, north of the notch on Rte 16. Restaurants are detailed under White Mountains Circuit, p. 227.

OUTDOOR RECREATION

Hiking and climbing

Mt Washington, at 6288 ft, is the highest peak in the north-eastern US and is renowned for its severe weather, in which many climbers and hikers have met their end. The Indians called it **Agiochook**, 'the dwelling place of the Great Spirit', and they helped a white settler make the first ascent in 1642.

Ascents in any season may have to be abandoned due to a change in the weather. *The AMC Guide* makes the point early on: 'The highest wind velocities ever recorded were attained on Mt Washington. Since *the worst is yet to come*, turn back without shame, before it is too late'. Be informed and prepared for any type of weather when heading into these mountains. (The record-setting winds: 231 mph. Lowest recorded temperature: ⁻47°F. Maximum snowfall: 566 inches.)

The *AMC Guide* is one of a hiker's most valuable companions. If you feel your plans don't warrant the investment, the AMC folder *So You Want to Take a Hike* is concise and is required reading. In the cold months, cross-country skiing, snowshoeing (hiking with snowshoes) and winter camping here require an understanding and respect for the risks involved. **Mt Washington Observatory**, at the summit, contains displays about geology, botany and meteorology. *tel: (603) 466-3388.* Open daily 0900-1800 weather permitting (mid-May to mid-Oct), $1. **Tuckerman Ravine**, a glacial cirque named for a botanist, is about 4 miles up a well-worn path. Daring skiers and spectators make spring pilgrimages. Heed avalanche warnings *at all times*.

An AMC shelter is 2.4 miles up the **Tuckerman Ravine Trail**. The summit of Mt Washington is at 4.1 miles. The **International Mountain Climbing School**, *P.O. Box 1666H, N. Conway, NH 03860; tel: (603) 356-7064*, teaches you how to climb rocks, ice and mountains.

The Great Outdoors Walking & Hiking Vacations, *P.O. Box 1937, N. Conway, NH 03860; tel: (603) 356-3113 or (800) 525-9100*, are two- to five-day hiking or mountain biking programs, based at **Stonehurst Manor**, where you'll lay your weary bones each night. Holidays range in price from $154 to $582 per person, including all meals, lodging and the service of guides. Several hikes are accessed from the Kancamagus Highway: For a good 30-mile backpacking trip, walk from Hancock Campground to **Ice Pond**, then follow a counterclockwise loop on the **Wilderness, Bondcliff, Twinway, Garfield Ridge, Franconia Ridge** and **Osseo** trails.

Greeley Ponds were raised by beaver and are inhabited by brook trout. The upper pond is 1.75 miles from the highway; the lower is 0.5 mile further. The trail is a gradual climb. Climbing to **East Peak**, though, at 4156 ft, is strenuous. It takes 10 or 15 mins to walk to **Sabbaday Falls** from the road. The pools and falling water are well worth the trip. Sorry, no swimming. **Bear Notch Road**, which cuts north to **Bartlett** from the

Kancamagus after **Jigger Johnson Campground**, gets narrow in places but is a good road to follow during foliage season. It's closed in winter.

Hikers can follow **Moat Mountain Trail** nine miles north from *Dugway Rd* over several peaks to **Diana's Baths**, a series of falls with swimmable pools.

Near Pinkham Notch, don't bypass **Glen Ellis Falls**. The largest cascade is formed by the Ellis River plunging 64 ft from a glacial cirque. If you can't walk the 165 stairs (600 ft) to the bottom, you can stop at one of several vistas along the way. **The Imp** is a profile in rock and the trail that takes you to it from Dolly Copp campsite. The 6.3-mile route offers views of Mt Washington and the Dolly Copp area from the profile. It ends 0.2 mile south of the starting point. **North Carter** and **Moriah** trails lead onward to **Imp Mountain** and, further on, an AMC shelter. **Arethusa Falls** is over 200 ft high; in spring it's worth the 1.3-mile hike which begins just inside **Crawford Notch State Park**, *Rte 302, Harts Location; tel: (603) 374-2272*. **Silver Cascade**, at the northern end of the state park, is a waterfall not to be missed.

Skiing

Big-time resorts, with trails for all skiers, are scattered through the region. To the south, off I-93 Exit 28 or 31, is **Waterville Valley**, *Waterville Valley, NH 03215; tel: (603) 236-8311*. At the western end of the Kancamagus Higway stands **Loon Mountain**, *Rte 112, Lincoln; tel: (603) 745-8111*. **Cannon Mountain** is a few miles north in Franconia Notch, off Franconia Notch Pkwy Exit 3 or I-93 Exit 35; *tel: (603) 823-5563*.

To the east is **Cranmore**, *N. Conway, NH 03860; tel: (603) 356-5544*. Heading north you'll find **Black Mountain**, *Jackson, NH 03846; tel: (603) 383-4490*, and **Wildcat**, *Rte 16, Pinkham Notch (mailing address: Box R, Jackson, NH 03846); tel: (603) 466-3326*. Between Glen and Franconia Notch, off Rte 302, are **Attitash/Bear Peak**, *P.O. Box 308, Bartlett, NH 03812; tel: (603) 374-2368*, and **Bretton Woods**, *Rte 302, Bretton Woods, NH 03575; tel: (603) 278-5000*.

Most of these downhill areas also offer Nordic trails, some as an afterthought, but cross-country skiing is embraced in the village of **Jackson**, where you can ski onto trails from the door of many inns. **Jackson Ski Touring Foundation Inc.**, *Box 216, Rte 16A, Jackson, NH 03846; tel: (603) 383-9355 or (800) 927-6697*, maintains trails through town, into the woods, up the mountain. The cross-country ski centre at **Bretton Woods Resort** hosts events in biathlon and ski-arc, which combines cross-country with archery.

Canoeing and Swimming

Upper Lady's Bath is five-mins walk downstream from Hancock Campground. **Franconia Falls**, another popular swimming hole, is 3.2 miles up the **Wilderness Trail**, an abandoned railroad bed which begins at **Lincoln Woods** and follows the **Pemigewasset River** north into the **Pemigewasset Wilderness**, a protected area. Because it's an easy grade, the trail is also good for cross-country skiing.

You can walk along the Swift River or cross a wooden footbridge to **Rocky Gorge**, on Rte 112. Swimming is allowed above and below the gorge. **Lower Falls** offers more good swimming and fishing.

Saco Bound Canoe Base, *Rte 302, Center Conway, NH 03813; tel: (603) 447-2177 or 447-3801*, can take you on a guided canoe trip on the river or rent you a boat and let you go it alone. It's a gentle, flat-water ride.

WHITE MOUNTAINS CIRCUIT

The roads that meander through the White Mountains and their notches (mountain passes) see heavy traffic in the summer, during fall foliage time and in winter ski season. In a handful of villages, visitors congregate, lured by roadside attractions, old inns and a cluster of modern shopping outlets.

DIRECT ROUTE: 135 MILES

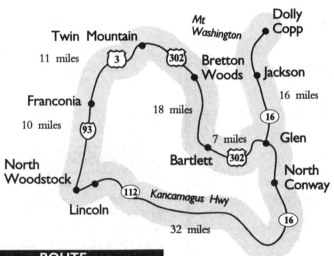

ROUTE

Start the loop, about 135 miles long, from North Woodstock and Lincoln (I-93 Exit 32), where you can gather brochures and maps on the whole region at the **White Mountains Visitor Center**. Turn right out of the centre's parking lot onto Rte 112 east, which becomes the 34.5-mile **Kancamagus Highway**. Top off with petrol as you pass through the centre of Lincoln; there are no filling stations for 32 miles along the Kancamagus. Petrol prices are comparable in all locations along this route. Follow the Kancamagus through the National Forest to its eastern end, near the Saco Ranger Station. Turn left onto Rtes 16/113 and follow Rte 16 north to **North Conway.**

The Appalachian Trail

In the early 1920s, Benton MacKaye, a Harvard-educated forester and regional planner, shared his idea of 'an Appalachian trail' with fellow planners and architects, several of whom were familiar with British garden cities and sensitive to the need for a place where the increasingly urban US population could maintain ties with primeval forests, the rivers and the hills. In myriad locations between Maine's Mt Katahdin and Springer Mountain in Georgia, an army of volunteers and government workers toiled to connect existing trails and to clear the way of what would become the Appalachian Trail.

From Baxter State Park in Maine, the trail stretches 2144 miles southward, It traces a route through New England's grandest forests – the White Mountains of New Hampshire, the Green Mountains of Vermont, the Berkshire Hills of Massachusetts and Connecticut – before reaching the Middle Atlantic and southern states.

It's doubtful that those early planners and volunteers could imagine the traffic on the trail today: about 200 hikers walk the entire route each year. Thousands more walk a part of the trail each year, following its white blazes, finding restoration and, on some of the less crowded stretches, solitude.

Autos and other vehicles under 8 ft, 2 inches tall may take a scenic turnoff after about 28 miles on the Kancamagus. Go 0.7 mile east of **Lower Falls Scenic Area** and turn left onto *Dugway Rd* at a sign to **Covered Bridge Campground**. After crossing **Albany Covered Bridge**, *Dugway Rd* follows the river east, narrowing after about two miles. Be prepared to stop or slow to let oncoming cars pass. *Dugway* becomes *Passaconaway Rd* and ends. Turn left onto *West Side Rd* and follow it 5.5 miles, then turn right onto *River Rd* to reach North Conway. From North Conway, head north along Rtes 16 and 302 for 5.3 miles; Rte 16 then diverts to **Jackson**, **Pinkham Notch** and **Mt Washington**. You can follow Rte 16 north 16 miles to the **Dolly Copp Area** for camping and access to nearby hiking trails (or continue north another 5 miles to Rte 2, an east-west highway skirting the forest's northern boundary).

Reverse direction, return south to Rte 302 and turn right, following it west through **Bartlett**, then north as it cuts through **Crawford Notch** on the way to **Bretton Woods** and **Twin Mountain**. At the junction of Rtes 302 and 3, turn left and follow Rte 3 until it joins I-93 south of Franconia Village as the **Franconia Notch Pkwy**. At Exit 1, take Rte 3 south to Rte 112 east and you'll return to the starting point at the White Mountains Visitor Center.

LINCOLN AND NORTH WOODSTOCK

Tourist Information: White Mountains Visitor Center, *Rte 112 at I-93 Exit 32, Lincoln, tel: (603) 745-8720*, open daily 0830–1700 (mid–Oct–late May), 0830–1730 (rest of year), has details on the whole region, good maps of the Kancamagus Highway; rangers can give tips for easy day hikes. **Lincoln-Woodstock Chamber of Commerce**, *P.O. Box 358, Lincoln, NH 03251; tel: (603) 745-6621; reservations, tel: (800) 227-4191.*

ACCOMMODATION

Woodstock Inn, *P.O. Box 118, Rte 3, Main St, N. Woodstock, NH 03262; tel:*

228

(603) 745-3951 or *(800) 321-3985*, is a moderate–expensive 19-room in-town inn with expensive dining on the porch and budget brewpub meals in a restored train station.
Wilderness Inn Bed & Breakfast, *Rte 3, N. Woodstock, NH 03262; tel: (603) 745-3890,* just outside the town centre, has seven rooms and awesome home-made breakfasts; moderate. There's an *Ma* near Loon Mountain; camping, cabins, motels, resort hotels and condominiums cover all prices ranges.

EATING AND DRINKING

Cheap eateries are easy to find along Rte 112 in Lincoln centre. **Café Lafayette Dinner Train**, *P.O. Box 9, Lincoln, NH 03251; tel: (603) 745-3500*, is a restored Pullman car and a moveable feast. Dinner is served while the train rides along the **Pemigewasset River**. Reservations required. Pricey. You can sit in the pub and watch the brewmaster at work in budget **Woodstock Station & Stock Room**, *Main St (Rte 3)* at the Woodstock Inn, *N. Woodstock; tel: (603) 745-3951*, or walk to several other eateries along *Main St.*

SIGHTSEEING AND RECREATION

Loon Mountain, *Rte 112, Lincoln; tel: (603) 745-8111*, offers downhill and cross-country skiing in winter; mountain biking, horseback riding and rollerblading in summer.

Ride the **Hobo Railroad**, *Rte 112, Lincoln; tel: (603) 745-2135*, along the Pemigewasset River, a 75-min excursion. Open daily 1000–1900 (June–mid-Oct); weekends only (mid-Mar–May and mid-Oct–Dec), $4.50–$7.

Some pity the captive performing bears at **Clark's Trading Post**, *Rte 3, Lincoln; tel: (603) 745-8913*. Others say the bears

are well cared for and live longer than their cousins in the wild. Only the bears know for sure. Open daily 1000–1800 (mid-June–early Sept); weekends 1000–1800 (late May–mid-June and early Sept–mid-Oct, $1–$7.

Boardwalks guide you through **Lost River Gorge**, *Rte 112* at *Kinsman Notch, N. Woodstock; tel: (603) 745-8031*. Open daily 0900–1700 (May–Jun and Sept–Oct), weather permitting; daily 0900–1800 (July–Aug), $4–$7.

Wear your bathing suit to **The Whale's Tale**, *Rte 3, Lincoln; tel: (603) 745-8810*, a water park with lots of splashing. Open daily 1000–1800 (June–early Sept), $9–$15. Free for kids under 36 inches and for senior citizens.

LINCOLN TO NORTH CONWAY

It's National Forest all the way along the Kancamagus Highway, the only national 'scenic byway' in New England. Parking areas give motorists access to scenic over-looks, picnic areas and trailheads for hiking (see p. 225). There are several National Forest campsites (see pp. 223–224), but no hotels, restaurants or filling stations for 32 miles east of Lincoln. Watch out for moose.

NORTH CONWAY

Tourist Information: Mt Washington Valley Chamber of Commerce, *N. Conway, NH 03860; tel: (603) 356-3171*; for reservations, *tel: (800) 367-3364*. Visit the **information booth** on the east side of Rtes 16 and 302 in the centre of town, open Mon–Fri 1000–1800, Sat 0900–2000, Sun 0900–1500. A **state booth** is two miles north at the scenic vista on Rte 16; *tel: (603) 356-3961*, open Mon–Thur 1000–1700, Fri–Sun 0700–1030.

ACCOMMODATION

The **1785 Inn**, *P.O. Box 1785, 3582 White Mountain Hwy, N. Conway, NH 03860; tel: (603) 356-9025 or (800) 421-1785*, has exceptional mountain views and a pub. Full breakfast included. Expensive. The **Forest**, *Box 37, Rte 16A, Intervale, NH 03845; tel: (603) 356-9772 or (800) 448-3534*, serves afternoon tea to British visitors; formal during fall foliage. Moderate. It's also the starting point for a non-guided inn-to-inn bicycle tour. For about $250 per person, **Bike the Whites**, *Box 189, Tamworth, NH 03886*, provides cyclists with three nights lodging, country breakfasts, candlelit dinners and maps, and transports their luggage to the next night's lodgings. Call The Forest for information. *Sh* and *BW*, among others, are nearby.

EATING AND DRINKING

Scottish Lion Inn & Restaurant, *Rte 16; tel: (603) 356-6381*, serves a Highland game pie, roast beef with Yorkshire pudding, Finnan Haddie and – what's this? – Thai pork loin and Bali chicken. Have a Scotch at the Inn's **Black Watch Pub**. Moderate.

SIGHTSEEING AND SHOPPING

Conway Scenic Railroad, *depot: Rte 16; mailing address: 38 Norcross Circle, N. Conway, NH 03860; tel: (603) 356-5251 or (800) 232-5251*, gives hour-long rides by steam or diesel engines; longer hauls over Crawford Notch to Bretton Woods. Weekends (mid-April–mid-May and late Oct–late Dec); daily (mid-May–late Oct). Call for ticket prices.

If you'd rather shop, turn off the suggested route at the junction of *River Rd* and Rtes 16/302 and head about 2 miles south to a strip of famous brand **outlet stores**; traffic can become congested there. The centre of North Conway, also

south of the junction, has a few nice shops. The **Mt Washington Observatory Resource Center and Museum Shop**, *Rte 16, Box 2310, N. Conway 03860; tel: (603) 356-8345*, is a good place to talk about the weather. Exhibits on meteorology and mountain history. Open daily 1000-1700 (late May–mid-Oct), free.

JACKSON TO GLEN

Tourist Information: Jackson Chamber of Commerce, *Rte 16, Jackson, NH 03846; tel: (603) 383-9356*, just south of the covered bridge that leads into the village, is open daily 0900–1500 all year. **Jackson Lodging Central Reservations**, *tel: (800) 866-3334*, can book stays at bed and breakfasts, inns, resorts, condominiums and motels.

ACCOMMODATION AND FOOD

Thorn Hill Inn, *P.O. Box A, Thorn Hill Rd, Jackson, NH 03846; tel: (603) 383-4242 or (800) 289-8990*, is a Victorian inn. Expensive–pricey. **Glen Ellis Family Campground**, *Rte 302 west of Rte 16, P.O. Box 397, Glen, NH 03838; tel: (603) 383-4567*, is a gem, a cut above all other private campsites. Budget. **Thompson House Eatery**, *Rte 16A, Jackson; tel: (603) 383-9341*, has an inventive menu, an ice-cream parlour, a wonderful view and a farm stand. Moderate.

SIGHTSEEING

Heritage, *Rte 16, Box 1776, Glen, NH 03838; tel: (603) 383-9776*, takes a journey through 350 years of New England history, all under one roof; excellent for rainy days. It begins with a taste of switchel and a sea biscuit. Open daily 0900–1700 (mid-May–mid-June); 0900–1800 (mid-June–early Sept), $7.50.

Story Land, *same address; tel: (603) 383-4293*, offering fun and fantasy, is next door. $15 per person, children under 4 free. Open daily 0900–1800 (mid-June–early Sept); weekends 1000–1700 to mid-Oct.

PINKHAM NOTCH

Climbing to the top of Mt Washington requires preparation and stamina. Driving up on the **Mt Washington Auto Road**, *Box 278, Gorham, NH 03581; tel: (603) 466-3988*, is easier and requires $14 per vehicle and driver, additional $3–$5 for passengers. Guided tour by van $10–$18. The start of the road is 2.6 miles north of the AMC lodge. Open daily 0730–1800 (mid-May–late Oct), weather permitting; shorter hours early and late in season. **The Presidential Range** can be seen from here: **Mt Madison, Mt Adams, Mt Jefferson and Mt Washington**, all named for early US presidents. For hiking and camping, here and at Dolly Copp, see White Mountain National Forest p. 222.

GLEN TO BRETTON WOODS

Road Kill Cafe, *Rte 302, Bartlett; tel: (603) 374-6116*, garnishes its dishes with country-blackened humor. Try the 'chish and fips'. You'll mingle with locals and smell like a cigarette when you leave. Moderate. There's no smoking **The Notchland Inn**, *Rte 302, Harts Location, NH 03812; tel: (800) 866-6131*, a grand granite mansion built in 1862 at the base of **Mt Bemis**. Pricey.

Bartlett is the location of **Attitash** ski resort, with activities and accommodation year-round.

BRETTON WOODS TO FRANCONIA NOTCH

The Mount Washington Hotel and Resort, *Rte 302, Bretton Woods, NH 03575; tel: (603) 278-1000 or (800) 258-0330*, is the last of several grand hotels that once attracted the wealthy and leisurely to these mountains. 'The Mount Wash', struggles to uphold its name, but has faded around the edges. Pricey. There's a great view of the resort and Mt Washington from atop **Bretton Woods** ski resort.

Mount Washington Cog Railway, *Base Rd, Mt Washington, NH 03589; tel: (603) 846-5404 or (800) 922-8825*, climbs a steep route to the summit, powered by steam engines. Open daily 0715–1830 (mid-May–mid-Oct), occasionally thereafter. Last train departs 1600; $24–$35 for the three-hour round trip, with 20 mins on top. Advance ticket purchase suggested. The station is 6 miles off Rte 302.

FRANCONIA NOTCH

Tourist Information: Take Exit 1 off the Franconia Notch Pkwy to the **Flume Visitor Center** for tourist information. **The Flume Gorge**; *tel: (603) 745-8391*, provides a safe walk through an 800-ft chasm. Open daily 0900–1730 (mid-May–mid-Sept), 0900–1700 to mid-Oct, $3–$6. The **Franconia Notch State Park Bike Path**, which runs 9 miles the length of the Notch, provides an easy, mostly level route for casual strollers, including children. From the Franconia Notch Pkwy, take Exit 2 to reach the **Cannon Aerial Tramway**; *tel: (603) 823-5563*, and ride up the mountain, $4.50–$9, in summer; skiers rule the slopes in winter.

The Old Man of the Mountains is a profile formed by three ledges of granite jutting out of the southeast side of **Profile Mountain;** best visibility of the 'great stone face' is from a well-marked scenic turnout along the highway (and cycle path). You can also see the Old Man on every New Hampshire licence plate – his face is the heraldic crest of New Hampshire.

BURLINGTON AND LAKE CHAMPLAIN

Vermont's biggest city, population a bit less than 40,000, is scarcely big at all. Visitors get the impression they're in a spacious college town, its openness enhanced by parkland frontage along Lake Champlain's shoreline. Here in the region's only landlocked state, witty citizens refer to Burlington as being on New England's West Coast. Cultural refinements combined with college-student effervescence contribute to its image as a small-scale, up-North version of Boston.

TOURIST INFORMATION

Lake Champlain Regional Chamber of Commerce, *60 Main St, Burlington, VT 05401; tel: (802) 863-3489,* open Mon–Fri 0830–1700, Sat–Sun 1000–1400.

WEATHER

The lake exerts a moderating influence, generally causing cooler summer temperatures and less winter snowfall and deep freezes than elsewhere in Vermont. But since all of New England is subject to unpredictabilities, a call to the regional National Weather Service office can be useful for next-day and short-term forecasts; *tel: (802) 862-2475.*

ARRIVING AND DEPARTING

Lake Champlain Transportation Co., *King St Dock, Burlington, VT 05401; tel:* *(802) 864-9804,* operates one-hour car-ferry crossings between Port Kent, N.Y., and Burlington mid-May–mid-Oct. Ferries make the 12-min voyage between Plattsburgh, N.Y., and Grand Isle, Vt. (north of Burlington in the Lake Champlain Islands) year-round.

Montréal is about 100 miles north; take I-89 north to Exit 17, then Rte 2 to Rte 314 for the Plattsburgh ferry, then follow I-87 north into Canada, where it becomes Rte 15.

Vermont Transit Lines, *135 St. Paul St, Burlington, VT 05401; tel: (802) 864-6811,* has regional motorcoach service to Boston and other destinations throughout New England, plus New York City and Montréal. Although Burlington isn't directly on the **Amtrak** network, there's a station in suburban Essex Junction for Amtrak's Vermonter connection to and from Manhattan; *tel: toll-free (800) 872-7245.*

PUBLIC TRANSPORT

The **Chittenden County Transportation Authority (CCTA)** serves metro Burlington including such adjacent communities as Winooski and Shelburne for a basic $0.75 adult fare; *tel: (802) 864-0211.* CCTA's free *College St* Shuttle connects this downtown thoroughfare and the University of Vermont campus on the east side of town, daily 1100–2100.

DRIVING

Good signage and a grid street pattern make modest-size Burlington easy to

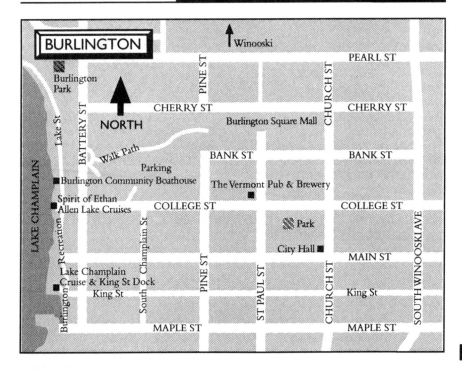

BURLINGTON

Winooski

Burlington Park

NORTH

PINE ST

CHERRY ST

PEARL ST

CHURCH ST

CHERRY ST

Lake St

BATTERY ST

Walk Path

Burlington Square Mall

BANK ST

BANK ST

Parking

LAKE CHAMPLAIN

Burlington Community Boathouse

The Vermont Pub & Brewery

COLLEGE ST

COLLEGE ST

Spirit of Ethan Allen Lake Cruises

Recreation

South Champlain St

Park

SOUTH WINOOSKI AVE

City Hall

MAIN ST

Lake Champlain Cruise & King St Dock

King St

Burlington

PINE ST

ST PAUL ST

CHURCH ST

King St

MAPLE ST

MAPLE ST

233

negotiate, especially if you've already sur-vived Boston's obstacle course. Take I-89 Exit 14 onto Rte 2, which becomes *Main St* heading straight through the city centre. On-street downtown parking is at two- and three-hour meters. Two city-man-aged garages (entrances on *Cherry St* and *Bank St*) offer a convenient alternative; full-day use costs $5.

STAYING IN BURLINGTON

Accommodation

RA, Burlington's only downtown hotel, overlooks the lake. Outlying hotels and motor inns include a huge *Sh,* plus *CI, EL, Hd, QI, RI, Rm* and *S8.* The New England Culinary Institute's surburban **Inn at Essex,** *70 Essex Way, Essex Junction, VT 05452; tel: (800) 727-4295,* is elegant and expensive–pricey. **Howden**

Cottage, *32 N. Champlain St, Burlington, VT 05401; tel: (802) 864-7198,* is a mod-erate, centrally located bed and breakfast. Time spent at tourist attractions in Shelburne, 7 miles south of Burlington centre, could be combined with a lakeshore stay at the moderate– expensive, 24-room **Inn at Shelburne Farms,** *102 Harbor Rd, Shelburne, VT 05482; tel: (802) 985-8498,* originally an 1880s summer mansion.

There's budget camping south of Burlington along the lake at **DAR State Park,** *Rte 17, Addison; tel: (802) 759-2354,* and **Button Bay State Park** on country roads in Vergennes; *tel: (802) 475-2377.*

Eating and Drinking

Newcomers strolling downtown's *Church St Marketplace* and immediate vicinity might wonder how such a small city could sustain so many restaurants and cafés, most with sidewalk terraces. Moderate choices amidst the electic abundance include **Leunig's,** *115 Church St; tel: (802) 863-3759,* a Euro-type bistro, and **Sakura,** *2 Church St; tel: (802) 863-1988,* for Japanese sushi and tempura. Moderate **Sweetwaters,** *120 Church St; tel: (802) 864-9800,* in a recycled bank building, serves such esoterica as bison burgers and bison chilli. Also moderate:

Bourbon Street Grill, *213 College St; tel: (802) 865-2800,* for Louisiana Cajun specialties, and the **Cactus Café,** *1 Lawson Lane; tel: (802) 862-6900,* for Tex-Mex.

The 16-page menu at antique-bedecked **Carbur's,** *115 St. Paul St; tel: (802) 862-4106,* covers a wide price spectrum. Best for Italian pizzas and full meals is **Sweet Tomatoes,** *83 Church St; tel: (802) 660-95 33.*

Lakefront proximity makes **Dockside,** *209 Battery St; tel: (802) 864-5266,* a satisfying choice for fresh seafood. Moderate–pricey **Isabel's,** *112 Lake St; tel: (802) 865-2522,* also close to the water, is the posh occupant of what used to be a sawmill.

The budget–moderate **Vermont Pub & Brewery,** *144 College St; tel: (802) 865-0500,* does a respectable job of emulating 'Brit' ambiance.

ENTERTAINMENT

Each Thursday's *Weekend* section of the *Burlington Free Press* is a handy guide to goings-on; weekly, free *Vox* tabloids are another such resource. You can, moreover, get a monthly summary of events by phoning Burlington City Arts' 24-hour Arts Line; *tel: (802) 865-9163.*

The **Flynn Theatre,** *153 Main St; tel: (802) 863-5966,* a restored Art Deco oldie, has become Burlington's all-purpose performing arts centre. **Toast,** *165 Church St; tel: (802) 660-2088,* is a hip downtown hang-out for live-music fans.

Amongst others are **Buddahs Hard Rock Café,** *75 Main St; tel: (802) 660-2832,* and **Java Blues,** *197 College St; tel: (802) 860-6050.* Another of the young crowd's popular hot spots is **Nectar's,** *188 Main St; tel: (802) 658-4771,* which doubles as a budget– moderate cafeteria, open 18 hours daily. Upstairs **Club Metronome,** offering heavy metal and acid rock, is high-decibel too; *tel: (802) 865-4563.*

Various downtown locations swing to early June's week-long **Discover Jazz Festival;** *tel: (802) 863-7992.*

Classical music has an avid following. The Burlington-based **Vermont Symphony Orchestra** performs in the Flynn Theatre and University of Vermont's Recital Hall, also at Shelburne Farms, on the meadow at Stowe's Trapp Family Lodge and other out-of-town venues; *tel: (802) 864-5741.*

Each year's **Vermont Mozart Festival,** three weeks in July–Aug, is a comparably far-ranging event that even includes concerts on Lake Champlain ferries; *tel: (802) 862-7352.*

In addition to what's on at the Flynn, enquire about stage productions at Champlain College's **Hauke Auditorium;** *tel: (802) 863-5966,* the **McCarthy Arts Center** at St. Michael's College; *tel: (802) 654-2281,* and **Contois Auditorium** in City Hall (home of the Green Candle theatrical company); *tel: (802) 893-7333.*

Event

Vermont's largest country fair is the all-American **Champlain Valley Fair,** *Champlain Valley Exposition Fairgrounds,*

Essex Junction, VT 05452; tel: (802) 878-5545, $6, late Aug–early Sept.

Recreation

The **Burlington Bike Path** extends 8.2 miles through three city parks along the lakefront. Rentals available from **North Star Cyclery**, *100 Main St; tel: (802) 863-3832*. **Winds of Ireland**, Burlington Community Boathouse (foot of *College St*); *tel: (802) 863-5090*, offers sailboat and Sea-Doo rentals. Golfers have several outlying choices that include pro shops for equipment rentals. One is the **Essex Country Club**, *Old Stage Rd, Essex Junction, VT 05452; tel: (802) 879-3232*, with its 18-hole, par 72 course in a pastoral setting, open May–Nov.

SHOPPING

Burlington's prime hunting ground is the **Church St Marketplace**, a pedestrian corridor extending four blocks between *Main* and *Pearl Sts* – inner-city vibrancy with pushcart vendors, entertainers and fountains. Dozens of speciality stores, plus the street's Burlington Square Mall retail enclosure, are intermingled with the eating and drinking establishments. You'll also find tempting rows of storefronts on intersecting *College St*.

SIGHTSEEING

The *Spirit of Ethan Allen II* embarks from the Burlington Boathouse dock on 90-min narrated lake cruises, with food and beverages available on board as passengers catch the breeze and view New York's Adirondack mountain ranges looming beyond the western shore.

It's inevitable that you'll be told about 'Champ', akin to Scotland's Loch Ness Monster. The last supposed sighting of Lake Champlain's mythical sea serpent occurred in 1984. **Lake Champlain**

Shoreline Cruises; *tel: (802) 862-8300*. Departures at 1000, 1200, 1400 and 1600 daily, late May–mid-Oct.

Shelburne Farms, *Harbor and Bay Rds, Shelburne, VT 05482; tel: (802) 985-8442*, is a 1,400-acre working farm reliant on turn-of-the-century methods, equipment and buildings, embellished by a beautiful agricultural landscape and perennial gardens. Walking trails looping 6 miles through meadows and woodlands open onto views of Lake Champlain and the Adirondacks from **Lone Tree Hill**. Picnic spots are plentiful, a cottage farm store stocks Vermont specialities and youngsters commune with goats, cows, sheep, pigs and chickens in the **Children's Farmyard**. Open daily 0930–1700 (mid-May–mid-Oct), $4 plus $2.50 for 90-min guided tour.

Families with children might enjoy watching cuddly cubs being stuffed and stitched on the production line at **Vermont Teddy Bear Co.**, *1126 Shelburne Rd, Shelburne, VT 05482; tel: (802) 985-3001*, open Mon–Sat 1000–1600, Sun 1100–1600, free.

The **Sugarbush/Vermont Express**; *tel: (802) 864-7277*, pulls six coaches and a 1917 Pullman lounge car on June–Oct rail excursions between Burlington's waterfront and Middlebury, with in-between stops at Shelburne and Vergennes; $8 round-trip. Passengers disembarking in Shelburne can board CCTA's **Shelburne Shuttle**, making a 20-min loop between the *Harbor Rd* public-transit station, Shelburne Farms and the **Vermont Teddy Bear factory**; *tel: (802) 864-2282*, all-day ticket $1, all-day family pass $3.

Museums

The amazing **Shelburne Museum**, *Rte 7, Shelburne, VT 05482; tel: (802) 985-3346*, bursts with miscellaneous outdoor-

235

Shelburne Museum
Electra Havemeyer Webb's 'Collectibles'

Electra Havemeyer Webb was a wealthy lady with a fervent interest in early New Englanders' ingenuity and craftsmanship. This prompted her lifelong passion for collecting all manner of pertinent artifacts, which led ultimately to the establishment of the quirky and remarkably diverse Shelburne Museum. It's a distinctly countrified, Yankee version of Washington, D.C.'s famed Smithsonian Institution.

The word *museum* for Electra's legacy might incorrectly imply a single storehouse stuffed with displays and exhibits. Instead, her acquisitions fill 37 structures scattered over 45 acres of landscaped grounds and blooming lilac gardens. Opened in 1947 and subsequently expanded ever since, Shelburne's mixed bag of Americana now amounts to over 80,000 items.

Crafts and folk art predominate – ranging from quilts and weathervanes, scrimshaw (carved whalebone) and pewter to toys, dolls, portraits, shop signs, carved wooden cigar-store Indians, clocks, music boxes, duck decoys and wall stencilling. But there's much, much more. Nearly 200 buggies, carriages, wagons, sleighs and fire engines from the horse-drawn era fill the Horseshoe Barn. Printers, blacksmiths and weavers demonstrate old-time skills. Tools, trophies, furniture, patent medicines, canoes, kettles and crockery are amidst this 'collection of collections'. Also – in six rooms recreating Electra's Manhattan apartment – paintings by Rembrandt, Manet, Monet, Goya, Degas and Mary Cassatt.

A transplanted Vermont church, covered bridge, round barn and one-room schoolhouse, even a 1915 locomotive, mightn't come as a surprise considering Electra's eclectic clutter. Here on Champlain Valley dry land, however, the Colchester Reef lighthouse and definitely the 220-ft-long sidewheeler steamboat *Ticonderoga* are indeed startling to behold.

236

indoor Americana (see feature box), making it a microcosm of New England life. Events include pageants, concerts, special exhibits, an annual mid-Aug crafts fair and seasonal festivals and celebrations. Open daily 1000–1700 (late May–late Oct), Sun at 1300 for guided tour of selected buildings (late Oct–late May), $17.50 for two consecutive days.

The Justin Morgan Memorial Museum, *Bostwick Rd, Shelburne, VT 05482 (adjacent to the Shelburne Museum); tel: (802) 985-8665,* devotes modernistic space to the Morgan horse, Vermont's beloved thoroughbred line. Open Mon–Fri 0800–1700, Sat 1000–1400, $1.

Learn all about the state's 'founding

father' and Revolutionary War hero in the **Ethan Allen Homestead,** first exit off *Rte 127 North, Burlington, VT 05401; tel: (802) 865-4556,* with exhibits and a multimedia show in Allen's 1787 farmhouse. Open Tues–Sun 1300–1700 (mid-May–mid-June); Mon–Sat 1000–1700, Sun 1300–1700 (mid-June–early Sept); daily 1300–1700 early Sept–mid-Oct, $3.50.

The University of Vermont's **Robert Hull Fleming Museum,** *61 Colchester Ave, Burlington, VT 05405; tel: (802) 656-2090,* open Tues–Fri 0900–1600, Sat–Sun 1300–1700, $2, houses an extraordinary array of more than 17,000 objects from worldwide cultures, including decorative and fine arts, anthropological artifacts, Japanese Samurai armour, Chinese imperial robes and an important collection of Northern Plains Native American art from the 1880s.

CHAMPLAIN ISLANDS

Vermont's portion of Lake Champlain (sixth biggest US fresh-water lake, despite spreading north into Québec) encompasses three islands and a peninsula. They're collectively bunched into little, offshore Grand Isle County, farm and orchard terrain that's also popular for boating, biking and camping. Getting there from Burlington is just a matter of driving 8 miles north on I-89, then following Rte 2 across bridges that tie the county together. 'Doing' all of the Champlain Islands would amount to about 40 miles.

Tourist Information: Lake Champlain Islands Chamber of Commerce, *P.O. Box 213, North Hero, VT 05474; tel: (802) 372-3826,* Mon–Fri 0800–1600. The chamber maintains an **information booth** on Rte 2 in South Hero; *tel: (802) 372-5683,* open Fri–Mon 1000–1800, Tue–Thur 1400–1800 (early July–early Sept).

ACCOMMODATION AND FOOD

Lodgings and meals are moderate at **North Hero House,** *North Hero, VT 05474; tel: (802) 372-8237,* with across-the-lake views of Mt Mansfield. Nearby is a moderate bed and breakfast overlooking Wilcox Cove: **Farmhouse on the Lake,** *116 West Shore Rd, Grand Isle, VT 05458; tel: (802) 372-8849.* Another recommendable, moderate bed and breakfast is the lakefront **Thomas Mott Homestead,** *Blue Rock Rd, Arlburg, VT 05440; tel: (802) 796-3736.*

Also attractive and moderate for lakeview meals and accommodation:

Ruthcliffe Lodge & Restaurant, *Old Quarry Rd, Isle La Motte, VT 05463; tel: (802) 928-3200.* **Margo's Café,** *Rte 2, Grand Isle; tel: (802) 372-6112,* is a pleasant stopping-off place for light meals and pastries. One of half a dozen county campsites is **Apple Tree Bay Resort,** *Sand Bar Bridge, South Hero, VT 05486; tel: (802) 372-5398.*

SIGHTSEEING

Two historic attractions are noteworthy. Built in 1783 and furnished with 18th-century artifacts, the **Hyde Log Cabin,** *Rte 2, Grand Isle, VT 05458; tel: (802) 372-5440,* Wed–Sun 1100–1700 (July–Aug), $1, is believed to be the oldest such dwelling in the US.

Catholic **St. Anne's Shrine,** *Rte 129, Isle La Motte, VT 05463; tel: (802) 928-3362,* free, is where Fort St. Anne, Vermont's first white settlement, stood in 1666. A statue of Samuel de Champlain commemorates the explorer's landing here in 1606.

ENTERTAINMENT AND RECREATION

Descendants of Austria's elite **Royal Lipizzan Stallions** perform in summertime: *Rte 2, North Hero, VT 05474; tel: (802) 372-5683,* open Thur–Fri 1800, Sat–Sun 1430, mid-July–Sept, $15.

The pancake-flat islands are ideal for bicycling. Hourly and full-day rentals are available at **Hero's Welcome** in North Hero; *tel: (802) 372-4161;* it's also a folksy store, bakery and café.

The **Missiquoi National Wildlife Refuge**; *tel: (802) 868-4781,* is a blissfully idyllic patch of woods and marshland on Lake Champlain's northeastern shore, near Swanton and a few miles below the US-Canadian border. Two marked trails put you in close touch with wide-open, unspoiled nature.

NORTHEAST KINGDOM LOOP

Geographically, 'the Kingdom' comprises Vermont's three north-eastern counties: Orleans, Caledonia and Essex. Why such a regal name for Vermont's most remote, rural area? Credit that to a senator's boastful flight of oratory in 1949. Remoteness can be advantageous. This 2000-sq-mile corner is less commercialised and mass-consumerised than any other part of New England. It's often scenically compared with the Scottish Highlands and – not coincidentally – a strong streak of Scottish Presbyterianism has prevailed since colonial times.

238

DIRECT ROUTE: 155 MILES

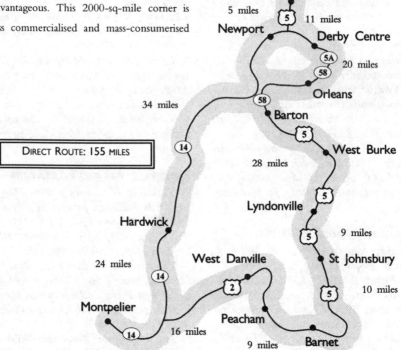

ROUTE

Montpelier is a suggested starting point for the 155- to 170-mile loop. Take Rte 14 north for 24 miles to **Hardwick** near the Northeast Kingdom's southern fringe, than another 24 miles to **Irasburg**. From there, continue 10 miles north via Rte 5 to **Newport** on the largest of the region's many lakes, Memphremagog. After an additional 4.5 miles on Rte 5, you'll arrive in **Derby Line**.

Backtrack by driving 11 miles on Rte 5 to **Derby Center** then take Rtes 5A/105 south to **West Charleston**, after which a 7-mile journey down Rte 5A brings you to **Lake Willoughby**. Turning onto Rte 58, go 7 miles west through **Evansville** to reach **Orleans**. Follow that with a 28.5-mile southward drive on Rte 5 via **Barton, Glover** (actually a short diversion down Rte 16 to Rte 122) and **West Burke** to **Lyndonville**.

If you'd rather rush things, I-91 can be accessed near Derby Line for travel directly south to Lyndonville and on to St. Johnsbury. (At St. Johnsbury, you can transfer to the Portland–New Hampshire Loop, p. 259; take I-91 south, then I-93 south to Littleton, N.H.). The distance between Lyndonville and sizable **St. Johnsbury** amounts to 9 miles via scenic Rte 5 or the speedier interstate. Continue south by either means from St. Johnsbury to **Barnet** (9.5 miles) on the Connecticut River. Then follow signs on the back roads leading to **West Barnet, South Peacham** and **Peacham** – overall a 9-mile ramble that curves west and then north to **Danville** on Rte 2. Close the loop by driving 16 miles to **Plainfield**, from there onto Rte 14 and back to Vermont's capital city, Montpelier.

TOURIST INFORMATION

Northeast Kingdom Chamber of Commerce, *30 Western Ave, St. Johnsbury, VT 05819; tel: (802) 748-3678 or toll-free (800) 639-6379,* open Mon–Fri 0830–1700, is an all-purpose resource covering the entire region.

HARDWICK

Budget–moderate **Carolyn's Bed & Breakfast**, *15 Church St, Hardwick, VT 05843; tel: (802) 472-6338,* is an appealing 1890s building near the town centre.

Moderate **Elliott's**, *Main St; tel: (802) 472-6770,* is best locally for family-style lunches and dinners. Linger over coffee or tea with fresh-baked scones at the budget **Renaissance Café**, *Main St; tel: (802) 472-9002,* next door to the well-stocked **Galaxy Bookshop**; *tel: (802) 472-5533.* Hardwick hosts the **Fiddlers' Contest**, a jamboree with a chicken barbecue, at Shephard's Field on the last Sat in July.

THE CRAFTSBURYS

Your Rte 14 drive north from Hardwick passes **Lake Elligo**; a mile beyond, watch for signs indicating a right-hand turn towards **Craftsbury, Craftsbury Common** and **East Craftsbury** – three outstandingly charming hamlets tucked amidst hills and farm fields. East Craftsbury's library, originally its 1830s general store, epitomises rural but bookish Vermont.

ACCOMMODATION AND FOOD

Top-priced amongst lodgings is hilltop **Inn on the Common**, *Craftsbury Common, VT 05827; tel: (802) 586-9619 or (800) 521-2233,* with meals prepared by a French chef. The circa-1850 **Craftsbury Inn**, *Craftsbury, VT 05826; tel: (802) 586-2848,* is expensive–pricey with both morning and evening meals included. **Finchingfield Farm**, *East Craftsbury, VT 05826; tel: (802) 586-7763,* a moderate bed and breakfast, features a tranquil setting and English furnishings and heirlooms. Moderate lodgings can be combined with bicycling, hiking or Catamount Trail cross-country skiing at **The Craftsbury Center**, *Craftsbury Common, VT 05827; tel: (800) 729-7751.* Four-seasons recreational amenities also augment **Highland Lodge**, *RR 1, Greensboro, VT 05841; tel: (802) 533-2647,* 5 miles down the road from East Craftsbury, overlooking Caspian

239

Lake, serving excellent meals and favoured mainly by families on holiday with children. In Greensboro centre, delve into **Willey's**, quite possibly Vermont's most crammed-to-the-rafters general store.

ENTERTAINMENT

The **Craftsbury Chamber Players** present classical concerts July–Aug primarily in three locations: Craftsbury's Town Hall, Hardwick's Town House and Greensboro's Fellowship Hall (plus the University of Vermont's Recital Hall in Burlington). For advance ticket purchases: *Box 37, Craftsbury, VT 05826; tel: (800) 639-3443.*

BLACK RIVER VALLEY

Lofty rolling hills, ponds, farms with red barns, tall silos and inevitable herds of grazing Holsteins are prevalent as Rte 14 wends its way north. You'll see flamboyant examples of Victorian domestic architecture in tiny **Albany**. One is a moderate bed and breakfast, the **Village House Inn**, *Rte 14, Albany, VT 05820; tel: (802) 755-6722*. Similar atmosphere on a slightly larger scale in **Irasburg**, with every village essential: central green, bandstand, white-steepled church, sturdy library and post office/general store – plus the past-century bed and breakfast, **Brick House**, *Rte 14, Irasburg, VT 05845; tel: (802) 754-2108*; moderate.

NEWPORT

Tourist Information: North Country Chamber of Commerce, *The Causeway, Newport, VT 05855; tel: (802) 334-7782*, open daily 0900–1700. Focuses on the region's upper tier, with a midtown information booth. Although there's nothing 'postcard cute' about this former railroading and sawmill town, it's impressively situated on Lake Memphremagog (most of which spreads into Québec and

has its own mythical sea serpent, Memphré). Newport, moreover, is useful for getting petrol and holiday supplies.

ACCOMMODATION AND FOOD

Moderate **Top of the Hills**, *Rtes 5/105, Newport, VT 05855; tel: (802) 334-6748*, is both a motel and bed and breakfast on the south edge of town. Enquire at the NCCC booth about **Prouty Beach** tent-pitch and RV campsites. Casual dining amidst movie memorabilia makes downtown's **Nickelodeon Café**, *41 Main St; tel: (802) 334-8055*, recommendable. Budget–moderate. **Newport Natural Foods**, *66 Main St; tel: (802) 334-2626*, is great for deli and bakery take-aways.

RECREATION

Newport Marine Services, *Farrant St; tel: (802) 334-5911*, offers boat rentals. To arrange a golf outing on fairways overlooking the lake, call the **Newport Country Club**; *tel: (802) 334-7751*.

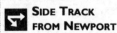
**SIDE TRACK
FROM NEWPORT**

This is a worthwhile 23- to 25-mile (one-way) westerly diversion if you'd like to track down six 19th-century covered bridges spanning the Trout River and Black Falls Creek in and around Montgomery Center and Montgomery Village. From Newport, take Rtes 105/100 to Troy, from there Rte 101 to Jay, then Rte 242 to Montgomery Center. All six bridges are along Rte 118.

This takes you to **Jay Peak**, *Rte 242, Jay, VT 05859; tel: (802) 988-2611*, a popular downhill ski area. In summer and autumn, Vermont's only aerial tramway reaches the 3861-ft summit for panoramic views and mountain-bike descents. ▨

DERBY LINE

While northerly Newport is close to the US-Canadian border, this town is right *on* it, adjoining Rock Island, Québec. Derby Line's turn-of-the-century **Haskell Free Library and Opera House,** *Caswell Ave; tel: (802) 873-3022,* exemplifies this dual nationality. The library's front entrance is in the US, the circulation desk in Canada. In the opera house upstairs, stage and front-row seats are in US territory, whilst most seats and the balcony are on the Québec side.

Enquire at the NCCC in Newport about opera-house performances. Library open Tues–Sat 1000–1700, also Thurs 1000–2000.

DERBY LINE TO LAKE WILLOUGHBY

The Northeast Kingdom's lakes, ponds and hump-backed hills reach to the horizon as motorists follow ridgetop roads towards West Charleston and then south to **Lake Willoughby**. With Mt Pisgah and Mt Hor's cliffsides rising from opposite shores, this long and narrow body of water resembles a Scottish loch. Twelve-plus miles of **Willoughby State Forest** hiking trails reach high-altitude vantage points.

WilloughVale Inn, *Rte 5A, Westmore, VT 05860; tel: (802) 525-4123 or (800) 541-0588,* combines an upmarket main building with lakeside housekeeping cottages, moderate–expensive.

LAKE WILLOUGHBY TO ORLEANS

Orleans is only 3 miles via rustic *Tarbox Rd* from **Brownington,** secluded in the hills and scarcely changed since the early 1800s. Stop by the **Old Stone House Museum,** *Brownington, VT 05860; tel: (802) 754-2022,* open daily 1100–1700

(July–Aug), Fri–Tues (mid-May–July and Sept–mid-Oct), $3, for a walking-tour guide to the village's historic district. Built as an academy dormitory, the granite-block museum provides insights into past-century village life. Do not conclude this diversion from Orleans before climbing the stairs of Brownington's **Prospect Hill Observatory** for 'Kingdom' panoramas.

BARTON AND GLOVER

Unpretentious and working-class like Orleans, **Barton** is similarly favourable for supplies and petrol fill-up. It's near the highest elevation of I-91 (more than 1800 ft) – at the dividing point of St. Lawrence River and Connecticut River watersheds. Result: Streams flow north instead of south in this uppermost part of Vermont.

Barton's **Crystal Lake State Park;** *tel: (802) 525-6206* has summertime appeal for swimming and picnics. **Sugarmill Farm,** *Rte 16 South, Barton, VT 05822; tel: (802) 525-3701,* demonstrates the traditional method of maple syrup production in a relaxed setting that includes sugar maples, trout ponds and a dairy bar; open daily 0800–2000 all year-round.

A diversion from Rte 5 south of Glover gets you to the **Bread & Puppet Museum,** *Rte 122, Glover, VT 05839; tel: (802) 525-3031,* open daily 1000–1700 mid-May–Nov, free – a century-old hay barn housing bizarre, gigantic puppets and masks used in the countercultural troupe's pageants and parades.

241

EAST BURKE AND LYNDONVILLE

Tourist Information: Lyndon Area Chamber of Commerce, *Lyndonville, VT 05851; tel: (802) 626-9696.* The town-centre visitors' booth is open daily 1000–1600 (early July–early Sept), Sat–Sun (early Sept–early Oct).

ACCOMMODATION AND FOOD

DI of Lyndonville is just off an I-91 exit. The moderate–expensive **Wildflower Inn**, *Darling Hill Rd, Lyndonville, VT 05851; tel: (802) 626-8310*, perches atop another of the 'Kingdom's' glorious highland ridge roads; very fine lodgings and meals, excellent for families. Nearby, also moderate–expensive, more for adults-only and part of an exceptionally beautiful farm is the bed and breakfast at **Mountain View Creamery**, *Darling Hill Rd, East Burke, VT 05832; tel: (802) 626-9924*. The area's trendiest restaurant is East Burke's **River Garden Café**, *Main St; tel: (802) 626-3514*.

SIGHTSEEING AND RECREATION

Ask at the LACC booth for a folder pinpointing the where-abouts of five covered bridges clustered in Lyndon, Lyndon Corner and Lyndonville. **Burke Mountain**; *tel: (802) 626-3305* draws downhill and cross-country skiers. Rent mountain bikes from **East Burke Sports**, *Main St; tel: (802) 626-3215*.

ST. JOHNSBURY

Tourist Information: The NKCC provides city as well as all-Northeast Kingdom information. Seasonal schedules at a visitors' booth, *Main St; no phone*, are comparable to the one in Lyndonville.

ACCOMMODATION AND FOOD

Budget–moderate motels at I-91 exits on the western outskirts of 'St. Jay' are fairly plentiful. Two in-town choices for budget–moderate lunches and dinners are **Anthony's**, *50 Railroad St; tel: (802) 748-3613*, and the **Grist Mill Tavern**, *2 Perkins St; tel: (802) 748-1989*. The topnotch **Northern Lights Bookstore**, *79 Railroad St; tel: (802) 748-4463*, also serves breakfasts, lunches and light dinners.

SIGHTSEEING

The **Fairbanks Museum and Planetarium**, *Main* and *Prospect Sts, St. Johnsbury, VT 05819; tel: (802) 748-2372*, contains northern New England's largest natural-science collections, beneath a barrel roof in a grandiose building. Open Mon–Sat 1000–1800, Sun 1300–1700 (July–Aug); Mon–Sat 1000–1600, Sun 1300–1700 (rest of year), $4. Planetarium shows daily 1330 (July–Aug); Sat–Sun only (rest of year), $1.50.)

Imposing enough as a High Victorian public library, the **St. Johnsbury Athenaeum**, *30 Main St, St. Johnsbury, VT 05819; tel: (802) 748-8291*, is also a skylit gallery of 19th-century art, well-nigh overwhelmed by Albert Bierstadt's 10-ft by 15-ft *Domes of Yosemite* canvas. Library and gallery open Mon and Wed 1000–2000, Tues and Thur–Fri 1000–1730, Sat 0930–1400, free.

PEACHAM

Here's another tucked-away, stopped-in-time village reached by an unnumbered roller-coaster road. When the movie adaptation of Edith Wharton's novel *Ethan Frome* was filmed in **Peacham** during a recent winter, only a few automobiles had to be moved out of sight for period authenticity.

Ha'Penny Gourmet, *Peacham, VT 05862; tel: (802) 592-3310*, triples as a food store, crafts shop and budget four-room bed and breakfast.

DANVILLE

Befitting Vermontish quirkiness, little **Danville** is home of the American Society of Dowsers – believers who aim forked sticks or prongs in search of water. Visitors welcomed at headquarters in the village centre, *tel: (802) 684-3417*, Mon–Fri 0900–1700.

PORTLAND

Portland is Maine's vibrant cultural and financial hub, which may explain why a city of fewer than 65,000 inhabitants boasts the amenities of a place thrice its size. Often treated as a jumping-off spot to Maine's interior for winter skiing or its coastal villages for summer sightseeing, Portland is very much a worthwhile destination in itself, not just a turn in the road. Intelligent city planning has salvaged the architectural remains of the city's Victorian heyday as a shipping and shipbuilding centre, and a recent influx of young professionals has transformed the once rather dreary city centre and port districts into a lively, engaging city. Situated on a peninsula in the focal point of sheltered Casco Bay, Portland is central to good beaches and islands and only minutes from the woodlands of Maine.

TOURIST INFORMATION

Convention and Visitors Bureau of Greater Portland (CVB), *305 Commercial St, Portland, ME 04101; tel: (207) 772-5800,* is a resource for advance materials.

The **Visitor Information Center of Greater Portland,** *at the same address,* open Mon–Fri 0800–1700, Sat, Sun and holidays 1000–1500 with extended hours in the summer, tracks the availability of rooms during high season, and provides a telephone for direct contact. The centre also displays members brochures and sells inexpensive but excellent architectural walking tour booklets. A smaller Visitor Information Center at the Portland Jetport provides the same services during the same hours.

WEATHER

The sea tempers Portland's climate, making for mild winters and cool summer breezes. Temperatures range from daytime summer highs of 60–85°F to daytime winter highs of 20–40°F. Winter snowfall in Casco Bay tends to be the heaviest on the New England coast.

ARRIVING AND DEPARTING

Airport

Portland International Jetport, *tel: (207) 874-8300,* is ten minutes from downtown Portland in South Portland. Taxi to downtown, $10. METRO bus service to downtown, $1.25. Mid-Coast Limo, *44 Elm St, Camden ME 04843; tel: (207) 236-2424,* provides a daily van service between the Portland Jetport bus station and midcoast towns north of the city between Brunswick and Camden.

International Ferry Service

Prince of Fundy Cruises, Ltd, *International Marine Terminal, 468 Commercial St, Portland ME 04101; tel: (207) 775-5616, (800) 341-7540 in USA, (800) 482-0955 in Maine,* sails daily early May–late Oct between Portland, Maine, and Yarmouth, Nova Scotia. Trip takes approximately 11 hours; many travellers spend the time in the on-board casino. Package options include nonstop 23-hour

243

roundtrip cruise, or one or two nights in Nova Scotia before return.

Ski Train

Silver Bullet Express Ski Train, *tel: (207) 824-RAIL or (207) 824-3000,* provides weekend service to and from Sunday River ski slopes from Christmas until early Apr. Train departs from old Portland North terminal on *Presumpscot St.*

Bus

Concord Trailways, *161 Marginal Way, Portland ME 04101; tel: (207) 828-1151,* provides service to Boston, Bangor and daily roundtrip service through the coastal Maine towns of Bath, Wiscasset, Damariscotta, Waldoboro, Rockland, Camden, Belfast and Searsport. **The Shuttle Bus,** *tel: (207) 282-5408,* provides daily service between Portland and Biddeford/Saco.

GETTING AROUND

City maps and bus routes are available free at the Visitors Information Center. Most attractions are concentrated in the downtown and Old Port areas, where it's easiest to park at a peripheral lot or garage and navigate on foot. But even some of the in-town attractions are a bit of a hike in the city's hilly terrain, and recent highway construction has effectively separated the waterfront and residential sections of the city, making a private automobile highly desirable for thorough touring.

Public Transport

Greater Portland Transit District (METRO), *114 Valley St; tel: (207) 774-0351,* buses run daily. All METRO lines provide service from 0600–1800 Mon–Sat except some holidays with some routes until midnight. Exact change of $1.25 required; discount passes available.

Contrary to the system name, these are *not* trains.

STAYING IN PORTLAND

Accommodation

Because Portland is a centre for business as well as for tourism, it has a wide variety of lodgings, with the greatest availability at the cusp of the moderate and expensive ranges. Budget lodging is sparse. Advance reservations are recommended in May and June, essential July–Oct. Motel prices are slightly lower in South Portland than in Portland, but location is less convenient.

Hotel chains in Portland include *HI* (summer only), *Hd, HJ, ES, Rm, Su*; South Portland also has *BW, CI, HJ, Ma, Sh.* **Portland Regency,** *20 Milk St, Portland ME 04101; tel: (207) 774-4200, (800) 727-3436,* in an historic armoury building in the centre of the Old Port is posh but not unreasonable; expensive. For a treat, try one of the several grand bed and breakfasts in the posh West End: the moderate **Inn on Carleton,** *46 Carleton St, Portland ME 04102; tel: (207) 775-1910,* or the moderate–expensive **Pomegranate Inn,** *49 Neal St, Portland, ME 04102; tel: (207) 772-1006,* or **West End Inn,** *146 Pine St, Portland ME 04102; tel: (207) 772-1377.*

Other bed and breakfasts are scattered throughout the city in gracious older homes; prices decline with distance from the city centre and waterfront. A superb choice can be found at the moderate **Andrews Lodging,** *417 Auburn St (Rte 26), Portland ME 04103; tel: (207) 797-9167,* with shared cooking and limited laundry facilities.

Nearest campsites for tent, trailer and RV camping are **Wassamki Springs,** *855 Saco St, Westbrook, ME 04092; (207) 839-4276,* on a private 30-acre lake, open

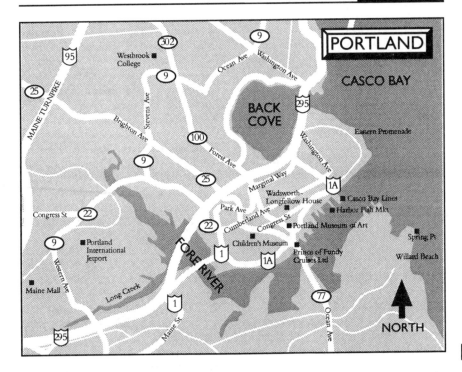

May–mid-Oct, and **Bailey's Pine Point,** *Rte 9, Pine Point, West Scarborough ME 04074; tel: (207) 883-6043,* with shuttle bus to beaches.

HI: *Portland Hall, University of Southern Maine, 645 Congress St, Portland, ME 04101; tel: (207) 874-3281, (207) 731-8096 (off season).* Open June–Aug, the Portland Summer Hostel offers double rooms with private bath; budget.

Eating and Drinking

With more than 100 restaurants, Portland is neither a capital of haute cuisine nor a wasteland of fast food. Local seafood – especially shellfish – is almost uniformly good if steamed, less dependable if fried. A broad variety of restaurants and cafés cluster in the Old Port, spilling over into Downtown. Restaurants with serious culinary aspirations require reservations.

Portland has led New England in the 'real ale' movement, first with Geary's Pale Ale and more recently with **Gritty McDuff's,** *396 Fore St; tel: (207) 772-BREW,* which offers budget English pub fare.

Best bets for informed, often elegant cooking in the moderate range are the bistro **Street & Co.,** *33 Wharf St; tel: (207) 775-0887,* modern American fare in a romantic setting at **Café Always,** *47 Middle St; tel: (207) 774-9399,* and trattoria-style Italian at **Perfetto,** *28 Exchange St; tel: (207) 828-0001.* Vegetarians should check out **The Pepperclub,** *78 Middle St; tel: (207) 772-0521,* budget.

Portland *is* Maine, and at mealtime, Maine means fish. On the casual side, **The Village Café,** *112 Newbury St; tel: (207) 772-5320,* consistently wins local polls for best fried clams, while **Gilbert's**

Chowder House, *92 Commercial St; tel: (207) 871-5636*, right near the fish docks is a good choice for chowder and baked fish as well as a broad selection of draft beers and ales. The city's best fishmonger is **Harbor Fish Market** on Custom House Wharf. (Walk down this street for local colour, whether you're buying or not.) Dining literally on the water makes an institution of **DeMillo's Floating Restaurant**, *25 Long Wharf; tel: (207) 772-2216.*

Fresh Market Pasta, *43 Exchange St/60 Market St, tel: (207) 773-7156*, has the best deal on a meal to eat in or take away; budget. To assemble your own gourmet picnic (perhaps to eat on the overlooks at either Eastern or Western Promenade), head to the back of **The Whip and Spoon**, *161 Commercial St; tel: (207) 774-6262.* This cooking utensil and appliance store stocks excellent wine, cheese and caviar for take-away.

246

Communications
Main post office is the **US Post Office Downtown Station** at *400 Congress St*, open on Mon–Fri 0800–1900, and Sat 0900–1300.

Pick up a copy of the free *Casco Bay Weekly* or *Go*, a Thur supplement to the *Portland Press Herald*, for complete listings of stage, concerts, clubs, galleries, dance, film, performing arts, comedy, etc. The **State Theatre**, *609 Congress St; tel: (207) 879-1111* for 24-hour concert hotline, Portland's chief venue for live pop, country and rock music (and also big-screen repertory films), closed its doors recently, but is expected to open under new ownership. The hippest night spots in town are alleged to be Gritty McDuff's, *396 Fore St*, and **Java Joe's**, *29 Exchange St*, which has

live music and poetry. The **Portland Performing Arts Center**, *25A Forest Ave; tel: (207) 774-0465*, hosts performances by the **Portland Stage Company**. The **Portland Symphony Orchestra**, *30 Myrtle St; tel: (207) 773-8191*, performs classical, pops and chamber concerts in City Hall Auditorium. From late June–early Aug, the city sponsors free outdoor band concerts on Tues evenings at Deering Oaks Park – a beautifully landscaped park (bounded by *Forest, Park* and *Brighton Aves*) with duck pond and playgrounds. The city also sponsors free folk concerts Wed evenings at Western Promenade. **The Movies**, *10 Exchange St; tel: (207) 772-9600*, shows international and art films. **Nickelodeon** cinema complex, *Temple* and *Middle Sts; tel: (207) 772-9751*, shows current films on six screens at half of standard ticket prices.

Spectator Sports
The **Portland Sea Dogs**, a minor-league baseball affiliate of the Florida Marlins, play at 6000-seat ballpark, **Hadlock Stadium**, *271 Park Ave; tel: (207) 874-9300*, from early Apr–early Sept. The **Portland Pirates**, *One Civic Center Sq., tel: (207) 828-4665*, a minor-league hockey team affiliated with the Washington Capitals, plays early Oct–early April at the **Cumberland County Civic Center** on *Spring St*.

Events
For ten days spread across the middle weekends of March, Portland goes nautical with **Aucocisco**, a festival that celebrates Casco Bay with events emphasizing local history, environmental concerns, arts and food. The **Maine Boatbuilders Show**, takes place on the second weekend of Mar.

SHOPPING

Most of the best shops, galleries and boutiques are found in the Old Port area bounded by *Commercial, Franklin, Congress* and *Union Sts.* Portland is rich in fine crafts. Two superb galleries with all media are **Nancy Margolis Gallery,** *367 Fore St; tel: (207) 775-3822,* and **Abacus,** *44 Exchange St; tel: (207) 772-4880.* **Stein Gallery,** *20 Milk St; tel: (207) 772-9072,* represents 65 of the best US glass artists. **Maine Potters Market,** *376 Fore St; tel: (207) 774-1633,* is a cooperative gallery of the state's ceramic artists.

A 3.5-million carat find of the pink and green semi-precious stone, tourmaline, in 1972 has made it the gem of choice for Maine jewellers. An especially good selection is available weekdays only at **Cross Jewelers,** *570 Congress St; tel: (207) 773-3107.*

Less precious but still very local are the Maine-only products at **Just Me.,** *510 Congress St; (207) 775-4860,* including canned chowders and bisques, clam spread, crab dip and almost anything made from blueberries.

SIGHTSEEING

Whether behind the wheel or on foot, your best orientation to Portland's human topography are the inexpensive brochures of self-guided architectural tours of four Portland neighbourhoods available from the Visitor Information Center. The **Western Promenade** highlights the architecture of one of America's best-preserved Victorian residential neighbourhoods. The Promenade itself, a public walk 175 feet above sea level, offers views to the White Mountains and beyond. The **State St** tour emphasizes architecture of the Federal-period and Greek Revival mansions, including the grandest dame of all, **Victoria Mansion. Congress St** is

the commercial and transportation spine of the Portland peninsula, and this tour continues from the shops and civic buildings eastward to the Portland Observatory lookout and the city's oldest graveyard. The **Old Port Exchange** brochure is especially worth picking up, since you'll probably shop and dine in the district. The tour highlights architecture and history in this neighbourhood; Old Port is the oldest part of the city but was largely destroyed by British bombardment during the American Revolution and again by the Great Fire of 1866. Although it was immediately rebuilt, the district had declined by the 1960s but was redeveloped in the 1970s.

Not graced with a Portland Landmarks Inc. brochure, the **waterfront** holds equal interest if less distinguished architecture. Be sure to walk **Custom House Wharf** (directly across from the Portland Regency Hotel) to see a working fishing port in action. There's also a public fish auction at 1300 Mon–Thur on **Portland Fish Pier.**

From the Water

Casco Bay Lines ferries depart from Casco Bay Ferry Terminal, *Commercial and Franklin Sts; tel: (207) 774-7871,* with many scenic rides at various times. Two scenic routes are offered in all seasons: The **Mail Boat Run** (the longest operating service of its kind in the USA) stops at the islands of Cliff, Chebeague, Long, and Little and Great Diamond. Ferries depart 1000 and 1400 mid-June–early Sept, 1000 and 1445 the rest of the year; adult fare is $9.50.

The **Sunset Run** follows the same route, departing daily all year at 1745; adult fare is $9.50. There is also regular roundtrip ferry service to Peaks Island ($3), a Portland bedroom island community with a good beach.

247

Museums and Historic Sites

Most museums charge $4 adult admission. The **Portland Museum of Art,** 7 *Congress Sq.; tel: (207) 775-6148,* open Tues–Sat 1000–1700, Thurs 1000–2100, Sun 1200–1700, closed Mon, occupies an award-winning building erected in 1983. The American galleries have works by Winslow Homer, Andrew and N.C. Wyeth, Edward Hopper, Rockwell Kent and other American notables as well as an excellent collection of 19th century American commercial glass. The prize collection of Homer watercolours tends only to be on view in the summer.

Next door, **The Children's Museum,** *142 Free St; tel: (207) 828-1234,* is open Mon, Wed, Thur and Sat 1000–1700, Tues and Sun 1200–1700, Fri 1000–2000, with extended summer hours. It's a must-see if you have small children and the weather's too damp for the beach. Most amazing exhibit? The camera obscura offers a panoramic view of Portland rooftops.

The **Wadsworth Longfellow House,** *485–489 Congress St; tel: (207) 879-0427,* was the childhood home of poet, scholar and translator Henry Wadsworth Longfellow; open Tues–Sun 1000–1600 (June–Oct), limited Sat hours (Jan–May). Built in 1786 of brick, it represented the outskirts of town. Volunteer guides vary in their interpretative skills.

The most-visited house in Maine is **Victoria Mansion,** *109 Danforth St; tel: (207) 772-4841.* Built 1858–1862 by one of the first Mainers to go out into the wide world and make a fortune, this Italianate villa has its original over-the-top interiors and ornate furnishings created by an operatic set designer. Open Tues–Sat 1000–1600, Sun 1300–1700 (end May–early Sept), Sat 1000–1600 and Sun 1300–1700 (early Sept–mid-Oct).

The **Maine Narrow Gauge Railroad Company and Museum,** *58 Fore St; tel: (207) 828-0814,* open daily 1000–1600, tells the story of Maine's five lines of two-foot railroads that operated 1870s–1940s. The narrow gauge allowed the lines to penetrate countryside inaccessible for standard-gauge railroads. Engines and many of the cars were built in the museum building. Admission is free, but if you take the half-mile ride along the waterfront, it will cost you $3.

OUT OF TOWN

Portland's lighthouses and beaches are actually not in Portland at all, but in the communities of Cape Elizabeth and Scarborough south of the city. Some maps give directions that only locals can follow. Instead, take Rte 77 south from the waterfront. After crossing the bridge to South Portland, follow the left arrow toward Cape Elizabeth. Turn right at first traffic light onto *Ocean Rd,* which is also Rte 77. In about three miles, turn left onto *Shore Rd,* following the signs to **Portland Head Light.** One of the most photographed lighthouses in the world, Portland Head has a lighthouse and historical museum (Admission $2); open Sat–Sun 1000–1600 (Apr–May), daily 1000–1600 (June–Oct). The park – the Revolutionary War **Fort Williams** – has grand views out to sea and is perfect for flying kites.

Retrace *Shore Rd* back to Rte 77, turn left, continue 1.6 miles then turn left to **Two Lights State Park.** The park is a knobby lookout, but the lighthouses of its name are a mile further down the road, with the **Lobster Shack Restaurant** between them on the dunes. Another mile south on Rte 77 is **Crescent State Beach,** considered Portland's finest but often very crowded. Three miles further is the less cramped **Higgins Beach.**

PORTLAND–BAR HARBOR

The coastal route between Portland and Bar Harbor is slow in the summer and fall but passes through or near most of the scenic villages for which Maine is justly famed. This is the region of photographic cliché – a ragged coast of peninsulas and archipelagos with rocky shorelines and few swimming beaches. Most of Maine's lobstering waters and fish farming operations (mussels and Atlantic salmon) lie along this stretch, so the dining is good if simple. Independent motels and bed and breakfasts, sometimes known as 'tourist homes', are the chief lodging choices.

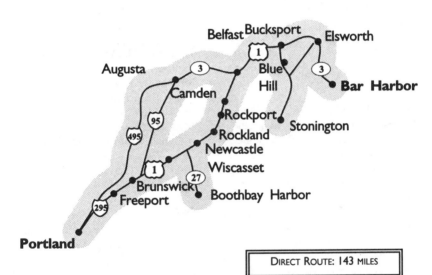

249

DIRECT ROUTE: 143 MILES

DIRECT ROUTE

The direct route follows interstate highways from downtown Portland to **Augusta,** then the mostly two-lane Rte 3 from Augusta to **Belfast** to merge with the slow coastal Rte 1 to **Ellsworth.** The entire route covers 143 miles and takes about 3.5 hours with light traffic, up to five hours July–Sept.

From *Commercial St* in Portland, proceed north along Rte 1A (a left turn onto Franklin Arterial) then onto I-295 North, following it 4 miles to the merger with I-95. Continue 53 miles to Augusta and exit onto Rte 3 east.

Follow Rte 3 for 47 miles to Belfast and junction with Rte 1. Continue on Rtes 1 and 3 North (actually eastward) for 39 miles through Ellsworth to the split of Rtes 1 and 3. Turn right for Rte 3: Bar Harbor is 19 miles south.

SCENIC ROUTE

▶ The scenic route largely follows coastal Rte 1 with forays down three scenic peninsulas (**Pemaquid, Boothbay** and **Castine**) on narrow, two-lane roads. Total distance is approximately 230 miles. Driving time in off-season is about five hours; from July–Sept, at least eight hours.

From *Commercial St* in Portland, proceed north along Rte 1A (a left turn onto Franklin Arterial) onto I-295 north and go 0.5 mile to Exit 9 (Rte 1).

Continue north on Rte 1 through **Brunswick** and Bath for 50 miles through **Wiscasset**. After the bridge, turn right on Rte 27 and drive south for 11 miles to **Boothbay Harbor**.

Double back 4 miles and turn right onto The *River Rd*. Continue north 9 miles to rejoin Rte 1 in Newcastle. Cross the bridge into Damariscotta and turn right to head south for 3 miles on Rtes 129 and 130 (*Bristol Rd*). Veer left at fork (Rte 130) and continue 13.5 miles to Pemaquid Point. Double back via Rte 130 for 3.5 miles, then turn right onto Rte 32 for 20 miles to rejoin Rte 1 in **Waldoboro**.

Continue 73 miles on Rte 1 through **Rockland, Rockport, Camden, Lincolnville Beach, Belfast, Searsport** and **Bucksport**. Two miles outside of Bucksport, turn right onto Rte 175. When Rte 175 splits left in 7.8 miles, continue straight on Rte 166, which leads into Castine.

Leave Castine by Rte 166 North, turning right on Rte 199, then right again on Rte 175 South, which is joined after about 200 yards, by Rte 15 South. The high point of the road provides perhaps the best panoramic view on the coast: a foreground of blueberry barrens, a midground of **Penobscot Bay** and its islands and a background of the **Camden Hills**.

Rte 15 leads across the Eggemoggin Reach to Little Deer Isle, Deer Isle and, at the tip of the island, **Stonington**. Double back on Rte 15 to Blue Hill. Take Rte 172 from the town centre north to **Ellsworth** and Rtes 1 and 3. One mile east of Ellsworth the routes split. Turn right for Rte 3: **Bar Harbor** is 19 miles away.

FREEPORT

Tourist Information: Freeport Merchants Association, *P.O. Box 452, Freeport, ME 04032; tel: (207) 865-1212* or toll-free *(800) 865-1994,* open Mon–Fri 0900–1700.

Tourist Information Center, *Depot St* at *Fashion Outlet Mall,* open daily 0900–1700 (late May–mid-Oct), infrequently otherwise.

ACCOMMODATION

Freeport has *S8* on Rte 1 at I-95 Exit 17 and a variety of charming Victorian bed and breakfasts along upper *Main St* (Rte 1) in Freeport Village.

You will find RV hookups at **Flying Point Campground,** *Lower Flying Point Rd, RR1, Box 155, Freeport, ME 04032; tel: (207) 865-4569,* along the shore west of town; tent campers will be happier at nearby **Recompence Shore Campsites,** *10 Burnett Rd; tel: (207) 865-9307,* open mid-May–mid-Oct, adjacent to the state park; budget.

SHOPPING

Besides being the model for Castle Rock in Stephen King's horror fiction (he grew up in adjacent Durham), Freeport is New England's original 'outlet mall center'. Sports outfitter **L.L. Bean** has long been open around the clock in Freeport, attracting hunters, sport fishermen and shoppers. Enterprising merchandisers tested the concept of direct-factory shops selling discontinued goods and 'factory seconds' (goods that failed quality inspection standards), leading to more than 100 such 'outlet stores' and a subsidiary local attraction of gawking at free-spending tourists.

Stores are generally open Mon–Sat 0900–2100, Sun 1000–1800.

SIGHTSEEING

The Desert of Maine, *Desert Rd; tel: (207) 865-6962*, open daily 0900–1700 (early May–late Oct); $4.75, is a geological peculiarity that has been a tourist trap since the mid-1920s.

Enjoy picnicking and 4 miles of wooded hiking trails along Casco Bay in 200-acre **Wolf Neck Woods State Park**, *Wolf Neck Rd; tel: (207) 865-4465*.

BRUNSWICK

Bowdoin College, founded in 1794, gives Brunswick most of its culture and much of its flavour. **Bowdoin College Museum of Art**, *Walker Art Bldg, Bowdoin Campus, Main St, Brunswick, ME 04011; tel: (207) 725-3275*, open Tues–Sat 1000–1700, Sun 1400–1700, free, is noted for its collection of Winslow Homer, Andrew Wyeth and late 19th- and early 20th-century American paintings. The **Peary-MacMillan Arctic Museum**, *Hubbard Hall, Bowdoin Campus, Main St; tel: (207) 725-3416*, open Tues–Sat 1000–1700, Sun 1400–1700, free, celebrates two

Bowdoin-educated polar explorers with artifacts from their 1909 North Pole mission.

BATH

Tourist Information: Bath-Brunswick Region Chamber of Commerce Tourist Information Center, *Rte 1 North, Bath, ME 04530; tel: (207) 443-9751*, open Fri–Sun 1000–1700 (May–mid-June), daily 1000–1900 (mid-June–early Sept), daily 1000-1800 (Sept–mid-Oct). Bath has a *Hd*.

From 1862–1902, Bath was the fifth-largest seaport in the US, and its 200 shipyards built more than half the country's fleet of wooden ships. Bath Iron Works still constructs ships for the US Navy. **Maine Maritime Museum**, *243 Washington St; tel: (207) 443-1316*, open daily 0930–1700, $6, occupies three acres where ships have been built for nearly 300 years. Its elaborate models and boatbuilding shop give a flavour of Bath's past.

> ⤴ **SIDE TRACK**
> **FROM BATH**
>
> A detour down Rte 127 (just across the bridge from Bath heading north) leads 14 miles down the Georgetown Peninsula to **Reid State Park**, where Mile Beach features a six-acre saltwater lagoon offering the warmest swimming on the Maine coast. 🏖

WISCASSET

Wiscasset bills itself as 'The Prettiest Village in Maine' and few contest the designation. It's a veritable museum of 18th- and 19th-century mansions with a downtown full of antiques shops, fine arts potters and cafés.

Le Garage, *Water St; tel: (207) 882-5409*, is a dramatic dining spot with a windowed porch overlooking the half-sunken

251

four-masted schooners *Hester* and *Luther Little* on the west bank of Sheepscot River. **Musical Wonder House**, *8 High St, Wiscasset, ME 04578; tel: (207) 882-7163*, is an eccentric 1852 mansion/museum showcasing 400 music boxes and other automata; full house tour $30; ground-floor tour $10; tours by appointment only Sept–mid-Oct. **Nickels-Sortwell House**, *Main and Federal Sts; tel: (207) 882-6218*, open Wed–Sun 1200–1700, adults $2, is a Federal-era manse built by a shipmaster in 1807.

A complete change of pace (and era) is Maine Yankee nuclear power plant's exhibit at **Maine Yankee Information Center**, *Rte 144, off Rte 1; tel: (207) 882-6321 or (800) 458-0066*, tours Mon–Sat 1000-1700, Sun 1200–1700; free.

BOOTHBAY HARBOR

252

Tourist Information: The Boothbay Harbor Region Chamber of Commerce, *Rte 27, P.O. Box 356, Boothbay Harbor, ME 04538; tel: (207) 633-2353*, open Mon–Fri 0800–1700.

The Boothbay region has been a summer resort community since 1870, when travellers arrived by steamship rather than automobile. Its snug harbour amid numerous inlets and coves makes the region a yachtsman's delight and a centre for deep-sea fishing (mostly tuna, shark and bass).

ACCOMMODATION AND FOOD

The **Spruce Point Inn**, *Grandview Ave (Atlantic Ave Extension), Boothbay Harbor, ME 04568; tel: (207) 633-4152 or (800) 553-0289*, is a turn-of-the-century inn on its own 100-acre peninsula; pricey, as is its fine modernist restaurant. The **Black Orchid**, *5 Byway; tel: (207) 633-6659*, offers Mediterranean-style preparations of Maine seafood; moderate.

For a budget meal, try **Ebb Tide**, *67*

Commercial St; tel: (207) 633-5692, a diner with home-style cooking for all three meals. **Lobsterman's Wharf**, *Rte 96, East Boothbay; tel: (207) 633-3443*, serves quintessential waterfront grub on a waterfront deck; open daily May–mid-Oct; budget–moderate.

SIGHTSEEING

Fishing charter boats charge $20–$40 per person and may be found in profusion at the town piers. Sightseeing boats range $8–$20, same location. Landlubbers might prefer **Boothbay Railway Village**, *Rte 27, Boothbay; tel: (207) 633-4727*, open 0930–1700 mid-June– mid-Oct, $6, a re-created circa-1900 village where you can view more than 50 antique autos and lorries or take a ride on a 1.5-mile narrow-gauge steam train. Maine State Ferry Service; *tel: (207) 596-2203*, provides summer service to Monhegan Island here.

NEWCASTLE AND DAMARISCOTTA

These two towns occupy facing banks of the Damariscotta River. Damariscotta was home port for Metcalf and Norris, pioneer clipper ship builders who became famous in the mid-1800s when their ship, *The Flying Scud*, made an unheard-of 76-day passage to Melbourne, Australia.

ACCOMMODATION AND FOOD

For a secluded retreat where the river becomes a lake, it's hard to beat **Mill Pond Inn**, *Main St, Damariscotta Mills, ME 04555; tel: (207) 563-8014*; moderate. The **Newcastle Inn**, *River Rd, Damariscotta, ME 04553; tel: (207) 563-5685 or (800) 83-BUNNY*, offers both peaceful lodging (expensive) and sumptuous dining that's discovered every few years by big-city food critics. Good budget family-style dining is available at

Backstreet Landing, *Elm St Plaza, Damariscotta; tel: (207) 563-5666*, and **Salt Bay Café**, *Main St, Damariscotta; tel: (207) 563-1666*, where the crab cakes are especially good.

Damariscotta Lake State Park, *Rte 32, Jefferson, ME 04348; tel: (207) 549-7600*, has pleasant activities such as swimming and boating.

PEMAQUID PENINSULA

The villages of the Town of Bristol – New Harbor, Pemaquid and Pemaquid Beach – constitute the lacy coast of the Pemaquid Peninsula. **Shaw's Fish and Lobster Wharf**, *Rte 32 (Northside Rd), New Harbor; tel: (207) 677-2200*, open mid-May–early Oct, is a dockside fish shack that's as much a local attraction as a fine place to eat steamed lobster and clams, shrimp, scallops and seafood stews; budget–moderate.

The leading attraction in these parts, however, is **Pemaquid Point Light** and the **Fisherman's Museum**, *Rte 32, Pemaquid Point, ME 04558; tel: (207) 677-2726*, open Mon–Sat 1000–1700, Sun 1100–1700 (end May–mid-Oct), free, in the keeper's house next to the lighthouse. This dramatic scene – where high rocks drop swiftly to crashing surf – is one of the most photographed sights along the Maine coast.

About 10 miles offshore is Monhegan Island, accessible only by passenger boat from New Harbor and Boothbay Harbor in the summer and mail boat from Port Clyde. (For Monhegan schedule and rates, call the **Maine State Ferry Service**; *tel: (207) 596-2203*.) **Colonial Pemaquid State Historic Site**, *Rte 130, Pemaquid Point; tel: (207) 677-2423*, open 0900–1700 (late May–early Sept), $2, is a small archaeological museum that shows results from excavations of the early 17th-century English fishing settlement, which may be the earliest English settlement in New England.

WALDOBORO

Waldoboro isn't much to look at from Rte 1. Few traces remain of its once-lofty status as the 19th century's No. 2 port in New England (after Boston). But you'll want to stop anyway for **Moody's Diner**, *Rte 1; tel: (207) 832-7468*, for such classic fare as deep-fried chicken with mashed potatoes and gravy, followed by peanut-butter pie; budget.

THOMASTON

Thomaston was the original settlement of mid-coast Maine, though it's been eclipsed by neighbours who once were part of the community. These days it's best known for the Maine State Prison, right downtown on Rte 1.

Once a major lime-burning and shipping port, it was home to the first US secretary of war, Gen Henry Knox. His house was razed in 1870, then rebuilt from the original plans in 1931 and refurnished with the original furnishings. Now it's a museum showing the life of rural gentry circa 1800: **Gen. Henry Knox Mansion**, *Rte 1, Thomaston, ME 04861*; no telephone, open 0900–1700 late-May–Aug, $2.

Take a right from *Main St* onto *High St* (Rte 131) and meander down the St George peninsula roads dotted with inns and antiques shops. The same road also leads to the village of Owls Head and the **Owls Head Transportation Museum**, *Rte 73, Owls Head, ME 04854; tel: (207) 594-4418*, open daily 1000–1700, $4, which displays autos, horse-drawn carriages, wagons, motorcycles and bicycles.

ROCKLAND

Tourist Information: The Rockland-

Maine Lobster

Until around 1950, Maine Lobsters were usually given to poorhouses and orphanages because this delectable crustacean was considered a trash fish. Today the misnamed 'lobster bake' is a massive summer industry. In truth, sweet and succulent lobster is always boiled or steamed live, when it turns from black to red. 'Baked stuffed' lobster is often stringy and flavourless.

Lobsters reach legal size at about 1 pound, which makes for a light meal; a 2 pound lobster is too much for most people to finish. Choose a 1¼–1½ pound lobster. Lobsters taste best before they moult their shells in July, after which they are somewhat soft and less sweet until late September.

The rocky coastline and freezing waters of Maine are said to be ideal conditions for producing the best lobsters in the world. Further north, Mainers believe that the water is too cold and deep to produce anything other than sluggish lobsters with inferior meat.

The quintessential Maine souvenir is an old wooden lobster trap – increasingly hard to find because most fishermen now use wire traps. Don't touch one that's washed up on a beach – 'molesting a trap' carries a $50 fine. Roadside stands charge an arm and a leg for traps. The best way to find one is to head to an inshore fishing town such as Spruce Head, Owls Head, Stonington or Jonesport and look for a pile on the dock. Chances are the owner will sell you one cheap if he's around. Even better, talk to his wife. She'll be glad to unload one for a buck and pocket the cash.

254

Thomaston Area Chamber of Commerce, *Harbor Park, P.O. Box 508, Rockland, ME 04841; tel: (207) 596-0376* or *(800) 562-2529*, open Mon–Sat 0900–1700; also Sun (May–Sept).

Rockland is the economic centre of midcoast Maine and its most important fishing port. Although not as quaint as surrounding communities, Rockland is home port to a substantial 'windjammer' fleet of former coastal freight sail craft (mostly schooners) refitted for weeklong sightseeing sails. Most cruises are booked a year ahead, although the motor yacht **M/V Pauline**; *tel: (207) 596-6528*, does have spots now and then on shorter cruises.

The **Rockport-Camden-Lincolnville Chamber of Commerce** (see below) lists all the ships and how to book them in its annual guide. Less pricey and always available are the Vinalhaven or North Haven island ferries from Rockland

Public Landing, both operated by the **Maine State Ferry Service**; *tel: (207) 596-2203*. Rockland also features a gem of a small art museum: the **Farnsworth Library and Art Museum**, *19 Elm St; tel: (207) 596-6457*, open Mon–Sat 1000–1700, Sun 1300–1700, $5, with work by three generations of Wyeths, Winslow Homer and native daughter Louise Nevelson.

Quirkier but genuinely charming, the **Shore Village Museum**, *104 Limerock St; tel: (207) 594-0311*, open 1000–1600 (June–mid-Oct), free, is both Maine's lighthouse museum (the largest in the US) and a repository for memorabilia from the local regiments of the Civil War and odd bits (a giant lobster shell, for example) that have collected in town over the centuries. It's one of those rare museums that encourages photographs.

The **Maine Lobster Festival**, *P.O.*

Box 552, Rockland, ME 04841; tel: (207) 596-0376, takes place at the town docks the first weekend of Aug; more lobsters are landed at Rockland than anywhere else in the US, and the celebration attracts several thousand people.

ROCKPORT

Rockport has all the scenery that Rockland lacks, which is why it's home to **Maine Coast Artists Gallery**, *Russell Ave, Rockport, ME 04856; tel: (207) 236-2875*, and the renowned **Maine Photographic Workshop**, *2 Central St; tel: (207) 236-8581*, open 0900–1700; call for exhibit information.

For a modern-day taste of the boat-building skills so important to this area, stop by **The Artisans School**, *9 Elm St; tel: (207) 236-6071*, to see small wooden boats in progress; follow *Russell Ave* toward Beauchamp Point. To set out on the water for yourself, rent canoes and kayaks from **Maine Sport**, *Rte 1; tel: (207) 236-8797*.

Reasonable camping is available at **Megunticook by the Sea**, *Rte 1, Rockport, ME 04856; tel: (207) 594-2428* or *(800) 884-2428*, which has 85 pitches with full RV hookups.

CAMDEN

Tourist Information: Rockport-Camden-Lincolnville Chamber of Commerce, Public Landing, *P.O. Box 919, Camden, ME 04843; tel: (207) 236-4404*, office open Mon–Fri 0900–1700, information centre daily 0900–1700. **Camden Accommodations & Reservations**, *77 Elm St, Camden, ME 04843; tel: (207) 236-2090* or *(800) 236-1920*, handles all forms of lodging in Camden and surrounding communities, including season-long rentals.

ACCOMMODATION AND FOOD

Among the several fine old inns along *High St*, aka 'B&B Row', is **Whitehall Inn**, *52 High St, Camden, ME 04843; tel: (207) 236-3391*, open mid-May–Oct; expensive. **The Belmont**, *6 Belmont Ave; tel: (207) 236-8053* or *(800) 238-8053*, is the local leader for fancy contemporary cuisine; pricey.

For lobster and clams to make a shore dinner, try **Ayer's Fish Market**, *43 Main St; tel: (207) 236-3509*. Gather picnic fixings at **French and Brawn**, *Main St; tel: (207) 236-3361*.

Although Camden tends to be expensive, there are also a few good budget dining options. **Mama & Leenie's**, *27 Elm St; tel: (207) 236-6300*, is a tiny café with an abundance of great baked goods and good soups, salads and sandwiches. **Sea Dog Brewing Co.**, *43 Mechanic St; tel: (207) 236-6863*, is a brewpub with good beer and conventional pub grub.

SIGHTSEEING

Without traffic, Camden would be the ideal picture of a Maine coastal village. Its protected harbour attracts sailors from around the Atlantic, including such celebrities as retired television newscaster Walter Cronkite.

The narrow *Main St* often backs up into metropolitan-sized traffic jams in mid-summer, but people keep coming for the restaurants, stunning scenery and gift shops. The most venerable of this final category is **Smiling Cow**, *41 Main St; tel: (207) 236-3551*, open daily 0800–2100 Apr–Nov.

Part of Camden's charm is the backdrop of mountains; the Camden Hills rise 1400 feet above the harbour. Two miles north of the village is **Camden Hills State Park**, *Rte 1, Camden; tel: (207) 236-3109*, open mid-May–mid-Oct 0830–

255

sunset, $2, offers 5000 acres of woodlands at the foot of Mount Battie and a 900-foot summit with panoramic views of Penobscot Bay and surrounding towns.

To see Camden and the bay from the water, take an afternoon sail on one of the local schooners: **Appledore**; *tel: (207) 236-8353*, 2 hr $20; or **Olad**; *tel: (207) 236-2323*, 2–6 hr, $12–$15. For getting around by land, **Fred's Bikes**, *53 Chestnut St; tel: (207) 236-6664*, not only rents bicycles, but delivers to motels, hotels and Bed and Breakfasts in the Camden-Rockport-Lincolnville area.

LINCOLNVILLE BEACH

The town of Lincolnville lies inland, but Lincolnville Beach is a wonderfully peculiar sliver of sand along an otherwise rocky coast. It's frequented almost entirely by locals who know that the long sandy tidal flats make for warm swimming at high tide.

This is also the spot to catch the **Islesboro Ferry**, *Maine State Ferry Service; tel: (207) 789-5611*, to the most accessible of Penobscot Bay islands.

BELFAST

Tourist Information: Belfast Area Chamber of Commerce, *31 Front St, Belfast, ME 04915; tel: (207) 338-5900*, open Mon–Fri 0900–1700. Once a chicken-processing and fish-canning town, Belfast was a good place to avoid at low tide.

With the food industries gone, it's become a haven of artists and craftspeople (who often show at the *lower Main St* galleries) and a summer place for people 'from away' (i.e., anyone not born there) who want the look of Camden without the crowds.

Rte 1 in East Belfast is lined with some of the coast's least expensive motels, most

dating from the 1940s–50s. Downtown, The **Jewelled Turret Inn**, *16 Pearl St, Belfast, ME 04915; tel: (207) 338-2304* or *(800) 696-2304*, typifies the handful of the city's grand homes that have been converted to bed and breakfast operations; some rooms have fireplaces; moderate.

Located on the road into town from Lincolnville, **Ducktrap River Fish Farm**, *57 Little River Dr., Belfast, ME 04915; tel: (207) 338-6280*, is nationally famed for its smoked fish and supplies fancy restaurants as far away as New York.

The **Belfast & Moosehead Lake Rail Road Company**, *Town Landing; tel: (207) 948-5500* or *338-2330*, toll-free *(800) 392-5500*, does 90-min train rides with a staged 'train robbery' on one of the old timber shipping lines: twice daily June–Aug, weekends from mid-May and Sept–late-Oct; $14. The same company also offers 'riverboat' cruises from Bangor Landing on the same schedule; $14.

SEARSPORT

Tourist Information: Searsport & Stockton Springs Chamber of Commerce, *Main St, P.O. Box 139, Searsport, ME 04974; tel: (207) 548-6510*, open Mon–Fri 1000–1700, Sat 1000–1500 (late May–mid-Sept only).

ACCOMMODATION AND FOOD

In the last half of the 19th century, more deep-water shipping captains hailed from Searsport than from any other US port. The village still recalls its halcyon days, with former captains' homes converted to inns and restaurants. Among them, the **Capt. A.V. Nickels Inn**, *Rte 1, Searsport, ME 04974; tel: (207) 548-6691* or *(800) 343-5001*, has ocean frontage on Penobscot Bay and a big front porch; moderate. Another former sea captain's home, the **Nickerson Tavern**, *Rte 1; tel:*

(207) 548-2220, open Tues–Sun, serves unpretentious but outstanding contemporary cuisine in genial surroundings; moderate–pricey.

SHOPPING AND SIGHTSEEING

Searsport's seafaring hegemony is told in thorough detail at the **Penobscot Marine Museum**, *Church St* (off Rte 1); *tel: (207) 548-2529*, open Mon–Sat 1000–1700, Sun 1300–1700 (late May–mid-Oct), $5. More than a collection of historic boats, models, nautical artifacts and portraits, the museum does a remarkable job of re-creating both 19th-century life on the Penobscot Bay and the danger and romance of rounding Cape Horn on the great sailing ships of the day, including the Downeasters, the largest shipping vessels under sail ever built. Rte 1 in Searsport is also lined with antiques shops and flea markets.

BUCKSPORT

Just before Rte 1 crosses the Penobscot River on the Waldo-Hancock suspension bridge, park at one of the turnouts for a good view of the river's gorge. On most days, you'll see osprey, golden eagles and (occasionally) bald eagles fishing in the river. Bucksport itself is a sleepy town with a pleasant waterfront promenade and some adequate if unexciting restaurants. For an overnight stop, there's a *BW*.

CASTINE

Unlike much of the Maine coast, Castine is a place you go to, not through. At the tip of a peninsula with an excellent harbour and pre-European routes to the inland forests, it was established as a 1600s fur-trading centre by the Pilgrims from Plymouth Colony.

Over the next century and a half, Castine changed hands nine times among

the French, British, Dutch and, finally, the Americans.

About 100 historical markers around town designate sites of battles, forts and battlements. The town was a Loyalist stronghold during the American Revolution, and when the peace was concluded many residents placed their homes on barges and floated them up the coast to St Stephen, New Brunswick, to remain under British rule. As a result, the grandest buildings mostly date from the early 1800s.

ACCOMMODATION AND FOOD

A rambling old building in the centre of town, the **Castine Inn**, *Main St, Castine, ME 04421; tel: (207) 326-4365*, has the best rooms in town; moderate–expensive; the best view is room 12. **Village Inn**, *Main St, Castine, ME 04421; tel: (207) 326-9510*, is smaller and more casual; moderate.

Downstairs is **Bah's Bakehouse**, *Water St; tel: (207) 326-9510*, which has earthy baked goods and makes custom picnic meals. Great pasta salads are available at **Mainstay Pasta**, *Main St; tel: (207) 326-8085*. Castine has one of the area's best Independence Day (4 July) celebrations, with salmon dinners and fireworks in the harbour. Castine is home to the Maine Maritime Academy and its training vessel, the State of Maine. If it's docked in the harbour, ask about a free tour.

DEER ISLE/STONINGTON

Tourist Information: Chamber of Commerce Information Center, *Rte 15, Little Deer Isle; no telephone*, open daily 0900–1800 (June–Sept only). A half-mile suspension bridge on Rte 15 spans Eggemoggin Reach to Little Deer Isle and the 9-mile-long Deer Isle, which together have a year-round population of about 3000.

257

ACCOMMODATION AND FOOD

For lodging in the midst of the briny atmosphere, try **Inn on the Habor**, *Main St, Stonington, ME 04681; tel: (207) 367-2420*; moderate.

Slightly removed but still in sight of the docks is **Près du Port Bed and Breakfast**, *W. Main St and Highland Ave, Stonington, ME 04681; tel: (207) 367-5007 July–Aug or (203) 869-1342* (in Connecticut) *Sept–June.*

Some fine seafood is available around Deer Isle, but the down-home style of **Bay View Restaurant**, *Seabreeze Ave, Stonington; tel: (207) 367-2274*, offers the best local colour. Try Nellie's Sautéed Lobster Meat à la Nova Scotia on toast points.

SIGHTSEEING

Haystack Mountain School of Crafts has helped make Deer Isle home for many jewellers, weavers, potters, carvers and blacksmiths. Stop in Deer Isle village to see excellent crafts at **Turtle Gallery**, *Rte 15; tel: (207) 348-9977*, open June–Sept, and stunning photographs at **Terrell S. Lester Photography Gallery**, *Rte 15; tel: (207) 348-2676.*

Lobstering and fishing are principal livelihoods in Stonington, as attested by the boats in the harbour. As one Stonington local puts it, 'The fellows in gum boots still pretty much run things' in this fishing village, which has made an uneasy peace with an influx of summer visitors.

Look out for piles of weathered lobster traps for sale, perhaps labelled 'Tourist Traps'.

Stonington is also the jump-off point via **mail boat**; *tel: (207) 367-5193* days, *367-2355* evenings, to Isle au Haut, half of which belongs to Acadia National Park. The island has 17.5 miles of hiking trails

and five lean-tos for camping in the Acadia section by reservation only: **Acadia National Park**, *Box 177, Bar Harbor, ME 04609.*

BLUE HILL

Blue Hill is best known for its potters (especially **Rowantrees Pottery**, *Rte 177; tel: (207) 374-5535*) and its writers – essayist and children's author E.B. White, (*Charlotte's Web*), among others, but these days it's an enclave of equal parts organic farmers and cultural mavens (painters, chamber musicians, etc.) in exile from New York.

Top dining and lodging in town is the antiques-filled **Blue Hill Inn**, *Rte 177, Blue Hill, ME 04614; tel: (207) 374-2844*, where the rooms are expensive and the five-course dinner pricey.

Homely and moderate, the best rooms in the **Blue Hill Farm Country Inn**, *Rte 15, Blue Hill, ME 04614; tel: (207) 374-5126*, are in the renovated barn. For food and nightly entertainment, try the **Left Bank Bakery & Café**, *Rte 172; tel: (207) 374-2201*; budget. On Sun and Fri nights in July and Aug, there's chamber music at **Kneisel Hall** in the centre of town.

ELLSWORTH

The last wide place in the road before reaching Mount Desert Island, Ellsworth advertises itself as 'centrally located', which is sort of true. Because this handsome town has few tourist attractions, its motels and grocery stores are somewhat less expensive than those closer to the action.

The area's chief industry was raising broiler chickens until about 1975. One remnant is the **Big Chicken Coop**, *Rte 1; tel: (207) 667-7308*, a combination antiques barn, flea market and jumble sale overflowing with castoffs of American consumer culture.

PORTLAND–
NEW HAMPSHIRE LOOP

This sampler of inland New England landscapes covers busy playgrounds along New Hampshire's Lake Winnepesaukee, exquisite foliage views on uncrowded roads, 18th-century village greens, dramatic mountain passes, the legendary wilds of Maine's Rangeley Lakes and the well-tamed landscape of the Sebago Lakes. Allow at least a week to meander this 420-mile loop of well-marked secondary roads in its entirety. Or use pieces of it to connect with excursions into the White Mountains National Forest in New Hampshire or Vermont's Northeast Kingdom, Green Mountains and Lake Champlain.

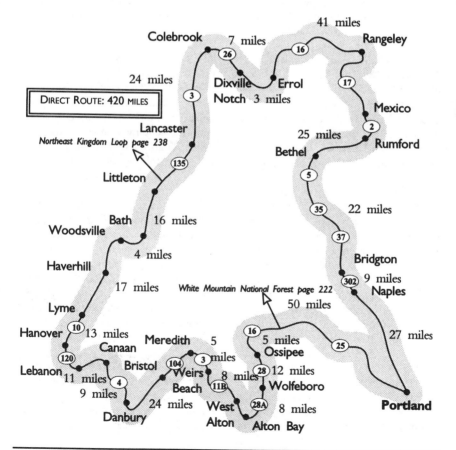

41 miles

Colebrook   7 miles   Rangeley
26   16

24 miles   Dixville   Errol   17
DIRECT ROUTE: 420 MILES   3   Notch   3 miles
Mexico   259
Lancaster   25 miles   2
Northeast Kingdom Loop page 238   Bethel   Rumford
135
Littleton   5

Bath   16 miles   35   22 miles
Woodsville   37

4 miles   Bridgton
Haverhill   302   9 miles
17 miles   White Mountain National Forest page 222   Naples
Lyme   50 miles

Hanover   10   13 miles   16   27 miles
Canaan   Meredith   5   5 miles   Ossipee   25
120   Bristol   104   3 miles   28   12 miles
Lebanon   11 miles   4   Weirs   8 miles   Wolfeboro
9 miles   Beach   11B
24 miles   West   28A   8 miles   Portland
Danbury   Alton   Alton Bay

ROUTE

Leave Portland on Rte 25 West (*Forest Ave*, a right turn from the Franklin Arterial) for 50 miles to Rte 16 in Center Ossipee, N.H., and turn left (south) onto Rte 16. (Heading north on Rte 16 would take you to North Conway and Pinkham Notch in the White Mountains, see p. 222). In 5 miles, turn right onto Rte 28 south and go 12 miles to **Wolfeboro** on the east side of Lake Winnepesaukee.

Continue on Rte 28 south toward Alton, turning right in 8 miles onto Rte 28A to **Alton Bay**. In 3 miles, Rte 28A joins Rte 11 west (turn right) through Alton Bay. Rte 11A (a left-hand spur) leads to **Gunstock** in 6 miles. Otherwise, continue 8 miles and turn right on Rte 11B to **Weirs Beach** on the lake's western shore. Continue north 5 miles on Rte 3 to **Meredith** at junction of Rtes 3 and 25. From Meredith, head south 1 mile on Rte 3 to Rte 104 west (crossing I-93, which leads north to Lincoln in the White Mountains, see p. 222, and south to Boston) toward **Bristol,** staying on Rte 104 in Bristol toward Danbury for a total of 24 miles.

Turn right onto Rte 4 west toward **Grafton** for a 4-mile roundtrip to Ruggles Mine (left turn, follow signs). Continue on Rte 4 for 9 miles to **Canaan.** Turn right at Jesse's Market onto *Canaan St* and proceed 2 miles to historic village centre.

New pavement abruptly turns to dirt; continue 9 miles to return to pavement, then 2 miles to **Lyme.** If you prefer paved roads, follow Rte 4 west another 11 miles from Canaan to Lebanon; get on I-89 for 2 miles to Exit 18, then follow Rte 120 into **Hanover** (see Boston–Hanover, p. 99), then Rte 10 north 11 miles to Lyme.

In Lyme, turn right onto Rte 10 north through **Haverhill** for 17 miles to **Woodsville** at the junction of Rtes 10 and 302. Three miles north is the junction with Rte 112 west toward Lincoln and North Woodstock (See White Mountains, p. 222). Continue 1 mile on Rtes 10 and 302 to **Bath;** 16 miles farther is **Littleton** (where you can join the Northeast Kingdom Loop, p. 238, by following I-93, then I-91 into St. Johnsbury).

Leaving Littleton, backtrack south 1 mile on Rte 302 to follow Rte 18 north 1.5 miles to Rte 135 north. Continue 20 miles to junction with Rtes 2 and 3 in **Lancaster.**

Turn left, then right onto Rte 3 in 1 mile. Continue north on Rte 3 for 20 miles to the turnoff for Columbia *Bridge Rd* on the left. Proceed 4 more miles on Rte 3 to **Colebrook.** Turn right onto Rte 26. The turn off for Coleman State Park is 7 miles on left. Proceed 3 more miles on Rte 26 to **Dixville Notch.**

From Dixville Notch, continue 7 miles to Errol and make a left turn onto Rte 16 north and continue 41 miles to **Rangeley,** Maine. Follow Rte 4 south; 1 mile past the centre of town, turn right onto *South Shore Dr.* and proceed 7 miles to Rte 17. Turn left onto Rte 17 south and drive 31 miles to Mexico and junction with Rte 2.

Turn right on Rte 2 through Rumford and continue 25 miles to **Bethel.** Leave Bethel by Rte 5 south for 7 miles to Rte 35 for 6 miles, where it is joined by Rte 37. Follow Rte 37 for 9 miles into **Bridgton,** turning left onto Rte 302. Follow Rte 302 for 9 miles through **Naples,** near Sebago Lake. It's another 27 miles on Rte 302 back to Portland.

PORTLAND TO WOLFEBORO

The drive across western Maine to the New Hampshire lakes region crosses a marshy landscape before following the Ossipee River. Many villages offer summer camp rentals (private cabins) but lack services for transient visitors.

WOLFEBORO

Tourist Information: Wolfeboro Chamber of Commerce, *Depot Building, Depot St, P.O. Box 547, Wolfeboro, NH 03894; tel: (603) 569-2200,* open Mon–Fri 1000–1500, Sat–Sun 1000–1300 all year. **Information Booth,** *South Main St* on Common, *no telephone,* open Mon–Sat 1000–1700, Sun 1100–1500 (July–early Sept); Sat 1000–1700, Sun 1100–1500 (late May–June).

ACCOMMODATION

Allen A. Motor Inn, *P.O. Box 1914, Rte 28, Wolfeboro, NH 03894; tel: (603) 569-1700 or (800) 732-8507,* moderate, sits near Allen H. Albee Beach on Lake Wentworth. **The Lake Motel,** *Rte 28, Box 887-B, Wolfeboro, NH 03894; tel: (603) 569-1100,* moderate–expensive, has a private beach on Lake Winniipesaukee, dock facilities and tennis courts.

The Wolfeboro Inn, *44 North Main St, Wolfeboro, NH 03894; tel: (603) 569-3016 or (800) 451-2389,* dates from 1812, though many parts of this expensive, roomy lodging are new; from here you can walk anywhere in town or ski 14 miles of cross-country trails in winter.

Wolfeboro Campground, *Rte 28 North, RR2, Box 500, Wolfeboro, NH 03894; tel: (603) 569-9881,* 5.5 miles from town, has 50 wooded pitches for tents and trailers with hookups.

EATING AND DRINKING

Wolfe's Tavern (budget) and **The Dining Room at the Wolfeboro Inn** (moderate), *44 North Main St; tel: (603) 569-3016,* deliver credible pub fare and unpretentious contemporary American dining, respectively.

P.J.'s Dockside, *Town Wharf; tel: (603) 569-6747,* has grilled food to eat in or take away; budget.

SIGHTSEEING AND RECREATION

Wolfeboro has been 'America's First Summer Resort' since the colonial governor built a Lake Winnipesaukee retreat in the mid-1700s. **Wolfeboro Trolley Company;** *tel: (603) 569-5257,* leaves from Town Dock with a 45-min narrated tour of the town; $3 for a one-day pass.

Wolfeboro Historical Society Museum, *South Main St; tel: (603) 569-4997,* open Mon–Fri 1000–1600, Sat 1000–1400 (early July–early Sept), has an 18th-century farmhouse, school house and firehouse replica; $3.

Wolfeboro is one of the main stops of the *M/S Mt. Washington* scenic cruises of Lake Winnipesaukee, late May–mid-Oct, from $12; *tel: (603) 366-2628.* The US Mail boat *Blue Ghost* sails Mon–Sat mornings for 3-hour, 60-mile trip; $16; *tel: (603) 569-2100.*

Wolfeboro has three public swimming beaches: Allen H. Albee Beach on Lake Wentworth about 4 miles north of the village centre on Rte 28; **Carry Beach** on *Forest Rd* on Lake Winnipesaukee; and **Brewster Beach** on *Clarke Rd* on Lake Winnipesaukee's Wolfeboro Bay. Area streams, ponds and lakes offer rich fishing. Five hiking trails range from 10-min walks to scenic overlooks to a 12-mile former railroad corridor across lakes and trestles.

Abenaki Ski Area has downhill skiing, a skating rink and 20 miles of groomed cross-country trails; snow phones, *tel: (603) 569-3151 or 569-8234.* Certified divers may rent scuba equipment from **Dive Winnipesaukee,** *4 North Main St, Box 2198, Wolfeboro, NH 03894; tel: (603) 569-8080,* which arranges trips to sunken ships; $39.

261

ALTON BAY

The village of Alton Bay lies at the head of a narrow arm of Winnipesaukee. Most inhabitants come for the whole summer, but good quarters may be found, including **Sandy Point Beach Resort**, *Box 6, Rte 11, Alton Bay, NH 03810; tel: (603) 875-6000*, with motel units or self-catering cottages open May–mid-Oct; moderate.

GILFORD/GUNSTOCK

Gunstock Recreation Area, *Rte 11A, Gilford, NH 03246; tel: (603) 293-4341*, lies within Gilford, but is a community unto itself, with alpine and nordic skiing in winter, horseback riding, hiking and mountain biking in summer.

Gunstock Campground, *Rte 1A, P.O. Box 1307, Laconia, NH 03247; tel: (603) 293-4344*, has 250 year-round pitches on 2000 acres.

Ames Farm Inn, *2800 Lake Shore Rd, Gilford, NH 03246; tel: (603) 293-4321 or 742-3962*, has self-catering apartments and lakefront cabins with individual boat slips, but rents only by the week July–Aug; moderate.

Ellacoya State RV Park, *Rte 11, P.O. Box 7277, Laconia, NH 03247; tel: (603) 271-3627 (Jan–May), (603) 293-7821 (June–mid-Oct))* has 38 pitches with full hook-ups. Next door is **Ellacoya State Beach** on Winnipesaukee's southwest shore; $2.50.

WEIRS BEACH

Tourist Information: Weirs Beach Information Center; *tel: (603) 366-4770*, open 1000–1800 daily (late June–early Sept), Sat–Sun 1000-1800 (early Sept–mid-Oct). **The Greater Laconia/Weirs Beach Chamber of Commerce,** *11 Veterans Sq, Laconia, NH 03246; tel: (603) 524-5531 or (800) 531-2347*.

ACCOMMODATION

Weirs Beach has the greatest concentration of lodging on Lake Winnipesaukee, mostly moderate.

Grand View Motel, *Rte 3, P.O. 5051, Weirs Beach, NH 03247; tel: (603) 366-4973*, has a view of Lake Winnipesaukee and mountains and offers self-catering cottages at almost the same rate; moderate.

RECREATION

Forget pristine, forget placid: This destination features go-carts, batting cages for baseball practice, water slides and miniature golf.

Weirs Beach/Endicott Beach, *Rte 3 near junction of Rte 11B*, is a fine swimming beach. **Weirs Drive-In Theater**, *Rte 3*, open mid-June–early Sept, shows double bills on four screens.

Funspot, *Rte 3; tel: (603) 366-4377*, a 1960s miniature golf course of New Hampshire landmarks, captures a daft side of American ingenuity.

Three sightseeing boats that dock at Weirs Beach may be booked at one number; *tel: (603) 366-BOAT (366-2628)*. The *Sophie C*, a US Mail boat, departs Mon–Sat mid-June–early Sept; $10. The *Doris E* cruises the northern end of Winnipesaukee and Meredith Bay daily July–early Sept; from $7. The *M/S Mt Washington* also picks up passengers at Weirs Beach. *Queen of Winnipesaukee*, a 46-ft sailing boat, departs from the public dock; *tel: (603) 366-5005*; from $12.

Thurston's Marina, *at the bridge, Rte 3; tel: (603) 366-4811*, rents ski boats, pontoon boats, water-ski equipment and two-person jet-skis. **The Winnipesaukee Scenic Railroad**, *Boardwalk; tel: (603) 279-5253*, offers one-hour ($6.50) and two-hour ($7.50) rides on vintage trains.

262

MEREDITH

Tourist Information: Meredith Chamber of Commerce Visitor Information Booth, *Rte 3, P.O. Box 732, Meredith, NH 03253; tel: (603) 279-6121,* open daily 0900–1700 (late June–early Sept), Fri–Sun 0900–1700 (late May–late June and early Sept–mid-Oct).

ACCOMMODATION

The Inn at Bay Point, *Bay Point, Meredith, NH 03253; tel: (603) 279-5400 or (800) 729-5253,* has 24 rooms with spectacular views of Lake Winnipesaukee; expensive. **Inn at Mills Falls,** *Mills Falls Marketplace, Meredith, NH 03253; tel: (603) 279-7006 or (800) 622-6455,* offers designer rooms a in shopping/dining complex across Rte 3 from Lake Winnipesaukee; moderate–expensive. **Olmec Motor Lodge,** *Meredith Neck, 95 Pleasant St, Meredith, NH 03253; tel: (603) 279-8584,* open mid-May–mid-Oct, offers rustic lakeside lodgings with access to all forms of boating; moderate.

Three campsites lie near the lake: **Clearwater Campground,** *Rte 104, 26 Campground Rd, Meredith, NH 03253; tel: (603) 279-7761;* **Meredith Woods 4 Season Camping Area,** *Rte 104, 26 Campground Rd, Meredith, NH 03253; tel: (603) 279-5449;* and **Harbor Hill Camping Area,** *189 Rte 125, Meredith, NH 03253; tel: (603) 279-6910.*

EATING AND DRINKING

The Boathouse Grille, *The Inn at Bay Point; tel: (603) 279-2253,* has steaks, chops and fish; moderate. **George's Diner,** *Plymouth St; tel: (603) 279-8723,* is known for for all-you-can-eat specials; budget. **K.C.'s Cafe & Soda Shoppe,** *379 Daniel Webster Hwy (Rtes 3 and 125); tel: (603) 279-4833,* has a genuine soda fountain; budget.

ENTERTAINMENT

Lakes Region Summer Theatre, *Rte 25; tel: (603) 279-9933,* a professional summer stock company, performs Tues–Sun late June–early Sept. **Meredith Marina & Boating Center,** *Bay Shore Dr; tel: (603) 279-7921,* rents power boats by the day, week or month.

MEREDITH TO LYME

This 60-mile drive through the uplands features some stretches of great fall foliage scenery (mid-Sept–mid-Oct). Bristol village is one of the few places to eat. In Grafton, the detour up a rough dirt road to a mountaintop feldspar mine is worth the trip: **Ruggles Mine;** *tel: (603) 523-4275,* open Sat–Sun 0900–1700 (mid-May–mid June), daily 0900–1700 (mid-June–mid-Oct) except 0900–1800 July–Aug; $10. (The view is free.)

Cardigan State Park in Canaan has a mountain road to a picnic spot on west slope of Mt Cardigan (elevation 3121 ft) with hiking trails to the summit.

Canaan's historic district is a mile of mostly 18th- and early 19th-century white clapboard churches and houses in typical 'add-on' style. The dirt road between Grafton and Lyme blazes with colour in the fall. Pavement recommences at an alpine ski area with low prices: **Dartmouth Skiway,** *Canaan Rd, Lyme Center; tel: (603) 795-2143.*

LYME

The nearest **Tourist Information** is in Hanover. **Alden Country Inn,** *On the Common, P.O. Box 60, Lyme, NH 03768; tel: (603) 795-2222 or (800) 794-2296,* has 14 guest rooms in a former stagecoach inn; moderate–expensive; the inn also serves traditional country dinners; moderate.

The Dowds' Country Inn, *On the Common, P.O. Box 58, Lyme, NH 03768;*

263

tel: (603) 795-4712 or (800) 482-4712, is a classic 1780 New England house converted to a bed and breakfast; expensive.

LYME TO WOODSVILLE

This 17-mile stretch rides a ridge above the Connecticut River valley. **Haverhill's** picturesque village centre has two town greens fenced with white paddocks. Clapboard houses date mostly from circa 1800, but the brick church and school bespeak a failed brick industry in the upper Connecticut River valley.

WOODSVILLE AND BATH

Woodsville marks the intersection of east-west roads between the White and Green Mountains and north-south roads along the Connecticut River; it lies about half an hour from four major ski areas. An exceptional lodging here is **Nootka Lodge,** *Rtes 10 and 302, RR2, Box 75, Woodsville, NH 03785; tel: (603) 747-2418 or (800) 626-9105,* which has 12 large units in a full log structure and 11 conventional units; moderate. Moderate dining choices include New American fare at **Blue Heron Cafe,** *23 Central St; tel: (603) 747-3670,* or a German-accented menu at **Chalet Schaefer,** *85 Central St; tel: (603) 747-2071.* The **Haverhill-Bath covered bridge,** built in 1832, is New Hampshire's oldest authenticated covered bridge. It lies along Rte 135, 0.2 mile north of Rte 302 at the Ammonoosuc River. The **Bath burr truss covered bridge,** built in 1832, lies west of Rte 302 at Bath Village by the **Brick Store,** a bona fide tourist trap that specialises in smoked meats and cheese.

LITTLETON AND LANCASTER

Tourist Information: Littleton Chamber of Commerce, *120 Main St,* *P.O. Box 105, Littleton, NH 03561; tel: (603) 444-6561,* daily 0900–1800 (July–Aug); Fri–Sun only (mid-May–mid-June and early Sept–mid-Oct). This 19th-century industrial town has striking public buildings featured on a walking tour map.

The Littleton Motel, *Main St, Littleton, NH 03561; tel: (603) 444-5780,* is in the heart of town; moderate. **Thayer Inn,** *Main St, Littleton, NH 03561; tel: (603) 444-6469,* is one of the state's oldest surviving inns, built in 1850; moderate. The **Littleton Diner,** *170 Main St; tel: (603) 444-3994,* was established in 1930; budget.

Tiny Lancaster is a major stop on the cross-country snowmobile paths. It also has two covered bridges. The **Mt Orne Bridge** on Rte 135, 5 miles west of village, spans an especially scenic section of the Connecticut River. The **Lancaster-Mechanic St covered bridge** over the Israel River dates from 1862 and lies east of Rtes 2 and 3 in the village.

LANCASTER TO DIXVILLE NOTCH

The **Columbia-Lemington covered bridge** spans the Connecticut River between New Hampshire and Vermont west of Rte 153 in Columbia Village; it may be reached from Rte 3 by the *Columbia Bridge Rd.*

North Country Chamber of Commerce, *Colebrook, NH 03576; tel: (603) 237-8939,* has information about outfitters and backwoods rentals. **Coleman State Park,** *12 miles east of Colebrook off Rte 26; tel: (603) 271-3627 (Jan–May), (603) 237-4520 (June–mid-Oct),* is situated on Little Diamond Pond in the Connecticut Lakes, and has trout fishing access, a picnic area and 30 tent pitches and field sites for RVs (but no hookups).

DIXVILLE NOTCH

Tourist Information: Dixville Notch Information Center, *Dixville Notch, NH 03576; tel: (603) 255-4255,* open daily 1100–1800 (July and Aug), weekends 1100–1800 (late May–mid-Oct).

Dixville Notch is the first place in the US to report its vote in presidential primaries and elections. About 30 voters cast their ballots at the stroke of midnight. It's also a striking bit of alpine scenery.

The Balsams, *Dixville Notch, NH 03576; tel: (603) 255-3400 or (800) 255-0600,* is a grand resort hotel from the Gilded Age that sits high in the mountains on an almost private lake. Pricey, but includes all meals and activities including boating, golf, tennis, hiking, biking and flyfishing in summer and nordic and alpine skiing in winter. Few such properties are left. **Dixville Notch State Park,** *Rte 26,* features a network of mountainous hiking trails, picnic areas and two waterfalls.

DIXVILLE NOTCH TO RANGELEY

Errol, N.H., marks a crossroads where turning south on Rte 16 would follow the Androscoggin River to Pinkham Notch and North Conway in the White Mountains (see p. 222). The same river is also perfect for learning kayak technique and taking half-day tours with **Umbagog Outfitters Kayak Touring and Whitewater School;** *tel: (603) 356-3292.* **Azicoos Valley Camping Area,** *Rte 16, HCR 10, Box 302, Wilson's Mills, ME 03579; tel: (207) 486-3271,* is about halfway between the White Mountains and the Rangeley Lakes.

RANGELEY

Tourist Information: Rangeley Lakes Chamber of Commerce, *Public Landing, P.O. Box 317, Rangeley, ME 04970; tel: (800) MT-LAKES (685-2537),* open Mon–Sat 0900–1700 (all year), also Sun 0930–1330 (July–Aug).

ACCOMMODATION AND FOOD

Rangeley Inn, *Main St, P.O. Box 398, Rangeley, ME 04970; tel: (207) 864-3341,* is the most venerable hostelry of the town; moderate. **Northwoods Bed & Breakfast,** *Main St, P.O. Box 79, Rangeley, ME 04970; tel: (207) 864-2440,* is a charming 1912 structure where frilly dolls supply a genteel alternative to the local 'fur-and-fin' backwoods mentality. **Town & Lake Motel,** *Main St, P.O. Box 47, Rangeley, ME 04970; tel: (207) 864-3755,* lies directly on the lake; moderate.

For housekeeping cottages and lakeside cabins, try either **Sam-o-Set,** *Box 562, Rangeley, ME 04970; tel: (207) 864-3657,* or **Samoset Four Seasons,** *Box 1006, Rangeley, ME 04970; tel: (207) 864-5137.* **Rock Ridge Bakery & Deli,** *Main St; tel: (207) 864-5880,* provides packed lunches.

RECREATION

Fishing, hunting and hiking are legendary at Rangeley, which lies at the edge of wilderness but is readily accessible by road. In recent years, Rangeley has become a snowmobiling mecca, connecting to 140 miles of trails sometimes shared by nordic skiers.

For airlifts to remote fishing areas as well as scenic rides beginning at $25, contact **Mountain Air Services,** *Main St, P.O. Box 367, Rangeley, ME 04970; tel: (207) 864-5307.* Enquire about fishing guides at the Chamber of Commerce or **Rangeley Region Sport Shop,** *85 Main St; tel: (207) 864-5615,* which also rents canoes and kayaks. **Dockside Sports Center,** *Town Cove; tel: (207) 864-2424,* rents canoes, powerboats, Sea-Doos (jet

265

skis) and is one of the few dealers to rent snowmobiles.

Rangeley Mountain Bike Touring Co, *53 Main St; tel: (207) 864-5799*, rents mountain bikes and kayaks in summer, nordic ski packages in winter. The company provides a route map where one might see bear and moose without being run over by log trucks.

Forty trails of alpine skiing and 50 km of ski touring are available at **Saddleback Ski Area,** *Dallas Hill Rd, Box 490; tel: (207) 864-5671.* Hiking trails range from 1.5-mile saunters to 17-mile rugged expeditions.

BETHEL

Tourist Information: The Bethel Area Chamber of Commerce, *Train Station, Cross St, P.O. Box 439, Bethel, ME 04217; tel: (207) 824-2282,* open Mon–Sat 0900–1700. Reservation service, *tel: (207) 824-3585 or (800) 442-5826* (late Nov–Mar).

Evans Notch Visitor Center, White Mountains National Forest, *Rte 2, RFD #2, Box 2270, Bethel, ME 04217; tel: (207) 824-2134;* open Mon–Fri 0830–1630, provides hiking maps and camping information.

Sunday River Ski Area, *Bethel, ME 04217; tel: (207) 824-3000 or (800) 543-2754,* provides information on skiing and mountain-biking as well as a dizzying array of lodging. The local newspaper, *Bethel Citizen,* publishes free seasonal tourism tabloids.

ARRIVING AND DEPARTING

Silver Bullet Express Ski Train, *tel: (207) 824-RAIL (824-7245) or 824-3000,* provides a weekend service between Bethel and Portland from Christmas–early Apr. The Station is on *Cross St,* just off Rte 2 which is north of the village.

ACCOMMODATION

Bethel Inn & Country Club, *Broad St, Bethel, ME 04217; tel: (207) 824-2175 or (800) 654-0125,* expensive–pricey, but includes meals and unlimited golf.

Moderate options along Rte 2 include **Briar Lea B&B,** *Rte 2, Bethel, ME 04217; tel: (207) 824-4717,* and **The Norseman Inn & Motel,** *Rte 2, Bethel, ME 04217; tel: (207) 824-2002.*

Sunday River Inn, *RFD2, Box 1688, Bethel, ME 04217; tel: (207) 824-2410,* offers accommodation ranging from dormitories to private rooms with baths. Rates (moderate–expensive) include meals and cross-country trail passes.

For camping, **Littlefield Beaches,** *RR2, Box 4300, Bryant Pond, ME 04219; tel: (207) 875-3290,* lies 6 miles south of Bethel on the shores of South Pond on Rte 26.

Stony Brook Campground, *HCR 61, Box 130, Hanover, ME 04237; tel: (207) 824-2836,* on Rte 2 north of Bethel, emphasises summer and winter sports.

There are five primitive camping areas in the White Mountain National Forest near Bethel; contact Evans Notch Visitor Center.

EATING AND DRINKING

Casual dining predominates. **Moose's Tale at Sunday River Brewing Company,** *Rte 2; tel: (207) 824-4253,* is the local microbrewery with general pub food.

The Iron Horse Bar and Grill, *Bethel Train Station; tel: (207) 824-0961,* occupies vintage rail dining cars, open Wed–Sun (Dec–Mar).

The Sudbury Inn, *Main St; tel: (207) 834-2174,* and **The Bethel Inn,** *Main St; tel: (207) 824-2175,* offer traditional meals in a rather more formal environment; moderate– pricey.

RECREATION

Founded in 1774, Bethel has evolved into a sporting centre. Most people visit to hike, canoe, mountain-bike or ski (nordic, alpine and telemark) at **Sunday River Ski Area.**

In summer, the ski area has mountain bike trails; bike rental with all-day lift $45, lift for hiker $8. **Great American Biking Company,** *Sunday River Rd; tel: (207) 824-3092*, rents mountain bikes and provides guided shuttle to **Grafton State Park** for $35 per person including bike; also rents canoes. The 18-hole golf course of the **Bethel Inn & Country Club;** *tel: (800) 654-0125*, is considered one of New England's best; greens fees $26–$33.

Speckled Mountain Ranch, *RR2, Box 717, Bethel, ME 04217; tel: (207) 836-2908*, on Flat Rd 6 miles west of Bethel village offers guided horseback trail rides on a network of forested trails and old logging roads; $20 per hour; also has accommodation; moderate. **The Telemark Inn,** *RFD2, Box 800, Bethel, ME 04217; tel: (207) 836-2703*, at the base of Caribou Mountain offers llama trekking starting at $60 for day hikes; also has accommodation; high moderate.

BRIDGTON

Tourist Information: Bridgton-Lakes Region Chamber of Commerce, *Rte 302, P.O. Box 236, Bridgton, ME 04009; tel: (207) 647-3472* (July–early Sept), *(207) 647-2533* (early Sept–June), open Mon–Sat 1000–1700, Sun 1000–1500 (July–early Sept), Fri–Sat 1000–1700, Sun 1000–1500 (late May–June and early Sept–mid-Oct).

Bridgton is the shopping town for rural villages and summer lakeside cottages. Lodgings on Highland Lake with private beaches include **Tarry-a-While Bed and Breakfast Resort,** *RR3, Box 1067,* *Bridgton, ME 04009; tel: (207) 647-2522*, moderate–expensive, and **Grady's West Shore Motel,** *RR3, Box 39, Bridgton, ME 04009; tel: (207) 647-2284*, moderate. Kramer's Landing public beach is near the town centre. *Main St* has extensive casual dining.

The Bridgton Drive-In, *Rte 302*, at the edge of town, is one of a vanishing breed of outdoor movie theatres.

NAPLES

Tourist Information: Naples Business Association, *Rte 302, Naples, ME 04055; tel: (207) 693-3825*, open daily 1000–1600 (late June–early Sept).

ACCOMMODATION

Inn at Long Lake, *Lakehouse Rd, P.O. Box 806, Naples, ME 04055; tel: (207) 693-6226*, moderate–expensive, is a bargain for its combination of elegance and convenience.

West Shore Motel, *Rte 302, P.O. Box 869, Naples, ME 04055; tel: (207) 693-9277*, has its own beach on Long Lake 1 mile west of the causeway, moderate–expensive.

Steamboat Landing, *P.O. Box 384, Naples, ME 04055; tel: (207) 693-6782*, is a family cottage resort on Brandy Pond with nine cottages starting at $685 per week; reservations taken after Jan 1 for mid-June–mid-Sept. **The Augustus Bove House Bed & Breakfast,** *Rtes 302 and 114, Naples, ME 04055; tel: (207) 693-6365*, was one of the first summer hotels in the area; moderate.

Two campsites with sandy beaches are **Bay of Naples Family Camping,** *Rte 11/114, Box 240, Naples, ME 04055; tel: (207) 693-6429*, and **Four Seasons Camping Area,** *Long Lake, Rte 302, Naples, ME 04055; tel: (207) 693-6797*. Limited public camping is also available at

267

Sebago Lake State Park, *Rte 114; tel: (207) 693-6613.* Principal daylight dining often involves ice cream or hotdogs from seasonal shacks.

EATING AND DRINKING

Rick's Cafe, *Rte 302; tel: (207) 693-3759,* has casual food, budget–moderate. **Charlie's on the Causeway,** *Rte 302; tel: (207) 693-3826,* emphasises seafood and serves eight microbrews on tap, moderate.

The Epicurean Inn, *Rte 302; tel: (207) 693-3839,* is aptly named for its classic French and New American fare; pricey.

SIGHTSEEING AND RECREATION

Most of Naples occupies a causeway between Long Lake and Brandy Pond, part of the lock system that connects the Sebago Lakes. It is easily the best place on this loop to bring young children.

The **Songo River Queen II**, *The Causeway; tel: (603) 693-6861,* makes one-hour sightseeing tours of Long Lake ($6) and 2.5-hour tours of the Songo River lock system ($9) daily (July–Aug) or Sat–Sun (June and Sept).

Motorboat rentals are available from several marinas, including **Causeway Marina,** *Rte 302; tel: (207) 693-6832,* and **Long Lake Leasing,** *Rte 302; tel: (207) 693-3159.*

Aqua-Bikes (plastic pedal-boats) may be rented at The Causeway. **JCA Leasing,** *the causeway; tel: (207) 693-3888,* rents power boats, bumper boats (a whirling powered inner tube) and Sea-Doo vehicles. JCA also offers parasail rides at 300–400 ft above the lake at $35 per person.

Rent lightweight touring bicycles from **Speed Cycle,** *Rte 302; tel: (207) 693-6118.*

Watch on the Wild Side

The northern tier of this loop is more densley inhabited by wildlife than by human beings. During daylight hours, large birds are among the easiest creatures to spot. Look for large raptors – especially golden eagles and red-tailed and red-shouldered hawks – riding the afternoon thermal currents along hillsides and above bodies of water.

Most other forms of wildlife are most active at dawn and dusk. Frequent signs warn of moose, which can weigh in excess of a metric tonne and are the unwitting participants in several auto accidents each year. They are seen most often in boggy areas.

White-tailed deer abound in this region despite their ill-timed attempts to cross backwoods roads just when visibility is poorest. Watch for these creatures (nearly twice the size of European red and fallow deer) crossing the road from a break in the woods to an open field on the opposite side. In the fall, virtually every abandoned orchard attracts a deer at dusk.

Overnight campers might encounter raccoons, porcupines and even the docile but large black bear – especially if they fail to secure all foodstuffs in their vehicles. Hikers traversing abandoned farmland might also see bushy-tailed red foxes and, at the edge of the woods, bobcats hunting rabbits, squirrels and voles. To observe beaver, sit very quietly near a beaver pond at dusk and wait for the families to surface.

PORTLAND– MOOSEHEAD LAKE

This 530- to 600-mile route encompasses the wilderness lakes, forests and mountains of northwestern Maine. Chief impediments to quick touring are washboard roads and the prospect of encountering *Alces americana*, the American moose. Moose spotting is a leading spectator sport, but many of the 5000 monthly sightings involve moose in the middle of what passes for highway in northern Maine. Field-and-stream aficionados will find outstanding fishing for trout and landlocked salmon and one of the last great bear hunting grounds in North America. Hikers, canoeists and rafters can enjoy the northernmost mountain of the Appalachian Trail and two of the most fabled rivers in American whitewater lore, the Allagash Wilderness Waterway and the West Branch Penobscot River.

Québec City page 339

Bar Harbor to Fort Kent Loop page 282

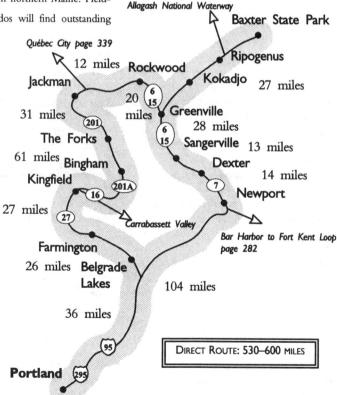

Allagash National Waterway

Baxter State Park

Ripogenus

12 miles Rockwood Kokadjo 27 miles

Jackman

20 **6** **15**

31 miles **201** miles Greenville 28 miles

The Forks **6** **15** Sangerville 13 miles

61 miles Bingham Dexter

Kingfield **201A** 14 miles

16 **7** Newport

27 miles **27**

Carrabassett Valley

Farmington

26 miles Belgrade Lakes 104 miles

36 miles

95

DIRECT ROUTE: 530–600 MILES

Portland **295**

269

ROUTES

DIRECT ROUTE

➡ To borrow the punchline from an old Maine joke, 'You can't get there from here', at least not by a direct route.

SCENIC ROUTE

➠ From Portland, follow I-295 north to its conclusion, where it joins I-95. Continue on I-95 north 104 miles to Exit 40 (Newport) to pick up Rte 7 North. (To connect instead with the Bar Harbor to Fort Kent Loop see (pp.282–285), continue on I-95 north 27 miles to Bangor.)

From Exit 40, follow Rte 7 for 14 miles to **Dexter,** where you veer left for Rte 23 for 13 miles to **Sangerville.** A half mile beyond Sangerville, turn left onto Rtes 6 and 15 and follow the road 28 miles to **Greenville,** the base for outfitters and guides for wilderness trips.

For an arduous side-track to **Baxter State Park,** bear right on *Lily Pond Rd,* which becomes an unnamed Great Northern Paper Company road ($8 road fee) at **Kokadjo.** Pavement ends soon, but follow the dirt road (left fork) 27 miles to Ripogenus Dam.

From 'Rip,' *Golden Pond Rd* leads southeast 24 miles to *Perimeter Rd* to enter **Baxter State Park** and the trails to 5267-ft Mt Katahdin. The truly hardy may drive for three hours over semi-washed-out logging roads to reach the headwaters of the **Allagash National Waterway** (bring extra petrol).

Back at Greenville, the main route continues north on Rtes 6 and 15 through Greenville Junction for 20 miles to **Rockwood,** continuing another 12 miles to **Jackman.** A right turn on Rte 201 leads toward Québec City, about two hours away; instead, turn south on Rte 201. In 31 miles at **The Forks** (pop. 30),

the road parallels the Kennebec River. In 34 miles, cross the river to Rte 201A and, in 11 more miles, turn right on Rte 16 West for 16 miles to **Kingfield.** Here, you can easily side-track on Rte 16 for 23 miles to **Carrabassett Valley.** Afterward, follow Rte 27 south for 27 miles to **Farmington,** then another 26 miles to **Belgrade Lakes.** Follow Rte 27 another 16 miles to I-95 South for 36 miles to I-295, then 4 miles to Portland.

PORTLAND TO GREENVILLE

The interstate offers many exits to towns, including **Brunswick** (see p. 251) and the state capital, **Augusta,** where restaurants and petrol are available. **Maine State Museum,** *Statehouse Complex, Rte 27, Augusta, ME 04330; tel: (207) 287-2301,* open Mon–Fri 0900–1700, Sat 1000–1600, Sun 1300–1600, chronicles Maine history and industry from 10,000 BC to present; free. The village of Sangerville is the birth-place of the only two Mainers knighted by the British Crown: Sir Hiram Maxim, inventor of the machine gun, and Sir Harry Oakes, gold baron and philathropist.

GREENVILLE

Tourist Information: Moosehead Lake Region Chamber of Commerce, *P.O. Box 581 (Rtes 6 and 15), Greenville, ME 04441; tel: (207) 695-2702 or 695-2026 (24-hour message line),* open daily 0900–1700 (May–June and Sept–Oct); daily 0800–1800 (July–Aug); Mon–Fri 1000–1700 (Nov–Apr). The Chamber publishes a directory of accommodation, camps, outfitters and expeditions in the region.

ACCOMMODATION AND FOOD

Most visitors camp or stay at hunting or fishing camps. But there are options for those who prefer more comfort, including the **Greenville Inn,** *P.O. Box 1194, Norris St, Greenville, ME 04441; tel: (207) 695-2206,* where half the ten rooms share baths, expensive; and **The Lodge at Moosehead,** *Lily Bay Rd, Greenville, ME 04441; tel: (207) 695-4400,* with breathtaking views, expensive.

Indian Hill Motel, *Rtes 6 and 15, P.O. Box 1181, Greenville, ME 04441; tel: (207) 695-2623 or toll-free (800) 771-4620,* has lake views; moderate.

Sporting camps range from rustic but accessible to very rustic and deep in the bush. **Beaver Cove Camps,** *Black Point Rd, P.O. Box 1233, Greenville, ME 04441; tel: (207) 695-3717 or (800) 577-3717,* is close to Greenville, moderate. Remote budget options (i.e., bring food for a week) north of Kokadjo include plumbing-free **Spencer Pond Camps,** *Star Rte 76, Box 580, Greenville, ME 04441; tel: (207) 695-2821* (leave message for radio relay), and plumbed **Medawisla on Second Roach Pond,** *Star Rte 76, Box 592, Greenville, ME 04441; tel: (207) 695-2690.* Campsites also vary in rusticity. On Rte 15 near Greenville is **Moosehead Family Campground,** *P.O. Box 1244, Greenville, ME 04441; tel: (207) 695-2210.* **Lily Bay State Park;** *tel: (207) 287-3834 for reservations,* offers 93 pitches, 9 miles north of Greenville on east side of Moosehead Lake. **Greenville Inn** and **The Lodge at Moosehead** (Nov–May only) offer white-linen dining; pricey. There are also several budget restaurants.

EVENTS

Moosemania, late May–late June, is a sequence of moose-themed events.

HUNTING AND FISHING

Hunting and fishing licenses, $17–$121 and $7–$66 respectively, are available in Greenville at the Department of Wildlife Management, *Lily Pond Rd.* Many camps have Maine Guides and will arrange hunting trips for deer, bear and moose.

Among the more accessible is **Foster's Maine Bush Sporting Camps,** *Lily Bay Rd, P.O. Box 1230, Greenville, ME 04441; tel: (207) 695-2845.* For fishing guides contact **Maine Guide Fly Shop & Guide Service,** *Main St, P.O. Box 1202, Greenville, ME 04441; tel: (207) 695-2266.*

CANOEING AND RAFTING

Canoes are almost a public utility, available for rental at most docks and piers. **Backwoods Adventure,** *Main St, P.O. Box 415, Greenville, ME 04441; tel: (207) 695-0977,* rents canoes and kayaks. Whitewater rafting (Class II–IV) on the

Moose on the loose

Keep an eye out for moose when driving through this region. They can often be seen in swampy areas or 'wallows', muddy areas marked by cloven hoof prints, and even next to the highway,

Especially at night, drive with caution through areas marked for moose crossings. Adult moose stand 6 ft tall at the shoulder, and their eyes may be too high to reflect the light of your car's headlights. Because of their mass, colliding with a moose often proves fatal to moose and motorists. During the day, beware of motorists stopping suddenly when they spot a moose. Either species can cause serious accidents.

It's best to watch the animals from the safety of your vehicle. Their movements cannot be predicted, especially the bulls in rut.

Penobscot, Dead and Kennebec rivers is available from **Eastern River Expeditions**, *Box 1173, Greenville, ME 04441; tel: (800) 634-7238.*

SIGHTSEEING

Greenville, a wide spot in the road at the southern tip of Moosehead Lake (the largest lake within a single state border), is the most sophisticated base for exploring the region.

Cruise the lake on the former steamship **Katahdin,** *Moosehead Marine Museum, Lily Pond Rd; tel: (207) 695-2716,* 3 hours ($13), late May–Sept.

The largest seaplane operator in the Northeast, **Folsom's Air Service,** *P.O. Box 507, Greenville, ME 04441; tel: (207) 695-2821,* flies into remote camps and fishing lakes and offers sightseeing flights from $20 per person.

MOOSE TRIPS

Moose are easily spotted at roadside bogs near dusk and dawn, but several operators arrange safaris for $30 per person and up, including **Main St Station,** *Main St, Greenville; tel: (207) 695-2375,* and the **Maine Guide Fly Shop & Guide Service,** which will fit moose-watchers with camouflage belly boats (floating platforms) to paddle eye-to-eye with moose.

SIDE TRACK TO BAXTER STATE PARK

Greenville gives access to the 'back route' to Baxter State Park's southern gate, which is more directly reached from Millinocket (see p. 283).

KOKADJO

Kokadjo Camps, *P.O. Box 1210 Greenville, ME 04441; tel: (207) 695-3993,* budget, and **Northern Pride Lodge,** *HC76, Box 588, Greenville,*

ME 04441; tel: (207) 695-2890, moderate, offer good bases for hunting and fishing. It might be useful to note that **Kokadjo General Store** has the last petrol for many miles.

BAXTER STATE PARK

Autos enter Baxter's **Perimeter Rd** by Togue Pond Gate off *Millinocket Rd* (an extension of *Golden Pond Rd*), or by Matagmon Gate west of Patten (See p. 282); non-resident vehicle fee $8 a day.

Accommodation in eight campsites include lean-tos, cabins and tent pitches. Reservations are advised. After Jan 1 write to **Baxter State Park HQ,** *Reservations Clerk, 64 Balsam Dr, Millinocket, ME 04462; tel: (207) 723-5140;* $7–$17. The best guide for hiking and rock-climbing is the *AMC Guide,* followed by the *DeLorme Map & Guide to Baxter State Park & Mount Katahdin,* both available from Moosehead Lake Region Chamber of Commerce (see Travel Essentials for other sources pp. 14–35). **Katahdin Air Service,** *P.O. Box 171, Millinocket, ME 04462; tel: (207) 723-8378,* arranges flights to remote parts of the Appalachian Trail to hike back to your vehicle.

ALLAGASH WILDERNESS WATERWAY

The waterway begins at Telos and Chamberlain lakes northwest of Baxter and runs 92 miles through a chain of lakes and rivers to the town of Allagash. Some logging roads skirt the waterway, but it's only passable by canoe, kayak or raft. Prepared sites for primitive camping dot the banks every dozen miles or so. Most of the route is flatwater, with some Class II rapids in the Allagash River. Two speciality outfitters are

Allagash Wilderness Outfitters, *Box 620, Star Rte 76, Greenville, ME 04441; radio relay tel: (207) 695-2821,* and **Allagash Canoe Trips,** *P.O. Box 713, Greenville, ME 04441; tel: (207) 695-3668.* [image]

ROCKWOOD

On the western shore of Moosehead Lake, Rockwood is Greenville with better hunting, less wit and closer proximity to the great flyfishing of the Kennebec River outlet from Moosehead Lake. Sightseeing and charter trips are available from **Jolly Roger's Moosehead Cruises;** *tel: (207) 534-8827.* Many wilderness camps use the Rockwood post office, including **The Birches,** *P.O. Box 41, Rockwood, ME 04478; tel: (207) 534-7305,* moderate, (which also runs raft trips as **Wilderness Expeditions**) and **Gray Ghost Camps,** *P.O. Box 35, Rockwood, ME 04478; tel: (207) 534-7362.* Self-catering cottages near village and lake include **Sundown Cabins & Cottages,** *P.O. Box 129, Rockwood, ME 04478; tel: (207) 534-7357.* **Old Mill Campground,** *Rte 15, Rockwood, ME 04478; tel: (207) 534-7333,* has great sites and views.

Bear and deer trophy hunters should contact **Russell Pond Outfitters,** *P.O. Box 386, Rockwood, ME 04478; tel: (207) 277-3353* or **Bob Lawrence,** *P.O. Box 101, Rockwood, ME 04478; tel: (207) 534-7709.*

JACKMAN

Tourist Information: **Jackman Chamber of Commerce,** *Main St, P.O. Box 368, Jackman, ME 04945; tel: (207) 668-4171,* open Wed–Sun 1000–1800 (mid-June–early Sept). Only 18 scenic miles from the Québec border, Jackman thrives on wilderness camping, hunting and fishing. **Sally Mountain Cabins,**

Box 50, Jackman, ME 04945; tel: (207) 668-5621, handles everything from lodging to licenses; budget.

THE FORKS

This village is the best place to put in a raft or canoe for Class II–III whitewater down a 12-mile gorge on the Kennebec River. **Northern Outdoors,** *Rte 201, P.O. Box 100, The Forks, ME 04985; tel: (800) 765-7238,* is on the spot.

KINGFIELD

The Stanley Museum, *School St; tel: (207) 265-2769,* open Tues–Sun 1300–1600, is filled with memorabilia of the brothers who invented the Stanley Steamer automobile, $2. **The Inn on Winter's Hill,** *Winter Hill Rd, RR 1, Box 1272, Kingfield, ME 04947; tel: (800) 233-9687,* moderate–expensive, has cross-counntry ski trails and is also site of **Julia's;** *tel: (207) 265-5426,* for fine dining, moderate–pricey. Good simple fare is available at **Longfellow's,** *Main St; tel: (207) 265-4394,* budget–moderate.

SIDE TRACK TO CARRABASSETT VALLEY
Sugarloaf/USA; *tel: (207) 235-2100,* is the ski mecca of Maine with 45 miles of trails, used for mountain biking off-season. **Tourist Information** (by mail): **Sugarloaf Area Chamber of Commerce,** *RR #1, Box 2151, Carrabassett Valley, ME 04947.* Lodging information; *tel: (800) 843-2732.* [image]

FARMINGTON TO PORTLAND

Farmington was a wealthy lumber and farming community and has a legacy of grand old homes. The drive through the summer cabin communities of **Belgrade Lakes** is a breather before the interstate.

273

BAR HARBOR AND ACADIA NATIONAL PARK

Bar Harbor and Acadia National Park are on 108-sq-mile Mt Desert (pronounced 'dessert') Island, the third largest island on the US Atlantic coast. Covered with rocky bald peaks, Mt Desert gives fresh meaning to the hoary tourism phrase, 'the rocky coast of Maine'.

The island is shaped like a lobster claw divided by Somes Sound, the only natural fjord on the US East Coast. It is a region of great natural beauty with occasional enclaves of human activity. The eastern half includes Bar Harbor, the major shopping and lodging town as well as Northeast Harbor, where the rich rebuilt their 'cottages' after an apocalyptic 1947 fire.

The 'quiet side' is west of the sound, anchored by Southwest Harbor, which struggles to maintain the fishing village identity that Bar Harbor surrendered years ago. Next door is Bass Harbor, a genuine fishing community. The 41,000-acre Acadia National Park dominates the island and is visited by more than 1 million people each year.

274

BAR HARBOR

TOURIST INFORMATION

Bar Harbor Chamber of Commerce, *93 Cottage St, P.O. Box 158, Bar Harbor,*

ME 04609; tel: (207) 288-5103, open daily 0800–1700 (mid-May–mid-Oct); Mon–Fri 0800–1630 (mid-Oct–mid-May), operates an **information booth** at **Marine Atlantic Terminal;** *tel: (207) 288-2404,* open daily 0900–2300 (mid-May–mid-Oct). **Mt Desert Chamber of Commerce,** *P.O. Box 675, Northeast Harbor, ME 04662; tel: (207) 276-5040,* has an **Information Bureau** at Sea St Marina, Northeast Harbor, open daily 0900–1700 (mid-June–Sept). **Southwest Harbor-Trenton Chamber of Commerce,** *Main St, Southwest Harbor, ME 04679; tel: (207) 244-9264 or toll-free (800) 423-9264,* open daily 0930–1230 and 1315–1700 (late May–mid-Oct), closed Tues 1500–1700.

Acadia National Park Headquarters, *Rte 233* (near northern edge of Eagle Lake), *P.O. Box 177, Bar Harbor, ME 04609; tel: (207) 288-3338* (general information) or *(207) 288-5262* for naturalist activities and reservations, operates the **Hulls Cove Visitor Center,** just off *Rte* 3 at the head of *Park Loop Rd,* open daily 0800–1630 (May–June, Sept–Oct); daily 0800–1800 (July–Aug), which has an introductory film, maps of roads and trails, and schedule of ranger-led programs including excusions and flora and fauna identification. The headquarters serve as the visitor centre Nov–Apr.

WEATHER

July–Aug daytime highs reach the low–mid-80s°F, evenings cool to mid-50s and lower. Autumn temperatures range into the 60s for daytime highs, the low 40s at night. The average winter low temperature is 14°F, with heavy snow. Radio station WDEA (1370 AM) broadcasts marine weather every half hour and provides a weather phone; *tel: (207) 667-8910.* WMDI (107.7 FM) broadcasts local and marine weather at 10 and 20 mins before and after each hour.

ARRIVING AND DEPARTING

Airport
Hancock County Airport, *tel: (207) 874-8300,* is 12 miles from Bar Harbor. **Colgan Air;** *tel: (207) 667-7171 or (800) 272-5488,* provides daily services between Bar Harbor and Boston.

By Ferry
Bluenose Ferry, *Hull Cove Terminal, Bar Harbor; tel: (207) 288-3395 or (800) 341-7981 in US; Marine Atlantic Reservations Bureau, P.O. Box 250, North Sydney, NS B2A 3M3, Canada; tel: (902) 564-7480.* International car and passenger ferry service to Nova Scotia; the 6-hour return passenger crossing is $39.95.

By Bus
Greyhound/Vermont Transit; *tel: (207) 772-6587,* operates from Bar Harbor to Boston and other cities, mid-June–early Sept.

GETTING AROUND

Public Transport
Downeast Transportation; *tel: (207) 667-5796,* provides a shuttle bus service late June–early Sept from Agarmont Park in central Bar Harbor to Sieur de Monts, Sand Beach and Blackwoods campsite in Acadia National Park. Fee is $2 in Bar Harbor, free at Acadia stops.

Driving
The eastern half of Mt Desert Island is circled by Rte 3. The western lobe is circled by Rte 102. The 'short cut' going cross-island is Rte 233, which also connects at the head of Somes Sound with Rtes 102/198 leading north to the mainland.

The other major road system is the *Park Loop Rd,* a 27-mile scenic road through the most-visited areas of Acadia on the eastern lobe of the island.

Another 57 miles of carriage roads wander through the eastern section of Acadia but autos are banned. Parking is scarce June–Oct, but is free, when you find it, on most streets and at town piers. RV parking allowed in designated areas only.

STAYING ON MT DESERT ISLAND

Accommodation
Once crowded with summer homes for the wealthy, the island now has a variety of accommodation. Prices range from budget to the outlandishly pricey, with most inns, larger motels and bed and breakfasts at the dividing line between moderate and expensive.

Many places require a three-day minimum stay in July and Aug; reservations essential. Most lodgings close mid-Oct–mid-May. Chain hotels include *BW, DI, Hd, Ma, QI.*

Bar Harbor has the largest concentration and greatest variety of lodgings. Motels along Rte 3 have the lowest rates. Moderate choices north of town include **The Colony,** *Rte 3, Box 66, Hulls Cove, ME 04644; tel: (207) 288-3383 or (800) 524-1159,* and **Edenbrook Motel,** *Rte 3, 96 Eden St, Bar Harbor, ME 04609; tel: (207) 288-4975 or (800) 323-7819.* Moderate choices south of town include **Cadillac Motor Inn,** *336 Main St, Bar*

275

Harbor, ME 04609; tel: (207) 288-3831; and **Cromwell Harbor Motel,** *359 Main St, Bar Harbor, ME 04609; tel: (207) 288-3201 or (800) 544-3201.* Larger rooms, better views and closer proximity to the village centre come at prices ranging from high moderate to expensive.

Atlantic Oakes-By-The-Sea, *119 Eden St (Rte 3), P.O. Box 3, Bar Harbor, ME 04069; tel: (207) 288-5801 or (800) 33-MAINE (336-2463),* incorporates the summer mansion of Sir Harry Oakes, a Canadian mining magnate and Jazz Age socialite, and views of Frenchman Bay. **The Atlantic Eyrie,** *Highbrook Rd, Bar Harbor, ME 04069; tel: (207) 288-9786 or (800) HABA-VUE (422-2883),* has an eagle's-eye view of Frenchman Bay and offers some self-catering suites.

Bed and breakfasts occupy the remaining grand cottages built by the wealthy in the late 19th century along *West St* and *Mt Desert St*, including **Kedge,** *112 West St, Bar Harbor, ME 04069; tel: (207) 288-5180 or (800) 597-8306,* expensive; **Manor House Inn,** *106 West St, Bar Harbor, ME 04069; tel: (207) 288-3759 or (800) 437-0088,* moderate–expensive; and **Primrose Inn,** *73 Mt Desert St, Bar Harbor, ME 04609; tel: (207) 288-4031 or (800) 543-7842,* moderate–expensive.

A few minutes' drive from Bar Harbor and close to Acadia is the **Lighthouse Inn and Restaurant,** *Main St (Rte 3), Seal Cove, ME 04674; tel: (207) 276-3958,* with rooms at low moderate, as well as moderate self-catering rooms.

A moderate–expensive option in Northeast Harbor is **The Maison Suisse Inn,** *Main St, P.O. Box 1090, Northeast Harbor, ME 04662; tel: (207) 276-5223 or (800) MAISONS (624-7667).*

In Southwest Harbor at the moderate end, the comfortably rumpled **Penury Hall Bed 'n' Breakfast,** *Main St, Box*

68, *Southwest Harbor, ME 04679; tel: (207) 244-7102,* has three rooms sharing two baths. **The Inn at Southwest,** *Main St, Box 93, Southwest Harbor, ME 04679; tel: (207) 244-3835,* is Victorian with a grand wrap-around porch; moderate– expensive. **The Claremont Hotel,** *Rte 102, P.O. Box 137, Southwest Harbor, ME 04679; tel: (207) 244-5036,* is Mt Desert Island's oldest summer resort hotel; moderate–expensive, no credit cards.

Camping

There are more than 500 woodland tent pitches in Acadia National Park, but no RV utility hookups. **Blackwoods Campground,** 6 miles east of Bar Harbor on *Rte 3*, has 310 pitches, which must be reserved in advance mid-June–mid-Sept by telephone only via **Destinet;** *tel: (800) 365-2267.*

Seawall Campground, 4 miles south of Southwest Harbor on *Rte 102A*, has more than 200 pitches on a first-come, first-served basis. A dozen private campsites also ring Mt Desert Island with rates $14–$35 per night.

Well-located campsites with oceanfront camping include **Smugglers Den Campground,** *Box 787, Rte 102, Southwest Harbor, ME 04679; tel: (207) 244-3944,* and **Bass Harbor Campground,** *Box 122, Bass Harbor, ME 04653; tel: (207) 244-5857.* Close to the Acadia Visitor Center is **Bar Harbor Campground,** *RFD #1, Box 1125 (Rte 3), Bar Harbor, ME 04609; tel: (207) 288-5185.*

Eating and Drinking

Rule of thumb is that the smaller the village, the fresher the lobster. A budget choice in Trenton (near the bridge from the mainland) is **Oak Point Lobster Pound Restaurant,** *off Rte 230, Trenton;*

tel: (207) 667-8548. On the opposite side of the island, a funky outdoor bar accompanies **Head of the Harbor Lobster Pound,** *Rte 102, Southwest Harbor; tel: (207) 244-3508,* budget.

Markets are readily available. **Don's Shop 'n Save,** *86 Cottage St, Bar Harbor; tel: (207) 288-3621,* is the island's best stocked food centre. Both Northeast and Southwest Harbors have upmarket grocers with good deli sections: **Pine Tree Market,** *Main St, Northeast Harbor; tel: (207) 276-3335;* and **Sawyer's Market,** *Main St, Southwest Harbor; tel: (207) 244-3315.* Don's opens at 0700 most days, Sawyer's at 0530.

Bar Harbor has the widest selection of dining. **Acadia Restaurant,** *62 Main St; tel: (207) 288-4881,* has sandwiches and locally favoured fish chowder in low-rent ambience; budget. Locals favour **West Street Café,** *comer of West and Rodick Sts; tel: (207) 288-5242,* for a quintessential Downeast meal of fish chowder, french fries, lobster and blueberry pie; budget–moderate.

Lompoc Café & Brewpub, *36 Rodick St; tel: (207) 288-9392,* has homemade beers and British ales on tap along with predictable bar food; budget–moderate. The **FinBack,** *78 West St; tel: (207) 288-4193,* combines an inventive international style with fresh local ingredients; moderate.

For bold cooking, the best bet is the moderate **Porcupine Grill,** *123 Cottage St; tel: (207) 288-3884.* For perhaps too much of a good thing, sample the lobster ice-cream at **Ben & Bill's Chocolate Emporium,** *80 Main St; tel: (207) 288-3281.* **Jordan Pond House,** *Park Loop Rd, Acadia National Park* (near Seal Harbor); *tel: (207) 276-3316,* is renowned for afternoon tea on the lawn; dinner is budget–moderate.

Redfield's, *Main St, Northeast Harbor; tel: (207) 276-5283,* serves light gourmet fare; moderate. **Preble Grille,** *14 Clark Point Rd, Southwest Harbor; tel: (207) 244-3034,* tends to contemporary Italian with New American styling and some excellent vegetarian dishes; moderate. **Keenan's,** *Rte 102, Tremont* (south of Southwest Harbor); *tel: (207) 244-3403,* is a roadhouse dive with baby back ribs, seafood gumbo and lobster; moderate.

Communications

Main post office in Bar Harbor is at 55 Cottage St, open Mon–Fri 0800–1700, Sat 0900–1200; *tel: (207) 288-3122.*

ENTERTAINMENT

Acadia Weekly is a free guide to Acadia National Park schedules, entertainment, activities and events throughout Mt Desert Island.

Acadia Repertory Theatre performs in summer and winter in *Masonic Hall, Rte 102, Somesville; tel: (207) 244-7260.* **Bar Harbor Music Festival,** *The Rodick Bldg, 59 Cottage St, Bar Harbor; tel: (207) 288-5744,* performs recitals, chamber music, pop and orchestral concerts early July–early Aug.

277

SHOPPING

Cottage and *Main Sts* in Bar Harbor are lined with souvenir shops of all levels of taste (or lack thereof). Some galleries and craft shops feature local artists, including **Island Artisans,** *99 Main St; tel: (207) 288-4214.*

OUTDOOR RECREATION

A state licence is required for **freshwater fishing** – available at town offices in Bar Harbor and other communities and at most hardware stores. Saltwater fishing requires no licence.

Originally established for croquet, **Kebo Valley Golf Club,** *Eagle Lake Rd, Bar Harbor; tel: (207) 288-5000,* is more than 100 years old. The 18-hole PGA championship course is open to the public; greens fee $30. The more modest **Bar Harbor Golf Course,** *Rtes 3 and 204, Trenton; tel: (207) 667-7505,* has nine-hole play; greens fees $12–$20.

Outdoor hard-surface and classic clay tennis courts are available at **Atlantic Oakes-by-the-Sea,** *Rte 3, Bar Harbor; tel: (207) 288-5218;* $3 per half hour.

Bar Harbor Bicycle Shop, *141 Cottage St, Bar Harbor; tel: (207) 288-3886,* rents mountain bikes and accessories. **Acadia Outfitters,** *106 Cottage St, Bar Harbor; tel: (207) 288-8118,* rents bicycles, canoes and sea kayaks and offers guided sea kayak tours. **Acadia Bike & Canoe,** *48 Cottage St, Bar Harbor; tel: (207) 288-9605 or (800) 526-8615,* rents mountain bikes, Old Town canoes (the local brand) and touring kayaks; they also offer a guided sunrise bicycle descent of Cadillac Mountain and guided sea kayak tours. **National Park Sea Kayak Tours,** *137 Cottage St, Bar Harbor; tel: (207) 288-0342,* offers half-day tandem kayak tours. **Southwest Cycle,** *Main St, Southwest Harbor; tel: (207) 244-5856,* rents mountain bikes. **National Park Canoe,** *Pond's End, Mt Desert; tel: (207) 244-5854,* rents canoes from the north end of Long Pond and provides free instruction.

Dive Maine, *Rte 102A, Bass Harbor; tel: (207) 244-5751,* rents snorkeling and SCUBA equipment and provides morning and afternoon dive trips as well as day-long charters.

Harbor Boat Rentals, *1 West St, Bar Harbor; tel: (207) 288-3747,* provides 13- and 17-foot Boston whalers.

Birdwatching tours at different proficiency levels can be booked with **Down**

East Nature Tours, *P.O. Box 521, Bar Harbor; tel: (207) 288-8128.*

SIGHTSEEING

Narrated tour buses jockey for parking along *Main St* near the Bar Harbor Town Pier, including **Jolly Roger's Trolley,** $10, which passes some of the mansions and takes in Cadillac Mountain summit in one hour, and the 2.5-hour **National Park Bus Tour,** $15. Tickets are sold at **Testa's Restaurant,** *53 Main St.* A budget choice for more autonomous touring is the **Acadia Tape Tour,** with directions covering a 56-mile driving tour of *Park Loop Rd* and Northeast Harbor, available at Hulls Cove Visitor Center; $8.95 rental, $11.95 purchase.

From the Water

Cruise schedules vary, but none are available before early May or after late Oct. State ferries run year-round.

Bar Harbor wildlife-watching cruises – for whales, seals and puffins – leave from the Holiday Inn Marina, the Bluenose Ferry Terminal and the Town Pier, with prices $15–$30. **Frenchman Bay Company,** *1 West St, Bar Harbor; tel: (207) 288-3322,* offers a wide variety.

For graceful sail cruising, book the **Natalie Todd,** *27 Main St, Bar Harbor; tel: (207) 288-4585 or 288-2373,* a 129-ft former Grand Banks fishing schooner, $17.50. The Town Marina in Northeast Harbor is a prime spot for touring boats and small island ferries. **Sea Princess Cruises,** *tel: (207) 276-5352,* offers naturalist cruises in Somes Sound and to the Cranberry Isles, $11–13. **The Islesford Ferry Company,** *tel: (207) 276-3717,* has several cruises, including a scenic island cruise with stopover on Little Cranberry Island, $10. Mail boat ferry service is available all year from the municipal pier to all

278

five Cranberry Isles, $8 return trip, from **Beal & Bunker Inc.;** *tel: (207) 244-3575.* The most colourful trip is the **Somes Sound Lobster Tour;** *tel: (207) 276-5352;* Captain Dave Hyde pulls his lobster traps, cruises up Somes Sound and boils a lobster on board; limited to six passengers, $25.

From Southwest Harbor, **Cranberry Cove Boating,** *Upper Town Dock; tel: (207) 244-5882,* provides ferry service to the Cranberry Isles, $9 return trip.

The **Masako Queen,** *Beal's Wharf; tel: (207) 288-5927,* offers deep-sea fishing trips, $28. Nearby Bass Harbor has the **Maine State Ferry Service;** *tel: (207) 596-2202,* to Swan's Island to see the lighthouse, walk the sand beaches or swim in the quarry, $8 return trip.

Island Cruises, *Little Island Marine, Bass Harbor; tel: (207) 244-5785,* traverses the islands of Blue Hill Bay; the lunch tour goes to Frenchboro, a 170-year-old fishing village on Long Island, $15.

Museums

Natural History Museum, *College of the Atlantic, Turrets Bldg, Rte 3, Bar Harbor; tel: (207) 288-5015,* open daily 0900–1700 (mid-June–early Sept); 1000–1600 (early Sept–mid-Oct), has exhibits of plant and animal life on the island and a self-guided nature trail, $2.50.

Oceanarium/Lobster Hatchery, *1 Harbor Pl, Bar Harbor; tel: (207) 288-2334,* open Mon–Sat 0900–1700 (mid-May–late Oct), shows how and why lobster are raised, $3.50, or as part of $9.75 pass to all three oceanariums on island. **Ocean-arium/Bar Harbor,** *Rte 3, Bar Harbor; tel: (207) 288-5005,* has seals and fish, $4. **Oceanarium/ Southwest Harbor,** *Clark Point Rd, Southwest Harbor; tel: (207) 244-7330,* has more than 20 tanks and many hands-on exhibits; $5.50.

Wendell Gilley Museum of Bird-Carving, *Main St* and *Herrick Rd, Southwest Harbor; tel: (207) 244-7555,* open Tues–Sun 1000–1600 (June and Sept–Oct); Tues–Sun 1000–1700 (July–Aug); Fri–Sun 1000–1600 (May and Nov–Christmas), features the best of the American bird carvers, $3. **Abbe Museum,** *Sieur de Monts Spring, Acadia National Park; tel: (207) 288-3519,* open daily 1000–1600 (May–June and Sept–Oct), daily 0900–1700 (July–Aug), has exhibits and artifacts of Maine Native Americans, $2.

This is why you came. Fees: One-to-seven-day automobile pass $5, seasonal pass $15, bicycle pass $3. *Park Loop Rd,* approximately 27 miles, offers a sampler of the coast and interior of Mt Desert Island and is the most accessible way to visit.

Highlights include: **Sieur de Monts Spring** with a Nature Center and wild-flower gardens; **Sand Beach,** swimming beach with 54°F water (at the warmest); **Thunder Hole,** where wave motion and hollow rocks create thunderclaps at a three-quarter rising tide with rough seas, but otherwise it's much ado about nothing; **Otter Cliff,** with pounding surf and wonderful waves; **Otter Point,** with superb tidepooling at low tide; **Jordan Pond House,** once a farm, now a tea house with beautiful gardens; and **Bubble Pond** and the **Bubble Erratics,** easy hiking to see geological anomalies.

Cadillac Mountain, at the end of a 3.5-mile road, is the island's highest peak with 360-degree views. **Blue Hill Parking Lot** is a great vantage for sunsets. **Champlain Mountain** is where peregrine falcons nest May–Aug.

Park Loop Rd will not satisfy those seeking uncrowded wilderness experiences.

279

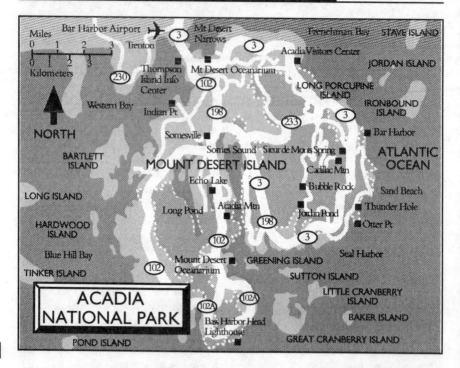

But Acadia has more than 120 miles of hiking trails and 57 miles of car-free carriage roads. (Pockets of land within the park are privately owned, and bicycles are banned on the carriage roads in these sections.) Scenic overlooks with parking are frequent along Acadia roads, and hiking trails radiate from these spots. Because much of the eastern park burned in 1947, the climactic spruce and fir forest is patchy but the replacement deciduous forest offers outstanding foliage and superior wildlife habitat.

While most visitors come in summer and autumn, the roads and carriage roads are open to cross-country skiing in the winter (skiers must share the park roads with snowmobiles).

The western side of Acadia is less visited and also has outstanding hiking, especially the **Acadia Mountain loop hike,** 2.5 easy miles overlooking Somes Sound and small islands. Park on the west side of Rte 102 at Echo Lake, 3 miles south of Somesville and pick up the trailhead across the road.

Swimming

Within Acadia National Park, hardy types can brave the salt water of **Sand Beach,** *Park Loop Rd,* while normal humans bathe at the freshwater beach of **Echo Lake,** *Rte 102,* north of Southwest Harbor.

Outside the park, there's an ocean beach at **Seal Harbor,** *Rte 3,* and several small freshwater beaches at the northern end of **Great Long Pond,** *Rte 198, Somesville.*

Other Outdoor Activities

The **Shore Walk** is an underutilised mile-long pathway which takes you along the edge of Frenchman Bay and past some grand summer cottages in Bar Harbor; the path begins near Agarmont Park at the town pier. **Bar Island** lies about a quarter of a mile offshore from Bar Harbor but is accessible for two hours before and after low tide at the foot of *Bridge St* via the sand bar that gave the town its name.

Blagden Preserve, *Indian Point Rd,* off Rte 198, is a 110-acre Nature Conservancy area on Mt Desert's northwest shoulder, with a trail network and scenic overlooks of Western Bay.

SIDETRACK TO CAMPOBELLO ISLAND

For the trip to US President Franklin Delano Roosevelt's summer home at Campobello Island (in Canada), return to Ellsworth and set off on Rtes 1 and 189 for 95 miles northeast through the spruce and blueberry barrens of Washington County.

At Gouldsboro, 23 miles east of Ellsworth, there's a diversion right at the signs for a tour and tasting of fruit and honey wines at **Bartlett Maine Estate Winery;** *tel: (207) 546-2408,* open Tues–Sat 1000–1700, Sun 1200–1700 (June–mid-Oct); Sat 1000–1700, Sun 1200–1700 (May).

In another 22 miles, turn off for the village of **Columbia Falls** to visit **Ruggles House,** *no telephone,* an early-1800s home known for an astonishing staircase and carved woodwork, open Mon–Sat 0930–1630, Sun 1100–1630 (June–mid-Oct), $2, and the **Columbia Falls Pottery;** *tel: (207) 483-4075.*

In 4 miles, turn right onto Rte 187 for **Jonesport and Beals Island,** fishing communities picturesque in their authenticity; they stonily ignore tourists and have almost no amenities.

Rejoin Rte 1 after 29 miles and continue 10 miles into **Machias,** the historic county seat and hotbed of the American Revolution (the first naval battle involved scuttling a moderately armed British schooner in 1775). The **Burnham Tavern Museum,** *Main St, Machias; tel: (207) 255-4432,* open Mon–Fri 0900–1700 (mid-June–Sept), $2, chronicles the 'Lexington of the Sea' amid Revolutionary-era furnishings. On the third weekend of Aug, the **Machias Blueberry Festival** combines a craft fair with athletic, artistic and blueberry baking and eating events.

Another 40 miles east along Rte 1, then Rte 189, lies **Lubec,** the easternmost town in the US, with 96 miles of coastline, including great views of Campobello and Grand Manan islands. **West Quoddy Head State Park,** is adjacent to the candy-striped West Quoddy Head Light.

A bridge leads from Lubec to Campobello Island, New Brunswick, which means passing through Customs to visit **Roosevelt Campobello International Park,** open daily 1000–1800 Atlantic Time (Eastern Time plus one hour) May–mid-Oct; free. The 34-room 'cottage' was FDR's summer home and is surrounded by nature trails. Extensive interpretive exhibits tell of Roosevelt's life and the US-Canadian friendship.

Visitors who come this far are often heading into Canada's Atlantic provinces. There's a ferry from Campobello to the mainland at St Andrews, but the more usual crossing is reached by following Rte 189 back to Rte 1, then Rte 1 north 47 miles to **Calais** (pronounced CAL-ess) and over the St John River to St Stephen, New Brunswick. ◣

281

BAR HARBOR– FORT KENT LOOP

Maine's enormity becomes evident in this 523-mile loop, which embarks from the shoreline through the forested interior on roads that parallel the lumber trade. At the far end of the loop, the St John River Valley opens into flat country resembling the English Midlands without industry. Canada and the USA contested this northerly region in the 1840s in the 'Aroostook War', but neither side cared strongly enough to fire a shot. This world of potato farms is most beautiful in July during the blossom season. The route is best undertaken in daylight; long stretches of two-lane blacktop unpunctuated by any sign of life, make night-time driving hazardous.

282

20 miles
Fort 9 miles
Kent Madawaska
17 miles ① Grande Isle
Van Buren 16 miles
Eagle Lake
42 miles 22 miles
Ashland Caribou 13 miles
Presque Isle

43 miles
60 miles
Baxter State Park Houlton
page 272 Patten
32 miles ⑪ ②A 55 miles
Millinocket ②
10 miles Mattawmkeag
Medway 13 miles
Lincoln
65 miles 13 miles
⑨⑤ Old Town
Bangor 8 miles
Portland to ①A Ellsworth
Moosehead Lake
page 269 26 miles
21 miles ③ **Bar Harbor**

ROUTE

From Bar Harbor, take Rte 3 west for 21 miles through Ellsworth to the junction with Rte 1A, then Rte 1A to **Bangor** 26 miles away. At Bangor, take I-95 north 65 miles to **Medway**. Here you can exit to Rtes 11 and 157 south and go 10 miles to **Millinocket**, the southern access point to Baxter State Park. Alternatively, head north on Rte 11 for 32 miles to **Patten**, the park's northern access point. From here it's 60 miles to **Ashland**, another 42 quite scenic miles to **Eagle Lake** and a final 17 miles to **Fort Kent**.

DIRECT ROUTE: 523 MILES

Turn south on Rte 1 (the only direction!) and proceed along the St John River, which forms the US-Canada border, 20 miles to **Madawaska**, 9 more miles to **Grand Isle**, then 16 miles to **Van**

Buren. It's another 22 miles inland to Caribou, 13 miles more to **Presque Isle** and 43 miles to **Houlton**. At Houlton, take Rte 2A west for 55 miles through the notorious Haynesville Woods ('If they buried every trucker lost on that road there'd be a tombstone every mile', sang Dick Curless) to rejoin Rte 2 just before **Mattawamkeag**. Continue 13 miles into Lincoln, another 37 miles to **Old Town**, and 8 more miles into Bangor. (At Bangor, you have the choice of taking I-95 south 27 miles to join the Portland to Moosehead Lake route or 146 miles to Portland). To head back to Bar Harbor, pick up Rte 1A to Ellsworth, then Rte 3.

BANGOR

Tourist Information: Greater Bangor Chamber of Commerce, *519 Main St, Bangor, ME 04401; tel: (207) 947-0307,* operates an **information centre** beneath the statue of legendary woodsman Paul Bunyan, open Mon–Fri 0800–1800, Sat–Sun 1000–1700 (late May–mid-Oct); Mon–Fri 0800–1700 (mid-Oct–late May).

AIRPORT

Bangor International Airport, *Rte 2; tel: (207) 947-0384,* has daily flights by major US carriers and many stops by European charter carriers.

ACCOMMODATION AND SIGHTSEEING

Chain hotels include *BW, CI, DI, Hd, HJ, Ma, M6, QI, Rm, S8* and **Scottish Inns**; *tel: (800) 251-1962.* As a cargo rail, air and highway hub, Bangor is the commercial centre for much of central Maine. Late 19th-century lumber wealth persists in some of the finer houses, including *45 W. Broadway*; girdled by a gargoyle-bedecked wrought-iron fence, this is the home of Stephen King, the horror-fiction writer, and his wife, author Tabitha King.

MEDWAY

The east and west branches of the Penobscot River join here, which made Medway a bustling centre in the log-running days. Now it's quiet and the rivers are full of fish again. Soak it all in by staying at **Katahdin Shadows Campground**, *Medway, ME 04460; tel: (207) 746-9349.*

MILLINOCKET

Tourist Information: Millinocket Area Chamber of Commerce, *1029 Central St, Millinocket, ME 04462; tel: (207) 723-4443,* open Mon–Fri 0900–1700.

ACCOMMODATION AND RECREATION

Great Northern Paper Company more or less built Millinocket in 1901 to house its employees. Paper remains the main industry, rivalled only by outdoor sports. Most hikers and mountain climbers heading to Mt Katahdin and Baxter State Park (see p. 272) use Millinocket as the jump-off to the southern gate.

Big Moose Inn, Cabins & Campground, *Box 98, Millinocket, ME 04462, tel: (207) 732-8391,* near Baxter and surrounded by lakes, has a restaurant and direct access to international snowmobile trails; moderate. Hikers favour **Katahdin Area Bed and Breakfast**, *94–96 Oxford St, Milliinocket, ME 04462; tel: (207) 723-5220,* budget–moderate. **Katahdin Lake Wilderness Camps**, *Box 398, Millinocket, ME 04462; tel: (207) 723-4050,* a remote camp in Township 3, Range 8, has pack horses to help haul big game from the woods; moderate.

To hike along one of the region's most striking natural wonders, drive west on Rte 11 to the turnoff for Katahdin Iron Works and continue 13 miles to **Gulf Hagas**, known locally as 'The Grand Canyon of the East'. This 3-mile canyon

283

contains five major waterfalls and has nearly vertical walls up to 40 metres high. The Appalachian Trail follows the rim.

PATTEN TO FORT KENT

The lumber and pulpwood town of Patten is the northern access for Baxter State Park for visitors seeking ponds and streams rather than the big lakes, rivers and mountains of the southern park. Access roads connecting north and south gates are in dire need of repair; ask locally about conditions before proceeding. Fishing around Patten is said to be among the best in North America.

Mt Chase Lodge, *Rte 1, Box 281D, Patten, ME 04765; tel: (207) 528-2183*, offers cabins and lodge rooms for hunting and fishing with family-style dining in a secluded spot on Shin Pond near the north entrance to Baxter State Park; moderate–expensive. **Macannamac**, *Box B, Patten, ME 04765; radio tel: (207) 528-2855*, budget–moderate, features a series of wilderness cabins in unnamed townships in the Allagash Lakes region.

Patten Lumberman's Museum, *Rte 159; tel: (207) 528-2650*, open Tues–Sat 0900–1600, Sun 1100–1600 (late May–Sept); Sat, Sun only (first half Oct), $2.50, has 3000 artifacts from the lumbering days collected in nine buildings, including an 1820 logging camp.

Ashland Logging Museum, *Hacker Rd, Ashland, ME 04732; no telephone*, is an outdoor exhibit of early 20th-century logging equipment as well as a machine shed and blacksmith shop; free. Eagle Lake, a key destination for big-game hunters, still has good hunting, but ecotourism (wildlife-watching) rivals its popularity. **Camps of Acadia**, *Box 202, Eagle Lake, ME 04739; tel: (207) 444-5207*, has eight cottages on the lake which is known for eagles, loons and moose; moderate.

FORT KENT

Tourist Information: Greater Fort Kent Area Chamber of Commerce, *Main St, P.O. Box 430F, Fort Kent, ME 04743; tel: (207) 834-5354 or toll-free (800) SEE-FKME (733-3563)*, open Mon–Fri 0900–1700.

ACCOMMODATION

Rock's Motel and Diner, *91 W. Main St, Fort Kent, ME 04743; tel: (207) 834-3133 or 834-6194*, has 200 miles of snowmobile trails beginning behind the motel; moderate. **Daigle's Bed & Breakfast,** *96 East Main St, Fort Kent, ME 04743; tel: (207) 834-5803* emphasises its 'gourmet' breakfasts and comforting fireplace.

SIGHTSEEING AND ENTERTAINMENT

US Rte 1 begins here and ends 2209 miles south in Key West, Florida. The town of 4400 virtually doubles during the third week of Feb, when the **Can-Am Dogsled Races** take over.

The **Fort Kent Blockhouse**, *Block House St, off Rte 1; tel: (207) 834-3866*, open Mon–Sat 0900–1700 (late-May–early Sept), is an 1840 relic of the Aroostook War.

Rte 11 crosses the St John River into Canada here at Clair, New Brunswick, then Rte 120 heads into Québec to the northeast of Québec City.

MADAWASKA TO VAN BUREN

Tourist Information: Madawaska Area Chamber of Commerce, *378 Main St, Madawaska, ME 04756; tel: (207) 728-7000*, open Mon–Fri 0900–1600.

The most northeasterly town in the USA, Madawaska carries the flame for the vanished Acadian culture in Aroostook County and is perhaps the closest to a truly bilingual town in Maine. The **Acadian**

Festival dominates everything in town 28 June–4 July with parades, historic re-enactments, Acadian Mass and many events involving food.

At Madawaska there's a border crossing to Edmundston, New Brunswick; Rte 2 heads into northern Québec.

At Grand Isle, the **Musée et Centre Culturel du Mont-Carmel**, *Rte 1, Lille-sur-St-Jean, Grand Isle, ME 04746; tel: (207) 895-3339 (curator's home)*, is one of the region's earliest French Catholic churches, now restored as a museum and cultural centre; limited hours, donation requested.

For an overnight stop-over in elegant comfort, try **The Farrell-Michaud House**, *231 Main St, Van Buren, ME 04785; tel: (207) 868-5209*, a bed-and-breakfast inn in a turreted Victorian manse; moderate. **Acadia Village**, *Rte 1* north of Van Buren; *tel: (207) 868-5042* or *868-2691*, open daily 1200–1700 (mid-June–mid-Sept), $2.50, a complex of a dozen reconstructed or relocated buildings circa 1785–1900, illustrates Francophone life in the St John Valley.

CARIBOU

Tourist Information: Caribou Chamber of Commerce, *111 High St, P.O. Box 357, Caribou, ME 04736; tel: (207) 498-6156*, is open Mon–Fri 0730–1600. Its population of almost 10,000 makes Caribou an Aroostook metropolis. For overnight stops, there's a *DI.* **Nylander Museum**, *393 Main St; tel: (207) 493-4209*, has extensive collections of natural history and of Native American artifacts; free.

PRESQUE ISLE

Tourist Information: Presque Isle Area Chamber of Commerce, *3 Houlton Rd, P.O. Box 672, Presque Isle,*

ME 04769; tel: (207) 764-6561, open Mon–Fri 0900–1700.

Maine's northernmost state park, **Aroostook State Park**, *off Rte 1; tel: (207) 768-8341*, has outstanding camping and hiking. Park admission is $2; non-resident camping $14. Boat and canoe rentals are available for use on Echo Lake ($10 per day). Within the park, **Quaggy Joe Mountain** has two peaks, with the three-quarter-mile direct hike to the north peak providing the best lake views.

HOULTON TO BAR HARBOR

Tourist Information: Greater Houlton Chamber of Commerce, *109 Main St, Houlton, ME 04730; tel: (207) 532-4216*, is open from Mon–Fri 0900–1700.

At the northern terminus of I-95, Houlton is the shire town for Aroostook County and a major border crossing into New Brunswick; from here it's about 200 miles to Fredericton.

There's a **Scottish Inns**; *tel: (800) 251-1962*. South of the infamous Haynesville Woods, **Mattawamkeag Wilderness Park**, *Rte 2, Box 5, Mattawamkeag, ME 04459; tel: (207) 736-4881*, has 15 miles of wilderness trails, access to the Mattawamkeag River and camping at tent pitches or lean-to cabins.

This town-operated site brags about being undiscovered; it is.

Almost back to Bangor, **Old Town Canoe**, *58 Middle St; tel: (207) 827-5513*, sells factory 'blems' (seconds) and shows a video on canoe-building, open Mon–Sat 0900–1800, Sun 0900–1500 (March–Dec); Mon–Fri 0900–1700 (Jan–Feb). **Penobscot Nation Museum**, *Indian Island; tel: (207) 827-6545*, open limited hours, valiantly tries to tell the tribe's story with a handful of old-time artifacts and several reproductions; $2.

285

NEW YORK CITY

New York is a tonic, a stimulant, an energiser – the ultimate vacation trip. With skyscrapers and slums, it's both fascinating and frustrating. Everything's bigger in this global city called The Big Apple, and nothing is done half-heartedly. It's certainly more expensive than places in New England, so don't even try to apply your Vermont budget to the New York experience. Still, you don't need a fortune to have a memorable stay here. If you budget wisely and realistically, it can be exceedingly good value.

TOURIST INFORMATION

The **New York Convention & Visitors Bureau (NYCVB)** operates a **Visitor Information Center,** *2 Columbus Circle* (southwest Central Park), *New York, NY 10019; tel: (212) 397-8222* or toll-free *(800) NYC-VISIT (692-8474),* open Mon–Fri 0900–1800, Sat–Sun and holidays 1000–1500.

When calling, choose the **New York by Phone** option for automated information about hotels, restaurants, sightseeing attractions, events, theatre, shopping and services. Multilingual counsellors are available Mon–Fri 0900–1800, Sat, Sun and holidays 1000–1500.

Bronx Tourism Council, *880 River Ave, Suite 3, Bronx, NY 10452; tel: (718) 590-3518.* **Meet Me in Brooklyn,** *30 Flatbush Ave, Suite 427, Brooklyn, NY 11217; tel: (718) 855-7882.* **Queens Tourism Council,** *P.O. Box 555, Queens Borough Hall, Queens, NY 11424; tel: (718) 647-3387* or *(800) 454-1329.* **Staten**

Island Chamber of Commerce, *130 Bay St, Staten Island, NY 10301; tel: (718) 727-1900.*

WEATHER

New York is just about at sea level and its coastal weather can be fairly unpredictable. Summers can be hot and relatively humid, though the once predictable 'August heat wave' is now apt to come at any time during the summer months. The average July temperature is 68–85°F. Winters may not be consistently freezing, though cold snaps are to be expected. There's never a guarantee of snow, which also, except in rare blizzard cases, does not last for long. The average Jan temperature is 26–38°F.

Daily weather reports include wind chill in the winter and humidity index in the summer, with occasional air quality advisories for those with a respiratory condition.

Radio and TV stations provide regular updates on weather and traffic conditions. Some TV channels keep the temperature of the moment in constant view on the screen. There is an an all-weather TV channel (Ch 36); *tel: (212) 976-1122.*

Since New York's hot weather is often accompanied by frigid air-conditioning and the cold days come with sometimes oppressive central heating, layering is the key when deciding what clothes to pack.

ARRIVING AND DEPARTING

Airports
John F. Kennedy International Airport (JFK), the main airport for international flights as well as many domestic

connections, is about 15 miles southeast of New York City. Several US airlines handle all flights from their own terminals; most non-US airlines use the international terminal. Ground transportation, *tel: (800) 247-7433;* parking information, *tel: (718) 656-5699.*

By yellow (metered) cab, it's 5–10 mins from airport hotels and 25 mins to an hour or more from midtown Manhattan, depending on traffic, weather, time of day and day of week. Average fare $35, includes $3 tunnel/bridge toll and tip. Car/limo service, $25, plus toll and tip.

Bus connections: **Carey Airport Express** buses, $13, depart every half hour from airport terminals; travel time one hour minimum. Stops in Manhattan are **Grand Central Terminal,** *Park Ave* and *42nd St* (on Manhattan's East Side) and **Port Authority Bus Terminal,** *42nd St* and *Eighth Ave* (West Side); *tel: (718) 632-0500.* Some of the large chain hotels (*HL, Sh, MA*) run shuttle buses (ask at Ground Transportation Centre).

Connections from JFK to other area airports: To LaGuardia, there's a Carey bus every 30 mins, $10. To Newark International, take the **Princeton Airporter;** *tel: (609) 587-6600,* $19 per person.

LaGuardia Airport, serving domestic destinations only – including hourly shuttle flights to Boston and Washington, D.C. – is about 8 miles northeast of New York City. Ground transportation, *tel: (800) 247-7433;* parking information, *tel: (718) 533-3400.*

By yellow cab, it's 10–30 mins from midtown Manhattan with an average fare of $20. Car/limo service is $15.

Bus connections: **Carey Airport Express buses,** $9, depart every half hour from airport terminals; travel time half an hour minimum. Stops in Manhattan are on the East Side at *Park Ave* and *42nd St*

near Grand Central Terminal and on the West Side at **Port Authority Bus Terminal,** *42nd St* and *Eighth Ave*; *tel: (718) 632-0500.* A variety of hotels run shuttle buses and Gray Line runs shuttle buses from the airports to your hotel.

Bus connections to other area airports: To JFK – Carey bus every 30 mins, $9.50. To Newark International – Princeton Airporter, $19 per person; *tel: (609) 587-6600.*

Newark International Airport, which has one international and two domestic terminals, is in New Jersey about 16 miles southwest of New York City. Ground transportation, *tel: (800) 247-7433;* parking information, *tel: (201) 961-4751.*

By taxi, it's 30–45 mins from midtown Manhattan. Average fare $30–$40. Car/limo service is $25.

Bus connections: **Olympia Trails Express Bus,** *tel: (212) 964-6233,* departs every 20–30 mins for Manhattan, $8, with stops downtown at World Trade Center, midtown at Grand Central and at Penn. Station (frequency varies with time of day and day of week). **NJ Transit,** *tel: (201) 762-5100,* runs an express bus, $7, about every 15 mins to Port Authority Bus Terminal, *Eighth Ave* and *42nd St.*

Bus connections to other area airports: To JFK, take the Princeton Airporter, $19 per person, *tel: (609) 587-6600.*

By car

Leaving Manhattan from the West Side to New Jersey and points west: Take either the **Henry Hudson Pkwy** (Rte 9A) north along the Hudson River to the **George Washington Bridge** and connect to **I-95.** Or, drive via the **Lincoln Tunnel** midtown (entrance Ninth Ave at 41st St) to **I-495,** or the **Holland Tunnel** downtown (entrance at Canal St) to **Rte 1** and eventually **I-78.** From Manhattan's lower tip, take the **Brooklyn Battery Tunnel** to Brooklyn and along **I-278** south, across the **Verrazano Narrows Bridge** and through Staten Island.

Leaving Manhattan from the East Side: Take the **Manhattan, Brooklyn** or **Williamsburg** bridges to Brooklyn and pick up **I-278,** either south to the Verrazano Bridge or north to Connecticut. Or take the **Queens Midtown Tunnel** (toll) entrance at 38th St and Second Ave to **I-495** east to **Long Island.**

Getting to the airports: For JFK, leave Manhattan via the **Queens Midtown Tunnel** (entrance at *38th St* and *Second Ave*), then take the **Long Island Expressway**. If there is no traffic, take Exit 22 **(Grand Central Parkway)**, then Exit 13 to **Van Wyck Expressway** to JFK. In heavy traffic, take Exit 19 **(Woodhaven Blvd)** to Belt Parkway and follow signs to JFK.

For LaGuardia, take the Queens Midtown Tunnel to the Long Island Expressway to **Brooklyn-Queens Expressway** to Grand Central Parkway to the airport. For Newark, take the Lincoln Tunnel (entrance *Ninth Ave* at *41st St*), follow signs to **New Jersey Turnpike** and then to Newark airport (Exit 13A).

By helicopter
New York Helicopter, *tel: (800) 645-3494*. Manhattan heliports: Downtown; *tel: (212) 248-7240*. E. *34th St; tel: (212) 889-0986*. W. *30th St; tel: (212) 563-4442*.

By train
There are two main rail stations. In midtown, Grand Central, a landmark terminal with restaurants, news-stands, fast-food stands and shops, runs a frequent schedule of Metro-North commuter trains; *tel:*

(212) 532-4900. The Hudson, Harlem and New Haven lines cover the suburban metro area and Connecticut.

Pennsylvania (Penn.) Station, between *Seventh* and *Eighth Ave* and *31st–33rd St (West Side)*, serves commuters to New Jersey and Long Island and train travellers to other US cities. For New Jersey, take **PATH** trains to Newark or Hoboken, or **NJ Transit;** *tel: (212) 564-8484* (bus only), *tel: (201) 762-5100* (bus or train). For Long Island, take **Long Island Rail Road (LIRR)**; *tel: (718) 217-5477*. The rest of the country is served from here by **Amtrak**, *tel: (212) 582-6875*. In the Northeast corridor, a speedy Metroliner, *tel: (800) 523-8720*, services Washington, D.C. A club car seat costs extra, but you get meal and beverage service and more comfort.

By bus
Port Authority Bus Terminal, *Eighth Ave* and *42nd St* (near the theatre district); *tel: (212) 564-8484*, is where buses to other parts of the country, on major lines, arrive and depart. The two major long-haul bus lines are **Greyhound**; *tel: (212) 971-6300* or *(800) 231-2222*, and **Adirondack Trailways**; *tel: (212) 967-2900* or *(800) 225-6815*. The two major short-haul lines are **New Jersey Transit**; *tel: (201) 762-5100*, and **Rockland Coaches**; *tel: (212) 279-6526*.

GETTING AROUND
With a population of 7 million and growing, metro New York is congested with traffic and pedestrians. Driving to attractions is not advised. With the aid of public tranport for longer distances, the best way to see the city and feel its energy is on foot.

A long and narrow island (12.5 miles long and 2.5 miles wide), Manhattan's streets and avenues are relatively simple to navigate – providing you know some basic facts and the lingo that goes with them: *Fifth Ave* runs north-south and divides Manhattan into **East Side** and **West Side.** Avenues run north and south, with mostly one-way traffic; even-numbered streets tend to run east and odd-numbered ones west. **Uptown** is an area – from the 60s on up – as well as a direction, as in going with the ascending street numbers. **Downtown** is the lower (southern-most) part of Manhattan and also refers to travelling in the direction of descending street numbers. Both are invaluable when using the subway. **Midtown** is the middle part of Manhattan – from the 30s to the 60s, between the East River and the Hudson River. **Crosstown** is a direction, as in travelling across the island (east or west). If you're walking, remember that crosstown blocks are twice as long as up or down-town ones.

Manhattan neighbourhoods

The Battery, at the lowest tip of the island, is where the city was founded. **Battery Park City** is residential, and the area is also where the terminals are located for ferries that serve Staten Island, Governors Island, the Statue of Liberty and Ellis island. The **Lower Broadway** area, just north of the Battery, encompasses the World Trade Center and the World Financial Center complexes. **Wall St** is a specific street as well as a generic name for the financial district, which at its northern boundary includes *Fulton St* (and the famous fish market) and the South St Seaport.

Next come City Hall and the court buildings and **Chinatown,** where the narrow, winding streets yield butchers, bakers and Chinese greengrocers. There are news-stands and souvenir shops as well as unmistakably Chinese-style public tele-

phone booths. **Canal St** divides Chinatown and **Little Italy,** which shows off its cultural heritage, mainly now with restaurants, cafés, bakeries and some grocers.

Proceding uptown, there is the **Lower East Side,** an area known as a burgeoning ghetto for late 19th-century and early 20th-century immigrants of all kinds, but mostly Jews from Eastern Europe. **Orchard St** is famous for bargain shopping, with many restaurants and businesses still retaining their ethnic flavour. The **SoHo Cast-Iron District** was designated a historic district by the New York City Landmarks Preservation commission in 1973 and is an architectural treasure trove; SoHo is short for 'South of Houston St' (pronounced HOW-ston).

Gramercy Park is a beautiful European style square and its surroundings have a fascinating history of famous former residents (architect Stanford White) and establishments such as **Pete's Tavern,** *66 Irving Pl* (which claims to have been a favoured haunt of author O. Henry), and the private **Players Club,** *16 Gramercy Park South.* **Greenwich Village,** with its distinctive Washington Arch, was originally the bohemian home of writers and artists, with residents such as O. Henry, Edgar Allan Poe and Mark Twain. At the southeast corner of **Washington Square** is the main building of New York University and nearby the small clubs and cafés of *Macdougal* and *Bleecker Sts.*

Central Park separates the **Upper East Side** from the **Upper West Side** (Central Park West, the gentrified *Columbus* and *Amsterdam Aves* and, at *110th St,* the Columbia University campus). **Morningside Heights** and **Harlem** have some of the city's poorer residential neighbourhoods, though Harlem also has historic points of interest (See Sightseeing).

From Greenwich Village's **Washington Square** upwards, the streets are laid out on a strict grid. In lower Manhattan, keep your street map handy, because the older streets are a jumble of names and directions.

Public Transport

If you're weary, time is short or distances great, use the city's very efficient public transportation system. Buses and subways are, by far, the most expedient and recommended method for getting around Manhattan and to the other boroughs. The major lines on the network are the **IRT**, **IND** and **BMT**, plus the **Shuttle** between Grand Central (East Side) and Times Square (West Side). The **No. 7 (Flushing) Line**, also serves as a shuttle between *Grand Central, Fifth Ave* and *Times Square,* but then it continues into the borough of Queens.

Free maps are available and 24-hour subway and bus information is provided by the **New York City Transit Authority,** *tel: (718) 330-1234.*

Use subways to cover the greater distances, say from your midtown lodgings to attractions at the lower tip of Manhattan (*Wall St*, South St Seaport, World Trade Center or the Statue of Liberty, via Battery Park). **Express trains** stop only at major stations, sometimes as far as 30 blocks apart); **Local trains** are not practical for longer distances, as they stop at major stations as well as everywhere in between, on an average of every eight blocks.

Drawbacks: the subway system is very extensive (more than 400 stations) and can be confusing, though markings are now colour-coded and vastly improved).

Avoid using subways during rush-hours (0730–0900 or 1700–1830) when they can be unpleasantly hectic and crowded or – very important! – late at night, after 2300.

Another caveat: Be prepared to climb lots of steep steps.

Tokens can be purchased in booths in the station. A single token costs $1.25, but may also be purchased in a ten-pack, which comes in handy, depending on the length of your visit. The same tokens are used on city buses.

Buses are a more scenic way of getting from point to point. The fare – a token or $1.25 in exact change – is deposited as you board. If your journey requires you to go uptown/downtown as well as crosstown, ask the driver for a (free) **transfer,** but mind that you re-board at a transfer point (marked on the back of the transfer). Most buses have wheelchair lifts. The Express version of a city bus is marked 'Limited Stops'. Otherwise buses stop every other block. Maps are available and frequency is noted on signs at bus stops. Again, be prepared for crowding and jostling (and standing) during rush hours.

Taxis are more expensive (fares increase with distance covered, plus a $0.50 evening surcharge) but are a more comfortable and convenient alternative if three or more are travelling together. (A typical door-to-door taxi fare might be $3 from midtown to the Broadway theatres. Individually, by bus or subway, the total cost for four – at $1.25 each – would be $5 for the same trip). Specific attractions outside Manhattan are best reached by subway, bus or train.

Driving in New York City

The best advice for holiday drivers is: DON'T. Free parking is practically non-existent, and garages are expensive or inconveniently located. Local drivers can be erratic, impatient and discourteous and, with frequent gridlock, it can take up to half an hour just to get across town.

If bringing a car into Manhattan is

unavoidable, here are two of the largest parking garages: **GMC (Garage Management Corp.)** has 53 locations; *tel: (212) 888-7400*, **Kinney System** has over 130 facilities; *tel: (800) 836-6666*. Or look under Parking Stations and Garages in Manhattan's Yellow Pages. For information about current street parking regulations, *tel: (212) 442-7080*.

STAYING IN NEW YORK CITY

Accommodation

Manhattan's 100,000-plus rooms include the most luxurious and elegant, the moderate and the safe-and-affordable. The biggest concentration of hotels is in midtown, both East and West Sides, but there are also several near Lincoln Center's operas, ballets and symphony concerts and, for business types, the downtown area. They range from the 'Y' (YMCA) to 5-star (which sometimes have special off-season or weekend rates worth checking out).

At the high end are the pricey **Four Seasons**, *57 E. 57th St, New York, NY 10022; tel (212) 758-5700*; the **Peninsula**, *700 Fifth Ave, New York, NY 10019; tel: (212) 247-2200*; **The Mark**, *25 E. 77th St, New York, NY 10021; tel: (212) 744-4300*, and the **Ritz Carlton**, *112 Central Park South, New York, NY 10019, tel: (212) 757-1900*. There are expensive *BW* and *HJ* and a variety of budget choices. All rooms are probably more expensive than elsewhere in New England.

If location is key, theatre district hotels include the pricey **Macklowe**, *141 W. 44th St, New York, NY 10036; tel. (212) 768-4400*, two *Sh* and *RM*. Near Lincoln Center are the pricey *RA* and expensive **Mayflower**, *15 Central Park West, New York, NY 10023; tel: (212) 265-066*. On

the Museum Mile, is the pricey **Stanhope**, *995 Fifth Ave, New York, NY 10028; tel: (212) 288-5800*, as well as the moderate–expensive **Wales**, *1295 Madison Ave, New York, NY 10028; tel: (212) 876-6000*. In the financial district are the expensive **Vista**, *3 World Trade Center, New York, NY 10048; tel: (212) 938-9100*, **Millenium**, *55 Church St, New York, NY 10007; tel: (212) 693-2001*, and *Hd*.

Two moderate finds on the East Side, midtown, are the **Pickwick Arms**, *230 E. 51st St, New York, NY 10022; tel: (212) 355-0300*, and **Quality Hotel Fifth Ave**, *3 E. 40th St, New York, NY 10016; tel: (800) 228-5151*.

There are all-suite hotels for families and some that offer a weekly rate. Consider apartment swapping or sharing a hotel/apartment that includes a kitchen with friends.

The YMCA offers group rates and package programs, including room, breakfast and a variety of meals; sightseeing and exursions are available, with an Airport Hospitality Service – The Y's Way Student Information Desk – on the ground floor of the International Arrivals Building at Kennedy Airport. Two locations in Manhattan are **YMCA-Vanderbilt**, *224 E. 47th St, New York, NY 10017; tel: (212) 756-9600*, and **YMCA-West Side**, *5 W. 63rd St, New York, NY 10023; tel: (212) 787-4400*. Students may request a multilingual catalogue from **The Y's Way International**, *224 E 47th St, New York, NY 10017, tel: (212) 308-2899*.

Another budget alternative is **HI**, *891 Amsterdam Ave at W. 103rd St, New York, NY 10025; tel: (212) 932-2300*. Rates for members of Hostelling International start at $20 and include use of garden, library, laundry room, coffee bar and cafeteria. For

291

non-members, rates are slightly higher.

Some words of wisdom for adventurous camping-types: Whatever you do, DON'T camp in the city parks. The nearest urban camp site, **New Yorker Trailer City,** *4901 Tonnelle Ave, North Bergen, NJ 07047; tel: (201) 866-0999,* is across the Hudson River in New Jersey; take bus no. 127 from Port Authority, via the Lincoln Tunnel (Note: no credit cards accepted). For New York State, a general number to call for Campsite and Cabin information is **New York State Reservations System;** *tel: (800) 456-2267.*

The New York Visitors Information Center has a handy, comprehensive hotel guide (with map indicating locations), prices and services available at up to 100 hotels in every price range.

Eating and Drinking

New York restaurants comprise the most sophisticated international blend with authentic ethnic ingredients from all over the world. As higher prices don't always dictate quality, be wary of expensive 'name' restaurants in busy tourist areas that provide heavy ambience while skimping on quality. Like most things in New York, a meal can be costly.

For an extensive, up-to-date listing of restaurants (by location and price) consult local newspapers, *New York* magazine, *WHERE* (available free in hotel lobbies) and *Times Square Restaurant Guide* (listing more than 200 establishments).

Always start with as fortifying a breakfast as possible. If it isn't included in your room rate then it will probably be cheaper to visit a deli or a café for a breakfast special. While sightseeing or shopping you may want to skip lingering over a big lunch, which may even slow you down. It's also the perfect opportunity to sample New York's famous **Street Food:** Grab 'a

slice' (pizza) and eat it while walking or sitting on a park bench. Other must-trys: big, soft pretzels (with mustard), chestnuts (seasonal), hot dogs (with sauerkraut, onions, mustard and ketchup), meat shish-kebabs, souvlaki, refreshing Italian ices or super-creamy ice-cream Dove Bars.

The **Deli** is short for delicatessen, but no one calls it that. It's a good source for takeout – generous sandwiches, with side orders of coleslaw or macaroni salad and a hot or cold beverage. Eat your meal in a charming, off-the-street pocket park, maybe at a table near a mini-waterfall. Some of the most authentic delis can be found on the Lower East Side, which also has the famous Jewish kosher eatery, moderate **Ratner's Dairy Restaurant,** *138 Delancey St; tel: (212) 677-5588,* (closed Fri evening and Sat for Sabbath). Other standouts: budget **Katz's** (since 1888), *205 E. Houston St; tel: (212) 254-2246,* and the moderate **Carnegie,** *854 Seventh Ave; tel: (212) 757-2245,* and **Stage Deli,** *834 Seventh Ave* near *53rd St; tel: (212) 245-7850.*

Near the financial district, the **South St Seaport** has good quality sit-down restaurants as well as take-away opportunities. For a great view of the Brooklyn and Manhattan bridges, sit on one of the long deckchairs overlooking the East River. In the main seaport complex, the moderate **North Star Pub** serves English meat pies, pasties and bangers, homemade by Peter Myers in his shop. **Myers of Keswick,** *634 Hudson St* (near *Jane St),* is well known for its ex-pat British clientele.

Some restaurants are more memorable than others and, though sometimes more expensive, are worth it. One, the **Tavern on the Green,** at the edge of Central Park at *67th St; tel: (212) 873-3200,* is as affordable as you want it to be for an à la carte Sunday Brunch (book ahead for the

Crystal Room). A nice spot to linger over a drink in the summertime is the restaurant's garden. A reasonable outdoor meal, with a lovely view of the Lincoln Center complex and fountain, can be had at one of the sidewalk restaurants along **Broadway**, between *64th* and *66th Sts.* People watchers may spot celebrities or lithe dancers from the New York City Ballet or guest companies strolling in the neighbourhood, post-rehearsal or pre-performance.

A fun, interactive place for dinner is moderate–pricey **Asti's**, *13 E. 12th St off Fifth Ave; tel: (212) 242-9868.* The waiters and bartenders at the family-owned restaurant entertain customers with opera arias. A nightly treat: Lights are lowered to the accompaniment of tinkling spoons against bar bottles as service staff sing a rousing *Anvil Chorus.* Selected restaurant patrons don hooded robes and march single-file among the tables while holding a small flashlight that eerily illuminates the face. Open early Sept–late June (closed summers).

In the theatre district, near the **Palace Theater** and the most popular show *Beauty and the Beast,* are two family-style restaurants, **The Olive Garden** is across the street at *47th St and Broadway; tel: (212) 246-4517* (café) or *(212) 333-3254* (restaurant), and **Langan's,** around the corner at *150 W. 47th St; tel: (212) 869-5482.*

Some fabulous aerial views can be enjoyed over pre- or post-theatre cocktails. **The View**, on the 48th floor (accessed by glass-walled elevators) of the **Marriott Marquis Hotel**, *1535 Broadway at 45th St, New York, NY 10036; tel: (212) 398-1900*, in the heart of the theatre district, is a revolving cocktail bar from which to see glowing sunsets over the Hudson River and the neon lights of Times Square. A complete revolution takes about one hour. There's a modest buffet, $9.95, and live music at designated times. The somewhat pricey **View** restaurant is one floor below.

A pleasant indoor and outdoor view of the Manhattan skyline, United Nations gardens, UN Plaza and the East River can be had from the **Top of the Tower** 26th-floor cocktail lounge in the **Beekman Tower Hotel**, *49th St* and *First Ave; tel: (212) 355-7300.* Also in Midtown, lower to the ground, are the glass walled **Sun Garden** and **Crystal Fountain** bar/restaurant at the **Grand Hyatt Hotel**, *E. 42nd St; tel: (212) 883-1234*, overhanging the sidewalk next to Grand Central Station.

In Chinatown, **20 Mott**, *20 Mott St; tel: (212) 964-0380*, for *Dim Sum* or dinner, and **Golden Unicorn**, *18 E. Broadway; tel: (212) 941-0911*, are a good starting point among the many possibilities. In Little Italy, there's **Joey Paesano**, *136 Mulberry St; tel: (212) 966-3337*, budget, for good value, and **SPQR**, *133 Mulberry St; tel: (212) 925-3120*, moderate. Also explore the offerings of **Little India**, a district on Lexington Ave between *27th* and *29th Sts*, where **Madras Mahal**, *104 Lexington Ave; tel: (212) 684-4010*, is a standout.

SoHo has upscale art galleries, luxury lofts and in-crowd restaurants for those who want to see and be seen. You may need to save up for a dining experience, but the fascinating area is worth a walk-through. Moderate American meals are at **American Renaissance**, *260 W. Broadway; tel: (212) 343-0049.*

Gourmet foods can be purchased at: **Balducci's**, *6th Ave and 9th St; tel: (212) 673-2600*, **Dean and Deluca**, *560 Broadway at Prince St; tel: (212) 254-8776*, **Macy's Cellar**, *Herald Sq. and 34th St; tel:*

293

MANHATTAN

UPPER WEST SIDE   CENTRAL PK

NORTH

Guggenheim Museum
Metropolitan Museum of Art

American Museum
of Natural History

UPPER EAST SIDE

York Ave

The Lake

Whitney Museum

Roosevelt
Island

West End Ave
Amsterdam Ave
Columbus Ave
BROADWAY
WEST SIDE HIGHWAY

Strawberry
Fields

Central Park
Visitor Center

The Pond

Park Ave
Lexington Ave
Third Ave
Second Ave
First Ave
Madison Ave

F.D.R. DRIVE

Museum of
American Folk Art

W. 63rd
Lincoln Center
W. 57th St

N.Y. Convention &
Visitors Bureau

Carnegie Hall

Fifth Ave

Queensboro Bridge

QUEENS

Gray Line Bus Tours
Museum of Modern Art

Intrepid Sea-Air-
Space Museum

THEATRE DISTRICT

E. 51st St

Circle Line Boat Tours

Rockfeller Center

E. 47th St

United Nations

Lincoln
Tunnel

Eleventh Ave
Tenth Ave
Ninth Ave
Eighth Ave

Times Square
Port Authority Bus Terminal

Bryant
Park

Grand Central Station

Queens Midtown
Tunnel

TWELFTH AVE

E. 40th St
Murray Hill

Ave of the Americas (Sixth Ave)

Pierpont Morgan Library

Garment
District

Penn Station

Empire State Building

F.D.R. DRIVE

EAST RIVER

Madison
Square Garden

Seventh Ave

Flatiron Building

E. 23rd St

CHELSEA

BROADWAY

Union Square Park
East Village   E. 9th St
Tompkins Square Park

GREENWICH VILLAGE

Washington
Square Park

HUDSON RIVER

WEST SIDE HIGHWAY

Houston St

SOHO

LITTLE
ITALY

Delancey St

Williamsburg
Bridge

Holland Tunnel

Canal St

CHINATOWN

NEW JERSEY

World Trade Center
World Financial Center

F.D.R. DRIVE

Manhattan Bridge

0   1/2 Mile

1/2 Kilometre

294

(212) 494-2647, **Manganaro's,** *488 Ninth Ave at 37th St; tel: (212) 563-5331,* originators of the six-ft 'hero' sandwich , and **Todaro Bros.**, *555 2nd Ave at 30th St tel: (212) 532-0633,* and **Zabar's,** *Broadway* and *80th St; tel: (212) 787-2000.*

Communications

Post offices are found throughout the city. Manhattan's main office is at *Eighth Ave and 33rd St,* near Penn. Station. More central, sizeable ones are also at *44th St and Lexington Ave* near Grand Central, and *55th St and Third Ave.* Mail can also be addressed to hotels.

Money

Thomas Cook Currency Services are Midtown at *630 Fifth Ave; tel: (212) 757-6915; 41 E. 42nd St; tel: (212) 883-0400; 101 Park Ave; tel: (212) 697-5285,* and *Herald Centre, 1 Herald Sq.; tel: (212) 736-9790;* downtown at *1590 Broadway; tel: 265-6049,* and *South St Seaport; tel: (212) 766-1064.*

ENTERTAINMENT

New York is IT – THE place – when it comes to entertainment. 'If you can make it here, you'll make it anywhere' affirm the lyrics of the song *New York, New York,* made popular by Frank Sinatra. For complete listings and current best bets, consult the entertainment sections of local newspapers or pick up a copy of *New York* magazine or *WHERE* comprehensive and free in hotel lobbies). Free theatre brochures are available at the ticket offices of the Broadway theatres. Some hotel lobbies have ticket agencies.

Entertainment can be expensive in New York. Seats at a **Broadway** show go for an average of $25 (balcony seat) to $75 (stalls). Half-price, same-day tickets (cash only) are available at two locations of

TKTS, *W 47th St and Broadway* (in the theatre district), open Mon–Sat 1500–2000, Wed and Sat matinees 1200–1400, Sun 1200–1900, and downtown, where lines are shorter, at *2 World Trade Center,* open Mon–Fri 1100-1730, Sat 1100-1530. This can either be time-consuming (but worth it) if you get 'on line' (New York-ese for queueing) early in the afternoon. Or arrive at 1945, when lines have usually gone, and see what's left: Sometimes the only available seats are in the stalls.

Excellent entertainment is also found at less centrally located **Off-Broadway,** where theatres are smaller and seats generally less expensive.

Three major performance halls are part of the **Lincoln Center** for the Performing Arts complex, *62nd to 65th Sts,* between *Broadway* and *Amsterdam Ave.* There's opera and ballet at **The Metropolitan Opera House,** *tel: (212) 362-6000,* and **New York State Theater,** *tel: (212) 870-5570.* **Avery Fisher Hall,** *tel: (212) 875-5030,* is home to the New York Philharmonic Orchestra and the Mostly Mozart Festival.

Two legendary entertainment halls are **Carnegie Hall,** *Seventh Ave and 57th St; tel: (212) 247-7800,* and **Radio City Music Hall,** *50th St and Sixth Ave; tel: (212) 247-4777,* while **Town Hall,** *123 W. 43rd St; tel: (212) 840-2824,* and **City Center,** *131 W. 55th St; tel: (212) 581-1212,* are both popular for music, dance and drama.

Nightlife

There are many other ways to stay entertained in Manhattan.

Live shows with dinner: **Michael's Pub,** *211 E. 55th St; tel: (212) 758-2272;* Harlem's **Cotton Club,** *West Side Highway at W. 125th St; tel: (212) 663-*

295

7980; **Tatou,** *151 E. 50th St; tel: (212) 753-1144.*

Jazz: **Bradley's,** *70 University Place at 10th St; tel: (212) 228-6440;* **Blue Note,** *131 W. Third St near Sixth Ave; tel: (212) 475-8592;* **Village Vanguard,** *178 Seventh Ave South at 11th St; tel: (212) 255-4037.*

Comedy: **Caroline's,** *1626 Broadway near 50th St; tel: (212) 757-4100.* **The Improvisation,** *433 W 34th St; tel: (212) 279-3446;* **Dangerfield's,** *1118 First Ave at 61st St; tel: (212) 593-1650).*

Events

The Metropolitan Opera holds outdoor concerts in city parks in all five boroughs during June, the New York Philharmonic holds its free summer parks concerts in Aug and **Shakespeare in the Park** events are held July–Aug at Delacorte Theater in Central Park. The **US Open Tennis Championships** are held late Aug–early Sept at Flushing Meadow Park, Queens.

The **New York Film Festival** takes place at Lincoln Center in late Sept–early Oct. The **New York Marathon** fills the streets (and hotels) with runners in early Nov. Radio City Music Hall holds its **Christmas Spectacular** early Nov–Jan, with the lighting of a giant Christmas tree at Rockefeller Center early Dec. On **New Year's Eve,** Times Square is jammed with revellers.

Sports

Madison Square Garden, *Seventh Ave and 33rd St; tel: (212) 465-6000,* is the home of the New York Knickerbockers (Knicks) basketball team and New York Rangers hockey team. Tickets are sold out well in advance of games; for schedules and information: **Knicks,** *tel: (212) 465-JUMP.* **Rangers,** *tel: (212) 308-NYRS.*

New York has two professional baseball teams, which play Apr–Oct. The Mets play at **Shea Stadium,** *126th St and Roosevelt Ave, Flushing, Queens; tel: (718) 507-8499* (subway: *Willets Point/No. 7 Flushing line*). The Yankees play at **Yankee Stadium,** *161 St and River Ave, Bronx; tel: (718) 293-6000* (subway: *IND D or C local trains or the Lexington Ave IRT No. 4 train*).

Both the New York Giants and the New York Jets professional football teams play Sept–Dec at **Giants Stadium Meadowlands Sports Complex** in Rutherford, N.J.; *tel: (201) 935-3900* (Buses leave from Port Authority Bus Terminal).

SHOPPING

New York tempts shoppers at every turn with all kinds of merchandise. The main shopping artery is *Fifth Ave,* with fashionable stores such as F.A.O. Schwarz, Bergdorf Goodman, Tiffany's, Bally, Steuben, Saks Fifth Avenue, Barnes & Noble and Lord & Taylor. Other notables are **Bloomingdale's,** *Lexington Ave and 59th St,* **Macy's** – the world's largest department store at *Herald Square, 34th St and Broadway* – and the popular **Barney's,** one at *Seventh Ave and 17th St* and the other at *61st St and Madison Ave.*

Shopping centres include the glitz and marble **Trump Tower,** *Fifth Ave off 57th St,* **A&S Plaza,** *33rd St and Sixth Ave* near *Herald Square,* and the **SoHo Emporium,** *375 W. Broadway* in lower Manhattan. Some of Manhattan's most stylish shops (Georg Jensen, Polo) are found along *Madison Ave* and there are designer showrooms (by appointment only) on *Seventh Ave (34th St to 42nd St).* **The Diamond District** is on *47th St* between *Fifth* and *Sixth Aves.*

Discounted merchandise can be found

in the **Orchard St Bargain District** on the Lower East Side; *tel: (212) 995-VALU;* **Daffy's** (two), *Madison and 44th St* and *Fifth Ave and 18th St.* Also, downtown, near the World Trade Center, and **Century 21**, *22 Cortland St.*

The two most popular and convenient discount outlets are the 150-shop **Woodbury Common**, *Route 32, Central Valley, NY; tel: (914) 928-7467, (NY State Thruway Exit 16)* with public transportation available from Port Authority bus terminal, *tel: (800) 631-8405*, and **Secaucus Outlet Center**, *Secaucus, NJ; tel: (800) 86-OUTLETS*, best accessed by car.

SIGHTSEEING

This ambitious undertaking is best approached methodically – from the bottom up.

Lower Manhattan

There is great concentration of attractions here: Take a Circle Line ferry from Battery Park to Liberty Island in New York Harbor. You can climb the 300 steps into the **Statue of Liberty's** crown, and learn how she was constructed, but be aware that it takes several hours to reach the top. Take an earlier boat if you're planning to make the climb.

Stop at **Ellis Island Immigration Museum**; *tel: (212) 363-3200*. Stroll through the stone canyons of narrow *Wall St*, see the **New York Stock Exchange** and **Trinity Church**. Walk around the informative observation deck at the **World Trade Center**, 110 floors up. Check out the beautiful lobby, shops and restaurants in the World Financial Center.

The **South St Seaport**, with its fleet of historic ships, is also in the area, as are City Hall and the courts, Chinatown and Little Italy.

Midtown

Here are such wonders as the **Empire State Building**, *Fifth Ave and 34th St; tel: (212) 736-3100*, where not only do you have views from the 86th- and 102nd-floor observatories, $2–$4, you can take the Skyride, a flight-simulator where visitors (wearing seatbelts) feel as if they are in a plane that takes off from the top of the building. Highlights are a 'crash landing' on *Wall St* and an 'out-of-control' detour through the faymous toyshop FAO Schwarz. Take a multilingual tour of the **United Nations**, *E. 46nd St and United Nations Plaza (First Ave); tel: (212) 963-7713*, open daily 0915–1645, $3.50–$6.50 (subway: *Grand Central*). Visit **Rockefeller Center** with its ice-skating rink and towering Christmas tree in the cold weather months and an open-air café when temperatures rise. **Tour NBC Studios**; *tel: (212) 664-4000*, open daily 0930–1630, $8.25, and nearby **Radio City Music Hall**, *tel: (212) 632-4041*, open daily 1000–1700, tours every 30–45 min, $6–$12, before resting up at at **St. Patrick's Cathedral**, *Fifth Ave* and *50th St*, regardless of your religious beliefs.

Uptown

On the upper West Side, visit **The Cloisters** at Fort Tryon Park on the Hudson River. At *West 122nd St*, is **Riverside Church** with its 400-ft high tower. Take a **Harlem Gospel** or **Soul Food and Jazz** tour, *tel: (212) 757-0425*.

Methods of touring vary. For a legitimate bird's-eye view, there's Air Pegasus Heliport, **Liberty Helicopter**, *W. 30th St and 12th Ave; tel: (212) 967-6464*, $49–$139. Since Manhattan is an island, water tours are among the most popular. The **Circle Line** boats, with frequent sailings from *Pier 83 at West 43rd St; tel: (212) 563-3200*, $9–$18, have been taking visitors on guided tours around Manhattan for 50 years. On board is a snack bar with cocktails, souvenirs, guidebooks and film. Extra special are Harbor Lights cruises and music cruises.

Along the streets of New York, **Gray Line** tours have double-decker buses or trolleys, *900 Eighth Ave at 53rd St, tel: (212) 397-2600;* impromptu horse and buggy rides through Central Park from *59th St* and *Fifth Ave* in a **Hansom carriage**, and – just because it's New York – **Olympia 'Rent-a-limo – Drive it yourself'** with hourly rates from $30 to $60 – for a 10-passenger super-stretch limo, *tel: (212) 995-1200.*

MUSEUMS

New York is a cultural centre and for passionate museum goers, there is much to see.

298

Upper West Side

The **American Museum of Natural History and Hayden Planetarium**, *Central Park West at 79th St, New York, NY 10024; tel: (212) 769-5100,* open Sun–Thur 1000–1745, Fri–Sat 1000–2045, $4–$6, the most child-friendly museum in the city, has two new dinosaur halls and a NatureMax Theatre presenting large-screen (70mm) IMAX films that make you part of the action. The **Children's Museum of Manhattan**, *212 W. 83rd St, New York, NY 10024; tel: (212) 721-1234,* open Mon, Wed, Thur 1530–1730, Fri, Sat, Sun 1000–1700, $5, has 'please touch' exhibits and special events of interest to children.

Studio Museum in Harlem, *144 W. 125th St, New York, NY 10027; tel: (212) 864-4500,* open Wed–Fri 1000– 1700, Sat–Sun 1300–1600, $1–$5, has changing exhibits of art and artifacts of black America and the African Diaspora. The

Black Fashion Museum, *155 W. 126th St, New York, NY 10027; tel: (212) 666-1320,* open daily 1200–2000, by appointment only, $2, has exhibits changing every six months. The **Museum of American Folk Art**, *Columbus Ave and 66th St, New York, NY 10023; tel: (212) 977-7298,* open Tues–Sun 1330–1930, free, shows quilts and old folk art, including paintings, sculpture and textiles from the 18th– 20th centuries.

Upper East Side

The **Metropolitan Museum of Art**, *Fifth Ave and 82nd St, New York, NY 10028; tel: (212) 979-5500,* open Tues–Thur, Sun 0930–1715, Fri, Sat 0930–2045, $3.50–$7, is the the *grande dame* of museums, with the Temple of Dendur as its centrepiece. The **Solomon R. Guggenheim Museum**, *Fifth Ave at 88th St, New York, NY 10128; tel: (212) 423-3500,* open Sun–Wed 1000–1800, Fri, Sat 1000–2000, $4–$7, is a designated landmark building, designed by US architect Frank Lloyd Wright in 1950 and known for its grand spiral ramp, where the art is displayed. This is modern art at its most contemporary. The Guggenheim has a **branch** at *575 Broadway, downtown; tel: (212) 423-3500,* open Wed–Fri, Sun 1100–1800, Sat 1100–2000, $3–$5, with changing avant-garde exhibits.

Housed in the mansion of 19th-century industrialist Andrew Carnegie is the **Cooper-Hewitt National Museum of Design** of the Smithsonian Institution, *2 E. 91st St, New York, NY 10128; tel: (212) 860-6868,* open Tue 1000–2100, Wed–Sat 1000–1700, Sun 1200–1700, $3, with exhibits on design from wallpaper to jewellery. The only museum that has the feel of being a private home is is **The Frick Collection**, *1 E. 70th St, New York, NY 10021 tel: (212) 288-0700,* open

Tue–Sat 1000–1800, Sun 1300–1800, $5, a permanent collection of Henry Clay Frick's art collection in his house. The **Whitney Museum of American Art**, *Madison Ave and 75th St, New York, NY 10021; tel: (212) 570-3676*, open Wed 1100–1800, Thur 1300–2000, Fri–Sun 1100–1800, $7, devotes itself solely to 20th-century US art, with the biggest collection of works by living artists. Alexander Calder's *Circus* sculpture plays in the main lobby.

The Jewish Museum, *1109 Fifth Ave at 92nd St, New York, NY 10128; tel: (212) 423-3200*, open Sun–Thur 1100–1745, Tue 1100–2000, $6, covers 4000 years of Jewish history. **The Asia Society**, *725 Park Ave at 70th St, New York, NY 10021; tel: (212) 517-6397 or 288-6400*, open Tue–Sat 1100–1800, Thur 1100–2000, Sun 1200–1700, $3, houses the collection of John D. Rockefeller III and teaches visitors about South and Southeast Asia. **El Museo del Barrio**, *1230 Fifth Ave at 104th St, New York, NY 10029; tel: (212) 831-7272*, open Wed–Sun 1100–1700, $4, is one of the foremost Latin American cultural institutions in the USA, specialising in Puerto Rican arts.

The Museum of the City of New York, *Fifth Ave at 103rd St, New York, NY 10029; tel: (212) 534-1672*, open Wed–Sat 1000–1700, Sun 1300–1700, founded in 1933, spans New York history from its settlement to the present.

The National Academy of Design, *1083 Fifth Ave, New York, NY 10128; tel: (212) 369-4880*, open Tues 1200–2000, Wed–Sun 1300–1700, $2.50, Tues 1700–2000, free, with a grand marble staircase, features US artists.

Midtown West Side

Aboard a World War II aircraft carrier, **The Intrepid Sea-Air-Space Museum**, *Pier 86, 12th Ave and W. 46th St, New York, NY 10036; tel: (212) 245-2533*, open Wed–Sun 1000–1700, $5–$10, showcases early aviation and World War II history.

The **Museum of Modern Art**, *11 W. 53rd St, New York, NY 10019; tel: (212) 708-9400*, open Sat–Tues 1100– 1800, Thur–Fri 1200–2030, $5–$8, has a comprehensive collection of 20th-century paintings, drawings, photos, sculpture, film and video, including works by Picasso and Matisse. You can hear and watch more than 70 years of radio and TV at the **Museum of Television and Radio**, *25 W. 52nd St, New York, NY 10019; tel: (212) 621-6800*, open Tue–Sun 1200–1800, Thur 1200–2000, $5.

China Institute of America, *125 E. 65th St, New York, NY 100021; tel: (212) 744-8181*, open Mon–Sat 1000-1700, $3, is the only museum in New York specialising in Chinese Art.

Midtown East Side

The Pierpont Morgan Library, *29 E. 36th St, New York, NY 10016; tel: (212) 685-0610*, Tue–Sat 1030–1700, Sun 1300–1700, $5, is a gem on the inside and out. The pink marble, Renaissance-style building contains books, manuscripts, paintings and art objects. **The Museum of American Illustration**, *128 E. 63rd St, New York, NY 10021; tel: (212) 838-2560*, open Sat 1200–1600, Tue 1000–2000, Wed–Fri 1000–1700, free, has a collection of contemporary and historic magazine, book and advertising illustrations. Near the United Nations, the **Japan Society Gallery**, *E. 47th St, New York, NY 10017; tel: (212) 832-1155*, open Tue–Sun 1100–1700, Fri 1100–1830, which, with its reflecting pool, is like a little corner of Japan.

299

Downtown

Lower East Side Tenement Museum, *90 Orchard St, New York, NY 10002; tel: (212) 431-0233,* open Tue–Fri 1100–1700, 1100–1800, $5–$7, shows New York's colourful immigrant history, with renovated tenement apartments and photos. **New York City Fire Museum**, *278 Spring St, New York, NY 10013; tel: (212) 691-1303,* open Tue–Sat 1000– 1600, $0.50–$3, is a renovated 1904 firehouse with all the trimmings. The **New York Police Museum**, same address; *tel: (212) 477-9753,* open by appointment only, free, has police-related paintings, photos, uniforms and firearms dating back to Colonial times.

The **New Museum of Contemporary Art**, *583 Broadway, New York, NY 10012; tel: (212) 219-1222,* open Wed–Sun 1200–1800, $3.50, has exhibits of contemporary art.

National Museum of the American Indian, *Alexander Hamilton US Customs House near Battery Park, New York, NY 10004; tel: (212) 668-6624,* open daily 1000–1700, free, has the world's largest collection of Native American artifacts, including Iroquois silver jewellery, paintings, ceremonial robes and headdresses.

The **Museum for African Art**, *593 Broadway, New York, NY 10012; tel: (212) 966-1313,* open Tues–Fri 1030–1730, Sat 1200–2000, Sun 1200–1800, $4, has a permanent collection like no other, especially on sub-Saharan art.

OUT OF MANHATTAN

Manhattan is one of five boroughs that comprise New York. The other four:

The Bronx

North of Manhattan, the many parks of **The Bronx** make it New York's greenest borough. Although its greatest notoriety once came from the rubble-strewn South Bronx (Fort Apache), the borough has undergone a remarkable renaissance. **The Bronx Museum of the Arts**, *1040 Grand Concourse; tel: (718) 681-6000,* open Wed 1500–2100, Thu–Fri 1000–1700, Sat–Sun 1000–1800, $3, reflects the cultural diversity.

Another major attraction is **The Bronx Zoo**, *Bronx River Pkwy (Exit 6) at Fordham Rd, Bronx, NY 10460; tel: (718) 367-1010,* (take Liberty Bus; *tel: (718) 652-8400,* or Metro North trains; *tel: (212) 532-4900,* from Grand Central Station), open Mon–Fri 1000–1700, Sat, Sun, holidays 1000–1730; $3–$6.75. This is probably the best-designed urban zoo in the country, with a monorail system, The World of Darkness, the World of Birds, Mouse House and children's petting zoo.

Adjacent to the zoo is the vast **New York Botanical Garden**, *Southern Blvd at Mosholu Pkwy, Bronx, NY 10458; tel: (718) 220-8700,* whose ornate centrepiece, a domed crystal palace, houses seasonal floral displays.

At the tip of Pelham Bay Park is **City Island** (tour departures from NYCVB, $12), its streets, buildings and sailboats creating an unexpectedly New England-like atmosphere.

The **Museum of Bronx History**, *3266 Bainbridge Ave (mailing address: 3309 Bainbridge Ave, Bronx, NY 10467); tel: (718) 881-8900,* open Sat 1000–1600, Sun 1300–1700, is a stop on the **Bronx Heritage Trail** *(same address for information),* which also includes **Edgar Allan Poe's Cottage**, *Grand Concourse and E. Kingsbridge Rd.*

Sports enthusiasts should catch a baseball game at **Yankee Stadium** (see Sports), whether or not they understand the rules of the 'national pastime'.

The best public transport access to The

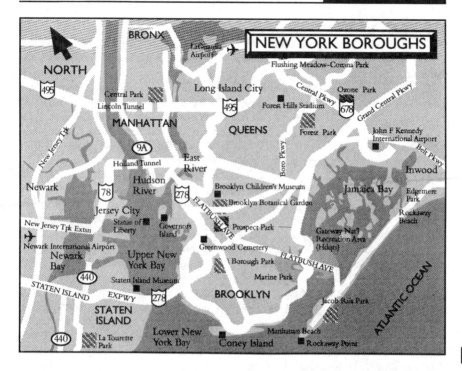

NEW YORK BOROUGHS

301

Bronx is via subway (IRT), bus or Metro North commuter train.

Brooklyn

At the other end of the **Brooklyn Bridge** (built in 1883), is the most populated (2.5 million) of the boroughs. It's rich in ethnic communities and accents — it's the land of 'dese and dose' (these and those) and 'toidy toid and toid' (33rd and Third). Brooklyn's immigrant population used to come mainly from Italy, Germany and Eastern Europe, but some of its newest arrivals are from the Caribbean, Africa and the Soviet Union. Woody Allen and Barbra Streisand were born here.

For family outings, there is the **Brooklyn Botanic Garden**, *1000 Washington Ave, Brooklyn, NY 11225; tel: (718) 941-4044*, open Tue–Fri 0800–1800, Sun and holidays 1000–1800,

free. Brooklyn also has museums and parks and, on the Atlantic Ocean, the **Coney Island** amusement park, *tel: (718) 266-1234*, with the Cyclone, boardwalk and famous Nathan's hot dogs. Also, the **Brooklyn Children's Museum**, *145 Brooklyn Ave, Brooklyn, NY 11217; tel: (718) 735-4400*, open Wed–Fri 1400–1700, Sat–Sun 1200–1700, and **The New York Aquarium**, *W. 8th St and Surf Ave, Brooklyn, NY 11224; tel: (718) 265-FISH*, open daily 1000–1645, $3–$6.75.

One of the most beautiful sights of all can be seen only from this borough, from the promenade in Brooklyn Heights: the spectacular **Manhattan skyline**, including the magnificent Williamsburg, Manhattan and Brooklyn bridges. Famous restaurants: **Junior's** (for cheesecake), *386 Flatbush Ave; tel: (718) 852-5257;* **Peter**

Luger Steak House, *175 Broadway*, near the Williamsburg Bridge, *tel: (718) 387-7400;* and the romantic **River Café**, on a barge at *1 Water St, tel: (718) 522-5200*.

Best public transport access to Brooklyn is by bus, subway or the Long Island Railroad.

Queens

You'll get your best overview of New York's 'bedroom community' as your plane is about to land at either Kennedy or LaGuardia airports. The largest of the boroughs area-wise, it consists mostly of one- and two-family homes.

Queens is well known as the site for the **1939 and 1964 World's Fairs**, in Flushing Meadow's Corona Park, where some of the exposition structures still remain, and its tennis centres – the formerly used **Forest Hills** and the modern **National Tennis Center**, *Flushing Meadow Park* (subway: *Willets Point*/No. 7 *Flushing Line); (718) 760-6200,* where US Open Tennis Championships are held every Sept. The complex is a 30-min subway ride from Grand Central in Manhattan and shares the same stop with **Shea Stadium,** home of the city's other famous baseball team, The 1986 World Champion New York Mets (see Sports). And for horse racing aficionados, **Aqueduct Racetrack** is on *Rockaway Boulevard and 108th St in Ozone Park; tel: (718) 641-4700.*

Queens, sometimes called the gateway to Long Island, has good beaches, golf courses, wildlife refuges and museums. Of note are **The Queens Botanical Garden**, *43–50 Main St, Flushing, NY 11355; tel: (718) 886-3800,* **The Museum of the Moving Image**, *35th Ave and 36th St, Astoria, NY 11106; tel: (718) 784-0077,* and **Kaufman-Astoria Studios**, *34–12 36th St, Astoria, Queens,*

NY 11106, where hit movies such as *Wall Street* and *Fatal Attraction* were made.

Astoria has the largest Greek population outside Athens. This borough also has its share of ethnic restaurants, among them, **Waters Edge** (French), *44th Dr. and the East River* in Long Island City, *tel: (718) 326-0717,* and **Altadonna** (Italian), *137-03 Cross Bay Blvd, Ozone Park, tel: (718) 848-6895.*

Queens is linked to Manhattan by four bridges and the Queens Midtown Tunnel, with public transportation provided by bus, subway and Long Island Railroad.

Staten Island

The only other island borough, Staten Island is a pleasant 20-min ride by car/passenger-ferry from downtown Manhattan. Don't forget your camera as you'll have one of the best views of the downtown skyscrapers as you depart from the aft deck of the **Staten Island Ferry**, *Whitehall St, next to Battery Park in Manhattan; tel: (212) 806-6940,* which runs daily every 20–30 mins, $0.50. It's as close as you can get to Ellis Island and the Statue of Liberty without stopping. Once ashore, you have a choice of bus or train (or car) to get around this largely residential borough. Points of interest include **Snug Harbor Cultural Center**, *1000 Richmond Terrace, Staten Island, NY 10301; tel: (718) 448-2500,* the **Museum of Staten Island**, *75 Stuyvesant Pl, Staten Island, NY 10301; tel: (718) 727-1135,* open Mon–Sat 0900–1700, Sun 1300–1700, $2.50, the botanical gardens and **The Greenbelt**, a vast wooded park used for hiking, golf, tennis and skiing. On the eastern shore are historic homes, beaches, and a marina. Besides the ferry from Battery Park, Staten Island can be accessed from Manhattan by car, via Brooklyn and the Verrazano-Narrows Bridge.

Niagara Falls

Niagara Falls is a honeymoon haven, a natural phenomenon, an American icon. It's millions of gallons of water crashing nearly 200 feet, exploding with a thunderous roar in clouds of mist and spray. Or, in the frigid upstate winters, a sculpture with massive stalactites and stalagmites of gleaming ice and snow. A poet once decreed the necessity of 'new combinations of language' to describe its magnificence. Any time of year, it's a sight to take your breath away.

Three cascades – American, Bridal Veil and, on the Canadian side, Horseshoe – make up the 3600-foot wide Falls at Niagara. The awsome sights are best seen on foot (wearing flat-heeled shoes) or via a canopied Viewmobile.

The half-hour Maid of the Mist boat tour, in operation since 1846, goes under the Bridal Veil and American Falls – so close you can touch them. Access is via Observation Tower elevator ($0.50) at Prospect Point. Waterproof clothing is provided for the tours, which run from mid-May–late Oct. The Cave of the Winds Trip to Goat Island Park lets visitors venture onto the Hurricane Deck at the base of Bridal Veil Falls. Excellent views from the 202-ft high Observation Tower.

The area has activities for the whole family: theatre, dinner cruises, rodeos, historic villages, museums and galleries. There are artisans shops, a Super Flea and Farmer's Market, shopping malls and factory outlets. Niagara is also apple-growing country and a year-round sport-fishing mecca for rainbow and brown trout, salmon, large and smallmouth bass, walleye and northern pike, muskelunge, pan fish and smelt. A free fishing guide provides maps and all the information you need for a successful fishing trip; tel: (800) 338-7890.

The falls are surrounded by parks, and outside the parks is the city of Niagara Falls. Downtown or 'the South End' is within walking distance and has hotels, motels, restaurants, shops and attractions. A pedestrian mall runs east from the falls through the heart of the city encompassing the oasis-like **Wintergarden,** and finally – 1,800 feet from the edge of the Falls – to the **Niagara Falls Convention & Civic Center.** The centre houses an arena, a ballroom, Greek theatre, Skylounge, meeting and banquet rooms. The Wintergarden is a greenhouse-like tropical park that becomes the centrepiece of Niagara Falls' **'Festival of Lights'** between Thanksgiving in late Nov and the New Year.

There are nearly 20 campsites in the area, plus hotels, motels, and bed and breakfasts. For tourist information: The **Niagara Falls Convention & Visitors Bureau,** 345 Third St, Suite 101, Niagara Falls, NY 14303; tel: (716) 285-2400.

Naiagara Falls is approximately a nine-hour drive from New York City, whichever route you choose. The simplest way, beginning from Mahattan's West Side, is to follow the Henry Hudson Pkwy (Rte 9A) north onto the Saw Mill River Pkwy. Take Exit 20 onto the New York Sate Thruway (I-87) and head north 120 mile to Albany. Here, the Thruway becomes I-90, continuing another 300 miles to Buffalo, where you can change to I-90 for another 22 miles to Naigara Falls.

A map of New York State reveals a few alternative routes, such as following Rte 17 to Binghampton, then I-81 north to Syracuse and I-90 west to Buffalo; or Rte 17 to the Finger Lakes region, then I-390 to I-90. These routes will save on Thruway tolls, but they aren't much faster or scenic.

Safety Tips for Tourists

All visitors, but especially first-timers, should keep in mind the following safety tips. They're not meant to frighten you. They are really only simple, common sense. Refer to p. 30 of Travel Essentials for further information.

1. If arriving by Carey airport bus at 42nd St and Park Ave, you may be approached by persons offering to help with your luggage or get you a taxi, and then asking for money. Do not accept help from them, as they are not affiliated with Carey Transportation. There are two official taxi dispatch stations across the street at *42nd St* and *Vanderbilt Ave.*

3. Petty thieves often work in pairs. If you see someone fall, do not immediately rush to help, as it may be a deliberate distraction. If someone appears to be genuinely hurt, fetch the nearest police officer or dial 911 from a public phone.

4. Avoid taking the subways very late at night or very early in the morning. If you do find yourself on a deserted platform in the 'off-hours', stand in the designated safety zone.

5. In a taxi, keep windows up and door locked.

6. If someone 'accidentally' squirts a substance (such as mustard) on you, step back and do not allow them to 'help' clean you up. Keep moving and check your purse or wallet.

7. Stay away from 'manufactured' crowds, such as those around a loud argument or commotion in the street or three-card Monte games (which are only set up to look like an easy way to win money).

8. If someone behind you bumps your car, do not get out. Ask them to follow you to the nearest police station for an accident report. This can be done with a pre-prepared sign.

LONG ISLAND LOOP

Less than a three-hour drive from New York City's steel spires and jangling traffic noise exists total serenity. More than 150 white sand beaches, sweeping dunes, steep cliffs, mansions and lighthouses.

Much of the summertime action is concentrated on the twin forks of the East End of the island. The North Fork is wine country. The South Fork holds the historic resort area of seaside towns called The Hamptons, where the rich and famous are found in summertime.

> **DIRECT ROUTE: 70 MILES**

305

ROUTE

Leave Manhattan via the Midtown Tunnel (entrance at *38th St* and *Second Ave*) and exit on the other side of the East River onto the **Long Island Expressway** (I-495) East. Avoid suburban traffic tangles by staying on the LIE until Exit 70. Take the exit and go south through **Manorville** 4 miles on Rte 111,

then turn left onto Rte 27 (*Sunrise Hwy*). After 4 miles, turn right at Exit 63 onto Rte 31 (*Old Riverhead Rd*), and go south 4 miles to **Westhampton Beach.** Backtrack 1 mile north to Rtes 27A/80 (*Montauk Hwy*) and go east 3 miles through **East Quogue,** another 3 miles into **Hampton Bays** and 6 miles more into **Southampton.** After about 1 mile, Rte 27A joins Rte 27 (*Montauk Hwy*) east.

From there it's 4 miles to **Bridge-hampton**, 6 miles to **East Hampton**, 4 miles to **Amagansett** and 11 miles into **Montauk**.

From Montauk, backtrack on Rte 27 14 miles west to **East Hampton**, then turn right onto Rte 114 north 7 miles to **Sag Harbor** and its port (North Haven) to take the car ferry to **Shelter Island**. Stay on Rte 114 for 3 miles to the northern tip of Shelter Island and board another ferry to **Greenport** on the North Fork. The beaches of **Orient Point** are 5 miles to the east.

From Orient Point, drive west on Rte 25 *(Main Rd)* and proceed through the North Fork **wine country**. After the wine route, it is 3 miles to Riverhead and 3 miles more to I-495 (Exit 72) and a straight road back into the Midtown Tunnel.

In summer, the South Fork is best visited either on weekdays or early/late in the season. Massive traffic jams are a given on summer weekends in and out of Manhattan.

TOURIST INFORMATION

Long Island Convention and Visitors Bureau, *350 Vanderbilt Motor Pkwy, Suite 103, Hyde Park, NY 11788; tel: (516) 794-4222* or *toll-free (800) 441-4601 (24 hours),* open Mon–Fri 0900–1700, has sightseeing, dining and lodging information, but does not make bookings.

NEW YORK CITY TO SOUTHAMPTON

The dense pattern of Long Island family homes, apartment blocks, schools, churches, shops and side streets repeats itself at the I-495 roadside for nearly half the length of the island, gradually thinning out and becoming more green and open and welcoming.

 SIDE TRACK TO JONES BEACH AND FIRE ISLAND

Jones Beach, one of the largest state parks along the Atlantic Ocean on Long Island's southern shore, is the cleanest and safest bathing beach in metropolitan New York. The 2400-acre park has a boardwalk and 6 miles of white sand beaches, bathhouses, a restaurant, tennis courts and two swimming pools. There is no overnight accommodation.

East of Jones Beach is **Fire Island,** a 32-mile-long, half-mile-wide strip of splendid beaches, with nightlife and a historic lighthouse. Park your car at Field 5 in **Robert Moses State Park;** *tel: (516) 669-1000,* and walk east 2 miles to Kismet, which along with Ocean Beach, Saltaire, Sailor's Haven and Cherry Grove (popular with the gay community) make up the towns on Fire Island.

To get there, follow I-495 about 33 miles east of New York City, take Exit 38 onto Northern State Pkwy east; then take Exit 31 onto Meadowbrook State Pkwy south about 14 miles to the entrance of Jones Beach State Park. From Jones Beach drive 16 miles east on Ocean Pkwy to Robert Moses Causeway and Robert Moses State Park at Fire Island.

(To go directly to Fire Island, take I-495 Exit 53 onto Sagtikos State Pkwy, then go south 7 miles to Robert Moses Causeway.) ◪

At Exit 70 make a right turn at Manorville. Proceed south for 2 miles along *Westhampton Rd,* then turn right again at **The Animal Farm Petting Zoo and Exotic Game Farm,** *184A Wading River Rd, Manorville, NY 11949; tel: (516) 878-1785,* open daily 1000–1700 (Mar–end

Oct), $8–$6. There are kiddy rides, exotic animals, reptiles, game and farm animals.

Westhampton Beach has a mix of fine shops and restaurants as well as a resort area with fishing, water sports and nature trails for hiking. For a moderate Italian dinner amid outdoor sculptures try **Rene's Casa Basso**, *Montauk Hwy; tel: (516) 288-1841,* open Tues–Sun 1700–2400.

A couple of miles east of Westhampton, offering yachtsmen peaceful harbours off the Atlantic Ocean is rural **East Quogue**. Check out the plentiful farm stands for healthy road snacks. The town of **Hampton Bays** has 25 miles of shoreline for swimming, sunbathing and water sports, with varied accommodation.

SOUTHAMPTON

Tourist Information: Southampton Chamber of Commerce, *76 Main St, Southampton, NY 11968; tel: (516) 283-0402;* open Mon–Fri 1000–1600, Sat–Sun 1100–1600.

ACCOMMODATION AND FOOD

Mainstay Bed & Breakfast, *579 Hill St; tel: (516) 283-4375,* moderate–pricey, is right in the historical village.

Motels only minutes from the village and beaches are the pricey **Bayberry Inn,** *County Rd 39; tel: (516) 283-4220,* and the moderate–expensive **Concord Resorts**, *161 Hill Station Rd; tel: (516) 283-6100.* **Horizon Hills,** *520 Montauk; tel: (516) 283-0458,* is a secluded Victorian manor house with a view of bay and ocean; moderate–pricey.

A budget family-style place to eat is **John Duck Jr.,** *15 Prospect St at N. Main; tel: (516) 283-0311,* where the speciality is Long Island duckling. The moderate **Coast Grill,** *Noyack Rd; tel: (516) 283-2277,* has a view over Wooley Pond.

SIGHTSEEING

The home of some of the wealthy and socially prominent, Southampton is the oldest (1640) English settlement in New York. A farming and fishing village in the early days, it now boasts luxury estates, elegant boutiques, antiques shops, fine restaurants, art galleries and museums.

Off *Main St,* **Southampton Historical Museum,** *17 Meeting House Lane; tel: (516) 283-1612,* open Tues–Sun 1100–1700 (June–Sept), $2, used to be a whaling captain's home in 1843. The grounds, which resemble a 19th-century village street scene, feature shops and a barn converted to a country store. Pick up a map and guide yourself on Southampton's Historic Walking Tour, which starts at the Chamber of Commerce and has such highlights as **Monument Square,** a memorial to all soldiers and sailors of all wars, a re-created old British fort, an early cemetery and the Silversmith Shop of Elias Pelletreau, a prominent craftsmen.

The 1648 **Halsey Homestead**, *South Main St; tel: (516) 283-3527,* open Tues–Sat 1100–1630, Sun 1400–1630 (mid-June–mid-Sept), $0.50–$2, is the oldest English-type saltbox house in the state, with authentic 17th- and 18th-century furnishings.

SOUTHAMPTON TO EAST HAMPTON

Proceeding east on Rte 27, you'll enter horse country. Low-key **Bridgehampton** hosts the annual Hampton Classic equestrian championship. Also known for wine, some of the best restaurants and antiques, it has been the haven for well-known writers such as Truman Capote and George Plimpton.

Most of Long Island's wine country (see feature box p. 310) are located on the

307

North Fork, but three vineyards are here, offering tours, tastings and wine sales. **Duck Walk Vineyards,** *Montauk Hwy (Rte 27), Water Mill; tel: (516) 726-7555,* is open daily 1100–1800. **Bridgehampton Winery,** *Box 979, Sag Harbor Turnpike, Bridgehampton; tel: (516) 537-3155,* open daily 1100–1700. In the next town is **Sag Pond Vineyards,** *Sagg Rd, Sagaponack; tel: (516) 537-5106,* open Thurs–Mon 1200–1700.

EAST HAMPTON

Tourist Information: East Hampton Chamber of Commerce, *4 Main St, East Hampton, NY 11937; tel: (516) 324-0362.*

ACCOMMODATION AND FOOD

The choices here are expensive–pricey. **East Hampton House,** *226 Pantigo Rd; tel: (516) 324-4300,* open July–Sept, is a motel with a heated pool, tennis, private patios. **Bassett House Inn,** *128 Montauk Hwy; tel: (516) 324-6127,* is a comfortable place with a rural inn atmosphere. The 19-room **Huntting Inn,** *94 Main St (Rte 27); tel: (516) 324-0410,* open May–Sept, has an English country garden and a restaurant serving steak and seafood amid turn-of-the-century decor.

Pricey restaurants include **1770 House,** *143 Main St; tel: (516) 324-1770,* with its own baked goods and antique furnishings, and **James Lane Cafe,** *74 James Lane; tel: (516) 324-7100,* which offers outdoor dining under canvas.

SIGHTSEEING

Fashionable and sophisticated East Hampton is sometimes called 'Hollywood East'. Its town pond, village green and elegant architecture make a perfect setting for its celebrity residents.

Homesick or not, take a tour of the **Home, Sweet Home House and Windmill,** *14 James Lane; tel: (516) 324-0713,* open daily Mon–Sat 1000–1600, Sun 1400–1600 (closed Wed–Thurs in winter), $4. On display at the childhood home of John Howard Payne, who wrote the song *Home, Sweet Home,* are English china and three centuries of American furniture and mementos. Adjacent to the Payne house is historic **Mulford Farm;** *tel: (516) 324-6850,* a living history farm museum with 18th-century New England architecture and costumed guides. Open daily 1000–1700 (June–Sept); weekends 1100–1700 (Sept–May).

AMAGANSETT

Between windswept dunes and rolling farmland lies tiny **Amagansett.** Though small, it has a couple of notable museums: **Miss Amelia Cottage Museum,** *Main St and Windmill Lane; tel: (516) 267-3020,* open Sat afternoons (June–Sept), offers a glimpse of how people lived from 1725 to the early 19th century. Donation requested. The **Town Marine Museum,** *Bluff Rd,* half a mile south of Rte 27; *tel: (516) 267-6544,* open daily 1000–1700 (July–Aug); weekends only (June and Sept), offers exhibits on fishing and whaling since colonial times, underwater archaeology and aquaculture.

MONTAUK

Tourist Information: Montauk Chamber of Commerce, *PO Box 5029, Montauk, NY 11954; tel: (516) 668-2428.*

ACCOMMODATION

Depending on the season, the popular resorts here vary from moderate to pricey. Many have beach views. The glitziest is **Gurney's Inn Resort & Spa,** *Old Montauk Hwy; tel: (516) 668-2345.* Across the road and more family oriented is

Lenhart's Cottages, *Sherman Rd at Old Montauk Hwy; tel: (516) 668-2356.* The sprawling **Panoramic View,** *Old Montauk Hwy, tel: (516) 668-3000,* has good off-season deals.

There's oceanfront camping at **Hither Hills State Park,** *Rte 27; tel: (516) 668-2554,* open end Apr–mid-Nov. Facilities include the beach and bathhouse, cycling, restaurant, showers and a store.

EATING AND DRINKING

Gosman's Dock, *W. Lake Drive, tel: (516) 668-5330,* has the best seafood, à la carte and children's portions; moderate.

A favourite for budget Sunday brunch or just to schmooze around the bar is **Shagwong Tavern,** *774 Montauk Hwy, tel: (516) 668-3050.* A hand-lettered sign in its front window says, 'Piano player wanted, Must know how to shuck clams'. Yes, it's a joke. Regulars gather at the **Dock,** *Montauk Harbor; tel: (516) 668-9778,* where the credo is: No cheques, no credit cards and 'Take screaming children outside'.

SIGHTSEEING

At the easternmost point of Long Island's South Fork, lively Montauk is a mecca for sports fishing, boating, marinas, hotels, motels, condos and guesthouses. Its reputation as one of the 'fishing capitals of the world' is well earned. Party boats, carrying 35 or more passengers, run on a schedule and do not require reservations; charter boats are booked individually for groups of up to six. Fishing tackle is supplied. Rates are $800 full day, $350 half day for a boat hire. Deep sea fishing can be booked at Montauk Marine Basin; *tel: (516) 668-5900.*

At **Montauk Point State Park,** 6 miles east on Rte 27, with the Atlantic Ocean on one side and Long Island Sound

to the north, there is the famous lighthouse, museum and a tourist centre; *tel: (516) 668-2461.*

SAG HARBOR

Tourist Information: Sag Harbor Chamber of Commerce, *P.O. Box 116, Sag Harbor, NY 11963; tel: (516) 725-0011.*

ACCOMMODATION AND FOOD

Sag Harbor Barons Cove Inn, *W. Water St; tel: (516) 725-2100,* is expensive, while **Royal Oaks Motels,** *Rte 144; tel: (516) 725-0714,* is moderate–expensive. **Il Capuccino,** *Madison St; tel: (516) 725-2747,* a moderate family restaurant, serves northern Italian food.

SIGHTSEEING

Once an important whaling port, Sag Harbor is now a port of entry for yachts. It is also favoured by writers and other creative types from the worlds of art and publishing.

Sag Harbor Whaling and Historical Museum, *Garden and Main Sts; tel: (516) 725-0770,* open Mon–Sat 1000–1700, Sun 1300–1700 (mid-May–Sept), houses artifacts from the town's whaling days. **Morton National Wildlife Refuge;** *tel: (516) 286-0485,* a few miles west on *Noyack Rd,* provides a sandy, wooded sanctuary to study wildlife and the environment. Free.

SHELTER ISLAND

Tourist Information: Shelter Island Chamber of Commerce, *Box 598, Shelter Island, NY 11964; tel: (516) 749-0399.*

Shelter Island, true to its name, is a tiny, ultra-relaxed world unto itself. It is reachable only by car/passenger ferry ($6 car and driver; $1 per passenger) from North

309

Haven (South Ferry, north of Sag Harbor) or Greenport (North Ferry). Ferries depart every ten minutes 0600–2400 all year round. At busy times, you may have to wait.

The island was settled by Quakers fleeing persecution by the Puritans in New England. There are plenty of outdoor activities – swimming, biking, hiking, tennis and golf. Sightseers can enjoy the Victorian homes in the Shelter Island Heights or explore Mahomack Preserve's woodland, beaches and manor house.

ORIENT BEACH

Montauk's more tranquil counterpart on the North Fork is renowned for lovely beaches and maritime activities. On Village Lane, the **Oysterponds Historical Society;** *tel: (516) 323-2480,* has a complex of buildings overflowing with artifacts. Its aim is to preserve the rural quality of the North Fork region.

NORTH FORK WINE COUNTRY

Heading eastward from Orient Beach, you enter wine country, a residential stretch of roads and farms decorated by farm stands and orderly rows of grape vines – a lovely scene that changes with each season. The first vineyard, **Corey Creek,** *Main Rd, Southold; tel: (516) 323-1224,* does not yet offer tours, but its wines can be sampled at area restaurants and wine shops.

Further west on Rte 25 *(Main Rd)* in Peconic are **Osprey's Dominion;** *tel: (516) 765-6188.* **The Lenz Winery;** *tel: (516) 734-6010,* open daily 1100–1700, weekends 1000–1800, has tours, tastings and sales. **Pindar Vineyards;** *tel: (516) 734-6200,* open daily 1100–1800, has tours before 1600, tastings, sales.

In Cutchogue, six of the seven vineyards offer tours as well as tastings and

sales: On Rte 25 *(Main Rd)* are **Bedell Cellars;** *tel: (516) 734-7537,* **Pugliese;** *tel: (516) 734-4057,* **Pellegrini Vineyards;** *tel: (516) 734-4111,* **Gristina Vineyards;** *tel: (516) 734-7089,* and **Peconic Bay Vineyards;** *tel: (516) 734-7361,* with tastings and sales only. On Rte 48 are **Bidwell Vineyards;** *tel: (516) 734-5200,* and **Hargrave Vineyard;** *tel: (516) 734-5111.*

In nearby Mattituck is **Mattituck Hills Winery,** *4250 Bergen Ave and Sound Ave; tel: (516) 298-9150,* open daily 1100–1800. Heading westward is **Jamesport Vineyards,** *Main Rd, Jamesport; tel: (516) 722-5256.* Two wineries in Aquebogue finish out the northern route: **Palmer Vineyards,** *Sound; tel: (516) 722-WINE,* open daily 1100–1800, and **Paumanok Vineyards,** *Rte 25, Main Rd; tel: (516) 722-8800.*

The Wine Route

A mong the beaches, fishing villages, inns and reastaurants, hundreds of acres of sheltered vines nurture one of Long Island's most pleasant surprises – its wineries. Seen by experts as 'the East Coast's answer to Napa Valley', there are 18 of them, enough to produce several million bottles a year. All but three are in the North Fork, which has a longer season and more favourable growing conditions.

Wine aficionados and the general public can sample Chardonnay, Riesling, Pinot Noir, Merlot and Cabernet Sauvignon wines in tasting rooms. Most of the wineries have tours Green 'Wine Trail' road signs help guide you along the way. For information, contact the **Long Island Wine Council,** *1281 Old Country Rd, Riverhead, NY 11901; tel: (516) 369-5887.*

NEW YORK CITY– BURLINGTON

This route follows waterways north of New York City, just beyond the western edge of the six-state New England region. First it traces the east bank of the historic Hudson River, which inspired a school of landscape artists, then it crosses the river to Albany, the capital of New York State. The northern half of the route follows the western shores of Lake George, gateway to the vast Adirondack Mountains, then Lake Champlain, an inland sea 121 miles long. It ends with a ferry crossing into northern Vermont – or a superhighway straight up to Montréal.

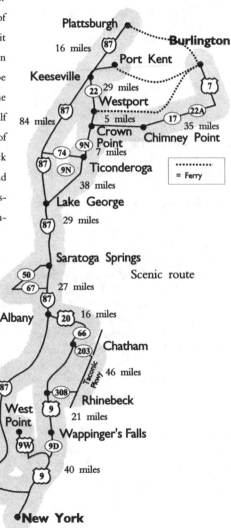

311

DIRECT ROUTE: 302 MILES

ROUTES

DIRECT ROUTE

→ From Times Sq., drive west on *42nd St* to *12th Ave*, then north on Rte 9A (the **Henry Hudson Pkwy**), which becomes the **Saw Mill River Pkwy** through **Yonkers**. From the Saw Mill take Exit 20 onto the **New York State Thruway** (I-87) north, which will join I-287 west.

Cross the Hudson River via the **Tappan Zee Bridge;** 17 miles west of the bridge, follow **I-87** north. *Do not stay on I-287.* I-87 is the New York Thruway to **Albany** (toll $4), then continues as the toll-free **Adirondack Northway** all the way to the Canadian border.

For Burlington, Vt.: By land, take I-87 Exit 28 onto Rte 74 west to **Ticonderoga**, then Rte 9N north to Crown Point. Cross the bridge to Chimney Point, Vt., then take Rte 17 west to Rte 22A north to Rte 7 north.

By ferry, take I-87 Exit 34 onto Rte 9N and Rte 9 to **Ausable Chasm**, then follow Rte 373 to the ferry landing at Port Kent (open mid-May–mid-Oct; $12 car, $3 per person); there's a year-round ferry ($6.75 car, $2 per person) farther north at **Plattsburgh** (Exit 39).

For Montréal: I-87 continues in Québec province as Rte 15. From New York City to the Canadian border is about 340 miles.

SCENIC ROUTE

▶ Follow direct route onto I-87 but do not cross the Tappan Zee Bridge. Instead, take Exit 9 onto Rte 9 north along the Hudson River's east bank.

After 17.5 miles, in Peekskill, Rte 9 turns left, crosses a bridge and comes to a traffic circle. Circle two-thirds of the rotary and take Rte 6 west, which leads 4 miles uphill, offering great scenic views of the river.

To visit **West Point**, cross the Bear Mountain Bridge westbound, then go north on Rte 9W. Afterwards, backtrack across the bridge and follow Rte 9D north 16.7 miles into **Wappinger's Falls**, where it turns sharply left, continues 1.5 miles, then meets Rte 9. Follow Rte 9 north through **Hyde Park** on the way into **Rhinebeck**. Here, take Rte 308 6 miles to the junction of Rte 199, and continue along Rte 199 east 7 miles to the **Taconic State Pkwy**.

Follow the Taconic north 32 miles, then Rte 203 west for 1.5 miles to **Chatham**. Turn right onto Rte 66 north to visit **Old Chatham**; Rte 66 makes several twists and turns for 11 miles on the way to Rte 20 west, which will offer a view 16 miles farther along, of the **Albany** skyline.

Visitors wishing to see the **Empire State Plaza** and Albany museums can drive straight into a parking garage beneath the plaza. To bypass the city, take I-787 north, then Rte 7 west onto I-87 north.

Follow I-87 22 miles to Exit 12, then Rte 67 west for 3.2 miles, turning north onto Rte 50 into **Ballston Spa**. After 6.4 miles, take Rtes 9 and 50 north through **Saratoga Springs**. Beyond the town centre, Rte 50 returns to I-87 at Exit 15. Follow I-87 north 24 miles to Exit 22 for **Lake George**; from here, to reach historic **Ticonderoga** either follow Rte 9N for 39 miles along Lake George or take I-87 another 23 miles to Exit 26, Rte 9 north to scenic Schroon Lake, then Rte 74 east.

From Ticonderoga, follow Rte 9N north through Crown Point (which gives land access to Burlington; see direct route). At Westport, take Rte 22 until it joins Rte

9 north into Keeseville. Stay on Rte 9 past **Ausable Chasm,** then take Rte 373 to Port Kent for the ferry to Burlington.

Along the route, pay careful attention to the distinction between Rte 9 and its numerous branches, which include 9A, 9D, 9N and 9W.

NEW YORK CITY TO RHINEBECK

Tourist Information: Dutchess County Tourism Promotion Agency, *3 Neptune Rd, Poughkeepsie, NY 12601; tel: (914) 463-4000* or toll-free *(800) 445-3131,* publishes self-guided, historical driving tours of the county and runs an information booth at the Roosevelt homestead, open daily 0900–1700 (early May–Oct). **Westchester Convention and Visitors Bureau,** *235 Mamaroneck Ave, White Plains, NY 10605; tel: (800) 833-9282,* has a lodging reservation line.

ACCOMMODATION

Hotel Thayer, *Thayer Rd, US Military Academy at West Point, NY 10996; tel: (800) 247-5047,* is moderate–expensive. Chain hotels are scattered along Rte 9 at Tarrytown, Poughkeepsie and Hyde Park.

Learned chefs from the world over teach their art to students at **The Culinary Institute of America,** *Rte 9, Hyde Park, NY 12538; tel: (914) 471-6608.* Sample their course work. Reservations suggested. Moderate–pricey.

SIGHTSEEING

The Hudson River Museum of Westchester, *511 Warburton Ave, Yonkers, NY 10701; tel: (914) 963-4550,* features landscape artists of the Hudson River School, a Victorian mansion and a planetarium. Open Wed, Thurs, Sat 1000–1700, Fri 1000–2100, Sun 1200–1700, $3.

The pageantry is rich at the **US Military Academy** at **West Point,** on the west bank of the Hudson River, reached via Bear Mountain Bridge to Rte 9W. Besides great river views, see cadets on parade in spring and fall, weather permitting. **West Point Tours,** *Box 268, Highland Falls, NY 10928; tel: (914) 446-4724,* gives tours of the academy daily 0800–1630, $2–$6. A **visitors centre,** *at Thayer Gate,* is open daily 0900–1645; *tel: (914) 938-2638.*

Hyde Park was FDR's home town. The **Franklin Delano Roosevelt National Historic Site,** on Rte 9 (mailing address: *National Park Service, 519 Albany Post Rd, Hyde Park, NY 12538); tel: (914) 229-9115,* shows the president's 1826 home, open daily 0900–1700 (May–Oct); closed Tues, Wed rest of year; the **Museum and Library** are open daily 0900–1800, $5.

President Roosevelt (1882-1945) and his wife, Eleanor, are buried in the Rose Garden. Eleanor's private retreat was **Val-Kill,** 2 miles to the east, off Rte 9G; *tel: (914) 229-9115.*

RHINEBECK

Tourist Information: Rhinebeck Chamber of Commerce, *19 Mill St, P.O. Box 42, Rhinebeck, NY 12572; tel: (914) 876-4778,* runs an information booth just south of Rtes 9 and 308 in the centre of town. Open Mon–Sat 1000–1600, Sun 1100–1500 (May–Oct).

ACCOMMODATION AND FOOD

Whistle Wood, *11 Pells Rd, Rhinebeck, NY 12572; tel: (914) 876-6838,* is a friendly, pastoral bed and breakfast. Horses are boarded here – in the stables, of course. Moderate–pricey. A variety of hotels can be found across the river in **Kingston,** including *Hd, HJ, S8* and *DI.* **Le Petit**

313

Bistro, *8 E. Market St; tel: (914) 876-7400*, is just as it sounds, with impressive fare and French proprietors; moderate.

If a French bistro doesn't interest you, try **China Rose**, *100 Schatzel Ave, Rhinecliff; tel: (914) 876-7442*, a Chinese bistro with Victorian atmosphere; moderate.

Rhinebeck's claim to fame is the **Old Rhinebeck Aerodrome**, *42 Stone Church Rd; tel: (914) 758-8610*, stages airshows with vintage planes, barnstormers, damsels in distress and much melodrama. Ride in an open-cockpit biplane before or after the shows; museum open daily 1000–1700 (mid-May to Oct), $4; shows Sat and Sun at 1430, $9.

SIDE TRACK TO THE CATSKILLS

The **Catskill Mountains** region, west of the Hudson River, is a popular holiday destination due to its natural beauty and a variety of lodgings, from campsites to elegant mountain resorts. It includes a 287,989-acre forest preserve, the well-known **Catskill Game Farm** (12 miles off I-87 Exit 21) and legendary rock music haven **Woodstock**. Access is from I-87 Exits 19–21, from Rhinebeck via Rte 9 to 199 to 28, or from the scenic route via Rtes 23 to 23A.

Mohonk Mountain House, *1000 Mountain Rest Rd, New Paltz, NY 12561; tel: (914) 255-1000*, is a landmark resort, built above **Lake Mohonk** in 1869. Pricey. Tom Wright grew up at Wimbledon and was a chef on the Queen Mary before he bought an inn called **Redcoat's Return**, *Dale Lane, Elka Park, NY 12427; tel: (518)*

589-9858 or *589-6379*. Closed Apr–May. Moderate.

North-South Lake Campground, *County Rte 18, Haines Falls; (518) 589-5058*, has two lakes, two beaches, access to hiking trails and lots of tent pitches. It's close to **Kaaterskill Falls**, with cascades of 250 and 260 ft. In the winter ski season, **Hunter Mountain**, *Hunter, NY 12442; tel: (518) 263-4223*, offers a two-mile downhill ski run, the longest you'll find in these parts.

Take one of 33 trails to the bottom of the 1600-foot mountain at **Ski Windham**, *CD Lane Rd, Windham, NY 12496; tel: (518) 734-4300 or (800) 729-7549*.

Nearby, the town of **Catskill**, where the fictional Rip Van Winkle had his lengthy sleep, was home to the painter **Thomas Cole**, artist Frederick Edwin Church's teacher, and the early training ground of world heavyweight champion boxer Mike Tyson.

RHINEBECK TO ALBANY

See **Rhinebeck Chamber of Commerce** (p. 313) or **Albany County Convention and Visitors Bureau** (p. 315) for tourist information.

Lake Taghkanic State Park, *1528 Rte 82, Ancram, NY 12502; tel: (518) 851-3631*, has tent pitches and lakeside cabins, budget. **Dingman's Family Campground**, *Rte 66, Nassau, NY 12123; tel: (518) 766-2310*, is also budget.

Olana, *Rte 9G, RD 2, Hudson, NY 12534; tel: (518) 828-0135*, was the home of **Frederick Edwin Church**, the most famous US Hudson River School artist during the mid-1800s. He painted landscapes, some without leaving the Persian-style house on this hilltop. House and visitor centre open Mon–Sat 1000–1600 (mid-Apr–early Sept); Wed–Sun 1200–1600 (early Sept–Oct), tour $3.

The **Shaker Museum and Library**, *151 Shaker Museum Rd, Old Chatham, NY 12136; tel: (518) 794-9100*, has displays on more than 200 years of the religious sect's history, along with Shaker furniture and pre-1850 tools. Open daily 1000-1700 (May–Oct), $6. Down the road is **A Country Garden at Antinore**, *tel: (518) 766-6088*, with a garden shop, butterfly gardens and walking trails along **Kinderhook Creek**; $4.

ALBANY

Tourist information: Albany County Convention and Visitors Bureau, *52 S. Pearl St, Albany, NY 12207; tel: (518) 434-1217 or (800) 258-3582*. Visitor centres are at *Broadway* and *Clinton Ave; tel: (518) 434-6311*, open Mon–Fri 0900–1700, and Empire State Plaza, Room 106 on the Concourse; *tel: (518) 474-2418*, open Mon–Fri 0900–1700.

ACCOMMODATION AND FOOD

Chain hotels include *BW, DI, Hd, HJ, Ma, QI, Rm, Su* and *S8*.

Restaurants to suit a range of tastes can be found at the intersection of *Western Ave* and *Quail St*. British authors are sketched and quoted on the walls at **The Ginger Man**, *234 Western Ave; tel: (518) 427-5963*, named for J.P. Dunleavy's novel. Moderate.

SIGHTSEEING

New York State's capital city, Albany, began as a Dutch fur trading center and fort on the Hudson River in 1609. It boomed with the opening of the Albany-to-Buffalo Erie Canal in 1825. More recently, author William Kennedy's novels, including *Ironweed*, have showed its grittier side.

The main sights cluster around the massive, 96-acre Empire State Plaza, built by Gov. Nelson Rockefeller and derided as 'Rockefeller's Edifice Complex'.

The late-1800s **New York State Capitol,** between *Washington Ave* and *State St; tel: (518) 474-2418*, where the state legislature meets, has tours Mon–Fri 0900–1600. **New York State Museum,** *Empire State Plaza; tel: (518) 474-5877*, open daily 1000–1700, shows the state's history, culture and environment.

The Albany Institute of History & Art, *125 Washington Ave; tel: (518) 463-4478*, showcases the art, culture and history of the Upper Hudson Valley. Open Wed– Sun 1200–1700, donation suggested.

The 1761 Georgian **Schuyler Mansion**, *32 Catherine St; tel: (518) 434-0834*, was the home of Revolutionary War Gen Peter Schuyler. Tours by appointment (Nov–Apr), $1. **The Mohawk-Hudson Bikeway** is a 35-mile route along the rivers of those names, connecting Albany, Schenectady and Troy. For information, *tel: (518) 447-5660*.

BALLSTON SPA

The National Bottle Museum, *76 Milton Ave, P.O. Box 621, Ballston Spa, NY 12020; tel: (518) 885-7589*, in a store-front on Rte 50, celebrates the region's role in the glass industry. Open daily 1000–1600 (June–Sept); Mon–Fri (rest of year), donation requested.

SARATOGA SPRINGS

Tourist Information: Saratoga Springs Urban Cultural Park Visitor Center at 'Drink Hall', *297 Broadway at*

Congress, Saratoga Springs, NY 12866; tel: (518) 587-3241, gives a museum-quality overview of the city's history and society, both of which sprang from the presence of mineral waters bubbling up from the ground. Open daily 0900–1600; closed Sun (Nov–Mar). Saratoga Springs is renowned for its racecourses and polo ground, attracting many visiors each year.

Erie Canal

Farmers, axmen, ex-slaves, Irish labourers fresh off the boat – about 3500 'canawlers' – cleared land and dug the Erie Canal, a seven-year project.

Climbing and descending 688 vertical feet over a distance of 363 miles, it linked the Great Lakes to the Hudson River and, thus, the American frontier to the port of New York City.

After it opened in 1825, thousands more men, women, boys ('hoggees') and mules helped move the freight barges up and down the canal.

Today, waterways along the route of the original Erie Canal have been reborn for leisure, not work. Where hoggees and mules once toiled along the tow-paths, bicyclists ride; and pleasure boats make their way through the locks.

Marinas, restaurants, inns and historic sites dot the banks, and nature preserves, parks and campsites have replaced mills and factories. The historic corridor, an engineering milestone that opened a path to the settlement of the West, is now a playground.

For information on recreation, cruises and boat rentals, contact **New York State Canal Corp.**, P.O. Box 189, Albany, NY 12201; tel: (800) 422-6254.

ACCOMMODATION AND FOOD

Batcheller Mansion Inn, 20 Circular St; tel: (518) 584-7012 or (800) 616-7012, is a Victorian refuge, recently restored; expensive–pricey. Chain hotels can be found on Rtes 50 and 9, including BW, Hd. During racing season, room rates jump by $100.

The walls of **Professor Moriarty's Dining & Drinking Saloon**, 430 Broadway; tel: (518) 587-5981, are hung with photos of his nemesis, Basil Rathbone, and other pretenders to the Sherlock Holmes throne.

Moderate. **Hattie's**, 45 Philadelphia St; tel: (518) 584-4790, offers New Orleans and Southern fare, homemade desserts, budget–moderate. **9 Maple Avenue**, tel: 583-2582, is an intimate bar but can get crowded Fri, Sat nights when live jazz can be heard.

ENTERTAINMENT

The Drink Hall exhibits lend perspective to the past for your visit to the **Roosevelt** or **Lincoln bathhouses** in **Saratoga Spa State Park**, S. Broadway, Saratoga Springs, NY 12866; tel: (518) 584-2011 or 583-2880, where you can soak in a tub of the mineral spring water. After your bath, an attendant wraps you in warm sheets and leaves you in quiet reflection. Call for appointments, $11–17.

Saratoga Race Course, Union Ave; tel: (718) 641-4700 off season, (518) 584-6200 in season, presents thoroughbred horse-racing mid-July–Aug and may be the most civilised course in the US: Dresses, jackets and ties are 'appreciated' in the clubhouse. First race 1300; closed Tues.

Breakfast is served at a trackside café 0700–0930. **Saratoga Raceway**, Crescent Ave; tel: (518) 584-2110, offers a much longer season of harness racing, mid-

Jan–late Nov, except for a break in Apr. The **Saratoga Performing Arts Center**, in the park, is the summer home of the New York City Ballet, New York City Opera and the Philadelphia Orchestra. Popular music concerts are also staged here. Open June–Sept; *tel: (518) 587-3330* (summer) or *(518) 584-9330* (off-season).

Saratoga News Stand, *382 Broadway; tel: (518) 581-0133*, carries *The Times, The Sun* and other tabloids. If the kids aren't interested in the *News of the World*, let them play video games at the arcade next door while you read.

SIGHTSEEING

Saratoga Battlefield, *Rtes 32 and 4, Stillwater, NY 12170; tel: (518) 664-9821*, is where Major Gen John Burgoyne's 1777 campaign south from Canada was finally stopped. He surrendered on the heights here 17 Oct, a decisive defeat in the Revolution. Admission $2, or $4 per car.

SARATOGA SPRINGS TO BURLINGTON

Tourist Information: Lake George Regional Chamber of Commerce, *P.O. Box 272, Lake George, NY 12845; tel: (518) 668-5755*, operates a booth at **Shepard Park**, downtown on the waterfront, open daily 0900–1700 (July and Aug). **The Hyde Collection**, *161 Warren St, Glens Falls, NY 12801; tel: (518) 792-1761*, is a gem – a must for art lovers – housed in a small mansion in the Italian Renaissance style. Among its facets are small works of Van Dyck, Tintoretto and Botticelli.

You'll know you've reached **Lake George** when the kids demand a stop at **Great Escape Fun Park**, They'll spot the roller coaster, easily visible from the

Northway (I-87) just before Exit 20, unless you can distract their gaze to the west. East of the park, the downtown is a honky-tonk strip of shops, restaurants with pedestrian fare and fast-food stops.

Further north along the lake you'll find more hotels and motels than homes.

SIDE TRACK TO THE ADIRONDACKS

The **Adirondack Mountains** may not be pure wilderness, but the region does contain vast numbers of trees, peaks, lakes and streams among its 6 million acres. Adirondack history encompasses old trains, wooden boats, rustic furniture and forest estates in addition to logging, hunting and fishing.

The Northway (I-87) crosses the Adirondacks' eastern edge, giving access from Exits 21, 22 (Lake George), 25, 29, 30 and 34.

The life of the region is captured best at **The Adirondack Museum**, *Blue Mountain Lake, NY 12812; tel: (518) 352-7311*, open daily 0930–1730 (late May–mid-Oct).

The Adirondack Mountain Club, *RR 3, Box 3055, Lake George, NY 12845; tel: (518) 668-4447*, provides information on hiking, camping, canoeing and more. It operates information booths at its Lake George headquarters on Rte 9, south of I-87 Exit 21, open Mon–Sat 0830–1700 (May–mid-Oct); Mon–Fri 0830–1630 (rest of year), and at **High Peaks Lodge**, *Adirondack Loj Rd, P.O. Box 867, Lake Placid, NY 12946; tel: (518) 523-3441*, which also provides overnight lodging and breakfast, budget.

Lake Placid was the site of the 1932 and 1980 Winter Olympics. With New York State's highest mountain, Mt

317

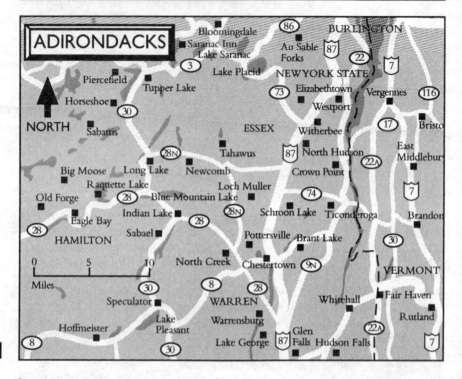

Marcy, looming in the background, Lake Placid draws visitors in both summer and winter. US ski jumpers practice in summer on the 90-metre **Intervale Ski Jumps**, *Rte 73; tel: (518) 532-1655.* **The Olympic Center ice-rink**, *Main St; tel: (518) 523-1655,* is open in summer for public ice-skating Mon–Fri 1945–2115, $4.

Ride a bobsled, a horse, a mountain bike or go cross-country skiing at the **Olympic Sports Complex at Mount Van Hoevenberg**, *Rte 73; tel: (518) 523-4436.*

Cannons still boom – just for show – and fife and drums are played at **Fort Ticonderoga**, *P.O. Box 390, Ticonderoga, NY 12883; tel: (518) 585-2821,* on the shores of Lake Champlain, the site of sev-

eral battles before and during the American Revolution. It was built by the French in 1755 under the name of Fort Carillon and destroyed by the British in 1777, after its occupation by Ethan Allen and his Green Mountain Boys in May 1775.

Following its restoration to its original condition, it has been converted into a military museum, a must for all history buffs. Historical cruises on the lake are also on offer. Open daily 0900–1700 (mid-May–mid-Oct), $7.

Ausable Chasm, *Rte 9, Ausable Chasm, NY 12911; tel: (518) 834-7454 or (800) 537-1211,* is a 1.5-mile river gorge cut through sandstone, which is explored on steps, steel bridges or in boats. Open daily 0900–1600 (late May–mid-Oct), walking tour $9, boat ride $13.

NEW YORK CITY–HARTFORD

Leave the city behind and head for quieter Connecticut. While I-84 is a routine highway, there are plenty of places to pick and choose from along the way to take you off the beaten track. Take side trips for adventures about local history, art, food or to stay at an inn. There are a variety of small-town activities plus the small industrial cities of Waterbury and New Britain. Some surprisingly good museums are along this route.

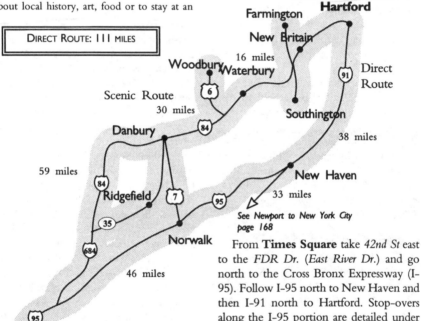

DIRECT ROUTE: 111 MILES

12 miles
Farmington   **Hartford**
New Britain
16 miles
Woodbury Waterbury   Direct
Scenic Route   Route
30 miles
Southington
Danbury
38 miles
59 miles
New Haven
Ridgefield
33 miles
See Newport to New York City
page 168
Norwalk
46 miles
New York

319

From **Times Square** take *42nd St* east to the *FDR Dr.* (*East River Dr.*) and go north to the Cross Bronx Expressway (I-95). Follow I-95 north to New Haven and then I-91 north to Hartford. Stop-overs along the I-95 portion are detailed under Newport to New York City (see p. 168).

ROUTES

DIRECT ROUTE

Depending on traffic, weather and the presence (or absence) of Connecticut State Police patrols, midtown Manhattan to Hartford is a very mundane direct drive of from a little more than two hours, up to three full hours.

SCENIC ROUTE

Follow the direct route out of New York City to the Cross Bronx Expressway (I-95), then the Hutchinson River Pkwy north. From there, you can choose to 'fast-forward' along I-684 north to I-84 north into **Danbury** and onward to Hartford. Or you can continue along the Hutchinson River Pkwy, which becomes the more scenic Merritt Pkwy after crossing into Connecticut; then at Norwalk take Exit 39 onto Rte 7 north to hit **Ridgefield** (via Rte 102 to Rte 35) on the way to Danbury. Either way, from Danbury to Hartford you follow I-84 north, getting off and returning to the highway for specific towns.

If you fast-forward to Danbury: Make your first diversion from I-84 by taking Exit 3 onto Rte 7 and following it south 4.4 miles. Bear right onto Rte 35 and follow for 3 miles into Ridgefield. This is an affluent area outside of Danbury that is popular among Manhattanites eager for a taste of country life. Ridgefield is especially known for some lovely but expensive inns and restaurants. The town was the site of the Battle of Ridgefield, 27 Apr 1777, in the American Revolution.

RIDGEFIELD AND DANBURY

Tourist Information: Housatonic Valley Tourism Commission, *P.O. Box 406, 72 West St, Danbury, CT 06813; tel: (203) 743-0546* or toll-free *(800) 841-4488.*

ACCOMMODATION

Danbury has a *DI, Hd, Hn, QI* and *Rm,* while Ridgefield offers three more interesting lodgings. The **Elms Inn**, *500 Main St, Ridgefield, CT 06877; tel: (203) 438-2541,* with 20 rooms, built in 1760, stands near the Revolutionary battle site and includes an adjacent 1850 building; expensive. Meals are elegant and moderate–pricey. **West Lane Inn**, *22 West Lane, Ridgefield, CT 06877; tel: (203) 438-7323,* is a beautiful early 1800s home with 20 rooms; expensive–pricey. The 16-room **Stonehenge**, *Rte 7 (P.O. Box 667), Ridgefield, CT 06877; tel: (203) 438-6511,* is located alongside a trout-filled lake; expensive–pricey. Its well-known restaurant is pricey.

EATING AND DRINKING

In Ridgefield, try out the moderate–pricey **Hay Day Café**, *21 Governor St, tel: (203) 438-2344,* which offers fresh, creative meals with an extensive wine list. The café also has a gourmet grocery store next door for take-away meals.

SIGHTSEEING

Aldrich Museum of Contemporary Art, *258 Main St, Ridgefield, CT 06877; tel: (203) 438-4519,* open Tues–Sun 1300–1700, tours Sun 1500, $3, has not only an impressive art collection but also a beautiful sculpture garden. **Keeler Tavern Museum**, *132 Main St, Ridgefield, CT 06877; tel: (203) 438-5485,* open Wed, Sat and Sun 1300–1600 (closed Jan), tours every half-hour, $3, is a historic inn boasting a British cannonball embedded in its exterior.

Danbury was once the home of a thriving hat manufacturing business. In 1904, the city was responsible for nearly a quarter of the total value of all hats produced in the US. It is also the birthplace of 20th-century composer Charles Ives, whose innovative, sometimes cacophonous music was so difficult that some of it was never performed in his lifetime. Take Exit 5 and follow signs to the business center for the **Scott-Fanton Museum and Historical Society**, *43 Main St, Danbury, CT 06810; tel: (203) 743-5200,* open Wed–Sun 1400–1700, which includes exhibits on local industry; no fee, but a donation requested. Nearby is the **Charles Ives Birthplace**, *5 Mountainville Ave, Danbury, CT 06810; same telephone,* open Wed–Sun 1400–1700, free.

SHOPPING

For sheer size, nothing can beat the **Danbury Fair Mall**, *7 Backus Ave, Danbury, CT 06810; tel: (203) 743-3247,* open Mon–Sat 1000–1930, Sun 1100–1800, New England's largest shopping mall with 230 stores. It's visible from I-84; take Exit 3.

Further along at Exit 7, **Stew Leonard's**, *99 Federal Rd, Danbury, CT 06811, tel: (203) 790-8030*, is a unique dairy and grocery store listed in the Guinness Book of Records as having the greatest sales per unit area in the US. You'll see why as you taste the free samples, watch the singing milk cartons, and enjoy the ice cream and take-away food. Kids love it.

Take Exit 15 and follow beautiful, tree-lined Rte 6 4 miles north and east into **Woodbury**, which has gracious Revolutionary War-era homes lining the route along with plenty of antique shops.

WOODBURY

Tourist Information: Litchfield Hills Travel Council, *P.O. Box 968, Litchfield, CT 06759; tel: (860) 567-4506*.

ACCOMMODATION AND FOOD

The Curtis House, *506 Main St, Woodbury, CT 06798; tel: (860) 263-2101*, is Connecticut's oldest inn. It's not fancy, but it's comfortable and budget-priced. The **Good News Café**, *694 Main St South; tel: (860) 266-4663*, features exotic meals made from local ingredients and fabulous desserts; moderate.

SHOPPING

Try **Monique Shay Antiques & Design**, *920 Main St South; tel: (860) 263-3186*, **Gerald Murphy Antiques Ltd**, *60 Main St; tel: (860) 266-4211*, There's also the **Woodbury Pewter Factory Outlet**, *860 Main St South; tel: (800) 648-2014* for colonial style pitchers, candlesticks, serving pieces and factory seconds at reduced prices.

SIGHTSEEING

Glebe House, *Hollow Rd, Woodbury, CT 06798; tel: (860) 263-2855*, open Wed–Sun 1300–1600 (Apr–Nov) or by appointment, $3, is an 18th-century farmhouse considered the birthplace of the American Episcopal church. The house has lush gardens designed by English horticulturalist Gertrude Jekyll.

WOODBURY TO WATERBURY

From Rte 6 in Woodbury, take Rte 64 2.8 miles east for a rural drive to **Quassy Amusement Park**, *P.O. Box 1085 (Rte 65) Middlebury, CT 06762; tel: (203) 758-2913* or *(800) FOR-PARK*, beach and picnic grounds on Lake Quassapaug open daily 0800–1900 (end May–early Sept); rides operate daily 1100–1900 (end May–early Sept); parking $3, all-day ride pass $9.95. Continue along Rte 64 to return to I-84.

WATERBURY

Tourist Information: Waterbury Region Convention and Visitors Bureau, *P.O. Box 1469, 83 Bank St, Waterbury, CT 06721; tel: (203) 597-9527*.

ACCOMMODATION

There is a Hd, HJ, QI and Sh. There are also two historic homes. **House on the Hill**, *92 Woodlawn Terrace, Waterbury, CT 06710; tel: (203) 757-9901*, is an 1888 Victorian home with five rooms furnished with antiques and has six fireplaces and a wraparound porch; expensive. **Seventy Hillside**, *70 Hillside Ave, Waterbury, CT 06710; tel: (203) 596-7070*, is a 1901 mansion with three suites located in a park-like setting; expensive.

SIGHTSEEING

Waterbury was known as the brass capital

of the world in the late 19th-century and was a major supplier of metal products, clocks and rubber goods. It retained much of its 19th-century architecture. A brochure describing a self-guided walking tour is available from the visitors bureau.

At I-84 Exit 21, the **Mattatuck Museum**, *144 W. Main St, Waterbury, CT 06702; tel: (203) 753-0381,* open Tues–Sat 1000–1700, Sun 1200–1700 (Sept–June); Tues–Sat 1000–1700 (rest of year), free, presents the industrial history of Waterbury from 1800 to 1950 that earned it the nickname 'Brass City'. Note the rubber desk owned by Charles Goodyear of Goodyear tyre company fame.

SOUTHINGTON TO NEW BRITAIN

Tourist Information: Central Connecticut Tourism District (CCTD), *One Central Park Plaza, Suite A201, New Britain, CT 06051; tel: (860) 225-3901.* **Greater Southington Chamber of Commerce**, *51 N. Main St, Southington, CT 06489; tel: (860) 628-8036.* For Bristol, contact **Litchfield Hills Travel Council**, *P.O. Box 968, Litchfield, CT 06759: tel: (860) 567-4506.*

ACCOMMODATION

Southington has plenty of accommodation, ranging from *CI, DI, M6* and the 149-room *Su* to the two-room **Captain Josiah Cowles Place**, *184 Marion Ave, Southington, CT 06479; tel: (860) 276-0227,* a 1740 bed and breakfast with lovely gardens; moderate.

EVENTS

Each year Southington hosts an Apple Harvest Festival on two consecutive weekends, at the end of Sept and beginning of Oct. Featuring a parade, a carnival and every apple product you can imagine:

fritters, caramel apples, apple cake, pie, cider and apple pie sundaes.

SIGHTSEEING

If you're truly adventurous **Berkshire Balloons**, *P.O. Box 706, Southington, CT 06489; tel: (860) 250-8441,* offer year-round, daily hot air balloons over the Southington, central Connecticut and Farmington River valleys. There are overnight packages including Bed and Breakfast and a balloon trip. Flights cost $200 and last about an hour. A flight for two and an overnight stay at a nearby inn is $495. Reservations are required.

From I-84 Exit 31 take Rte 229 to reach three sites of interest in Bristol, a community that used to be a major manufacturer of clocks. The **New England Carousel Museum**, *95 Riverside Ave (Rte 72), Bristol, CT 06010; tel: (860) 585-5411,* open Mon–Sat 1000–1700, Sun 1200–1700 (Apr–Oct); closed Mon (Nov–Mar) $4, has a large collection of carousel art along with guided tours explaining the history and development of the carousel. **The American Clock and Watch Museum**, *100 Maple St, Bristol, CT 06010; tel: (860) 583-6070,* open daily 1000–1700 (Apr–Nov), $3.50, has a fascinating collection of 3000 clocks and watches dating from 1590. Just off Rte 72 is **Lake Compounce Theme Park**, *822 Lake Ave, Bristol, CT 06010; tel: (860) 583-3631,* open Tues–Thur and Sun 1100–2100, Fri–Sat 1100–2300 (end May–early Sept), $12.95, featuring 25 attractions including roller coasters, a 1911 carousel and live entertainment.

NEW BRITAIN

Tourist Information: New Britain Chamber of Commerce, *One Central Park Plaza, New Britain, CT 06051; tel: (860) 229- 1665.*

ACCOMMODATION AND FOOD

If you plan an overnight stop, there's an RI. The city is known for its Polish food. One of the best known restaurants is the budget **Fatherland**, *450 South Main St; tel: (860) 224-3345.*

EVENTS

New Britain spices it up with its annual Italian-American Feast sponsored by a local church parish during a mid-July weekend. Some 15,000 people attend and dine on pasta, fried dough, Italian sausage and more.

SIGHTSEEING

The 'hardware city' earned its nickname during the 19th- and early 20th-century when metal-working industries predominated and the city grew into an industrial and architecturally rich environment. A self-guiding booklet, *Architectural Walking Tour*, pointing out the Art Deco architecture downtown, is available from the CCTD. The **New Britain Museum of American Art**, *5 Lexington St, New Britain, CT 06052; tel: (860) 229-0257*, open Tues–Sun 1300–1700, free, boasts more than 5000 works including paintings by realist Andrew Wyeth, 19th-century portraitist John Singer Sargent and southwest contemporary artist Georgia O'Keeffe. Don't miss muralist Thomas Hart Benton's *Arts of Life in America*.

The **New Britain Youth Museum**, *30 High St, New Britain, CT 06051; tel: (860) 225-3020*, open Tues–Fri 1300–1700, Sat 1000–1600, donation requested, has dolls, miniatures and activities for youngsters. Take Exit 35.

FARMINGTON AND WEST HARTFORD

Tourist Information: Greater Hartford Tourism District, *One Civic Center Plaza, Hartford, CT 06103; tel: (860) 520-4480 or toll-free (800) 793-4480.*

SIGHTSEEING

Farmington is an affluent community with attractions in three historic homes, all reached from I-84 Exit 39. The best is the **Hill-Stead Museum**, *35 Mountain Rd, Farmington, CT 06032; tel: (860) 677-9064*, open Tues–Sun 1000–1600 (May–Oct); 1100–1600 rest of year, $6, with paintings by impressionists Mary Cassatt, Monet, Degas and Manet and other art objects. The house was designed in 1900 by Theodate Pope, one of the first American women architects. The grounds include a sunken garden.

The **Day-Lewis Museum**, *158 Main St, Farmington, CT 06032; tel: (860) 678-1645*, open Wed 1400–1600, closed Aug and Dec–Feb, $2, is an Indian archaeology museum housed in a Tunxis Indian home. The **Stanley-Whitman House**, *37 High St, Farmington, CT 06032; tel: (860) 677-9222*, open Wed–Sun 1300–1600 (May–end Oct); Sun 1200–1600 (March, Apr and Nov–Dec), $3, is a 1720 colonial homestead, with authentic period furnishings and exhibits.

West Hartford, though right next door to gritty Hartford, is very much a suburban community. If your interested in language take Exit 41 to visit the **Noah Webster House**, *227 S. Main St, West Hartford, CT 06107; tel: (860) 521-5362*, open Mon, Tues, Thurs, Fri 1000–1600; Sat and Sun 1300–1600 (mid-June–end Sept); Thurs–Tues 1300–1600 (rest of year), where lexicographer Noah Webster was born in 1758. His first dictionary of American English was published in 1806. This restored 18th-century farmhouse has early editions of the dictionary and local history exhibits.

323

NEW YORK CITY-LENOX

Most natives consider northwestern Connecticut the most scenic part of the state. Small country towns, covered bridges, horse farms and quiet inns are among its attractions. It's also known for its affluence. Restaurants, shops and inns reflect New York sophistication – and prices. Actors Dustin Hoffman and Meryl Streep have homes here, as do playwright Arthur Miller (*Death of a Salesman*), novelist William Styron (*Sophie's Choice*) and former US Secretary of State Henry Kissinger. Don't expect to bump into them, but you will see what brings them here. Although small, the area invites an overnight stay in order to spend time rambling about.

While there is a scenic route with some detours worth taking, this is one instance in which the direct route (Rte 7) is also unusually lovely, winding through country towns and along the Housatonic River. This is a popular region to visit in fall 'leaf-peeping' season.

324

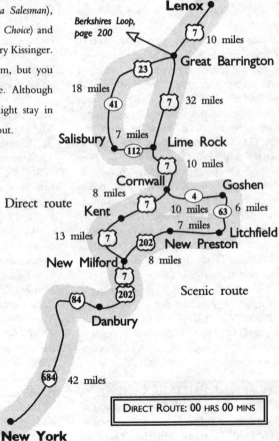

Berkshires Loop, page 200

Lenox

7 10 miles

Great Barrington

23

18 miles

41   7 32 miles

Salisbury 7 miles   Lime Rock

112

7 10 miles

Cornwall   Goshen

8 miles   4

Direct route   Kent   7   10 miles 63 6 miles

7 miles

13 miles 7   Litchfield

202 New Preston

New Milford   8 miles

7

84   202   Scenic route

Danbury

684 42 miles

DIRECT ROUTE: 00 HRS 00 MINS

New York

ROUTES

DIRECT ROUTE

From Times Square, take 42nd St east to FDR Drive (East River Drive) and go north to the Cross Bronx Expressway (I-95). Follow the expressway east, then take the Hutchinson River Pkwy north to I-684, which connects to I-84 north. Continue to **Danbury**, where you exit onto Rte 7 north, driving about 50 miles to the border of Massachusetts. After **New Milford**, the drive is beautiful, especially the section along the Housatonic River.

Continue on Rte 7 north about 10 miles into Massachusetts to Great Barrington (see p. 201) and another 10 miles to complete the trip to Lenox (detailed on pp. 192–199).

SCENIC ROUTE

Rte 7 north in Danbury will start out as a dull drive. At New Milford follow Rte 202 east on a pleasant 8-mile diversion to **New Preston**; then, at the junction of Rte 45, turn left for a picturesque 8-mile ramble around **Lake Waramaug**. Returning to Rte 202, continue for about 7 miles and visit **Litchfield**, a model New England village. From there take rural Rte 63 north 6 miles to **Goshen**, then follow Rte 4 west about 10 miles along a leafy, pleasant road back to Rte 7 in **Cornwall**.

From here you can side-track 3 miles to Kent Falls State Park and another 4 miles to **Kent**, a beautiful section of Rte 7 that parallels a piece of the Maine-to-Georgia Appalachian Trail, and continue on to the covered bridge at Bulls Bridge.

Otherwise, continue north on Rte 7 to West Cornwall with its own covered bridge and through the **Housatonic State Forest**, which affords views of the unspoiled Housatonic River. Continue to Rte 112 west, going past Lime Rock racetrack for a view of rolling hills and country homes. In posh Salisbury take Rte 41 north past views of the Litchfield Hills and 2380-ft Mt. Frissell, the highest point in Connecticut, and north into Massachusetts. Follow Rte 41, then Rtes 41 and 23 until you rejoin Rte 7 at Great Barrington; it's another 10 miles into Lenox.

DANBURY TO LITCHFIELD

New Milford is a transition between the sprawl that has overtaken the Danbury area and the more rural northwest. There is a large town green and several good places to stay.

ACCOMMODATION AND FOOD

Heritage Inn, *34 Bridge St, New Milford, CT 06776; tel: (860) 354-8883,* has 20 rooms in a historic 19th-century building that was once a tobacco warehouse; moderate. **Homestead Inn**, *5 Elm St, New Milford, CT 06776; tel: (860) 354-4080,* has eight rooms in a comfortable Victorian homestead and six other less interesting rooms in a motel; moderate.

The **Maple Leaf Motor Lodge**, *244 Kent Rd (Rte 7) New Milford, CT 06776; tel: (860) 350-2766,* is located on the Housatonic River and has 35 moderate units.

Four miles north of New Milford on Rte 202 is **The Silo**, *44 Upland Rd, tel: (860) 355-0300,* a silo and barn owned by band leader Skitch Henderson and his wife, Ruth, with gourmet treats and crafts.

NEW PRESTON

New Preston is a charming small town with antique shops and several outstanding inns well known for their good food, comfort and lakeside views.

ACCOMMODATION AND FOOD

The noted **Inn on Lake Waramaug**, *North Shore Rd, New Preston, CT 06777; tel: (860) 868-0563* or toll-free *(800) LAKE-INN*, with 23 rooms, is in a 1790s building and has a private beach. Rooms are expensive–pricey and meals pricey.

The outstanding 17-room **Boulders Inn**, *East Shore Rd (Rte 45), New Preston, CT 06777; tel: (860) 868-0541*, is a former private home built in 1895 overlooking Lake Waramaug and the Litchfield Hills. Plenty of antiques and charm make this a cosy retreat with an excellent restaurant. Meals and rooms are pricey.

Hopkins Inn, *22 Hopkins Rd, New Preston, CT 06777, tel: (860) 868-7295*, has 13 rooms and overlooks the lake. The restaurant features Austrian and Swiss food. Rooms are moderate and meals moderate–pricey.

SHOPPING AND SIGHTSEEING

Adjacent to the inn is the **Hopkins Vineyard**, *Hopkins Rd, New Preston, CT 06777; tel: (860) 868-7954*, open daily 1000–1700 (May–end Dec); Fri–Sun 1000–1700 (Jan–end Apr), for free tasting and self-guided tours. Amidst antiques shops is **J. Seitz & Co.**, *Main St (Rte 45); tel: (860) 868-0119*, which has US Southwest furniture and Native American crafts.

Five miles at the other end of the lake from New Preston is **Lake Waramaug State Park**, *30 Lake Waramaug Rd, New Preston, CT 06777; tel: (860) 8868-0220*, open mid-May–end Sept, parking $5–$8, with a public beach, picnic areas and a budget–moderate campsite.

↴ SIDE TRACK TO WASHINGTON

After leaving New Preston on Rte 202, take Rte 47 south 4 miles to Washington Depot and then 1 mile to Washington, a pretty town boasting an unusually grand and expensive inn. The **Mayflower Inn**, *118 Woodbury Rd (Rte 47), Washington, CT 06793; tel: (860) 868-9466*, is set on 28.5 acres of gardens and manicured lawns and has 25 rooms, a health club, sauna, pool and tennis. Rooms are very pricey ($225–$350), as are meals. Among other comforts are marble bathrooms, mahogany wainscoting and sumptuous four-poster beds. Check out the classy gift shop.

From Washington, take Rte 199 south 1.25 miles to *Curtis Rd* and make a right for the **Institute for American Indian Studies**, *Curtis Rd, Washington, CT 06793; tel: (860) 868-0518*, open Mon–Sat 1000–1700, Sun 1200–1700, films shown Sat–Mon 1430, $4, which has artifacts and art from 10,000 years ago to the present as well as a 17th-century Algonquian village. ▣

LITCHFIELD

Tourist Information: Litchfield Hills Travel Council, *P.O. Box 968, Litchfield, CT 06759; tel: (860) 567-4506*. The **Litchfield Hills Information Booth**, *Rte 202 On-the-Green, Litchfield; no telephone*, is open daily 0930–1630 (July–Sept); 1000–1630 (early Oct).

Litchfield is the heart of northwest Connecticut with fine shops, restaurants and the idyllic notion of what a New England village should look like. Take a brief drive up and down Rte 63 north and south through town to see beautifully kept Colonial houses surrounded by impeccably groomed lawns and gardens.

ACCOMMODATION

Tollgate Hill Inn and Restaurant, *P.O. Box 1339, Rte 202 Litchfield, CT*

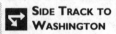

06759; tel: (860) 567-4545, was originally built as a tavern in 1745 and has 20 rooms; expensive–pricey. The restaurant serves grilled meats and seafood; moderate.

The **Litchfield Inn**, *Rte202, Litchfield, CT 06759; tel: (860) 567-4503*, just outside the centre of town, has 30 rooms, moderate–expensive.

EATING AND DRINKING

The **West Street Grill**, *West St, On-the-Green, Litchfield, CT 06759; tel: (860) 567-3885*, is a popular local hangout serving excellent food; moderate. For a more informal or take-away meal there's **Spinell's Litchfield Food Company**, *39 West St, tel: (860) 567-3113*, with gourmet sandwiches, salads and entrées; budget.

SHOPPING

Litchfield is known to gardeners throughout the US as the home of **White Flower Farm**, *Rte 63, Litchfield, CT 06759; tel: (860) 567-8789*, open Mon–Fri 1000–1700, Sat, Sun and holidays 0900–1730 (mid-Apr–mid-Dec); free. This garden centre is famous for the quality of its catalogues offering enticing plants and flowers. Visit 10 acres of display gardens, 30 acres of growing fields and the store.

The town boasts several excellent bookshops including **Barnidge & McEnroe**, *7 West St; tel: (860) 567-4670*, with three stories of books and gifts in a 19th-century Victorian setting along with an espresso bar.

SIGHTSEEING

About 8 miles before entering Litchfield from Rte 202 is **Mt. Tom State Park**, with swimming and hiking and a one-mile trail to a tower at the 1325-ft summit with excellent views. For pre-trip information,

contact **Bureau of Parks & Forests**, *Connecticut Department of Environmental Protection, 79 Elm St, Hartford, CT 06106-5127; tel: (860) 566-2305*.

In town, visit **Tapping Reeve House and Law School**, *South St (Rte 63), Litchfield, CT 06759; tel: (860) 567-4501*, open Tues–Sat 1100–1700, Sun 1300–1700 (mid-May–mid-Oct), $2, America's first law school, founded in 1773. Among its graduates were US Cabinet members, senators, congressmen and other politicians.

The **Congregational Church**, at the junction of *Rtes 202* and *181*, is a gleaming, white, spare building built in 1828 and often photographed.

SIDE TRACK
TO KENT

The direct route sends you right through this lovely town; it's a side-track for those on the scenic route:

After returning to Rte 7 via Rte 4, drive south to **Kent Falls State Park** on Rte 7, open daily Apr–Nov, weekend and holiday parking $5–$8; weekdays free. For information contact **Macedonia Brook State Park**, *159 Macedonia Brook Rd, Kent, CT 06757; tel: (860) 927-3238*.

This series of waterfalls includes a 200-ft cascade and a steep, quarter-mile hiking trail. Continue south to the bustling town of Kent where you'll find shopping, cafés and art galleries.

The **Fife 'n Drum Restaurant and Inn**, *Rte 7, 59 North Main St, Kent, CT 06757; tel: (860) 927-3509*, has good seafood and lamb; pricey. The seven-room inn is moderate to expensive.

The **Sloane-Stanley Museum**, *Rte 7, Kent, CT 06757; tel: (860) 927-3849*, open Wed–Sun 1000–1600 (mid-May–end Oct), $1.50, features works by artist and author Eric Sloane as well as early American tools and implements and the remains of the Kent Iron Furnace, which operated from 1826–92.

For sweets there is the **Kent Coffee and Chocolate Company**, *8 Main St; tel: (860) 927-1445,* featuring 50 varieties of coffees and teas as well as fudge, truffels and assorted chocolates.

For ice-cream try **Stosh's Ice-Cream**, *Kent Station Sq., Rte 7; tel: (860) 927-4495.* There are numerous art galleries. The **Heron American Craft Gallery**, *Main St, Kent, CT 06757; tel: (860) 927-4804,* features contemporary New England crafts.

Continue south on Rte 7 about 3 more miles to Bulls Bridge to see a rustic covered bridge over the Housatonic River, which carries drivers heading into New York State.

CORNWALL BRIDGE TO MASSACHUSETTS BORDER

Drive north on Rte 7 through Cornwall Bridge. Despite the name, don't look for a covered bridge here; instead travel along the river through the Housatonic Meadows State Park to **West Cornwall**. At the junction with Rte 128 is the one-lane, red covered bridge that has been in continuous service since 1837.

Just before the bridge, across from the river, is **Clarke Outdoors**, *163 Rte 7, West Cornwall, CT 06796: tel: (860) 672-6365,* where you can rent canoes for $45 a day, rafts for $22 or kayaks ($35) or take lessons.

The Housatonic River is not only beautiful but has an area of easy, flatwater canoeing. For the adventurous, there are whitewater raft trips in the spring.

Reservations are suggested for all rentals and trips. On the drive along Rte 112, note on the left **Lime Rock Park**, *Lime Rock, CT 06039; tel: (860) 435-0896* or toll-free *(800) RACE-LRP,* where sports car and stock car racing takes place Apr–Oct, $12–$60. It's known as the place where actor Paul Newman occasionally tries out his racing skills.

In **Lakeville**, the **Wake Robin Inn**, *Rte 41, Lakeville, CT 06039, tel: (860) 435-2515,* is a Georgian colonial-style building on 15 acres with 40 units; expensive. It houses the **Savarin Restaurant**, serving excellent French food; pricey.

The **Interlaken Inn**, *74 Interlaken Rd, Lakeville, CT 06039, tel: (860) 435-9878,* with a total of 79 rooms in Victorian and Tudor houses as well as a larger, modern building, is more of a resort than an inn. It's on **Wononskopomuc Lake** and there are plenty of rowing boats, canoes and sailing boats along with a pool and golf course. Rooms are expensive–pricey, meals pricey.

SALISBURY

Salisbury, with its attractive main street and fine shops, provides the moneyed New England atmosphere the region is known for. Its peacefulness belies its past: During the 18th and 19th centuries, the town was a major iron-producing centre with forges, blast furnaces and hundreds of workers. Trees were cut down to make charcoal, leaving forests bare. During the American Revolution, the government of Connecticut took over the town's largest furnace, whose ore was used to make one of every three cannons used by the Continental Army. Today Salisbury is a quiet, leafy town. The **Hotchkiss School**, one of Connecticut's many 'prep schools' (which prepare affluent adolescents for college), makes its home here.

Covered Bridges

Covered bridges summon the romance of an earlier, slower time when the clip-clop of horses' hooves could be heard crossing wooden planks over a stream or river. At one time there were some 10,000 covered bridges in the US; today only about 1000 remain.

While the best-selling novel and hit movie, *The Bridges of Madison County*, popularised such bridges in the Midwestern US, covered bridges are more often associated with New England, where they dot the countryside, adding a picturesque rural flavour to the landscape. While the largest number are in Vermont, Connecticut boasts two in the western part of the state that are easily accessible to travellers; Bulls Bridge in Kent, built in 1858, and the West Cornwall Bridge, built in 1837.

The bridges were built using the same construction that farmers employed to erect barns. In fact, they've been described as barns with openings at either end. They were popular as a means of protecting the wooden floor timbers from the harsh climate. Pitched roofs meant snow could slide down the sides, and wide openings made it easier for horses and horse-drawn carriages to drive through.

One of the appeals of the covered bridge is the fine craftsmanship that went into their construction, using different types of portals and trusses, or framework. The grandfather of the covered bridge was Andrea Palladio, a 16th-century Italian architect whose published drawings of such structures became known in New England. The most popular truss was known as the Howe truss. The Connecticut bridges use the Town Lattice truss, designed by Ethiel Town in 1820. The entries to the bridges, known as portals, are equally varied, adding individual character to each bridge.

Unfortunately, many bridges have been neglected in recent times. Many were too small for modern traffic or could not bear the weight of large trucks. The dwindling number of remaining covered bridges are a special reminder of life in earlier times.

329

ACCOMMODATION AND FOOD

To buy excellent tea, try **John Harney and Sons Ltd.**, *11 East Main St, Rte 44; tel: (800) TEA-TIME (832-8463)*, a mail order business that sells to hotels and restaurants. There's a small showroom in which to buy teas and gifts. Call ahead for a free tour of the plant or for tea tasting.

For lunch or dessert in a serene atmosphere, there's **Chaiwalla**, *One Main St; tel: (860) 435-9758*, which also features exotic Asian teas; budget. Across the street is the 26-room **White Hart Inn**, *Box 385, Salisbury, CT 06068; tel: (860) 435-0030*, a rambling 19th-century inn; mod-erate–expensive. It has two restaurants, the casual Tap Room, with pizza, soups, salads and entrées, budget–moderate, and the pricey Sea Grill.

The seven-room **Under Mountain Inn**, *482 Under Mountain Rd (Rte 41), Salisbury, CT 06068, tel: (860) 435-0242*, is a white, 18th-century farmhouse with a British accent; pricey. Meals feature full English breakfasts, imported ales and a proper cup of tea.

Ragamont Inn, *Main St, Salisbury, CT 06068; tel: (860) 435-2372*, is a building dating back to 1830, with nine rooms; moderate–expensive.

ACROSS THE BORDER

You can combine a tour of New England with a visit to eastern Canada, and the two principal cities of French-speaking Québec province, Montréal and Québec City, described on the pages that follow.

Details of roads between the Canadian cities and northern points in New England are given in the table below.

If Montréal is your gateway into North America, then you may prefer to take a bus/train ride into New England (passengers for 'The Vermonter' take a bus from Montréal to St Albans, Vt, then the train, which goes as far as New York City), or even fly down to Boston, rather than hire a car in Canada to drive into the USA. If going into Canada, check that this is permitted under the terms of your US car rental. If you have entered the USA on a Visa Waiver scheme (see p. 28), you are normally entitled to one trip into Canada and back.

Public transport links between Montréal and Québec City themselves are good: VIA Rail runs several trains a day between the two cities, journey time under 3 hrs, and Orleans Express Coach Lines buses take 3½–4 hrs. Driving between the two cities is also straightforward, taking Rte 40, 257 km (160 miles).

Connections to Montréal and Québec City

From	To	By	Route	Distance/Time
Burlington, Vt	Montréal	Car	I-89 to border; then Rtes 133, 35, 10 and 134	97 miles
Burlington, Vt	Montréal	Bus/Train	From Essex Junction 'The Vermonter'. Once daily.	3 hrs
Montpelier, Vt	Montréal	Bus/Train	'The Vermonter'. Once daily.	4 hrs
Colebrook, NH	Montréal	Car	Rtes 3 then 114 to border; then Rte 147 to Sherbrooke, then Rte 10	144 miles
Colebrook, NH	Québec City	Car	As above to Sherbrooke, then Rte 55 to Drummondsville, turn east on Rte 20	160 miles
Littleton, NH	Montréal	Car	I-93/I-91 to the border; Rte 55 to Magog, then Rte 10	152 miles
Hanover, NH	Montréal	Bus/Train	From White River Junction 'The Vermonter'. Once daily.	5½ hrs
Hanover, NH	Montréal	Car	I-91 to Magog, then as for Littleton above	191 miles
Jackman, ME	Québec City	Car	Rte 201 to the border; then Rtes 173 and 73 to Q. C.	115 miles

NB Train journey times and frequencies are approx. and subject to seasonal and other changes. Schedules should be checked locally.

MONTRÉAL

Although it is the second largest French-speaking city in the world, Montréal is as decisively North American as it is Francophone. Its early fortunes were made in furs and shipping as the most inland navigable port on the St. Lawrence River, but today Montréal is a banking, manufacturing and world trade centre. It emerged as an international city with the Expo '67 world fair, which left behind the Métro system and Underground City as well as harbour islands as recreational and exposition resources. The 1976 summer Olympiad prompted massive public works to create open spaces and the Olympic Park.

An economic dynamo, Montréal has been an immigration magnet for Francophones, creating a city of great ethnic diversity. Perhaps no industry has so benefitted from this immigration as food service. It is hard to find a better place to eat in all of North America, and Montréal enjoys nothing so much as a good party combined with a good meal.

TOURIST INFORMATION

Greater Montréal Convention and Tourism Bureau, 1555 r. Peel, Bureau 600, Montréal, PQ H3A 1X6; tel: (514) 844-5400, produces superb maps and brochures available at the main **Infotouriste Centre**, 1001 r. du sq.-Dorchester (Métro: Peel); tel: (514) 873-2015; open daily 0830–1930 (June–early Sept); daily 0900–1800 (early Sept–May). **Montréal Reservation Centre;** tel: (514) 284-2277 or (800) 567-8687, handles lodging, event and tour reservations.

WEATHER

Summer is humid and can be hot (up to 90°F). Winter is cold and snowy; the average Jan high is 18°F.

ARRIVING AND DEPARTING

Airports
Montréal International Airport (Dorval) handles flights from USA and Canada; tel: (514) 633-3105. It is 20 km from downtown Montréal. Airport buses C$9, C$17 return. Taxi approximately C$24. **Montréal International Airport (Mirabel)** handles international flights from outside North America; tel: (514) 476-3010. It lies about 50 km from Montréal. Airport buses C$15, C$22 return. Taxi about C$58. Airport buses serve the downtown air terminal, 777 r. de la Gauchetière; tel: (514) 394-7369.

Rail and Bus
VIA Rail, Gare Central, 895 r. de la Gauchetière Ouest (beneath Hotel La Reine Elizabeth); tel: (514) 871-1331 or (800) 361-5390, connects daily to Ottawa, Toronto and Québec and frequently to Atlantic Canada and Vancouver. All buses use **Terminus Voyageurs,** 505 blvd de Maisonneuve Est (Métro: Berri-UQAM); tel: (514) 842-2281. **Orleans Express Coach Lines** connects to Québec city and elsewhere in the province. **Voyageur Colonial** connects to Atlantic Canada and

331

Ontario. **Greyhound** connects to New York via Albany and Boston via Burlington, Vt.

Communications

Canada Post offices are open Mon-Fri 0800–1745. The two main offices are at *1250 r. University; tel: (514) 395-4909,* and *1250 r. Ste-Catherine Ouest; tel: (514) 522-5191.*

GETTING AROUND

The island of Montréal is large, but most areas of interest lie on the south and east side of the mountain that gave the city its name. **Vieux Montréal** has most of the historic buildings and colourful, narrow streets dating from the 17th and 18th centuries. (The 1642 town lies beneath the Point-à-Callière museum.) **Vieux Port,** the waterfront area of Vieux Montréal, has been recently redeveloped to create a promenade and pier entertainments. The definition of **Downtown** varies, but covers the business and shopping district from *av. St-Laurent* west to *r. du Fort,* from *r. Sherbrooke Ouest* down to Vieux Montréal. It contains many museums, all the major shopping centres and most large hotels.

Av. St-Laurent bisects the city: cross streets are designated east or west. *Av. St-Laurent* and the nearby parallel **av. St-Denis** are the most lively streets in Montréal for restaurants, nightlife and boutique shopping. **Maisonneuve**, in the east end of the city, is predominantly residential but includes the complex of attractions around the Olympic Park and Botanical Gardens. The **Underground City** is a 29-km network of underground passageways linked to the Métro system. It was begun in the 1960s and provides access to 1700 boutiques, department stores, restaurants, movie houses, theatres and seven major hotels.

Public Transport

Société de transport de la Communauté urbaine de Montréal; *tel: (514) 288-6287,* operates the bus and Métro system. Tickets are C$1.75 or six for C$7.50. *La carte touristique* provides unlimited travel for one day for C$5, three consecutive days for C$12; available at Infotouriste Centre and some hotels. Passenger and bicycle ferry service between Vieux Port (Quai Jacques-Cartier) and Île Ste-Hélène runs late May–early Oct; C$2.75; *tel: (514) 281-8000.*

Driving and Cycling

Driving in Montréal follows the aggressive North American style. Right turns on red are prohibited and pedestrians have the right-of-way. Limited parking is available at street meters (C$1.50 per hr), but most visitors park at garages for C$7–C$12 per day. A bicycle path network covers the island; ask for map at Infotouriste Centre.

STAYING IN MONTRÉAL

Accommodation

Hotel chains include *BW, CP, DI, Hn, Hd, HJ, Ma, Rd, Sh* and *TL,* as well as **Kempinski;** *tel: (800) 426-3135,* **Loews;** *tel: (800) 235-6397,* **Quality Hotel/ Journey's End;** *tel: (800) 268-6116,* and **Westin;** *tel: (800) 228-3000.* **Montréal Youth Hostel,** *1030 r. Mackay (Métro: Lucien-L'Allier); tel: (514) 843-3317.* Largest of the city's bed and breakfast reservation services is **bed and breakfast Downtown Network,** *3458 av. Laval, Montréal, PQ H2X 3C8; tel: (514) 289-9749* or *(800) 267-5180.*

An outstanding Bed and Breakfast attached to an art gallery in Vieux Montréal is **Les Passants du Sans Soucy,** *171 r. St-Paul Ouest, Montréal, PQ H2Y 1Z5; tel: (514) 842-2634;* moderate.

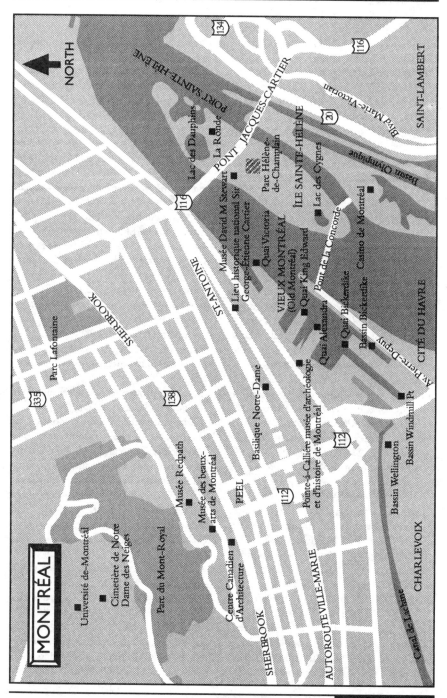

The least expensive (budget–moderate) small hotels lie on r. *St-Hubert* uphill from the bus station, including the cozy **Hotel Bon Accueil**, *1601 r. St-Hubert, Montréal, PQ H2L 3Z1; tel: (514) 527-9655*, and the classier **Hotel L'Emérillon**, *1600 r. St-Hubert, Montréal, PQ H2L 3Z3; tel: (514) 849-3214 or (800) 613-3383*.

Three moderate self-catering options downtown are **Château Royal Hotel Suites**, *1420 r. Crescent, Montréal, PQ H3G 2B7; tel: (514) 848-0999 or (800) 363-0335*, **L'Appartement-in-Montréal**, *455 r. Sherbrooke Ouest, Montréal, PQ H3A 1B7; tel: (514) 284-3634 or (800) 363-3010*, and **Tours Richelieu**, *2045 r. Peel, Montréal, PQ H3A 1T6; tel: (514) 844-3381 or (800) 567-0190*. **Hotel La Reine Elizabeth**, *900 blvd René-Lévesque Ouest, Montréal, PQ H3B 4A5; tel: (514) 861-3511 or (800) 441-1414*, is the largest and grandest hotel in Montréal. Many good business hotels also offer large discounts on weekends and shoulder seasons (Apr–mid-May and mid-Sept–Oct) including the **Le Château Champlain**, *1 Place du Canada, Montréal, PQ H3B 439; tel: (514) 878-9000 or (800) 200-5909*, and **Hotel Inter-Continental**, *360 r. St-Antoine Ouest, Montréal, PQ H2Y 3X4; tel: (514) 987-9900 or (800) 361-3600*.

EATING AND DRINKING

There are more than 5000 restaurants in Montréal. French and North American cuisines dominate, followed closely by cuisines from former French colonies (Indochina, West Africa, Lebanon) and central Europe. Two local specialties are roasted chicken dinners as pioneered in 1936 by **Rôtisserie Laurier**, *381 r. Laurier Ouest; tel: (514) 273-3671*, and 'smoked meat', a pickled-smoked brisket introduced in 1908 at **Ben's Delicatessen**, *990 blvd de Maisonneuve Ouest; tel: (514) 844-1000*. To dine most economically on the finest food, choose the fixed midday menu.

In the Downtown area near the hotels, many restaurants on *Crescent, Bishop* and *de la Montagne Sts* are overblown pubs, but the exceptions are exceptional. The best French meal in Downtown is at **Les Halles**, *1450 r. Crescent; tel: (514) 844-2328*; pricey but worth it. Elegant power breakfasts and cozy French bourgeois dinners are the order at **Le Caveau**, *2063 r. Victoria; tel: (514) 844-1624*; moderate. For haute cuisine, try **The Beaver Club** at the Queen Elizabeth Hotel, *900 blvd René-Lévesque Ouest; tel: (514) 861-3511*; pricey. A surprisingly excellent steak-frites meal is the only menu item at **L'entrecôte St-Jean**, *2022 r. Peel; tel: (514) 281-6492*; moderate. Take-away desserts and gourmet salad-sandwich fare are superb at **La Tulipe Noire**, *2100 r. Stanley* (in Maison Alcan); *tel: (514) 285-1225*. **Le Faubourg shopping centre**, *1616 r. Ste-Catherine Ouest (Métro: Guy-Concordia)*, proffers a wide selection of ethnic foods and sundry snacks.

The restaurants of Vieux Montréal fall in extremes of the fast-food terraces of *Place Jacques-Cartier* and wonderful provincial French spots like the masterful eponymous **Claude Postel**, *443 r. St-Vincent; tel: (514) 875-5067*, pricey. Inexpensive Chinese food is available near Vieux Montréal in Chinatown on *r. de la Gauchetière* between *av. St-Urbain* and *av. St-Laurent*.

The most lively dining in the city is along *avs. St-Laurent* and *St-Denis* north of *r. Sherbrooke*. *St-Laurent* features the cuisines of Central Europe and speciality stores where you can buy sausages, spices and other imports. *St-Denis* is action-central for sidewalk dining and young chefs' own restaurants, of which the brightest star is Normand Laprise at the eccentric and witty **Toqué**, *3842 r. St-Denis; tel: (514) 499-2084;* moderate–pricey. A less eclectic, more locally rooted style shows up at **Allumette**, *3434 r. St-Denis; tel: (514) 284-4239,* moderate–pricey. St-Denis is also the home of many often-excellent ethnic eateries from Ethiopian and Algerian to Cambodian and Thai. They are typically budget–moderate.

ENTERTAINMENT

Schedules of performances, exhibitions and club dates appear in the Friday *Gazette.* Montréal's bars range from discos (the largest is **Métropolis**, *59 r. Ste-Catherine,* downtown) to the cool jazz strains of **L'Air du Temps**, *194 r. St-Paul Ouest* in Vieux Montréal. **Centre Info-Arts Bell**, *Places-des-Arts; tel: (514) 790-ARTS,* provides information, open Mon–Sat 1100–2000, Sun 1200–1700.

Locally based performing arts include **Orchestre Symphonique de Mont-réal**; *tel: (514) 842-9951,* **Les Grandes Ballets Canadiens**; *tel: (514) 849-8681,* and **L'Opéra de Montréal**; *tel: (514) 985-2258.* **Office National du Film Montréal**, *1564 r. St-Denis; tel: (514) 283-4823,* has movie and video theatres as well as 21 cinescope stations (individual viewing stations) to view Canadian and Quebecois films.

La Ronde amusement park, *Île Ste-Hélène* (Métro: *Île Ste-Hélène*/bus no. 167 or Métro: *Papineau*/bus no. 169); *tel: (514) 872-6100,* open late May–early Sept, is the largest of its kind in the region; day pass C$18.87. The **Casino de Montréal**; *tel: (514) 392-2746,* open daily 1100–0300, occupies the former French pavilion from Expo '67 on Île Notre-Dame; with 86 gaming tables and 1500 slot machines, the Casino cultivates a decorum expressed in its dress code ban-

ning casual attire. Free casino shuttle bus departs *sq.-Dorchester* on the hour from 1100–1800.

IMAX, *Quai King-Edward, Vieux Port; tel: (514) 496-4629,* is Montréal's version of the seven-storey-high wrap-around cinema screen, creating a full immersion cinema experience; adults C$11.75. **Café Electronique**, *85 r. St-Paul Ouest; tel: (514) 849-1612,* serves food but the main attractions are the computers loaded with CD-ROMs and the Internet connection (C$5 per half hour).

Although the **Cirque du Soleil** is based in Montréal, it performs shows of acrobatics and mime only on even-numbered years at Quai Jacques-Cartier. **Indoor ice skating** is available all year at *Bell Amphitheatre, 1000 de la Gauchetière Ouest; tel: (514) 395-0555.*

Spectator Sports

The **Montréal Canadiens** hockey team plays at the *Forum, 2313 r. Ste-Catherine Ouest; tel: (514) 932-2582,* Oct–mid-June, and has won the Stanley Cup 24 times. The **Montréal Expos** baseball team plays Apr–Sept at *Olympic Stadium, 4549 av. Pierre-de-Coubertin; tel: (514) 846-3976.*

Events

Montréal celebrates a festival with the slightest provocation. The **Festival International de Jazz de Montréal**, late June–early July, is one of the five largest jazz festivals in the world with more than 350 shows.

The **Festival Juste Pour Rire**, late July, with more than 300 shows – some in French, some in English – is the world's largest festival of humour. **L'International Benson & Hedges Inc.**, mid-June–late July, the world's largest fireworks competition, takes place at La

Ronde amusement park on Île Ste-Helène but can be viewed for free from the Pont Jacques-Cartier.

The **Grand Prix Molson du Canada,** early–mid-June, is the only North American stop on this prestigious auto racing circuit. **La Fête de St-Jean-Baptiste,** June 24, is Québec province's 'national' day and is celebrated in Montréal with non-stop parties in the streets, homes and bars.

SHOPPING

Vieux Montréal is rife with souvenir shops, but the edges of the district are in flux, with new art galleries opening. Although portions have become seedy, r. Ste-Catherine Ouest is the traditional shopping street with the grand old department stores and entrances to many of the shopping centres that also link to the Underground City.

The three largest shopping centres in the city are along r. Ste-Catherine (Métro: McGill): **Place Montréal Trust** and **Le Centre Eaton de Montréal,** both at the corners with r. McGill College, and **Les Promenades de la Cathédrale,** a half-block west. (The most important shopping centres of the Underground not directly on r. Ste-Catherine are **Place Ville-Marie** and **Place Bonaventure.**)

Montréal is perhaps the best place in North America to buy stylish clothes for cold weather. The 1800 block of r. Notre-Dame Ouest is lined with antiques and collectibles dealers, including a combination antiques shop and tearoom, **Ambiance,** 1874 r. Notre-Dame Ouest; tel: (514) 939-2609. **Davidoff,** 1452 r. Sherbrooke Ouest; tel: (514) 289-9118, carries fine Cuban cigars. Several galleries featuring graphic arts, painting and crafts lie on r. Sherbrooke Ouest in the two blocks west of the Musée des Beaux-Arts.

Tax Rebates

Vistors to Canada may apply for rebates on the 7% goods and services tax (GST) on goods purchased and removed from Canada. Rebates are also available for GST paid on short-term lodging. Refund forms are readily available from merchants and the Infotouriste Centre (see Travel Essentials).

SIGHTSEEING

By Bus

Bus tours leave from Infotouriste Centre, 1001 r. sq.-Dorchester; tickets sold at centre and many hotels; C$23.50–C$25. Several bus tours allow reboarding, late June–early Oct: **Murray Hill Trolley Bus;** tel: (514) 871-4733, and **Royal City Tour;** tel: (514) 871-4733. **Amphi-Bus Tour;** tel: (514) 849-5181, leaves from Quai King-Edward, Vieux Port, to tour city and adjacent river in amphibious vehicle; reservations required; May–Oct, C$18.

From the Water

Closest Métro for all boat tours: Champs-de-Mars. **Le Bateau-Mouche,** Quai Jacques-Cartier, Vieux Port; tel: (514) 849-9952, modelled on the Parisian tour ships, cruises upstream through ancient locks, under bridges and around the islands of Expo '67, May–Oct; C$19.95 adults for 1.5-hour scenic cruise, C$59.75 for three-hour dinner cruise, on weekday tours at 1000 children under 12 travel free with an adult. **Croisières du Port de Montréal,** Quai Victoria, Vieux Port; tel: (514) 842-3871 or (800) 667-3131, cruises two hours around Vieux Port and nearby islands including Île Ste-Helène; mid-May–early Oct; adults C$19.75. **Croisières Nouvelle Orléans,** Quai Jacques-Cartier, Vieux Port; tel: (514) 842-7655 or (800) 667-3131, offers a 1.5-hour cruise on a replica of a Mississippi river-boat; mid-May–early Oct; adults C$15.75. **Saute moutons, Jet St-Laurent,** *Quai de l'Horologe, Vieux Port; tel: (514) 284-9607,* shoots the Lachine rapids upstream twice on a jet boat with passengers riding back down on rafts; adults C$48.

Walks

Ask at the main Infotouriste Centre for various walking tours, including the detailed booklet, *Old Montreal: A Walking Tour,* which pokes into obvious and less obvious corners of Vieux Montréal. High points for many visitors are the Notre-Dame church and a *calèche* (horse-drawn carriage) tour (C$30 for half hour, C$50 for hour). Less documented but fascinating in its own right is the **Vieux Port;** *tel: (514) 496-PORT,* which was reclaimed as a recreational area in time for the 350th anniversary in 1992. The piers have many entertainments, but the highlight is the green promenade from the Clocktower lookout westward to the old lock system.

Parks

The vast green space of **Parc du Mont-Royal** in the centre of the island was designed by Frederick Law Olmsted and has been a recreational resource since the 1870s. Footpaths and bicycle paths become cross-country ski trails in winter. Lac aux Castors at the west end of the park becomes a skating rink.

Parc des Îles (Métro: *Île Ste-Hélène*) in the middle of the St. Lawrence River comprises the natural island of Île Ste-Hélène and the man-made Île Notre-Dame. The islands were developed for Expo '67 and the city has adapted the site for La Ronde amusement park, the Casino de Montréal and **La Biosphère,** *160 Tour d'Isle, Île Ste-Hélène* (Métro: *Île Ste-Hélène*); *tel: (514) 283-5000,* open daily 1000–2000 (early June–Sept); 0900–1800 (Oct–May), adults C$6.50. Occupying Buckminster Fuller's landmark geodesic dome that was the USA pavilion at Expo '67, La Biosphère is an environmental educational centre about the St. Lawrence River and the Great Lakes. The park's beach and swimming pools are popular in the summer. In winter it has toboggan slides and 14 km of cross-country ski trails. The former Olympic rowing basin becomes a 2-km-long ice-skating rink.

Olympic Park (Métro: *Viau*) dates from the 1976 summer Olympiad. **La Tour de Montréal** arches above the stadium and provides a panoramic view of the city and St. Lawrence valley, open Mon 1200–2100, Tues–Thur 1000–2100, Fri–Sun 1000–2300 (mid-June–early Sept); Mon 1200–1800 and Tues–Sun 1000–1800 (early Sept–mid-June), adults C$7.25.

Olympic Stadium is home to the Montréal Expos baseball team. At its base is the Sports Centre with pools where visitors may train, swim, dive, scuba dive or work out. Tours of the stadium are C$5.25. The nearby **Jardins Botaniques** and **Insectarium,** *4101 r. Sherbrooke Est; tel: (514) 872-1400,* open daily 0900–1700 (Sept–late June); 0800–2000 (late June–Aug), adults C$7 (C$13.50 with Biodôme), are beautiful and creepy, respectively.

Biodôme de Montréal, *4777 r. Pierre-de-Coubertin* (Métro: *Viau*); *tel: (514) 868-3000,* open daily 0900–1800 (Sept–late June); 0900–2000 (late June–Aug), adults C$9.50 (C$13.50 with Jardins Botaniques and Insectaritarium), contains four distinct environments complete with flora and fauna.

Museums and Historic Sites

The Montréal Museums Pass, available at

Infotouriste Centre and most participating museums, provides entrance to 19 museums: 1 day C$15, 3 days C$28. **Musée des Beaux-Arts,** *1379 r. Sherbrooke Ouest* (Métro: *Peel or Guy-Concordia*); *tel: (514) 285-1600,* open Tues–Sun 1100–1800, Wed 1100–2100, adults C$12, has superb collections of Canadian and Arctic art and hosts touring exhibitions often unseen elsewhere in North America. **Musée des Arts Decoratifs,** *2929 av. Jeanne-d'arc* (Métro: *Pie IX*/bus nos 185/139); *tel: (514) 259-2575,* open Wed–Sun 1100–1700, adults C$3, emphasises decorative art and industrial design 1935-present.

Centre Canadien d'Architecture, *1920 r. Baile* (Métro: *Atwater/Guy-Concordia*); *tel: (514) 939-7026,* open Wed and Fri 1100–1800, Thur 1100–2000, Sat–Sun 1100–1700 (Oct–May); Tues–Sun 1100–1800, Thur 1100–2000 (June–Sept), adults C$5, is devoted to great world architecture. **Musée d'Art Contemporain de Montréal,** *185 r. Ste-Catherine* (Métro: *Place-des-Arts*); *tel: (514) 847-6212,* emphasises Québec and international art after 1940; adults C$5, free Wed evenings.

Pointe-à-Callière, Montréal Museum of Archaeology and History, *350 Place Royale* (Métro: *Place d'Armes*/bus no. 26); *tel: (514) 872-9150,* open Tues–Sun 1000–2000 (July–Aug); Tues–Sun 1000–1700 and Wed 1000–2000 (Sept–June), adults C$7, stands on the site of the original city settlement. Clever interactive exhibits tell the more conventional tale of civic growth at the **Centre d'Histoire de Montréal,** *335 place d'Youville* (Métro: *sq.-Victoria*); *tel: (514) 872-3207,* open daily 0900–1700 (early May–mid-June), daily 1000–1800 (mid-June–early Sept), Tues–Sun 1000–1700 (early Sept–mid-Dec), non-resident adults

C$4.50. A feel for Montréal's role as the economic and political centre of Canada in the 19th century comes through at the **Sir George-Étienne Cartier National Historic Site,** *458 r. Notre-Dame Est* (Métro: *Champs-de-Mars*); *tel: (514) 283-2282,* open Wed–Sun 1000–1700 (Sept–mid-May); daily 0900–1700 (mid-May–Aug), adults C$3.

Basilique Notre-Dame, *110 r. Notre-Dame Ouest; tel: (514) 842-2925,* open daily 0700–1800 (early Sept–late June); daily 0700–2000 (late June–early Sept), is a masterpiece of neo-Gothic architecture constructed 1824–29. The **McCord Museum of Canadian History,** *690 r. Sherbrooke Ouest* (Métro: *McGill*/bus no. 24); *tel: (514) 398-7100,* open Tues, Wed and Fri 1000–1800, Thur 1000–2100, Sat–Sun 1000–1700, adults C$5, is the grand dame of national history museums in Canada.

Musée des Hospitalières de l'Hôtel de Montréal, *201 av. des Pins Ouest* (Métro: *Sherbrooke*/bus no. 144); *tel: (514) 849-2919,* open Tues–Fri 1000–1700 and Sat–Sun 1300–1700 (mid-June–mid-Oct); Wed–Sun 1300–1700 (mid-Oct–mid-June), adults C$5, relates the tale of a key influence in Montréal history, the Hospitalières de St-Joseph, who first arrived in 1659. **David M. Stewart Museum, Museum of Discoveries,** *Le Fort, Île Ste-Hélène* (Métro: *Île Ste-Hélène*); *tel: (514) 861-6701,* open daily 1000–1800 (late June–early Sept), Wed–Mon 1000–1700 (early Sept–late June), adults C$5, is a repository of early maps and documents of exploration.

Musée Juste Pour Rire, *2111 blvd St-Laurent* (Métro: *St-Laurent*); *tel: (514) 845-4000,* open Tues–Sun 1300–2000, adults C$9.95, is about humour – as well as spectacle, sensation and a peculiarly French-Canadian take on cinema.

QUÉBEC CITY

Perched atop an escarpment over the St. Lawrence River, the fortified city of Québec was the first North American site chosen for the UNESCO World Heritage list. Within the 17th-century walls, Québec remains a picuresque low-rise city built chiefly of local grey stone, dominated on the bluff overlooking the river by the Loire Valley-style Château Frontenac hotel. The vigorous industrial city outside the walls is more mundane, although the wooden homes of residential districts are tended with obvious pride.

Besieged six times since its founding in 1608, Québec fell twice to the British – temporarily in 1629 and decisively in 1759. But the French won the peace; Québec is the North American centre of French language and culture. Speaking French can be an advantage when visiting Québec as it may open a few doors to the least expensive dining and lodging, but a fluency in French is not essential.

TOURIST INFORMATION

Greater Québec Area Tourism and Convention Bureau, *60 r. D'Auteuil, Québec, PQ G1R 4C4; tel: (418) 692-2471 or 651-2882,* provides a superb tourist guide and detailed map. The **Maison du Tourisme de Québec,** *12 r. Ste-Anne,* across from Le Château Frontenac; *tel: (418) 873-2015* or toll-free *(800) 363-7777,* open daily 0830–1930

(late June–early Sept), 0900–1700 (early Sept–late June), has an automated cash dispenser, a bureau de change and stations for car hire and hotel reservations in addition to literature.

WEATHER

Summer is humid and can be hot (up to 90°F). Winter is cold and snowy; the average Jan high is 18°F.

ARRIVING AND DEPARTING

Airport

Jean-Lesage International Airport; *tel: (418) 874-8333,* is in Sainte-Foy, 16 km from downtown. Taxi to downtown is about C$25. Airport shuttle service is C$8.75 one way or C$16.50 round trip. Shuttles run only every few hours. Local bus service is limited to 0800 and 1700.

Rail and Bus

VIA Rail; *tel: (418) 692-3940,* offers a daily service between Montréal and Québec, arriving at **Gare du Palais,** *450 r. de la Gare-du-Palais; tel: (418) 524-4161.* **Orleans Express Coach Lines** (connecting to other major Canadian cities) and **Intercar Côte-Nord** (provincial transport) also use the Gare du Palais, but a different entrance, *320 r. Abraham-Martin; tel: (418) 525-3000.*

GETTING AROUND

Québec is a walking city despite being built above and below a cliff. The easiest way to negotiate this division is the **Funiculaire,** C$1, from the *Terrasse Dufferin* to *Le Quartier Petit Champlain.*

Public Transport

City buses cost C$1.80 in change or C$1.45 with the purchase of tickets from a *tabagerie*. For information, *tel: (418) 627-2511*, or inquire at the Maison du Tourisme. Buses to suburban shopping and sights use *Place d'Youville* as a main terminus.

Driving

Driving is awkward in Old Québec and on-street parking is sparse. Meters are C$1.25 per hour. Park at an underground lot when you arrive and use your car only for excursions. Even many small hotels have parking.

Accommodation

Hotel chains include *CP, Rd, Rm. Hn* and **Loews Concorde Hotel,** *1225 Place Montcalm; tel: (418) 647-2222* or toll-free in Canada *(800) 463-5256,* have tower hotels just outside the city walls with remarkable views. Chains in neighbouring Sainte-Foy include *BW, DI, Hd.* **Le Château Frontenac,** *1 r. des Carrières, Québec, PQ G1R 4P5; tel: (418) 692-3861,* the most prominent sight in town, celebrated its 100th anniversary in 1993; pricey. Québec has several stylish hotels in the moderate–expensive range: the Art Nouveau **Hôtel Clarendon,** *57 r. Ste-Anne, Québec, PQ G1R 3X4; tel: (418) 692-2480;* the contemporary chic **Le Priori,** *5 r. Sault-au-Matelot, Québec, PQ G1K 3Y7; tel: (418) 692-3992;* and the Beaux-Arts exterior, Art Deco interior **Hôtel du Théâtre Capitole,** *972 r. St-Jean, Québec, PQ G1R 1R5; tel: (418) 694-4040* or *(800) 363-4040.* Moderate options include **Hôtel Au Jardin du Gouverneur,** *16 r. Mont-Carmel, Québec, PQ G1R 4A3; tel: (418) 692-1704;* the

Cap Diamant Maison de Touristes, *39 av. Ste-Geneviève, Québec, PQ G1R 4B3; tel: (418) 694-0313;* **Auberge La Caravelle,** *68½ r. St-Louis, Québec, PQ G1R 3Z3; tel: (418) 694-0656* or *(800)*, *267-0656.* **Le Château Bonne Entemps,** *3400 Chemin Ste-Foy, Sainte-Foy, PQ G1X 1S6; tel: (418) 653-5221* or *(800) 463-4390,* lies at the suburban edge of the city on the bus line. Main hotel rooms are expensive– pricey, but the cabins (with complete housekeeping) are moderate.

The nearest campsite is **Camping Municipal de Beauport,** *95 r. Sérénité, Beauport, PQ G13 3L1; tel: (418) 666-2228,* about 20 mins from downtown and close to Montmorency Falls. **Centre International de Séjour de Québec,** *19 r. Ste-Ursule, Québec, PQ G1R 4E1; tel: (418) 694-0755,* is the city's youth hostel; membership (available on site) mandatory for non-Canadian visitors; budget. The street has many other inexpensive places to stay.

Eating and Drinking

Québec's restaurants are generally more expensive inside the city walls than outside, except along **Grand Allée.** Table d'hôte midday meals Mon–Fri are usually the best value. The area around **r. St-Louis** and the **Quartier Petit Champlain** are perhaps the most tourist-oriented. **R. St-Jean** between *Côte de la Fabrique* and the city walls hops with small spots catering to a young crowd. *Grand Allée* between *George V* and *Place Montcalm* is blessed with broad terraces and a plethora of pretty good dining. For a nice mix of inexpensive, mostly ethnic restaurants as well as good grocery and take-away shops, try the stretch of *r. St-Jean* on the other side of *Autoroute Dufferin* from the *Place d'Youville*. Predictably, food with

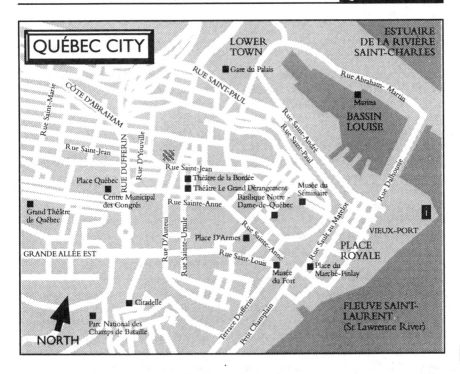

a French accent is the most interesting. **Restaurant Aux Anciens Canadiens,** *34 r. St-Louis; tel: (418) 692-1627,* specialises in traditional Québecois dishes with upmarket treatment; moderate–pricey. **Serge Bruyère,** *1200 r. St-Jean; tel: (418) 694-0618,* pioneered serious modern cuisine in Québec and still sets the local standard; pricey. Bistro-like and *très français* is **Paris–Brest Restaurant Française,** *590 Grand-Allée est; tel: (418) 529-2243;* moderate. In the lower city, **Bistro Belge Môss,** *255 r. St-Paul; tel: (418) 692-0233,* has wonderful local mussels (moderate), and **Restaurant Asia,** *89 Sault-au-Matelot; tel: (418) 692-3799,* exemplifies colonial French with elegant Indochinese cuisine (grilled shrimp, for example) at sidewalk prices; budget. The **Bar-Restaurant Rotatif L'Astral** at the Loews Concorde Hotel has a splendid view of the Plains of Abraham and the old walled city; best is the Sunday brunch buffet at C$21.75. **Le Commensal,** *860 r. St-Jean; tel: (418) 647-3733,* is a vegetarian buffet in the St-Jean–Baptiste neighbourhood.

Communications

Canada Post offices are open Mon–Fri 0800–1745. **Main Post Office** is at *300 r. St-Paul; tel: (418) 694-6176;* the upper city office is at *3 r. Buade; tel: (418) 694-6102.*

ENTERTAINMENT

Québec has world-class street performers. Musicians, acrobats and quirky circus acts congregate on the *Terrasse Dufferin,* the *Place d'Armes* and the end of *r. St-Jean* near *Porte St-Jean.* Parks and amphitheatres have free evening performances. *The Québec*

Chronicle-Telegraph, the English-language newspaper, carries listings.

The **Québec Symphony Orchestra,** the oldest in Canada, performs at the **Grand Théâtre de Québec,** *269 blvd René-Lévesque est; tel: (418) 643-8131.* The theatre is also a venue for other music, variety shows, theatre and dance. Many churches offer concerts of both sacred and secular music. Jazz buffs congregate for performances at **l'Emprise at the Hotel Clarendon,** *57 r. Ste-Anne; tel: (418) 692-2480;* no cover, one drink minimum. Local singer-songwriters hold forth at **La Boîte aux Chansons Chez son Père,** *24 r. Stanislas; tel: (418) 692-5308.*

Sports

The **Québec Nordiques** play professional hockey mid-Sept–Apr at the **Colisée de Québec,** *2205 av. du Colisée, Parc de l'Exposition, Québec, PQ G1L 4W7; tel: (418) 523-3333 or (800) 463-3333* (bus nos 4 or 12). Harness racing takes place all year at the **Hippodrome de Québec,** *C.P. 2053, Parc de l'Exposition, Québec, PQ G1K 7M9; tel: (418) 524-5283* (bus nos 4 or 12).

Events

Two ten-day seasonal events celebrate Québec's position as the centre of French culture in North America. **Festival d'été international de Québec** in July, is the summer party, while **Carnival d'hiver,** Feb, marks the distinctly Québecois love for their daunting winter. The summer festival emphasises food and music; the winter festival, food and outdoor sports.

SHOPPING

R. St–Paul between *r. Rioux* and *r. du Sault-au-Matelot* in the Old Port is best for antiques shopping. Artists hawk picturesque city scenes and portraits at *r.*

Trésor near *Place d'Armes.* Many stores throughout *Le Quartier Petit Champlain* and the main streets of Old Québec cater to tourists; the best sell leather goods, Native arts and French goods. Québec's largest shopping centre, **Place Laurier,** is in Sainte-Foy, a 10-min ride on bus no. 800 from *Place d'Youville.*

Non-residents visiting Canada may apply for **rebates** on the 7% goods and services tax (GST) on goods purchased and removed from Canada. Rebates are also available for GST paid on short-term accommodation. Refund forms are readily available, see Travel Essentials p. 17.

SIGHTSEEING

For a sweeping vantage of Québec City from the St. Lawrence River, take the **Lévis ferry,** C\$1.25 each way, terminal opposite *Place Royale.* For a bird's-eye view, visit the free art gallery and observation deck on the 31st floor of a government building: **Anima G,** *Édifice Marie-Guyart, 1037 r. de la Chevrotière,* open Mon–Fri 1000-1600, Sat–Sun 1300–1700.

The classic tour of Old Québec is by horse-drawn carriage, or calèche, C\$50 for a minimum of 35 mins, available at *Place d'Armes* or along *r. d'Auteuil.* Several companies offer bus tours of the city and countryside. You can get on and off all day from the narrated trolley City Tour: **Maple Leaf Sightseeing Tours & Dupont,** *36½ r. St-Louis; tel: (418) 649-9226 or (800) 267-0616,* C\$19.95. Tours leave from *Place d'Armes.*

The **Ligue de Taxis Québec;** *tel: (418) 648-9199,* has 125 drivers certified as tour guides who have completed 105 hours of courses; rates vary. Several sightseeing boats offer cruises of 1–1½ hours from the Old Port to Montmorency Falls and back; C\$15–C\$20. The Paris-style hydrofoil **Le Bateau-Mouche;** *tel: (418) 692-4949 or (800) 361-0130,* does four daytime cruises and a dinner cruise daily May–Oct, departing from Bassin Louise; day tours C$19.75; dinner cruise C$58.75; children under 13 free with an adult, Mon–Fri on the 1000 tour.

Québec's walls are the physical manifestation of the fortified civic spirit as defender of the French faith, and strolling the ramparts is the best way to begin to comprehend the city and its moods. Without doubt, Québec is most charming on the *Terrasse Dufferin,* a wooden boardwalk next to the Château Frontenac overlooking the St. Lawrence River. Both Québecois and visitors enjoy strolling amid the musicians and performers.

Historic Sites

Nestled between the Cap Diamant escarpment and the St. Lawrence River, **Place Royale** is where, in 1608, Samuel de Champlain began the fortified fur-trading post that would become Québec. Restored to reveal the 17th- and 18th-century city, the district bustles with modern commerce amid interpretive sites.

The **Information Centre,** *215 Marché Finley; tel: (418) 643-6631,* open daily 1000–1700 (June–Sept), has slide shows in French and English. The **Interpretation Centre,** *25 r. St-Pierre, no telephone,* open daily 1000–1800 (June–Sept), traces Québec history from the Native period to present. Admission to both centres and a few historic buildings is free.

Musée du Fort, *20 r. Ste-Anne; tel: (418) 692-2175,* open daily 1000–1800 (late June–Aug), 1000–1700 (April–May and Sept–Oct); weekdays 1100–1500, weekends 1100–1700 (Nov–Mar), C$5.50, interprets the six sieges of Québec with sound and light shows on dioramas and a maquette.

Atop Cap Diamant, the **Citadelle;** *tel: (418) 648-3563,* was the eastern flank of Québec's fortress under the British. Built in 1820, it is the largest group of fortified buildings in North America still occupied by troops, though their tasks are largely ceremonial. Guided tours – on the hour daily 0900–1800 in summer, shorter hours in fall and spring, by reservation only Nov–Mar, C$4.50 – include the **Royal 22nd Regiment Museum** and, when timing is right, **Changing of the Guard** or **Beating of Retreat.**

For deeper understanding of Québec's original fortifications, visit the **Artillery National Historic Park,** *2 r. d'Auteuil; tel: (418) 648-4205,* open daily 1000–1700, C$2.50. The buildings are still being restored, but the chief attraction is a scale model of the fortifications created in 1806–08. Near the St-Louis gate is the old powder magazine building, now the visitors' centre for the **Fortifications of Québec National Historic Site,** *100 r. St-Louis; tel: (418) 648-7016,* open daily 1000–1700, C$2.50. Guided tours of the ramparts can be arranged here. The **National Battlefields Park Interpretation Centre,** *Musée du Québec, Baillairgé Building, level 1; tel: (418) 648-4071,* open daily 1000–1700, C$2 basic admission, extra for multimedia shows and driving tour, explains the Plains of Abraham, where the British conquered the French to seize Québec as part of Lower Canada. Or simply walk the rolling 250-acre battlefield above the river and read the plaques and statues.

Colonial powers fought over Québec because it was a strategic shipping point, and **The Port of Québec in the 19th Century National Historic Park Centre,** *100 r. St-André; tel: (418) 648-3300,* open daily 1000–1700, C$2.50 adults, C$1.25 children 6–16, does a

343

dynamic job of telling the port's tale. The roofdeck has a good view of today's working port.

Québec's complex politics is embodied in **Hôtel du Parlement**, *av. Dufferin and Grand Allée est; tel: (418) 643-7239*, a French Renaissance Revival structure 100 m square housing a British form of government conducted in French. Half-hour free guided tours in French and English depart from Door 3, Mon–Fri 0900-1630.

Religious History

Religious orders have played central roles in Québec's story and the Roman Catholic Church still has a looming presence. The richly decorated **Basilique-cathédrale Notre-Dame-de-Québec**, *16 r. Buade; (418) 692-2533*, open daily 0630–1730, dates from 1650. The basilica also runs a sound-and-light show (C$6) on French missions in North America. Guided tours of the basilica and crypt are given Mon–Sat 0900–1630, Sun 1230–1630 (mid-May–Oct) by the **Corporation of Religious Tourism**; *tel: (418) 694-0665*; the corporation also arranges tours to other churches, convents and the Québec seminary. The **Musée des Ursulines**, *12 r. Donnacona; tel: (418) 694-0694*, open Tues–Sat 0930–1200 and 1300–1630, Sun 1230– 1700, C$3, outlines this cloistered teaching order's history in Québec. As you pass churches, peek in if they're open. **Notre-Dame-des-Victoires,** *Place Royale,* dating from 1688, has a magnificent high altar sculpted in the form of a castle.

Art and Culture

The 1992 remake of the **Musée de Québec**, *Parc des Champs-de-bataille; tel: (418) 643-2150*, open daily 1000–1745, Wed 1000–2145 (late June–mid-Oct); Tues–Sun 1200–1745, Wed 1200-2045 (rest of year), C$4.75, beautifully merges the original museum building with a 19th-century prison (a youth hostel in the 1970s!). Similar imagination informs the exhibitions. Some of Québec's best religious sculpture is here and some terrific paintings by Canada's leading artists.

The **Musée de la Civilisation,** *85 r. Dalhousie; tel: (418) 643-2158,* open daily 1000–1900 (late June–early Sept); Tues–Sun 1000–1700, Wed 1000–2100 (early Sept–late June), C$6, Tues free except summer, has permanent exhibits that include the history of Québec and a 250-year-old boat unearthed at the museum site. Clever temporary exhibitions deal with all aspects of modern and pop culture.

OUT OF TOWN

Montmorency Falls is an 83-m natural waterfall (1.5 times the height of Niagara Falls but not as dramatic) a few kilometres east of the city. The falls have always been a popular natural wonder – recently developed to create a genuine attraction.

Pick up Autoroute Dufferin just outside the walls of the city in front of Place Québec, veering left at the major interchange to Rte 175 (Autoroute Laurentienne). At the cloverleaf interchange, take Rte 138 east about 15 km to Parc de la Chute-Montmorency parking lot. Or take the bus no. 800, with a change at *Terminus Beauport* to Rte 50. Most scenic tours also include the falls. A cable car (C$4.50 one way, C$7 round trip) running every few minutes connects the lower falls with the upper cliffs, where the Manoir Montmorency stands. Once the home of the Duke of Kent, the restaurant complex is the region's favourite spot for wedding receptions. A narrow footbridge crosses the falls to steps down the cliffs of the eastern side through the mists to the parking area.

DRIVING DISTANCES AND TIMES

These distances between main cities generally follow the fastest roads, not necessarily the most direct routes. Timings are approximate and assume good driving conditions.

Bangor, ME, to . . .	Miles	Hours
Boston, MA	249	4
Burlington, VT	285	5½
Concord, NH	230	4
Montréal	290	7
New York, NY	470	8½

Boston, MA, to . . .		
Bangor, ME	249	4
Burlington, VT	209	4½
Concord, NH	75	1½
Hartford, CT	109	2
Montréal	335	5½
New Haven, CT	135	2½
New York, NY	220	4½
Portland, ME	115	2
Providence, RI	51	1

Burlington, VT, to . . .		
Bangor, ME	285	5½
Boston, MA	209	4½
Concord, NH	150	3
Hartford, CT	241	5
Montréal	98	2
New York, NY	349	7

Concord, NH, to . . .		
Bangor, ME	230	4
Boston, MA	75	1½
Burlington, VT	150	3
Hartford, CT	165	3½
New Haven, CT	207	4
New York, NY	300	6½
Providence, RI	126	2½

Hartford, CT, to . . .	Miles	Hours
Boston, MA	109	2
Burlington, VT	241	5
Concord, NH	165	3½
New Haven, CT	42	1
New York, NY	119	2
Providence, RI	74	1½

Montréal to . . .		
Bangor, ME	290	7
Boston, MA	335	5½
Burlington, VT	98	2
New York, NY	380	8
Portland, ME	290	5½

New Haven, CT, to . . .		
Boston, MA	135	2½
Concord, NH	207	4
Hartford, CT	42	1
New York, NY	77	1½
Providence, RI	110	2

New York, NY, to . . .		
Bangor, ME	470	8½
Boston, MA	220	4½
Burlington, VT	349	7
Concord, NH	300	6½
Hartford, CT	119	2
Montréal	380	8
New Haven, CT	77	1½
Providence, RI	183	3½

Portland, ME, to . . .		
Boston, MA	115	2
Montréal	290	5½

Providence, RI, to . . .		
Boston, MA	51	1
Concord, NH	126	2½
Hartford, CT	74	1½
New Haven, CT	110	2
New York, NY	183	3½

345

HOTEL CODES
AND CENTRAL BOOKING NUMBERS

The following abbreviations have been used throughout the book to show which chains are represented in a particular town. Cities and large towns have most except *Hl*. Central booking numbers are shown in bold – use these numbers whilst in the USA to make reservations at any hotel in the chain. Where available, numbers that can be called in your own country are also noted. (Aus = Australia, Can = Canada, Ire = Ireland, NZ = New Zealand, SA = South Africa, UK = United Kingdom, USA = United States of America.), WW = World wide.

Bl	**Budgetel Inn**	Aus *(800) 221 066*			**(800) 228 5151**
	(800) 428 3438	Can *(800) 465 4329*	*Rd*	**Radisson**	
BW	**Best Western**	Ire *(800) 553 155*		**(800) 333 3333**	
	(800) 528 1234	NZ *(0800) 442 222*		Ire *(800) 557 474*	
	Aus *(1 800) 222 422*	SA *(011) 482 3500*		NZ *(800) 443 333*	
	Can *(800) 528 1234*	UK *(0800) 897121*		UK *(800) 191991*	
	Ire *(800) 709 101*	*Hl*	**Hostelling International**	*Rm*	**Ramada**
	NZ *(09) 520 5418*	**202 783 6161**		**(800) 228 2828**	
	SA *(011) 339 4865*	(information only)		Aus *(800) 222 431*	
	UK *(0800) 393130*	UK *(0171) 248 6547*		Can *(800) 854 7854*	
Cl	**Comfort Inn**	*HJ*	**Howard Johnson**	Ire *(800) 252 627*	
	(800) 228 5150	(HoJo)		NZ *(800) 441 111*	
	Aus *(008)090 600*	**(800) 654 2000**		UK *(800) 181737*	
	Can *(800) 888 4747*	Aus *02 262 4918*	*Rl*	**Residence Inn**	
	Ire *(800) 500 600*	UK *(0181) 688 1418*		**(800) 331 3131**	
	NZ *(800) 808 228*	*Hn*	**Hilton**	Aus *(800) 251 259*	
	UK *(0800) 181591*	**(800) 445 8667**		Ire *(800) 409929*	
	USA *(800) 888 4747*	Aus *(800) 222 255*		NZ *(800) 441035*	
CM	**Courtyard by Marriott**	Can *(800) 445 8667*		US *(800) 221222*	
	(800) 321 2211	NZ *(800) 448 002*	*Sh*	**Sheraton**	
CP	**Canadian Pacific**	SA *(011) 880 3108*		**(800) 325 3535** or	
	(800) 325 2525	UK *(0345) 581595*		*(800) 325 1717*	
DI	**Days Inn**	*Hy*	**Hyatt**	(hearing impaired)	
	(800) 325 2525	**(800) 233 1234**		Aus *(008) 073 535*	
	UK *(01483) 440470*	Aus *(800) 131 234*		Can *(800) 325 3535*	
EL	**Econolodge**	Can/USA *(800) 233 1234*		Ire *(800) 535 353*	
	(800) 424 6423	Ire *(800) 535 500*		NZ *(0800) 443 535*	
	WW *(800) 221 2222*	NZ *(800) 441 234*		UK *(0800) 353535*	
ES	**Embassy Suites**	SA *(011) 773 9888*	*Su*	**Susse Chalet**	
	(800) 362 2779	UK *(0345) 581666*		**(800) 524 2538**	
	Aus *02 959 3922*	*Ma*	**Marriott**	*S8*	**Super 8**
	Can *416 626 3974*	**(800) 228 9290**		WW *(800) 800 8000*	
	NZ *09 623 4294*	Aus *(800) 251 259*	*TL*	**Travelodge**	
	SA *11 789 6706*	Can *(800) 228 9290*		**(800) 578 7878**	
	UK *(01992) 441517*	NZ *(800) 441 035*		Aus *(800) 622 240*	
Ha	**Hampton Inn**	UK *(800) 221222*		Ire *(800) 409 040*	
	(800) 426 7866	*M6*	**Motel 6**		NZ *(800) 801 111*
Hd	**Holiday Inn**	**(800) 437 7486**		SA *(011) 442 9201*	
	(800) 465 4329	*Ql*	**Quality Inn**		UK *(0345) 404040*

CONVERSION TABLES

DISTANCE

km	miles	km	miles
1	0.62	30	21.75
2	1.24	40	24.85
3	1.86	45	27.96
4	2.49	50	31.07
5	3.11	55	34.18
6	3.73	60	37.28
7	4.35	65	40.39
8	4.97	70	43.50
9	5.59	75	46.60
10	6.21	80	49.71
15	9.32	90	55.92
20	12.43	100	62.14
25	15.53	125	77.67

1km = 0.6214 miles
1mile = 1.609 km

METRES AND FEET

Unit	Metres	Feet
1	0.30	3.281
2	0.61	6.563
3	0.91	9.843
4	1.22	13.124
5	1.52	16.403
6	1.83	19.686
7	2.13	22.967
8	2.4	26.248
9	2.74	29.529
10	3.05	32.810
14	4.27	45.934
18	5.49	59.058
20	6.10	65.520
50	15.24	164.046
75	22.8	246.069
100	30.48	328.092

WEIGHT

Unit	kg	Pounds
1	0.45	2.205
2	0.90	4.405
3	1.35	6.614
4	1.80	8.818
5	2.25	11.023
10	4.50	22.045
15	6.75	33.068
20	9.00	44.889
25	11.25	55.113
50	22.50	110.225
75	33.75	165.338
100	45.00	220.450

1kg	=	1000g
100g	=	3.5oz
1oz	=	28.35g
1lb	=	453.60g

FLUID MEASURES

Litres	Imp.gal.	US gal.
5	1.1	1.3
10	2.2	2.6
15	3.3	3.9
20	4.4	5.2
25	5.5	6.5
30	6.6	7.8
35	7.7	9.1
40	8.8	10.4
45	9.9	11.7
50	11.0	13.0

1 litre(l)=0.88 imp.quarts
1 litre(l)=1.06 US quarts
1 imp. quart = 1.141
1 imp. gallon= 4.55 l
1 US quart = 0.95 l
1 US gallon = 3.81 l

MENS' SHIRTS

UK	Europe	US
14	36	14
15	38	15
15.5	39	15.5
16	41	16
16.5	42	16.5
17	43	17

MENS' SHOES

UK	Europe	US
6	40	7
7	41	8
8	42	9
9	43	10
10	44	11
11	45	12

Unit	mm	cm	metres
1 inch	25.4	2.54	0.025
1 foot	304.8	30.48	0.304
1 yard	914.4	91.44	0.914

To convert cms to inches, multiply by 0.3937
To convert inches to cms, multiply by 2.54

MENS' CLOTHES

UK	Europe	US
36	46	36
38	48	38
40	50	40
42	52	42
44	54	44
46	56	46

LADIES' SHOES

UK	Europe	US
3	36	4.5
4	37	5.5
5	38	6.5
6	39	7.5
7	40	8.5
8	41	9.5

TYPICAL COSTS

Roll of 35 mm print film	$6.50
Can of cola	75 cents
Local morning newspaper	50 cents
Bottle of beer In liquor store	$1.50
Small beer in bar	$2.50
Glass of wine, gin & tonic	$3.00
Glass of whisky	$3.00
Cup of coffee	85 cents
Burger	$4.00
Sandwich	$4.00
Chocolate ('candy') bar	$1.00

LADIES' CLOTHES

UK	France	Italy	Rest of Europe	US
10	36	38	34	8
12	38	40	36	10
14	40	42	38	12
16	42	44	40	14
18	44	46	42	16
20	46	48	44	18

INDEX

READER SURVEY

If you enjoyed using this book, or even if you didn't, please help us improve future editions by taking part in our reader survey. Every returned form will be acknowledged, and to show our appreciation we will give you £1 off your next purchase of a Thomas Cook guidebook. Just take a few minutes to complete and return this form to us.

When did you buy this book? _____

Where did you buy it? (Please give town/city and if possible name of retailer)
_____

When did you/do you intend to travel in New England?

    For how long (approx.)? _____
    How many people in your party? _____

Which cities, national parks and other locations did you/do you intend mainly to visit?
_____
_____
_____

Did you/will you:
    ☐ Make all your travel arrangements independently?
    ☐ Travel on a fly-drive package?
Please give brief details: _____
_____

Did you/do you intend to use this book:
    ☐ For planning your trip?
    ☐ During the trip itself?
    ☐ Both?

Did you/do you intend also to purchase any of the following travel publications for your trip?
Thomas Cook Travellers: Boston and New England/New York
A road map/atlas (please specify) _____
Other guidebooks (please specify) _____
_____

Have you used any other Thomas Cook guidebooks in the past? If so, which?
_____

Please rate the following features of On the Road around New England for their value to you (Circle VU for 'very useful', U for 'useful', NU for 'little or no use'):

The 'Travel Essentials'section on pages 14–35	VU	U	NU
The 'Driving in New England' section on pages 36–43	VU	U	NU
The 'Touring Itineraries' on pages 54–59	VU	U	NU
The recommended driving routes throughout the book	VU	U	NU
Information on towns and cities, National Parks, etc	VU	U	NU
The maps of towns and cities, parks, etc	VU	U	NU
The colour planning map	VU	U	NU

Please use this space to tell us about any features that in your opinion could be changed, improved, or added in future editions of the book, or any other comments you would like to make concerning the book:

Your age category: ☐ 21-30   ☐ 31-40   ☐ 41–50   ☐ over 50

Your name: Mr/Mrs/Miss/Ms
(First name or initials)
(Last name)

Your full address: (Please include postal or zip code)

Your daytime telephone number:

Please detach this page and send it to: The Project Editor, On the Road around New England, Thomas Cook Publishing, PO Box 227, Peterborough PE3 8BQ, United Kingdom.

We will be pleased to send you details of how to claim your discount upon receipt of this questionnaire.

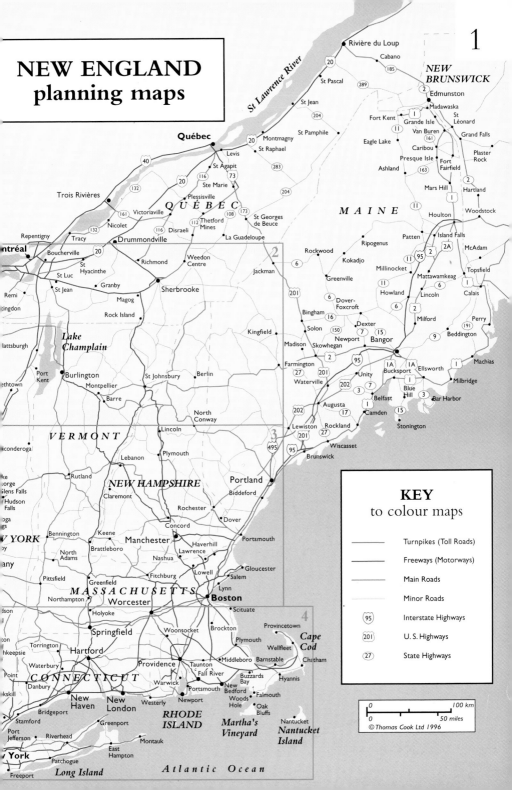

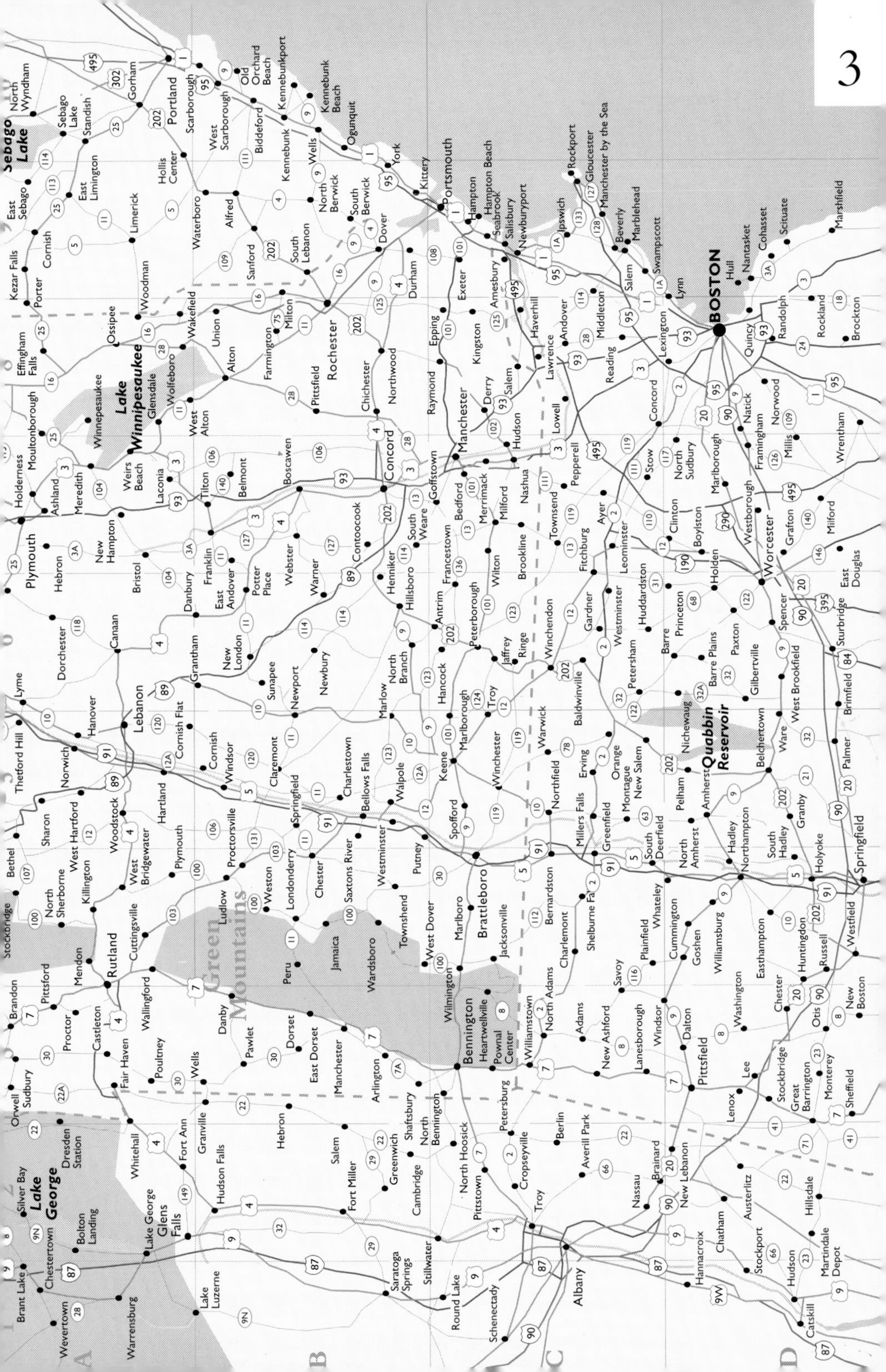

Sebago Lake
North Wyndham
Sebago Lake
Standish
Gorham
Portland
Scarborough
Old Orchard Beach
Kennebunkport
Kennebunk Beach
Biddeford
Kennebunk
West Scarborough
Hollis Center
East Sebago
East Limington
Limerick
Cornish
Kezar Falls
Porter
Waterboro
Alfred
Sanford
Wells
Ogunquit
York
Kittery
North Berwick
South Berwick
South Lebanon
Dover
Durham
Portsmouth
Hampton
Hampton Beach
Seabrook
Salisbury
Newburyport
Rockport
Gloucester
Manchester by the Sea
Ipswich
Beverly
Marblehead
Swampscott
Salem
Lynn
BOSTON
Hull
Nantasket
Cohasset
Scituate
Marshfield
Woodman
Ossipee
Effingham Falls
Wakefield
Union
Milton
Farmington
Rochester
Wolfeboro
Alton
Lake Winnipesaukee
Winnepesaukee
Glendale
West Alton
Pittsfield
Chichester
Northwood
Moultonborough
Holderness
Ashland
Meredith
Weirs Beach
Laconia
Tilton
Belmont
Boscawen
Concord
Epping
Exeter
Kingston
Amesbury
Haverhill
Andover
Middleton
Raymond
Manchester
Derry
Salem
Lawrence
Reading
Lexington
Quincy
Randolph
Rockland
Brockton
Plymouth
Hebron
New Hampton
Bristol
Franklin
Danbury
East Andover
Potter Place
Webster
Warner
Contoocook
Henniker
South Weare
Goffstown
Bedford
Merrimack
Hudson
Nashua
Lowell
Pepperell
Concord
Stow
North Sudbury
Marlborough
Natick
Framingham
Norwood
Millis
Wrentham
Hillsboro
Francestown
Milford
Wilton
Brookline
Townsend
Fitchburg
Ayer
Leominster
Clinton
Boylston
Westborough
Grafton
Milford
Worcester
Holden
Dorchester
Canaan
Lebanon
Grantham
New London
Sunapee
Newport
Newbury
Antrim
Peterborough
Hancock
Jaffrey
Rindge
Winchendon
Gardner
Westminster
Huddardston
Princeton
Barre
Barre Plains
Paxton
Spencer
East Douglas
Sturbridge
Lyme
Hanover
Cornish Flat
Cornish
Windsor
Claremont
Charlestown
Marlow
North Branch
Troy
Marlborough
Keene
Walpole
Bellows Falls
Winchester
Warwick
Baldwinville
Petersham
Gilbertville
West Brookfield
Brimfield
Quabbin Reservoir
Nichewaug
Belchertown
Ware
Palmer
Thetford Hill
Norwich
Sharon
West Hartford
Hartland
Woodstock
Springfield
Saxtons River
Westminster
Putney
Spofford
Brattleboro
Northfield
Erving
Orange
New Salem
Montague
Pelham
Amherst
Greenfield
Millers Falls
South Deerfield
North Amherst
Hadley
Northampton
Granby
South Hadley
Holyoke
Springfield
Bethel
North Sherborne
Killington
West Bridgewater
Plymouth
Proctorsville
Ludlow
Weston
Londonderry
Chester
Townshend
West Dover
Marlboro
Jacksonville
Bernardston
Shelburne Falls
Whateley
Plainfield
Cummington
Goshen
Williamsburg
Easthampton
Huntingdon
Westfield
Russell
Stockbridge
Rutland
Cuttingsville
Green Mountains
Jamaica
Wardsboro
Peru
Wilmington
Charlemont
Savoy
Windsor
Washington
Chester
New Boston
Otis
Mendon
Pittsford
Brandon
Proctor
Castleton
Wallingford
Danby
Pawlet
Dorset
East Dorset
Manchester
Arlington
Bennington
Heartwellville
Pownal Center
Williamstown
North Adams
Adams
New Ashford
Lanesborough
Dalton
Pittsfield
Lee
Stockbridge
Great Barrington
Monterey
Sheffield
Orwell
Sudbury
Fair Haven
Poultney
Wells
Hebron
Salem
Shaftsbury
North Bennington
Petersburg
Berlin
Averill Park
Lenox
Dresden Station
Whitehall
Fort Ann
Granville
Hudson Falls
Greenwich
Cambridge
North Hoosick
Cropseyville
Brainard
New Lebanon
Austerlitz
Hillsdale
Silver Bay
Lake George
Bolton Landing
Chestertown
Lake George
Glens Falls
Fort Miller
Pittstown
Troy
Nassau
Chatham
Hannacroix
Stockport
Hudson
Martindale Depot
Brant Lake
Wevertown
Warrensburg
Lake Luzerne
Saratoga Springs
Stillwater
Round Lake
Schenectady
Albany
Catskill
A
B
C
D